GUIN

SOCCER

WHO'S WHO

Jack Rollin

Cover design: Ad Vantage Studios

©Jack Rollin and Guinness Publishing Ltd, 1984, 1986, 1989, 1990, 1991, 1992, 1993

First Published in 1984
Second edition 1986
Third edition 1989
Fourth edition 1990
Fifth edition 1991
Sixth edition 1992

Published in Great Britain by Guinness Publishing Ltd,
33 London Road, Enfield, Middlesex

Typeset in Monotype Times Roman by BPCC Whitefriars
Printed and bound in Great Britain by
BPCC Paperbacks Ltd

Member of BPCC Ltd

'Guinness' is a registered trade mark of Guinness Publishing Ltd

A catalogue record for this book is
available from the British Library

ISBN 0-85112-718-5

THE AUTHOR

Jack Rollin was born in London in 1932 and educated at King's, Harrow. There he played soccer, while later at Westcliff-on-Sea High School it was rugby. Within ten days of joining the Royal Air Force he was playing in a Welsh Cup tie for RAF Bridgnorth and in the services he learned shorthand and typing, resuming his career in journalism and covering the 1954 World Cup in Switzerland in a freelance capacity.

In 1958 an ankle injury ended his own career during which, at the age of 14, he had been offered a trial with the United States club Chicago Maroons. He wisely declined a one-off re-appearance in 1971 against the European cup finalists Panathinaikos of Greece.

For ten years Jack Rollin was Editor of the weekly magazine *Soccer Star* and its companion monthly *World Soccer* before becoming a freelance again in 1970. Since then he has researched football for BBC Television, acted as an assistant to commentators on 'Match of the Day', spoken on radio and appeared on television programmes. He has contributed to *What's on in London* and *Radio Times* and in 1975 he won the Designers and Art Directors Association Silver Award for *Radio Times World Cup Special* for the most outstanding specialist feature of the year.

In 1972 he became one of the compilers of the *Rothmans Football Yearbook* and later became its Editor. He has provided advice on the football sections of the *Encyclopaedia Britannica* and *Guinness Book of Records*. He is a football columnist for the *Sunday Telegraph*.

Jack Rollin contributed to three part-works: *The Game* (8 vols. 1970); *Book of Football* (6 vols. 1972) and *Football Handbook* (1979–80). His articles have appeared in programmes for matches at Wembley Stadium since 1963. He has produced handbooks which include *World Soccer Digest* 1961, 1962 and 1963 and *World Cup Digest* 1966.

In 1978 he carried out the international research for the BBC Television Series 'The Game of the Century' and produced the first edition of *The Guinness Book of Soccer Facts and Feats*.

Other books he has written: *England's World Cup Triumph* (1966), *A Source Book of Football* (1971), *The History of Aldershot Football Club* (1975), *World Cup Guide* (1982), *Soccer at War 1939–45* (1985), *Soccer: The Records* (1985), *Soccer: Records, Facts and Champions* (1988), *Soccer Shorts* (1988) and *More Soccer Shorts* (1991), *The World Cup 1930–1990* (1990), *The Football Fact Book* (1990 and 1993). In 1974 he contributed the South American section for John Moynihan's *Football Fever*.

The author is married to June and has a daughter Glenda.

FOREWORD

I am delighted to welcome the seventh edition of the *Guinness Soccer Who's Who* by Jack Rollin. It is certainly on a par with all the quality reference books in the Guinness library and will prove an invaluable help to all administrators, managers, soccer writers and supporters of football throughout the United Kingdom.

It is a difficult task to keep abreast of the changing face of personnel at clubs and Jack Rollin is to be congratulated on achieving this task successfully. There are precise details of professional players in England, Wales and Scotland which can be found by quick and easy alphabetical reference and it provides all the information necessary for a football fact-finder.

The book will occupy a prominent place on my desk and I do not hesitate to recommend it.

Gordon Taylor

Gordon Taylor,
Chief Executive, The Professional Footballers' Association

Front cover, from left:
Gavin Peacock (Newcastle United), Paul Merson (Arsenal), Mark Robins (Norwich City), Alan Shearer (Blackburn Rovers), Stephen Wright (Aberdeen)

INTRODUCTION

This book features the statistical League careers of all players who made FA Premier and Barclays League appearances during the 1992–93 season as well as those in the Scottish Premier Division and Raith Rovers and Kilmarnock the promoted teams from the First Division.

Club names in italics indicate temporary transfers where they have not become permanent moves in the same season. Italic figures refer to Colchester United, Lincoln City and Darlington in the GM Vauxhall Conference as well as Aldershot in 1991–92. All appearances include those as substitute.

The Editor would like to thank Alan Elliott for providing details of Scottish League players and also acknowledge the co-operation and assistance of the FA Premier League and Football League in the compilation of this book. In particular Mike Foster of the FA Premier League and Sheila Murphy and Debbie Birch of the Football League.

Bibliography: *Rothmans Football Yearbook*

Also published by Guinness:
European Soccer Who's Who
The Guinness Record of World Soccer
The Guinness Record of the FA Cup
The Football Fact Book
More Soccer Shorts
The Football Encyclopedia
Chelsea Player by Player
Tottenham Hotspur Player by Player
Arsenal Player by Player
Leeds United Player by Player
Everton Player by Player
Liverpool in Europe

ABBOTT, Greg

Born Coventry 14.12.63. Ht 5 9
Wt 10 07
Midfield. From Apprentice.

Season	Club	App	Goals
1981–82	Coventry C	—	—
1982–83	Bradford C	11	—
1983–84		35	3
1984–85		42	6
1985–86		39	10
1986–87		33	7
1987–88		32	5
1988–89		28	4
1989–90		35	3
1990–91		26	—
1991–92	Halifax T	28	1
From Guiseley			
1992–93	Hull C	27	1

ABEL, Graham

Born Runcorn 17.9.60. Ht 6 2 Wt 13 00
Defender. From Northwich V and
Runcorn.

Season	Club	App	Goals
1985–86	Chester C	23	2
1986–87		41	1
1987–88		45	2
1988–89		40	3
1989–90		41	7
1990–91		29	4
1991–92	Chester C	44	9
1992–93		33	1

ABLETT, Gary

Born Liverpool 19.11.65. Ht 6 0
Wt 11 04
Defender. From Apprentice. England B,
Under-21.

Season	Club	App	Goals
1983–84	Liverpool	—	—
1984–85		—	—
1984–85	*Derby Co*	6	—
1985–86	Liverpool	—	—
1986–87	*Hull C*	5	—
1986–87	Liverpool	5	1
1987–88		17	—
1988–89		35	—

Season	Club	App	Goals
1989–90		15	—
1990–91		23	—
1991–92		14	—
1991–92	Everton	17	1
1992–93		40	—

ABRAHAM, Gareth

Born Merthyr Tydfil 13.2.69. Ht 6 4
Wt 12 11
Defender. From Trainee.

Season	Club	App	Goals
1987–88	Cardiff C	2	1
1988–89		31	2
1989–90		37	1
1990–91		2	—
1991–92		15	—
1992–93		—	—
1992–93	Hereford U	19	1

ABRAHAMS, Paul

Born Colchester 31.10.73 Ht 5 8
Wt 10 06
Forward. From Trainee.

Season	Club	App	Goals
1991–92	Colchester U	7	—
1992–93		23	6

ACHAMPONG, Kenny

Born London 26.6.66. Ht 5 9 Wt 11 01
Midfield. From Apprentice.

Season	Club	App	Goals
1984–85	Fulham	10	3
1985–86		35	3
1986–87		21	6
1987–88		15	3
1988–89		—	—
1988–89	*West Ham U*	—	—
1989–90	Charlton Ath	10	—
1990–91		—	—
1990–91	Leyton Orient	34	4
1991–92		24	2
1992–93		25	1

ADAMS, Mick

Born Sheffield 8.11.61. Ht 5 8 Wt 11 03
Defender. From Apprentice. England
Youth.

Season	Club	App	Goals
1979–80	Gillingham	4	—

Season	Club	League Appearances/Goals
1980–81	....	13 —
1981–82	....	31 2
1982–83	....	44 3
1983–84	Coventry C	17 1
1984–85	....	31 3
1985–86	....	31 3
1986–87	....	11 2
1986–87	Leeds U	17 1
1987–88	....	40 —
1988–89	....	16 1
1988–89	Southampton	8 —
1989–90	....	15 —
1990–91	....	30 —
1991–92	....	34 3
1992–93	....	38 4

ADAMS, Neil

Born Stoke 23.11.65. Ht 5 7 Wt 10 06
Forward. From Local. England Under-21.

Season	Club	League Appearances/Goals
1985–86	Stoke C	32 4
1986–87	Everton	12 —
1987–88	....	8 —
1988–89	....	— —
1988–89	*Oldham Ath*...............	9 —
1989–90	Oldham Ath................	27 4
1990–91	....	31 6
1991–92	....	26 4
1992–93	....	32 9

ADAMS, Tony

Born London 10.10.66. Ht 6 3 Wt 13 11
Defender. From Apprentice. England
Youth, B, Under-21, 26 full caps.

Season	Club	League Appearances/Goals
1983–84	Arsenal......................	3 —
1984–85	....	16 —
1985–86	....	10 —
1986–87	....	42 6
1987–88	....	39 2
1988–89	....	36 4
1989–90	....	38 5
1990–91	....	30 1
1991–92	....	35 2
1992–93	....	35 —

ADCOCK, Paul

Born Ilminster 2.5.72. Ht 5 8 Wt 10 02
Forward. From Trainee.

Season	Club	League Appearances/Goals
1990–91	Plymouth Arg.............	12 —
1991–92	....	— —
1992–93	....	9 2

ADCOCK, Tony

Born Bethnal Green 27.2.63. Ht 5 11
Wt 11 09
Forward. From Apprentice.

Season	Club	League Appearances/Goals
1980–81	Colchester U...............	1 —
1981–82	....	40 5
1982–83	....	30 17
1983–84	....	43 26
1984–85	....	28 24
1985–86	....	33 15
1986–87	....	35 11
1987–88	Manchester C	15 5
1987–88	Northampton T..........	18 10
1988–89	....	46 17
1989–90	....	8 3
1989–90	Bradford C	28 5
1990–91	....	10 1
1990–91	Northampton T..........	21 3
1991–92	....	14 7
1991–92	Peterborough U..........	24 7
1992–93	....	45 16

ADEBOLA, Dele

Born Liverpool 23.6.75.
Forward. From Trainee.

Season	Club	League Appearances/Goals
1992–93	Crewe Alex	6 —

ADEKOLA, David

Born Nigeria 18.5.68. Ht 6 0 Wt 12 02
Forward.

Season	Club	League Appearances/Goals
1992–93	Bury	16 8

ADKINS, Nigel

Born Birkenhead 11.3.65.   Ht 5 11
Wt 13 04
Goalkeeper. From Apprentice. England
Schools.

1982–83	Tranmere R	10	—
1983–84		4	—
1984–85		38	—
1985–86		34	—
1986–87	Wigan Ath	8	—
1987–88		2	—
1988–89		30	—
1989–90		13	—
1990–91		18	—
1991–92		46	—
1992–93		38	—

AGANA, Tony

Born London 2.10.63.   Ht 6 0   Wt 12 02
Forward. From Weymouth.

1987–88	Watford	15	1
1987–88	Sheffield U	12	2
1988–89		46	24
1989–90		31	10
1990–91		16	2
1991–92		13	4
1991–92	Notts C	13	1
1991–92	*Leeds U*	2	—
1992–93	Notts Co	29	2

AGBOOLA, Reuben

Born London 30.5.62.   Ht 5 10   Wt 11 09
Defender. From Apprentice.

1979–80	Southampton	—	—
1980–81		6	—
1981–82		5	—
1982–83		37	—
1983–84		33	—
1984–85		9	—
1984–85	Sunderland	8	—
1985–86		12	—
1986–87	*Charlton Ath*	1	—
1986–87	Sunderland	11	—
1987–88		38	—
1988–89		29	—

1989–90		36	—
1990–91		5	—
1990–91	*Port Vale*	9	—
1991–92	Sunderland	1	—
1991–92	Swansea C	21	—
1992–93		7	—

AGNEW, Paul

Born Lisburn 15.8.65.   Ht 5 9   Wt 10 07
Defender. From Cliftonville. Northern
Ireland Schools, Youth, Under-23.

1983–84	Grimsby T	1	—
1984–85		12	—
1985–86		16	—
1986–87		29	—
1987–88		38	1
1988–89		34	—
1989–90		24	2
1990–91		7	—
1991–92		24	—
1992–93		23	—

AGNEW, Steve

Born Shipley 9.11.65.   Ht 5 8   Wt 11 10
Midfield. From Apprentice.

1983–84	Barnsley	1	—
1984–85		10	1
1985–86		2	—
1986–87		33	—
1987–88		25	6
1988–89		39	6
1989–90		46	8
1990–91		38	8
1991–92	Blackburn R	2	—
1992–93		—	—
1992–93	*Portsmouth*	5	—
1992–93	Leicester C	9	1

AINSWORTH, Gareth

Born Blackburn 10.5.73.   Ht 5 9
Wt 11 09
Forward. From Blackburn R Trainee.

1991–92	Preston NE	5	—
1992–93	Cambridge U	4	1

1992–93	Preston NE	26	—

AITKEN, Roy

Born Irvine 24.11.58. Ht 6 0 Wt 13 00
Midfield. From Celtic BC. Scotland
Schools, Under-21, 57 full caps.

1975–76	Celtic	12	—
1976–77		33	5
1977–78		33	2
1978–79		36	5
1979–80		35	3
1980–81		33	4
1981–82		33	3
1982–83		33	6
1983–84		31	5
1984–85		33	3
1985–86		36	—
1986–87		42	1
1987–88		43	1
1988–89		32	—
1989–90		18	2
1989–90	Newcastle U	22	1
1990–91		32	—
1991–92	St Mirren	34	1
1992–93	Aberdeen	26	2

AIZLEWOOD, Mark

Born Newport 1.10.59. Ht 6 0 Wt 13 03
Midfield. From Apprentice. Wales Under-
21, 36 full caps.

1975–76	Newport Co	6	—
1976–77		5	—
1977–78		27	1
1977–78	Luton T	—	—
1978–79		39	—
1979–80		10	—
1980–81		23	—
1981–82		26	3
1982–83		—	—
1982–83	Charlton Ath	22	1
1983–84		31	1
1984–85		38	3
1985–86		35	3
1986–87		26	1
1986–87	Leeds U	15	—
1987–88		17	—

1988–89		38	3
1989–90	Bradford C	39	1
1990–91	Bristol C	42	2
1991–92		34	1
1992–93		20	—

ALBISTON, Arthur

Born Edinburgh 14.7.57. Ht 5 7
Wt 11 03
Defender. From Apprentice. Scotland
Schoolboy, Under-21, 14 full caps.

1974–75	Manchester U	2	—
1975–76		3	—
1976–77		17	—
1977–78		28	—
1978–79		33	—
1979–80		25	—
1980–81		42	1
1981–82		42	1
1982–83		38	1
1983–84		40	2
1984–85		39	—
1985–86		37	1
1986–87		22	—
1987–88		11	—
1988–89	WBA	43	2
1989–90	Dundee	10	—
1990–91		—	—
1990–91	Chesterfield	3	1
1991–92	Chester C	44	—
1992–93		24	—

ALDRIDGE, John

Born Liverpool 18.9.58. Ht 5 11
Wt 11 10
Forward. From South Liverpool. Eire 54
caps.

1978–79	Newport Co	—	—
1979–80		38	14
1980–81		27	7
1981–82		36	11
1982–83		41	17
1983–84		28	20
1983–84	Oxford U	8	4
1984–85		42	30
1985–86		39	23

1986–87		25	15
1986–87	Liverpool	10	2
1987–88		36	26
1988–89		35	21
1989–90		2	1
1989–90	Real Sociedad	28	16
1990–91		35	17
1991–92	Tranmere R	43	22
1992–93		30	21

ALDRIDGE, Martin

Born Northampton 6.12.74.
Forward. From Trainee.

| 1991–92 | Northampton T | 5 | — |
| 1992–93 | | 9 | 2 |

ALEXANDER, Graham

Born Coventry 10.10.71. Ht 5 10
Wt 11 08
Defender. From Trainee.

1989–90	Scunthorpe U	—	—
1990–91		1	—
1991–92		36	5
1992–93		41	5

ALEXANDER, Ian

Born Glasgow 26.1.63. Ht 5 8 Wt 10 07
Defender. From Leicester J.

1981–82	Rotherham U	8	—
1982–83		3	—
1983–84	Motherwell	16	1
1984–85		8	1
1984–85	Morton	7	1
From Pezoporikos			
1986–87	Bristol R	22	1
1987–88		45	1
1988–89		42	—
1989–90		43	1
1990–91		39	1
1991–92		41	1
1992–93		41	1

ALEXANDER, Keith

Born Nottingham 14.11.58. Ht 6 4
Wt 13 06
Forward. From Barnet.

1988–89	Grimsby T	44	14
1989–90		38	12
1990–91		1	—
1990–91	Stockport Co	11	—
1990–91	Lincoln C	23	3
1991–92		15	1
1992–93		7	—

ALLAN, Derek

Born Irving 24.12.74. Ht 6 0 Wt 10 13
Defender. From Ayr United BC.

| 1992–93 | Ayr U | 5 | — |
| 1992–93 | Southampton | 1 | — |

ALLARDYCE, Craig

Born Bolton 9.6.75 Ht 6 2 Wt 13 06
Defender. From Trainee.

| 1992–93 | Preston NE | 1 | — |

ALLARDYCE, Sam

Born Dudley 19.10.54 Ht 6 2 Wt 14 00
Defender. From Apprentice.

1971–72	Bolton W	—	—
1972–73			
1973–74		7	—
1974–75		18	3
1975–76		40	5
1976–77		41	6
1977–78		41	4
1978–79		20	1
1979–80		17	2
1980–81	Sunderland	25	2
1981–82		—	—
1981–82	Millwall	36	1
1982–83		27	1
1983–84	Coventry C	28	1
1984–85	Huddersfield T	37	—
1985–86	Bolton W	14	—
1986–87	Preston NE	37	2

Season	Club	App	Goals
1987–88		39	—
1988–89		14	—
1989–90	WBA	1	—
From Ireland			
1992–93	Preston NE	3	—

ALLEN, Bradley

Born Harold Wood 13.9.71. Ht 5 7
Wt 10 00
Forward. From Schoolboys. England
Youth, Under-21.

Season	Club	App	Goals
1988–89	QPR	1	—
1989–90		—	—
1990–91		10	2
1991–92		11	5
1992–93		25	10

ALLEN, Chris

Born Oxford 18.11.72. Ht 5 11 Wt 12 02
Forward. From Trainee.

Season	Club	App	Goals
1990–91	Oxford U	—	—
1991–92		14	1
1992–93		31	3

ALLEN, Clive

Born London 20.5.61. Ht 5 10 Wt 12 03
Forward. From Apprentice. England
Schools, Youth, Under-21, 3 full caps.
Football League.

Season	Club	App	Goals
1978–79	QPR	10	4
1979–80		39	28
1980–81	Arsenal	—	—
1980–81	Crystal Palace	25	9
1981–82	QPR	37	13
1982–83		25	13
1983–84		25	14
1984–85	Tottenham H	13	7
1985–86		19	9
1986–87		39	33
1987–88		34	11
From Bordeaux			
1989–90	Manchester C	30	10
1990–91		20	4
1991–92		3	2

Season	Club	App	Goals
1991–92	Chelsea	16	7
1991–92	West Ham U	4	1
1992–93		27	14

ALLEN, Malcolm

Born Dioniolen 21.3.67. Ht 5 8 Wt 11 10
Forward. From Apprentice. Wales Youth,
B, 13 full caps.

Season	Club	App	Goals
1984–85	Watford	—	—
1985–86		13	2
1986–87		4	—
1987–88		22	3
1987–88	*Aston Villa*	4	—
1988–89	Norwich C	23	5
1989–90		12	3
1989–90	Millwall	8	2
1990–91		21	7
1991–92		11	5
1992–93		41	10

ALLEN, Martin

Born Reading 14.8.65. Ht 5 10 Wt 11 00
Midfield. From school. England Youth,
Under-21 Football League.

Season	Club	App	Goals
1983–84	QPR	—	—
1984–85		5	—
1985–86		31	3
1986–87		32	5
1987–88		38	4
1988–89		28	4
1989–90		2	—
1989–90	West Ham U	39	9
1990–91		40	3
1991–92		19	—
1992–93		34	4

ALLEN, Paul

Born Aveley 28.8.62. Ht 5 7 Wt 10 10
Midfield. From Apprentice. England
Youth, Under-21.

Season	Club	App	Goals
1979–80	West Ham U	31	2
1980–81		3	1
1981–82		28	—
1982–83		33	—

Season	Club	App	Goals
1983–84		19	—
1984–85		38	3
1985–86	Tottenham H	33	1
1986–87		37	3
1987–88		39	3
1988–89		37	1
1989–90		32	6
1990–91		36	3
1991–92		39	3
1992–93		38	3

ALLISON, Neil

Born Hull 20.10.73. Ht 6 2 Wt 11 10
Defender. From Trainee.

Season	Club	App	Goals
1990–91	Hull C	1	—
1991–92		7	—
1992–93		11	—

ALLISON, Wayne

Born Huddersfield 16.10.68. Ht 6 1
Wt 12 06
Forward.

Season	Club	App	Goals
1986–87	Halifax T	8	4
1987–88		35	4
1988–89		41	15
1989–90	Watford	7	—
1990–91	Bristol C	37	6
1991–92		43	10
1992–93		39	4

ALLON, Joe

Born Gateshead 12.11.66. Ht 5 10
Wt 11 12
Forward. From Trainee. England Youth.

Season	Club	App	Goals
1984–85	Newcastle U	1	—
1985–86		3	1
1986–87		5	1
1987–88	Swansea C	32	11
1988–89		2	—
1988–89	Hartlepool U	21	4
1989–90		45	18
1990–91		46	28
1991–92	Chelsea	11	2
1991–92	*Port Vale*	6	—

Season	Club	App	Goals
1992–93	Chelsea	3	—
1992–93	Brentford	24	6

ALSFORD, Julian

Born Poole 24.12.72 Ht 6 2 Wt 12 11
Defender.

Season	Club	App	Goals
1991–92	Watford	—	—
1992–93		5	—

AMPADU, Kwame

Born Bradford 20.12.70. Ht 5 10
Wt 10 13
Forward. From Trainee. Eire Youth,
Under-21.

Season	Club	App	Goals
1988–89	Arsenal	—	—
1989–90		2	—
1990–91		—	—
1990–91	*Plymouth Arg*	6	1
1990–91	*WBA*	7	1
1991–92	WBA	21	3
1992–93		10	—

ANDERS, Jason

Born Rochdale 13.3.74. Ht 5 10
Wt 10 06
Forward. From Trainee.

Season	Club	App	Goals
1990–91	Rochdale	2	—
1991–92		—	—
1992–93		15	1

ANDERSON, Colin

Born Newcastle 26.4.62. Ht 5 8
Wt 10 08
Midfield. From Apprentice.

Season	Club	App	Goals
1979–80	Burnley	—	—
1980–81		2	—
1981–82		4	—
1982–83	Torquay U	42	5
1983–84		39	4
1984–85		28	2
1984–85	*QPR*	—	—
1984–85	WBA	—	—

Season	Club	App	Goals
1985–86		11	—
1986–87		28	1
1987–88		23	1
1988–89		42	6
1989–90		13	—
1990–91		23	2
1991–92	Walsall	26	2
1992–93	Hereford U	35	—

ANDERSON, Lee

Born Bury 4.10.73. Ht 5 9 Wt 10 07
Defender. From Trainee.

Season	Club	App	Goals
1991–92	Bury	5	—
1992–93		13	—

ANDERSON, Viv

Born Nottingham 29.8.56. Ht 6 0
Wt 11 08
Defender. From Apprentice. England
Under-21 B, 30 full caps, Football League.

Season	Club	App	Goals
1974–75	Nottingham F	16	—
1975–76		21	—
1976–77		38	1
1977–78		37	3
1978–79		40	1
1979–80		41	3
1980–81		31	—
1981–82		39	—
1982–83		25	1
1983–84		40	6
1984–85	Arsenal	41	3
1985–86		39	2
1986–87		40	4
1987–88	Manchester U	31	2
1988–89		6	—
1989–90		16	—
1990–91		1	—
1990–91	Sheffield W	22	2
1991–92		22	3
1992–93		26	3

ANDERSSON, Patrik

Born Borgeby 18.8.71
Defender. From Malmo. Sweden full caps.

Season	Club	App	Goals
1992–93	Blackburn R	11	—

ANDERTON, Darren

Born Southampton 3.3.72. Ht 6 1
Wt 11 12 00
Forward. From Trainee. England Youth,
Under-21 .

Season	Club	App	Goals
1989–90	Portsmouth	—	—
1990–91		20	—
1991–92		42	7
1992–93	Tottenham H	34	6

ANDREWS, Ian

Born Nottingham 1.12.64. Ht 6 2
Wt 12 13
Goalkeeper. From Apprentice. England
Youth.

Season	Club	App	Goals
1982–83	Leicester C	—	—
1983–84		2	—
1983–84	*Swindon T*	1	—
1984–85	Leicester C	31	—
1985–86		39	—
1986–87		42	—
1987–88		12	—
1988–89	Celtic	5	—
1988–89	*Leeds U*	1	—
1989–90	Celtic	—	—
1989–90	Southampton	3	—
1990–91		1	—
1991–92		1	—
1992–93		—	—

ANGELL, Brett

Born Marlborough 20.8.68. Ht 6 2
Wt 13 12
Forward. From Portsmouth and
Cheltenham T.

Season	Club	App	Goals
1987–88	Derby Co	—	—
1988–89	Stockport Co	26	5
1989–90		44	23
1990–91	Southend U	42	15
1991–92		43	21
1992–93		13	5

ANGUS, Ian

Born Glasgow 19.11.61. Ht 5 10
Wt 10 03
Midfield. From Eastercraigs.

1979–80	Aberdeen	—	—
1980–81		19	1
1981–82		1	1
1982–83		5	3
1983–84		12	—
1984–85		28	2
1985–86		17	2
1986–87		2	1
1986–87	Dundee	29	4
1987–88		40	6
1988–89		15	—
1989–90		4	—
1989–90	*Plymouth Arg*	—	—
1990–91	Motherwell	20	2
1991–92		25	3
1992–93		31	3

ANGUS, Terry

Born Coventry 14.1.66. Ht 5 11
Wt 12 00
Defender. From VS Rugby.

1990–91	Northampton T	42	2
1991–92		37	2
1992–93		37	2

ANNAN, Richard

Born Leeds 4.12.68   Ht 5 8   Wt 11 00
Defender. From Guiseley.

1991–92	Crewe Alex	—	—
1992–93		9	—

ANSAH, Andy

Born Lewisham 19.3.69. Ht 5 10
Wt 11 01
Forward. From Crystal Palace.

1988–89	Brentford	7	2
1989–90		1	—
1989–90	Southend U	7	1
1990–91		40	9

1991–92		40	9
1992–93		30	7

ANTHROBUS, Steve

Born Lewisham 10.11.68. Ht 6 2
Wt 12 13
Forward.

1986–87	Millwall	—	—
1987–88		3	—
1988–89		3	—
1989–90		15	4
1989–90	*Southend U*	—	—
1989–90	Wimbledon	10	—
1990–91		3	—
1991–92		10	—
1992–93		5	—

APPLEBY, Matthew

Born Middlesbrough 16.4.72. Ht 5 10
Wt 11 02
Defender. From Trainee.

1989–90	Newcastle U	—	—
1990–91		1	—
1991–92		18	—
1992–93		—	—

APPLETON, Steve

Born Liverpool 27.7.73. Ht 5 11
Wt 10 09
Defender. From Trainee.

1990–91	Wigan Ath	10	—
1991–92		9	—
1992–93		29	1

ARCHDEACON, Owen

Born Greenock 4.3.66. Ht 5 9   Wt 10 08
Forward. From Gourock United. Scotland
Youth, Under-21.

1982–83	Celtic	—	—
1983–84		1	—
1984–85		3	1
1985–86		23	3

1986–87		29	2
1987–88		10	1
1988–89		10	—
1989–90	Barnsley	21	3
1990–91		45	2
1991–92		40	6
1992–93		38	6

ARCHER, Lee

Born Bristol 6.11.72. Ht 5 6 Wt 9 04
Midfield. From Trainee.

1991–92	Bristol R	5	—
1992–93		2	1

ARCHIBALD, Steve

Born Glasgow 27.9.56. Ht 5 10 Wt 11 02
Forward. From Fernhill Ath. Scotland
Under-21, 27 full caps.

1974–75	Clyde	4	—
1975–76		16	2
1976–77		31	3
1977–78		14	2
1977–78	Aberdeen	10	4
1978–79		32	13
1979–80		34	12
1980–81	Tottenham H	41	20
1981–82		27	6
1982–83		31	11
1983–84		32	21
From Barcelona			
1987–88	Blackburn R	20	6
1988–89	Hibernian	31	13
1989–90		13	2
1990–91	St Mirren	16	2
1991–92	Reading	1	—
1992–93	Fulham	2	—

ARDLEY, Neil

Born Epsom 1.9.72. Ht 5 9 Wt 12 02
Forward. From Trainee. England
Under-21.

1990–91	Wimbledon	1	—
1991–92		8	—
1992–93		26	4

ARKINS, Vinny

Born Dublin 18.9.70. Ht 6 1 Wt 11 07
Forward. From Home Farm. Eire Youth,
Under-21.

1987–88	Dundee Utd	—	—
1988–89		—	—
From Shamrock R			
1991–92	St Johnstone	21	5
1992–93		26	6

ARMSTRONG, Chris

Born Newcastle 19.6.71. Ht 6 0
Wt 11 00
Forward.

1988–89	Wrexham	—	—
1989–90		22	3
1990–91		38	10
1991–92	Millwall	25	4
1992–93		3	1
1992–93	Crystal Palace	35	15

ARMSTRONG, Gordon

Born Newcastle 15.7.67. Ht 6 0
Wt 11 10
Midfield. From Apprentice.

1984–85	Sunderland	4	—
1985–86		14	2
1986–87		41	5
1987–88		37	5
1988–89		45	8
1989–90		46	8
1990–91		35	6
1991–92		40	10
1992–93		45	3

ARMSTRONG, Lachlan

Born Melbourne 22.4.73. Ht 5 9 Wt 10 8
Forward. From Hamilton Th.

1990–91	Dundee	—	—
1991–92		—	—
1992–93		1	—

ARNOLD, Ian

Born Durham City 4.7.72. Ht 5 9
Wt 11 00
Forward. From Trainee.

1989–90	Middlesbrough	—	—
1990–91		2	—
1991–92		1	—
1992–93	Carlisle U	29	6

ARNOTT, Andy

Born Chatham 18.10.73. Ht 5 11
Wt 12 07
Forward. From Trainee.

1990–91	Gillingham	—	—
1991–92		19	2
1992–93		15	6
1992–93	*Manchester U*	—	—

ARNOTT, Doug

Born Lanark 5.8.64. Ht 5 7 Wt 10 07
Forward. From Pollok Juniors.

1986–87	Motherwell	1	—
1987–88		2	—
1988–89		14	1
1989–90		30	5
1990–91		29	14
1991–92		26	8
1992–93		33	6

ARTHUR, Gordon

Born Kirkcaldy 30.5.58 Ht 5 11 Wt 12 0
Goalkeeper. From Dundonald Bluebell.

1977–78	Stirling Albion	1	—
1978–79		2	—
1979–80		39	—
1980–81		39	—
1981–82		34	—
1982–83		35	—
1983–84		34	—
1984–85	Dumbarton	35	—
1985–86		38	—
1986–87		31	—
1987–88		40	—

1988–89	Raith R	39	—
1989–90		39	—
1990–91		34	—
1991–92		44	—
1992–93		17	—

ASHBY, Barry

Born London 21.11.70. Ht 6 2 Wt 12 03
Defender. From Trainee.

1988–89	Watford	—	—
1989–90		18	1
1990–91		23	—
1991–92		21	—
1992–93		35	—

ASHCROFT, Lee

Born Preston 7.9.72. Ht 5 10 Wt 11 00
Forward. From Trainee. England
Under-21.

1990–91	Preston NE	14	1
1991–92		38	5
1992–93		39	7

ASHDJIAN, John

Born Hackney 13.9.72.
Forward. From Northampton T Trainee.

1991–92	Scarborough	32	9
1992–93		28	5

ASHENDEN, Scott

Born Basildon 3.2.74 Ht 6 0 Wt 11 00
Midfield. From Trainee.

1992–93	Southend U	5	—

ASHLEY, Kevin

Born Birmingham 31.12.68. Ht 5 7
Wt 10 04
Defender. From Apprentice.

1986–87	Birmingham C	7	—
1987–88		1	—

Season	Club	Apps	Goals
1988–89		15	—
1989–90		31	1
1990–91		3	—
1990–91	Wolverhampton W	16	—
1991–92		44	1
1992–93		28	—

ASHURST, Jack

Born Coatbridge 12.10.54.   Ht 6 0
Wt 12 04
Defender. From Apprentice.

Season	Club	Apps	Goals
1971–72	Sunderland	—	—
1972–73		11	—
1973–74		19	1
1974–75		6	—
1975–76		21	—
1976–77		31	—
1977–78		38	2
1978–79		11	1
1979–80		3	—
1979–80	Blackpool	25	—
1980–81		28	3
1981–82	Carlisle U	46	1
1982–83		30	—
1983–84		41	1
1984–85		42	—
1985–86		35	—
1986–87	Leeds U	41	1
1987–88		41	—
1988–89		7	—
1988–89	Doncaster R	30	1
1989–90		43	—
From Bridlington			
1990–91	Doncaster R	29	1
1991–92		37	—
1992–93	Rochdale	1	—

ASPIN, Neil

Born Gateshead 12.4.65.   Ht 6 0   Wt 12 3
Defender. From Apprentice.

Season	Club	Apps	Goals
1981–82	Leeds U	1	—
1982–83		15	—
1983–84		21	1
1984–85		32	1
1985–86		38	2
1986–87		41	1

Season	Club	Apps	Goals
1987–88		26	—
1988–89		33	—
1989–90	Port Vale	42	—
1990–91		41	1
1991–92		42	—
1992–93		35	—

ASPINALL, Warren

Born Wigan 13.9.67.   Ht 5 8   Wt 10 6
Forward. From Apprentice. England
Youth.

Season	Club	Apps	Goals
1984–85	Wigan Ath	10	1
1985–86		—	—
1985–86	Everton	1	—
1985–86	*Wigan Ath*	41	21
1986–87	Everton	6	—
1986–87	Aston Villa	12	3
1987–88		32	11
1988–89	Portsmouth	40	11
1989–90		3	—
1990–91		33	4
1991–92		24	4
1992–93		27	2

ATHERTON, Peter

Born Orrell 6.4.70.   Ht 5 11   Wt 12 03
Defender. From Trainee. England
Under-21.

Season	Club	Apps	Goals
1987–88	Wigan Ath	16	—
1988–89		40	1
1989–90		46	—
1990–91		46	—
1991–92		1	—
1991–92	Coventry C	35	—
1992–93		39	—

ATKIN, Paul

Born Nottingham 3.9.69.   Ht 6 0
Wt 12 11
Defender. From Trainee. England Youth.

Season	Club	Apps	Goals
1987–88	Notts Co	—	—
1988–89		—	—
1988–89	Bury	1	—
1989–90		9	1

1990–91	....	11	—
1991–92	York C........................	33	1
1992–93	....	31	2

ATKINS, Ian

Born Birmingham 16.1.57.   Ht 6 0
Wt 12 03
Midfield. From Apprentice.

1974–75	Shrewsbury T..............	—	—
1975–76	....	32	4
1976–77	....	43	7
1977–78	....	41	10
1978–79	....	44	11
1979–80	....	39	3
1980–81	....	39	6
1981–82	....	40	17
1982–83	Sunderland..................	37	4
1983–84	....	40	2
1984–85	....	—	—
1984–85	Everton	6	1
1985–86	....	1	—
1985–86	Ipswich T....................	21	2
1986–87	....	40	1
1987–88	....	16	1
1987–88	Birmingham C.............	8	1
1988–89	....	40	3
1989–90	....	45	2
1990–91	Colchester U...............	41	7
1991–92	Birmingham C.............	8	—
1992–93	....	—	—
1992–93	Cambridge U..............	2	—

ATKINS, Mark

Born Doncaster 14.8.68.   Ht 6 1
Wt 12 00
Defender.

1986–87	Scunthorpe U	26	—
1987–88	....	22	2
1988–89	Blackburn R	46	6
1989–90	....	41	7
1990–91	....	42	4
1991–92	....	44	6
1992–93	....	31	5

ATKINSON, Brian

Born Darlington 19.1.71.   Ht 5 10
Wt 12 00
Midfield. From Trainee. England
Under-21.

1988–89	Sunderland..................	3	—
1989–90	....	13	—
1990–91	....	6	—
1991–92	....	30	2
1992–93	....	36	2

ATKINSON, Dalian

Born Shrewsbury 21.3.68.   Ht 6 0
Wt 13 10
Forward. England B.

1985–86	Ipswich T....................	1	—
1986–87	....	8	—
1987–88	....	17	8
1988–89	....	34	10
1989–90	Sheffield W..................	38	10
To Real Sociedad			
1991–92	Aston Villa..................	14	1
1992–93	....	28	11

ATKINSON, Graeme

Born Hull 11.11.71.   Ht 5 10   Wt 10 02
Forward. From Trainee.

1989–90	Hull C........................	13	1
1990–91	....	16	—
1991–92	....	25	8
1992–93	....	46	6

ATTEVELD, Ray

Born Amsterdam 8.9.66.   Ht 5 10
Wt 12 00
Midfield. From Haarlem.

1989–90	Everton	18	1
1990–91	....	20	—
1991–92	....	13	—
1991–92	*West Ham U*...............	1	—
1991–92	Bristol C	7	1
1992–93	....	7	—

AUSTIN, Dean

Born Hemel Hempstead 26.4.70. Ht 6 0
Wt 12 04
Defender. From St. Albans C.

1989–90	Southend U	7	—
1990–91		44	—
1991–92		45	2
1992–93	Tottenham H	34	—

AWFORD, Andy

Born Worcester 14.7.72.   Ht 5 9
Wt 11 09
Defender. From Worcester C, Portsmouth
Trainee. England Youth, Under-21.
Football League.

1988–89	Portsmouth	4	—
1989–90		—	—
1990–91		14	—
1991–92		45	—
1992–93		44	—

AYLOTT, Trevor

Born London 26.11.57.   Ht 6 1   Wt 14 00
Forward. From Apprentice.

1976–77	Chelsea	—	—
1976–77	*QPR*	—	—
1977–78	Chelsea	11	2
1978–79		15	—
1979–80		3	—
1979–80	Barnsley	18	4
1980–81		37	11
1981–82		41	11
1982–83	Millwall	32	5
1982–83	Luton T	12	2
1983–84		20	8
1984–85	Crystal Palace	35	8
1985–86		18	4
1985–86	*Barnsley*	9	—
1986–87	Bournemouth	37	10
1987–88		43	9
1988–89		40	6
1989–90		18	2
1990–91		9	—
1990–91	Birmingham C	25	—
1991–92		2	—

1991–92	Oxford U	37	6
1992–93	Gillingham	10	2

BAAH, Peter

Born Littleborough 1.5.73.   Ht 5 9
Wt 10 04
Forward. From Trainee.

Season	Club	Apps	Goals
1991–92	Blackburn R	1	—
1992–93	Fulham	16	—

BABB, Phil

Born Lambeth 30.11.70.   Ht 6 0
Wt 12 03
Midfield.

Season	Club	Apps	Goals
1988–89	Millwall	—	—
1989–90		—	—
1990–91	Bradford C	34	10
1991–92		46	4
1992–93	Coventry C	34	—

BACON, Paul

Born London 20.12.70.   Ht 5 9   Wt 10 04
Midfield. From Trainee.

Season	Club	Apps	Goals
1988–89	Charlton Ath	—	—
1989–90		—	—
1990–91		1	—
1991–92		14	—
1992–93		18	—

BADDELEY, Lee

Born Cardiff 12.7.74.   Ht 6 1   Wt 12 10
Defender. From Trainee.

Season	Club	Apps	Goals
1990–91	Cardiff C	2	—
1991–92		18	—
1992–93		8	—

BAILEY, Danny

Born Leyton 21.5.64.   Ht 5 7   Wt 12 07
Midfield. From Apprentice.

Season	Club	Apps	Goals
1980–81	Bournemouth	2	—
From Local			
1983–84	Torquay U	1	—
From Wealdstone			
1989–90	Exeter C	46	1

Season	Club	Apps	Goals
1990–91		18	1
1990–91	Reading	26	2
1991–92		24	—
1992–93		—	—
1992–93	*Fulham*	3	—
1992–93	Exeter C	27	—

BAILEY, Dennis

Born Lambeth 13.11.65.   Ht 5 10
Wt 11 06
Forward. From Fulham, Farnborough T.

Season	Club	Apps	Goals
1987–88	Crystal Palace	5	1
1988–89		—	—
1988–89	*Bristol R*	17	9
1989–90	Birmingham C	43	18
1990–91		32	5
1990–91	*Bristol R*	6	1
1991–92	QPR	24	9
1992–93		15	1

BAILEY, Neil

Born Wigan 26.9.58
Defender. From Apprentice.

Season	Club	Apps	Goals
1976–77	Burnley	—	—
1977–78		—	—
1978–79	Newport Co	21	1
1979–80		29	1
1980–81		21	1
1981–82		18	—
1982–83		40	4
1983–84		5	—
1983–84	Wigan Ath	23	1
1984–85		12	—
1985–86		6	1
1986–87	Stockport Co	17	—
1986–87	*Newport Co*	9	1
1987–88	Stockport Co	34	—
1988–89		—	—
Retired			
1992–93	Blackpool	8	—

BAIN, Kevin

Born Kirkcaldy 19.9.72   Ht 6 0   Wt 11 9
Defender. From Abbey Star. Scotland U-16, U-21.

Season	Club	Apps	Goals
1989–90	Dundee	1	—

Season	Club	Apps	Goals
1990–91		—	—
1991–92		—	—
1992–93		24	—

BAIRD, Ian

Born Rotherham 1.4.64.   Ht 6 0
Wt 12 10
Forward. From Apprentice. England
Schools.

Season	Club	Apps	Goals
1981–82	Southampton	—	—
1982–83		11	2
1983–84		6	1
1983–84	*Cardiff C*	12	6
1984–85	Southampton	5	2
1984–85	*Newcastle U*	5	1
1984–85	Leeds U	10	6
1985–86		35	12
1986–87		40	15
1987–88	Portsmouth	20	1
1987–88	Leeds U	10	3
1988–89		43	10
1989–90		24	4
1989–90	Middlesbrough	19	5
1990–91		44	14
1991–92	Hearts	30	6
1992–93		34	9

BAKER, Clive

Born North Walsham 14.3.59   Ht 5 9
Wt 11 00
Goalkeeper. From Amateur.

Season	Club	Apps	Goals
1977–78	Norwich C	2	—
1978–79		2	—
1979–80		—	—
1980–81		—	—
1981–82		—	—
1982–83		—	—
1983–84		—	—
1984–85	Barnsley	37	—
1985–86		42	—
1986–87		39	—
1987–88		44	—
1988–89		46	—
1989–90		37	—
1990–91		46	—
1991–92	Coventry C	—	—

Season	Club	Apps	Goals
1992–93	Ipswich T	31	—

BAKER, Paul

Born Newcastle 5.1.63.   Ht 6 1   Wt 13 06
Midfield. From Bishop Auckland.

Season	Club	Apps	Goals
1984–85	Southampton	—	—
1985–86	Carlisle U	35	2
1986–87		36	9
1987–88	Hartlepool U	39	19
1988–89		40	7
1989–90		43	16
1990–91		46	12
1991–92		29	13
1992–93	Motherwell	9	1
1992–93	Gillingham	21	6

BALFOUR, Evan

Born Edinburgh 9.9.65.   Ht 5 11   Wt 12 6
Midfield. From Whitburn J.

Season	Club	Apps	Goals
1989–90	Airdrieonians	36	5
1990–91		33	6
1991–92		41	2
1992–93		27	1

BALL, Kevin

Born Hastings 12.11.64.   Ht 5 9   Wt 12 00
Defender. From Apprentice.

Season	Club	Apps	Goals
1983–84	Portsmouth	1	—
1984–85		—	—
1985–86		9	—
1986–87		16	—
1987–88		29	1
1988–89		14	1
1989–90		36	2
1990–91	Sunderland	33	3
1991–92		33	1
1992–93		43	3

BALL, Steve

Born Colchester 2.9.69.   Ht 6 0   Wt 12 01
Midfield. From Trainee.

Season	Club	Apps	Goals
1987–88	Arsenal	—	—
1988–89		—	—

Season	Club	App	Goals
1989–90	Colchester U	4	—
1990–91	Norwich C	—	—
1991–92		2	—
1992–93	Colchester U	24	4

BALL, Steve

Born Leeds 22.11.73   Ht 5 7   Wt 11 00
Defender. From Leeds U trainee.

Season	Club	App	Goals
1992–93	Darlington	22	2

BALMER, Stuart

Born Falkirk 20.6.69.   Ht 6 1   Wt 12 04
Defender. From Celtic BC.

Season	Club	App	Goals
1987–88	Celtic	—	—
1988–89		—	—
1989–90		—	—
1990–91	Charlton Ath	24	—
1991–92		18	—
1992–93		45	2

BALTACHA, Sergei

Born Ukraine 17.2.58.   Ht 6 0   Wt 12 00
Defender. From Dynamo Kiev. USSR full caps.

Season	Club	App	Goals
1988–89	Ipswich T	20	1
1989–90		8	—
1990–91	St Johnstone	34	—
1991–92		31	1
1992–93		25	—

BAMBER, Dave

Born St. Helens 1.2.59.   Ht 6 3   Wt 13 10
Forward. From Manchester Univ.

Season	Club	App	Goals
1979–80	Blackpool	7	1
1980–81		15	3
1981–82		38	15
1982–83		26	10
1983–84	Coventry C	19	3
1983–84	Walsall	10	3
1984–85		10	4
1984–85	Portsmouth	4	1
1985–86		—	—

Season	Club	App	Goals
1985–86	Swindon T	23	9
1986–87		42	9
1987–88		41	13
1988–89	Watford	18	3
1988–89	Stoke C	23	6
1989–90		20	2
1989–90	Hull C	19	3
1990–91		9	2
1990–91	Blackpool	23	17
1991–92		42	26
1992–93		24	13

BANGER, Nicky

Born Southampton 25.2.71.   Ht 5 9
Wt 10 11
Forward. From Trainee.

Season	Club	App	Goals
1988–89	Southampton	—	—
1989–90		—	—
1990–91		6	—
1991–92		4	—
1992–93		27	6

BANKS, Ian

Born Mexborough 9.1.61.   Ht 5 10
Wt 13 07
Midfield. From Apprentice.

Season	Club	App	Goals
1978–79	Barnsley	2	—
1979–80		38	3
1980–81		45	14
1981–82		42	15
1982–83		37	5
1983–84	Leicester C	26	3
1984–85		33	9
1985–86		31	2
1986–87		3	—
1986–87	Huddersfield T	37	8
1987–88		41	9
1988–89	Bradford C	30	3
1988–89	WBA	4	—
1989–90	Barnsley	37	3
1990–91		33	2
1991–92		26	2
1992–93	Rotherham U	45	5

BANNISTER, Gary

Born Warrington 22.7.60.   Ht 5 10
Wt 11 08
Forward. From Apprentice. England
Under-21.

1978–79	Coventry C	4	1
1979–80		7	—
1980–81		11	2
1981–82	Sheffield W	42	21
1982–83		39	20
1983–84		37	14
1984–85	QPR	42	17
1985–86		36	16
1986–87		34	15
1987–88		24	8
1987–88	Coventry C	8	1
1988–89		24	8
1989–90		11	2
1989–90	WBA	13	2
1990–91		44	13
1991–92		15	3
1991–92	*Oxford U*	10	2
1992–93	Nottingham F	31	8

BANNON, Eamonn

Born Edinburgh 18.4.58.   Ht 5 9
Wt 11 11
Midfield. From Links BC. Scotland
Schools, Under-21, 9 full caps.

1976–77	Hearts	13	1
1977–78		39	12
1978–79		19	5
1978–79	Chelsea	19	1
1979–80		6	—
1979–80	Dundee U	24	4
1980–81		34	8
1981–82		36	12
1982–83		32	10
1983–84		33	7
1984–85		35	10
1985–86		31	11
1986–87		39	9
1987–88		26	1
1988–89	Hearts	30	2
1989–90		33	2
1990–91		19	2

1991–92		13	2
1992–93		19	1

BAPTIE, Crawford

Born Glasgow 24.2.59.   Ht 6 1   Wt 11 7
Midfield. From Baillieston.

1984–85	Falkirk	26	4
1985–86		19	2
1985–86	Motherwell	16	3
1986–87		17	—
1986–87	Falkirk	8	—
1987–88		35	9
1988–89		28	2
1989–90		34	8
1990–91		26	3
1991–92		38	7
1992–93		9	2

BARACLOUGH, Ian

Born Leicester 4.12.70.   Ht 6 1   Wt 12 00
Midfield. From Trainee.

1988–89	Leicester C	—	—
1989–90		—	—
1989–90	*Wigan Ath*	9	2
1990–91	Leicester C	—	—
1990–91	*Grimsby T*	4	—
1991–92	Grimsby T	—	—
1992–93		1	—
1992–93	Lincoln C	36	5

BARBER, Fred

Born Ferryhill 26.8.63.   Ht 5 10   Wt 12 00
Goalkeeper. From Apprentice.

1981–82	Darlington	—	—
1982–83		12	—
1983–84		46	—
1984–85		45	—
1985–86		32	—
1985–86	Everton	—	—
1986–87		—	—
1986–87	Walsall	36	—
1987–88		46	—
1988–89		44	—
1989–90		25	—

Season	Club	Apps	Goals
1989–90	Peterborough U	6	—
1990–91	Walsall	2	—
1990–91	Chester	8	—
1990–91	Blackpool	2	—
1991–92	Peterborough U	39	—
1992–93		—	—
1992–93	Colchester U	10	—
1992–93	Chesterfield	—	—

BARBER, Philip

Born Tring 10.6.65. Ht 5 11 Wt 12 12
Forward. From Aylesbury.

Season	Club	Apps	Goals
1983–84	Crystal Palace	9	2
1984–85		23	4
1985–86		39	9
1986–87		31	5
1987–88		37	7
1988–89		46	6
1989–90		30	1
1990–91		19	1
1991–92	Millwall	29	4
1992–93		46	8

BARDSLEY, David

Born Manchester 11.9.64. Ht 5 10
Wt 11 00
Defender. From Apprentice. England
Youth, 2 full caps.

Season	Club	Apps	Goals
1981–82	Blackpool	1	—
1982–83		28	—
1983–84		16	—
1983–84	Watford	25	—
1984–85		17	—
1985–86		13	2
1986–87		41	5
1987–88		4	—
1987–88	Oxford U	34	1
1988–89		37	6
1989–90		3	—
1989–90	QPR	31	1
1990–91		38	—
1991–92		41	—
1992–93		40	3

BARHAM, Mark

Born Folkestone 12.7.62. Ht 5 7
Wt 11 00
Midfield. From Apprentice. England
Youth, 2 full caps.

Season	Club	Apps	Goals
1979–80	Norwich C	4	—
1980–81		35	1
1981–82		27	4
1982–83		38	4
1983–84		11	2
1984–85		14	1
1985–86		35	9
1986–87		13	2
1987–88	Huddersfield T	26	1
1988–89		1	—
1988–89	Middlesbrough	4	—
1989–90	WBA	4	—
1989–90	Brighton	17	2
1990–91		32	4
1991–92		24	2
1992–93	Shrewsbury T	8	1

BARKER, Simon

Born Farnworth 4.11.64. Ht 5 9
Wt 11 00
Midfield. From Apprentice. England
Under-21.

Season	Club	Apps	Goals
1982–83	Blackburn R	—	—
1983–84		28	3
1984–85		38	2
1985–86		41	10
1986–87		42	11
1987–88		33	9
1988–89	QPR	25	1
1989–90		28	3
1990–91		35	1
1991–92		34	6
1992–93		25	1

BARKUS, Lea

Born Reading 7.12.74. Ht 5 6 Wt 9 13
Forward. From Trainee.

Season	Club	Apps	Goals
1991–92	Reading	6	1
1992–93		9	—

BARLOW, Andy

Born Oldham 24.11.65. Ht 5 9 Wt 11 01
Defender.

Season	Club	App	Goals
1984–85	Oldham Ath	33	—
1985–86		26	—
1986–87		29	2
1987–88		26	—
1988–89		15	—
1989–90		44	1
1990–91		46	—
1991–92		28	2
1992–93		6	—

BARLOW, Martin

Born Barnstable 25.6.71. Ht 5 7
Wt 10 03
Midfield. From Trainee.

Season	Club	App	Goals
1988–89	Plymouth Arg	1	—
1989–90		1	—
1990–91		30	1
1991–92		28	3
1992–93		24	1

BARLOW, Stuart

Born Liverpool 16.7.68. Ht 5 10
Wt 11 01
Forward.

Season	Club	App	Goals
1990–91	Everton	2	—
1991–92		7	—
1991–92	*Rotherham U*	—	—
1992–93	Everton	26	5

BARMBY, Nick

Born Hull 11.2.74 Ht 5 6 Wt 11 04
Forward. From Trainee. England Youth.

Season	Club	App	Goals
1991–92	Tottenham H	—	—
1992–93		22	6

BARNARD, Darren

Born Rinteln 30.11.71. Ht 5 9 Wt 11 00
Defender. From Wokingham.

Season	Club	App	Goals
1990–91	Chelsea	—	—

Season	Club	App	Goals
1991–92		4	—
1992–93		13	1

BARNES, Bobby

Born Kingston 17.12.62. Ht 5 7
Wt 10 09
Forward. From Apprentice.

Season	Club	App	Goals
1980–81	West Ham	6	1
1981–82		3	—
1982–83		—	—
1983–84		13	2
1984–85		20	2
1985–86		1	—
1985–86	*Scunthorpe U*	6	—
1985–86	Aldershot	14	8
1986–87		25	11
1987–88		10	7
1987–88	Swindon T	28	10
1988–89		17	3
1988–89	Bournemouth	10	—
1989–90		4	—
1989–90	Northampton T	37	18
1990–91		43	13
1991–92		18	6
1991–92	Peterborough U	15	5
1992–93		26	3

BARNES, David

Born London 16.11.61. Ht 5 10
Wt 11 01
Defender. From Apprentice. England
Youth.

Season	Club	App	Goals
1979–80	Coventry C	3	—
1980–81		—	—
1981–82		6	—
1981–82	Ipswich T	—	—
1982–83		6	—
1983–84		11	—
1984–85		—	—
1984–85	Wolves	23	1
1985–86		38	1
1986–87		26	2
1987–88		1	—
1987–88	Aldershot	30	—
1988–89		39	1
1989–90	Sheffield U	24	—

Season	Club	App	Goals
1990–91		28	1
1991–92		15	—
1992–93		13	—

BARNES, John

Born Jamaica 7.11.63.   Ht 5 11   Wt 12 07
Forward. From Sudbury Court. England
Under-21, 73 full caps.

Season	Club	App	Goals
1981–82	Watford	36	13
1982–83		42	10
1983–84		39	11
1984–85		40	12
1985–86		39	9
1986–87		37	10
1987–88	Liverpool	38	15
1988–89		33	8
1989–90		34	22
1990–91		35	16
1991–92		12	1
1992–93		27	5

BARNES, Paul

Born Leicester 16.11.67.   Ht 5 10
Wt 12 09
Forward. From Apprentice.

Season	Club	App	Goals
1985–86	Notts Co	14	4
1986–87		—	—
1987–88		11	2
1988–89		15	7
1989–90		13	1
1989–90	Stoke C	5	—
1990–91		6	—
1990–91	*Chesterfield*	1	—
1991–92	Stoke C	13	3
1992–93	York C	40	21

BARNESS, Anthony

Born London 25.3.72.   Ht 5 10   Wt 10 12
Defender. From Trainee.

Season	Club	App	Goals
1990–91	Charlton Ath	—	—
1991–92		22	1
1992–93		5	—
1992–93	Chelsea	2	—

BARNETT, Dave

Born London 16.4.67.   Ht 6 0   Wt 12 08
Defender. From Windsor & Eton.

Season	Club	App	Goals
1988–89	Colchester U	20	—
1989–90	WBA	—	—
1990–91	Walsall	5	—
From Kidderminster H			
1991–92	Barnet	4	—
1992–93		36	2

BARNETT, Gary

Born Stratford 11.3.63.   Ht 5 6   Wt 9 13
Forward. From Apprentice.

Season	Club	App	Goals
1980–81	Coventry C	—	—
1990–91	Huddersfield T	22	1
1981–82		—	—
1982–83	Oxford U	22	2
1982–83	*Wimbledon*	5	1
1983–84	Oxford U	19	7
1984–85		2	—
1984–85	*Fulham*	2	1
1985–86	Oxford U	2	—
1985–86	Fulham	36	6
1986–87		42	9
1987–88		42	9
1988–89		28	5
1989–90		32	1
1990–91	Huddersfield T	22	1
1991–92		31	3
1992–93		46	7

BARNSLEY, Andy

Born Sheffield 9.6.62.   Ht 6 0   Wt 11 11
Defender. From Denaby U.

Season	Club	App	Goals
1984–85	Rotherham U	—	—
1985–86		28	—
1986–87	Sheffield U	42	1
1987–88		32	—
1988–89		3	—
1988–89	Rotherham U	27	—
1989–90		37	3
1990–91		19	—
1991–92	Carlisle U	28	3
1992–93		27	2

BARR, Billy

Born Halifax 21.1.69.   Ht 5 11   Wt 11 07
Defender. From Trainee.

Season	Club		
1987–88	Halifax T	30	—
1988–89		43	4
1989–90		23	2
1990–91		37	1
1991–92		35	3
1992–93		28	3

BARRAS, Tony

Born Teesside 29.3.71.   Ht 6 0   Wt 12 03
Forward. From Trainee.

Season	Club		
1988–89	Hartlepool U	3	—
1989–90		9	—
1990–91	Stockport Co	40	—
1991–92		42	5
1992–93		14	—

BARRATT, Tony

Born Salford 18.10.65.   Ht 5 8   Wt 11 01
Defender. From Billingham T.

Season	Club		
1985–86	Grimsby T	22	—
	From Billingham T		
1986–87	Hartlepool U	23	—
1987–88		43	3
1988–89		32	1
1988–89	York C	12	—
1989–90		46	4
1990–91		29	1
1991–92		21	3
1992–93		10	—

BARRETT, Earl

Born Rochdale 28.4.67.   Ht 5 11
Wt 11 00
Defender. From Apprentice. England B,
Under-21, 3 full caps.

Season	Club		
1984–85	Manchester C	—	—
1985–86		1	—
1985–86	*Chester C*	12	—
1986–87	Manchester C	2	—
1987–88		—	—

1987–88	Oldham Ath	18	—
1988–89		44	—
1989–90		46	2
1990–91		46	3
1991–92		29	2
1991–92	Aston Villa	13	—
1992–93		42	1

BARRETT, Scott

Born Derby 2.4.63   Ht 5 10   Wt 14 02
Goalkeeper. From Ilkeston T.

Season	Club		
1984–85	Wolverhampton W	4	—
1985–86		21	—
1986–87		5	—
1987–88	Stoke C	27	—
1988–89		17	—
1989–90		7	—
1989–90	*Colchester U*	13	—
1989–90	*Stockport Co*	10	—
1990–91	Colchester U	*42*	—
1991–92		*42*	*1*
1992–93	Gillingham	34	—

BARRICK, Dean

Born Hemsworth 30.9.69.   Ht 5 8
Wt 11 07
Midfield. From Trainee.

Season	Club		
1987–88	Sheffield W	—	—
1988–89		8	2
1989–90		3	—
1990–91		—	—
1990–91	Rotherham U	19	2
1991–92		34	1
1992–93		46	4

BARROW, Graham

Born Chorley 13.6.54.   Ht 6 2   Wt 13 07
Midfield. From Altrincham.

Season	Club		
1981–82	Wigan Ath	41	12
1982–83		28	3
1983–84		42	5
1984–85		38	9
1985–86		30	7
1986–87	Chester C	41	5

1987–88	....	38	4
1988–89	....	35	3
1989–90	....	28	1
1990–91	....	20	—
1991–92	....	40	2
1992–93	....	33	2

BARROW, Lee

Born Belper 1.5.73
Defender. From Trainee.

1991–92	Notts Co.....................	—	—
1992–93	Scarborough................	11	—
1992–93	Torquay U.................	15	2

BARTLETT, Kevin

Born Portsmouth 12.10.62.   Ht 5 9
Wt 10 12
Forward. From Apprentice.

| 1980–81 | Portsmouth .... | 2 | — |
| 1981–82 | .... | 1 | — |
| From Fareham |
1986–87	Cardiff C.....................	23	4
1987–88	....	37	12
1988–89	....	22	9
1988–89	WBA..........................	17	3
1989–90	....	20	7
1989–90	Notts Co	14	8
1990–91	....	40	13
1991–92	....	29	7
1992–93	....	16	5
1992–93	*Port Vale*..................	5	1
1992–93	Cambridge U..............	8	1

BARTLETT, Neal

Born Southampton 7.4.75   Ht 5 10
Wt 12 00
Midfield. From Trainee.

| 1992–93 | Southampton .... | 1 | — |

BARTON, Warren

Born London 19.3.69.   Ht 6 0   Wt 11 00
Defender. From Leytonstone/Ilford.
England B.

| 1989–90 | Maidstone U.............. | 42 | — |

1990–91	Wimbledon	37	3
1991–92	....	42	1
1992–93	....	23	2

BARTRAM, Vince

Born Birmingham 7.8.68.   Ht 6 2
Wt 13 04
Goalkeeper. From Local.

1985–86	Wolverhampton W	—	—
1986–87	....	1	—
1987–88	....	—	—
1988–89	....	—	—
1989–90	....	—	—
1989–90	*Blackpool*	9	—
1990–91	Wolverhampton W	4	—
1990–91	*WBA*	—	—
1991–92	Bournemouth..............	46	—
1992–93	....	45	—

BART-WILLIAMS, Chris

Born Freetown 16.6.74.   Ht 5 11
Wt 11 00
Midfield. From Trainee. England Youth,
Under-21.

1990–91	Leyton Orient	21	2
1991–92	....	15	—
1991–92	Sheffield W.................	15	—
1992–93	....	34	6

BASS, David

Born Frimley 29.11.74.   Ht 6 0   Wt 11 04
Forward. From Trainee.

| 1991–92 | Reading....................... | 3 | — |
| 1992–93 | .... | 5 | — |

BATES, Jamie

Born London 24.2.68.   Ht 6 1   Wt 12 12
Defender. From Trainee.

1986–87	Brentford	24	1
1987–88	....	23	1
1988–89	....	36	1
1989–90	....	15	—

Season	Club	League Appearances/Goals
1990–91		32 2
1991–92		42 1
1992–93		24 —

BATTY, David

Born Leeds 2.12.68. Ht 5 7 Wt 10 07
Midfield. From Trainee. England B,
Under-21, 14 full caps.

Season	Club	League Appearances/Goals
1987–88	Leeds U	23 1
1988–89		30 —
1989–90		42 —
1990–91		37 —
1991–92		40 2
1992–93		30 1

BAYES, Ashley

Born Lincoln 19.4.72. Ht 6 1 Wt 12 12
Goalkeeper. From Trainee.

Season	Club	League Appearances/Goals
1989–90	Brentford	1 —
1990–91		— —
1991–92		1 —
1992–93		2 —

BAZELEY, Darren

Born Northampton 5.10.72. Ht 5 10
Wt 10 09
Forward. From Trainee. England
Under-21.

Season	Club	League Appearances/Goals
1989–90	Watford	1 —
1990–91		7 —
1991–92		34 6
1992–93		22 1

BEADLE, Peter

Born London 13.5.72. Ht 6 0 Wt 11 12
Forward. From Trainee.

Season	Club	League Appearances/Goals
1988–89	Gillingham	2 —
1989–90		10 2
1990–91		22 7
1991–92		33 5
1992–93	Tottenham H	— —
1992–93	*Bournemouth*	9 2

BEAGRIE, Peter

Born Middlesbrough 28.11.65. Ht 5 8
Wt 9 10
Midfield. From Local. England B,
Under-21.

Season	Club	League Appearances/Goals
1983–84	Middlesbrough	— —
1984–85		7 1
1985–86		26 1
1986–87	Sheffield U	41 9
1987–88		43 2
1988–89	Stoke C	41 7
1989–90		13 —
1989–90	Everton	19 —
1990–91		17 2
1991–92		27 3
1991–92	*Sunderland*	5 1
1992–93	Everton	22 3

BEARDSLEY, Peter

Born Newcastle 18.1.61. Ht 5 8
Wt 11 07
Forward. From Wallsend BC. England B,
49 full caps. Football League.

Season	Club	League Appearances/Goals
1979–80	Carlisle U	37 8
1980–81		43 10
1981–82		22 4
From Vancouver Whitecaps		
1982–83	Manchester U	— —
From Vancouver Whitecaps		
1983–84	Newcastle U	35 20
1984–85		38 17
1985–86		42 19
1986–87		32 5
1987–88	Liverpool	38 15
1988–89		37 10
1989–90		29 10
1990–91		27 11
1991–92	Everton	42 15
1992–93		39 10

BEASANT, Dave

Born Willesden 20.3.59. Ht 6 4 Wt 13 00
Goalkeeper. From Edgware T. England B,
2 full caps.

Season	Club	League Appearances/Goals
1979–80	Wimbledon	2 —

24

Season	Club	League Appearances/Goals
1980–81	....	34 —
1981–82	....	46 —
1982–83	....	46 —
1983–84	....	46 —
1984–85	....	42 —
1985–86	....	42 —
1986–87	....	42 —
1987–88	....	40 —
1988–89	Newcastle U...............	20 —
1988–89	Chelsea......................	22 —
1989–90	....	38 —
1990–91	....	35 —
1991–92	....	21 —
1992–93	....	17 —
1992–93	*Grimsby T*	6 —
1992–93	*Wolverhampton W*	4 —

BEASLEY, Andy

Born Sedgley 5.2.64.   Ht 6 2   Wt 13 02
Goalkeeper. From Apprentice.

Season	Club	League Appearances/Goals
1981–82	Luton T.	— —
1982–83	....	— —
1983–84	....	— —
1983–84	*Mansfield T*	— —
1983–84	*Gillingham*	— —
1984–85	Mansfield T................	3 —
1985–86	....	— —
1986–87	....	— —
1986–87	*Peterborough U*	7 —
1987–88	Mansfield T................	8 —
1987–88	*Scarborough*	4 —
1988–89	Mansfield T................	6 —
1989–90	....	26 —
1990–91	....	42 —
1991–92	....	9 —
1992–93	....	— —
1992–93	*Bristol R*....................	1 —

BEAUCHAMP, Joe

Born Oxford 13.3.71.   Ht 5 11   Wt 11 10
Forward. From Trainee.

Season	Club	League Appearances/Goals
1988–89	Oxford U	1 —
1989–90	....	3 —
1990–91	....	4 —
1991–92	....	27 7
1991–92	*Swansea C*..................	5 2

Season	Club	League Appearances/Goals
1992–93	Oxford U	44 7

BEAUMONT, Chris

Born Sheffield 5.12.65.   Ht 5 11   Wt 11 07
Forward. From Denaby.

Season	Club	League Appearances/Goals
1988–89	Rochdale......................	34 7
1989–90	Stockport Co	22 5
1990–91	....	45 15
1991–92	....	34 2
1992–93	....	44 14

BEAUMONT, David

Born Edinburgh 10.12.63.   Ht 5 10
Wt 11 05
Midfield. 'S' Form. Scotland Youth,
Under-21.

Season	Club	League Appearances/Goals
1980–81	Dundee U	— —
1981–82	....	— —
1982–83	....	— —
1983–84	....	2 —
1984–85	....	18 1
1985–86	....	13 —
1986–87	....	28 —
1987–88	....	10 1
1988–89	....	18 1
1988–89	Luton T	15 —
1989–90	....	19 —
1990–91	....	33 —
1991–92	....	9 —
1991–92	Hibernian...................	21 —
1992–93	....	16 —

BEAVON, Stuart

Born Wolverhampton 30.11.58.   Ht 5 6
Wt 10 04
Midfield. From Apprentice.

Season	Club	League Appearances/Goals
1976–77	Tottenham H	— —
1977–78	....	— —
1978–79	....	1 —
1979–80	....	3 —
1979–80	*Notts Co*......................	6 —
1980–81	Reading......................	37 6
1981–82	....	40 5
1982–83	....	46 4

Season	Club	App	Goals
1983–84	....	36	7
1984–85	....	46	2
1985–86	....	44	3
1986–87	....	42	3
1987–88	....	34	2
1988–89	....	39	9
1989–90	....	32	3
1990–91	Northampton T	41	10
1991–92	....	33	3
1992–93	....	24	1

BECKFORD, Darren

Born Manchester 12.5.67. Ht 6 1
Wt 11 01
Forward. From Apprentice. England
Youth.

Season	Club	App	Goals
1984–85	Manchester C	4	—
1985–86	....	3	—
1985–86	*Bury*	12	5
1986–87	Manchester C	4	—
1986–87	*Port Vale*	11	4
1987–88	Port Vale	40	9
1988–89	....	42	20
1989–90	....	42	17
1990–91	....	43	22
1991–92	Norwich C	30	7
1992–93	....	8	1
1992–93	Oldham Ath.................	7	3

BECKFORD, Jason

Born Manchester 14.2.70. Ht 5 9
Wt 12 04
Midfield. From Trainee. England Youth.

Season	Club	App	Goals
1987–88	Manchester C	5	—
1988–89	....	8	1
1989–90	....	5	—
1990–91	....	2	—
1990–91	*Blackburn R*	4	—
1991–92	Manchester C	—	—
1991–92	*Port Vale*.....................	5	1
1991–92	Birmingham C	4	1
1992–93	....	3	1

BEDROSSIAN, Ara

Born Cyprus 2.6.67 Ht 5 9 Wt 10 00
Midfield.

Season	Club	App	Goals
1992–93	Fulham	9	—

BEECH, Chris

Born Blackpool 16.9.74
Forward. From Trainee.

Season	Club	App	Goals
1992–93	Blackpool....................	1	—

BEEDIE, Stuart

Born Aberdeen 16.8.60 Ht 5 10
Wt 11 00
Midfield. From Sunnybank A.

Season	Club	App	Goals
1978–79	Montrose	10	—
1979–80	....	34	4
1980–81	....	36	9
1981–82	St Johnstone	26	5
1982–83	....	34	2
1983–84	....	34	2
1984–85	Dundee U	28	3
1985–86	....	18	3
1986–87	Hibernian...................	9	2
1986–87	Dunfermline Ath	6	—
1987–88	....	36	2
1988–89	....	23	2
1989–90	Dundee........................	21	3
1990–91	....	9	—
1991–92	....	40	4
1992–93	....	14	—

BEENEY, Mark

Born Pembury 30.12.67. Ht 6 4
Wt 14 07
Goalkeeper.

Season	Club	App	Goals
1986–87	Gillingham	2	—
1987–88	Maidstone U................	—	—
1988–89	....	—	—
1989–90	....	33	—
1989–90	*Aldershot*	7	—
1990–91	Maidstone U................	17	—
1990–91	Brighton & HA............	2	—
1991–92	....	25	—

1992–93	....	42	—
1992–93	Leeds U	1	—

BEESLEY, Paul

Born Wigan 21.7.65.   Ht 6 1   Wt 11 11
Defender. From Marine.

1984–85	Wigan Ath	2	—
1985–86	....	17	—
1986–87	....	39	—
1987–88	....	42	1
1988–89	....	44	2
1989–90	....	11	—
1989–90	Leyton Orient	32	1
1990–91	Sheffield U	37	1
1991–92	....	40	2
1992–93	....	39	2

BEESTON, Carl

Born Stoke 30.6.67.   Ht 5 9   Wt 12 04
Midfield. From Apprentice. England
Under-21.

1984–85	Stoke C	1	—
1985–86	....	5	—
1986–87	....	—	—
1987–88	....	12	—
1988–89	....	23	2
1989–90	....	38	2
1990–91	....	37	2
1991–92	....	43	3
1992–93	....	27	3

BEEVER, Anthony

Born Huddersfield 18.9.74   Ht 6 0
Wt 12 05
Forward. From Trainee.

1992–93	Rochdale	1	—

BEINLICH, Stefan

Born Berlin 13.1.72.   Ht 5 11   Wt 11 02
Forward. From Bergmann Borsig.

1991–92	Aston Villa	2	—
1992–93	....	7	—

BELL, Michael

Born Newcastle 15.11.71.   Ht 5 8
Wt 10 04
Midfield. From Trainee.

1989–90	Northampton T	6	—
1990–91	....	28	—
1991–92	....	30	4
1992–93	....	39	5

BELLAMY, Gary

Born Worksop 4.7.62.   Ht 6 2   Wt 11 05
Defender. From Apprentice.

1980–81	Chesterfield	3	—
1981–82	....	25	—
1982–83	....	42	—
1983–84	....	38	1
1984–85	....	22	2
1985–86	....	12	2
1986–87	....	42	2
1987–88	Wolverhampton W	24	2
1988–89	....	43	1
1989–90	....	39	3
1990–91	....	26	3
1991–92	....	4	—
1991–92	*Cardiff*	9	—
1992–93	Wolverhampton W	—	—
1992–93	Leyton Orient	39	4

BENALI, Francis

Born Southampton 30.12.68.   Ht 5 10
Wt 11 00
Forward. From Apprentice.

1986–87	Southampton	—	—
1987–88	....	—	—
1988–89	....	7	—
1989–90	....	27	—
1990–91	....	12	—
1991–92	....	22	—
1992–93	....	33	—

BENJAMIN, Ian

Born Nottingham 11.12.61. Ht 5 11
Wt 13 01
Forward. From Apprentice. England
Youth.

1978–79	Sheffield U	2	2
1979–80		3	1
1979–80	WBA	—	—
1980–81		2	—
1981–82	Notts Co	—	—
1982–83	Peterborough U	46	6
1983–84		34	8
1984–85	Northampton T	44	18
1985–86		46	22
1986–87		46	18
1987–88		14	1
1987–88	Cambridge U	25	2
1988–89	Chester C	22	2
1988–89	Exeter C	20	3
1989–90		12	1
1989–90	Southend U	15	4
1990–91		46	13
1991–92		45	9
1992–93		16	7
1992–93	Luton T	10	1

BENNETT, Craig

Born Doncaster 29.8.73. Ht 6 0
Wt 12 00
Forward. From Trainee.

1990–91	Doncaster R	2	—
1991–92		5	—
1992–93		1	—

BENNETT, Gary

Born Liverpool 20.9.63. Ht 5 11
Wt 12 00
Forward. From Local.

1984–85	Wigan Ath	20	3
1985–86	Chester C	43	13
1986–87		33	13
1987–88		43	10
1988–89		7	—
1988–89	Southend U	17	2
1989–90		25	4

1989–90	Chester C	8	1
1990–91		30	3
1991–92		42	11
1992–93	Wrexham	35	16

BENNETT, Gary

Born Manchester 4.12.61. Ht 6 1
Wt 12 01
Defender. From Amateur.

1979–80	Manchester C	—	—
1980–81		—	—
1981–82	Cardiff C	19	1
1982–83		36	8
1983–84		32	2
1984–85	Sunderland	37	3
1985–86		28	3
1986–87		41	4
1987–88		38	2
1988–89		40	3
1989–90		36	3
1990–91		37	2
1991–92		39	3
1992–93		15	—

BENNETT, Gary

Born Enfield 2.9.69 Ht 5 7 Wt 10 06
Midfield. From Trainee.

1988–89	Colchester U	9	1
1989–90		36	4
1990–91		*36*	*9*
1991–92		*39*	*16*
1992–93		38	8

BENNETT, Ian

Born Worksop 10.10.71. Ht 6 0
Goalkeeper. From Newcastle U Trainee.

| 1991–92 | Peterborough U | 7 | — |
| 1992–93 | | 46 | — |

BENNETT, Mickey

Born London 27.7.69. Ht 5 10 Wt 11 11
Midfield. From Apprentice. England
Youth.

| 1986–87 | Charlton Ath | 2 | — |

Season	Club	App	Goals
1987–88		16	1
1988–89		11	—
1989–90		6	1
1989–90	Wimbledon	7	1
1990–91		6	—
1991–92		5	1
1992–93	Brentford	38	4

BENNETT, Tom

Born Falkirk 12.12.69. Ht 5 11 Wt 11 08
Defender. From Trainee.

Season	Club	App	Goals
1987–88	Aston Villa	—	—
1988–89	Wolverhampton W	2	—
1989–90		30	—
1990–91		26	—
1991–92		38	2
1992–93		1	—

BENNETT, Troy

Born Barnsley 25.12.75
Midfield. From Trainee.

Season	Club	App	Goals
1992–93	Barnsley	2	—

BENSTEAD, Graham

Born Aldershot 20.8.63. Ht 6 2 Wt 12 04
Goalkeeper. From Apprentice. England
Youth.

Season	Club	App	Goals
1981–82	QPR	—	—
1982–83		—	—
1983–84		—	—
1984–85		—	—
1984–85	*Norwich C*	1	—
1985–86	Norwich C	—	—
1986–87		13	—
1987–88		2	—
1987–88	*Colchester U*	18	—
1987–88	*Sheffield U*	8	—
1988–89	Sheffield U	39	—
1989–90		—	—
1990–91	Brentford	45	—
1991–92		37	—
1992–93		25	—

BENSTOCK, Danny

Born London 10.7.70
Defender. From Barking.

Season	Club	App	Goals
1992–93	Leyton Orient	9	—

BENT, Junior

Born Huddersfield 1.3.70. Ht 5 5
Wt 10 06
Forward. From Trainee.

Season	Club	App	Goals
1987–88	Huddersfield T	7	—
1988–89		22	5
1989–90		7	1
1989–90	*Burnley*	9	3
1989–90	Bristol C	1	—
1990–91		20	2
1991–92		17	2
1991–92	*Stoke C*	1	—
1992–93	Bristol C	20	3

BENTON, James

Born Wexford 9.4.75.
Defender. From Trainee.

Season	Club	App	Goals
1991–92	Northampton T	5	1
1992–93		5	—

BERESFORD, John

Born Sheffield 4.9.66. Ht 5 5 Wt 10 04
Midfield. From Apprentice. England
Schools, Youth.

Season	Club	App	Goals
1983–84	Manchester C	—	—
1984–85		—	—
1985–86		—	—
1986–87	Barnsley	27	1
1987–88		34	3
1988–89		27	1
1988–89	Portsmouth	2	—
1989–90		28	—
1990–91		42	2
1991–92		35	6
1992–93	Newcastle U	42	1

BERESFORD, Marlon

Born Lincoln 2.9.69.   Ht 6 1   Wt 12 06
Goalkeeper. From Trainee.

Season	Club	App	Goals
61987–88	Sheffield W	—	—
1988–89		—	—
1989–90		—	—
1989–90	*Bury*	1	—
1989–90	*Ipswich T*	—	—
1990–91	Sheffield W	—	—
1990–91	*Northampton T*	13	—
1990–91	*Crewe Alex*	3	—
1991–92	Sheffield W	—	—
1991–92	*Northampton T*	15	—
1992–93	Burnley	44	—

BERG, Henning

Born Eidsvell 1.9.69
Defender. From Lillestrom. Norway full caps.

Season	Club	App	Goals
1992–93	Blackburn R	4	—

BERGSSON, Gudni

Born Iceland 21.7.65.   Ht 6 01   Wt 12 03
Defender. From Valur. Iceland Youth, Under-21, full caps.

Season	Club	App	Goals
1988–89	Tottenham H	8	—
1989–90		18	—
1990–91		12	1
1991–92		28	1
1992–93		5	—

BERNARD, Paul

Born Edinburgh 30.12.72.   Ht 5 11
Wt 11 08
Midfield. From Trainee. Scotland Under-21.

Season	Club	App	Goals
1990–91	Oldham Ath	2	1
1991–92		21	5
1992–93		33	4

BERRY, Greg

Born Essex 5.3.71.   Ht 5 10   Wt 12 00
Forward. From East Thurrock.

Season	Club	App	Goals
1989–90	Leyton Orient	9	1

Season	Club	App	Goals
1990–91		35	5
1991–92		36	8
1992–93	Wimbledon	3	—

BERRY, Neil

Born Edinburgh 6.4.63   Ht 6 0   Wt 12 0
Defender. From Apprentice. Scotland Youth.

Season	Club	App	Goals
1980–81	Bolton W	—	—
1981–82		3	—
1982–83		9	—
1983–84		14	—
1984–85		6	—
1984–85	Hearts	3	—
1985–86		32	2
1986–87		30	3
1987–88		35	—
1988–89		32	1
1989–90		10	1
1990–91		19	1
1991–92		—	—
1992–93		17	1

BETT, Jim

Born Hamilton 25.11.59.   Ht 5 11
Wt 12 03
Midfield. From school. Scotland Schools, Under-21, 25 full caps.

Season	Club	App	Goals
1976–77	Airdrieonians	1	—
1977–78		7	—
From Iceland and Lokeren			
1980–81	Rangers	34	4
1981–82		35	11
1982–83		35	6
From Lokeren			
1985–86	Aberdeen	24	3
1986–87		38	4
1987–88		38	10
1988–89		31	5
1989–90		30	3
1990–91		36	7
1991–92		38	1
1992–93		17	—

BETTS, Simon

Born Middlesbrough 3.3.73   Ht 5 8
Wt 10 07
Defender. From Trainee.

Season	Club		
1991–92	Ipswich T	—	—
1992–93	Scarborough	—	—
1992–93	Colchester U	23	—

BIGGINS, Wayne

Born Sheffield 20.11.61.   Ht 5 10
Wt 11 00
Forward. From Apprentice.

Season	Club		
1979–80	Lincoln C	—	—
1980–81		8	1
From Matlock Town and King's Lynn			
1983–84	Burnley	20	8
1984–85		46	18
1985–86		12	3
1985–86	Norwich C	28	7
1986–87		31	4
1987–88		20	5
1988–89	Manchester C	32	9
1989–90	Stoke C	35	10
1990–91		38	12
1991–92		41	22
1992–93		8	2
1992–93	Barnsley	34	14

BILLING, Peter

Born Liverpool 24.10.64.   Ht 6 2
Wt 13 00
Defender. From South Liverpool.

Season	Club		
1985–86	Everton	1	—
1986–87		—	—
1986–87	Crewe Alex	19	—
1987–88		32	—
1988–89		37	1
1989–90	Coventry C	18	—
1990–91		15	—
1991–92		22	1
1992–93		3	—
1992–93	Port Vale	12	—

BILLY, Chris

Born Huddersfield 2.1.73.   Ht 5 11
Wt 11 08
Forward. From Trainee.

Season	Club		
1991–92	Huddersfield T	10	2
1992–93		13	—

BIRCH, Paul

Born West Bromwich 20.11.62.   Ht 5 6
Wt 10 04
Midfield. From Apprentice.

Season	Club		
1980–81	Aston Villa	—	—
1981–82		—	—
1982–83		—	—
1983–84		22	2
1984–85		25	3
1985–86		27	2
1986–87		29	3
1987–88		38	6
1988–89		12	—
1989–90		12	—
1990–91		8	—
1990–91	Wolverhampton W	20	2
1991–92		45	8
1992–93		28	3

BIRD, Anthony

Born Cardiff 1.9.74   Ht 5 10   Wt 11 09
Forward. From Trainee. Wales Under-21.

Season	Club		
1991–92	Cardiff C	—	—
1992–93		9	1

BISHOP, Charlie

Born Nottingham 16.2.68.   Ht 6 0
Wt 12 01
Defender. From Stoke C Apprentice.

Season	Club		
1986–87	Watford	—	—
1987–88	Bury	17	—
1988–89		38	3
1989–90		30	1
1990–91		29	2
1991–92	Barnsley	28	—
1992–93		43	—

BISHOP, Eddie

Born Liverpool 28.11.62.   Ht 5 8
Wt 11 07
Midfield. From Winsford U, Northwich
Vic, Altrincham, Runcorn.

Season	Club		
1987–88	Tranmere R	5	1
1988–89		35	8
1989–90		28	7
1990–91		8	3
1990–91	Chester C	19	7
1991–92		21	4
1991–92	*Crewe Alex*	3	—
1992–93	Chester C	29	6

BISHOP, Ian

Born Liverpool 29.5.65.   Ht 5 9   Wt 10 12
Midfield. From Apprentice. England B.

Season	Club		
1983–84	Everton	1	—
1983–84	*Crewe Alex*	4	—
1984–85	Everton	—	—
1984–85	Carlisle U	30	2
1985–86		36	6
1986–87		42	3
1987–88	Bournemouth	24	3
1988–89		44	2
1989–90	Manchester C	19	2
1989–90	West Ham U	17	2
1990–91		40	4
1991–92		41	1
1992–93		22	1

BISSETT, Nicky

Born Fulham 5.4.64.   Ht 6 2   Wt 12 10
Defender. From Barnet.

Season	Club		
1988–89	Brighton	16	—
1989–90		29	6
1990–91		3	—
1991–92		13	1
1992–93		12	—

BJORNEBYE, Stig Inge

Born Norway 11.12.69.   Ht 5 10   Wt 11 09
Defender. From Rosenborg. Norway full
caps.

Season	Club		
1992–93	Liverpool	11	—

BLACK, Kenny

Born Stenhousemuir 29.11.63.   Ht 5 8
Wt 10 11
Midfield. From Linlithgow Rose. Scotland
Schools, Youth.

Season	Club		
1980–81	Rangers	—	—
1981–82		8	—
1982–83		14	1
1983–84	Motherwell	17	—
1984–85	Hearts	32	7
1985–86		29	2
1986–87		42	1
1987–88		42	4
1988–89		33	1
1989–90	Portsmouth	41	2
1990–91		21	1
1991–92		—	—
1991–92	Airdrieonians	33	2
1992–93		33	1

BLACK, Kingsley

Born Luton 22.6.68.   Ht 5 8   Wt 10 11
Midfield. From school. Northern Ireland,
27 full caps.

Season	Club		
1986–87	Luton T	—	—
1987–88		13	—
1988–89		37	8
1989–90		36	11
1990–91		37	7
1991–92		4	—
1991–92	Nottingham F	25	4
1992–93		24	5

BLACK, Tom

Born Lanark 11.10.62.   Ht 5 8   Wt 10 12
Defender. From Bellshill YM.

Season	Club		
1980–81	Airdrieonians	—	—
1981–82		—	—
1982–83		5	—
1983–84		32	4
1984–85		37	1
1985–86		12	—
1986–87		24	1
1987–88		29	1
1988–89		37	4

Season	Club	App	Goals
1989–90	St Mirren	31	1
1990–91		34	2
1991–92		9	1
1992–93	Kilmarnock	10	1

BLACKMORE, Clayton

Born Neath 23.9.64.   Ht 5 9   Wt 11 06
Midfield. From Apprentice. Wales Schools,
Youth, Under-21, 37 full caps.

Season	Club	App	Goals
1982–83	Manchester U	—	—
1983–84		1	—
1984–85		1	—
1985–86		12	3
1986–87		12	1
1987–88		22	3
1988–89		28	3
1989–90		28	2
1990–91		35	4
1991–92		33	3
1992–93		14	—

BLACKSTONE, Ian

Born Harrogate 7.8.64.   Ht 6 0   Wt 13 00
Forward. From Harrogate T.

Season	Club	App	Goals
1990–91	York C	28	6
1991–92		30	8
1992–93		39	16

BLACKWELL, Dean

Born London 5.12.69.   Ht 6 1   Wt 12 10
Defender. From Trainee. England
Under-21.

Season	Club	App	Goals
1988–89	Wimbledon	—	—
1989–90		3	—
1989–90	*Plymouth Arg*	7	—
1990–91	Wimbledon	35	—
1991–92		4	1
1992–93		24	—

BLACKWELL, Kevin

Born Luton 21.12.58   Ht 5 11   Wt 12 10
Goalkeeper. From Boston U, Barnet.

Season	Club	App	Goals
1987–88	Scarborough	21	—

Season	Club	App	Goals
1988–89		15	—
1989–90		8	—
1989–90	Notts Co	—	—
1990–91		—	—
1991–92		—	—
1992–93		—	—
1992–93	Torquay U	18	—

BLADES, Paul

Born Peterborough 5.1.65.   Ht 6 0
Wt 10 12
Defender. From Apprentice. England
Youth.

Season	Club	App	Goals
1982–83	Derby Co	6	—
1983–84		4	—
1984–85		22	—
1985–86		30	—
1986–87		16	—
1987–88		31	—
1988–89		38	1
1989–90		19	—
1990–91	Norwich C	21	—
1991–92		26	—
1992–93	Wolverhampton W	40	1

BLAKE, Mark

Born Portsmouth 19.12.67.   Ht 6 1
Wt 12 08
Defender. From Apprentice. England
Youth.

Season	Club	App	Goals
1985–86	Southampton	1	—
1986–87		8	1
1987–88		6	1
1988–89		3	—
1989–90		—	—
1989–90	*Colchester U*	4	1
1989–90	*Shrewsbury T*	10	—
1990–91	Shrewsbury T	46	2
1991–92		39	—
1992–93		32	1

BLAKE, Mark

Born Nottingham 16.12.70.   Ht 5 11
Wt 12 07
Midfield. From Trainee. England Schools,
Youth, Under-21.

1989–90	Aston Villa	9	—
1990–91		7	—
1990–91	*Wolverhampton W*	2	—
1991–92	Aston Villa	14	2
1992–93		1	—

BLAKE, Nathan

Born Cardiff 27.1.72.   Ht 5 10   Wt 12 00
Defender. From Chelsea Trainee and
Cardiff C Trainee. Wales B, Under-21.

1989–90	Cardiff C	6	—
1990–91		40	4
1991–92		31	6
1992–93		34	11

BLAKE, Noel

Born Jamaica 12.1.62.   Ht 6 0   Wt 13 11
Defender. From Walsall Amateur and
Sutton Coldfield T.

1979–80	Aston Villa	3	—
1980–81		—	—
1981–82		1	—
1981–82	*Shrewsbury T*	6	—
1982–83	Aston Villa	—	—
1982–83	Birmingham C	37	3
1983–84		39	2
1984–85	Portsmouth	42	3
1985–86		42	4
1986–87		41	3
1987–88		19	—
1988–89	Leeds U	44	4
1989–90		7	—
1989–90	Stoke C	18	—
1990–91		44	3
1991–92		13	—
1991–92	*Bradford C*	6	—
1992–93	Bradford C	32	3

BLISSETT, Gary

Born Manchester 29.6.64.   Ht 6 1
Wt 11 13
Forward. From Manchester C, Manchester
U. Amateur and Altrincham.

1983–84	Crewe Alex	22	3
1984–85		29	9
1985–86		38	11
1986–87		33	16
1986–87	Brentford	10	5
1987–88		41	9
1988–89		36	6
1989–90		37	11
1990–91		26	10
1991–92		37	17
1992–93		46	21

BLISSETT, Luther

Born W. Indies 1.2.58.   Ht 5 10   Wt 12 03
Forward. From Juniors. England Under-
21, B, 14 full caps.

1975–76	Watford	3	1
1976–77		4	—
1977–78		33	6
1978–79		41	21
1979–80		42	10
1980–81		42	11
1981–82		40	19
1982–83		41	27
1983–84	AC Milan	30	5
1984–85	Watford	41	21
1985–86		23	7
1986–87		35	11
1987–88		25	4
1988–89		3	1
1988–89	Bournemouth	30	19
1989–90		46	18
1990–91		45	19
1991–92	Watford	42	10
1992–93		—	—
1992–93	*WBA*	3	1

BOARDMAN, Paul

Born Tottenham 6.11.67   Ht 6 0
Wt 11 02
Forward.

Season	Club		
1992–93	Plymouth Arg	2	1

BODIN, Paul

Born Cardiff 13.9.64.   Ht 6 0   Wt 13 01
Midfield. From Chelsea Amateur. Wales
Youth, Under-21, 19 full caps.

Season	Club		
1981–82	Newport Co	—	—
1982–83	Cardiff C	31	—
1983–84		26	3
From Bath C			
1987–88	Newport Co	6	1
1987–88	Swindon T	5	1
1988–89		16	1
1989–90		41	5
1990–91		31	2
1990–91	Crystal Palace	5	—
1991–92		4	—
1991–92	*Newcastle U*	6	—
1991–92	Swindon T	21	2
1992–93		35	11

BODLEY, Mick

Born Hayes 14.9.67.   Ht 5 11   Wt 12 00
Defender. From Apprentice.

Season	Club		
1985–86	Chelsea	—	—
1986–87		—	—
1987–88		6	1
1988–89		—	—
1988–89	Northampton T	20	—
1989–90		—	—
1990–91	Barnet	—	—
1991–92		36	1
1992–93		33	2

BOGIE, Ian

Born Newcastle 6.12.67.   Ht 5 7
Wt 12 00
Midfield. From Apprentice. England
Schools.

Season	Club		
1985–86	Newcastle U	—	—

Season	Club		
1986–87		1	—
1987–88		7	—
1988–89		6	—
1988–89	Preston NE	13	1
1989–90		35	3
1990–91		31	8
1991–92	Millwall	25	—
1992–93		22	—

BOLAND, Willie

Born Ennis 6.8.75   Ht 5 9   Wt 11 02
Midfield.

Season	Club		
1992–93	Coventry C	1	—

BOLDER, Bob

Born Dover 2.10.58.   Ht 6 3   Wt 14 06
Goalkeeper. From Dover.

Season	Club		
1976–77	Sheffield W	—	—
1977–78		23	—
1978–79		19	—
1979–80		31	—
1980–81		39	—
1981–82		42	—
1982–83		42	—
1983–84	Liverpool	—	—
1984–85		—	—
1985–86		—	—
1985–86	Sunderland	22	—
1985–86	*Luton T*	—	—
1986–87	Charlton Ath	26	—
1987–88		35	—
1988–89		38	—
1989–90		38	—
1990–91		39	—
1991–92		46	—
1992–93		27	—

BOLLAN, Gary

Born Dundee 24.3.73.   Ht 5 11   Wt 12 4
Midfield. From Celtic BC. Scotland
Under-21.

Season	Club		
1987–88	Celtic	—	—
1988–89		—	—
1989–90		—	—

Season	Club	App	Goals
1990–91	Dundee U	2	—
1991–92		10	1
1992–93		15	3

BOND, Kevin

Born London 22.6.57. Ht 6 2 Wt 13 10
Defender. From Bournemouth Apprentice.
England B.

Season	Club	App	Goals
1974–75	Norwich C	—	—
1975–76		1	—
1976–77		3	—
1977–78		28	—
1978–79		42	2
1979–80		40	9
1980–81		28	1
From Seattle S			
1981–82	Manchester C	33	3
1982–83		40	3
1983–84		34	4
1984–85		3	1
1984–85	Southampton	33	1
1985–86		34	1
1986–87		34	1
1987–88		39	3
1988–89	Bournemouth	27	1
1989–90		31	—
1990–91		30	2
1991–92		38	1
1992–93	Exeter C	18	—

BOND, Richie

Born Blyth 27.10.65 Ht 5 11 Wt 11 06
Forward. From Blyth Spartans.

Season	Club	App	Goals
1991–92	Blackpool	—	—
1992–93		1	—

BONNER, Mark

Born Ormskirk 7.6.74. Ht 5 10 Wt 11 00
Midfield. From Trainee.

Season	Club	App	Goals
1991–92	Blackpool	3	—
1992–93		15	—

BONNER, Pat

Born Donegal 25.5.60. Ht 6 2 Wt 13 01
Goalkeeper. From Keadie Rovers. Eire
Youth, Under-21, 66 full caps.

Season	Club	App	Goals
1978–79	Celtic	2	—
1979–80		—	—
1980–81		36	—
1981–82		36	—
1982–83		36	—
1983–84		33	—
1984–85		34	—
1985–86		30	—
1986–87		43	—
1987–88		32	—
1988–89		26	—
1989–90		36	—
1990–91		36	—
1991–92		19	—
1992–93		33	—

BOOKER, Bob

Born Watford 25.1.58. Ht 6 3 Wt 13 03
Midfield. From Bedmond Sports.

Season	Club	App	Goals
1978–79	Brentford	3	—
1979–80		12	6
1980–81		26	7
1981–82		38	4
1982–83		39	6
1983–84		29	4
1984–85		38	7
1985–86		44	7
1986–87		2	—
1987–88		12	—
1988–89		8	—
1988–89	Sheffield U	26	2
1989–90		42	8
1990–91		29	3
1991–92		12	—
1991–92	Brentford	16	2
1992–93		3	—

BOOTH, Andrew

Born Huddersfield 17.3.73. Ht 5 10
Wt 10 03
Forward. From Trainee.

Season	Club	App	Goals
1991–92	Huddersfield T	3	—

1992–93		5	2

BOOTH, Scott

Born Aberdeen 16.12.71.   Ht 5 7
Wt 10 03
Forward. From Schools. Scotland Under-21, 3 full caps.

1988–89	Aberdeen	—	—
1989–90		2	—
1990–91		19	6
1991–92		33	5
1992–93		29	13

BOOTHROYD, Adrian

Born Bradford 8.2.71.   Ht 5 8   Wt 10 12
Defender. From Trainee.

1989–90	Huddersfield T	10	—
1990–91	Bristol R	3	—
1991–92		13	—
1992–93	Hearts	4	—

BORROWS, Brian

Born Liverpool 20.12.60.   Ht 5 10
Wt 10 12
Defender. From Amateur. England B.

1979–80	Everton	—	—
1980–81		—	—
1981–82		15	—
1982–83		12	—
1982–83	Bolton W	9	—
1983–84		44	—
1984–85		42	—
1985–86	Coventry C	41	—
1986–87		41	1
1987–88		33	—
1988–89		38	1
1989–90		37	1
1990–91		38	6
1991–92		35	—
1992–93		38	2

BORTHWICK, John

Born Hartlepool 24.3.64.   Ht 6 1
Wt 12 05
Forward. From Local.

1982–83	Hartlepool U	2	—
1983–84		10	—
1984–85		6	1
1985–86		32	8
1986–87		14	—
1987–88		34	5
1988–89		19	1
1989–90	Darlington	*42*	*19*
1990–91		46	10
1991–92		29	5
1992–93	York C	33	8

BOSNICH, Mark

Born Fairfield 13.1.72.   Ht 6 1   Wt 13 07
Goalkeeper. From Croatia Sydney.

1989–90	Manchester U	1	—
1990–91		2	—
1991–92	Aston Villa	1	—
1992–93		17	—

BOULD, Stephen

Born Stoke 16.11.62.   Ht 6 4   Wt 14 02
Defender. From Apprentice.

1980–81	Stoke C	—	—
1981–82		2	—
1982–83		14	—
1982–83	*Torquay U*	9	—
1983–84	Stoke C	38	2
1984–85		38	3
1985–86		33	—
1986–87		28	1
1987–88		30	—
1988–89	Arsenal	30	2
1989–90		19	—
1990–91		38	—
1991–92		25	1
1992–93		24	1

BOUND, Matthew

Born Trowbridge 9.11.72. Ht 6 2
Wt 13 12
Defender. From Trainee.

1990–91	Southampton	1	—
1991–92		—	—
1992–93		3	—

BOWDEN, Jon

Born Stockport 21.1.63. Ht 6 10
Wt 11 07
Midfield. From Local.

1979–80	Oldham Ath	—	—
1980–81		—	—
1981–82		5	2
1982–83		31	2
1983–84		31	1
1984–85		15	—
1985–86		—	—
1985–86	Port Vale	36	3
1986–87		34	4
1987–88	Wrexham	26	1
1988–89		42	10
1989–90		33	1
1990–91		40	5
1991–92		6	3
1991–92	Rochdale	31	6
1992–93		35	8

BOWEN, Jason

Born Merthyr 24.8.72. Ht 5 6   Wt 10 07
Midfield. From Trainee. Wales Under-21.

1990–91	Swansea C	3	—
1991–92		11	—
1992–93		38	10

BOWEN, Mark

Born Neath 7.12.63. Ht 5 8   Wt 11 13
Defender. From Apprentice. Wales
Schools, Youth, Under-21, 24 full caps.

1981–82	Tottenham H	—	—
1982–83		—	—
1983–84		7	—

1984–85		6	—
1985–86		2	1
1986–87		2	1
1987–88	Norwich C	24	1
1988–89		35	2
1989–90		38	7
1990–91		37	1
1991–92		36	3
1992–93		42	1

BOWLING, Ian

Born Sheffield 27.7.65. Ht 6 3   Wt 14 08
Goalkeeper. From Gainsborough T.

1988–89	Lincoln C	8	—
1989–90		—	—
1989–90	*Hartlepool U*	1	—
1990–91	Lincoln C	16	—
1991–92		20	—
1992–93		15	—
1992–93	*Bradford C*	7	—

BOWMAN, David

Born Tunbridge Wells 10.3.64. Ht 5 10
Wt 11 02
Midfield. From Salvesen BC. Scotland
Under-21, 4 full caps.

1980–81	Hearts	17	1
1981–82		16	1
1982–83		39	5
1983–84		33	—
1984–85		11	1
1984–85	Coventry C	10	—
1985–86		30	2
1986–87	Dundee U	29	—
1987–88		39	1
1988–89		29	1
1989–90		24	1
1990–91		20	1
1991–92		41	3
1992–93		24	—

BOWMAN, Robert

Born Durham 21.11.75.
Defender. From Trainee.

1992–93	Leeds U	4	—

BOWRY, Bobby

Born Croydon 19.5.71   Ht 5 8   Wt 10 00
Midfield.

Season	Club		
1991–92	Crystal Palace	—	—
1992–93		11	1

BOYD, Tom

Born Glasgow 24.11.65.   Ht 5 11
Wt 11 04
Defender. 'S' Form. Scotland Youth, B, Under-21, 17 full caps.

Season	Club		
1983–84	Motherwell	13	—
1984–85		36	—
1985–86		31	—
1986–87		31	—
1987–88		42	2
1988–89		36	1
1989–90		33	1
1990–91		30	2
1991–92	Chelsea	23	—
1991–92	Celtic	13	1
1992–93		42	—

BOYLE, Jimmy

Born Glasgow 19.2.67.   Ht 5 6   Wt 11 2
Defender. From Celtic BC.

Season	Club		
1985–86	Queen's Park	30	1
1986–87		39	3
1987–88		39	8
1988–89		39	4
1989–90	Airdrieonians	31	1
1990–91		11	—
1991–92		37	3
1992–93		40	4

BOZINOSKI, Vlado

Born Macedonia 30.3.64   Ht 5 10
Wt 11 03
Midfield. From Hellas, FC Brugge, Beira Mar, Sporting Lisbon.

Season	Club		
1992–93	Ipswich T	9	—

BRACEWELL, Paul

Born Stoke 19.7.62.   Ht 5 8   Wt 10 09
Midfield. From Apprentice. England Under-21, 3 full caps.

Season	Club		
1979–80	Stoke C	6	—
1980–81		40	2
1981–82		42	1
1982–83		41	2
1983–84	Sunderland	38	4
1984–85	Everton	37	2
1985–86		38	3
1986–87		—	—
1987–88		—	—
1988–89		20	2
1989–90		—	—
1989–90	Sunderland	37	2
1990–91		37	—
1991–92		39	—
1992–93	Newcastle U	25	2

BRACEY, Lee

Born Ashford 11.9.68.   Ht 6 1   Wt 12 08
Goalkeeper. From Trainee.

Season	Club		
1987–88	West Ham U	—	—
1988–89	Swansea C	30	—
1989–90		31	—
1990–91		35	—
1991–92		3	—
1991–92	Halifax T	32	—
1992–93		41	—

BRADBURY, Shaun

Born Birmingham 11.2.74   Ht 5 10
Wt 11 00
Forward. From Trainee.

Season	Club		
1992–93	Wolverhampton W	2	2

BRADLEY, Darren

Born Birmingham 24.11.65.   Ht 5 7
Wt 11 12
Defender. From Apprentice. England Youth.

Season	Club		
1983–84	Aston Villa	—	—

Season	Club	League Appearances/Goals
1984–85		2 —
1985–86		18 —
1985–86	WBA	10 —
1986–87		14 1
1987–88		19 —
1988–89		26 —
1989–90		27 2
1990–91		39 1
1991–92		37 2
1992–93		42 1

BRADLEY, Russell

Born Birmingham 28.3.66.   Ht 6 0
Wt 12 05
Midfield. From Dudley T.

Season	Club	League Appearances/Goals
1987–88	Nottingham F	— —
1988–89		— —
1988–89	*Hereford U*	12 1
1989–90	Hereford U	33 1
1990–91		41 2
1991–92		3 —
1991–92	Halifax T	26 2
1992–93		30 1

BRADSHAW, Carl

Born Sheffield 2.10.68.   Ht 6 0   Wt 11 00
Forward. From Apprentice. England
Youth.

Season	Club	League Appearances/Goals
1986–87	Sheffield W	9 2
1986–87	*Barnsley*	6 1
1987–88	Sheffield W	20 2
1988–89		3 —
1988–89	Manchester C	5 —
1989–90		— —
1989–90	Sheffield U	30 3
1990–91		27 1
1991–92		18 2
1992–93		32 1

BRADSHAW, Darren

Born Sheffield 19.3.67.   Ht 5 11   Wt 11 04
Midfield. From Matlock T.

Season	Club	League Appearances/Goals
1987–88	Chesterfield	18 —
1987–88	York C	25 1

Season	Club	League Appearances/Goals
1988–89		34 2
1989–90		— —
1989–90	Newcastle U	12 —
1990–91		7 —
1991–92		19 —
1992–93	Peterborough	34 —

BRADY, Kieron

Born Glasgow 17.9.71.   Ht 5 9   Wt 11 13
Midfield. From Trainee. Eire Youth,
Under-21.

Season	Club	League Appearances/Goals
1989–90	Sunderland	11 2
1990–91		14 2
1991–92		8 3
1992–93		— —
1992–93	*Doncaster R*	4 3

BRAIN, Simon

Born Evesham 31.3.66.   Ht 5 6   Wt 10 08
Forward. From Cheltenham T.

Season	Club	League Appearances/Goals
1990–91	Hereford U	22 8
1991–92		41 10
1992–93		21 2

BRAMMER, David

Born Bromborough 28.2.75   Ht 5 9
Wt 10 05
Midfield. From Trainee.

Season	Club	League Appearances/Goals
1992–93	Wrexham	2 —

BRANAGAN, Keith

Born Fulham 10.7.66.   Ht 6 1   Wt 13 00
Goalkeeper.

Season	Club	League Appearances/Goals
1983–84	Cambridge U	1 —
1984–85		19 —
1985–86		9 —
1986–87		46 —
1987–88		35 —
1987–88	Millwall	— —
1988–89		— —
1989–90		16 —
1989–90	*Brentford*	2 —

Season	Club	App	Goals	Season	Club	App	Goals
1990–91	Millwall	18	—	1983–84		19	2
1991–92		12	—	1984–85		6	2
1991–92	*Gillingham*	1	—	1984–85	*Port Vale*	6	3
1991–92	*Fulham*	—	—	1984–85	Preston NE	17	3
1992–93	Bolton W	46	—	1985–86		43	14
				1986–87		45	18
				1987–88		36	14

BRANCH, Graham

Born Heswall 12.2.72.   Ht 6 2   Wt 13 00
Forward. From Heswall Ath.

Season	Club	App	Goals
1991–92	Tranmere R	4	—
1992–93		3	—
1992–93	*Bury*	4	1

Season	Club	App	Goals
1988–89		25	9
1988–89	Newcastle U	7	—
1989–90		16	2
1990–91	Fulham	41	4
1991–92		46	14
1992–93		30	7

BRANNAN, Ged

Born Liverpool 15.1.72.   Ht 6 0   Wt 13 03
Defender. From Trainee.

Season	Club	App	Goals
1990–91	Tranmere R	18	1
1991–92		18	1
1992–93		38	1

BREACKER, Tim

Born Bicester 2.7.65.   Ht 5 11   Wt 13 00
Defender. England Under-21.

Season	Club	App	Goals
1983–84	Luton T	2	—
1984–85		35	—
1985–86		36	—
1986–87		29	1
1987–88		40	1
1988–89		22	—
1989–90		38	1
1990–91		8	—
1990–91	West Ham U	24	1
1991–92		34	2
1992–93		39	2

BRAZIL, Derek

Born Dublin 14.12.68.   Ht 5 11   Wt 10 05
Defender. From Rivermount BC. Eire
Youth, B, Under-21, Under-23.

Season	Club	App	Goals
1985–86	Manchester U	—	—
1986–87		—	—
1987–88		—	—
1988–89		1	—
1989–90		1	—
1990–91		—	—
1990–91	*Oldham Ath*	1	—
1991–92	Manchester U	—	—
1991–92	*Swansea C*	12	1
1992–93	Cardiff C	34	—

BREEN, Gary

Born London 12.12.73.   Ht 6 1   Wt 12 07
Defender. From Charlton Ath.

Season	Club	App	Goals
1991–92	Maidstone U	19	—
1992–93	Gillingham	29	—

BRAZIL, Gary

Born Tunbridge Wells 19.9.62.   Ht 5 11
Wt 10 02
Forward. From Crystal Palace Apprentice.

Season	Club	App	Goals
1980–81	Sheffield U	3	—
1981–82		1	—
1982–83		33	5

BREITKREUTZ, Matthias

Born Crivitz 12.5.71.   Ht 5 9   Wt 11 03
Midfield. From Bergmann Borsig.

Season	Club	App	Goals
1991–92	Aston Villa	8	—
1992–93		3	—

BRENNAN, Mark

Born Rossendale 4.10.65. Ht 5 10
Wt 10 13
Midfield. From Apprentice. England
Youth, Under-21.

Season	Club	App	Goals
1982–83	Ipswich T	—	—
1983–84		19	1
1984–85		36	2
1985–86		40	3
1986–87		37	7
1987–88		36	6
1988–89	Middlesbrough	25	3
1989–90		40	3
1990–91	Manchester C	16	3
1991–92		13	3
1992–93		—	—
1992–93	Oldham Ath	14	3

BRESSINGTON, Graham

Born Eton 8.7.66. Wt 12 00
Defender. From Wycombe W.

Season	Club	App	Goals
1987–88	Lincoln C	*12*	—
1988–89		30	1
1989–90		43	2
1990–91		37	—
1991–92		3	—
1992–93		28	4

BREVETT, Rufus

Born Derby 24.9.69. Ht 5 8 Wt 11 00
Defender. From Trainee.

Season	Club	App	Goals
1987–88	Doncaster R	17	—
1988–89		23	—
1989–90		42	—
1990–91		27	3
1990–91	QPR	10	—
1991–92		7	—
1992–93		15	—

BREWSTER, Craig

Born Dundee 13.12.66 Ht 5 11 Wt 10 7
Midfield. From Stobwell J.

Season	Club	App	Goals
1985–86	Forfar Ath	16	2

Season	Club	App	Goals
1986–87		32	3
1987–88		39	2
1988–89		37	9
1989–90		38	8
1990–91		29	11
1991–92	Raith R	42	12
1992–93		44	22

BRIEN, Tony

Born Dublin 10.2.69. Ht 5 11 Wt 11 09
Defender. From Apprentice.

Season	Club	App	Goals
1986–87	Leicester C	—	—
1987–88		15	1
1988–89		1	—
1988–89	Chesterfield	29	1
1989–90		43	3
1990–91		43	3
1991–92		41	—
1992–93		39	1

BRIGGS, Gary

Born Leeds 8.5.58. Ht 6 3 Wt 12 10
Defender. From Apprentice.

Season	Club	App	Goals
1977–78	Middlesbrough	—	—
1977–78	Oxford U	20	2
1978–79		39	—
1979–80		46	1
1980–81		42	1
1981–82		45	1
1982–83		37	1
1983–84		38	3
1984–85		42	4
1985–86		38	—
1986–87		40	3
1987–88		18	1
1988–89		15	1
1989–90	Blackpool	17	2
1990–91		30	—
1991–92		24	—
1992–93		33	1

BRIGHT, Mark

Born Stoke 6.6.62. Ht 6 0 Wt 13 00
Forward. From Leek T.

Season	Club	App	Goals
1981–82	Port Vale	2	—

Season	Club	Apps	Goals
1982–83		1	1
1983–84		26	9
1984–85	Leicester C	16	—
1985–86		24	6
1986–87		2	—
1986–87	Crystal Palace	28	8
1987–88		38	25
1988–89		46	20
1989–90		36	12
1990–91		32	9
1991–92		42	17
1992–93		5	1
1992–93	Sheffield W	30	11

BRIGHTWELL, David

Born Lutterworth 7.1.71. Ht 6 1
Wt 13 05
Midfield. From Trainee.

Season	Club	Apps	Goals
1987–88	Manchester C	—	—
1988–89		—	—
1989–90		—	—
1990–91		—	—
1990–91	*Chester C*	6	—
1991–92	Manchester C	4	—
1992–93		8	—

BRIGHTWELL, Ian

Born Lutterworth 9.4.68. Ht 5 10
Wt 11 07
Midfield. From Congleton T. England
Schools, Youth, Under-21.

Season	Club	Apps	Goals
1986–87	Manchester C	16	1
1987–88		33	5
1988–89		26	6
1989–90		28	2
1990–91		33	—
1991–92		40	1
1992–93		21	1

BRITTON, Gerard

Born Glasgow 20.10.70. Ht 6 1 Wt 11 0
Forward. From Celtic BC.

Season	Club	Apps	Goals
1987–88	Celtic	—	—
1988–89		—	—

Season	Club	Apps	Goals
1989–90		—	—
1990–91		2	—
1991–92		—	—
1991–92	*Reading*	2	—
1992–93	Partick T	40	12

BROCK, Kevin

Born Middleton Stoney 9.9.62. Ht 5 9
Wt 10 12
Midfield. From Apprentice. England
Schools, Under-21.

Season	Club	Apps	Goals
1979–80	Oxford U	19	2
1980–81		26	5
1981–82		28	5
1982–83		37	4
1983–84		45	3
1984–85		37	6
1985–86		23	—
1986–87		31	1
1987–88	QPR	26	2
1988–89		14	—
1988–89	Newcastle U	21	2
1989–90		44	2
1990–91		38	5
1991–92		35	4
1992–93		7	2

BRODDLE, Julian

Born Laughton 1.11.64. Ht 5 9 Wt 11 07
Midfield. From Apprentice.

Season	Club	Apps	Goals
1981–82	Sheffield U	1	—
1982–83		—	—
1983–84	Scunthorpe U	13	1
1984–85		45	14
1985–86		41	7
1986–87		38	10
1987–88		7	—
1987–88	Barnsley	19	1
1988–89		38	3
1989–90		20	—
1989–90	Plymouth Arg	9	—
1990–91		—	—
1990–91	*Bradford C*	—	—
1990–91	St Mirren	10	—
1991–92		35	2
1992–93	Partick T	6	—

1992–93 *Scunthorpe U* .... 5 —

BROLLY, Richard

Born York 5.10.69 Ht 6 0 Wt 11 03
Midfield. From Illinois Univ.

1992–93 Wigan Ath 2   1

BROOKS, Chris

Born Sutton-in-Ashfield 6.6.72 Ht 5 10
Wt 11 10
Forward. From Luton T.

1992–93 Shrewsbury T 1   —

BROOKS, Shaun

Born London 9.10.62. Ht 5 7 Wt 11 00
Midfield. From Apprentice. England
Schools, Youth.

1979–80	Crystal Palace	1	—
1980–81	....	17	—
1981–82	....	25	2
1982–83	....	7	2
1983–84	....	4	—
1983–84	Orient	36	9
1984–85	....	29	5
1985–86	....	38	7
1986–87	....	45	5
1987–88	Bournemouth	37	6
1988–89	....	36	3
1989–90	....	35	4
1990–91	....	13	—
1991–92	....	7	—
1992–93	....	—	—
1992–93	*Stockport Co*	—	—

BROUGH, John

Born Heanor 8.1.73 Ht 6 1 Wt 12 07
Forward. From Trainee.

1991–92	Notts Co	—	—
1992–93	Shrewsbury T	14	1

BROWN, Grant

Born Sunderland 19.11.69. Ht 6 0
Wt 11 12
Defender. From Trainee.

1987–88	Leicester C	2	—
1988–89	....	12	—
1989–90	Lincoln C	34	2
1990–91	....	32	1
1991–92	....	37	1
1992–93	....	40	1

BROWN, John

Born Stirling 26.1.62. Ht 5 11 Wt 10 02
Defender. From Blantyre Welfare.

1979–80	Hamilton A	19	—
1980–81	....	38	6
1981–82	....	28	5
1982–83	....	9	—
1983–84	....	39	—
1984–85	Dundee	34	7
1985–86	....	29	11
1986–87	....	31	10
1987–88	....	20	3
1987–88	Rangers	9	2
1988–89	....	29	1
1989–90	....	27	1
1990–91	....	27	1
1991–92	....	25	4
1992–93	....	39	4

BROWN, Jon

Born Barnsley 8.9.66. Ht 5 10 Wt 11 03
Defender. From Denaby U.

1990–91	Exeter C	29	
1991–92	....	35	
1992–93	....	40	1

BROWN, Kenny

Born Barking 11.7.67. Ht 5 8 Wt 11 06
Defender. From Apprentice.

1984–85	Norwich C	—	
1985–86	....	—	
1986–87	....	18	

Season	Club	App	Goals
1987–88		7	—
1988–89	Plymouth Arg	39	1
1989–90		44	—
1990–91		43	3
1991–92	West Ham U	27	3
1992–93		15	2

BROWN, Linton

Born Driffield 12.4.68 Ht 5 9 Wt 11 00
Midfield. From Guiseley.

Season	Club	App	Goals
1992–93	Halifax T	3	—
1992–93	Hull C	23	1

BROWN, Mike

Born Birmingham 8.2.68. Ht 5 9
Wt 10 12
Forward. From Apprentice.

Season	Club	App	Goals
1985–86	Shrewsbury T	—	—
1986–87		22	2
1987–88		41	5
1988–89		41	—
1989–90		43	1
1990–91		43	1
1991–92	Bolton W	27	3
1992–93		6	—
1992–93	Shrewsbury T	17	1

BROWN, Nicky

Born Northampton 25.1.73.
Goalkeeper. From Norwich C Trainee.

Season	Club	App	Goals
1991–92	Halifax T	1	—
1992–93		1	—

BROWN, Phil

Born South Shields 30.5.59. Ht 5 11
Wt 11 06
Defender. From Local.

Season	Club	App	Goals
1978–79	Hartlepool U	—	—
1979–80		10	—
1980–81		46	1
1981–82		44	4
1982–83		44	2

Season	Club	App	Goals
1983–84		31	—
1984–85		42	1
1985–86	Halifax T	45	2
1986–87		46	12
1987–88		44	5
1988–89	Bolton W	46	4
1989–90		46	1
1990–91		45	—
1991–92		37	2
1992–93		40	5

BROWN, Richard

Born Nottingham 13.1.67. Ht 5 10
Wt 11 02
Defender. From Derby Co, Ilkeston T.

Season	Club	App	Goals
1984–85	Sheffield W	—	—
1985–86		—	—
From Kettering T			
1990–91	Blackburn R	—	—
1990–91	*Maidstone U*	3	—
1991–92	Blackburn R	26	—
1992–93		2	—

BROWN, Steve

Born Northampton 6.7.66. Ht 5 9
Wt 10 12
Forward.

Season	Club	App	Goals
1985–86	Northampton T	—	—
From Irthlingborough D			
1989–90	Northampton T	21	1
1990–91		40	2
1991–92		35	3
1992–93		38	9

BROWN, Steve

Born Brighton 13.5.72. Ht 6 1 Wt 12 08
Defender. From Trainee.

Season	Club	App	Goals
1990–91	Charlton Ath		—
1991–92		1	—
1992–93		—	—

BROWN, Steve

Born Southend 6.12.73 Ht 5 11
Wt 11 10
Forward. From Trainee.

1992–93	Southend U	10	2

BROWN, Tony

Born Bradford 17.9.58. Ht 6 2 Wt 12 07
Defender. From Thackley.

1982–83	Leeds U	1	—
1983–84		22	1
1984–85		1	—
1984–85	*Doncaster R*	14	—
1985–86	Doncaster R	38	2
1986–87		35	—
1986–87	Scunthorpe U	22	—
1988–89		32	2
1989–90	Rochdale	43	—
1990–91		26	—
1991–92		40	—
1992–93		5	—

BROWNING, Marcus

Born Bristol 22.4.71. Ht 5 11 Wt 12 00
Forward. From Trainee.

1989–90	Bristol R	1	—
1990–91		—	—
1991–92		11	—
1992–93		19	1
1992–93	*Hereford U*	7	5

BRUCE, Steve

Born Newcastle 31.12.60. Ht 6 0
Wt 12 6
Defender. From Apprentice. England
Youth.

1978–79	Gillingham	—	—
1979–80		40	6
1980–81		41	4
1981–82		45	6
1982–83		39	7
1983–84		40	6
1984–85	Norwich C	39	1

1985–86		42	8
1986–87		41	3
1987–88		19	2
1987–88	Manchester U	21	2
1988–89		38	2
1989–90		34	3
1990–91		31	13
1991–92		37	5
1992–93		42	5

BRYANT, Matthew

Born Bristol 21.9.70. Ht 6 1 Wt 12 11
Defender. From Trainee.

1989–90	Bristol C	—	—
1990–91		22	1
1990–91	*Walsall*	13	—
1991–92	Bristol C	43	2
1992–93		41	1

BRYCE, Steven

Born Shotts 30.6.69. Ht 5 8 Wt 10 07
Forward. From Motherwell BC.

1987–88	Motherwell	—	—
1988–89		9	—
1989–90		3	—
1990–91		4	1
1991–92		5	—
1992–93		1	—

BRYSON, Ian

Born Kilmarnock 26.11.62. Ht 5 11
Wt 11 11
Midfield.

1981–82	Kilmarnock	14	3
1982–83		28	1
1983–84		25	4
1984–85		36	3
1985–86		38	14
1986–87		32	10
1987–88		42	5
1988–89	Sheffield U	37	8
1989–90		39	9
1990–91		29	7
1991–92		34	9

46

Season	Club		Apps	Goals
1992–93			16	3

BUCKLE, Paul

Born Hatfield 16.12.70.   Ht 5 8   Wt 10 08
Midfield. From Trainee.

Season	Club		Apps	Goals
1987–88	Brentford		1	—
1988–89			—	—
1989–90			10	—
1990–91			26	—
1991–92			15	1
1992–93			5	—

BUCKLEY, John

Born Glasgow 10.5.62.   Ht 5 9   Wt 11 00
Forward. From Queen's Park and Celtic.

Season	Club		Apps	Goals
1982–83	Partick T		8	1
1983–84			37	4
1984–85	Doncaster R		39	6
1985–86			45	5
1986–87	Leeds U		9	1
1986–87	*Leicester C*		5	—
1987–88	Leeds U		1	—
1987–88	*Doncaster R*		6	—
1987–88	Rotherham U		26	—
1988–89			36	5
1989–90			40	7
1990–91			3	1
1990–91	Partick Th		26	5
1991–92	Scunthorpe U		28	6
1992–93			15	2
1992–93	Rotherham U		4	—

BUGLIONE, Martin

Born London 19.6.68   Ht 6 1   Wt 11 9
Forward. From Margate.

Season	Club		Apps	Goals
1992–93	St Johnstone		7	2

BULL, Gary

Born West Bromwich 12.6.66.   Ht 5 9
Wt 11 07
Forward.

Season	Club		Apps	Goals
1986–87	Southampton		—	—
1987–88			—	—

Season	Club		Apps	Goals
1987–88	Cambridge U		9	3
1988–89			10	1
To Barnet				
1991–92	Barnet		42	20
1992–93			41	17

BULL, Steve

Born Tipton 28.3.65.   Ht 5 11   Wt 11 04
Forward. From Apprentice. England
Under-21, B, 13 full caps.

Season	Club		Apps	Goals
1985–86	WBA		1	—
1986–87			3	2
1986–87	Wolverhampton W		30	14
1987–88			44	34
1988–89			45	37
1989–90			42	24
1990–91			43	26
1991–92			43	20
1992–93			36	16

BULLIMORE, Wayne

Born Sutton-in-Ashfield 12.9.70.   Ht 5 9
Wt 10 06
Midfield. From Trainee. FA Schools.

Season	Club		Apps	Goals
1988–89	Manchester U		—	—
1989–90			—	—
1990–91			—	—
1990–91	Barnsley		—	—
1991–92			18	1
1992–93			17	—

BUMSTEAD, John

Born Rotherhithe 27.11.58.   Ht 5 7
Wt 10 05
Midfield. From Apprentice.

Season	Club		Apps	Goals
1977–78	Chelsea		—	—
1978–79			8	1
1979–80			28	3
1980–81			41	1
1981–82			21	4
1982–83			36	4
1983–84			31	7
1984–85			25	3
1985–86			32	1

Season	Club	Apps	Goals
1986–87		29	8
1987–88		17	1
1988–89		29	2
1989–90		29	2
1990–91		13	1
1991–92	Charlton Ath	36	—
1992–93		20	3

BUNBURY, Alex

Born British Guyana 18.6.67   Ht 5 10
Wt 11 00
Forward. From Montreal Supra. Canada
full caps.

Season	Club	Apps	Goals
1992–93	West Ham U	4	—

BURGESS, Daryl

Born Birmingham 20.4.71.   Ht 5 11
Wt 12 03
Defender. From Trainee.

Season	Club	Apps	Goals
1989–90	WBA	34	—
1990–91		25	—
1991–92		36	2
1992–93		18	1

BURGESS, Dave

Born Liverpool. 20.1.60.   Ht 5 10
Wt 11 04
Defender. From Local.

Season	Club	Apps	Goals
1981–82	Tranmere R	46	1
1982–83		46	—
1983–84		44	—
1984–85		41	—
1985–86		41	—
1986–87	Grimsby T	31	—
1987–88		38	—
1988–89	Blackpool	46	—
1989–90		19	1
1990–91		—	—
1991–92		16	—
1992–93		20	—
1992–93	Carlisle U	6	—

BURKE, David

Born Liverpool 6.8.60.   Ht 5 10   Wt 11 00
Defender. From Apprentice. England
Youth.

Season	Club	Apps	Goals
1977–78	Bolton W	—	—
1978–79		20	1
1979–80		27	—
1980–81		22	—
1981–82	Huddersfield T	41	1
1982–83		44	1
1983–84		42	—
1984–85		31	1
1985–86		—	—
1986–87		21	—
1987–88		10	—
1987–88	Crystal Palace	31	—
1988–89		39	—
1989–90		11	—
1990–91	Bolton W	14	—
1991–92		37	—
1992–93		43	—

BURKE, Mark

Born Solihull 12.2.69.   Ht 5 10   Wt 11 08
Forward. From Apprentice. England
Youth.

Season	Club	Apps	Goals
1986–87	Aston Villa	1	—
1987–88		6	—
1987–88	Middlesbrough	16	—
1988–89		29	5
1989–90		12	1
1990–91		—	—
1990–91	Darlington	5	1
1990–91	Ipswich T	—	—
1990–91	Wolverhampton W	6	—
1991–92		18	2
1992–93		32	8

BURLEY, Craig

Born Ayr 24.9.71.   Ht 6 1   Wt 11 07
Midfield. From Trainee. Scotland
Under-21.

Season	Club	Apps	Goals
1989–90	Chelsea	—	—
1990–91		1	—
1991–92		8	—

| 1992–93 | | 3 — | 1991–92 | Kilmarnock | 31 4 |
| | | | 1992–93 | | 10 — |

BURNETT, Wayne

Born London 4.9.71. Ht 5 9 Wt 10 11
Midfield. From Trainee.

1989–90	Leyton Orient	3 —
1990–91		1 —
1991–92		36 —
1992–93	Blackburn R	— —

BURNHAM, Jason

Born Mansfield 8.5.73.
Defender. From Notts County Trainee,
Northampton T Trainee.

| 1991–92 | Northampton T | 40 2 |
| 1992–93 | | 31 — |

BURNS, Chris

Born Manchester 9.11.67. Ht 6 0
Wt 12 00
Midfield. From Cheltenham T.

1990–91	Portsmouth	— —
1991–92		46 8
1992–93		32 1

BURNS, Hugh

Born Lanark 13.12.65. Ht 6 0 Wt 11 7
Defender. From Cambuslang R.

1982–83	Rangers	— —
1983–84		4 —
1984–85		15 —
1985–86		28 3
1986–87		3 —
1986–87	Leeds U	— —
1986–87	Hamilton A	5 1
1987–88	Hearts	24 —
1988–89		— —
1988–89	Dunfermline Ath	15 —
1989–90		— —
1989–90	Fulham	6 —
1990–91	Hamilton A	24 6
1991–92		9 —

BURNS, Tommy

Born Glasgow 16.2.56 Ht 5 11 Wt 11 3
Midfield. From Maryhill J. Scotland U-21,
8 full caps.

1974–75	Celtic	1 —
1975–76		5 —
1976–77		22 1
1977–78		23 3
1978–79		29 3
1979–80		15 —
1980–81		33 4
1981–82		33 9
1982–83		17 7
1983–84		33 9
1984–85		27 7
1985–86		34 5
1986–87		17 —
1987–88		27 2
1988–89		32 2
1989–90		9 —
1989–90	Kilmarnock	22 3
1990–91		37 8
1991–92		41 3
1992–93		39 2

BURRIDGE, John

Born Workington 3.12.51. Ht 5 11
Wt 13 03
Goalkeeper. From Apprentice.

1968–69	Workington	1 —
1969–70		— —
1970–71		26 —
1970–71	Blackpool	3 —
1971–72		34 —
1972–73		22 —
1973–74		30 —
1974–75		38 —
1975–76		7 —
1975–76	Aston Villa	30 —
1976–77		35 —
1977–78		— —
1977–78	Southend U	6 —
1977–78	Crystal Palace	10 —

Season	Club	Apps	Goals
1978–79	....	42	—
1979–80	....	36	—
1980–81	....	—	—
1980–81	QPR..............	19	—
1981–82	....	20	—
1982–83	Wolverhampton W	42	—
1983–84	....	32	—
1984–85	....	—	—
1984–85	*Derby Co*............	6	—
1984–85	Sheffield U......	30	—
1985–86	....	42	—
1986–87	....	37	—
1987–88	Southampton	31	—
1988–89	....	31	—
1989–90	....	—	—
1989–90	Newcastle U........	28	—
1990–91	....	39	—
1991–92	Hibernian...........	35	—
1992–93	....	30	—

BURROWS, Adrian

Born Sutton 16.1.59. Ht 5 11 Wt 11 12
Defender. From Local.

Season	Club	Apps	Goals
1979–80	Mansfield T...........	17	—
1980–81	....	20	3
1981–82	....	41	2
1982–83	Northampton T........	43	4
1983–84	....	45	—
1984–85	Plymouth Arg........	39	—
1985–86	....	7	2
1986–87	....	17	1
1987–88	....	23	1
1987–88	*Southend U*	6	—
1988–89	Plymouth Arg........	43	1
1989–90	....	46	1
1990–91	....	45	4
1991–92	....	15	3
1992–93	....	20	1

BURROWS, David

Born Dudley 25.10.68. Ht 5 10 Wt 11 08
Defender. From Apprentice. England B,
Under-21.

Season	Club	Apps	Goals
1985–86	WBA............	1	—
1986–87	....	15	1
1987–88	....	21	—

Season	Club	Apps	Goals
1988–89	....	9	—
1988–89	Liverpool	21	—
1989–90	....	26	—
1990–91	....	35	—
1991–92	....	30	1
1992–93	....	30	2

BURTON, Mark

Born Barnsley 7.5.73. Ht 5 8 Wt 11 07
Midfield. From Trainee.

Season	Club	Apps	Goals
1991–92	Barnsley	—	—
1992–93	....	5	—

BURTON, Simon

Born Bolton 29.12.73. Ht 5 10 Wt 10 04
Forward. From Trainee.

Season	Club	Apps	Goals
1992–93	Preston NE............	21	3

BUSHELL, Steve

Born Manchester 28.12.72. Ht 5 9
Wt 11 00
Midfield. From Trainee.

Season	Club	Apps	Goals
1990–91	York C............	15	—
1991–92	....	16	—
1992–93	....	8	—

BUSST, Dave

Born Birmingham 30.6.67. Ht 6 1
Wt 12 10
Defender. From Moor Green.

Season	Club	Apps	Goals
1991–92	Coventry C............	—	—
1992–93	....	10	—

BUTCHER, Terry

Born Singapore 28.12.58. Ht 6 4
Wt 14 00
Defender. From Amateur. England Under-
21, B, 77 full caps.

Season	Club	Apps	Goals
1976–77	Ipswich T............	—	—
1977–78	....	3	—

Season	Club	Apps	Goals
1978–79	....	21	2
1979–80	....	36	2
1980–81	....	40	4
1981–82	....	27	1
1982–83	....	42	—
1983–84	....	34	1
1984–85	....	41	2
1985–86	....	27	4
1986–87	Rangers....................	43	3
1987–88	....	11	1
1988–89	....	34	2
1989–90	....	34	3
1990–91	....	5	—
1990–91	Coventry C	6	—
1991–92	....	—	—
1992–93	Sunderland....................	38	—

BUTLER, Barry

Born Farnworth 4.6.62.   Ht 6 2   Wt 13 0
Defender. From Atherton T.

Season	Club	Apps	Goals
1985–86	Chester C	14	—
1986–87	....	44	—
1987–88	....	16	—
1988–89	....	35	—
1989–90	....	44	4
1990–91	....	43	5
1991–92	....	41	6
1992–93	....	31	—

BUTLER, John

Born Liverpool 7.2.62.   Ht 5 11   Wt 11 07
Defender. From Prescot Cables.

Season	Club	Apps	Goals
1981–82	Wigan Ath	1	—
1982–83	....	40	5
1983–84	....	41	3
1984–85	....	45	3
1985–86	....	36	—
1986–87	....	36	—
1987–88	....	26	1
1988–89	....	20	3
1988–89	Stoke C	25	1
1989–90	....	44	—
1990–91	....	31	2
1991–92	....	42	3
1992–93	....	44	1

BUTLER, Lee

Born Sheffield 30.5.66.   Ht 6 2   Wt 14 02
Goalkeeper. From Haworth Colliery.

Season	Club	Apps	Goals
1986–87	Lincoln C....................	30	—
1987–88	Aston Villa....................	—	—
1988–89	....	4	—
1989–90	....	—	—
1990–91	....	4	—
1990–91	*Hull C*	4	—
1991–92	Barnsley	43	—
1992–93	....	28	—

BUTLER, Paul

Born Bradford 2.11.72.   Ht 6 2   Wt 13 00
Defender. From Trainee.

Season	Club	Apps	Goals
1990–91	Rochdale....................	2	—
1991–92	....	25	—
1992–93	....	16	2

BUTLER, Peter

Born Halifax 27.8.66.   Ht 5 9   Wt 11 02
Midfield. From Apprentice.

Season	Club	Apps	Goals
1984–85	Huddersfield T	4	—
1985–86	....	1	—
1985–86	*Cambridge U*	14	1
1986–87	Bury	11	—
1986–87	Cambridge U	29	4
1987–88	....	26	5
1987–88	Southend U	15	3
1988–89	....	35	2
1989–90	....	41	2
1990–91	....	42	2
1991–92	....	9	—
1991–92	*Huddersfield T*	7	—
1992–93	West Ham U	39	2

BUTLER, Steve

Born Birmingham 27.1.62.   Ht 6 2
Wt 13 00
Forward. From Windsor and Eton,
Wokingham.

Season	Club	Apps	Goals
1984–85	Brentford	3	1
1985–86	....	18	2

To Maidstone U (1986)

Season	Club	Apps	Goals
1989–90	....	44	21
1990–91	....	32	20
1990–91	Watford	10	1
1991–92	....	43	8
1992–93	....	9	—
1992–93	*Bournemouth*	1	—
1992–93	Cambridge U	23	6

BUTLER, Tony

Born Stockport 28.9.72.   Ht 6 2   Wt 11 12
Defender. From Trainee.

Season	Club	Apps	Goals
1990–91	Gillingham	6	—
1991–92	....	5	—
1992–93	....	41	—

BUTT, Nicky

Born Manchester 21.1.75   Ht 5 10
Wt 11 00
Midfield. From Trainee. England Youth.

Season	Club	Apps	Goals
1992–93	Manchester U	1	—

BUTTERS, Guy

Born Hillingdon 30.10.69.   Ht 6 3
Wt 13 00
Defender. From Trainee. England
Under-21.

Season	Club	Apps	Goals
1988–89	Tottenham H	28	1
1989–90	....	7	—
1989–90	*Southend U*	16	3
1990–91	Portsmouth	23	—
1991–92	....	33	2
1992–93	....	15	1

BUTTERWORTH, Ian

Born Crewe 25.1.65.   Ht 6 1   Wt 12 10
Defender. From Apprentice. England
Under-21.

Season	Club	Apps	Goals
1981–82	Coventry C	14	—
1982–83	....	30	—
1983–84	....	24	—
1984–85	....	22	—
1985–86	Nottingham F.............	23	—
1986–87	....	4	—
1986–87	Norwich C	28	—
1987–88	....	35	—
1988–89	....	37	2
1989–90	....	22	—
1990–91	....	31	—
1991–92	....	31	1
1992–93	....	26	1

BYRNE, David

Born London 5.3.61.   Ht 5 8   Wt 10 09
Forward. From Kingstonian.

Season	Club	Apps	Goals
1985–86	Gillingham	23	3
1986–87	Millwall......................	40	4
1987–88	....	23	2
1988–89	....	—	—
1988–89	*Cambridge U*	4	—
1988–89	*Blackburn R*	4	—
1988–89	Plymouth Arg	13	1
1989–90	....	32	1
1989–90	*Bristol R*......................	2	—
1990–91	Plymouth Arg	14	—
1990–91	Watford	17	2
1991–92	....	—	—
1991–92	*Reading*	7	2
1991–92	*Fulham*	5	—
1992–93	St Johnstone	12	—

BYRNE, John

Born Manchester 1.2.61.   Ht 5 11
Wt 13 01
Forward. From Apprentice. Eire 23 full
caps.

Season	Club	Apps	Goals
1978–79	York C........................	—	—
1979–80	....	9	2
1980–81	....	38	6
1981–82	....	29	6
1982–83	....	43	12
1983–84	....	46	27
1984–85	....	10	2
1984–85	QPR	23	3
1985–86	....	36	12
1986–87	....	40	11
1987–88	....	27	4
From Le Havre			
1990–91	Brighton.....................	38	9

Season	Club	League Appearances/Goals	
1991–92	....	13	5
1991–92	Sunderland..................	27	7
1992–93	....	6	1
1992–93	Millwall......................	13	1
1992–93	*Brighton*	7	2

CADETTE, Richard

Born Hammersmith 21.3.65. Ht 5 8
Wt 11 07
Forward. From Wembley.

Season	Club		
1984–85	Orient..........................	21	4
1985–86	Southend U.................	44	24
1986–87	....	46	24
1987–88	Sheffield U	28	7
1988–89	Brentford	32	12
1989–90	....	16	1
1989–90	*Bournemouth*	8	1
1990–91	Brentford	28	6
1991–92	....	11	1
1991–92	Falkirk	14	3
1992–93	....	31	8

CAESAR, Gus

Born London 5.3.66. Ht 6 0 Wt 12 00
Defender. From Apprentice. England
Under-21.

Season	Club		
1983–84	Arsenal........................	—	—
1984–85	....	—	—
1985–86	....	2	—
1986–87	....	15	—
1987–88	....	22	—
1988–89	....	2	—
1989–90	....	3	—
1990–91	....	—	—
1990–91	*QPR*...........................	5	—
1991–92	Cambridge U	—	—
1991–92	Bristol C	10	—
1991–92	Airdrieonians..............	12	—
1992–93	....	29	—

CAGIGAO, Francisco

Born London 10.11.69 Ht 5 9 Wt 12 00
Forward. From Arsenal, Barcelona.

Season	Club		
1991–92	Southend U.................	—	—
1992–93	....	1	—

CAIG, Anthony

Born Whitehaven 11.4.74 Ht 6 1
Wt 13 05
Goalkeeper. From Trainee.

Season	Club		
1992–93	Carlisle U....................	1	—

CALDERWOOD, Colin

Born Stranraer 20.1.65.   Ht 6 0   Wt 12 00
Defender. From Amateur. Football
League.

Season	Club	App	Goals
1981–82	Mansfield T	1	—
1982–83		28	—
1983–84		30	1
1984–85		41	—
1985–86	Swindon T	46	2
1986–87		46	1
1987–88		34	1
1988–89		43	4
1989–90		46	3
1990–91		23	2
1991–92		46	5
1992–93		46	2

CALLAGHAN, Aaron

Born Dublin 8.10.66.   Ht 5 11   Wt 11 02
Defender. From Apprentice. Eire Youth,
Under-21.

Season	Club	App	Goals
1984–85	Stoke C	5	—
1985–86		—	—
1985–86	*Crewe Alex*	8	—
1986–87	Stoke C	2	—
1986–87	Oldham Ath	5	—
1987–88		11	2
1988–89	Crewe Alex	41	4
1989–90		41	2
1990–91		39	—
1991–92		37	—
1992–93	Preston NE	35	2

CALVERT, Mark

Born Consett 11.9.70.   Ht 5 9   Wt 11 05
Forward. From Trainee.

Season	Club	App	Goals
1988–89	Hull C	5	—
1989–90		—	—
1990–91		7	—
1991–92		11	1
1992–93		7	—

CAME, Mark

Born Exeter 14.9.61.   Ht 6 0   Wt 12 13
Defender. From Winsford U.

Season	Club	App	Goals
1983–84	Bolton W	—	—
1984–85		23	1
1985–86		35	1
1986–87		43	—
1987–88		43	5
1988–89		2	—
1989–90		19	—
1990–91		8	—
1991–92		18	—
1992–93		4	—
1992–93	Chester C	17	—

CAMERON, Colin

Born Kirkcaldy 23.10.72   Ht 5 6   Wt 9 6
Forward. From Lochore Welfare.

Season	Club	App	Goals
1990–91	Raith R	—	—
1991–92	*Sligo R*	—	—
1992–93	Raith R	16	1

CAMERON, Ian

Born Glasgow 24.8.66.   Ht 5 9   Wt 10 04
Midfield. 'S' Form. Scotland Schools,
Youth.

Season	Club	App	Goals
1983–84	St Mirren	8	—
1984–85		9	1
1985–86		12	—
1986–87		31	6
1987–88		41	8
1988–89		26	2
1989–90	Aberdeen	11	—
1990–91		10	1
1991–92		6	—
1992–93	Partick T	41	5

CAMPBELL, Calum

Born Erskine 7.11.65   Ht 6 1   Wt 12 0
Forward. From Kilbirnie Ladeside.

Season	Club	App	Goals
1987–88	Airdrieonians	42	15
1988–89		36	14
1989–90	Partick T	34	18

Season	Club	Appearances	Goals
1990–91	....	26	4
1990–91	Kilmarnock.................	7	4
1991–92	....	38	10
1992–93	....	24	4

CAMPBELL, Dave

Born Eglinton 2.6.65 Ht 5 10 Wt 11 02
Midfield. From Oxford BC (Northern
Ireland). Northern Ireland 10 caps.

Season	Club	Appearances	Goals
1983–84	Nottingham F.............	—	—
1984–85	....	1	—
1985–86	....	18	3
1986–87	....	14	—
1986–87	*Notts Co*.....................	18	2
1987–88	Nottingham F.............	8	—
1987–88	Charlton Ath	21	1
1988–89	....	9	—
1988–89	*Plymouth Arg*..............	1	—
1988–89	Bradford C	12	1
1989–90	....	23	3
1990–91	....	—	—
1990–91	*Shamrock R*	9	3
1991–92	....	22	2
1991–92	Bradford C	—	—
1992–93	WBA	—	—
1992–93	Rotherham U	1	—
1992–93	Burnley	8	—

CAMPBELL, Duncan

Born Paisley 11.9.70. Ht 5 7 Wt 10 12
Forward. From Jerviston BC.

Season	Club	Appearances	Goals
1988–89	Dundee........................	8	1
1989–90	....	15	1
1990–91	....	16	—
1991–92	....	15	2
1992–93	....	4	—

CAMPBELL, Jamie

Born Birmingham 21.10.72. Ht 6 1
Wt 11 03
Forward. From Trainee.

Season	Club	Appearances	Goals
1991–92	Luton T	11	—
1992–93	....	9	1

CAMPBELL, Kevin

Born Lambeth 4.2.70. Ht 6 1 Wt 13 08
Forward. From Trainee. England Under-
21, B.

Season	Club	Appearances	Goals
1987–88	Arsenal........................	1	—
1988–89	....	—	—
1988–89	*Leyton Orient*..............	16	9
1989–90	Arsenal........................	15	2
1989–90	*Leicester C*..................	11	5
1990–91	Arsenal........................	22	9
1991–92	....	31	13
1992–93	....	37	4

CAMPBELL, Sol

Born Newham 18.9.74 Ht 6 0 Wt 12 00
Defender. From Trainee. England Youth.

Season	Club	Appearances	Goals
1992–93	Tottenham H	1	1

CAMPBELL, Stephen

Born Dundee 20.11.67. Ht 5 9 Wt 11 02
Midfield. From Downfield BC. Scotland
Under-21.

Season	Club	Appearances	Goals
1985–86	Dundee........................	5	—
1986–87	....	4	—
1987–88	....	7	1
1988–89	....	24	—
1989–90	....	2	—
1990–91	....	6	1
1991–92	....	30	3
1992–93	....	20	—

CANHAM, Tony

Born Leeds 8.6.60. Ht 5 8 Wt 11 05
Midfield. From Harrogate Railway.

Season	Club	Appearances	Goals
1984–85	York C........................	3	1
1985–86	....	41	13
1986–87	....	38	9
1987–88	....	18	2
1988–89	....	41	9
1989–90	....	34	4
1990–91	....	41	5
1991–92	....	31	5
1992–93	....	29	4

CANTONA, Eric

Born Paris 24.5.66   Ht 6 1   Wt 12 10
Forward. From Nimes. France full caps.

1983–84	Auxerre	2	—
1984–85		4	2
1985–86		7	—
1985–86	Martigues	—	—
1986–87	Auxerre	36	13
1987–88		32	8
1988–89	Marseille	22	5
1988–89	Bordeaux	11	6
1989–90	Montpellier	33	10
1990–91	Marseille	18	8
1991–92	Leeds U	15	3
1992–93		13	6
1992–93	Manchester U	22	9

CARBON, Matthew

Born Nottingham 8.6.75   Ht 6 2
Wt 11 13
Defender. From Trainee.

1992–93	Lincoln C	1	—

CAREY, Brian

Born Cork 31.5.68.   Ht 6 3   Wt 11 13
Defender. From Cork C. Eire 2 full caps.

1989–90	Manchester U	—	—
1990–91		—	—
1990–91	*Wrexham*	3	—
1991–92	Manchester U	—	—
1991–92	*Wrexham*	13	1
1992–93	Manchester U	—	—

CARMICHAEL, Matt

Born Singapore 13.5.64.   Ht 6 2
Wt 11 07
Forward. From Army.

1989–90	Lincoln C	26	5
1990–91		26	2
1991–92		40	7
1992–93		41	4

CARPENTER, Richard

Born Sheppey 30.9.72.   Ht 5 10   Wt 13 00
Midfield. From Trainee.

1990–91	Gillingham	9	1
1991–92		3	—
1992–93		28	—

CARR, Cliff

Born London 19.6.64.   Ht 5 8   Wt 10 12
Midfield. From Apprentice. England
Under-21.

1982–83	Fulham	6	1
1983–84		41	4
1984–85		38	4
1985–86		35	4
1986–87		25	—
1987–88	Stoke C	41	—
1988–89		41	—
1989–90		22	—
1990–91		20	—
1991–92	Shrewsbury T	1	1
1991–92	Mansfield T	20	—
1992–93	Chesterfield	42	1

CARR, Darren

Born Bristol 4.9.68.   Ht 6 2   Wt 13 00
Defender.

1985–86	Bristol R	1	—
1986–87		20	—
1987–88		9	—
1987–88	Newport Co	9	—
1987–88	Sheffield U	3	—
1988–89		10	1
1989–90		—	—
1990–91		—	—
1990–91	Crewe Alex	36	—
1991–92		36	3
1992–93		32	2

CARR, Franz

Born Preston 24.9.66.   Ht 5 7   Wt 10 12
Midfield. From Apprentice. England
Schools, Youth, Under-21.

1984–85	Blackburn R	—	—

Season	Club		
1985–86	Nottingham F	23	3
1986–87		36	4
1987–88		22	4
1988–89		23	3
1989–90		14	1
1989–90	*Sheffield W*	12	—
1990–91	Nottingham F	13	2
1990–91	*West Ham U*	3	—
1991–92	Newcastle U	15	2
1992–93		10	1
1992–93	*Sheffield U*	8	3

CARRUTHERS, Martin

Born Nottingham 7.8.72. Ht 5 11
Wt 11 07
Forward. From Trainee.

Season	Club		
1990–91	Aston Villa	—	—
1991–92		3	—
1992–93		1	—
1992–93	*Hull C*	13	6

CARSON, Tom

Born Alexandria 26.3.59   Ht 6 0   Wt 12 0
Goalkeeper. From Vale of Leven.

Season	Club		
1978–79	Dumbarton	—	—
1979–80		3	—
1980–81		33	—
1981–82		39	—
1982–83		37	—
1983–84		37	—
1984–85	Dundee	20	—
1985–86		—	—
1986–87	*Hibernian*	2	—
1987–88	*Partick T*	6	—
1987–88	*Queen of the S*	7	—
1987–88	*Dunfermline Ath*	5	—
1987–88	*Ipswich T*	1	—
1987–88	Dundee	6	—
1988–89		2	—
1989–90		16	—
1990–91		33	—
1991–92		—	—
1991–92	*Dumbarton*	6	—
1992–93	Raith R	27	—

CARSTAIRS, Jim

Born St. Andrews 29.1.71.   Ht 6 0
Wt 12 05
Defender. From Trainee.

Season	Club		
1988–89	Arsenal	—	—
1989–90		—	—
1990–91		—	—
1990–91	*Brentford*	8	—
1991–92	Cambridge U	—	—
1991–92	Stockport C	20	—
1992–93		14	1

CARTER, Danny

Born Hackney 29.6.69.   Ht 5 11
Wt 11 12
Midfield. From Billericay.

Season	Club		
1988–89	Leyton Orient	1	—
1989–90		31	5
1990–91		42	5
1991–92		20	2
1992–93		29	3

CARTER, Jimmy

Born London 9.11.65.   Ht 5 10   Wt 11 01
Midfield. From Apprentice.

Season	Club		
1983–84	Crystal Palace	—	—
1984–85		—	—
1985–86	QPR	—	—
1986–87	Millwall	12	1
1987–88		26	—
1988–89		20	5
1989–90		28	2
1990–91		24	2
1990–91	Liverpool	5	—
1991–92		—	—
1991–92	Arsenal	6	—
1992–93		16	2

CARTER, Mark

Born Liverpool 17.12.60.   Ht 5 9
Wt 11 06
Forward. From S. Liverpool, Bangor C,
Runcorn.

Season	Club		
1991–92	Barnet	36	19

1992–93	....	41	11

CARTER, Tim

Born Bristol 5.10.67.   Ht 6 2   Wt 13 11
Goalkeeper. From Apprentice. England
Youth.

Season	Club	App	Goals
1985–86	Bristol R	2	—
1986–87	....	38	—
1987–88	....	7	—
1987–88	*Newport Co*	1	—
1987–88	*Carlisle U*	4	—
1987–88	Sunderland	1	—
1988–89	....	2	—
1988–89	*Bristol C*	3	—
1989–90	Sunderland	18	—
1990–91	....	1	—
1991–92	....	2	—
1991–92	*Birmingham C*	2	—
1992–93	Sunderland	13	—

CARTWRIGHT, Lee

Born Rawtenstall 19.9.72.   Ht 5 8
Wt 10 06
Midfield. From Trainee.

1990–91	Preston NE	14	1
1991–92	....	33	4
1992–93	....	34	3

CASCARINO, Tony

Born St Paul's Cray 1.9.62.   Ht 6 2
Wt 13 12
Forward. From Crockenhill. Eire 43 full
caps.

1981–82	Gillingham	24	5
1982–83	....	38	15
1983–84	....	37	12
1984–85	....	43	16
1985–86	....	34	14
1986–87	....	43	16
1987–88	Millwall.......................	39	20
1988–89	....	38	13
1989–90	....	28	9
1989–90	Aston Villa..................	10	2
1990–91	....	36	9

1991–92	Celtic............................	24	4
1991–92	Chelsea........................	11	2
1992–93	....	9	2

CASE, Jimmy

Born Liverpool 18.5.54.   Ht 5 9   Wt 12 08
Midfield. From Sth Liverpool. England
Under-23.

1973–74	Liverpool	—	—
1974–75	....	1	—
1975–76	....	27	6
1976–77	....	27	1
1977–78	....	33	5
1978–79	....	37	7
1979–80	....	37	3
1980–81	....	24	1
1981–82	Brighton......................	33	3
1982–83	....	35	3
1983–84	....	35	4
1984–85	....	24	—
1984–85	Southampton	10	1
1985–86	....	36	2
1986–87	....	39	3
1987–88	....	38	—
1988–89	....	34	—
1989–90	....	33	3
1990–91	....	25	1
1991–92	Bournemouth	40	1
1992–93	Halifax T	21	2
1992–93	Wrexham	4	—

CASH, Stuart

Born Tipton 5.9.65.   Ht 5 10   Wt 11 11
Defender. From Halesowen.

1989–90	Nottingham F.............	—	—
1989–90	*Rotherham U*..............	8	1
1990–91	Nottingham F.............	—	—
1990–91	*Brentford*.....................	11	—
1991–92	Nottingham F.............	—	—
1991–92	*Shrewsbury T*	8	1
1992–93	Chesterfield.................	23	—

CASTLE, Steve

Born Barkingside 17.5.66. Ht 5 11
Wt 12 05
Midfield. From Apprentice.

Season	Club		
1984–85	Orient	21	1
1985–86		23	4
1986–87		24	5
1987–88		42	10
1988–89		24	6
1989–90		27	7
1990–91		45	12
1991–92		37	10
1992–93	Plymouth Arg	31	11

CASTLEDINE, Gary

Born Dumfries 27.3.70. Ht 5 8 Wt 11 04
Forward.

1990–91	Mansfield T	—	—
1991–92		7	—
1992–93		28	3

CASTLEDINE, Stewart

Born London 22.1.73. Ht 6 0 Wt 12 00
Midfield. From Trainee.

1991–92	Wimbledon	2	—
1992–93		—	—

CATLIN, Bob

Born London 22.6.65 Ht 6 2 Wt 14 00
Goalkeeper. From Marconi.

1992–93	Notts Co	2	—
1992–93	*Birmingham C*	8	—

CAWLEY, Peter

Born London 15.9.65. Ht 6 4 Wt 13 00
Defender. From Chertsey.

1986–87	Wimbledon	—	—
1986–87	*Bristol R*	10	—
1987–88	Wimbledon	—	—
1988–89		1	—
1988–89	*Fulham*	5	—

1989–90	Bristol R	3	—
1990–91	Southend U	7	1
1990–91	Exeter C	7	—
1991–92	Barnet	3	—
1992–93		—	—
1992–93	Colchester U	24	3

CAWTHORN, Paul

Born Pontefract 26.5.75
Midfield. From Trainee.

1992–93	Scarborough	3	—

CECERE, Michele

Born Chester 4.1.68. Ht 6 0 Wt 11 04
Forward. From Apprentice.

1985–86	Oldham Ath	—	—
1986–87		14	4
1987–88		25	2
1988–89		13	2
1988–89	Huddersfield T	31	4
1989–90		23	4
1989–90	*Stockport Co*	1	—
1990–91	Huddersfield T	—	—
1990–91	Walsall	32	6
1991–92		35	8
1992–93		39	16

CHALMERS, Grant

Born Guernsey 12.9.69 Ht 5 10
Wt 11 10
Midfield. From Northerners.

1992–93	Brentford	11	1

CHAMBERLAIN, Alec

Born March 20.6.64. Ht 6 2 Wt 13 01
Goalkeeper. From Ramsey T.

1981–82	Ipswich T	—	—
1982–83	Colchester U	—	—
1983–84		46	—
1984–85		46	—
1985–86		46	—
1986–87		46	—

Season	Club	App	Goals
1987–88	Everton	—	—
1987–88	*Tranmere R*	15	—
1988–89	Luton T	6	—
1989–90		38	—
1990–91		38	—
1991–92		24	—
1992–93		32	—
1992–93	*Chelsea*	—	—

CHAMBERLAIN, Mark

Born Stoke 19.11.61. Ht 5 9   Wt 10 07
Forward. From Apprentice. England
Schools, Under-21, 8 full caps.

Season	Club	App	Goals
1978–79	Port Vale	8	—
1979–80		11	—
1980–81		31	9
1981–82		46	8
1982–83	Stoke C	37	6
1983–84		40	7
1984–85		28	1
1985–86		7	3
1985–86	Sheffield W	21	2
1986–87		24	5
1987–88		21	1
1988–89	Portsmouth	28	6
1989–90		38	6
1990–91		25	2
1991–92		16	1
1992–93		41	4

CHANNING, Justin

Born Reading 19.11.68.   Ht 5 11
Wt 11 07
Defender. From Apprentice. England
Youth.

Season	Club	App	Goals
1986–87	QPR	2	—
1987–88		14	1
1988–89		9	1
1989–90		23	2
1990–91		5	—
1991–92		—	—
1992–93		2	1
1992–93	Bristol R	25	3

CHAPMAN, Gary

Born Bradford 1.5.64.   Ht 5 8   Wt 11 07
Forward. From Local.

Season	Club	App	Goals
1988–89	Bradford C	2	—
1989–90		3	—
1989–90	Notts Co	19	4
1990–91		6	—
1990–91	*Mansfield T*	6	—
1991–92	Notts Co	—	—
1991–92	Exeter C	20	4
1992–93		4	1
1992–93	Torquay U	8	—

CHAPMAN, Ian

Born Brighton 31.5.70.   Ht 5 9   Wt 12 05
Defender. FA Schools.

Season	Club	App	Goals
1986–87	Brighton	5	—
1987–88		—	—
1988–89		19	—
1989–90		42	1
1990–91		23	—
1991–92		37	2
1992–93		34	1

CHAPMAN, Lee

Born Lincoln 5.12.59.   Ht 6 2   Wt 13 00
Forward. From Amateur. England B,
Under-21.

Season	Club	App	Goals
1978–79	Stoke C	—	—
1978–79	*Plymouth Arg*	4	—
1979–80	Stoke C	17	3
1980–81		41	15
1981–82		41	16
1982–83	Arsenal	19	3
1983–84		4	1
1983–84	Sunderland	15	3
1984–85	Sheffield W	40	15
1985–86		31	10
1986–87		41	19
1987–88		37	19
From Niort			
1988–89	Nottingham F	30	8
1989–90		18	7
1989–90	Leeds U	21	12
1990–91		38	21

| 1991–92 | | 38 | 16 |
| 1992–93 | | 40 | 14 |

CHAPPLE, Phil

Born Norwich 26.11.66. Ht 6 2 Wt 12 07
Defender. From Apprentice.

1984–85	Norwich C	—	—
1985–86		—	—
1986–87		—	—
1987–88		—	—
1987–88	Cambridge U	6	1
1988–89		46	3
1989–90		45	5
1990–91		43	5
1991–92		29	3
1992–93		18	2

CHAPPLE, Shaun

Born Swansea 14.2.73. Ht 5 11 Wt 12 03
Midfield. From Trainee. Wales Under-21.

| 1991–92 | Swansea C | 21 | 2 |
| 1992–93 | | 4 | — |

CHARD, Phil

Born Corby 16.10.60. Ht 5 8 Wt 11 03
Midfield. From Nottingham F. Amateur.

1978–79	Peterborough U	6	1
1979–80		20	2
1980–81		—	—
1981–82		39	3
1982–83		44	4
1983–84		38	7
1984–85		25	1
1985–86	Northampton T	41	7
1986–87		40	12
1987–88		34	8
1987–88	Wolverhampton W	9	2
1988–89		19	3
1989–90		6	—
1989–90	Northampton T	29	2
1990–91		43	7
1991–92		29	3
1992–93		34	6

CHARLERY, Ken

Born Stepney 28.11.64. Ht 6 1 Wt 12 07
Forward. From Fisher Ath, Basildon U,
Beckton U (1989).

1989–90	Maidstone U	30	2
1990–91		29	9
1990–91	Peterborough U	4	—
1991–92		37	16
1992–93		10	3
1992–93	Watford	32	11

CHARLES, Gary

Born London 13.4.70. Ht 5 9 Wt 10 13
Defender. England Under-21, 2 full caps.

1987–88	Nottingham F	—	—
1988–89		1	—
1988–89	Leicester C	8	—
1989–90	Nottingham F	1	—
1990–91		10	—
1991–92		30	1
1992–93		14	—

CHARLES, Steve

Born Sheffield 10.5.60. Ht 5 9 Wt 10 07
Midfield. From Sheffield University.
England Schools.

1979–80	Sheffield U	14	1
1980–81		31	6
1981–82		30	1
1982–83		35	—
1983–84		11	1
1984–85		2	1
1984–85	Wrexham	32	7
1985–86		40	20
1986–87		41	10
1987–88	Mansfield T	46	12
1988–89		46	7
1989–90		43	7
1990–91		39	4
1991–92		40	6
1992–93		23	3
1992–93	Scunthorpe U	4	—
1992–93	Scarborough	16	3

CHARLTON, Simon

Born Huddersfield 25.10.71.   Ht 5 7
Wt 10 11
Defender. From Trainee. FA Schools.

1989–90	Huddersfield T............	3	—
1990–91	....	30	—
1991–92	....	45	—
1992–93	....	46	1

CHARNOCK, Phil

Born Southport 14.2.75   Ht 5 11
Wt 11 02
Midfield. From Trainee.

| 1992–93 | Liverpool .... | — | — |

CHEETHAM, Michael

Born Amsterdam 30.6.67.   Ht 5 11
Wt 11 05
Midfield. From Army.

1988–89	Ipswich T	3	—
1989–90	....	1	—
1989–90	Cambridge U	36	10
1990–91	....	44	7
1991–92	....	22	3
1992–93	....	17	—

CHERRY, Paul

Born Derby 14.10.64.   Ht 6 0   Wt 11 07
Midfield. From Salvesen BC.

1984–85	Hearts	3	—
1985–86	....	5	—
1986–87	Cowdenbeath	35	5
1987–88	....	35	8
1988–89	St Johnstone	39	2
1989–90	....	39	4
1990–91	....	20	—
1991–92	....	24	1
1992–93	....	16	1

CHERRY, Steve

Born Nottingham 5.8.60.   Ht 6 1
Wt 13 00
Goalkeeper. From Apprentice. England
Youth.

1977–78	Derby Co	—	—
1978–79	....	—	—
1979–80	....	4	—
1980–81	*Port Vale*.....................	4	—
1981–82	Derby Co	4	—
1982–83	....	31	—
1983–84	....	38	—
1984–85	Walsall	41	—
1985–86	....	30	—
1986–87	....	—	—
1986–87	Plymouth Arg..............	21	—
1987–88	....	37	—
1988–89	....	15	—
1988–89	*Chesterfield*	10	—
1988–89	Notts Co	18	—
1989–90	....	46	—
1990–91	....	46	—
1991–92	....	42	—
1992–93	....	44	—

CHETTLE, Steve

Born Nottingham 27.9.68.   Ht 6 1
Wt 12 00
Defender. From Apprentice. England
Under-21.

1986–87	Nottingham F.............	—	—
1987–88	....	30	—
1988–89	....	28	2
1989–90	....	22	1
1990–91	....	37	2
1991–92	....	22	1
1992–93	....	30	—

CHILDS, Gary

Born Birmingham 19.4.64.   Ht 5 7
Wt 10 08
Midfield. From Apprentice. England
Youth.

| 1981–82 | WBA........................... | 2 | — |
| 1982–83 | .... | — | — |

Season	Club	App	Goals
1983–84		1	—
1983–84	Walsall	30	2
1984–85		40	2
1985–86		33	5
1986–87		28	8
1987–88	Birmingham C	32	1
1988–89		23	1
1989–90	Grimsby T	44	5
1990–91		25	4
1991–92		29	3
1992–93		17	—

CHISHOLM, Gordon

Born Glasgow 8.4.60. Ht 6 0 Wt 12 09
Defender. From Apprentice.

Season	Club	App	Goals
1977–78	Sunderland	—	—
1978–79		27	1
1979–80		13	—
1980–81		34	3
1981–82		22	—
1982–83		32	1
1983–84		36	4
1984–85		32	1
1985–86		1	—
1985–86	Hibernian	29	2
1986–87		23	2
1987–88		7	—
1987–88	Dundee	15	—
1988–89		33	4
1989–90		34	3
1990–91		34	3
1991–92		39	5
1992–93	Partick T	9	—

CHIVERS, Gary

Born Stockwell 15.5.60. Ht 5 11
Wt 11 05
Defender. From Apprentice.

Season	Club	App	Goals
1978–79	Chelsea	5	—
1979–80		29	2
1980–81		40	2
1981–82		29	—
1982–83		30	—
1983–84	Swansea C	10	—
1983–84	QPR	—	—
1984–85		23	—

Season	Club	App	Goals
1985–86		14	—
1986–87		23	—
1987–88	Watford	14	—
1987–88	Brighton	10	—
1988–89		46	6
1989–90		41	3
1990–91		39	3
1991–92		38	1
1992–93		43	—

CHRISTIE, David

Born Salford 26.2.73. Ht 6 1 Wt 12 00
Forward. From Trainee.

Season	Club	App	Goals
1991–92	Preston NE	2	—
1992–93		2	—
1992–93	Halifax T	9	—

CHRISTIE, Max

Born Edinburgh 7.11.71. Ht 5 5
Wt 10 04
Midfield. From Hutcheson V. Scotland
Under-21.

Season	Club	App	Goals
1988–89	Hearts	—	—
1989–90		—	—
1990–91		—	—
1991–92	Meadowbank T	34	1
1991–92	Dundee	1	—
1992–93		3	—

CIRCUIT, Steve

Born Sheffield 11.4.72.
Defender. From Sheffield U trainee.

Season	Club	App	Goals
1992–93	Halifax T	1	—

CLARIDGE, Steve

Born Portsmouth 10.4.66. Ht 5 11
Wt 11 08
Forward. From Portsmouth, Fareham.

Season	Club	App	Goals
1984–85	Bournemouth	6	1
1985–86		1	—
From Weymouth			
1988–89	Crystal Palace	—	—

Season	Club	League Appearances/Goals		Season	Club	League Appearances/Goals	
1988–89	Aldershot	37	9	1984–85		10	3
1989–90		25	10	1985–86		11	1
1989–90	Cambridge U	20	4	1986–87		30	3
1990–91		30	12	1987–88		28	3
1991–92		29	12	1988–89		20	2
1992–93	Luton T	16	2	1989–90		29	1
1992–93	Cambridge U	29	7	1990–91		18	2
				1991–92		35	1
				1992–93		37	2

CLARK, Billy

Born Christchurch 19.5.67. Ht 6 0
Wt 12 03
Defender. From Local.

1984–85	Bournemouth	1	—
1985–86		1	—
1986–87		—	—
1987–88		2	—
1987–88	Bristol R	31	1
1988–89		11	—
1989–90		—	—
1990–91		14	1
1991–92		24	1
1992–93		24	1

CLARK, Howard

Born Coventry 19.9.68. Ht 5 11
Wt 11 01
Defender. From Apprentice.

1986–87	Coventry C	—	—
1987–88		—	—
1988–89		9	1
1989–90		9	—
1990–91		2	—
1991–92		—	—
1991–92	*Darlington*	5	—
1991–92	Shrewsbury T	23	—
1992–93		33	—

CLARK, John

Born Edinburgh 22.9.64. Ht 6 0
Wt 13 01
Defender. 'S' Form. Scotland Youth.

1981–82	Dundee U	—	—
1982–83		1	—
1983–84		9	1

CLARK, Lee

Born Wallsend 27.10.72. Ht 5 7
Wt 11 07
Midfield. From Trainee. England Youth,
Under-21.

1989–90	Newcastle U	—	—
1990–91		19	2
1991–92		29	5
1992–93		46	9

CLARK, Martin

Born Uddington 13.10.68. Ht 5 9
Wt 10 11
Defender. From Hamilton A.

1987–88	Clyde	26	—
1988–89		25	2
1988–89	Nottingham F	—	—
1989–90		—	—
1989–90	*Falkirk*	3	1
1989–90	*Mansfield T*	14	1
1990–91	Mansfield T	24	—
1991–92		9	—
1992–93	Partick T	8	—

CLARK, Paul

Born Benfleet 14.9.58. Ht 5 9 Wt 13 07
Midfield. From Apprentice. England
Schools, Youth.

1976–77	Southend U	25	—
1977–78		8	1
1977–78	Brighton	26	3
1978–79		33	4
1979–80		11	2
1980–81		9	—

Season	Club	App	Goals
1981–82	*Reading*	2	—
1982–83	Southend U	31	1
1983–84		20	—
1984–85		29	1
1985–86		39	1
1986–87		46	—
1987–88		30	—
1988–89		16	—
1989–90		25	—
1990–91		40	—
1991–92	Gillingham	42	—
1992–93		35	1

CLARKE, Andy

Born London 22.7.67.   Ht 5 10   Wt 11 07
Forward. From Barnet.

Season	Club	App	Goals
1990–91	Wimbledon	12	3
1991–92		34	3
1992–93		33	5

CLARKE, Colin

Born Newry 30.10.62.   Ht 6 0   Wt 13 06
Forward. From Apprentice. Northern
Ireland, 38 full caps.

Season	Club	App	Goals
1980–81	Ipswich T	—	—
1981–82	Peterborough	27	4
1982–83		37	9
1983–84		18	5
1983–84	*Gillingham*	8	1
1984–85	Tranmere R	45	22
1985–86	Bournemouth	46	26
1986–87	Southampton	33	20
1987–88		40	16
1988–89		9	—
1988–89	*Bournemouth*	4	2
1988–89	QPR	12	5
1989–90		34	6
1990–91	Portsmouth	42	13
1991–92		24	4
1992–93		19	1

CLARKE, David

Born Nottingham 3.12.64.   Ht 5 10
Wt 11 00
Midfield. From Apprentice. England
Youth.

Season	Club	App	Goals
1982–83	Notts Co	16	—
1983–84		20	—
1984–85		22	—
1985–86		42	1
1986–87		23	6
1987–88	Lincoln C	*30*	*5*
1988–89		36	4
1989–90		30	2
1990–91		15	—
1991–92		28	—
1992–93		31	2

CLARKE, Matthew

Born Sheffield 3.11.73   Ht 6 3   Wt 11 07
Goalkeeper. From Trainee.

Season	Club	App	Goals
1992–93	Rotherham U	9	—

CLARKE, Nicky

Born Walsall 20.8.67.   Ht 5 11   Wt 13 11
Defender. From Apprentice.

Season	Club	App	Goals
1984–85	Wolverhampton W	—	—
1985–86		23	1
1986–87		24	—
1987–88		8	—
1988–89		8	—
1989–90		3	—
1990–91		14	—
1991–92		1	—
1991–92	Mansfield T	16	1
1992–93		12	1
1992–93	*Chesterfield*	7	—

CLARKE, Simon

Born Chelmsford 23.9.71.   Ht 5 11
Wt 11 02
Forward. From Trainee.

Season	Club	App	Goals
1990–91	West Ham U	1	—
1991–92		1	—

Season	Club	Apps	Goals
1992–93		1	—

CLARKE, Stephen

Born Saltcoats 29.8.63.   Ht 5 10
Wt 10 02
Defender. From Beith Juniors. Scotland
Youth, Under-21, B. Football League.

Season	Club	Apps	Goals
1981–82	St Mirren	—	—
1982–83		31	—
1983–84		33	2
1984–85		33	—
1985–86		31	3
1986–87		23	1
1986–87	Chelsea	16	—
1987–88		38	1
1988–89		36	—
1989–90		24	3
1990–91		18	1
1991–92		31	1
1992–93		20	—

CLARKE, Tim

Born Stourbridge 19.9.68.   Ht 6 3
Wt 13 07
Goalkeeper. From Halesowen.

Season	Club	Apps	Goals
1990–91	Coventry C	—	—
1991–92	Huddersfield T	39	—
1992–93		31	—
1992–93	*Rochdale*	2	—

CLARKE, Wayne

Born Wolverhampton 28.2.61.   Ht 6 0
Wt 11 08
Forward. From Apprentice. England
Schools, Youth.

Season	Club	Apps	Goals
1977–78	Wolverhampton W	1	—
1978–79		8	1
1979–80		16	2
1980–81		24	3
1981–82		29	6
1982–83		39	12
1983–84		31	6
1984–85	Birmingham C	40	17
1985–86		28	5

Season	Club	Apps	Goals
1986–87		24	16
1986–87	Everton	10	5
1987–88		27	10
1988–89		20	3
1989–90	Leicester C	11	1
1989–90	Manchester C	9	—
1990–91		7	1
1990–91	*Shrewsbury T*	7	6
1990–91	*Stoke C*	9	3
1991–92	Manchester C	5	1
1991–92	*Wolverhampton W*	1	—
1992–93	Walsall	39	21

CLARKSON, Ian

Born Birmingham 4.12.70.   Ht 5 11
Wt 12 00
Defender. From Trainee.

Season	Club	Apps	Goals
1988–89	Birmingham C	9	—
1989–90		20	—
1990–91		37	—
1991–92		42	—
1992–93		28	—

CLARKSON, Phil

Born Hambleton 13.11.68.   Ht 5 10
Wt 10 08
Midfield. From Fleetwood.

Season	Club	Apps	Goals
1991–92	Crewe Alex	28	6
1992–93		35	13

CLAYTON, Gary

Born Sheffield 2.2.63.   Ht 5 11   Wt 12 08
Midfield. From Rotherham U Apprentice,
Burton Alb.

Season	Club	Apps	Goals
1986–87	Doncaster R	35	5
1987–88	Cambridge U	45	5
1988–89		46	1
1989–90		10	1
1990–91		6	—
1990–91	*Peterborough U*	4	—
1991–92	Cambridge U	11	3
1992–93		36	3

CLAYTON, John

Born Elgin 20.8.61.   Ht 5 11   Wt 11 07
Forward. From Apprentice.

1978–79	Derby C	1	—
1979–80		—	—
1980–81		9	1
1981–82		14	3
From Bulova, Hong Kong			
1983–84	Chesterfield	33	5
1984–85	Tranmere R	44	31
1985–86		3	4
1985–86	Plymouth Arg	36	12
1986–87		21	3
1987–88		20	6
1988–89	Fortuna Sittard	30	10
1989–90		17	6
1990–91	Volendam	34	8
1991–92		27	10
1992–93	Burnley	3	1

CLELAND, Alec

Born Glasgow 10.12.70.   Ht 5 8   Wt 10 00
Defender. From S Form. Scotland
Under-21.

1987–88	Dundee U	1	—
1988–89		9	—
1989–90		15	—
1990–91		20	2
1991–92		31	4
1992–93		24	—

CLOSE, Shaun

Born Islington 8.9.66.   Ht 5 8   Wt 10 01
Forward. From Trainee.

1984–85	Tottenham H	—	—
1985–86		—	—
1986–87		2	—
1987–88		7	—
1987–88	Bournemouth	16	6
1988–89		23	2
1989–90		—	—
1989–90	Swindon T	11	—
1990–91		14	—
1991–92		12	1
1992–93		7	—

CLOUGH, Nigel

Born Sunderland 19.3.66.   Ht 5 9
Wt 11 04
Forward. From AC Hunters England B,
Under-21, 14 full caps.

1984–85	Nottingham F	9	1
1985–86		39	15
1986–87		42	14
1987–88		34	19
1988–89		36	14
1989–90		38	9
1990–91		37	14
1991–92		34	5
1992–93		42	10

COATSWORTH, Gary

Born Sunderland 7.10.68.   Ht 6 0
Wt 13 02
Defender.

1986–87	Barnsley	—	—
1987–88		6	—
1988–89		—	—
1989–90	Darlington	3	1
1990–91		12	1
1991–92		10	1
1991–92	Leicester C	3	—
1992–93		10	2

COBB, Paul

Born Thurrock 13.12.72.   Ht 5 6
Wt 10 02
Forward. From Purfleet.

1990–91	Leyton Orient	4	—
1991–92		1	—
1992–93		—	—

COCKERILL, Glenn

Born Grimsby 25.8.59.   Ht 5 10   Wt 12 03
Midfield. From Louth U.

1976–77	Lincoln C	4	—
1977–78		13	1
1978–79		35	6
1979–80		19	3

Season	Club	Apps	Goals
1979–80	Swindon T	10	1
1980–81		16	—
1981–82	Lincoln C	44	11
1982–83		38	8
1983–84		33	6
1983–84	Sheffield U	10	1
1984–85		40	7
1985–86		12	2
1985–86	Southampton	30	7
1986–87		42	7
1987–88		39	2
1988–89		34	6
1989–90		36	4
1990–91		32	2
1991–92		37	4
1992–93		23	—

COCKERILL, John

Born Cleethorpes 12.7.61. Ht 6 0
Wt 12 07
Midfield. From Stafford R.

Season	Club	Apps	Goals
1988–89	Grimsby T	29	6
1989–90		33	5
1990–91		35	7
1991–92		10	1
1992–93		—	—

CODNER, Robert

Born Walthamstow 23.1.65. Ht 5 11
Wt 11 08
Midfield. From Leicester C, Barnet.

Season	Club	Apps	Goals
1988–89	Brighton	28	1
1989–90		45	9
1990–91		42	8
1991–92		45	6
1992–93		43	3

COLCOMBE, Scott

Born West Bromwich 15.12.71. Ht 5 6
Wt 10 00
Midfield. From Trainee.

Season	Club	Apps	Goals
1989–90	WBA	—	—
1990–91		—	—
1991–92	Torquay U	28	—

Season	Club	Apps	Goals
1992–93		24	1

COLDICOTT, Stacy

Born Worcester 29.4.74 Ht 5 11
Wt 11 02
Defender. From Trainee.

Season	Club	Apps	Goals
1991–92	WBA	—	—
1992–93		14	—

COLE, Andrew

Born Nottingham 15.10.71. Ht 5 11
Wt 11 02
Forward. From Trainee. England Youth,
Under-21. Football League.

Season	Club	Apps	Goals
1989–90	Arsenal	—	—
1990–91		1	—
1991–92		—	—
1991–92	*Fulham*	13	3
1991–92	*Bristol C*	12	8
1992–93	Bristol C	29	12
1992–93	Newcastle U	12	12

COLE, Anthony

Born Gateshead 18.9.72 Ht 6 1 Wt 12 13
Defender. From Middlesbrough trainee.

Season	Club	Apps	Goals
1992–93	St Johnstone	7	—

COLEMAN, Chris

Born Swansea 10.6.70. Ht 6 2 Wt 12 10
Defender. From Apprentice. Wales Under-
21, 2 full caps.

Season	Club	Apps	Goals
1987–88	Swansea C	30	—
1988–89		43	—
1989–90		46	2
1990–91		41	—
1991–92	Crystal Palace	18	4
1992–93		38	5

COLEMAN, Simon

Born Worksop 13.3.68. Ht 6 0 Wt 10 08
Midfield.

Season	Club	Apps	Goals
1985–86	Mansfield T	—	—

Season	Club	Apps	Goals
1986–87	....	2	—
1987–88	....	44	2
1988–89	....	45	5
1989–90	....	5	—
1989–90	Middlesbrough..............	36	1
1990–91	....	19	1
1991–92	Derby Co..................	43	2
1992–93	....	25	—

COLKIN, Lee

Born Nuneaton 15.7.74.
Defender. From Trainee.

Season	Club	Apps	Goals
1991–92	Northampton T..........	3	—
1992–93	....	13	—

COLLETT, Andy

Born Middlesbrough 28.10.73 Ht 5 11
Wt 12 00
Goalkeeper. From Trainee.

Season	Club	Apps	Goals
1991–92	Middlesbrough............	—	—
1992–93	....	2	—

COLLINS, David

Born Dublin 30.10.71. Ht 6 1 Wt 12 10
Defender. From Trainee. Eire Youth,
Under-21.

Season	Club	Apps	Goals
1989–90	Liverpool	—	—
1990–91	....	—	—
1991–92	....	—	—
1991–92	*Wigan Ath*..................	9	—
1992–93	Oxford U	13	—

COLLINS, Eamonn

Born Dublin 22.10.65 Ht 5 6 Wt 10 09
Midfield. From Blackpool and
Southampton apprentice. Eire Youth,
Under-21.

Season	Club	Apps	Goals
1982–83	Southampton	—	—
1983–84	....	—	—
1984–85	....	3	—
1985–86	....	—	—
1986–87	Portsmouth	5	—

Season	Club	Apps	Goals
1987–88	....	—	—
1987–88	*Exeter C*......................	9	—
1988–89	Portsmouth	—	—
1989–90	Colchester U..............	39	2
1990–91	....	*35*	*2*
1991–92	....	*33*	*2*
1992–93	Exeter C......................	11	—

COLLINS, John

Born Galashiels 31.1.68. Ht 5 7 Wt 9 10
Midfield. From Hutchison Vale BC.
Scotland Youth, Under-21, 14 full caps.

Season	Club	Apps	Goals
1984–85	Hibernian....................	—	—
1985–86	....	19	1
1986–87	....	30	1
1987–88	....	44	6
1988–89	....	35	2
1989–90	....	35	6
1990–91	Celtic..........................	35	1
1991–92	....	38	11
1992–93	....	43	8

COLLINS, Simon

Born Pontefract 16.12.73 Ht 6 0
Wt 11 02
Midfield. From Trainee.

Season	Club	Apps	Goals
1992–93	Huddersfield T............	1	—

COLLYMORE, Stan

Born Stone 22.1.71. Ht 6 2 Wt 14 00
Forward. From Stafford R.

Season	Club	Apps	Goals
1990–91	Crystal Palace.............	6	—
1991–92	....	12	1
1992–93	....	2	—
1992–93	Southend U.................	30	15

COLQUHOUN, John

Born Stirling 14.7.63. Ht 5 7 Wt 11 00
Forward. From Grangemouth Inter.

Season	Club	Apps	Goals
1980–81	Stirling Albion............	13	—
1981–82	....	37	13
1982–83	....	39	21

Season	Club	App	Goals
1983–84		15	11
1983–84	Celtic	12	2
1984–85		20	2
1985–86	Hearts	36	8
1986–87		43	13
1987–88		44	15
1988–89		36	5
1989–90		36	6
1990–91		36	7
1991–92	Millwall	27	3
1992–93	Sunderland	20	—

COMPTON, Paul

Born Stroud 6.6.61. Ht 6 1 Wt 13 01
Defender. From Trowbridge T.

Season	Club	App	Goals
1980–81	Bournemouth	31	—
1981–82		20	—
1982–83		13	—
1983–84		—	—
1983–84	Aldershot	13	—
1983–84	Torquay U	16	2
1984–85		22	1
1985–86		43	1
1986–87		14	—
From Youth Development Officer			
1991–92	Torquay U	19	—
1992–93		2	—

COMSTIVE, Paul

Born Southport 25.11.61. Ht 6 1
Wt 12 07
Midfield. From Amateur.

Season	Club	App	Goals
1979–80	Blackburn R	—	—
1980–81		3	—
1981–82		2	—
1982–83		1	—
1982–83	*Rochdale*	9	2
1983–84	Wigan Ath	29	2
1984–85		6	—
1984–85	Wrexham	28	3
1985–86		35	3
1986–87		36	2
1987–88	Burnley	44	8
1988–89		38	9
1989–90		—	—
1989–90	Bolton W	31	1

Season	Club	App	Goals
1990–91		18	2
1991–92		—	—
1991–92	Chester C	28	3
1992–93		29	3

COMYN, Andy

Born Manchester 2.6.68. Ht 6 1
Wt 12 00
Defender. From Alvechurch.

Season	Club	App	Goals
1989–90	Aston Villa	4	—
1990–91		11	—
1991–92	Derby Co	46	1
1992–93		17	—

CONN, Samuel

Born Lanark 26.10.61. Ht 5 11 Wt 12 0
Midfield. From Polkemmet J.

Season	Club	App	Goals
1980–81	Falkirk	17	1
1981–82		9	2
1982–83	Albion R	34	6
1983–84		30	5
1984–85		31	2
1985–86		33	6
1986–87		17	4
1986–87	Clydebank	19	1
1987–88	Falkirk	36	2
1988–89	Airdrieonians	31	8
1989–90		31	2
1990–91		21	1
1991–92		27	5
1992–93		14	—

CONNELLY, Dino

Born Glasgow 6.1.70. Ht 5 9 Wt 10 08
Midfield. From Celtic BC, Arsenal
Trainee. Scotland Schools, Youth.

Season	Club	App	Goals
1987–88	Arsenal	—	—
1988–89		—	—
1989–90		—	—
1990–91	Barnsley	9	—
1991–92		3	—
1991–92	*Wigan Ath*	12	2
1992–93	Barnsley	1	—
1992–93	*Carlisle U*	3	—

1992–93 Wigan Ath .... 7 —

CONNELLY, Sean

Born Sheffield 26.6.70
Defender. From Hallam.

1991–92 Stockport Co .... — —
1992–93 .... 7 —

CONNOLLY, Karl

Born Prescot 9.2.70. Ht 5 11 Wt 11 02
Midfield. From Napoli (Liverpool Sunday League).

1990–91 Wrexham .... — —
1991–92 .... 36 8
1992–93 .... 42 9

CONNOLLY, Patrick

Born Glasgow 25.6.70. Ht 5 8 Wt 9 04
Forward. From S Form. Scotland Under-21.

1986–87 Dundee U .... — —
1987–88 .... — —
1988–89 .... 2 —
1989–90 .... 15 5
1990–91 .... 10 2
1991–92 .... 5 —
1992–93 .... 42 16

CONNOR, Robert

Born Kilmarnock 4.8.60. Ht 5 11 Wt 11 04
Midfield. From Ayr U BC. Scotland Youth, B, Under-21, 4 full caps.

1977–78 Ayr U .... 9 —
1978–79 .... 29 —
1979–80 .... 38 9
1980–81 .... 39 8
1981–82 .... 30 —
1982–83 .... 39 4
1983–84 .... 39 7
1984–85 Dundee....................... 34 7
1985–86 .... 35 2

1986–87 .... 2 —
1986–87 Aberdeen.................... 32 4
1987–88 .... 34 1
1988–89 .... 36 4
1989–90 .... 34 1
1990–91 .... 29 6
1991–92 .... 11 —
1992–93 .... 6 —

CONNOR, Terry

Born Leeds 9.11.62. Ht 5 9 Wt 11 08
Forward. From Apprentice. England Youth, Under-21.

1979–80 Leeds U 23 6
1980–81 .... 27 4
1981–82 .... 27 4
1982–83 .... 19 5
1982–83 Brighton...................... 7 1
1983–84 .... 40 13
1984–85 .... 38 14
1985–86 .... 33 14
1986–87 .... 38 9
1987–88 Portsmouth 19 4
1988–89 .... 14 5
1989–90 .... 15 3
1990–91 Swansea C.................. 33 5
1991–92 .... 6 1
1991–92 Bristol C 11 1
1992–93 .... 5 —
1992–93 *Swansea C*................. 3 —

CONROY, Mike

Born Glasgow 31.12.65. Ht 6 0 Wt 11 00
Forward. From Apprentice.

1983–84 Coventry C .... — —
1983–84 Clydebank................... 2 —
1984–85 .... 26 11
1985–86 .... 28 7
1986–87 .... 36 9
1987–88 .... 22 11
1987–88 St Mirren 10 1
1988–89 Reading....................... 13 4
1989–90 .... 34 2
1990–91 .... 33 1
1991–92 Burnley 38 24
1992–93 .... 39 6

CONSTABLE, Shaun

Born Maidstone 21.3.68   Ht 5 11
Wt 12 00
Midfield.

1992–93	Scunthorpe U	7	—

COOK, Andy

Born Romsey 10.8.69.   Ht 5 9   Wt 10 12
Defender. From Apprentice.

1987–88	Southampton	2	—
1988–89		3	—
1989–90		4	1
1990–91		7	—
1991–92		—	—
1991–92	Exeter C	38	—
1992–93		32	1

COOK, Jason

Born Edmonton 29.12.69   Ht 5 7
Wt 10 06
Midfield. From Trainee.

1988–89	Tottenham H	—	—
1989–90	Southend U	29	1
1990–91		1	—
1991–92	Colchester U	*32*	*2*
1992–93		34	1

COOK, Mitch

Born Scarborough 15.10.61.   Ht 6 0
Wt 12 0
Midfield. From Scarborough.

1984–85	Darlington	31	3
1985–86		3	1
1985–86	Middlesbrough	6	—
1986–87	Scarborough	—	—
1987–88		38	5
1988–89		43	5
1989–90	Halifax T	37	2
1990–91		17	—
1990–91	*Scarborough*	9	1
1990–91	*Darlington*	9	—
1991–92	Darlington	27	3
1991–92	Blackpool	8	—

1992–93		9	—

COOK, Paul

Born Liverpool 22.2.67.   Ht 5 11
Wt 10 10
Midfield.

1984–85	Wigan Ath	2	—
1985–86		13	2
1986–87		27	4
1987–88		41	8
1988–89	Norwich C	4	—
1989–90		2	—
1989–90	Wolverhampton W	28	2
1990–91		42	6
1991–92		43	8
1992–93		44	1

COOKE, Richard

Born Islington 4.9.65.   Ht 5 6   Wt 9 00
Forward. From Apprentice. England
Youth, Under-21.

1982–83	Tottenham H	—	—
1983–84		9	1
1984–85		—	—
1985–86		2	1
1986–87		—	—
1986–87	*Birmingham C*	5	—
1986–87	Bournemouth	23	8
1987–88		34	5
1988–89		15	3
1988–89	Luton T	6	—
1989–90		11	1
1990–91		—	—
1990–91	Bournemouth	10	2
1991–92		31	—
1992–93		12	—

COOPER, Colin

Born Durham 28.2.67.   Ht 5 11   Wt 11 05
Defender. England Under-21.

1984–85	Middlesbrough	—	—
1985–86		11	—
1986–87		46	—
1987–88		43	2

Season	Club	Apps	Goals
1988–89	....	35	2
1989–90	....	21	2
1990–91	....	32	—
1991–92	Millwall.....................	36	2
1992–93	....	41	4

COOPER, David

Born Welwyn 7.3.73. Ht 6 0 Wt 12 00
Defender. From Luton T Trainee.

Season	Club	Apps	Goals
1991–92	Exeter C.....................	13	—
1992–93	....	20	—

COOPER, Davie

Born Hamilton 25.2.56. Ht 5 8 Wt 12 05
Forward. From Hamilton Avondale.
Scotland Under-21. 22 full caps.

Season	Club	Apps	Goals
1974–75	Clydebank.....................	26	4
1975–76	....	26	13
1976–77	....	38	11
1977–78	Rangers.....................	35	6
1978–79	....	30	5
1979–80	....	30	2
1980–81	....	25	3
1981–82	....	30	3
1982–83	....	31	5
1983–84	....	34	6
1984–85	....	32	5
1985–86	....	32	4
1986–87	....	42	8
1987–88	....	33	1
1988–89	....	23	1
1989–90	Motherwell.....................	31	6
1990–91	....	34	6
1991–92	....	39	3
1992–93	....	43	2

COOPER, Gary

Born Edgware 20.11.65. Ht 5 8 Wt 11 03
Defender. From Brentford, QPR and
Fisher Ath (1989).

Season	Club	Apps	Goals
1989–90	Maidstone U.....................	33	4
1990–91	....	27	3
1990–91	Peterborough U..........	6	1
1991–92	....	33	4

Season	Club	Apps	Goals
1992–93	....	35	3

COOPER, Geoff

Born Kingston 27.12.60. Ht 5 10
Wt 11 00
Midfield. From Bognor Regis.

Season	Club	Apps	Goals
1987–88	Brighton.....................	2	—
1988–89	....	5	—
To Barnet			
1991–92	Barnet..........................	14	1
1992–93	....	17	—

COOPER, Mark

Born Wakefield 18.12.68. Ht 5 8
Wt 11 04
Midfield. From Trainee.

Season	Club	Apps	Goals
1987–88	Bristol C.....................	—	—
1988–89	....	—	—
1989–90	Exeter C.....................	5	—
1989–90	*Southend U*.....................	5	—
1990–91	Exeter C.....................	42	11
1991–92	....	3	1
1991–92	Birmingham C............	33	4
1992–93	....	6	—
1992–93	Fulham	9	—
1992–93	*Huddersfield T*............	10	4

COOPER, Mark

Born Cambridge 5.4.67. Ht 6 2 Wt 13 04
Forward. From Apprentice.

Season	Club	Apps	Goals
1983–84	Cambridge U..............	2	—
1984–85	....	18	3
1985–86	....	19	1
1986–87	....	32	13
1986–87	Tottenham H..............	—	—
1987–88	....	—	—
1987–88	Shrewsbury T..............	6	2
1987–88	Gillingham..............	31	8
1988–89	....	18	3
1988–89	Leyton Orient..............	14	4
1989–90	....	39	11
1990–91	....	22	9
1991–92	....	18	6
1992–93	....	28	7

COOPER, Steve

Born Birmingham 22.6.64.   Ht 5 11
Wt 10 12
Forward.

Season	Club		
1983–84	Birmingham C	—	—
1983–84	*Halifax T*	7	1
1984–85	*Mansfield T*	—	—
1984–85	Newport Co	38	11
1985–86	Plymouth Arg	38	8
1986–87		12	4
1987–88		23	3
1988–89	Barnsley	35	6
1989–90		30	5
1990–91		12	2
1990–91	Tranmere R	17	2
1991–92		9	1
1991–92	*Peterborough U*	9	—
1992–93	Tranmere R	6	—
1992–93	*Wigan Ath*	4	—

CORK, Alan

Born Derby 4.3.59.   Ht 6 0   Wt 12 00
Forward. From Amateur.

Season	Club		
1977–78	Derby C	—	—
1977–78	*Lincoln C*	5	—
1977–78	Wimbledon	17	4
1978–79		45	22
1979–80		42	12
1980–81		41	23
1981–82		6	—
1982–83		7	5
1983–84		42	29
1984–85		28	11
1985–86		38	11
1986–87		30	5
1987–88		34	9
1988–89		25	2
1989–90		31	5
1990–91		25	5
1991–92		19	2
1991–92	Sheffield U	8	2
1992–93		27	2

CORNFORTH, John

Born Whitley Bay 7.10.67.   Ht 6 1
Wt 12 08
Defender. From Apprentice.

Season	Club		
1984–85	Sunderland	1	—
1985–86		—	—
1986–87		—	—
1986–87	*Doncaster R*	7	3
1987–88	Sunderland	12	2
1988–89		15	—
1989–90		2	—
1989–90	*Shrewsbury T*	3	—
1989–90	*Lincoln C*	9	1
1990–91	Sunderland	2	—
1991–92	Swansea C	17	—
1992–93		44	5

CORNWELL, John

Born Bethnal Green 13.10.64.   Ht 6 4
Wt 13 00
Midfield. From Apprentice.

Season	Club		
1981–82	Orient	3	—
1982–83		31	3
1983–84		42	7
1984–85		36	10
1985–86		44	8
1986–87		46	7
1987–88	Newcastle U	24	1
1988–89		9	—
1988–89	Swindon T	6	—
1989–90		19	—
1990–91	Southend U	19	2
1991–92		43	—
1992–93		39	3

COSTELLO, Peter

Born Halifax 31.10.69.   Ht 6 0   Wt 12 00
Forward. From Trainee.

Season	Club		
1988–89	Bradford C	8	2
1989–90		12	—
1990–91	Rochdale	34	10
1990–91	Peterborough U	5	—
1991–92		1	—
1991–92	*Lincoln C*	3	—
1992–93	Peterborough U	2	—

Season	Club	App	Goals
1992–93	Lincoln C	27	7

COTON, Tony

Born Tamworth 19.5.61.   Ht 6 2
Wt 13 07
Goalkeeper. From Mile Oak. England B.

Season	Club	App	Goals
1978–79	Birmingham C	—	—
1979–80		—	—
1979–80	*Hereford U*	—	—
1980–81	Birmingham C	3	—
1981–82		15	—
1982–83		28	—
1983–84		41	—
1984–85		7	—
1984–85	Watford	33	—
1985–86		40	—
1986–87		31	—
1987–88		37	—
1988–89		46	—
1989–90		46	—
1990–91	Manchester C	33	—
1991–92		37	—
1992–93		40	—

COTTEE, Tony

Born West Ham 11.7.65.   Ht 5 7
Wt 11 03
Forward. From Apprentice. England
Youth, Under-21, 7 full caps.

Season	Club	App	Goals
1982–83	West Ham U	8	5
1983–84		39	15
1984–85		41	17
1985–86		42	20
1986–87		42	22
1987–88		40	13
1988–89	Everton	36	13
1989–90		27	13
1990–91		29	10
1991–92		24	8
1992–93		26	12

COTTERILL, Steve

Born Cheltenham 20.7.64.   Ht 6 1
Wt 12 05
Forward. From Burton A.

Season	Club	App	Goals
1988–89	Wimbledon	4	1

Season	Club	App	Goals
1989–90		2	1
1990–91		4	1
1991–92		—	—
1992–93		7	3
1992–93	*Brighton*	11	4

COUGHLIN, Russell

Born Swansea 15.2.60.   Ht 5 8   Wt 11 12
Midfield. From Apprentice.

Season	Club	App	Goals
1977–78	Manchester C	—	—
1978–79		—	—
1978–79	Blackburn R	11	—
1979–80		10	—
1980–81		3	—
1980–81	Carlisle U	25	3
1981–82		37	5
1982–83		38	2
1983–84		30	3
1984–85	Plymouth Arg	38	3
1985–86		45	10
1986–87		40	5
1987–88		8	—
1987–88	Blackpool	24	2
1988–89		43	5
1989–90		35	1
1990–91		—	—
1990–91	*Shrewsbury T*	5	—
1990–91	Swansea C	29	—
1991–92		33	1
1992–93		39	1

COUSINS, Tony

Born Dublin 25.8.69.   Ht 5 9   Wt 11 10
Forward. From Dundalk.

Season	Club	App	Goals
1991–92	Liverpool	—	—
1992–93		—	—
1992–93	*Hereford U*	3	—

COWAN, Tom

Born Bellshill 28.8.69.   Ht 5 8   Wt 10 08
Defender. From Netherdale BC.

Season	Club	App	Goals
1988–89	Clyde	16	2
1988–89	Rangers	4	—
1989–90		3	—

Season	Club	App	Goals
1990–91		5	—
1991–92	Sheffield U	20	—
1992–93		21	—

COWANS, Gordon

Born Durham 27.10.58. Ht 5 7 Wt 9 8
Midfield. From Apprentice. England
Youth, Under-21, B, 10 full caps.

Season	Club	App	Goals
1975–76	Aston Villa	1	—
1976–77		18	3
1977–78		35	7
1978–79		34	4
1979–80		42	6
1980–81		42	5
1981–82		42	6
1982–83		42	10
1983–84		—	—
1984–85		30	1
1985–86	Bari	20	—
1986–87		38	3
1987–88		36	—
1988–89	Aston Villa	33	2
1989–90		34	4
1990–91		38	1
1991–92		12	—
1991–92	Blackburn R	26	1
1992–93		24	1

COX, Neil

Born Scunthorpe 8.10.71. Ht 6 00
Wt 12 10
Midfield. From Trainee. England
Under-21.

Season	Club	App	Goals
1989–90	Scunthorpe U	—	—
1990–91		17	1
1990–91	Aston Villa	—	—
1991–92		7	—
1992–93		15	1

COX, Paul

Born Nottingham 1.1.72. Ht 5 11
Wt 11 12
Defender. From Trainee.

Season	Club	App	Goals
1990–91	Notts Co	—	—

COYLE, Owen

Born Glasgow 14.7.66. Ht 5 11 Wt 10 5
Forward. From Renfrew YM. Eire Under-
21, B.

Season	Club	App	Goals
1984–85	Dumbarton	—	—
1985–86		16	5
1986–87		43	17
1987–88		41	14
1988–89		3	—
1988–89	Clydebank	36	16
1989–90		27	17
1989–90	Airdrieonians	10	10
1990–91		28	20
1991–92		43	11
1992–93		42	9

COYLE, Ronald

Born Glasgow 4.8.64 Ht 5 11 Wt 12 9
Midfield. From Celtic BC.

Season	Club	App	Goals
1983–84	Celtic	—	—
1984–85		1	—
1985–86		1	—
1986–87	Middlesbrough	3	—
1987–88	Rochdale	24	1
1987–88	Raith R	16	3
1988–89		36	1
1989–90		28	2
1990–91		35	1
1991–92		29	—
1992–93		35	1

COYNE, Danny

Born St Asaph 27.8.73
Goalkeeper. From Trainee.

Season	Club	App	Goals
1991–92	Tranmere R	—	—
1992–93		1	—

COYNE, Tommy

Born Glasgow 14.11.62. Ht 5 11
Wt 12 00
Forward. From Hillwood BC. Eire 8 full
caps.

1981–82	Clydebank	31	9
1982–83		38	18
1983–84		11	10
1983–84	Dundee U	18	3
1984–85		21	3
1985–86		13	2
1986–87	Dundee	20	9
1987–88		43	33
1988–89		26	9
1988–89	Celtic	7	—
1989–90		23	7
1990–91		26	18
1991–92		39	15
1992–93		10	3
1992–93	Tranmere R	12	1

CRABBE, Scott

Born Edinburgh 12.8.68. Ht 5 7
Wt 10 00
Midfield. From Tynecastle BC. Scotland
Under-21.

1986–87	Hearts	5	—
1987–88		5	—
1988–89		1	—
1989–90		35	12
1990–91		21	3
1991–92		41	15
1992–93		8	1
1992–93	Dundee U	27	4

CRAIG, Albert

Born Glasgow 3.1.62. Ht 5 8 Wt 11 03
Midfield. From Yoker Ath.

1981–82	Dumbarton	13	2
1982–83		32	7
1983–84		26	4
1984–85		35	4
1985–86		32	6
1986–87	Hamilton A	16	5
1986–87	Newcastle U	6	—

1987–88		3	—
1987–88	*Hamilton A*	6	1
1988–89	Newcastle U	1	—
1988–89	Northampton T	2	1
1988–89	Dundee	6	2
1989–90		20	2
1990–91		12	3
1991–92		25	7
1992–93	Partick T	29	1

CRAINIE, Danny

Born Kilsyth 24.5.62. Ht 5 8 Wt 10 11
Forward. From Celtic BC.

1979–80	Celtic	—	—
1980–81		—	—
1981–82		16	7
1982–83		7	—
1983–84		1	—
1983–84	Wolverhampton W	28	3
1984–85		13	—
1984–85	*Blackpool*	6	—
1985–86	Wolverhampton W	23	1
1985–86	Dundee	3	—
From Cork C, Wollongong C			
1990–91	Airdrieonians	28	1
1991–92		3	—
1992–93	Kilmarnock	9	1

CRANE, Steve

Born Essex 3.6.72 Ht 5 9 Wt 12 00
Forward. From USA.

1992–93	Gillingham	7	1

CRANSON, Ian

Born Easington 2.7.64. Ht 6 0 Wt 13 04
Defender. From Apprentice. England
Under-21.

1982–83	Ipswich T	—	—
1983–84		8	—
1984–85		20	1
1985–86		42	1
1986–87		32	2
1987–88		29	1
1987–88	Sheffield W	4	—

Season	Club	Apps	Goals
1988–89	....	26	—
1989–90	Stoke C	17	2
1990–91	....	9	—
1991–92	....	41	2
1992–93	....	45	3

CRAVEN, Peter

Born Hanover 30.6.68
Midfield. From Park Avenue.

Season	Club	Apps	Goals
1991–92	Bury	—	—
1992–93	Halifax T	7	—

CRAWFORD, Stephen

Born Dunfermline 9.1.74   Ht 5 10
Wt 10 7
Midfield. From Rosyth Recreation.

Season	Club	Apps	Goals
1992–93	Raith R	20	3

CREANEY, Gerard

Born Coatbridge 13.4.70.   Ht 5 10
Wt 10 07
Forward. From Celtic BC. Scotland
Under-21.

Season	Club	Apps	Goals
1987–88	Celtic	—	—
1988–89	....	—	—
1989–90	....	6	1
1990–91	....	31	7
1991–92	....	32	14
1992–93	....	26	9

CRICHTON, Paul

Born Pontefract 3.10.68.   Ht 6 1
Wt 12 05
Goalkeeper. From Apprentice.

Season	Club	Apps	Goals
1986–87	Nottingham F	—	—
1986–87	Notts Co	5	—
1986–87	Darlington	5	—
1986–87	Peterborough U	4	—
1987–88	Nottingham F	—	—
1987–88	Darlington	3	—
1987–88	Swindon T	4	—
1987–88	Rotherham U	6	—

Season	Club	Apps	Goals
1988–89	Nottingham F	—	—
1988–89	Torquay U	13	—
1988–89	Peterborough U	31	—
1989–90	....	16	—
1990–91	Doncaster R	20	—
1991–92	....	16	—
1992–93	....	41	—

CRISP, Richard

Born Wordsley 23.5.72   Ht 5 7   Wt 10 05
Midfield. From Trainee.

Season	Club	Apps	Goals
1991–92	Aston Villa	—	—
1992–93	....	—	—
1992–93	Scunthorpe U	8	—

CROCKER, Marcus

Born Plymouth 8.10.74   Ht 5 10
Wt 11 05
Forward. From Trainee.

Season	Club	Apps	Goals
1992–93	Plymouth Arg	4	—

CROFT, Brian

Born Chester 27.9.67.   Ht 5 9   Wt 10 10
Midfield.

Season	Club	Apps	Goals
1984–85	Chester C	—	—
1985–86	....	1	—
1986–87	....	21	1
1987–88	....	37	2
1988–89	Cambridge U	17	2
1989–90	Chester C	44	3
1990–91	....	38	—
1991–92	....	32	—
1992–93	QPR	—	—

CROFT, Gary

Born Burton-on-Trent 17.2.74.   Ht 5 9
Wt 10 08
Defender. From Trainee.

Season	Club	Apps	Goals
1990–91	Grimsby T	1	—
1991–92	....	—	—
1992–93	....	32	—

CROOK, Ian

Born Romford 18.1.63.   Ht 5 8   Wt 10 06
Midfield. From Apprentice. England B.

1980–81	Tottenham H	—	—
1981–82		4	—
1982–83		4	—
1983–84		3	—
1984–85		5	1
1985–86		4	—
1986–87	Norwich C	33	5
1987–88		23	1
1988–89		26	1
1989–90		35	—
1990–91		32	3
1991–92		21	1
1992–93		34	3

CROSBY, Andy

Born Rotherham 3.3.73.   Ht 6 2
Wt 13 00
Defender. From Leeds U Trainee.

1991–92	Doncaster R	22	—
1992–93		29	—

CROSBY, Gary

Born Sleaford 8.5.64.   Ht 5 7   Wt 9 11
Midfield. From Lincoln U.

1986–87	Lincoln C	7	—
From Grantham			
1987–88	Nottingham F	14	1
1988–89		13	—
1989–90		34	5
1990–91		29	2
1991–92		33	3
1992–93		23	1

CROSS, Jonathan

Born Wallasey 2.3.75.   Ht 5 10   Wt 11 04
Midfield. From Trainee.

1991–92	Wrexham	6	—
1992–93		37	7

CROSS, Mark

Born Abergavenny 6.5.76.
Forward. From Trainee.

1992–93	Hereford U	1	—

CROSS, Nicky

Born Birmingham 7.2.61.   Ht 5 9
Wt 11 12
Forward. From Apprentice.

1978–79	WBA	—	—
1979–80		—	—
1980–81		2	1
1981–82		22	2
1982–83		32	4
1983–84		25	3
1984–85		24	5
1985–86	Walsall	44	21
1986–87		39	16
1987–88		26	8
1987–88	Leicester C	17	6
1988–89		41	9
1989–90	Port Vale	42	13
1990–91		19	2
1991–92		8	—
1992–93		38	12

CROSS, Paul

Born Barnsley 31.10.65.   Ht 5 7   Wt 9 06
Midfield. From Apprentice.

1983–84	Barnsley	—	—
1984–85		1	—
1985–86		20	—
1986–87		18	—
1987–88		38	—
1988–89		—	—
1989–90		36	—
1990–91		2	—
1991–92		3	—
1991–92	*Preston NE*	5	—
1991–92	Hartlepool U	21	—
1992–93		37	1

CROSS, Ryan

Born Plymouth 11.10.72.   Ht 6 1
Wt 13 06
Defender. From Trainee.

Season	Club	App	Goals
1990–91	Plymouth Arg	7	—
1991–92		12	—
1992–93	Hartlepool U	33	2

CROSS, Steve

Born Wolverhampton 22.12.59.   Ht 5 10
Wt 11 05
Defender. From Apprentice.

Season	Club	App	Goals
1976–77	Shrewsbury T	5	—
1977–78		1	—
1978–79		19	2
1979–80		19	—
1980–81		35	2
1981–82		34	3
1982–83		33	5
1983–84		41	9
1984–85		40	5
1985–86		35	8
1986–87	Derby Co	6	—
1987–88		15	3
1988–89		19	—
1989–90		8	—
1990–91		21	—
1991–92		4	—
1991–92	Bristol R	32	2
1992–93		11	—

CROSSLEY, Mark

Born Barnsley 16.6.69.   Ht 6 0   Wt 13 09
Goalkeeper. England Under-21.

Season	Club	App	Goals
1987–88	Nottingham F	—	—
1988–89		2	—
1989–90		8	—
1989–90	Manchester U	—	—
1990–91	Nottingham F	38	—
1991–92		36	—
1992–93		37	—

CROWN, David

Born Enfield 16.2.58.   Ht 5 9   Wt 12 03
Forward. From Walthamstow Ave.

Season	Club	App	Goals
1980–81	Brentford	38	6
1981–82		8	2
1981–82	Portsmouth	27	2
1982–83		1	—
1982–83	Exeter C	7	3
1983–84	Reading	45	7
1984–85		43	8
1985–86	Cambridge U	43	24
1986–87		46	12
1987–88		17	9
1987–88	Southend U	28	17
1988–89		44	25
1989–90		41	19
1990–91	Gillingham	30	11
1991–92		36	22
1992–93		20	5

CRUMPLIN, John

Born Bath 26.5.67.   Ht 5 8   Wt 11 10
Midfield. From Bognor Regis.

Season	Club	App	Goals
1986–87	Brighton	5	—
1987–88		26	2
1988–89		12	—
1989–90		25	2
1990–91		46	—
1991–92		29	—
1992–93		32	1

CULLEN, Jon

Born Durham 10.1.73.
Defender. From Trainee.

Season	Club	App	Goals
1990–91	Doncaster R	1	—
1991–92		8	—
1992–93		—	—

CULLEN, Tony

Born Newcastle 30.9.69.   Ht 5 6
Wt 11 07
Forward. From Local.

Season	Club	App	Goals
1988–89	Sunderland	7	—

Season	Club	League Appearances/Goals
1989–90	....	16 —
1989–90	*Carlisle U*....................	2 1
1990–91	Sunderland..................	5 —
1990–91	*Rotherham U*..............	3 1
1991–92	Sunderland..................	1 —
1991–92	*Bury*	4 —
1992–93	Swansea C..................	27 3

CULVERHOUSE, Ian

Born Bishop's Stortford 22.9.64.
Ht 5 10   Wt 11 02
Defender. From Apprentice. England
Youth.

Season	Club	League Appearances/Goals
1982–83	Tottenham H..............	— —
1983–84	....	2 —
1984–85	....	— —
1985–86	....	— —
1985–86	Norwich C	30 —
1986–87	....	25 —
1987–88	....	33 —
1988–89	....	38 —
1989–90	....	32 —
1990–91	....	34 —
1991–92	....	21 —
1992–93	....	41 —

CUNDY, Jason

Born Wimbledon 12.11.69.   Ht 6 1
Wt 13 07
Defender. From Trainee. England
Under-21.

Season	Club	League Appearances/Goals
1988–89	Chelsea........................	— —
1989–90	....	— —
1990–91	....	29 —
1991–92	....	12 1
1991–92	*Tottenham H*..............	10 —
1992–93	Tottenham H	15 1

CUNNINGHAM, Ken

Born Dublin 28.6.71.   Ht 6 0   Wt 11 08
Defender. Eire Under-21, B.

Season	Club	League Appearances/Goals
1989–90	Millwall.......................	5 —
1990–91	....	23 —
1991–92	....	17 —

Season	Club	League Appearances/Goals
1992–93	....	37 —

CUNNINGHAM, Tony

Born Jamaica 12.11.57.   Ht 6 1   Wt 13 13
Forward. From Stourbridge.

Season	Club	League Appearances/Goals
1979–80	Lincoln C....................	38 12
1980–81	....	34 6
1981–82	....	46 11
1982–83	....	5 3
1982–83	Barnsley	29 7
1983–84	....	13 4
1983–84	Sheffield W.................	28 5
1984–85	Manchester C	18 1
1984–85	Newcastle U................	13 1
1985–86	....	17 1
1986–87	....	17 2
1987–88	Blackpool....................	40 10
1988–89	....	31 7
1989–90	Bury	25 8
1990–91	....	33 9
1990–91	Bolton W	9 4
1991–92	Rotherham U	36 18
1992–93	....	33 6

CUNNINGTON, Shaun

Born Bourne 4.1.66.   Ht 5 10   Wt 11 07
Defender. From Bourne T.

Season	Club	League Appearances/Goals
1982–83	Wrexham	4 —
1983–84	....	42 —
1984–85	....	41 6
1985–86	....	42 2
1986–87	....	46 1
1987–88	....	24 3
1987–88	Grimsby T	15 2
1988–89	....	44 1
1989–90	....	44 3
1990–91	....	46 2
1991–92	....	33 5
1992–93	Sunderland..................	39 7

CURBISHLEY, Alan

Born Forest Gate 8.11.57.   Ht 5 11
Wt 11 10
Midfield. From Apprentice. England
Schools, Youth, Under-21.

Season	Club	League Appearances/Goals
1974–75	West Ham U	2 —

Season	Club	Apps	Goals
1975–76	....	14	2
1976–77	....	10	1
1977–78	....	32	1
1978–79	....	27	1
1979–80	Birmingham C	42	3
1980–81	....	29	6
1981–82	....	29	1
1982–83	....	30	1
1982–83	Aston Villa..............	7	—
1983–84	....	26	1
1984–85	....	3	—
1984–85	Charlton Ath	23	2
1985–86	....	30	4
1986–87	....	10	—
1987–88	Brighton..............	34	6
1988–89	....	37	6
1989–90	....	45	1
1990–91	Charlton Ath	25	—
1991–92	....	1	—
1992–93	....	1	—

CURLE, Keith

Born Bristol 14.11.63.   Ht 6 0   Wt 12 07
Defender. From Apprentice. England B, 3
full caps.

Season	Club	Apps	Goals
1981–82	Bristol R	20	2
1982–83	....	12	2
1983–84	Bristol R	—	—
1983–84	Torquay U..................	16	5
1983–84	Bristol C..................	6	—
1984–85	....	40	—
1985–86	....	44	1
1986–87	....	28	—
1987–88	....	3	—
1987–88	Reading..................	30	—
1988–89	....	10	—
1988–89	Wimbledon	18	—
1989–90	....	38	2
1990–91	....	37	1
1991–92	Manchester C	40	5
1992–93	....	39	3

CURRAN, Chris

Born Manchester 6.1.71.   Ht 6 1
Wt 12 06
Forward. From Trainee.

Season	Club	Apps	Goals
1989–90	Crewe Alex	1	—

Season	Club	Apps	Goals
1990–91	....	4	—
1991–92	....	—	—
1991–92	Scarborough...............	8	2
1992–93	....	32	2

CURRAN, Chris

Born Birmingham 17.9.71.   Ht 5 11
Wt 11 09
Defender. From Trainee.

Season	Club	Apps	Goals
1989–90	Torquay U..................	1	—
1990–91	....	13	—
1991–92	....	17	—
1992–93	....	34	—

CURRAN, Henry

Born Glasgow 9.10.66.   Ht 5 8   Wt 11 04
Midfield. From Eastercraigs.

Season	Club	Apps	Goals
1984–85	Dumbarton	2	—
1985–86	....	6	—
1986–87	....	8	—
1986–87	Dundee U	3	—
1987–88	....	6	—
1988–89	....	6	—
1989–90	St Johnstone	31	3
1990–91	....	35	9
1991–92	....	39	8
1992–93	....	34	8

CURRIE, David

Born Stockton 27.11.62.   Ht 5 11
Wt 12 09
Forward. From Local.

Season	Club	Apps	Goals
1981–82	Middlesbrough............	1	—
1982–83	....	8	—
1983–84	....	39	15
1984–85	....	39	12
1985–86	....	26	4
1986–87	Darlington	45	12
1987–88	....	31	21
1987–88	Barnsley	15	7
1988–89	....	41	16
1989–90	....	24	7
1989–90	Nottingham F.............	8	1
1990–91	Oldham Ath................	27	2

1991–92	....	4	1
1991–92	Barnsley	37	7
1992–93	....	35	4
1992–93	*Rotherham U*..............	5	2

CURTIS, Andy

Born Doncaster 2.12.72. Ht 5 10
Wt 11 07
Midfield. From Trainee.

1990–91	York C........................	5	—
1991–92	....	7	—
1992–93	Peterborough U..........	11	1

CURTIS, Paul

Born London 1.7.63
Defender. From Corby.

1992–93	Northampton T..........	22	1

CUSACK, Nicky

Born Rotherham 24.12.65. Ht 6 0
Wt 11 13
Forward. From Alvechurch.

1987–88	Leicester C..................	16	1
1988–89	Peterborough U..........	44	10
1989–90	Motherwell..................	31	11
1990–91	....	29	4
1991–92	....	17	2
1991–92	Darlington	21	6
1992–93	Oxford U	39	4

CUSICK, John

Born Kirkcaldy 16.1.75 Ht 5 8 Wt 10 0
Forward. From Lochore Welfare.

1992–93	Raith R.......................	2	—

DAILLY, Christian

Born Dundee 23.10.73. Ht 5 10
Wt 10 11
Forward. S Form. Scotland Under-21.

1990–91	Dundee U	18	5
1991–92	....	8	—
1992–93	....	14	4

DAIR, Jason

Born Dunfermline 15.6.74 Ht 5 11
Wt 10 8
Forward. From Castlebridge.

1991–92	Raith R.......................	4	—
1992–93	....	15	1

DAISH, Liam

Born Portsmouth 23.9.68. Ht 6 2
Wt 13 05
Defender. From Apprentice. Eire Under-21, 1 full cap.

1986–87	Portsmouth	1	—
1987–88	....	—	—
1988–89	Cambridge U..............	28	—
1989–90	....	42	1
1990–91	....	13	1
1991–92	....	22	—
1992–93	....	16	—

DALE, Carl

Born Colwyn Bay 29.4.66. Ht 6 0
Wt 12 00
Forward. From Bangor C.

1987–88	Chester C....................	—	—
1988–89	....	41	22
1989–90	....	31	9
1990–91	....	44	10
1991–92	Cardiff C....................	41	22
1992–93	....	20	8

DALEY, Philip

Born Walton 12.4.67. Ht 6 2 Wt 12 09
Forward. From Newton.

1989–90	Wigan Ath	33	6

Season	Club	Apps	Goals
1990–91		41	10
1991–92		38	14
1992–93		31	6

DALEY, Tony

Born Birmingham 18.10.67.   Ht 5 8
Wt 10 08
Forward. From Apprentice. England
Youth, 7 full caps.

Season	Club	Apps	Goals
1984–85	Aston Villa	5	—
1985–86		23	2
1986–87		33	3
1987–88		14	3
1988–89		29	5
1989–90		32	6
1990–91		23	2
1991–92		34	7
1992–93		13	2

DALTON, Paul

Born Middlesbrough 25.4.67.   Ht 5 11
Wt 11 07
Midfield. From Brandon.

Season	Club	Apps	Goals
1987–88	Manchester U	—	—
1988–89		—	—
1988–89	Hartlepool U	17	2
1989–90		45	11
1990–91		46	11
1991–92		43	13
1992–93	Plymouth Arg	32	9

DALZIEL, Gordon

Born Motherwell 16.3.62   Ht 5 10
Wt 10 13
Forward. From Bonkle YC.

Season	Club	Apps	Goals
1978–79	Rangers	—	—
1979–80		1	—
1980–81		—	—
1981–82		17	6
1982–83		15	3
1983–84	Manchester C	5	—
1984–85	Partick T	25	6
1985–86		18	—
1986–87	East Stirling	10	2

Season	Club	Apps	Goals
1986–87	Raith R	11	7
1987–88		42	25
1988–89		36	11
1989–90		39	20
1990–91		39	25
1991–92		39	26
1992–93		44	32

DALZIEL, Ian

Born South Shields 24.10.62.   Ht 5 8
Wt 11 10
Defender. From Apprentice.

Season	Club	Apps	Goals
1979–80	Derby Co	—	—
1980–81		—	—
1981–82		4	—
1982–83		18	4
1983–84	Hereford U	30	4
1984–85		26	—
1985–86		41	3
1986–87		28	—
1987–88		25	1
1988–89	Carlisle U	42	1
1989–90		24	1
1990–91		13	—
1991–92		—	—
1992–93		12	—

DANIEL, Ray

Born Luton 10.12.64.   Ht 5 8   Wt 11 09
Midfield. From Apprentice.

Season	Club	Apps	Goals
1982–83	Luton T	3	—
1983–84		7	2
1983–84	*Gillingham*	5	—
1984–85	Luton T	7	1
1985–86		5	1
1986–87	Hull C	9	—
1987–88		26	2
1988–89		23	1
1989–90	Cardiff C	43	1
1990–91		13	—
1990–91	Portsmouth	14	—
1991–92		8	—
1992–93		40	4

DANIELS, Scott

Born Benfleet 22.11.69. Ht 6 1 Wt 11 09
Defender. From Trainee.

1987–88	Colchester U	1	—
1988–89		26	—
1989–90		46	—
1990–91		*40*	*1*
1991–92	Exeter C	43	3
1992–93		26	2

DANZEY, Michael

Born Widnes 8.2.71 Ht 6 1 Wt 12 00
Forward. From Trainee.

1988–89	Nottingham F	—	—
1989–90		—	—
1989–90	*Chester C*	2	—
1990–91	Peterborough U	1	—
From St Albans			
1992–93	Cambridge U	2	—

DARBY, Duane

Born West Midlands 17.10.73.
Forward. From Trainee.

1991–92	Torquay U	14	2
1992–93		34	12

DARBY, Julian

Born Bolton 3.10.67. Ht 6 0 Wt 11 04
Defender. England Schools.

1984–85	Bolton W	—	—
1985–86		2	—
1986–87		28	—
1987–88		35	2
1988–89		44	5
1989–90		46	10
1990–91		45	9
1991–92		44	6
1992–93		21	4

DARLINGTON, Jermaine

Born London 11.4.74. Ht 5 6 Wt 10 06
Midfield. From Trainee.

1991–92	Charlton Ath	2	—

1992–93		—	—

DARTON, Scott

Born Ipswich 27.3.75
Defender. From Trainee.

1992–93	WBA	2	—

DAVENPORT, Peter

Born Birkenhead 24.3.61. Ht 5 10
Wt 11 06
Forward. From Everton Amateur,
Cammell Laird. England B, 1 full cap.

1981–82	Nottingham F	5	4
1982–83		18	6
1983–84		33	15
1984–85		35	16
1985–86		27	13
1985–86	Manchester U	11	1
1986–87		39	14
1987–88		34	5
1988–89		8	2
1988–89	Middlesbrough	24	4
1989–90		35	3
1990–91	Sunderland	29	7
1991–92		36	4
1992–93		34	4

DAVEY, Simon

Born Swansea 1.10.70. Ht 5 10 Wt 11 02
Midfield. From Trainee.

1986–87	Swansea C	1	—
1987–88		4	—
1988–89		3	—
1989–90		18	2
1990–91		18	2
1991–92		5	—
1992–93	Carlisle U	38	5

DAVID, Lionel

Born Nantes 28.9.66 Ht 6 1 Wt 12 7
Midfield. From La Roche sur Yon.

1992–93	Dundee	8	—

DAVIDSON, Jonathan

Born Cheadle 1.3.70.   Ht 5 8   Wt 11 11
Defender. From Trainee.

1988–89	Derby Co	—	—
1989–90		6	—
1990–91		5	2
1991–92		1	—
1992–93	Preston NE	21	1
1992–93	*Chesterfield*	1	—

DAVIES, Andy

Born Wolverhampton 6.6.72.   Ht 6 0
Wt 11 06
Defender. From Trainee.

1988–89	Torquay U	3	—
1989–90		10	—
1990–91	Hartlepool U	4	—
1991–92		3	—
1992–93	Torquay U	3	—

DAVIES, Gareth

Born Hereford 11.12.73.
Defender. From Trainee. Wales Under-21.

1991–92	Hereford U	4	—
1992–93		32	1

DAVIES, John

Born Glasgow 25.9.66.   Ht 5 7   Wt 10 0
Midfield. From Anniesland U.

1985–86	Clydebank	3	—
1986–87		14	—
From Jonkoping			
1987–88	Clydebank	22	3
1988–89		38	3
1989–90		31	5
1990–91		14	1
1990–91	St Johnstone	21	1
1991–92		40	—
1992–93		38	4

DAVIES, Michael

Born Stretford 19.1.66.   Ht 5 8   Wt 10 07
Midfield. From Apprentice.

1983–84	Blackpool	3	—

1984–85		17	—
1985–86		36	5
1986–87		42	6
1987–88		38	—
1988–89		30	2
1989–90		23	—
1990–91		37	1
1991–92		29	1
1992–93		30	1

DAVIS, Aaron

Born London 11.2.72.
Defender.

1991–92	Torquay U	12	—
1992–93		12	—

DAVIS, Mike

Born Bristol 19.10.74
Forward. From Yate T.

1992–93	Bristol R	1	1

DAVIS, Paul

Born London 9.12.61.   Ht 5 10   Wt 10 13
Midfield. From Apprentice. England B,
Under-21.

1979–80	Arsenal	2	—
1980–81		10	1
1981–82		38	4
1982–83		41	4
1983–84		35	1
1984–85		24	1
1985–86		29	4
1986–87		39	4
1987–88		29	5
1988–89		12	1
1989–90		11	1
1990–91		37	3
1991–92		12	—
1992–93		6	—

DAVIS, Steve

Born Birmingham 26.7.65. Ht 6 0
Wt 12 07
Defender. From Stoke C. Apprentice.
England Youth.

1983–84	Crewe Alex	24	—
1984–85		40	—
1985–86		45	1
1986–87		33	—
1987–88		3	—
1987–88	Burnley	33	5
1988–89		37	—
1989–90		31	1
1990–91		46	5
1991–92	Barnsley	9	—
1992–93		11	—

DAVIS, Steve

Born Hexham 30.10.68. Ht 6 2 Wt 12 08
Defender. From Trainee.

1987–88	Southampton	—	—
1988–89		—	—
1989–90		4	—
1989–90	*Burnley*	9	—
1990–91	Southampton	3	—
1990–91	*Notts Co*	2	—
1991–92	Burnley	40	6
1992–93		37	2

DAVISON, Aidan

Born Sedgefield 11.5.68. Ht 6 2
Wt 13 11
Goalkeeper. From Billingham Syn.

1987–88	Notts Co	—	—
1988–89		1	—
1989–90		—	—
1989–90	*Leyton Orient*	—	—
1989–90	Bury	—	—
1989–90	*Chester C*	—	—
1990–91	Bury	—	—
1990–91	*Blackpool*	—	—
1991–92	Millwall	33	—
1992–93		1	—

DAVISON, Bobby

Born S. Shields 17.7.59 Ht 5 9 Wt 11 09
Forward. From Seaham C.W.

1980–81	Huddersfield T	2	—
1981–82	Halifax T	46	20
1982–83		17	9
1982–83	Derby Co	26	8
1983–84		40	14
1984–85		46	24
1985–86		41	17
1986–87		40	19
1987–88		13	1
1987–88	Leeds U	16	5
1988–89		39	14
1989–90		29	11
1990–91		5	1
1991–92		2	—
1991–92	*Derby Co*	10	8
1991–92	*Sheffield U*	11	4
1992–93	Leicester C	25	6

DAWES, Ian

Born Croydon 22.2.63. Ht 5 10
Wt 11 10
Defender. From Apprentice. England
Schools.

1980–81	QPR	—	—
1981–82		5	—
1982–83		42	—
1983–84		42	2
1984–85		42	—
1985–86		42	1
1986–87		23	—
1987–88		33	—
1988–89	Millwall	30	1
1989–90		38	4
1990–91		40	—
1991–92		36	—
1992–93		46	—

DAWS, Nick

Born Manchester 15.3.70 Ht 5 11
Wt 13 02
Midfield. From Altrincham.

1992–93	Bury	36	1

DAWS, Tony

Born Sheffield 10.9.66.   Ht 5 8   Wt 11 10
Forward. From Apprentice. England
Youth.

1984–85	Notts Co	7	1
1985–86		1	—
1986–87	Sheffield U	11	3
1987–88	Scunthorpe U	10	3
1988–89		46	24
1989–90		33	11
1990–91		34	14
1991–92		36	7
1992–93		24	4
1992–93	Grimsby T	6	1

DAY, Keith

Born Grays 29.11.62.   Ht 6 1   Wt 11 00
Defender. From Aveley.

1984–85	Colchester U	45	4
1985–86		30	5
1986–87		38	3
1987–88	Orient	41	3
1988–89		45	2
1989–90		39	1
1990–91		24	1
1991–92		33	1
1992–93		10	1

DAY, Mervyn

Born Chelmsford 26.6.55.   Ht 6 2
Wt 15 01
Goalkeeper. From Apprentice. England
Youth, Under-23.

1972–73	West Ham U	—	—
1973–74		33	—
1974–75		42	—
1975–76		41	—
1976–77		42	—
1977–78		23	—
1978–79		13	—
1979–80	Orient	42	—
1980–81		40	—
1981–82		42	—
1982–83		46	—
1983–84	Aston Villa	14	—

1984–85		16	—
1984–85	Leeds U	18	—
1985–86		40	—
1986–87		34	—
1987–88		44	—
1988–89		45	—
1989–90		44	—
1990–91		—	—
1990–91	*Coventry C*	—	—
1991–92	Leeds U	—	—
1991–92	*Luton T*	4	—
1991–92	*Sheffield U*	1	—
1992–93	Leeds U	2	—

DEANE, Brian

Born Leeds 7.2.68.   Ht 6 3   Wt 12 07
Forward. From Apprentice. England B, 3
full caps.

1985–86	Doncaster R	3	—
1986–87		20	2
1987–88		43	10
1988–89	Sheffield U	43	22
1989–90		45	21
1990–91		38	13
1991–92		30	12
1992–93		41	15

DEARDEN, Kevin

Born Luton 8.3.70.   Ht 5 11   Wt 12 08
Goalkeeper. From Trainee.

1988–89	Tottenham H	—	—
1988–89	*Cambridge U*	15	—
1989–90	Tottenham H	—	—
1989–90	*Hartlepool U*	10	—
1989–90	*Oxford U*	—	—
1989–90	*Swindon T*	1	—
1990–91	Tottenham H	—	—
1990–91	*Peterborough U*	7	—
1990–91	*Hull C*	3	—
1991–92	Tottenham H	—	—
1991–92	*Rochdale*	2	—
1991–92	*Birmingham C*	12	—
1992–93	Tottenham H	1	—
1992–93	*Portsmouth*	—	—

DEARY, John

Born Ormskirk 18.10.62.   Ht 5 10
Wt 12 04
Midfield. From Apprentice.

1979–80	Blackpool	—	—
1980–81		10	—
1981–82		27	—
1982–83		45	6
1983–84		31	6
1984–85		32	13
1985–86		40	7
1986–87		44	3
1987–88		37	3
1988–89		37	5
1989–90	Burnley	41	2
1990–91		43	7
1991–92		40	6
1992–93		32	3

DEAS, Paul

Born Perth 22.2.72.   Ht 5 11   Wt 11 00
Midfield. From Kinnoull J. Scotland
Under-21.

1990–91	St Johnstone	1	—
1991–92		18	—
1992–93		25	1

DELAP, Rory

Born Coaldfield 6.7.76
Midfield. From Trainee.

| 1992–93 | Carlisle U | 1 | — |

DEMETRIOS, Chris

Born Dudley 26.10.73   Ht 5 8   Wt 11 01
Midfield. From Trainee.

| 1992–93 | Walsall | 7 | 1 |

DEMPSEY, Mark

Born Dublin 10.12.72.   Ht 5 8   Wt 11 02
Midfield. From Trainee. Eire Under-21.

| 1990–91 | Gillingham | 2 | — |

| 1991–92 | | 30 | 2 |
| 1992–93 | | 16 | — |

DEMPSEY, Samuel

Born Airdrie 15.10.74
 From St Mungo's BC.

| 1992–93 | Airdrieonians | 1 | — |

DEN BIEMAN, Ivo

Born Wamel 4.2.67   Ht 6 2   Wt 13 0
Midfield. From SV Leones.

1990–91	Montrose	36	5
1991–92		42	6
1992–93	Dundee	24	3

DENNIS, Shaun

Born Kirkcaldy 20.12.69   Ht 6 1   Wt 13 7
Defender. From Lochgelly Albert.
Scotland U-21.

1988–89	Raith R	10	—
1989–90		18	—
1990–91		35	1
1991–92		42	—
1992–93		31	1

DENNIS, Tony

Born Eton 1.12.63.   Ht 5 7   Wt 10 02
Midfield. From Plymouth Arg, Bideford,
Taunton, Slough.

1988–89	Cambridge U	18	3
1989–90		17	2
1990–91		20	2
1991–92		40	2
1992–93		16	1

DENNISON, Robert

Born Banbridge 30.4.63.   Ht 5 7
Wt 11 00
Forward. From Glenavon. Northern
Ireland 16 full caps.

| 1985–86 | WBA | 12 | 1 |

Season	Club	League Appearances/Goals
1986–87	....	4 —
1986–87	Wolverhampton W	10 3
1987–88	....	43 3
1988–89	....	43 8
1989–90	....	46 8
1990–91	....	42 5
1991–92	....	22 1
1992–93	....	37 5

DEVEREUX, Robert

Born Gt Cornard 13.1.71 Ht 5 8
Wt 10 09
Midfield. From Ipswich T trainee.

1989–90	Colchester U	2 —
From local		
1992–93	Colchester U	6 —

DEVINE, Steve

Born Strabane 11.12.64. Ht 5 9
Wt 11 00
Midfield. From Apprentice. Northern
Ireland Youth.

1982–83	Wolverhampton W	— —
1983–84	Derby Co	10 —
1984–85	....	1 —
1985–86	Stockport Co	2 —
1985–86	Hereford U	11 1
1986–87	....	41 1
1987–88	....	43 —
1988–89	....	41 —
1989–90	....	34 1
1990–91	....	38 —
1991–92	....	37 1
1992–93	....	27 —

DEVLIN, Mark

Born Irvine 18.1.73. Ht 5 10 Wt 11 04
Midfield. From Trainee.

1990–91	Stoke C	21 2
1991–92	....	— —
1992–93	....	3 —

DEVLIN, Paul

Born Birmingham 14.4.72. Ht 5 8
Wt 10 05
Forward. From Stafford R.

1991–92	Notts Co	2 —
1992–93	....	32 3

DEWHURST, Robert

Born Keighley 10.9.71. Ht 6 3 Wt 13 01
Defender. From Trainee.

1990–91	Blackburn R	13 —
1991–92	....	— —
1991–92	*Darlington R*	11 1
1992–93	Blackburn R	— —
1992–93	*Huddersfield T*	7 —

DIBBLE, Andy

Born Cwmbran 8.5.65. Ht 6 2 Wt 13 07
Goalkeeper. From Apprentice. Wales
Schools, Youth, Under-21, 3 full caps.

1981–82	Cardiff C	1 —
1982–83	....	20 —
1983–84	....	41 —
1984–85	Luton T	13 —
1985–86	....	7 —
1985–86	*Sunderland*	12 —
1986–87	Luton T	1 —
1986–87	*Huddersfield T*	5 —
1987–88	Luton T	9 —
1988–89	Manchester C	38 —
1989–90	....	31 —
1990–91	....	3 —
1990–91	*Aberdeen*	5 —
1990–91	*Middlesbrough*	19 —
1991–92	Manchester C	2 —
1991–92	*Bolton W*	13 —
1991–92	*WBA*	9 —
1992–93	Manchester C	2 —
1992–93	*Oldham Ath*	— —

DICK, James

Born Bellshill 21.6.72 Ht 5 11 Wt 12 5
Midfield. From Royal Albert J.

1990–91	Airdrieonians	3 —

Season	Club	App	Goals
1991–92		—	—
1992–93		1	—

DICKENS, Alan

Born Plaistow 3.9.64. Ht 5 11 Wt 12 05
Midfield. From Apprentice. England
Youth, Under-21.

Season	Club	App	Goals
1982–83	West Ham U	15	6
1983–84		10	—
1984–85		25	2
1985–86		41	4
1986–87		36	3
1987–88		28	3
1988–89		37	5
1989–90	Chelsea	22	1
1990–91		16	—
1991–92		10	—
1992–93		—	—
1992–93	*WBA*	3	1
1992–93	Brentford	15	1

DICKINS, Matt

Born Sheffield 3.9.70. Ht 6 4 Wt 14 00
Goalkeeper. From Trainee.

Season	Club	App	Goals
1989–90	Sheffield U	—	—
1989–90	*Leyton Orient*	—	—
1990–91	Lincoln C	7	—
1991–92		20	—
1991–92	Blackburn R	1	—
1992–93		—	—
1992–93	*Blackpool*	19	—

DICKOV, Paul

Born Glasgow 1.11.72 Ht 5 5 Wt 11 05
Forward. From Trainee. Scotland
Under-21.

Season	Club	App	Goals
1992–93	Arsenal	3	2

DICKS, Julian

Born Bristol 8.8.68. Ht 5 7 Wt 11 07
Defender. From Apprentice. England
Under-21, B.

Season	Club	App	Goals
1985–86	Birmingham C	23	—

Season	Club	App	Goals
1986–87		34	—
1987–88		32	1
1987–88	West Ham U	8	—
1988–89		34	2
1989–90		40	9
1990–91		13	4
1991–92		23	3
1992–93		34	11

DIGBY, Fraser

Born Sheffield 23.4.67. Ht 6 1 Wt 12 12
Goalkeeper. From Apprentice. England
Youth, Under-21.

Season	Club	App	Goals
1984–85	Manchester U	—	—
1985–86		—	—
1985–86	*Oldham Ath*	—	—
1985–86	*Swindon T*	—	—
1986–87	Manchester U	—	—
1986–87	Swindon T	39	—
1987–88		31	—
1988–89		46	—
1989–90		45	—
1990–91		41	—
1991–92		21	—
1992–93		33	—
1992–93	*Manchester U*	—	—

DIGWEED, Perry

Born London 26.10.59. Ht 6 0 Wt 11 04
Goalkeeper. From Apprentice.

Season	Club	App	Goals
1976–77	Fulham	1	—
1977–78		—	—
1978–79		2	—
1979–80		11	—
1980–81		1	—
1980–81	Brighton	15	—
1981–82		12	—
1982–83		15	—
1983–84		4	—
1983–84	*WBA*	—	—
1984–85	Brighton	—	—
1984–85	*Charlton Ath*	—	—
1985–86	Brighton	33	—
1986–87		22	—
1987–88	*Newcastle U*	—	—
1987–88	*Chelsea*	3	—

Season	Club	App	Goals
1988–89	Brighton	1	—
1989–90		11	—
1990–91		42	—
1991–92		20	—
1992–93		4	—
1992–93	*Wimbledon*	—	—

DIJKSTRA, Meindert

Born Eindhoven 28.2.67   Ht 5 11
Wt 12 00
Defender. From Willem II.

Season	Club	App	Goals
1992–93	Notts Co	11	—

DILLON, Kevin

Born Sunderland 18.12.59.   Ht 6 0
Wt 12 07
Midfield. From Apprentice. England
Youth, Under-21.

Season	Club	App	Goals
1977–78	Birmingham C	17	1
1978–79		36	2
1979–80		31	6
1980–81		39	2
1981–82		36	1
1982–83		27	3
1982–83	Portsmouth	11	5
1983–84		36	9
1984–85		37	9
1985–86		31	5
1986–87		39	8
1987–88		32	9
1988–89		29	—
1989–90	Newcastle U	43	—
1990–91		19	—
1991–92	Reading	29	3
1992–93		40	1

DINNIE, Alan

Born Glasgow 14.5.63.   Ht 5 10   Wt 11 00
Defender. From Baillieston J.

Season	Club	App	Goals
1987–88	Partick T	37	1
1988–89		31	1
1989–90		14	2
1989–90	Dundee	22	—
1990–91		25	3

Season	Club	App	Goals
1991–92		29	—
1992–93		26	1

DIXON, Ben

Born Lincoln 16.9.74.   Ht 6 1   Wt 11 00
Forward. From Trainee.

Season	Club	App	Goals
1991–92	Lincoln C	3	—
1992–93		2	—

DIXON, Kerry

Born Luton 24.7.61.   Ht 6 0   Wt 14 01
Forward. From Tottenham H Apprentice
and Dunstable. England Under-21, 8 full
caps.

Season	Club	App	Goals
1980–81	Reading	39	13
1981–82		42	12
1982–83		35	26
1983–84	Chelsea	42	28
1984–85		41	24
1985–86		38	14
1986–87		36	10
1987–88		33	11
1988–89		39	25
1989–90		38	20
1990–91		33	10
1991–92		35	5
1992–93	Southampton	9	2
1992–93	*Luton T*	17	3

DIXON, Lee

Born Manchester 17.3.64.   Ht 5 8
Wt 11 08
Defender. From Local. England B, 20 full
caps.

Season	Club	App	Goals
1982–83	Burnley	3	—
1983–84		1	—
1983–84	Chester	16	1
1984–85		41	—
1985–86	Bury	45	5
1986–87	Stoke C	42	3
1987–88		29	2
1987–88	Arsenal	6	—
1988–89		33	1
1989–90		38	5

Season	Club	Apps	Goals
1990–91	....	38	5
1991–92	....	38	4
1992–93	....	29	—

DOBBIN, Jim

Born Dunfermline 17.9.63.   Ht 5 9
Wt 10 07
Midfield. From Whitburn BC. Scotland Youth.

Season	Club	Apps	Goals
1980–81	Celtic...........................	—	—
1981–82	....	—	—
1982–83	....	—	—
1983–84	....	2	—
1983–84	*Motherwell*	2	—
1983–84	Doncaster R...............	11	2
1984–85	....	17	1
1985–86	....	31	6
1986–87	....	5	4
1986–87	Barnsley	30	4
1987–88	....	16	2
1988–89	....	41	5
1989–90	....	28	1
1990–91	....	14	—
1991–92	Grimsby T	32	6
1992–93	....	39	6

DOBBS, Gerald

Born London 24.1.71.   Ht 5 8   Wt 11 07
Defender. From Trainee.

Season	Club	Apps	Goals
1990–91	Wimbledon	—	—
1991–92	....	4	—
1992–93	....	19	1

DOBIE, Mark

Born Carlisle 8.11.63.   Ht 5 11   Wt 11 07
Forward. From Gretna.

Season	Club	Apps	Goals
1990–91	Cambridge U	—	—
1991–92	Torquay U	20	2
1992–93	Darlington	36	8

DOBSON, Paul

Born Hartlepool 17.12.62.   Ht 5 11
Wt 10 02
Forward. From Newcastle U Amateur.

Season	Club	Apps	Goals
1981–82	Hartlepool U	5	—

Season	Club	Apps	Goals
1982–83	....	26	8

From Horden

Season	Club	Apps	Goals
1983–84	....	27	12
1984–85	....	38	10
1985–86	....	15	2
1986–87	Torquay U	39	16
1987–88	....	38	22
1988–89	Doncaster R...............	24	10
1988–89	Scarborough..............	18	5
1989–90	....	37	15
1990–91	....	6	2
1990–91	*Halifax T*	1	1
1990–91	*Hereford U*	6	1
1990–91	Lincoln C..................	10	1
1991–92	....	11	4
1992–93	Darlington	14	2

DOBSON, Tony

Born Coventry 5.2.69.   Ht 6 1   Wt 12 10
Defender. From Apprentice. England Under-21.

Season	Club	Apps	Goals
1986–87	Coventry C	1	—
1987–88	....	1	—
1988–89	....	16	—
1989–90	....	30	—
1990–91	....	6	1
1990–91	Blackburn R	17	—
1991–92	....	5	—
1992–93	....	19	—

DOCHERTY, Stephen

Born Glasgow 18.2.76.   Ht 5 8   Wt 10 10
Midfield. From St Roch's.

Season	Club	Apps	Goals
1992–93	Partick T....................	1	—

DODD, Jason

Born Bath 2.11.70.   Ht 5 10   Wt 11 13
Defender. England Under-21.

Season	Club	Apps	Goals
1988–89	Southampton	—	—
1989–90	....	22	—
1990–91	....	19	—
1991–92	....	28	—
1992–93	....	30	1

DODDS, Billy

Born New Cumnock 5.2.69.   Ht 5 8
Wt 10 10
Forward. From Apprentice.

Season	Club		
1986–87	Chelsea	1	—
1987–88		—	—
1987–88	*Partick T*	30	9
1988–89	Chelsea	2	—
1989–90	Dundee	30	13
1990–91		37	15
1991–92		42	19
1992–93		41	16

DOLAN, Eamonn

Born Dagenham 20.9.67.   Ht 5 10
Wt 12 01
Forward. From Apprentice. Eire Youth,
Under-21.

Season	Club		
1984–85	West Ham U	—	—
1985–86		—	—
1986–87		1	—
1987–88		4	—
1988–89		—	—
1988–89	*Bristol C*	3	—
1989–90	West Ham U	10	3
1990–91		—	—
1990–91	Birmingham C	10	1
1991–92		2	—
1991–92	Exeter C	7	—
1992–93		19	4

DOLAN, Jim

Born Salsburgh 22.2.69.   Ht 5 10
Wt 10 07
Forward. From Motherwell BC.

Season	Club		
1987–88	Motherwell	—	—
1988–89		5	—
1989–90		12	—
1990–91		8	1
1991–92		32	2
1992–93		25	2

DOLBY, Tony

Born Greenwich 16.4.74   Ht 5 10
Wt 12 02
Forward. From Trainee.

Season	Club		
1991–92	Millwall	—	—
1992–93		18	1

DOLING, Stuart

Born Newport, IOW 28.10.72.   Ht 5 6
Wt 10 06
Midfield. From Trainee.

Season	Club		
1990–91	Portsmouth	—	—
1991–92		13	2
1992–93		6	—

DONAGHY, Mal

Born Belfast 13.9.57.   Ht 5 9   Wt 10 00
Defender. From Larne. Northern Ireland
Under-21, 84 caps.

Season	Club		
1978–79	Luton T	40	—
1979–80		42	1
1980–81		42	—
1981–82		42	9
1982–83		40	3
1983–84		40	1
1984–85		42	1
1985–86		42	—
1986–87		42	—
1987–88		32	1
1988–89		6	—
1988–89	Manchester U	30	—
1989–90		14	—
1989–90	*Luton T*	5	—
1990–91	Manchester U	25	—
1991–92		20	—
1992–93	Chelsea	40	2

DONALD, Graeme

Born Stirling 14.4.74.   Ht 6 0   Wt 11 04
Forward. From Gairdoch U. Scotland
Under-21.

Season	Club		
1991–92	Hibernian	5	3
1992–93		4	—

DONALD, Warren

Born Hillingdon 7.10.64   Ht 5 7
Wt 10 03
Midfield. From Apprentice.

Season	Club		
1982–83	West Ham U	—	—
1983–84		2	—
1984–85		—	—
1984–85	*Northampton T*	11	2
1985–86	West Ham U	—	—
1985–86	Northampton T	32	3
1986–87		41	3
1987–88		40	2
1988–89		37	1
1989–90		27	2
1990–91	Colchester U	*38*	*1*
1991–92		*41*	—
1992–93		10	—

DONOVAN, Kevin

Born Halifax 17.12.71.   Ht 5 7   Wt 10 10
Forward. From Trainee.

Season	Club		
1989–90	Huddersfield T	1	—
1990–91		6	1
1991–92		10	—
1991–92	*Halifax T*	6	—
1992–93	Huddersfield T	3	—
1992–93	WBA	32	6

DONOWA, Lou

Born Ipswich 24.9.64.   Ht 5 9   Wt 11 00
Forward. From Apprentice. England
Under-21.

Season	Club		
1982–83	Norwich C	1	—
1983–84		25	4
1984–85		34	7
1985–86		2	—
1985–86	*Stoke C*	4	1
From Coruna, Willem II Tilburg			
1989–90	Ipswich T	23	1
1990–91	Bristol C	24	3
1991–92	Birmingham C	26	2
1992–93		21	2
1992–93	*Crystal Palace*	—	—
1992–93	*Burnley*	4	—

DOOLAN, John

Born South Liverpool 10.11.68.   Ht 5 10
Wt 10 12
Midfield. From Knowsley U.

Season	Club		
1991–92	Wigan Ath	2	—
1992–93		17	—

DORIGO, Tony

Born Australia 31.12.65.   Ht 5 10
Wt 10 09
Defender. From Apprentice. England B,
Under-21, 14 full caps.

Season	Club		
1983–84	Aston Villa	1	—
1984–85		31	—
1985–86		38	1
1986–87		41	—
1987–88	Chelsea	40	—
1988–89		40	6
1989–90		35	3
1990–91		31	2
1991–92	Leeds U	38	3
1992–93		33	1

DOUGLAS, Colin

Born Hurlford 9.9.62.   Ht 6 1   Wt 11 07
Defender. From Celtic.

Season	Club		
1981–82	Doncaster R	42	3
1982–83		38	7
1983–84		44	15
1984–85		46	10
1985–86		42	13
1986–87	Rotherham U	43	3
1987–88		40	1
1988–89	Doncaster R	46	2
1989–90		45	2
1990–91		46	—
1991–92		34	—
1992–93		21	1

DOW, Andrew

Born Dundee 7.2.73.   Ht 5 9   Wt 10 07
Midfield. From Sporting Club 85. Scotland
Under-21.

Season	Club		
1990–91	Dundee	—	—

Season	Club	Apps	Goals
1991–92		4	—
1992–93		14	1

DOWIE, Iain

Born Hatfield 9.1.65. Ht 6 1 Wt 13 07
Forward. From Hendon. Northern Ireland
Under-23, 18 full caps.

Season	Club	Apps	Goals
1988–89	Luton T	8	—
1989–90		29	9
1989–90	*Fulham*	5	1
1990–91	Luton T	29	7
1990–91	West Ham U	12	4
1991–92		—	—
1991–92	Southampton	30	9
1992–93		36	11

DOWNING, Keith

Born Oldbury 23.7.65. Ht 5 8 Wt 11 00
Midfield. From Mile Oak R.

Season	Club	Apps	Goals
1984–85	Notts Co	12	—
1985–86		3	—
1986–87		8	1
1987–88	Wolverhampton W	34	1
1988–89		32	1
1989–90		31	3
1990–91		31	1
1991–92		32	—
1992–93		31	2

DOWNS, Greg

Born Carlton 13.12.58. Ht 5 9 Wt 10 07
Defender. From Apprentice.

Season	Club	Apps	Goals
1976–77	Norwich C	—	—
1977–78		1	—
1977–78	*Torquay U*	1	1
1978–79	Norwich C	3	—
1979–80		18	—
1980–81		29	2
1981–82		28	1
1982–83		28	—
1983–84		42	4
1984–85		20	—
1985–86	Coventry C	41	—
1986–87		39	2

Season	Club	Apps	Goals
1987–88		27	2
1988–89		22	—
1989–90		17	—
1990–91	Birmingham C	17	—
1991–92	Hereford U	40	2
1992–93		38	—

DOWSON, Alan

Born Gateshead 17.6.70. Ht 5 10
Wt 11 02
Defender. From Trainee.

Season	Club	Apps	Goals
1988–89	Millwall	—	—
1989–90		—	—
1989–90	*Fulham*	4	—
1990–91	Millwall	1	—
1991–92	Bradford C	18	—
1992–93	Darlington	32	—

DOYLE, Maurice

Born Ellesmere Port 17.10.69. Ht 5 8
Wt 10 07
Forward. From Trainee.

Season	Club	Apps	Goals
1987–88	Crewe Alex	4	—
1988–89		4	2
1989–90	QPR	—	—
1990–91	*Crewe Alex*	7	2
1990–91	*Wolverhampton W*	—	—
1991–92	QPR	—	—
1992–93		5	—

DOYLE, Steve

Born Neath 2.6.58. Ht 5 9 Wt 11 01
Midfield. From Apprentice. Wales
Under-21.

Season	Club	Apps	Goals
1974–75	Preston NE	13	—
1975–76		24	1
1976–77		22	—
1977–78		32	1
1978–79		29	2
1979–80		14	—
1980–81		27	1
1981–82		36	3
1982–83	Huddersfield T	42	2
1983–84		36	2

Season	Club	Apps	Goals
1984–85		36	2
1985–86		42	—
1986–87		5	—
1986–87	Sunderland	33	—
1987–88		32	1
1988–89		35	1
1989–90	Hull C	36	2
1990–91		11	—
1990–91	Rochdale	31	—
1991–92		27	—
1992–93		18	—

DOZZELL, Jason

Born Ipswich 9.12.67.   Ht 6 1   Wt 12 13
Midfield. From school. England Youth,
Under-21.

Season	Club	Apps	Goals
1983–84	Ipswich T	5	1
1984–85		14	2
1985–86		41	3
1986–87		42	2
1987–88		39	1
1988–89		29	11
1989–90		46	8
1990–91		30	6
1991–92		45	11
1992–93		41	7

DRAPER, Mark

Born Derby 11.11.70.   Ht 5 10   Wt 11 00
Midfield. From Trainee. England
Under-21.

Season	Club	Apps	Goals
1988–89	Notts Co	20	3
1989–90		34	3
1990–91		45	9
1991–92		35	1
1992–93		44	11

DREYER, John

Born Alnwick 11.6.63.   Ht 6 1   Wt 11 06
Defender. From Wallingford T.

Season	Club	Apps	Goals
1984–85	Oxford U	—	—
1985–86		—	—
1985–86	*Torquay U*	5	—
1985–86	*Fulham*	12	2

Season	Club	Apps	Goals
1986–87	Oxford U	25	2
1987–88		35	—
1988–89	Luton T	18	1
1989–90		38	2
1990–91		38	3
1991–92		42	2
1992–93		38	2

DRINKELL, Kevin

Born Grimsby 18.6.60.   Ht 5 11   Wt 12 06
Forward. From Apprentice.

Season	Club	Apps	Goals
1976–77	Grimsby T	4	2
1977–78		26	5
1978–79		28	7
1979–80		33	16
1980–81		41	7
1981–82		28	6
1982–83		39	17
1983–84		36	15
1984–85		35	14
1985–86	Norwich C	41	22
1986–87		42	16
1987–88		38	12
1988–89	Rangers	32	12
1989–90		4	—
1989–90	Coventry C	22	5
1990–91		15	—
1991–92		4	—
1991–92	*Birmingham C*	5	2
1992–93	Falkirk	35	7

DRUCE, Mark

Born Oxford 3.3.74.   Ht 5 11   Wt 11 11
Forward. From Trainee.

Season	Club	Apps	Goals
1991–92	Oxford U	2	—
1992–93		4	1

DRYDEN, Richard

Born Stroud 14.6.69.   Ht 6 0   Wt 11 02
Defender.

Season	Club	Apps	Goals
1986–87	Bristol R	6	—
1987–88		6	—
1988–89		1	—
1988–89	Exeter C	21	—

Season	Club	Apps	Goals
1989–90	....	30	7
1990–91	*Manchester C*	—	—
1991–92	Notts Co	29	1
1992–93	....	2	—
1992–93	*Plymouth Arg*	5	—
1992–93	Birmingham C	11	—

DRYSDALE, Jason

Born Bristol 17.11.70. Ht 5 10 Wt 12 00
Defender. From Trainee. England Youth.
Football League.

Season	Club	Apps	Goals
1988–89	Watford	—	—
1989–90	....	20	—
1990–91	....	30	—
1991–92	....	37	5
1992–93	....	39	6

DUBLIN, Dion

Born Leicester 22.4.69. Ht 6 0 Wt 12 04
Forward.

Season	Club	Apps	Goals
1987–88	Norwich C	—	—
1988–89	Cambridge U	21	6
1989–90	....	46	15
1990–91	....	46	16
1991–92	....	43	15
1992–93	Manchester U	7	1

DUBLIN, Keith

Born Wycombe 29.1.66. Ht 6 0
Wt 12 10
Defender. From Apprentice. England
Youth.

Season	Club	Apps	Goals
1983–84	Chelsea	1	—
1984–85	....	11	—
1985–86	....	11	—
1986–87	....	28	—
1987–88	Brighton	46	5
1988–89	....	43	—
1989–90	....	43	—
1990–91	Watford	43	—
1991–92	....	46	—
1992–93	....	46	1

DUFFIELD, Peter

Born Middlesbrough 4.2.69. Ht 5 6
Wt 10 07
Forward.

Season	Club	Apps	Goals
1986–87	Middlesbrough	—	—
1987–88	Sheffield U	11	1
1987–88	*Halifax T*	12	6
1988–89	Sheffield U	38	11
1989–90	....	5	2
1990–91	....	2	—
1990–91	*Rotherham U*	17	4
1991–92	Sheffield U	2	—
1992–93	....	—	—
1992–93	*Blackpool*	5	1
1992–93	*Bournemouth*	—	—
1992–93	*Stockport Co*	7	4
1992–93	*Crewe Alex*	2	—

DUFFY, Darrell

Born Birmingham 18.1.71 Ht 6 0
Wt 12 04
Defender. From Trainee. FA Schools,
England Youth.

Season	Club	Apps	Goals
1988–89	Aston Villa	1	—
1989–90	....	—	—
1990–91	....	—	—
From Moor Green			
1992–93	Scunthorpe U	4	—

DUFFY, Jim

Born Glasgow 27.4.59. Ht 5 10 Wt 11 04
Defender. From Maryhill Jun.

Season	Club	Apps	Goals
1978–79	Celtic	—	—
1979–80	....	—	—
1980–81	....	—	—
1981–82	Morton	20	—
1982–83	....	27	—
1983–84	....	38	2
1984–85	....	34	1
1985–86	Dundee	36	—
1986–87	....	42	2
1987–88	....	5	—
1988–89	Falkirk manager		
1989–90	Dundee	8	—
1990–91	Partick T	34	2

1991–92	....	38	2
1992–93	Dundee..................	39	—

DUFFY, Neil (Cornelius)

Born Glasgow 5.6.67. Ht 6 1   Wt 11 13
Defender. From Shamrock (SA).

1989–90	Dundee U	—	—
1990–91	Falkirk	25	2
1991–92	....	39	2
1992–93	....	34	5

DUNN, Iain

Born Derwent 1.4.72.   Ht 5 11   Wt 10 10
Forward. From School. England Youth.

1988–89	York C..................	26	6
1989–90	....	18	2
1990–91	....	33	3
1991–92	Chesterfield	13	1
From Goole T			
1992–93	Huddersfield T............	28	3

DUNNE, Joe

Born Dublin 25.5.73.   Ht 5 8   Wt 11 06
Midfield. From Trainee. Eire Youth,
Under-21.

1990–91	Gillingham	26	—
1991–92	....	11	—
1992–93	....	4	—

DUNNE, Liam

Born Dublin 1.9.71.   Ht 5 7   Wt 10 09
Midfield. From Bohemians.

1991–92	St Johnstone	17	—
1992–93	....	8	2

DUNPHY, Sean

Born Rotherham 5.11.70.   Ht 6 3
Wt 13 05
Defender. From Trainee.

1989–90	Barnsley	6	—

1990–91	Lincoln C..................	—	—
1991–92	....	5	1
1992–93	....	31	1

DURIE, Gordon

Born Paisley 6.12.65.   Ht 6 0   Wt 12 00
Forward. From Hill of Beath Hawthorn.
Scotland B, Under-21, 23 full caps.

1981–82	East Fife	13	1
1982–83	....	25	2
1983–84	....	34	16
1984–85	....	9	7
1984–85	Hibernian..................	22	8
1985–86	....	25	6
1985–86	Chelsea..................	1	—
1986–87	....	25	5
1987–88	....	26	12
1988–89	....	32	17
1989–90	....	15	5
1990–91	....	24	12
1991–92	Tottenham H	31	7
1992–93	....	17	3

DURKAN, Kieron

Born Chester 1.12.73.   Ht 5 10   Wt 11 05
Midfield. From Trainee.

1991–92	Wrexham	1	—
1992–93	....	1	—

DURNIN, John

Born Bootle 18.8.65.   Ht 5 10   Wt 11 04
Forward. From Waterloo Dock.

1985–86	Liverpool	—	—
1986–87	....	—	—
1987–88	....	—	—
1988–89	....	—	—
1988–89	*WBA*	5	2
1988–89	Oxford U	19	3
1989–90	....	42	13
1990–91	....	26	9
1991–92	....	37	8
1992–93	....	37	11

DURRANT, Iain

Born Glasgow 29.10.66. Ht 5 8 Wt 9 07
Midfield. From Glasgow United. Scotland
Youth, Under-21, 9 full caps.

Season	Club	Apps	Goals
1984–85	Rangers	5	—
1985–86		30	2
1986–87		39	4
1987–88		40	10
1988–89		8	2
1989–90		—	—
1990–91		4	1
1991–92		13	—
1992–93		30	3

DUXBURY, Lee

Born Skipton 7.10.69. Ht 5 10 Wt 11 07
Midfield. From Trainee.

Season	Club	Apps	Goals
1988–89	Bradford C	1	—
1989–90		12	1
1989–90	*Rochdale*	10	—
1990–91	Bradford C	45	5
1991–92		46	5
1992–93		42	5

DUXBURY, Mike

Born Accrington 1.9.59. Ht 5 9
Wt 11 02
Defender. From Apprentice. England
Under-21, 10 full caps.

Season	Club	Apps	Goals
1976–77	Manchester U	—	—
1977–78		—	—
1978–79		—	—
1979–80		—	—
1980–81		33	2
1981–82		24	—
1982–83		42	1
1983–84		39	—
1984–85		30	1
1985–86		23	1
1986–87		32	1
1987–88		39	—
1988–89		18	—
1989–90		19	—
1990–91	Blackburn R	22	—
1991–92		5	—

Season	Club	Apps	Goals
1991–92	Bradford C	16	—
1992–93		36	—

DYCHE, Sean

Born Kettering 28.6.71. Ht 6 0 Wt 11 07
Midfield. From Trainee.

Season	Club	Apps	Goals
1988–89	Nottingham F	—	—
1989–90		—	—
1989–90	Chesterfield	22	2
1990–91		28	2
1991–92		42	3
1992–93		20	1

DYER, Alex

Born West Ham 14.11.65. Ht 5 11
Wt 11 12
Midfield. From Watford Apprentice.

Season	Club	Apps	Goals
1983–84	Blackpool	9	—
1984–85		36	8
1985–86		39	8
1986–87		24	3
1986–87	Hull C	17	4
1987–88		28	—
1988–89		15	2
1988–89	Crystal Palace	7	2
1989–90		10	—
1990–91	Charlton Ath	35	7
1991–92		13	—
1992–93		30	6

DYER, Bruce

Born Ilford 13.4.75
Forward. From Trainee.

Season	Club	Apps	Goals
1992–93	Watford	2	—

DYKSTRA, Sieb

Born Kerkrade 20.10.66. Ht 6 5
Wt 14 07
Goalkeeper. From Roda JC.

Season	Club	Apps	Goals
1991–92	Motherwell	1	—
1992–93		35	—

DYSON, Jon

Born Mirfield 18.12.71
Defender. From school.

Season	Club		
1991–92	Huddersfield T	—	—
1992–93		15	—

DZIEKANOWSKI, Dariusz

Born Warsaw 30.9.62. Ht 6 1 Wt 12 13
Forward. From Legia Warsaw. Poland full caps.

Season	Club		
1989–90	Celtic	33	8
1990–91		15	2
1991–92		1	—
1991–92	Bristol C	17	4
1992–93		26	3

EADEN, Nicky

Born Sheffield 12.12.72 Ht 6 0 Wt 12 00
Defender. From Trainee.

Season	Club		
1991–92	Barnsley	—	—
1992–93		2	—

EARLE, Robbie

Born Newcastle, Staffs. 27.1.65. Ht 5 9
Wt 10 10
Forward. From Stoke C.

Season	Club		
1981–82	Port Vale	—	—
1982–83		8	1
1983–84		12	—
1984–85		46	15
1985–86		46	15
1986–87		35	6
1987–88		25	4
1988–89		44	13
1989–90		43	12
1990–91		35	11
1991–92	Wimbledon	40	14
1992–93		42	7

EAVES, David

Born Blackpool 13.2.73. Ht 5 11
Wt 11 07
Forward. From Trainee.

Season	Club		
1990–91	Preston NE	3	—
1991–92		—	—
1992–93		4	—

EBBRELL, John

Born Bromborough 1.10.69. Ht 5 7
Wt 9 12
Midfield. FA Schools, England Youth, B, Under-21.

Season	Club		
1986–87	Everton	—	—
1987–88		—	—
1988–89		4	—
1989–90		17	—
1990–91		36	3
1991–92		39	1

1992–93 24   1

EBDON, Marcus

Born Pontypool 17.10.70.   Ht 5 9
Wt 11 00
Midfield. From Trainee. Wales Under-21.

1988–89	Everton	—	—
1989–90		—	—
1990–91		—	—
1991–92	Peterborough U	15	2
1992–93		28	4

ECKHARDT, Jeff

Born Sheffield 7.10.65.   Ht 6 0   Wt 11 07
Defender.

1984–85	Sheffield U	7	—
1985–86		33	2
1986–87		22	—
1987–88		12	—
1987–88	Fulham	29	1
1988–89		43	2
1989–90		40	2
1990–91		29	2
1991–92		43	7
1992–93		30	6

EDESON, Matthew

Born Beverley 11.8.76   Ht 5 10   Wt 11 00
Forward. From Trainee.

1992–93	Hull C	2	—

EDINBURGH, Justin

Born Brentwood 18.12.69.   Ht 5 10
Wt 11 08
Defender. From Trainee.

1988–89	Southend U	15	—
1989–90		22	—
1989–90	*Tottenham H*	—	—
1990–91	Tottenham H	16	1
1991–92		23	—
1992–93		32	—

EDMONDS, Darren

Born Watford 12.4.71.   Ht 5 9   Wt 11 06
Midfield. From Trainee.

1989–90	Leeds U	—	—
1990–91		—	—
1991–92	Ipswich T	2	—
1992–93	Scarborough	1	—
1992–93	Halifax T	2	—

EDMONDSON, Darren

Born Coniston 4.11.71.   Ht 6 0   Wt 12 02
Defender. From Trainee.

1990–91	Carlisle U	31	—
1991–92		27	2
1992–93		34	—

EDWARDS, Andy

Born Epping 17.9.71.   Ht 6 2   Wt 13 06
Midfield. From Trainee.

1988–89	Southend U	1	—
1989–90		8	—
1990–91		2	1
1991–92		9	—
1992–93		41	—

EDWARDS, David

Born Bridgnorth 13.1.74.   Ht 5 10
Wt 10 08
Midfield. From Trainee.

1991–92	Walsall	22	1
1992–93		5	—

EDWARDS, Matthew

Born Hammersmith 15.6.71   Ht 5 10
Wt 11 00
Midfield. From Trainee.

1989–90	Tottenham H	—	—
1990–91		—	—
1990–91	*Reading*	8	—
1991–92	Tottenham H	—	—
1992–93	Brighton	33	2

EDWARDS, Neil

Born Aberdare 5.12.70. Ht 5 8 Wt 11 02
Goalkeeper. From Trainee.

1988–89	Leeds U	—	—
1989–90		—	—
1990–91		—	—
1990–91	*Huddersfield T*	—	—
1991–92	Stockport Co	39	—
1992–93		35	—

EDWARDS, Paul

Born Liverpool 22.2.65. Ht 5 11
Wt 11 05
Goalkeeper. From St. Helens T.

1988–89	Crewe Alex	10	—
1989–90		8	—
1990–91		9	—
1991–92		2	—
1992–93	Shrewsbury T	42	—

EDWARDS, Paul R

Born Birkenhead 25.12.63. Ht 5 11
Wt 11 00
Defender. From Altrincham.

1987–88	Crewe Alex	13	1
1988–89		45	4
1989–90		28	1
1989–90	Coventry C	8	—
1990–91		23	—
1991–92		5	—
1992–93		—	—
1992–93	Wolverhampton W	35	—

EDWARDS, Robert

Born Manchester 23.2.70. Ht 5 8
Wt 11 07
Forward. From Trainee.

1987–88	Crewe Alex	6	1
1988–89		4	—
1989–90		4	—
1990–91		29	11
1991–92		28	6
1992–93		23	7

EDWARDS, Robert

Born Kendal 1.7.73. Ht 6 0 Wt 11 06
Defender. Wales Under-21.

1989–90	Carlisle U	12	—
1990–91		36	5
1990–91	Bristol C	—	—
1991–92		20	1
1992–93		18	—

EDWORTHY, Mark

Born Barnstaple 24.12.72. Ht 5 7
Wt 9 08
Midfield. From Trainee.

1990–91	Plymouth Arg	—	—
1991–92		15	—
1992–93		15	—

EELES, Tony

Born Chatham 15.11.70. Ht 5 6
Wt 10 08
Midfield. From Trainee.

1988–89	Gillingham	3	—
1989–90		33	2
1990–91		6	—
1991–92		17	1
1992–93		14	2

EHIOGU, Ugo

Born London 3.11.72. Ht 6 2 Wt 13 03
Defender. From Trainee. England
Under-21.

1990–91	WBA	2	—
1991–92	Aston Villa	8	—
1992–93		4	—

EKOKU, Efan

Born Manchester 8.6.67. Ht 6 1
Wt 12 00
Forward. From Sutton U.

1990–91	Bournemouth	20	3
1991–92		28	11

Season	Club	Apps	Goals
1992–93	....	14	7
1992–93	Norwich C	4	3

ELI, Roger

Born Bradford 11.9.65.   Ht 5 11
Wt 11 03
Defender. From Apprentice.

Season	Club	Apps	Goals
1983–84	Leeds U	—	—
1984–85	....	1	—
1985–86	....	1	—
1985–86	Wolverhampton W	14	—
1986–87	....	4	—
1987–88	Cambridge U	—	—
1987–88	Crewe Alex	27	1
1988–89	York C	4	1
1988–89	Bury	2	—
From Northwich Vic.			
1989–90	Burnley	29	—
1990–91	....	26	1
1991–92	....	33	10
1992–93	....	11	—

ELKINS, Gary

Born Wallingford 4.5.66.   Ht 5 09
Wt 11 12
Midfield. From Apprentice. England
Youth.

Season	Club	Apps	Goals
1983–84	Fulham	—	—
1984–85	....	21	—
1985–86	....	13	—
1986–87	....	9	—
1987–88	....	29	—
1988–89	....	22	1
1989–90	....	10	1
1989–90	Exeter C	5	—
1990–91	Wimbledon	10	—
1991–92	....	18	1
1992–93	....	18	—

ELLIOTT, Matthew

Born Surrey 1.11.68.   Ht 6 3   Wt 14 05
Defender. From Epsom & Ewell.

Season	Club	Apps	Goals
1988–89	Charlton Ath	—	—
1988–89	Torquay U	13	2

Season	Club	Apps	Goals
1989–90	....	33	2
1990–91	....	45	6
1991–92	....	33	5
1991–92	Scunthorpe U	8	1
1992–93	Scunthorpe U	39	6

ELLIOTT, Paul

Born London 18.3.64.   Ht 6 2   Wt 11 11
Defender. From Apprentice. England
Youth, Under-21.

Season	Club	Apps	Goals
1980–81	Charlton Ath	—	—
1981–82	....	38	1
1982–83	....	25	—
1982–83	Luton T	13	1
1983–84	....	38	2
1984–85	....	9	1
1985–86	....	6	—
1985–86	Aston Villa	23	2
1986–87	....	34	5
From Bari.			
1989–90	Celtic	27	—
1990–91	....	27	2
1991–92	Chelsea	35	3
1992–93	....	7	—

ELLIOTT, Tony

Born Nuneaton 30.11.69.   Ht 6 0
Wt 12 12
Goalkeeper. England Youth.

Season	Club	Apps	Goals
1986–87	Birmingham C	—	—
1987–88	....	—	—
1988–89	....	—	—
1988–89	Hereford U	23	—
1989–90	....	29	—
1990–91	....	5	—
1991–92	....	18	—
1992–93	Huddersfield T	15	—

ELLIS, Tony

Born Salford 20.10.64.   Ht 5 11   Wt 11 00
Forward. From Horwich RMI, Northwich
Vic.

Season	Club	Apps	Goals
1986–87	Oldham Ath	5	—
1987–88	....	3	—

Season	Club		League Appearances/Goals
1987–88	Preston NE	24	4
1988–89		45	19
1989–90		17	3
1989–90	Stoke C	24	6
1990–91		38	9
1991–92		15	4
1992–93	Preston NE	35	22

ELLISON, Tony

Born Bishop Auckland 13.1.73. Ht 6 0
Wt 12 00
Forward. From Trainee.

1990–91	Darlington	13	3
1991–92		27	10
1992–93		3	—
1992–93	*Hartlepool U*	4	1

ELSTRUP, Lars

Born Roby, Denmark 24.3.63. Ht 5 11
Wt 11 11
Forward. From OB Odense. Denmark full
caps.

1989–90	Luton T	23	4
1990–91		37	15
To Odense			

EMBERSON, Carl

Born Epsom 13.7.73 Ht 6 1 Wt 13 11
Goalkeeper. From Trainee.

1991–92	Millwall	—	—
1992–93		—	—
1992–93	*Colchester U*	13	—

EMERSON, Dean

Born Salford 27.12.62. Ht 5 9 Wt 12 11
Midfield. From Local.

1981–82	Stockport Co	23	1
1982–83		45	3
1983–84		44	1
1984–85		44	2
1985–86	Rotherham U	45	7
1986–87		10	1

Season	Club		League Appearances/Goals
1986–87	Coventry C	19	—
1987–88		20	—
1988–89		18	—
1989–90		12	—
1990–91		24	—
1991–92		21	—
1992–93	Hartlepool U	32	1

ENGLISH, Isaac

Born Paisley 12.11.71. Ht 5 8 Wt 10 00
Forward. From Gleniffer Th.

1989–90	St Mirren	—	—
1989–90	Partick T	6	2
1990–91		13	2
1991–92		26	5
1992–93		13	—

ENGLISH, Tony

Born Luton 19.10.66 Ht 6 0 Wt 12 04
Defender. From Coventry C apprentice.
England Youth.

1984–85	Colchester U	22	3
1985–86		45	13
1986–87		32	7
1987–88		43	2
1988–89		36	8
1989–90		44	2
1990–91		*40*	7
1991–92		*38*	6
1992–93		33	1

ESDAILLE, David

Born Manchester 22.7.63
Midfield.

1992–93	Wrexham	4	—
1992–93	Bury	6	—

EVANS, Ceri

Born Christchurch 2.10.63. Ht 6 1
Wt 14 02
Defender. From Otago Univ, Worcester
Coll. (Oxford). New Zealand full caps.

1988–89	Oxford U	4	—

1989–90	....	24	2
1990–91	....	18	1
1991–92	....	29	—
1992–93	....	41	—

EVANS, Gareth

Born Coventry 14.1.67. Ht 5 8 Wt 10 06
Forward. From Apprentice.

1984–85	Coventry C	—	—
1985–86	....	6	—
1986–87	....	1	—
1986–87	Rotherham U	34	9
1987–88	....	29	4
1987–88	Hibernian..................	12	2
1988–89	....	35	5
1989–90	....	28	3
1990–91	*Northampton T*...........	2	—
1990–91	*Stoke C*	5	1
1991–92	Hibernian..................	41	6
1992–93	....	39	6

EVANS, Jason

Born Cambridge 22.1.74 Ht 5 7
Wt 11 05
Midfield. From Trainee.

1992–93	Shrewsbury T.............	1	—

EVANS, Mark

Born Leeds 24.8.70. Ht 6 0 Wt 11 08
Goalkeeper. From Trainee.

1988–89	Bradford C	3	—
1989–90	....	5	—
1990–91	....	3	—
1991–92	....	1	—
1992–93	Scarborough..............	20	—

EVANS, Mike

Born Plymouth 1.1.73. Ht 6 0 Wt 11 02
Forward. From Trainee.

1990–91	Plymouth Arg.............	4	—
1991–92	....	13	—
1992–93	....	23	1

1992–93	*Blackburn R*	—	—

EVANS, Nicky

Born Bedford 6.7.58. Ht 6 0 Wt 11 10
Midfield. From Kettering T, QPR,
Peterborough U, Wycombe W.

1991–92	Barnet	9	1
1992–93	....	18	4

EVANS, Paul

Born Oswestry 1.9.74. Ht 5 6 Wt 10 08
Midfield. From Trainee.

1991–92	Shrewsbury T..............	2	—
1992–93	....	4	—

EVANS, Richard

Born Ebbw Vale 12.4.68. Ht 5 11
Wt 11 07
Midfield. From Weymouth.

1991–92	Bristol R	2	1
1992–93	....	11	—
1992–93	*Exeter C*.....................	5	2

EVANS, Stewart

Born Maltby 15.11.60. Ht 6 4 Wt 11 05
Forward. From Apprentice.

1978–79	Rotherham U	—	—
1979–80	....	—	—
From Gainsborough TH			
1980–81	Sheffield U	—	—
1981–82	Wimbledon	18	4
1982–83	....	42	14
1983–84	....	45	14
1984–85	....	40	14
1985–86	....	30	6
1986–87	WBA	14	1
1986–87	Plymouth Arg.............	5	—
1987–88	....	37	10
1988–89	....	3	—
1988–89	Rotherham U	25	6
1989–90	....	20	4
1990–91	....	20	4

Season	Club		App	Goals
1990–91	*Torquay U*		15	5
1991–92	Crewe Alex		17	4
1992–93			26	1

EVANS, Terry

Born London 12.4.65. Ht 6 5 Wt 15 01
Defender. From Hillingdon B.

1985–86	Brentford		19	1
1986–87			1	—
1987–88			29	4
1988–89			45	5
1989–90			44	3
1990–91			36	2
1991–92			44	8
1992–93			11	—

EVERINGHAM, Nick

Born Hull 11.2.73
Defender. From Oldham Ath trainee.

1992–93	Halifax T		2	—

EYRES, David

Born Liverpool 26.2.64. Ht 5 10
Wt 11 00
Forward. From Rhyl.

1989–90	Blackpool		35	7
1990–91			36	6
1991–92			41	9
1992–93			46	16

FAIRCLOUGH, Chris

Born Nottingham 12.4.64. Ht 5 11
Wt 11 02
Defender. From Apprentice. England
Under-21.

1981–82	Nottingham F		—	—
1982–83			15	—
1983–84			31	—
1984–85			35	—
1985–86			—	—
1986–87			26	1
1987–88	Tottenham H		40	4
1988–89			20	1
1988–89	Leeds U		11	—
1989–90			42	8
1990–91			34	4
1991–92			31	2
1992–93			30	3

FAIRCLOUGH, Wayne

Born Nottingham 27.4.68. Ht 5 10
Wt 12 02
Defender. From Apprentice.

1985–86	Notts Co		5	—
1986–87			9	—
1987–88			29	—
1988–89			20	—
1989–90			8	—
1989–90	Mansfield T		13	—
1990–91			41	6
1991–92			25	3
1992–93			33	1

FALANA, Wade

Born London 7.1.70
Forward.

1992–93	Doncaster R		4	—
1992–93	Scarborough		—	—
1992–93	Chesterfield		5	—

FALCONER, Willie

Born Aberdeen 5.4.66. Ht 6 1 Wt 11 09
Midfield. From Lewis United. Scotland
Schools, Youth.

1982–83	Aberdeen		1	—

Season	Club	Apps	Goals
1983–84		8	1
1984–85		16	4
1985–86		8	—
1986–87		8	—
1987–88		36	8
1988–89	Watford	33	5
1989–90		30	3
1990–91		35	4
1991–92	Middlesbrough	25	5
1992–93		28	5

FARNINGHAM, Ray

Born Dundee 10.4.61.   Ht 5 8   Wt 10 07
Forward. From Celtic BC.

Season	Club	Apps	Goals
1978–79	Forfar Ath	1	—
1979–80		38	5
1980–81		34	4
1981–82		39	5
1982–83		21	3
1983–84		37	6
1984–85		31	4
1985–86		37	2
1986–87		2	—
1986–87	Motherwell	29	3
1987–88		29	6
1988–89		18	3
1989–90	Dunfermline Ath	17	—
1990–91		10	—
1991–92		4	1
1991–92	Partick T	33	7
1992–93		37	8

FARNWORTH, Simon

Born Chorley 28.10.63.   Ht 6 0   Wt 11 13
Goalkeeper. From Apprentice. England
Schools.

Season	Club	Apps	Goals
1981–82	Bolton W	—	—
1982–83		—	—
1983–84		36	—
1984–85		46	—
1985–86		31	—
1986–87		—	—
1986–87	*Stockport Co*	10	—
1986–87	*Tranmere R*	7	—
1986–87	Bury	14	—
1987–88		39	—

Season	Club	Apps	Goals
1988–89		45	—
1989–90		7	—
1990–91	Preston NE	23	—
1991–92		23	—
1992–93		35	—

FARRELL, Andy

Born Colchester 7.10.65.   Ht 6 0
Wt 11 00
Defender. From School.

Season	Club	Apps	Goals
1983–84	Colchester U	15	—
1984–85		38	—
1985–86		24	1
1986–87		28	4
1987–88	Burnley	45	3
1988–89		36	4
1989–90		36	2
1990–91		37	2
1991–92		39	3
1992–93		42	4

FARRELL, David

Born Glasgow 29.10.69.   Ht 5 9   Wt 10 12
Midfield. From Oxford U Apprentice.

Season	Club	Apps	Goals
1988–89	Hibernian	—	—
1989–90		—	—
1990–91		2	—
1991–92		6	—
1992–93		12	—

FARRELL, David

Born Birmingham 11.11.71   Ht 5 11
Wt 11 02
Forward. From Redditch U.

Season	Club	Apps	Goals
1992–93	Aston Villa	2	—
1992–93	*Scunthorpe U*	5	1

FARRELL, Sean

Born Watford 28.2.69.   Ht 6 1   Wt 12 08
Midfield. From Apprentice.

Season	Club	Apps	Goals
1986–87	Luton T	—	—
1987–88		—	—

Season	Club	Appearances	Goals
1987–88	*Colchester U*	9	1
1988–89	Luton T	—	—
1989–90		1	—
1990–91		20	1
1991–92		4	—
1991–92	*Northampton T*	4	1
1991–92	Fulham	25	10
1992–93		35	12

FARRINGTON, Mark

Born Liverpool 15.6.65. Ht 5 10
Wt 11 12
Forward. From Everton Apprentice.

Season	Club	Appearances	Goals
1983–84	Norwich C	2	—
1984–85		12	2
1984–85	Cambridge U	10	1
1985–86	Cardiff C	31	3
From Feyenoord			
1991–92	Brighton	14	1
1992–93		8	2

FASHANU, John

Born Kensington 18.9.63. Ht 6 1
Wt 11 12
Forward. From Cambridge U. Amateur.
England 2 full caps.

Season	Club	Appearances	Goals
1979–80	Norwich C	—	—
1980–81		—	—
1981–82		5	1
1982–83		2	—
1983–84		—	—
1983–84	*Crystal Palace*	1	—
1983–84	Lincoln C	26	6
1984–85		10	4
1984–85	Millwall	25	4
1985–86		25	8
1985–86	Wimbledon	9	4
1986–87		37	11
1987–88		38	14
1988–89		30	12
1989–90		24	11
1990–91		35	20
1991–92		38	18
1992–93		29	6

FASHANU, Justin

Born Kensington 19.2.61. Ht 6 1
Wt 13 01
Forward. From Apprentice. England
Youth, Under-21, B.

Season	Club	Appearances	Goals
1978–79	Norwich C	16	5
1979–80		34	11
1980–81		40	19
1981–82	Nottingham F	32	3
1982–83	Southampton	9	3
1982–83	Nottingham F	—	—
1982–83	Notts Co	15	7
1983–84		17	5
1884–85		32	8
1985–86	Brighton	16	2
1986–87		—	—
From Edmonton			
1989–90	Manchester C	2	—
1989–90	West Ham U	2	—
1989–90	Leyton Orient	5	—
From Toronto B			
1991–92	Newcastle U	—	—
1991–92	Torquay U	21	10
1992–93		20	5
1992–93	Airdrie	16	5

FEAR, Peter

Born London 10.9.73 Ht 5 10 Wt 11 05
Defender. From Trainee.

Season	Club	Appearances	Goals
1992–93	Wimbledon	4	—

FEARON, Ron

Born Romford 19.11.60 Ht 6 0 Wt 11 12
Goalkeeper. From QPR Apprentice.

Season	Club	Appearances	Goals
1979–80	Reading	—	—
1980–81		6	—
1981–82		42	—
1982–83		13	—
From Sutton			
1987–88	Ipswich T	10	—
1988–89		18	—
1988–89	*Brighton*	7	—
1989–90		—	—
1990–91	Leyton Orient	—	—
1991–92	Ipswich T	—	—

1992–93	....	—	—	
1992–93	Walsall	1	—	

FEE, Greg

Born Halifax 24.6.64.   Ht 6 1   Wt 13 02
Defender.

1982–83	Bradford C	3	—
1983–84	....	4	—
From Boston UH			
1987–88	Sheffield W	16	—
1988–89	....	8	—
1989–90	....	2	—
1990–91	....	—	—
1990–91	*Preston NE*	15	—
1990–91	*Northampton T*	1	—
1990–91	*Leyton Orient*	5	—
1990–91	Mansfield T	10	—
1991–92	....	34	4
1992–93	....	10	3
1992–93	*Chesterfield*	10	—

FEENEY, Mark

Born Derry 26.7.74
Midfield. From Trainee.

1992–93	Barnsley	2	—

FELGATE, David

Born Blaenau Ffestiniog 4.3.60.   Ht 6 2
Wt 13 06
Goalkeeper. From Blaenau Ffestiniog.
Wales Schools, Under-21, 1 full cap.

1978–79	Bolton W	—	—
1978–79	*Rochdale*	35	—
1979–80	Bolton W	—	—
1979–80	*Bradford C*	—	—
1979–80	*Crewe Alex*	14	—
1979–80	*Rochdale*	12	—
1980–81	Bolton W	—	—
1980–81	Lincoln C	42	—
1981–82	....	43	—
1982–83	....	46	—
1983–84	....	46	—
1984–85	....	21	—
1984–85	*Cardiff C*	4	—

1984–85	*Grimsby T*	12	—
1985–86	Grimsby T	12	—
1985–86	Bolton W	15	—
1986–87	....	20	—
1986–87	*Rotherham U*	—	—
1987–88	Bolton W	46	—
1988–89	....	46	—
1989–90	....	40	—
1990–91	....	46	—
1991–92	....	25	—
1992–93	....	—	—

FELLENGER, David

Born Edinburgh 6.6.69.   Ht 5 8   Wt 10 02
Midfield. From Hutchinson Vale BC.

1987–88	Hibernian	—	—
1988–89	....	2	—
1989–90	....	12	1
1990–91	....	12	1
1991–92	....	6	—
1992–93	....	5	2

FENSOME, Andy

Born Northampton 18.2.69.   Ht 5 8
Wt 11 02
Midfield. From Trainee.

1986–87	Norwich C	—	—
1987–88	....	—	—
1988–89	....	—	—
1988–89	*Newcastle U*	—	—
1989–90	Cambridge U	24	—
1990–91	....	36	—
1991–92	....	34	1
1992–93	....	30	—

FENWICK, Paul

Born London 25.8.69
Defender. From Winnipeg Fury.

1992–93	Birmingham C	10	—

FENWICK, Terry

Born Camden, Co. Durham 17.11.59.
Ht 5 10   Wt 11 12
Defender. From Apprentice. England
Youth, Under-21, 20 full caps.

Season	Club		
1976–77	Crystal Palace	—	—
1977–78		10	—
1978–79		24	—
1979–80		15	—
1980–81		21	—
1980–81	QPR	19	2
1981–82		36	5
1982–83		39	3
1983–84		41	10
1984–85		41	2
1985–86		37	7
1986–87		21	1
1987–88		22	3
1987–88	Tottenham H	17	—
1988–89		34	8
1989–90		10	—
1990–91		4	—
1990–91	*Leicester C*	8	1
1991–92	Tottenham H	23	—
1992–93		5	—

FERDINAND, Les

Born London 18.12.66.   Ht 5 11
Wt 13 05
Forward. From Hayes. England 4 full
caps.

Season	Club		
1986–87	QPR	2	—
1987–88		1	—
1987–88	*Brentford*	3	—
1988–89	QPR	—	—
1988–89	*Besiktas*	—	—
1989–90	QPR	9	2
1990–91		18	8
1991–92		23	10
1992–93		37	20

FEREDAY, Wayne

Born Warley 16.6.63.   Ht 5 9   Wt 11 08
Midfield. From Apprentice. England
Under-21.

Season	Club		
1980–81	QPR	6	2

1981–82		4	—
1982–83		5	—
1983–84		17	4
1984–85		26	7
1985–86		34	2
1986–87		37	2
1987–88		37	4
1988–89		31	—
1989–90	Newcastle U	25	—
1990–91		8	—
1990–91	Bournemouth	18	—
1991–92		5	—
1991–92	WBA	22	2
1992–93		16	1

FERGUSON, Darren

Born Glasgow 9.2.72.   Ht 5 10   Wt 10 04
Midfield. From Trainee. Scotland
Under-21.

Season	Club		
1990–91	Manchester U	5	—
1991–92		4	—
1992–93		15	—

FERGUSON, Derek

Born Glasgow 31.7.67.   Ht 5 8   Wt 10 11
Midfield. From Gartcosh United. Scotland
Schools, Youth, Under-21, 2 full caps.

Season	Club		
1983–84	Rangers	1	—
1984–85		8	—
1985–86		19	—
1986–87		30	1
1987–88		32	4
1988–89		16	2
1989–90		5	—
1989–90	*Dundee*	4	—
1990–91	Hearts	28	2
1991–92		38	1
1992–93		37	1

FERGUSON, Duncan

Born Stirling 27.12.71   Ht 6 3   Wt 13 05
Forward. From Carse Thistle. Scotland
Under-21, 3 full caps.

Season	Club		
1990–91	Dundee U	9	1

Season	Club	League Appearances/Goals	
1991–92		38	15
1992–93		30	12

FERGUSON, Graeme

Born Stirling 3.3.71.   Ht 5 9   Wt 11 06
Midfield. From Gairdoch U.

Season	Club	App	Goals
1987–88	Aberdeen	—	—
1988–89		—	—
1989–90		—	—
1990–91		—	—
1991–92		4	—
1992–93		1	—

FERGUSON, Iain

Born Newarthill 4.8.62.   Ht 5 7   Wt 10 07
Forward. From Fir Park BC. Scotland
Youth, Under-21.

Season	Club	App	Goals
1979–80	Dundee	13	5
1980–81		11	1
1981–82		34	12
1982–83		29	9
1983–84		33	12
1984–85	Rangers	28	6
1985–86		4	—
1986–87	*Dundee*	3	2
1986–87	Dundee U	36	16
1987–88		39	11
1988–89	Hearts	29	5
1989–90		11	1
1989–90	*Charlton Ath*	1	—
1989–90	*Bristol C*	11	2
1990–91	Hearts	12	2
1990–91	Motherwell	15	8
1991–92		20	—
1992–93		15	2

FERGUSON, Ian

Born Glasgow 15.3.67.   Ht 5 10   Wt 10 11
Midfield. From Clyde BC. Scotland B,
Under-21, 6 full caps.

Season	Club	App	Goals
1984–85	Clyde	2	—
1985–86		19	4
1986–87		5	—
1986–87	St Mirren	35	4

Season	Club	App	Goals
1987–88		22	6
1987–88	Rangers	8	1
1988–89		30	6
1989–90		24	—
1990–91		11	1
1991–92		16	1
1992–93		30	4

FERGUSON, Ian

Born Dunfermline 5.8.68.   Ht 6 1
Wt 12 00
Forward. From Lochgelly Albert.

Season	Club	App	Goals
1987–88	Raith R	9	4
1988–89		28	4
1989–90		32	6
1990–91		33	8
1991–92		9	1
1991–92	Hearts	30	4
1992–93		24	4

FERNEY, Martin

Born Lambeth 8.11.71.   Ht 5 11
Wt 12 04
Defender. From Trainee.

Season	Club	App	Goals
1990–91	Fulham	14	—
1991–92		—	—
1992–93		16	1

FERREYRA, Victor

Born Buenos Aires 24.2.65.   Ht 5 11
Wt 12 05
Forward. From San Lorenzo. Argentina
full caps.

Season	Club	App	Goals
1991–92	Dundee U	23	4
1992–93		7	—

FETTIS, Alan

Born Newtonards 1.2.71.   Ht 6 1
Wt 11 04
Goalkeeper. From Ards. Northern Ireland
3 full caps.

Season	Club	App	Goals
1991–92	Hull C	43	—

1992–93		20	—

FICKLING, Ashley

Born Sheffield 15.11.72   Ht 5 10
Wt 11 08
Defender. From Trainee.

1991–92	Sheffield U	—	—
1992–93		—	—
1992–93	*Darlington*	14	—

FILAN, John

Born Sydney 8.2.70   Ht 5 11   Wt 12 10
Goalkeeper. From Budapest St George.

1992–93	Cambridge U	6	—

FINDLAY, William

Born Kilmarnock 29.8.70.   Ht 5 10
Wt 10 13
Midfield. From Kilmarnock BC. Scotland
Under-21.

1987–88	Hibernian	—	—
1988–89		3	1
1989–90		10	—
1990–91		26	2
1991–92		9	—
1992–93		7	—

FINLEY, Alan

Born Liverpool 10.12.67.   Ht 6 3
Wt 14 03
Defender. From Marine.

1988–89	Shrewsbury T	34	1
1989–90		29	1
1990–91	Stockport Co	19	3
1991–92		18	1
1992–93		22	1
1992–93	*Carlisle U*	1	—

FINNEY, Kevin

Born Newcastle-under-Lyme 19.10.69.
Ht 6 0   Wt 12 00
Midfield. From Apprentice.

1987–88	Port Vale	15	—

1988–89		14	1
1989–90		—	—
1990–91		—	—
1991–92	Lincoln C	23	2
1992–93		14	—

FINNEY, Stephen

Born Hexham 31.10.73.   Ht 5 10
Wt 12 00
Forward. From Trainee.

1991–92	Preston NE	2	1
1992–93		4	—

FIORE, Mark

Born Southwark 18.11.69.   Ht 5 10
Wt 11 10
Midfield. From Trainee.

1988–89	Wimbledon	1	—
1989–90		—	—
1989–90	Plymouth Arg	12	1
1990–91		38	3
1991–92		32	4
1992–93		1	—

FISHER, Neil

Born St Helens 7.11.70.   Ht 5 8   Wt 11 00
Midfield. From Trainee.

1990–91	Bolton W	—	—
1991–92		7	1
1992–93		4	—

FITZGERALD, Scott

Born London 13.8.69.   Ht 6 0   Wt 12 02
Defender. From Trainee. Eire Under-21,
B.

1988–89	Wimbledon	—	—
1989–90		1	—
1990–91		—	—
1991–92		36	1
1992–93		20	—

FITZPATRICK, Paul

Born Liverpool 5.10.65. Ht 6 4 Wt 12 00
Midfield.

Season	Club	App	Goals
1984–85	Tranmere R	—	—
1985–86	Liverpool	—	—
1984–85	Preston NE	—	—
1984–85	Bolton W	3	—
1985–86		11	—
1986–87	Bristol C	19	2
1987–88		24	5
1988–89		1	—
1988–89	Carlisle U	32	—
1988–89	*Preston NE*	2	—
1989–90	Carlisle U	45	4
1990–91		32	—
1991–92	Leicester C	26	4
1992–93		1	—
1992–93	Birmingham C	7	—
1992–93	*Bury*	9	—

FLATTS, Mark

Born Haringay 14.10.72 Ht 5 06 Wt 9 08
Midfield. From Trainee.

Season	Club	App	Goals
1992–93	Arsenal	10	—

FLECK, Robert

Born Glasgow 11.8.65. Ht 5 10 Wt 10 03
Forward. From Possil YM. Scotland
Youth, Under-21, 4 full caps.

Season	Club	App	Goals
1983–84	Partick T	2	1
1983–84	Rangers	1	—
1984–85		8	—
1985–86		15	3
1986–87		40	19
1987–88		21	7
1987–88	Norwich C	18	7
1988–89		33	10
1989–90		27	7
1990–91		29	5
1991–92		36	11
1992–93	Chelsea	31	2

FLEMING, Craig

Born Calder 6.10.71. Ht 6 0 Wt 11 07
Defender. From Trainee.

Season	Club	App	Goals
1988–89	Halifax T	1	—
1989–90		10	—
1990–91		46	—
1991–92	Oldham Ath	32	1
1992–93		24	—

FLEMING, Curtis

Born Manchester 8.10.68. Ht 5 8
Wt 11 04
Defender. From St Patrick's Ath. Eire
Youth, Under-21, B.

Season	Club	App	Goals
1988–89	Swindon T	—	—
	From St Patrick's Athletic		
1991–92	Middlesbrough	28	—
1992–93		24	—

FLEMING, Gary

Born Londonderry 17.2.67. Ht 5 9
Wt 11 03
Defender. From Apprentice. Northern
Ireland 21 full caps.

Season	Club	App	Goals
1984–85	Nottingham F	2	—
1985–86		16	—
1986–87		34	—
1987–88		22	—
1988–89		—	—
1989–90	Manchester C	14	—
1989–90	*Notts Co*	3	—
1989–90	Barnsley	12	—
1990–91		44	—
1991–92		42	—
1992–93		46	—

FLEMING, Paul

Born Halifax 6.9.67. Ht 5 7 Wt 11 08
Defender.

Season	Club	App	Goals
1985–86	Halifax T	13	—
1986–87		15	—
1987–88		9	—
1988–89		23	—

Season	Club	Apps	Goals
1989–90	....	40	1
1990–91	....	39	—
1991–92	Mansfield T.................	38	—
1992–93	....	—	—

FLEMING, Terry

Born Marston Green 5.1.73.   Ht 5 9
Wt 11 00
Forward. From Trainee.

Season	Club	Apps	Goals
1990–91	Coventry C	2	—
1991–92	....	—	—
1992–93	....	11	—

FLETCHER, Steve

Born Hartlepool 26.6.72.   Ht 6 2
Wt 14 00
Forward. From Trainee.

Season	Club	Apps	Goals
1990–91	Hartlepool U	14	2
1991–92	....	18	2
1992–93	Bournemouth..............	31	4

FLITCROFT, David

Born Bolton 14.1.74   Ht 6 0   Wt 13 09
Forward. From Trainee.

Season	Club	Apps	Goals
1991–92	Preston NE	—	—
1992–93	....	8	2

FLITCROFT, Gary

Born Bolton 6.11.72.   Ht 5 11   Wt 11 08
Defender. From Trainee. England
Under-21.

Season	Club	Apps	Goals
1991–92	Manchester C	—	—
1991–92	*Bury*	12	—
1992–93	Manchester C	32	5

FLOUNDERS, Andy

Born Hull 13.12.63.   Ht 5 11   Wt 11 06
Forward. From Apprentice.

Season	Club	Apps	Goals
1980–81	Hull C.........................	5	—
1981–82	....	13	5

Season	Club	Apps	Goals
1982–83	....	23	13
1983–84	....	30	9
1984–85	....	39	14
1985–86	....	25	10
1986–87	....	24	3
1986–87	Scunthorpe U	15	6
1987–88	....	45	24
1988–89	....	46	16
1989–90	....	44	18
1990–91	....	46	23
1991–92	Rochdale.....................	42	17
1992–93	....	32	14
1992–93	*Rotherham U*..............	6	2

FLOWERS, Paul

Born London 7.9.74   Ht 5 11   Wt 12 06
Defender. From Trainee.

Season	Club	Apps	Goals
1992–93	Colchester U..............	3	—

FLOWERS, Tim

Born Kenilworth 3.2.67.   Ht 6 2
Wt 14 01
Goalkeeper. From Apprentice. England
Youth, Under-21, 1 full cap.

Season	Club	Apps	Goals
1984–85	Wolverhampton W	38	—
1985–86	....	25	—
1985–86	*Southampton*	—	—
1986–87	Southampton	9	—
1986–87	*Swindon T*	2	—
1987–88	Southampton	9	—
1987–88	*Swindon T*	5	—
1988–89	Southampton	7	—
1989–90	....	35	—
1990–91	....	37	—
1991–92	....	41	—
1992–93	....	42	—

FLYNN, Brian

Born Port Talbot 12.10.55.   Ht 5 4
Wt 10 00
Midfield. From Apprentice. Wales Schools,
Under-23, 66 full caps.

Season	Club	Apps	Goals
1972–73	Burnley	—	—
1973–74	....	2	—

Season	Club	App	Goals
1974–75		26	—
1975–76		39	4
1976–77		41	2
1977–78		12	2
1977–78	Leeds U	29	1
1978–79		41	3
1979–80		24	3
1980–81		41	3
1981–82		17	1
1981–82	*Burnley*	2	—
1982–83	Leeds U	2	—
1982–83	Burnley	28	1
1983–84		43	9
1984–85		9	1
1984–85	Cardiff C	22	—
1985–86		10	—
1985–86	Doncaster R	27	—
1986–87	Bury	19	—
From Limerick H			
1987–88	Doncaster R	24	1
1987–88	Wrexham	17	1
1988–89		41	1
1989–90		23	2
1990–91		11	1
1991–92		6	—
1992–93		2	—

FLYNN, Mike

Born Oldham 23.2.69.   Ht 6 0   Wt 11 00
Defender. From Trainee.

Season	Club	App	Goals
1986–87	Oldham Ath	—	—
1987–88		31	1
1988–89		9	—
1988–89	Norwich C	—	—
1989–90		—	—
1989–90	Preston NE	23	1
1990–91		35	1
1991–92		43	3
1992–93		35	2
1992–93	Stockport Co	10	—

FLYNN, Sean

Born Birmingham 13.3.68.   Ht 5 8
Wt 11 08
Midfield. From Halesowen T.

Season	Club	App	Goals
1991–92	Coventry C	22	2

Season	Club	App	Goals
1992–93		7	—

FOLEY, Steve

Born Liverpool 4.10.62.   Ht 5 7   Wt 11 03
Midfield. From Apprentice.

Season	Club	App	Goals
1980–81	Liverpool	—	—
1981–82		—	—
1982–83		—	—
1983–84		—	—
1983–84	*Fulham*	3	—
1984–85	Grimsby T	31	2
1985–86	Sheffield U	28	5
1986–87		38	9
1987–88	Swindon T	35	4
1988–89		40	8
1989–90		23	4
1990–91		44	7
1991–92		9	—
1991–92	Stoke C	20	1
1992–93		44	7

FORD, Gary

Born York 8.2.61.   Ht 5 8   Wt 12 05
Midfield. From Apprentice.

Season	Club	App	Goals
1978–79	York C	33	4
1979–80		29	2
1980–81		43	4
1981–82		41	8
1982–83		45	11
1983–84		46	11
1984–85		44	5
1985–86		40	3
1986–87		45	4
1987–88	Leicester C	16	2
1987–88	Port Vale	23	3
1988–89		22	7
1989–90		—	—
1989–90	*Walsall*	13	2
1990–91	Port Vale	30	2
1990–91	Mansfield T	12	1
1991–92		39	4
1992–93		37	1

FORD, John

Born Birmingham 12.4.68.   Ht 6 1
Wt 13 01
Midfield. From Cradley T.

1991–92	Swansea C	44	—
1992–93		43	3

FORD, Mike

Born Bristol 9.2.66.   Ht 6 0   Wt 11 02
Defender. From Apprentice.

1983–84	Leicester C	—	—
	From DevizesH		
1984–85	Cardiff C	20	1
1985–86		44	4
1986–87		36	1
1987–88		45	7
1988–89	Oxford U	10	1
1989–90		31	2
1990–91		28	1
1991–92		9	1
1992–93		44	4

FORD, Stuart

Born Sheffield 20.7.71.   Ht 5 11   Wt 11 13
Goalkeeper. From Trainee.

1989–90	Rotherham U	1	—
1990–91		—	—
1991–92		4	—
1991–92	Scarborough	6	—
1992–93	Scarborough	22	—

FORD, Tony

Born Grimsby 14.5.59.   Ht 5 9   Wt 12 02
Forward. From Apprentice. England B.

1975–76	Grimsby T	14	—
1976–77		6	—
1977–78		34	2
1978–79		45	15
1979–80		37	5
1980–81		28	4
1981–82		35	7
1982–83		37	4
1983–84		42	8

1984–85		42	6
1985–86		34	3
1985–86	Sunderland	9	1
1986–87	Stoke C	41	6
1987–88		44	7
1988–89		27	—
1988–89	WBA	11	1
1989–90		42	8
1990–91		46	5
1991–92		15	—
1991–92	Grimsby T	22	1
1992–93		17	2

FOREMAN, Darren

Born Southampton 12.2.68.   Ht 5 10
Wt 10 08
Forward. England Schools.

1986–87	Barnsley	16	1
1987–88		9	4
1988–89		5	—
1989–90		17	3
1989–90	Crewe Alex	14	3
1990–91		9	1
1990–91	Scarborough	14	5
1991–92		24	2
1992–93		42	27

FORREST, Craig

Born Vancouver 20.9.67.   Ht 6 5
Wt 14 00
Goalkeeper. From Apprentice. Canada full
caps.

1985–86	Ipswich T	—	—
1986–87		—	—
1987–88		—	—
1987–88	Colchester U	11	—
1988–89	Ipswich T	28	—
1989–90		45	—
1990–91		43	—
1991–92		46	—
1992–93		11	—

FORRESTER, Jamie

Born Bradford 1.11.74
Forward. From Auxerre. England Youth.

1992–93	Leeds U	6	—

FORSTER, Nick

Born Oxted 8.9.73   Ht 5 9   Wt 11 05
Forward. From Horley T.

1992–93	Gillingham	26	6

FORSYTH, Mike

Born Liverpool 20.3.66.   Ht 5 11
Wt 12 02
Defender. From Apprentice. England
Youth, B, Under-21.

1983–84	WBA	8	—
1984–85		10	—
1985–86		11	—
1985–86	*Northampton T.*	—	—
1985–86	Derby Co	—	—
1986–87		41	1
1987–88		39	3
1988–89		38	—
1989–90		38	—
1990–91		35	—
1991–92		43	1
1992–93		41	1

FOSTER, Adrian

Born Kidderminster 20.7.71.   Ht 5 9
Wt 11 00
Forward. From Trainee.

1989–90	WBA	14	1
1990–91		5	—
1991–92		8	1
1992–93	Torquay U	36	9

FOSTER, Colin

Born Chislehurst 16.7.64.   Ht 6 4
Wt 14 01
Defender. From Apprentice.

1981–82	Orient	23	2
1982–83		43	2
1983–84		11	1
1984–85		42	1
1985–86		36	2
1986–87		19	2
1986–87	Nottingham F.	9	1

1987–88		39	2
1988–89		18	2
1989–90		6	—
1989–90	West Ham U	22	1
1990–91		36	3
1991–92		24	—
1992–93		6	1

FOSTER, George

Born Plymouth 26.9.56.   Ht 5 10
Wt 11 02
Defender. From Apprentice.

1973–74	Plymouth Arg	5	—
1974–75		—	—
1975–76		16	1
1976–77		15	2
1976–77	*Torquay U*	6	3
1977–78	Plymouth Arg	46	3
1978–79		28	—
1979–80		46	—
1980–81		46	—
1981–82		10	—
1981–82	*Exeter C*	28	—
1982–83	Derby Co	30	—
1983–84	Mansfield T	42	—
1984–85		44	—
1985–86		46	—
1986–87		45	—
1987–88		44	—
1988–89		42	—
1989–90		42	—
1990–91		34	—
1991–92		24	—
1992–93		10	—

FOSTER, Steve

Born Portsmouth 24.9.57.   Ht 6 1
Wt 14 00
Defender. From Apprentice. England
Under-21, 3 full caps.

1975–76	Portsmouth	11	—
1976–77		31	1
1977–78		31	3
1978–79		36	2
1979–80	Brighton	38	1
1980–81		42	1

Season	Club	Appearances	Goals
1981–82		40	2
1982–83		36	1
1983–84		16	1
1983–84	Aston Villa	7	1
1984–85		8	2
1984–85	Luton T	25	1
1985–86		35	3
1986–87		28	2
1987–88		39	2
1988–89		36	3
1989–90	Oxford U	35	4
1990–91		38	3
1991–92		22	2
1992–93	Brighton	35	4

FOSTER, Wayne

Born Leigh 11.9.63. Ht 5 8   Wt 11 00
Forward. From Apprentice. England
Youth.

Season	Club	Appearances	Goals
1981–82	Bolton W	23	2
1982–83		24	4
1983–84		30	3
1984–85		28	4
1985–86	Preston NE	31	3
1986–87	Hearts	31	4
1987–88		39	4
1988–89		9	1
1989–90		17	1
1990–91		28	1
1991–92		7	—
1992–93		11	—

FOWLER, Jason

Born Bristol 20.8.74
Midfield. From Trainee.

Season	Club	Appearances	Goals
1992–93	Bristol C	1	—

FOWLER, John

Born Preston 27.10.74   Ht 5 10   Wt 11 10
Midfield. From Trainee.

Season	Club	Appearances	Goals
1991–92	Cambridge U	—	—
1992–93		3	—
1992–93	*Preston NE*	6	—

FOWLER, Lee

Born Nottingham 26.1.69.   Ht 5 8
Wt 11 07
Forward. From Trainee.

Season	Club	Appearances	Goals
1987–88	Stoke C	1	—
1988–89		—	—
1989–90		15	—
1990–91		17	—
1991–92		16	—
1992–93	Preston NE	32	2

FOX, Matthew

Born Birmingham 13.7.71.   Ht 6 0
Wt 13 00
Defender. From Trainee.

Season	Club	Appearances	Goals
1988–89	Birmingham C	3	—
1989–90		—	—
1990–91		11	—
1991–92		—	—
1992–93	Northampton T	1	—

FOX, Peter

Born Scunthorpe 5.7.57.   Ht 5 10
Wt 12 04
Goalkeeper. From Apprentice.

Season	Club	Appearances	Goals
1972–73	Sheffield W	1	—
1973–74		—	—
1974–75		20	—
1975–76		27	—
1976–77		1	—
1976–77	*West Ham U*	—	—
1977–78	Sheffield W	—	—
1977–78	*Barnsley*	1	—
1977–78	Stoke C	—	—
1978–79		1	—
1979–80		23	—
1980–81		42	—
1981–82		38	—
1982–83		35	—
1983–84		42	—
1984–85		14	—
1985–86		37	—
1986–87		39	—
1987–88		17	—
1988–89		29	—

Season	Club	App	Goals
1989–90	....	38	—
1990–91	....	44	—
1991–92	....	—	—
1992–93	....	10	—
1992–93	*Wrexham*.....................	—	—

FOX, Ruel

Born Ipswich 14.1.68.   Ht 5 6   Wt 10 00
Midfield. From Apprentice.

Season	Club	App	Goals
1985–86	Norwich C	—	—
1986–87	....	3	—
1987–88	....	34	2
1988–89	....	4	—
1989–90	....	7	3
1990–91	....	28	4
1991–92	....	37	2
1992–93	....	34	4

FOY, David

Born Coventry 20.10.72   Ht 6 1   Wt 12 00
Midfield. From Trainee.

Season	Club	App	Goals
1991–92	Birmingham C	—	—
1992–93	....	3	—
1992–93	Scunthorpe U	3	—

FOYLE, Martin

Born Salisbury 2.5.63.   Ht 5 10   Wt 11 02
Forward. From Amateur.

Season	Club	App	Goals
1980–81	Southampton	—	—
1981–82	....	—	—
1982–83	....	7	1
1983–84	....	5	—
1983–84	*Blackburn R*	—	—
1984–85	Aldershot	44	15
1985–86	....	20	9
1986–87	....	34	11
1986–87	Oxford U	4	—
1987–88	....	33	10
1988–89	....	40	14
1989–90	....	13	2
1990–91	....	36	10
1991–92	Port Vale...................	43	11
1992–93	....	16	4

FRAIL, Stephen

Born Glasgow 10.8.69.   Ht 5 9   Wt 10.09
Midfield. From Possilpark YM.

Season	Club	App	Goals
1985–86	Dundee.....................	—	—
1986–87	....	—	—
1987–88	....	4	—
1988–89	....	23	1
1989–90	....	6	—
1990–91	....	26	—
1991–92	....	3	—
1992–93	....	7	—

FRAIN, David

Born Sheffield 11.10.62.   Ht 5 8   Wt 10 05
Forward. From Rowlinson YC.

Season	Club	App	Goals
1985–86	Sheffield U	7	1
1986–87	....	19	3
1987–88	....	18	1
1988–89	Rochdale.....................	42	12
1989–90	Stockport Co	29	2
1990–91	....	43	3
1991–92	....	39	4
1992–93	....	41	—

FRAIN, John

Born Birmingham 8.10.68.   Ht 5 7
Wt 11 10
Midfield. From Apprentice.

Season	Club	App	Goals
1985–86	Birmingham C	3	—
1986–87	....	3	1
1987–88	....	14	2
1988–89	....	28	3
1989–90	....	38	1
1990–91	....	42	3
1991–92	....	44	5
1992–93	....	45	6

FRANCE, Darren

Born Hull 8.8.67.   Ht 6 0   Wt 14 02
Forward. From North Ferriby.

Season	Club	App	Goals
1991–92	Hull C.......................	17	4
1992–93	....	26	3

FRANCIS, John

Born Dewsbury 21.11.63.   Ht 5 8
Wt 11 02
Forward. From Emley.

Season	Club		
1988–89	Sheffield U	22	1
1989–90		20	5
1989–90	Burnley	19	4
1990–91		45	14
1991–92		37	8
1992–93	Cambridge U	29	3
1992–93	Burnley	9	1

FRANCIS, Kevin

Born Moseley 6.12.67.   Ht 6 7   Wt 15 08
Forward. From Mile Oak R.

Season	Club		
1988–89	Derby Co	—	—
1989–90		8	—
1990–91		2	—
1990–91	Stockport Co	13	5
1991–92		35	15
1992–93		42	28

FRANCIS, Steve

Born Billericay 29.5.64.   Ht 5 11
Wt 11 05
Goalkeeper. From Apprentice. England
Youth.

Season	Club		
1981–82	Chelsea	29	—
1982–83		37	—
1983–84		—	—
1984–85		2	—
1985–86		3	—
1986–87		—	—
1986–87	Reading	14	—
1987–88		34	—
1988–89		22	—
1989–90		46	—
1990–91		34	—
1991–92		32	—
1992–93		34	—

FRANCIS, Trevor

Born Plymouth 19.4.54.   Ht 5 10
Wt 11 07
Forward. From Apprentice. England
Youth, Under-23, 52 full caps.

Season	Club		
1970–71	Birmingham C	22	15
1971–72		39	12
1972–73		31	6
1973–74		37	6
1974–75		23	13
1975–76		35	17
1976–77		42	21
1977–78		42	25
From Detroit E			
1978–79	Birmingham C	9	3
1978–79	Nottingham F	20	6
From Detroit E			
1979–80	Nottingham F	30	14
1980–81		18	6
1981–82		2	2
1981–82	Manchester C	26	12
1982–83	Sampdoria	14	7
1983–84		15	3
1984–85		24	6
1985–86		15	1
1986–87	Atalanta	21	1
1987–88	Rangers	18	—
1987–88	QPR	9	—
1988–89		19	7
1989–90		4	5
1989–90	Sheffield W	12	—
1990–91		38	4
1991–92		20	1
1992–93		5	—

FREESTONE, Roger

Born Newport 19.8.68.   Ht 6 2   Wt 12 03
Goalkeeper. Wales Under-21.

Season	Club		
1986–87	Newport Co	13	—
1986–87	Chelsea	6	—
1987–88		15	—
1988–89		21	—
1989–90		—	—
1989–90	*Swansea C*	14	—
1989–90	*Hereford U*	8	—
1990–91	Chelsea	—	—

1991–92	Swansea C	42	—
1992–93		46	—

FROGGATT, Steve

Born Lincoln 9.3.73. Ht 5 10 Wt 11 00
Midfield. From Trainee. England
Under-21.

1990–91	Aston Villa	—	—
1991–92		9	—
1992–93		17	1

FRY, Chris

Born Cardiff 23.10.69.   Ht 5 9   Wt 9 06
Forward. From Trainee.

1988–89	Cardiff C	9	—
1989–90		23	1
1990–91		23	—
1991–92	Hereford U	37	3
1992–93		37	4

FULTON, Stephen

Born Greenock 10.8.70. Ht 5 10
Wt 11 00
Midfield. From Celtic BC. Scotland
Under-21.

1986–87	Celtic	—	—
1987–88		—	—
1988–89		3	—
1989–90		16	—
1990–91		21	—
1991–92		30	2
1992–93		6	—

FUNNELL, Simon

Born Brighton 8.8.74.   Ht 6 0   Wt 12 08
Forward. From Trainee.

1991–92	Brighton	1	—
1992–93		2	—

FURLONG, Paul

Born London 1.10.68.   Ht 6 0   Wt 12 11
Forward. From Enfield.

1991–92	Coventry C	37	4

1992–93	Watford	41	19

FURPHY, Willie

Born London 7.5.66 Ht 5 1 Wt 11 7
Defender. From Eastern Villas.

1985–86	Ayr U	—	—
1986–87		36	1
1987–88		37	—
1988–89		34	—
1989–90		34	—
1990–91		24	—
1991–92		39	—
1992–93		6	—
1992–93	Kilmarnock	1	—
1992–93	Montrose	1	—

FUTCHER, Paul

Born Chester 25.9.56.   Ht 6 0   Wt 12 03
Defender. From Apprentice. England
Under-21. Football League.

1972–73	Chester	2	—
1973–74		18	—
1974–75	Luton T	19	—
1975–76		41	—
1976–77		40	1
1977–78		31	—
1978–79	Manchester C	24	—
1979–80		13	—
1980–81	Oldham Ath	36	1
1981–82		37	—
1982–83		25	—
1982–83	Derby Co	17	—
1983–84		18	—
1983–84	Barnsley	10	—
1984–85		36	—
1985–86		37	—
1986–87		36	—
1987–88		41	—
1988–89		41	—
1989–90		29	—
1990–91	Halifax T	15	—
1990–91	Grimsby T	22	—
1991–92		29	—
1992–93		35	—

GABBIADINI, Marco

Born Nottingham 20.1.68.   Ht 5 10
Wt 12 04
Forward. From Apprentice. England B,
Under-21.

1984–85	York C	1	—
1985–86		22	4
1986–87		29	9
1987–88		8	1
1987–88	Sunderland	35	21
1988–89		36	18
1989–90		46	21
1990–91		31	9
1991–92		9	5
1991–92	Crystal Palace	15	5
1991–92	Derby Co	20	6
1992–93		44	9

GABBIADINI, Ricardo

Born Newport 11.3.70.   Ht 5 11
Wt 13 06
Forward. From Trainee.

1987–88	York C	1	—
1988–89	Sunderland	—	—
1989–90		1	—
1989–90	*Blackpool*	5	3
1989–90	*Brighton*	1	—
1989–90	*Grimsby T*	3	1
1990–91	Sunderland	—	—
1990–91	*Crewe Alex*	2	—
1990–91	Hartlepool U	5	—
1991–92		9	2
1991–92	Scarborough	7	1
1992–93	Carlisle U	24	3

GAGE, Kevin

Born Chiswick 21.4.64.   Ht 5 9   Wt 11 02
Defender. From Apprentice. England
Youth.

1980–81	Wimbledon	1	—
1981–82		21	1
1982–83		26	4
1983–84		24	4
1984–85		37	2

1985–86		29	1
1986–87		30	3
1987–88	Aston Villa	44	2
1988–89		28	3
1989–90		22	3
1990–91		21	—
1991–92		—	—
1991–92	Sheffield U	22	2
1992–93		27	—

GALE, Tony

Born London 19.11.59.   Ht 6 1   Wt 13 07
Defender. From Apprentice. England
Youth, Under-21.

1977–78	Fulham	38	8
1978–79		36	2
1979–80		42	4
1980–81		40	1
1981–82		44	1
1982–83		42	2
1983–84		35	1
1984–85	West Ham U	37	—
1985–86		42	—
1986–87		32	2
1987–88		18	—
1988–89		31	—
1989–90		36	1
1990–91		24	1
1991–92		25	—
1992–93		23	1

GALLACHER, Bernard

Born Johnstone 22.3.67.   Ht 5 9
Wt 11 00
Defender. From Apprentice.

1984–85	Aston Villa	—	—
1985–86		—	—
1986–87		1	—
1987–88		43	—
1988–89		4	—
1989–90		7	—
1990–91		2	—
1990–91	*Blackburn R*	4	—
1991–92	Doncaster R	2	—
1991–92	Brighton	31	1
1992–93		14	—

GALLACHER, John

Born Glasgow 26.1.69 Ht 5 10 Wt 10 08
Forward.

1987–88	Falkirk	2	—
1988–89		16	5
1989–90	Newcastle U	28	6
1990–91		1	—
1991–92		—	—
1992–93	Hartlepool U	21	1

GALLACHER, Kevin

Born Clydebank 23.11.66. Ht 5 7
Wt 9 11
Forward. From Duntocher BC. Scotland
Youth, B, Under-21, 17 full caps.

1983–84	Dundee U	—	—
1984–85		—	—
1985–86		20	3
1986–87		37	10
1987–88		26	4
1988–89		31	9
1989–90		17	1
1989–90	Coventry C	15	3
1990–91		32	11
1991–92		33	8
1992–93		20	6
1992–93	Blackburn R	9	5

GALLAGHER, Eddie

Born Glasgow 21.11.64. Ht 5 9 Wt 10 06
Forward. From Campsie BW.

1985–86	Partick T	23	4
1986–87		30	5
1987–88		34	13
1988–89		3	2
1988–89	Hamilton A	14	3
1988–89	Dunfermline Ath	7	1
1989–90		14	1
1990–91		3	—
1991–92		4	—
1991–92	Dundee	22	11
1992–93		4	—
1992–93	St Mirren	19	12

GALLEN, Joe

Born Hammersmith 2.9.72 Ht 5 11
Wt 11 08
Forward. From Trainee.

1991–92	Watford	—	—
1992–93		—	—
1992–93	*Exeter C*	6	—

GALLIMORE, Tony

Born Crewe 21.2.72. Ht 5 10 Wt 11 10
Midfield. From Trainee.

1989–90	Stoke C	1	—
1990–91		7	—
1991–92		3	—
1991–92	*Carlisle U*	16	—
1992–93	Stoke C	—	—
1992–93	*Carlisle U*	8	1

GALLOWAY, Mick

Born Oswestry 30.5 65. Ht 5 11
Wt 11 07
Defender. From Amateur. Scotland
Youth, Under-21, 1 full cap.

1983–84	Mansfield T	17	—
1984–85		31	3
1985–86		6	—
1985–86	Halifax T	19	—
1986–87		43	3
1987–88		17	2
1987–88	Hearts	25	6
1988–89		31	2
1989–90	Celtic	33	2
1990–91		6	1
1991–92		34	2
1992–93		30	3

GANNON, Jim

Born London 7.9.68. Ht 6 2 Wt 13 00
Defender. From Dundalk.

1988–89	Sheffield U	—	—
1989–90		—	—
1989–90	*Halifax T*	2	—
1989–90	Stockport Co	7	1

1990–91	....	41	6
1991–92	....	43	16
1992–93	....	46	12

GANNON, John

Born Wimbledon 18.12.66. Ht 5 8
Wt 10 10
Midfield. From Apprentice.

1984–85	Wimbledon	—	—
1985–86		1	1
1986–87		2	—
1986–87	*Crewe Alex*	15	—
1987–88	Wimbledon	13	1
1988–89		—	—
1988–89	*Sheffield U*	16	1
1989–90	Sheffield U	39	3
1990–91		22	—
1991–92		32	1
1992–93		27	1

GARDINER, Mark

Born Cirencester 25.12.66. Ht 5 10
Wt 10 07
Forward. From Apprentice.

1983–84	Swindon T	1	—
1984–85		4	—
1985–86		1	—
1986–87		4	—
1986–87	Torquay U	22	3
1987–88		27	1
1988–89	Crewe Alex	38	10
1989–90		26	6
1990–91		33	10
1991–92		38	5
1992–93		13	1

GARDINER, Matthew

Born Birmingham 28.3.74 Ht 5 4
Wt 10 10
Defender. From Trainee.

| 1992–93 | Torquay U | 7 | — |

GARDNER, James

Born Dunfermline 27.9.67. Ht 5 10
Wt 10 02
Defender. From Ayresome North AFC.

1986–87	Queen's Park	1	—
1987–88		1	—
1988–89	Motherwell	—	—
1989–90		1	—
1990–91		—	—
1991–92		12	—
1992–93		3	—

GARDNER, Steve

Born Teeside 3.7.68. Ht 5 11 Wt 12 06
Defender. From Apprentice.

1986–87	Manchester U	—	—
1987–88	Burnley	42	—
1988–89		44	—
1989–90		9	—
From Glossop
1991–92	Bradford C	14	—
1992–93	Bury	1	—

GARLAND, Peter

Born Croydon 20.1.71. Ht 5 9 Wt 12 00
Midfield. From Trainee. England Youth.

1989–90	Tottenham H	—	—
1990–91		1	—
1991–92		—	—
1991–92	Newcastle U	2	—
1992–93		—	—
1992–93	Charlton Ath	13	1

GARNER, Andy

Born Chesterfield 8.3.66. Ht 6 0
Wt 12 01
Forward. From Apprentice.

1983–84	Derby Co	13	5
1984–85		16	3
1985–86		16	5
1986–87		2	—
1987–88		24	4
1988–89	Blackpool	42	11

Season	Club	Appearances	Goals
1989–90	....	46	8
1990–91	....	36	13
1991–92	....	30	5
1992–93	....	5	—

GARNER, Darren

Born Plymouth 10.12.71.   Ht 5 6
Wt 10 01
Midfield. From Trainee.

Season	Club	Appearances	Goals
1988–89	Plymouth Arg..............	1	—
1989–90	....	1	—
1990–91	....	5	1
1991–92	....	10	—
1992–93	....	10	—

GARNER, Simon

Born Boston 23.11.59.   Ht 5 9   Wt 11 12
Forward. From Apprentice.

Season	Club	Appearances	Goals
1978–79	Blackburn R	25	8
1979–80	....	28	6
1980–81	....	33	7
1981–82	....	36	14
1982–83	....	41	22
1983–84	....	42	19
1984–85	....	37	12
1985–86	....	38	12
1986–87	....	40	10
1987–88	....	40	14
1988–89	....	44	20
1989–90	....	43	18
1990–91	....	12	1
1991–92	....	25	5
1992–93	WBA	25	8

GARNETT, Shaun

Born Wallasey 22.11.69.   Ht 6 2
Wt 11 00
Midfield. From Trainee.

Season	Club	Appearances	Goals
1987–88	Tranmere R	1	—
1988–89	....	—	—
1989–90	....	4	—
1990–91	....	16	1
1991–92	....	8	—
1992–93	....	5	1

Season	Club	Appearances	Goals
1992–93	*Chester C*	9	—
1992–93	*Preston NE*	10	2
1992–93	*Wigan Ath*	13	1

GARVEY, Steve

Born Tameside 22.11.73.   Ht 5 9
Wt 11 01
Forward. From Trainee.

Season	Club	Appearances	Goals
1990–91	Crewe Alex	1	—
1991–92	....	11	—
1992–93	....	10	1

GASCOIGNE, Paul

Born Gateshead 27.5.67.   Ht 5 10
Wt 11 07
Midfield. From Apprentice. England B,
Under-21, 27 full caps.

Season	Club	Appearances	Goals
1984–85	Newcastle U................	2	—
1985–86	....	31	9
1986–87	....	24	5
1987–88	....	35	7
1988–89	Tottenham H	32	6
1989–90	....	34	6
1990–91	....	26	7
1991–92	....	—	—

To Lazio

GATTING, Steve

Born Park Royal 29.5.59.   Ht 5 11
Wt 11 11
Defender. From Apprentice.

Season	Club	Appearances	Goals
1976–77	Arsenal........................	—	—
1977–78	....	—	—
1978–79	....	21	1
1979–80	....	14	1
1980–81	....	23	3
1981–82	....	—	—
1981–82	Brighton......................	39	3
1982–83	....	40	4
1983–84	....	35	4
1984–85	....	8	—
1985–86	....	17	—
1986–87	....	40	1
1987–88	....	46	3

Season	Club	App	Goals
1988–89	....	29	3
1989–90	....	19	—
1990–91	....	43	1
1991–92	Charlton Ath	32	1
1992–93	....	32	2

GAUGHAN, Steve

Born Doncaster 14.4.70. Ht 5 11
Wt 11 02
Midfield.

Season	Club	App	Goals
1987–88	Doncaster R................	4	—
1988–89	....	34	2
1989–90	....	29	1
1990–91	Sunderland..................	—	—
1991–92	....	—	—
1991–92	Darlington	20	—
1992–93	....	37	1

GAVIN, Mark

Born Bailleston 10.12.63. Ht 5 8
Wt 10 07
Midfield. From Apprentice.

Season	Club	App	Goals
1981–82	Leeds U	—	—
1982–83	....	7	1
1983–84	....	12	1
1984–85	....	11	1
1984–85	*Hartlepool U*	7	—
1985–86	Carlisle U...................	13	1
1985–86	Bolton W	8	1
1986–87	....	41	2
1987–88	Rochdale.....................	23	6
1987–88	Hearts	7	—
1988–89	....	2	—
1988–89	Bristol C	29	3
1989–90	....	40	3
1990–91	Watford	13	—
1991–92	....	—	—
1991–92	Bristol C	14	1
1992–93	....	19	1

GAVIN, Pat

Born Hammersmith 5.6.67. Ht 6 0
Wt 12 00
Forward. From Hanwell T.

Season	Club	App	Goals
1988–89	Gillingham	13	7

Season	Club	App	Goals
1989–90	Leicester C................	—	—
1989–90	*Gillingham*	34	1
1990–91	Leicester C................	3	—
1990–91	Peterborough U	11	5
1991–92	....	11	—
1992–93	....	1	—
1992–93	Barnet	—	—
1992–93	Northampton T	14	4

GAYLE, Brian

Born London 6.3.65. Ht 6 1   Wt 12 07
Defender.

Season	Club	App	Goals
1984–85	Wimbledon	12	1
1985–86	....	13	—
1986–87	....	32	1
1987–88	....	26	1
1988–89	Manchester C	41	3
1989–90	....	14	—
1989–90	Ipswich T...................	20	—
1990–91	....	33	4
1991–92	....	5	—
1991–92	Sheffield U	33	3
1992–93	....	31	2

GAYLE, Howard

Born Liverpool 18.5.58. Ht 5 10
Wt 10 09
Midfield. Local. England Under-21.

Season	Club	App	Goals
1977–78	Liverpool	—	—
1978–79	....	—	—
1979–80	....	—	—
1979–80	*Fulham*	14	—
1980–81	Liverpool	4	1
1981–82	....	—	—
1982–83	Liverpool	—	—
1982–83	*Birmingham C*	13	1
1982–83	*Newcastle U*	8	2
1983–84	Birmingham C	33	8
1984–85	Sunderland..................	25	2
1985–86	....	23	2
1986–87	Stoke C	6	2
1987–88	Blackburn R	13	1
1988–89	....	45	19
1989–90	....	30	5
1990–91	....	24	4
1991–92	....	4	—

1992–93	Halifax T	5 —

GAYLE, John

Born Birmingham 30.7.64. Ht 6 4
Wt 13 01
Forward. From Burton Alb.

1988–89	Wimbledon	2	—
1989–90		11	1
1990–91		7	1
1990–91	Birmingham C	22	6
1991–92		3	1
1992–93		19	3

GAYLE, Marcus

Born Hammersmith 27.9.70. Ht 6 2
Wt 12 13
Midfield. From Trainee. England Youth.

1988–89	Brentford	3	—
1989–90		9	—
1990–91		33	6
1991–92		38	6
1992–93		38	4

GAYLE, Mark

Born Bromsgrove 21.10.69. Ht 6 0
Wt 12 00
Goalkeeper. From Trainee.

1988–89	Leicester C	—	—
1989–90	Blackpool	—	—
From Worcester C			
1991–92	Walsall	24	—
1992–93		41	—

GAYNOR, Tommy

Born Limerick 29.1.63. Ht 6 1   Wt 13 02
Forward. From Limerick.

1986–87	Doncaster R	23	4
1987–88		10	3
1987–88	Nottingham F	12	3
1988–89		19	4
1989–90		11	—
1990–91		11	3

1990–91	*Newcastle U*	4	1
1991–92	Nottingham F	4	—
1992–93		—	—
1992–93	Millwall	3	—

GEDDES, Bobby

Born Inverness 12.8.60. Ht 6 0   Wt 11 4
Goalkeeper. From Ross County. Scotland
U-21.

1977–78	Dundee	—	—
1978–79		—	—
1979–80		—	—
1980–81		20	—
1981–82		28	—
1982–83		1	—
1983–84		24	—
1984–85		16	—
1985–86		36	—
1986–87		44	—
1987–88		38	—
1988–89		34	—
1989–90		12	—
1990–91	Kilmarnock	38	—
1991–92		33	—
1992–93		44	—

GEE, Phil

Born Pelsall 19.12.64. Ht 6 0   Wt 12 01
Forward. From Riley Sports and Gresley
R.

1985–86	Derby Co	4	2
1986–87		41	15
1987–88		38	6
1988–89		12	1
1989–90		8	1
1990–91		2	—
1991–92		19	1
1991–92	Leicester C	14	2
1992–93		18	4

GEMMILL, Scot

Born Paisley 2.1.71. Ht 5 10   Wt 10 01
Midfield. From School. Scotland
Under-21.

1989–90	Nottingham F	—	—

Season	Club	League Appearances/Goals
1990–91		4 —
1991–92		39 8
1992–93		33 1

GERMAN, David

Born Sheffield 16.10.73.
Midfield. From Sheffield W Schoolboy.

1990–91	Halifax T	1 —
1991–92		3 —
1992–93		35 2

GERRARD, Paul

Born Heywood 22.1.73
Goalkeeper. From Trainee. England
Under-21.

1991–92	Oldham Ath	— —
1992–93		25 —

GIBBINS, Roger

Born Enfield 6.9.55. Ht 5 10 Wt 11 09
Forward. From Apprentice. England
Schools.

1972–73	Tottenham H	— —
1973–74		— —
1974–75		— —
1975–76	Oxford U	19 2
1976–77	Norwich C	20 5
1977–78		28 7
From New England Tea Men		
1979–80	Cambridge U	35 4
1980–81		30 4
1981–82		35 4
1981–82	Cardiff C	46 8
1982–83		42 4
1983–84		40 5
1984–85		11 —
1985–86	Swansea C	35 6
1986–87	Newport Co	46 8
1987–88		33 1
1987–88	Torquay U	12 2
1988–89		21 3
From Newport Co		
1988–89	Cardiff C	12 —
1989–90		38 1

Season	Club	League Appearances/Goals
1990–91		43 5
1991–92		41 1
1992–93		8 —

GIBBS, Nigel

Born St Albans 20.11.65. Ht 5 7
Wt 11 01
Defender. From Apprentice. England
Youth, Under-21.

1983–84	Watford	3 —
1984–85		12 —
1985–86		40 1
1986–87		15 —
1987–88		30 —
1988–89		46 1
1989–90		41 —
1990–91		34 —
1991–92		43 1
1992–93		7 —

GIBSON, Andrew

Born Dechmont 2.2.69. Ht 5 8 Wt 11 04
Midfield. From Gairdoch U.

1987–88	Stirling Albion	5 —
1988–89		12 1
1988–89	Aberdeen	— —
1989–90		— —
1990–91		— —
1991–92		5 —
1992–93		1 1

GIBSON, Colin

Born Bridport 6.4.60. Ht 5 8 Wt 11 01
Defender. From Apprentice. England
Under-21, B.

1977–78	Aston Villa	— —
1978–79		12 —
1979–80		31 2
1980–81		21 —
1981–82		23 —
1982–83		23 1
1983–84		28 1
1984–85		40 4
1985–86		7 2

Season	Club	Apps	Goals
1985–86	Manchester U	18	5
1986–87		24	1
1987–88		29	2
1988–89		2	—
1989–90		6	1
1990–91		—	—
1990–91	*Port Vale*	6	2
1990–91	Leicester C	18	1
1991–92		17	3
1992–93		9	—

GIBSON, Terry

Born Walthamstow 23.12.62. Ht 5 5
Wt 10 00
Forward. From Apprentice. England
Schools, Youth.

Season	Club	Apps	Goals
1979–80	Tottenham H	1	—
1980–81		—	—
1981–82		1	—
1982–83		16	4
1983–84	Coventry C	36	17
1984–85		38	15
1985–86		24	11
1985–86	Manchester U	7	—
1986–87		16	1
1987–88		—	—
1987–88	Wimbledon	17	6
1988–89		17	5
1989–90		18	5
1990–91		19	5
1991–92		7	—
1991–92	*Swindon T*	9	1
1992–93	Wimbledon	8	1

GIGGS, Ryan

Born Cardiff 29.11.73. Ht 5 11 Wt 10 10
Forward. From School. Wales Youth,
Under-21, 8 full caps.

Season	Club	Apps	Goals
1990–91	Manchester U	2	1
1991–92		38	4
1992–93		41	9

GILBERT, David

Born Lincoln 22.6.63. Ht 5 4 Wt 10 04
Midfield. From Apprentice.

Season	Club	Apps	Goals
1980–81	Lincoln C	1	—

Season	Club	Apps	Goals
1981–82		29	1
1982–83	Scunthorpe U	1	—
From Boston U			
1986–87	Northampton T	45	8
1987–88		41	6
1988–89		34	7
1988–89	Grimsby T	11	3
1989–90		45	10
1990–91		44	12
1991–92		41	2
1992–93		41	4

GILCHRIST, Philip

Born Stockton 25.8.73 Ht 6 0 Wt 11 12
Defender. From Trainee.

Season	Club	Apps	Goals
1990–91	Nottingham F	—	—
1991–92	Middlesbrough	—	—
1992–93	Hartlepool U	24	—

GILKES, Michael

Born Hackney 20.7.65. Ht 5 8 Wt 10 02
Forward.

Season	Club	Apps	Goals
1984–85	Reading	16	2
1985–86		9	2
1986–87		7	—
1987–88		39	4
1988–89		46	9
1989–90		42	2
1990–91		21	1
1991–92		20	—
1991–92	*Chelsea*	1	—
1991–92	*Southampton*	6	—
1992–93	Reading	38	12

GILLARD, Ken

Born Dublin 30.4.72 Ht 5 9 Wt 11 08
Defender. From Trainee.

Season	Club	Apps	Goals
1991–92	Luton T	—	—
1992–93		—	—
1992–93	*Northampton T*	9	—

GILLESPIE, Gary

Born Stirling 5.7.60. Ht 6 2 Wt 12 07
Defender. From school. Scotland Under-
21, 13 full caps.

1977–78	Falkirk	22	—
1978–79	Coventry C	15	—
1979–80		38	1
1980–81		37	1
1981–82		40	2
1982–83		42	2
1983–84	Liverpool	—	—
1984–85		12	1
1985–86		14	3
1986–87		37	—
1987–88		35	4
1988–89		15	1
1989–90		13	4
1990–91		30	1
1991–92	Celtic	24	2
1992–93		18	—

GILZEAN, Ian

Born London 10.12.69 Ht 6 1 Wt 12 10
Forward. From Tottenham H Trainee.

1991–92	Tottenham H	—	—
1992–93	Dundee	24	5
1992–93	Doncaster R	3	—

GINTER, Tony

Born Plymouth 6.11.74
Midfield. From Trainee.

1992–93	Torquay U	1	—

GITTENS, Jon

Born Moseley 22.1.64. Ht 6 0 Wt 12 06
Defender. From Paget R.

1985–86	Southampton	4	—
1986–87		14	—
1987–88	Swindon T	29	—
1988–89		29	1
1989–90		40	4
1990–91		28	1
1990–91	Southampton	8	—

1991–92		11	—
1991–92	Middlesbrough	12	1
1992–93	Middlesbrough	13	—

GLEGHORN, Nigel

Born Seaham 12.8.62. Ht 6 0 Wt 13 04
Midfield. From Seaham Red Star.

1985–86	Ipswich T	21	2
1986–87		29	7
1987–88		16	2
1988–89	Manchester C	32	6
1989–90		2	1
1989–90	Birmingham C	43	9
1990–91		42	6
1991–92		46	17
1992–93		11	1
1992–93	Stoke C	34	7

GLOVER, Dean

Born West Bromwich 29.12.63. Ht 5 10
Wt 11 13
Defender. From Apprentice.

1981–82	Aston Villa	—	—
1982–83		—	—
1983–84		—	—
1984–85		5	—
1985–86		18	—
1986–87		—	—
1986–87	Sheffield U	5	—
1987–88		5	—
1987–88	Middlesbrough	38	4
1988–89		12	1
1988–89	Port Vale	22	—
1989–90		44	4
1990–91		41	1
1991–92		46	1
1992–93		39	3

GLOVER, Lee

Born Kettering 24.4.70. Ht 5 10
Wt 12 01
Forward. From Trainee. Scotland
Under-21.

1986–87	Nottingham F	—	—

Season	Club	App	Goals
1987–88	....	20	3
1988–89	....	—	—
1989–90	....	—	—
1989–90	*Leicester C*	5	1
1989–90	*Barnsley*	8	—
1990–91	Nottingham F............	8	1
1991–92	....	16	—
1991–92	*Luton T*....................	1	—
1992–93	Nottingham F............	14	—

GOATER, Shaun

Born Bermuda 25.2.70. Ht 6 1 Wt 12 00
Forward. Bermuda full caps.

Season	Club	App	Goals
1988–89	Manchester U............	—	—
1989–90	....	—	—
1989–90	Rotherham U	12	2
1990–91	....	22	2
1991–92	....	24	9
1992–93	....	23	7

GODDARD, Paul

Born Harlington 12.10.59. Ht 5 7
Wt 12 00
Forward. From Apprentice. England
Under-21, 1 full cap.

Season	Club	App	Goals
1977–78	QPR	7	1
1978–79	....	23	6
1979–80	....	40	16
1980–81	West Ham U	37	17
1981–82	....	39	15
1982–83	....	39	10
1983–84	....	5	1
1984–85	....	40	9
1985–86	....	6	1
1986–87	....	4	1
1986–87	Newcastle U...............	26	11
1987–88	....	35	8
1988–89	Derby Co	31	7
1989–90	....	18	8
1989–90	Millwall	14	1
1990–91	....	6	—
1990–91	Ipswich T	19	6
1991–92	....	24	4
1992–93	....	25	3

GODFREY, Kevin

Born Kennington 24.2.60. Ht 5 10
Wt 10 11
Forward. From Apprentice.

Season	Club	App	Goals
1976–77	Orient....................	—	—
1977–78	....	11	—
1978–79	....	6	—
1979–80	....	5	1
1980–81	....	9	2
1981–82	....	42	8
1982–83	....	45	11
1983–84	....	41	10
1984–85	....	40	10
1985–86	....	16	4
1985–86	*Plymouth Arg*...............	7	1
1986–87	Orient	36	10
1987–88	....	34	7
1988–89	Brentford	29	8
1989–90	....	27	2
1990–91	....	32	4
1991–92	....	31	3
1992–93	....	21	—

GODFREY, Warren

Born Liverpool 31.3.73 Ht 5 11
Wt 11 02
Midfield. From Trainee.

Season	Club	App	Goals
1991–92	Liverpool	—	—
1992–93	Barnsley	8	—

GOLDRING, Mark

Born Brighton 17.9.72. Ht 6 2 Wt 13 00
Goalkeeper. From Trainee.

Season	Club	App	Goals
1991–92	Chesterfield	7	—
1992–93	....	—	—

GOODACRE, Sam

Born Sheffield 1.12.70 Ht 5 7 Wt 10 12
Forward. From school.

Season	Club	App	Goals
1989–90	Sheffield W.................	—	—
1990–91	....	—	—
1991–92	Scunthorpe U	—	—
1992–93	....	21	9

GOODING, Mick

Born Newcastle 12.4.59. Ht 5 7
Wt 10 13
Forward. From Bishop Auckland.

1979–80	Rotherham U	34	3
1980–81		37	4
1981–82		22	2
1982–83		9	1
1982–83	Chesterfield	12	—
1983–84		—	—
1983–84	Rotherham U	26	7
1984–85		44	10
1985–86		40	8
1986–87		46	8
1987–88	Peterborough U	44	18
1988–89		3	3
1988–89	Wolverhampton W	31	4
1989–90		13	—
1989–90	Reading	27	3
1990–91		44	7
1991–92		40	3
1992–93		40	3

GOODMAN, Don

Born Leeds 9.5.66. Ht 5 10 Wt 11 10
Forward. From School.

1983–84	Bradford C	2	—
1984–85		25	5
1985–86		20	4
1986–87		23	5
1986–87	WBA	10	2
1987–88		40	7
1988–89		36	15
1989–90		39	21
1990–91		22	8
1991–92		11	7
1991–92	Sunderland	22	11
1992–93		41	16

GOODMAN, Jon

Born Walthamstow 2.6.71. Ht 5 11
Wt 12 11
Forward. From Bromley. Football League.

1990–91	Millwall	23	5
1991–92		17	3

1992–93		35	12

GOODWIN, Craig

Born Wrexham 12.2.74
Defender. From Aston Villa trainee.

1992–93	Chester C	5	—

GOODWIN, Shaun

Born Rotherham 14.6.69. Ht 5 8
Wt 10 11
Midfield. From Trainee.

1987–88	Rotherham U	3	—
1988–89		41	4
1989–90		38	6
1990–91		34	3
1991–92		39	5
1992–93		30	1

GORAM, Andy

Born Bury 13.4.64. Ht 5 11 Wt 11 06
Goalkeeper. From West Bromwich
Apprentice. Scotland Under-21, 28 full
caps.

1981–82	Oldham Ath	3	—
1982–83		38	—
1983–84		22	—
1984–85		41	—
1985–86		41	—
1986–87		41	—
1987–88		9	—
1987–88	Hibernian	33	1
1988–89		36	—
1989–90		34	—
1990–91		35	—
1991–92	Rangers	44	—
1992–93		34	—

GORDON, Colin

Born Stourbridge 17.1.63. Ht 6 1
Wt 12 12
Forward. From Oldbury U.

1984–85	Swindon T	33	17

Season	Club		
1985–86	....	39	16
1986–87	Wimbledon	3	—
1986–87	*Gillingham*	4	2
1987–88	Reading......................	20	8
1987–88	*Bristol C*......................	8	4
1988–89	Reading......................	4	1
1988–89	Fulham	17	2
1989–90	Birmingham C	21	3
1990–91	....	5	—
1990–91	*Hereford U*................	6	—
1990–91	*Walsall*......................	6	1
1990–91	*Bristol R*....................	4	—
1991–92	Leicester C.................	21	5
1992–93	....	3	—

GORDON, Dale

Born Gt Yarmouth 9.1.67.   Ht 5 10
Wt 11 08
Forward. From Apprentice. England
Schools, Youth B, Under-21.

Season	Club		
1983–84	Norwich C	—	—
1984–85	....	23	3
1985–86	....	6	1
1986–87	....	41	5
1987–88	....	21	3
1988–89	....	38	5
1989–90	....	26	3
1990–91	....	36	7
1991–92	....	15	4
1991–92	Rangers......................	23	5
1992–93	....	22	1

GORDON, Dean

Born Croydon 10.2.73.   Ht 6 0   Wt 11 05
Midfield.

Season	Club		
1991–92	Crystal Palace.............	4	—
1992–93	....	10	—

GORE, Ian

Born Liverpool 10.1.68.   Ht 5 11
Wt 12 04
Midfield.

Season	Club		
1986–87	Birmingham C	—	—
From Southport			
1987–88	Blackpool......................	—	—

Season	Club		
1988–89	....	21	—
1989–90	....	34	—
1990–91	....	41	—
1991–92	....	41	—
1992–93	....	30	—

GORMAN, Andy

Born Cardiff 13.9.74.   Ht 5 11   Wt 13 03
Defender. From Trainee.

Season	Club		
1991–92	Cardiff C....................	11	—
1992–93	....	1	1

GORMAN, Paul

Born Macclesfield 18.9.68.   Ht 5 9
Wt 12 02
Forward.

Season	Club		
1987–88	Doncaster R................	7	1
1988–89	....	9	1
From Fisher Ath			
1990–91	Charlton Ath	8	2
1991–92	....	8	3
1992–93	....	10	2

GORMLEY, Eddie

Born Dublin 23.10.68.   Ht 5 7   Wt 10 07
Midfield. From Bray W. Eire Youth,
Under-21.

Season	Club		
1987–88	Tottenham H	—	—
1988–89	....	—	—
1988–89	*Chesterfield*	4	—
1988–89	*Motherwell*	—	—
1989–90	Tottenham H	—	—
1989–90	*Shrewsbury T*	—	—
1990–91	Doncaster R................	40	5
1991–92	....	37	5
1992–93	....	41	6

GOSNEY, Andy

Born Southampton 8.11.63.   Ht 6 4
Wt 13 02
Goalkeeper. From Apprentice. England
Youth.

Season	Club		
1981–82	Portsmouth	1	—

Season	Club	League Appearances/Goals	
1982–83		—	—
1983–84		—	—
1984–85		—	—
1985–86		4	—
1986–87		—	—
1987–88		4	—
1988–89		14	—
1989–90		—	—
1990–91		24	—
1991–92		1	—
1991–92	*York C*	5	—
1992–93	Birmingham C	21	—

GOSS, Jeremy

Born Cyprus 11.5.65.   Ht 5 9   Wt 10 09
Midfield. Amateur. England Youth, Wales
3 full caps.

Season	Club	League Appearances/Goals	
1982–83	Norwich C	—	—
1983–84		1	—
1984–85		5	—
1985–86		—	—
1986–87		1	—
1987–88		22	2
1988–89		—	—
1989–90		7	—
1990–91		19	1
1991–92		33	1
1992–93		25	1

GOUCK, Andy

Born Blackpool 8.6.72.   Ht 5 9   Wt 11 02
Midfield. From Trainee.

Season	Club	League Appearances/Goals	
1989–90	Blackpool	8	1
1990–91		5	—
1991–92		24	2
1992–93		29	4

GOUGH, Alan

Born Watford 10.3.71   Ht 5 11   Wt 12 13
Goalkeeper. From Shelbourne.

Season	Club	League Appearances/Goals	
1989–90	Portsmouth	—	—
1990–91		—	—
1991–92		—	—
1992–93	Fulham	3	—

GOUGH, Richard

Born Stockholm 5.4.62.   Ht 6 0   Wt 12 00
Defender. From Witz University. Scotland
Under-21, 61 full caps.

Season	Club	League Appearances/Goals	
1980–81	Dundee U	4	—
1981–82		30	1
1982–83		34	8
1983–84		33	3
1984–85		33	6
1985–86		31	5
1986–87	Tottenham H	40	2
1987–88		9	—
1987–88	Rangers	31	5
1988–89		35	4
1989–90		26	—
1990–91		26	—
1991–92		33	2
1992–93		25	2

GOULD, Jonathan

Born Paddington 18.7.68.   Ht 6 1
Wt 12 07
Goalkeeper.

Season	Club	League Appearances/Goals	
1990–91	Halifax T	23	—
1991–92		9	—
1991–92	WBA	—	—
1992–93	Coventry C	9	—

GOULOOZE, Richard

Born Holland 16.11.67
Defender. From SC Heerenveen.

Season	Club	League Appearances/Goals	
1992–93	Derby Co	12	—

GOURLAY, Archie

Born Greenock 29.6.69.   Ht 5 8   Wt 10 00
Midfield.

Season	Club	League Appearances/Goals	
1987–88	Morton	2	—
1987–88	Newcastle U	—	—
1988–89		1	—
1989–90		—	—
1989–90	*Morton*	4	—
1990–91	Newcastle U	2	—
1991–92		—	—

1991–92	Motherwell	1 —
1992–93		2 —

GRAHAM, Alastair

Born Glasgow 11.8.66   Ht 6 3   Wt 12 7
Forward. From Anniesland U.

1984–85	Clydebank	1 —
1985–86		2 —
1986–87		— —
1987–88	Albion R	28 10
1988–89		39 15
1989–90		31 7
1990–91	Ayr U	38 8
1991–92		40 14
1992–93		30 9
1992–93	Motherwell	4 1

GRAHAM, Deniol

Born Cannock 4.10.69.   Ht 5 10
Wt 10 05
Forward. From Trainee. Wales Under-21.

1987–88	Manchester U	1 —
1988–89		— —
1989–90		1 —
1990–91		— —
1991–92	Barnsley	21 1
1992–93		15 1
1992–93	*Preston NE*	8 —

GRAHAM, Jimmy

Born Glasgow 15.11.69.   Ht 5 11
Wt 11 00
Defender. From Trainee.

1988–89	Bradford C	1 —
1989–90		6 —
1989–90	*Rochdale*	11 —
1990–91	Rochdale	28 1
1991–92		31 —
1992–93		38 —

GRAINGER, Martin

Born Enfield 23.8.72   Ht 5 11   Wt 12 00
Defender. From Trainee.

1989–90	Colchester U	7 2

1990–91		5 —
1991–92		18 —
1992–93		31 3

GRANT, Brian

Born Bannockburn 19.6.64.   Ht 5 9
Wt 10 07
Midfield. From Fallin Violet.

1981–82	Stirling Alb	1 —
1982–83		1 —
1983–84		24 3
1984–85	Aberdeen	— —
1985–86		— —
1986–87		15 4
1987–88		7 1
1988–89		26 1
1989–90		31 6
1990–91		32 2
1991–92		33 6
1992–93		29 3

GRANT, Kim

Born Ghana 25.9.72.   Ht 5 10   Wt 10 12
Forward. From Trainee.

1990–91	Charlton Ath	12 2
1991–92		4 —
1992–93		21 2

GRANT, Peter

Born Bellshill 30.8.65.   Ht 5 9   Wt 10 03
Midfield. From Celtic BC. Scotland
Schools, Youth, B, Under-21, 2 full caps.

1982–83	Celtic	— —
1983–84		3 —
1984–85		20 4
1985–86		30 1
1986–87		37 1
1987–88		37 2
1988–89		21 —
1989–90		26 —
1990–91		27 —
1991–92		22 —
1992–93		31 2

GRAY, Andy

Born Lambeth 22.2.64.   Ht 5 11
Wt 13 03
Midfield. From Corinthian C. and
Dulwich H. England Under-21, 1 full cap.

Season	Club		
1984–85	Crystal Palace	21	5
1985–86		30	10
1986–87		30	6
1987–88		17	6
1987–88	Aston Villa	19	1
1988–89		18	3
1988–89	QPR	11	2
1989–90	Crystal Palace	35	6
1990–91		30	4
1991–92		25	2
1991–92	*Tottenham H*	14	1
1992–93	Tottenham H	17	1
1992–93	*Swindon T*	3	—

GRAY, Andy

Born Southampton 25.10.73.   Ht 5 6
Wt 10 10
Forward. From Trainee.

Season	Club		
1991–92	Reading	1	—
1992–93		11	3

GRAY, Kevin

Born Sheffield 7.1.72.   Ht 6 0   Wt 13 08
Midfield. From Trainee.

Season	Club		
1988–89	Mansfield T	1	—
1989–90		16	—
1990–91		31	1
1991–92		18	—
1992–93		33	—

GRAY, Martin

Born Stockton 17.8.71.   Ht 5 9   Wt 10 11
Midfield. From Trainee.

Season	Club		
1989–90	Sunderland	—	—
1990–91		—	—
1990–91	*Aldershot*	5	—
1991–92	Sunderland	1	—
1992–93		12	1

GRAY, Michael

Born Sunderland 3.8.74
Defender. From Trainee.

Season	Club		
1992–93	Sunderland	27	2

GRAY, Paul

Born Portsmouth 28.1.70.   Ht 5 9
Wt 11 08
Forward. From Trainee.

Season	Club		
1988–89	Luton T	—	—
1989–90		7	1
1990–91		—	—
1991–92	Wigan Ath	5	—
1992–93		—	—

GRAY, Philip

Born Belfast 2.10.68.   Ht 5 10   Wt 12 03
Forward. From Apprentice. Northern
Ireland Schools, Youth, Under-23, 4 full
caps.

Season	Club		
1986–87	Tottenham H	1	—
1987–88		1	—
1988–89		1	—
1989–90		—	—
1989–90	*Barnsley*	3	—
1990–91	Tottenham H	6	—
1990–91	*Fulham*	3	—
1991–92	Luton T	14	3
1992–93		45	19

GRAY, Stuart

Born Withernsea 19.4.60.   Ht 5 10
Wt 11 09
Defender. From Local.

Season	Club		
1980–81	Nottingham F	14	1
1981–82		33	2
1982–83		2	—
1982–83	*Bolton W*	10	—
1983–84	Barnsley	17	8
1984–85		7	—
1985–86		36	2
1986–87		40	11
1987–88		20	2

Season	Club	App	Goals
1987–88	Aston Villa	20	5
1988–89		35	4
1989–90		29	—
1990–91		22	—
1991–92		—	—
1991–92	Southampton	12	—
1992–93		—	—

GRAY, Stuart

Born Harrogate 18.12.73   Ht 5 11
Wt 11 0
Midfield. From Giffnock N.

Season	Club	App	Goals
1992–93	Celtic	1	0

GRAYSON, Simon

Born Ripon 16.12.69.   Ht 5 11   Wt 12 13
Defender. From Trainee.

Season	Club	App	Goals
1987–88	Leeds U	2	—
1988–89		—	—
1989–90		—	—
1990–91		—	—
1991–92		—	—
1991–92	Leicester C	13	—
1992–93		24	1

GREAVES, Steve

Born London 17.1.70   Ht 5 9   Wt 11 09
Midfield. From Trainee.

Season	Club	App	Goals
1987–88	Fulham	1	—
1988–89		—	—
1988–89	*Waterford*	—	—
1989–90	Fulham	—	—
1989–90	*Brighton*	—	—
1990–91	Preston NE	2	—
1991–92	Ipswich T	—	—
1992–93	Scunthorpe U	15	—

GREEN, Richard

Born Wolverhampton 22.11.67.   Ht 6 1
Wt 13 11
Defender.

Season	Club	App	Goals
1986–87	Shrewsbury T	15	—
1987–88		31	2

Season	Club	App	Goals
1988–89		39	3
1989–90		40	—
1990–91		—	—
1990–91	Swindon T	—	—
1991–92		—	—
1991–92	Gillingham	12	4
1992–93		39	3

GREEN, Ron

Born Birmingham 3.10.56   Ht 6 2
Wt 14 00
Goalkeeper. From Alvechurch.

Season	Club	App	Goals
1977–78	Walsall	1	—
1978–79		1	—
1979–80		39	—
1980–81		24	—
1981–82		46	—
1982–83		35	—
1983–84		17	—
1983–84	*WBA*	—	—
1984–85	Shrewsbury T	19	—
1984–85	*Bristol R.*	18	—
1985–86	Bristol R	38	—
1986–87	Scunthorpe U	43	—
1987–88		35	—
1988–89	Wimbledon	4	—
1988–89	*Shrewsbury T*	17	—
1988–89	*Manchester C*	—	—
1988–89	Walsall	2	—
1989–90		21	—
1990–91		44	—
From Local			
1992–93	Colchester U	4	—
1992–93	Cambridge U	—	—
1992–93	Shrewsbury T	—	—

GREEN, Scott

Born Walsall 15.1.70.   Ht 6 0   Wt 11 12
Forward. From Trainee.

Season	Club	App	Goals
1988–89	Derby Co	—	—
1989–90		—	—
1989–90	Bolton W	5	2
1990–91		41	6
1991–92		37	2
1992–93		41	6

GREENALL, Colin

Born Billinge 30.12.63. Ht 5 10 Wt 11 06
Defender. From Apprentice.

1980–81	Blackpool	12	—
1981–82		18	—
1982–83		24	1
1983–84		39	4
1984–85		44	3
1985–86		43	1
1986–87		3	—
1986–87	Gillingham	37	2
1987–88		25	2
1987–88	Oxford U	12	—
1988–89		40	2
1989–90		15	—
1989–90	*Bury*	3	—
1990–91	Bury	31	—
1991–92		37	5
1991–92	Preston NE	9	1
1992–93		20	—

GREENE, David

Born Luton 26.10.73 Ht 6 2 Wt 13 05
Defender. From Trainee.

1991–92	Luton T	—	—
1992–93		1	—

GREENHALGH, Laurie

Born Salford 2.4.74 Ht 5 10 Wt 11 00
Defender. From Trainee.

1992–93	Bury	2	—

GREENMAN, Chris

Born Bristol 22.12.68. Ht 5 10 Wt 11 06
Defender. From School.

1988–89	Coventry C	—	—
1989–90		—	—
1990–91		—	—
1991–92		4	—
1992–93		2	—
1992–93	Peterborough U	9	—

GREENWOOD, Nigel

Born Preston 27.11.66. Ht 5 11 Wt 12 00
Forward. From Apprentice.

1984–85	Preston NE	15	5
1985–86		30	9
1986–87	Bury	37	15
1987–88		30	4
1988–89		23	1
1989–90		20	5
1989–90	Preston NE	5	—
1990–91		5	1
1991–92		20	3
1992–93	Halifax T	25	5

GREGAN, Sean

Born Cleveland 29.3.74. Ht 6 2 Wt 13 7
Defender. From Trainee.

1991–92	Darlington	17	—
1992–93		17	1

GREGORY, David

Born Sudbury 23.1.70. Ht 5 11 Wt 11 10
Midfield. From Trainee.

1987–88	Ipswich T	—	—
1988–89		2	—
1989–90		4	—
1990–91		21	—
1991–92		1	—
1992–93		3	1

GREW, Mark

Born Bilston 15.2.58. Ht 5 11 Wt 12 08
Goalkeeper. From Amateur.

1976–77	WBA	—	—
1977–78		—	—
1978–79		—	—
1978–79	*Wigan Ath*	4	—
1978–79	*Notts Co*	—	—
1979–80	WBA	—	—
1980–81		—	—
1981–82		23	—
1982–83		10	—
1983–84	Leicester C	5	—

Season	Club	App	Goals
1983–84	Oldham Ath	5	—
1983–84	Ipswich T	—	—
1984–85		6	—
1985–86		—	—
1985–86	Fulham	4	—
1985–86	WBA	1	—
1985–86	Derby Co	—	—
1986–87	Port Vale	3	—
1987–88		41	—
1988–89		37	—
1989–90		43	—
1990–91		14	—
1990–91	Blackburn R	13	—
1991–92	Port Vale	46	—
1992–93	Cardiff C	10	—

GREYGOOSE, Dean

Born Thetford 18.12.64. Ht 5 11
Wt 11 05
Goalkeeper. From Apprentice. England
Youth.

Season	Club	App	Goals
1982–83	Cambridge U	—	—
1983–84		16	—
1984–85		10	—
1984–85	Orient	—	—
1985–86	Cambridge U	—	—
1985–86	Lincoln C	6	—
1985–86	Orient	1	—
1986–87		—	—
1986–87	C. Palace	—	—
1987–88		—	—
1987–88	Crewe Alex	43	—
1988–89		36	—
1989–90		32	—
1990–91		31	—
1991–92		33	—
1992–93		30	—

GRIDELET, Phil

Born Edgware 30.4.67. Ht 5 11 Wt 12 00
Midfield. From Watford, Hendon, Barnet.

Season	Club	App	Goals
1990–91	Barnsley	4	—
1991–92		—	—
1992–93		2	—
1992–93	Rotherham U	9	—

GRIFFIN, James

Born Hamilton 1.1.67. Ht 5 8 Wt 11 04
Defender. From Fir Park BC.

Season	Club	App	Goals
1985–86	Motherwell	1	—
1986–87		—	—
1987–88		6	—
1988–89		1	—
1989–90		11	—
1990–91		23	4
1991–92		22	1
1992–93		25	1

GRIFFITH, Cohen

Born Georgetown 26.12.62. Ht 5 10
Wt 11 07
Forward. From Kettering T.

Season	Club	App	Goals
1989–90	Cardiff C	38	9
1990–91		45	9
1991–92		37	1
1992–93		34	10

GRIFFITHS, Brian

Born Prescot 26.1.65. Ht 5 9 Wt 11 00
Forward. From St Helens T.

Season	Club	App	Goals
1988–89	Wigan Ath	29	8
1989–90		45	7
1990–91		43	12
1991–92		28	4
1992–93		44	13

GRIFFITHS, Carl

Born Coventry 15.7.71. Ht 5 9 Wt 10 06
Forward. From Trainee. Wales Youth,
Under-21.

Season	Club	App	Goals
1988–89	Shrewsbury T	28	6
1989–90		18	4
1990–91		19	4
1991–92		27	8
1992–93		42	27

GRIFFITHS, Neil

Born Halifax 4.9.72. Ht 6 1 Wt 12 00
Defender. From Trainee.

Season	Club	App	Goals
1990–91	Halifax T	1	—

Season	Club	Apps	Goals
1991–92	....	2	—
1992–93	....	1	—

GRITT, Steve

Born Bournemouth 31.10.57. Ht 5 9
Wt 10 10
Midfield. From Apprentice.

Season	Club	Apps	Goals
1976–77	Bournemouth..............	6	3
1977–78	Charlton Ath	34	3
1978–79	....	39	3
1979–80	....	31	7
1980–81	....	40	—
1981–82	....	34	3
1982–83	....	27	1
1983–84	....	33	1
1984–85	....	35	1
1985–86	....	11	2
1986–87	....	14	1
1987–88	....	27	—
1988–89	....	22	2
1989–90	Walsall.....................	20	1
1989–90	Charlton Ath	2	—
1990–91	....	10	—
1991–92	....	14	1
1992–93	....	7	—

GROBBELAAR, Bruce

Born Durban 6.10.57. Ht 6 1 Wt 13 00
Goalkeeper. From Vancouver Whitecaps.
Zimbabwe full caps.

Season	Club	Apps	Goals
1979–80	Crewe Alex	24	1
From Vancouver Whitecaps			
1980–81	Liverpool	—	—
1981–82	....	42	—
1982–83	....	42	—
1983–84	....	42	—
1984–85	....	42	—
1985–86	....	42	—
1986–87	....	31	—
1987–88	....	38	—
1988–89	....	21	—
1989–90	....	38	—
1990–91	....	31	—
1991–92	....	37	—
1992–93	....	5	—
1992–93	Stoke C	4	—

GROVES, Paul

Born Derby 28.2.66. Ht 5 11 Wt 11 05
Midfield. From Burton Alb.

Season	Club	Apps	Goals
1987–88	Leicester C..................	1	1
1988–89	....	15	—
1989–90	....	—	—
1989–90	Lincoln C	8	1
1989–90	Blackpool.....................	19	1
1990–91	....	46	11
1991–92	....	42	9
1992–93	Grimsby T	46	12

GROVES, Perry

Born London 19.4.65. Ht 5 10 Wt 12 08
Forward. From Apprentice.

Season	Club	Apps	Goals
1981–82	Colchester U	9	—
1982–83	....	17	2
1983–84	....	42	2
1984–85	....	44	10
1985–86	....	43	12
1986–87	....	1	—
1986–87	Arsenal......................	25	3
1987–88	....	34	6
1988–89	....	21	4
1989–90	....	30	4
1990–91	....	32	3
1991–92	....	13	1
1992–93	....	1	—
1992–93	Southampton	15	2

GUENTCHEV, Bontcho

Born Bulgaria 7.7.64. Ht 5 10 Wt 11 07
Forward. From Etar, Locomotiv, Sporting
Lisbon. Bulgaria full caps.

Season	Club	Apps	Goals
1992–93	Ipswich T...................	21	3

GUNN, Bryan

Born Thurso 22.12.63. Ht 6 2 Wt 13 13
Goalkeeper. From Invergordon BC.
Scotland Schools, Youth, Under-21, B, 3
full caps.

Season	Club	Apps	Goals
1980–81	Aberdeen.....................	—	—
1981–82	....	—	—

Season	Club	App	Goals
1982–83		1	—
1983–84		—	—
1984–85		2	—
1985–86		10	—
1986–87		2	—
1986–87	Norwich C	29	—
1987–88		38	—
1988–89		37	—
1989–90		37	—
1990–91		34	—
1991–92		25	—
1992–93		42	—

GYNN, Mick

Born Peterborough 19.8.61.   Ht 5 5
Wt 10 10
Midfield. From Apprentice.

Season	Club	App	Goals
1978–79	Peterborough U	11	2
1979–80		27	1
1980–81		29	7
1981–82		46	6
1982–83		43	17
1983–84	Coventry C	23	2
1984–85		39	4
1985–86		12	1
1986–87		22	5
1987–88		25	3
1988–89		8	1
1989–90		34	3
1990–91		35	8
1991–92		23	3
1992–93		20	2

HAAG, Kelly

Born Enfield 6.10.70.   Ht 6 0   Wt 12 03
Forward. From Trainee.

Season	Club	App	Goals
1989–90	Brentford	5	—
1990–91	Fulham	23	3
1991–92		34	6
1992–93		10	—

HACKETT, Gary

Born Stourbridge 11.10.62.   Ht 5 7
Wt 11 03
Forward. From Bromsgrove R.

Season	Club	App	Goals
1983–84	Shrewsbury T	31	3
1984–85		38	5
1985–86		42	6
1986–87		39	3
1987–88	Aberdeen	15	—
1987–88	Stoke C	1	—
1988–89		46	5
1989–90		26	2
1989–90	WBA	14	2
1990–91		5	—
1991–92		15	—
1992–93		10	1

HACKETT, Warren

Born Newham 16.12.71.   Ht 5 9
Wt 11 12
Defender. From Tottenham H Trainee.

Season	Club	App	Goals
1990–91	Leyton Orient	—	—
1991–92		22	—
1992–93		17	—

HAGEN, David

Born Edinburgh 5.5.73   Ht 5 11   Wt 13 0
Midfield. From Grahamston BC.

Season	Club	App	Goals
1989–90	Rangers	—	—
1990–91		—	—
1991–92		—	—
1992–93		8	2

HAGUE, Paul

Born Durham 16.9.72.   Ht 6 2   Wt 12 06
Defender. From Trainee.

Season	Club	Apps	Goals
1990–91	Gillingham	7	—
1991–92		—	—
1992–93		1	—

HAILS, Julian

Born Lincoln 20.11.67.   Ht 5 10
Wt 11 01
Forward.

Season	Club	Apps	Goals
1989–90	Fulham	—	—
1990–91		—	—
1991–92		18	1
1992–93		46	6

HALES, Kevin

Born Dartford 13.1.61.   Ht 5 7   Wt 10 04
Defender. From Apprentice.

Season	Club	Apps	Goals
1978–79	Chelsea	—	—
1979–80		7	—
1980–81		—	—
1981–82		10	2
1982–83		3	—
1983–84	Orient	43	2
1984–85		33	—
1985–86		31	2
1986–87		33	1
1987–88		42	6
1988–89		35	9
1989–90		39	2
1990–91		5	—
1991–92		10	—
1992–93		29	1

HALL, Derek

Born Manchester 5.1.65.   Ht 5 8
Wt 12 03
Midfield. From Apprentice.

Season	Club	Apps	Goals
1982–83	Coventry C	1	—
1983–84		—	—
1983–84	*Torquay U*	10	2
1984–85	Torquay U	45	4

Season	Club	Apps	Goals
1985–86	Swindon T	10	—
1986–87	Southend U	43	9
1987–88		40	3
1988–89		40	3
1989–90	Halifax T	41	4
1990–91		8	—
1991–92	Hereford U	20	—
1992–93		41	9

HALL, Gareth

Born Croydon 20.3.69.   Ht 5 8   Wt 10 07
Defender. Wales Under-21, 9 full caps.

Season	Club	Apps	Goals
1986–87	Chelsea	1	—
1987–88		13	—
1988–89		22	—
1989–90		13	1
1990–91		24	—
1991–92		10	—
1992–93		37	2

HALL, Mark

Born London 13.1.73.   Ht 5 6   Wt 10 12
Midfield. From Tottenham H Trainee.

Season	Club	Apps	Goals
1991–92	Southend U	3	—
1992–93		9	—

HALL, Paul

Born Manchester 3.7.72.   Ht 5 9
Wt 10 02
Forward. From Trainee.

Season	Club	Apps	Goals
1989–90	Torquay U	10	—
1990–91		17	—
1991–92		38	1
1992–93		28	—
1992–93	Portsmouth	—	—

HALL, Richard

Born Ipswich 14.3.72.   Ht 6 2   Wt 13 01
Defender. From Trainee. England
Under-21.

Season	Club	Apps	Goals
1989–90	Scunthorpe U	1	—
1990–91		21	3

1990–91	Southampton	1	—
1991–92		26	3
1992–93		28	4

HALL, Wayne

Born Rotherham 25.10.68 Ht 5 9
Wt 10 04
Midfield. From Darlington.

1988–89	York C	2	—
1989–90		27	3
1990–91		46	1
1991–92		37	3
1992–93		42	1

HALLE, Gunnar

Born Oslo 11.8.65. Ht 5 11 Wt 11 02
Defender. From Lillestrom. Norway full
caps.

1990–91	Oldham Ath	17	—
1991–92		10	—
1992–93		41	5

HALLWORTH, Jon

Born Stockport 26.10.65. Ht 6 1
Wt 14 03
Goalkeeper. From School.

1983–84	Ipswich T	—	—
1984–85		—	—
1984–85	*Swindon T*	—	—
1984–85	*Fulham*	—	—
1984–85	*Bristol R*	2	—
1985–86	Ipswich T	6	—
1986–87		6	—
1987–88		33	—
1988–89		—	—
1988–89	Oldham Ath	16	—
1989–90		15	—
1990–91		46	—
1991–92		41	—
1992–93		16	—

HALSALL, Mick

Born Bootle 21.7.61. Ht 5 10 Wt 11 04
Midfield. From Apprentice.

1979–80	Liverpool	—	—

1980–81		—	—
1981–82		—	—
1982–83		—	—
1982–83	Birmingham C	12	1
1983–84		21	2
1984–85		3	—
1984–85	Carlisle U	26	5
1985–86		41	4
1986–87		25	2
1986–87	Grimsby T	12	—
1987–88	Peterborough U	45	4
1988–89		42	1
1989–90		46	10
1990–91		45	6
1991–92		45	5
1992–93		25	2

HAMILTON, Brian

Born Paisley 5.8.67. Ht 6 0 Wt 11 07
Midfield. From Pollok United BC.
Scotland Schools, Under-21.

1985–86	St Mirren	8	—
1986–87		28	3
1987–88		27	—
1988–89		23	1
1989–90	Hibernian	28	1
1990–91		26	2
1991–92		40	3
1992–93		41	1

HAMILTON, Ian

Born Stevenage 14.12.67. Ht 5 9
Wt 11 03
Forward. From Apprentice.

1985–86	Southampton	—	—
1986–87		—	—
1987–88		—	—
1987–88	Cambridge U	9	1
1988–89		15	—
1988–89	Scunthorpe U	27	1
1989–90		43	6
1990–91		34	2
1991–92		41	9
1992–93	WBA	46	7

HAMMOND, Nicky

Born Hornchurch 7.9.67.   Ht 6 0
Wt 11 13
Goalkeeper. From Apprentice.

Season	Club	App	Goals
1985–86	Arsenal	—	—
1986–87		—	—
1986–87	*Bristol R*	3	—
1986–87	*Peterborough U*	—	—
1986–87	*Aberdeen*	—	—
1987–88	Swindon T	4	—
1988–89		—	—
1989–90		—	—
1990–91		5	—
1991–92		25	—
1992–93		13	—

HAMON, Chris

Born Jersey 27.4.70   Ht 6 1   Wt 13 07
Forward. From St Peter.

Season	Club	App	Goals
1992–93	Swindon T	2	—

HANCOX, Richard

Born Stourbridge 14.10.70
Midfield. From Stourbridge Swifts.

Season	Club	App	Goals
1992–93	Torquay U	7	—

HANDYSIDE, Peter

Born Dumfries 31.7.74   Ht 6 1   Wt 12 03
Defender. From Trainee. Scotland
Under-21.

Season	Club	App	Goals
1992–93	Grimsby T	11	—

HANNAH, David

Born Coatbridge 4.8.74   Ht 5 11   Wt 11 1
Midfield. From Hamilton Th.

Season	Club	App	Goals
1991–92	Dundee U	—	—
1992–93		5	—

HARBEY, Graham

Born Chesterfield 29.8.64.   Ht 5 8
Wt 11 08
Defender. From Apprentice.

Season	Club	App	Goals
1982–83	Derby Co	—	—

Season	Club	App	Goals
1983–84		19	—
1984–85		4	1
1985–86		3	—
1986–87		14	—
1987–88	Ipswich T	35	1
1988–89		23	—
1989–90		1	—
1989–90	WBA	30	—
1990–91		21	1
1991–92		46	1
1992–93	Stoke C	17	—

HARDING, Paul

Born Mitcham 6.3.64.   Ht 5 9   Wt 12 05
Midfield. From Barnet.

Season	Club	App	Goals
1990–91	Notts Co	24	—
1991–92		29	1
1992–93		1	—

HARDY, Jason

Born Burnley 14.12.69.   Ht 5 10
Wt 11 04
Midfield. From Trainee.

Season	Club	App	Goals
1986–87	Burnley	1	—
1987–88		—	—
1988–89		17	1
1989–90		22	—
1990–91		—	—
1991–92		3	—
1991–92	*Halifax T*	4	—
1992–93	Halifax T	22	2

HARDY, Phil

Born Chester 9.4.73.   Ht 5 8   Wt 11 00
Defender.

Season	Club	App	Goals
1989–90	Wrexham	1	—
1990–91		32	—
1991–92		42	—
1992–93		32	—

HARDYMAN, Paul

Born Portsmouth 11.3.64.   Ht 5 8
Wt 11 07
Defender. From Local. England Under-21.

Season	Club	App	Goals
1983–84	Portsmouth	3	—

Season	Club	Apps	Goals
1984–85		15	—
1985–86		21	1
1986–87		33	—
1987–88		20	1
1988–89		25	1
1989–90	Sunderland	42	7
1990–91		32	—
1991–92		32	2
1992–93	Bristol R	37	4

HARFORD, Mick

Born Sunderland 12.2.59. Ht 6 3
Wt 14 05
Forward. From Lambton St BC. England
B, 2 full caps.

Season	Club	Apps	Goals
1977–78	Lincoln C	27	9
1978–79		31	6
1979–80		36	16
1980–81		21	10
1980–81	Newcastle U	19	4
1981–82	Bristol C	30	11
1981–82	Birmingham C	12	9
1982–83		29	6
1983–84		39	8
1984–85		12	2
1984–85	Luton T	22	15
1985–86		37	22
1986–87		18	4
1987–88		25	9
1988–89		33	7
1989–90		4	—
1989–90	Derby Co	16	4
1990–91		36	8
1991–92		6	3
1991–92	Luton T	29	12
1992–93	Chelsea	28	9
1992–93	Sunderland	11	2

HARGREAVES, Christian

Born Cleethorpes 12.5.72. Ht 5 1
Wt 11 00
Forward. From Trainee.

Season	Club	Apps	Goals
1989–90	Grimsby T	19	2
1990–91		18	3
1991–92		10	—
1992–93		4	—

Season	Club	Apps	Goals
1992–93	*Scarborough*	3	—

HARKES, John

Born New Jersey 8.3.67. Ht 5 10
Wt 11 10
Midfield. From United States Soccer
Federation. USA full caps.

Season	Club	Apps	Goals
1990–91	Sheffield W	23	2
1991–92		29	3
1992–93		29	2

HARKNESS, Steve

Born Carlisle 27.8.71. Ht 5 10 Wt 11 02
Midfield. From Trainee. England Youth.

Season	Club	Apps	Goals
1988–89	Carlisle U	13	—
1989–90	Liverpool	—	—
1990–91		—	—
1991–92		11	—
1992–93		10	1

HARMON, Darren

Born Northampton 30.1.73. Ht 5 5
Wt 9 12
Midfield. From Trainee.

Season	Club	Apps	Goals
1991–92	Notts Co	—	—
1991–92	Shrewsbury T	5	2
1992–93		1	—
1992–93	Northampton T	25	1

HARPER, Alan

Born Liverpool 1.11.60. Ht 5 8 Wt 10 09
Defender. From Apprentice. England
Youth.

Season	Club	Apps	Goals
1977–78	Liverpool	—	—
1978–79		—	—
1979–80		—	—
1980–81		—	—
1981–82		—	—
1982–83		—	—
1983–84	Everton	29	1
1984–85		13	—
1985–86		21	—

1986–87		36	3
1987–88		28	—
1988–89	Sheffield W	24	—
1989–90		11	—
1989–90	Manchester C	21	—
1990–91		29	1
1991–92	Everton	33	—
1992–93		18	—

HARPER, Steve

Born Stoke 3.2.69. Ht 5 10 Wt 11 05
Forward. From Trainee.

1987–88	Port Vale	21	2
1988–89		7	—
1988–89	Preston NE	5	—
1989–90		36	10
1990–91		36	—
1991–92	Burnley	35	3
1992–93		34	5

HARRIOTT, Marvin

Born Dulwich 20.4.74.
Defender. From West Ham U trainee.
England Youth.

1991–92	Oldham Ath	—	—
1992–93		—	—
199s–93	Barnsley	—	—

HARRIS, Andy

Born Birmingham 17.11.70. Ht 5 10
Wt 12 02
Midfield. From Trainee.

1989–90	Birmingham C	1	—
1990–91		—	—
1991–92		—	—
1991–92	Oxford U	1	—
1991–92	Exeter C	6	—
1992–93		28	1

HARRIS, Mark

Born Reading 15.7.63. Ht 6 1 Wt 12 05
Defender. From Wokingham.

1987–88	Crystal Palace	—	—

HARRISON, Gerry

Born Lambeth 15.4.72. Ht 5 10
Wt 12 12
Midfield. From Trainee.

1988–89		2	—
1989–90		—	—
1989–90	Burnley	4	—
1989–90	Swansea C	41	2
1990–91		41	1
1991–92		44	3
1992–93		42	5

HARRISON, Gerry

Born Lambeth 15.4.72. Ht 5 10
Wt 12 12
Midfield. From Trainee.

1989–90	Watford	3	—
1990–91		6	—
1991–92	Bristol C	4	—
1991–92	Cardiff C	10	1
1992–93	Bristol C	33	1

HARRISON, Lee

Born Billericay 12.9.71. Ht 6 2 Wt 12 02
Goalkeeper. From Trainee.

1990–91	Charlton Ath	—	—
1991–92		—	—
1991–92	Fulham	—	—
1991–92	Gillingham	2	—
1992–93	Charlton Ath	—	—
1992–93	Fulham	—	—

HARRISON, Tom

Born Edinburgh 22.1.74 Ht 5 9 Wt 10 7
Midfield. From Salvesen BC.

1990–91	Hearts	3	—
1991–92		1	—
1992–93		4	1

HARTFIELD, Charles

Born London 4.9.71. Ht 6 0 Wt 12 02
Defender. From Trainee.

1989–90	Arsenal	—	—
1990–91		—	—
1991–92	Sheffield U	7	—
1992–93		17	—

HARVEY, Jimmy

Born Lurgan 2.5.58.   Ht 5 9   Wt 11 04
Midfield. From Glenavon. Northern
Ireland, Under-23.

Season	Club		
1977–78	Arsenal	1	—
1978–79		2	—
1979–80		—	—
1979–80	*Hereford U*	11	—
1980–81	Hereford U	30	1
1981–82		42	5
1982–83		41	5
1983–84		44	9
1984–85		34	5
1985–86		42	9
1986–87		34	5
1986–87	Bristol C	2	—
1987–88		1	—
1987–88	*Wrexham*	6	—
1987–88	Tranmere R	33	3
1988–89		42	4
1989–90		46	7
1990–91		39	3
1991–92		24	1
1992–93	Crewe Alex	17	—

HARVEY, Lee

Born Harlow 21.12.66.   Ht 5 11   Wt 11 07
Forward. From Local. England Youth.

Season	Club		
1983–84	Orient	4	—
1984–85		4	—
1985–86		12	2
1986–87		15	1
1987–88		23	1
1988–89		29	6
1989–90		37	6
1990–91		26	3
1991–92		13	—
1992–93		21	4

HARVEY, Richard

Born Letchworth 17.4.69.   Ht 5 10
Wt 11 10
Defender. From Apprentice. England
Schools, Youth.

Season	Club		
1986–87	Luton T	5	—

Season	Club		
1987–88		—	—
1988–89		12	—
1989–90		26	—
1990–91		29	—
1991–92		32	2
1992–93		1	—
1992–93	*Blackpool*	5	—

HATELEY, Mark

Born Liverpool 7.11.61.   Ht 6 1   Wt 11 07
Forward. From Apprentice. England
Youth, Under-21, 32 full caps.

Season	Club		
1978–79	Coventry C	1	—
1979–80		4	—
1980–81		19	3
1981–82		34	13
1982–83		35	9
1983–84	Portsmouth	38	22
1984–85	AC Milan	21	7
1985–86		22	8
1986–87		23	2
From Monaco			
1990–91	Rangers	33	10
1991–92		30	21
1992–93		37	19

HATHAWAY, Ian

Born Worsley 22.8.68   Ht 5 6   Wt 11 04
Forward. From WBA Apprentice,
Bedworth U.

Season	Club		
1988–89	Mansfield T	12	1
1989–90		22	1
1990–91		10	—
1990–91	Rotherham U	5	1
1991–92		8	—
1992–93		—	—

HAUSER, Thomas

Born West Germany 10.4.65.   Ht 6 3
Wt 12 06
Forward. From Berne OB.

Season	Club		
1988–89	Sunderland	13	2
1989–90		18	6
1990–91		10	1

Season	Club		
1991–92		12	—
1992–93		—	—
To Cambuur			

HAWKE, Warren

Born Durham 20.9.70.   Ht 5 10   Wt 10 11
Midfield. From Trainee.

Season	Club		
1988–89	Sunderland	4	—
1989–90		8	1
1990–91		7	—
1991–92		4	—
1991–92	*Chesterfield*	7	1
1992–93	Sunderland	2	—
1992–93	*Carlisle U*	8	2
1992–93	*Northampton T*	7	1

HAYES, Martin

Born Walthamstow 21.3.66.   Ht 5 10
Wt 11 12
Forward. From Apprentice. England B,
Under-21.

Season	Club		
1983–84	Arsenal	—	—
1984–85		—	—
1985–86		11	2
1986–87		35	19
1987–88		27	1
1988–89		17	1
1989–90		12	3
1990–91	Celtic	7	—
1991–92		—	—
1991–92	*Wimbledon*	2	—
1992–93	Swansea C	15	—

HAYLOCK, Paul

Born Lowestoft 24.3.63.   Ht 5 9
Wt 11 10
Defender. From Apprentice.

Season	Club		
1980–81	Norwich C	—	—
1981–82		21	—
1982–83		42	1
1983–84		39	—
1984–85		41	1
1985–86		12	1
1986–87	Gillingham	45	—

Season	Club		
1987–88		32	—
1988–89		31	—
1989–90		44	—
1990–91		—	—
1990–91	Maidstone U	16	—
1991–92		32	1
1992–93	Shrewsbury T	18	1

HAYRETTIN, Hakan

Born London 4.2.70.   Ht 5 9   Wt 11 02
Midfield. From Trainee.

Season	Club		
1988–89	Leyton Orient	—	—
From Barnet			
1991–92	Barnet	4	—
1992–93		2	—
1992–93	*Torquay U*	4	—

HAYWARD, Steve

Born Walsall 8.9.71.   Ht 5 10   Wt 11 07
Midfield. From Trainee. England Youth.

Season	Club		
1988–89	Derby Co	—	—
1989–90		3	—
1990–91		1	—
1991–92		7	—
1992–93		7	1

HAZARD, Mike

Born Sunderland 5.2.60.   Ht 5 7
Wt 10 05
Midfield. From Apprentice.

Season	Club		
1977–78	Tottenham H	—	—
1978–79		—	—
1979–80		3	—
1980–81		4	—
1981–82		28	5
1982–83		18	1
1983–84		11	2
1984–85		23	4
1985–86		4	1
1985–86	Chelsea	18	1
1986–87		18	6
1987–88		28	2
1988–89		4	—
1989–90		13	—

Season	Club	Apps	Goals
1989–90	Portsmouth	8	1
1990–91		—	—
1990–91	Swindon T	34	8
1991–92		44	6
1992–93		32	3

HAZEL, Desmond

Born Bradford 15.7.67. Ht 5 11
Wt 10 13
Midfield. From Apprentice.

Season	Club	Apps	Goals
1985–86	Sheffield W	—	—
1986–87		—	—
1986–87	*Grimsby T*	9	2
1987–88	Sheffield W	6	—
1988–89	Rotherham U	42	6
1989–90		33	2
1990–91		39	3
1991–92		38	8
1992–93		36	7

HAZEL, Julian

Born Luton 25.9.73
Forward. From Trainee.

Season	Club	Apps	Goals
1992–93	Colchester U	2	—

HEALD, Paul

Born Wath-on-Dearne 20.8.68. Ht 6 2
Wt 12 05
Goalkeeper. From Trainee.

Season	Club	Apps	Goals
1987–88	Sheffield U	—	—
1988–89		—	—
1988–89	Leyton Orient	28	—
1989–90		37	—
1990–91		38	—
1991–92		2	—
1991–92	*Coventry C*	2	—
1992–93	Leyton Orient	26	—
1992–93	*Crystal Palace*	—	—

HEANEY, Neil

Born Middlesbrough 3.11.71. Ht 5 9
Wt 11 09
Forward. From Trainee. England Youth,
Under-21.

Season	Club	Apps	Goals
1989–90	Arsenal	—	—
1990–91		—	—
1990–91	*Hartlepool U*	3	—
1991–92	Arsenal	1	—
1991–92	*Cambridge U*	13	2
1992–93	Arsenal	5	—

HEARD, Pat

Born Hull 17.3.60. Ht 5 10 Wt 11 00
Defender. From Apprentice. England
Youth.

Season	Club	Apps	Goals
1977–78	Everton	—	—
1978–79		10	—
1979–80		1	—
1979–80	Aston Villa	9	—
1980–81		—	—
1981–82		8	2
1982–83		7	—
1982–83	Sheffield W	19	2
1983–84		5	1
1984–85		1	—
1984–85	Newcastle U	34	2
1985–86		—	—
1985–86	Middlesbrough	25	2
1985–86	Hull C	8	—
1986–87		37	1
1987–88		35	4
1988–89	Rotherham U	30	4
1989–90		14	3
1990–91	Cardiff C	38	3
1991–92		8	1
1992–93	Hull C	4	—

HEATH, Adrian

Born Stoke 11.1.61. Ht 5 6 Wt 10 01
Forward. From Apprentice. England
Under-21, B.

Season	Club	Apps	Goals
1978–79	Stoke C	2	—
1979–80		38	5
1980–81		38	6
1981–82		17	5
1981–82	Everton	22	6
1982–83		38	10
1983–84		36	12
1984–85		17	11
1985–86		36	10
1986–87		41	11

Season	Club	Apps	Goals
1987–88		29	9
1988–89		7	2
From Espanol			
1989–90	Aston Villa	9	—
1989–90	Manchester C	12	2
1990–91		35	1
1991–92		28	1
1991–92	Stoke C	6	—
1992–93	Burnley	43	19

HEATHCOCK, Adrian

Born Dudley 26.1.75
Midfield. From Trainee.

Season	Club	Apps	Goals
1992–93	Hereford U	2	—

HEATHCOTE, Mike

Born Durham 10.9.65.   Ht 6 2   Wt 12 05
Defender. From Middlesbrough,
Spennymoor U.

Season	Club	Apps	Goals
1987–88	Sunderland	1	—
1987–88	*Halifax T*	7	1
1988–89	Sunderland	—	—
1989–90		8	—
1989–90	*York C*	3	—
1990–91	Shrewsbury T	39	6
1991–92		5	—
1991–92	Cambridge U	22	5
1992–93		42	2

HEBBERD, Trevor

Born Winchester 19.6.58.   Ht 6 0
Wt 11 04
Midfield. From Apprentice.

Season	Club	Apps	Goals
1976–77	Southampton	12	2
1977–78		12	1
1978–79		22	2
1979–80		36	2
1980–81		11	—
1981–82		4	—
1981–82	*Bolton W*	6	—
1981–82	*Leicester C*	4	1
1981–82	Oxford U	15	2
1982–83		39	10
1983–84		46	11

Season	Club	Apps	Goals
1984–85		42	6
1985–86		41	3
1986–87		38	2
1987–88		39	3
1988–89	Derby Co	37	5
1989–90		23	4
1990–91		21	1
1991–92		—	—
1991–92	Portsmouth	4	—
1991–92	Chesterfield	24	—
1992–93		32	1

HEGGS, Carl

Born Leicester 11.10.70.   Ht 6 0
Wt 11 08
Forward. From Doncaster R Trainee,
Paget R.

Season	Club	Apps	Goals
1991–92	WBA	3	—
1992–93		17	2

HELLIWELL, Ian

Born Rotherham 7.11.62.   Ht 6 3
Wt 14 02
Forward. From Matlock T.

Season	Club	Apps	Goals
1987–88	York C	32	8
1988–89		41	11
1989–90		46	14
1990–91		41	7
1991–92	Scunthorpe U	39	9
1992–93		41	13

HENDON, Ian

Born Ilford 5.12.71.   Ht 6 0   Wt 12 10
Defender. From Trainee. England Youth,
Under-21.

Season	Club	Apps	Goals
1989–90	Tottenham H	—	—
1990–91		2	—
1991–92		2	—
1991–92	*Portsmouth*	4	—
1991–92	*Leyton Orient*	6	—
1992–93	Tottenham H	—	—
1992–93	*Barnsley*	6	—

HENDRIE, John

Born Lennoxtown 24.10.63.   Ht 5 7
Wt 11 07
Forward. From Apprentice. Scotland
Youth.

Season	Club		
1981–82	Coventry C	6	—
1982–83		12	2
1983–84		3	—
1983–84	*Hereford U*	6	—
1984–85	Bradford C	46	9
1985–86		42	10
1986–87		42	14
1987–88		43	13
1988–89	Newcastle U	34	4
1989–90	Leeds U	27	5
1990–91	Middlesbrough	41	3
1991–92		38	3
1992–93		32	9

HENDRY, Colin

Born Keith 7.12.65.   Ht 6 1   Wt 12 00
Defender. From Islavale. Scotland B, 2 full
caps.

Season	Club		
1983–84	Dundee	4	—
1984–85		4	—
1985–86		20	—
1986–87		13	2
1986–87	Blackburn R	13	3
1987–88		44	12
1988–89		38	7
1989–90		7	—
1989–90	Manchester C	25	3
1990–91		32	1
1991–92		6	1
1991–92	Blackburn R	30	4
1992–93		41	1

HENDRY, John

Born Glasgow 6.1.70.   Ht 5 11   Wt 10 06
Forward. From Hillington YC. Scotland
Under-21.

Season	Club		
1988–89	Dundee	2	—
1989–90		—	—
1989–90	*Forfar Ath*	10	6
1990–91	Tottenham H	4	2

Season	Club		
1991–92		5	1
1991–92	*Charlton Ath*	5	1
1992–93	Tottenham H	5	2

HENRY, Liburd

Born Dominica 29.8.67.   Ht 5 11
Wt 12 09
Forward. From Colchester U, Rainham T,
Millwall, Leytonstone/Ilford.

Season	Club		
1987–88	Watford	—	—
1988–89		1	—
1988–89	*Halifax T*	5	—
1989–90	Watford	9	1
1990–91	Maidstone U	30	2
1991–92		37	7
1992–93	Gillingham	28	1

HENRY, Nick

Born Liverpool 21.2.69.   Ht 5 6   Wt 9 08
Midfield. From Trainee.

Season	Club		
1987–88	Oldham Ath	5	—
1988–89		18	—
1989–90		41	—
1990–91		43	4
1991–92		42	6
1992–93		32	6

HERD, Stuart

Born Tittensor 25.2.74
Midfield. From Norwich C.

Season	Club		
1992–93	Torquay U	7	—

HERITAGE, Peter

Born Bexhill 8.11.60.   Ht 6 1   Wt 13 00
Forward. From Hythe Town.

Season	Club		
1989–90	Gillingham	42	9
1990–91		15	2
1990–91	Hereford U	18	1
1991–92		39	8
1992–93	Doncaster R	31	2

HERRERA, Roberto

Born Torbay 12.6.70.   Ht 5 7   Wt 10 06
Defender. From Trainee.

Season	Club		
1987–88	QPR	—	—

Season	Club	App	Goals
1988–89		2	—
1989–90		1	—
1990–91		3	—
1991–92		—	—
1991–92	Torquay U	11	—
1992–93	QPR	—	—
1992–93	Torquay U	5	—

HESELTINE, Wayne

Born Bradford 3.12.69 Ht 5 9 Wt 11 06
Defender. From Trainee.

Season	Club	App	Goals
1987–88	Manchester U	—	—
1988–89		—	—
1989–90		—	—
1989–90	Oldham Ath	1	—
1990–91		—	—
1991–92		—	—
1992–93	Bradford C	42	1

HESSENTHALER, Andy

Born Gravesend 17.8.65. Ht 5 7
Wt 11 00
Midfield. From Redbridge Forest.

Season	Club	App	Goals
1991–92	Watford	35	1
1992–93		45	3

HETHERSTON, Peter

Born Bellshill 6.11.64 Ht 5 9 Wt 10 7
Midfield. From Bargeddie Ams.

Season	Club	App	Goals
1984–85	Falkirk	12	2
1985–86		22	2
1986–87		36	3
1987–88	Watford	5	—
1987–88	Sheffield U	11	—
1988–89	Falkirk	31	3
1989–90		22	2
1990–91		26	4
1991–92	Raith R	31	1
1992–93		44	4

HEWITT, Jamie

Born Chesterfield 17.5.68. Ht 5 11
Wt 11 07
Defender. From School.

Season	Club	App	Goals
1984–85	Chesterfield	—	—

Season	Club	App	Goals
1985–86		17	—
1986–87		42	2
1987–88		28	2
1988–89		40	1
1989–90		42	6
1990–91		43	—
1991–92		37	3
1992–93	Doncaster R	27	—

HICKS, Martin

Born Stratford-on-Avon 27.2.57. Ht 6 3
Wt 13 06
Defender. From Stratford T.

Season	Club	App	Goals
1976–77	Charlton Ath	—	—
1977–78		—	—
1977–78	Reading	19	1
1978–79		46	1
1979–80		1	1
1980–81		27	2
1981–82		44	3
1982–83		32	1
1983–84		46	1
1984–85		40	2
1985–86		34	2
1986–87		34	3
1987–88		44	1
1988–89		45	3
1989–90		44	2
1990–91		44	—
1991–92	Birmingham C	42	1
1992–93		18	—

HICKS, Stuart

Born Peterborough 30.5.67. Ht 6 1
Wt 13 00
Defender. From Peterborough U
Apprentice, Wisbech.

Season	Club	App	Goals
1987–88	Colchester U	7	—
1988–89		37	—
1989–90		20	—
1990–91	Scunthorpe U	46	1
1991–92		21	—
1992–93	Doncaster R	36	—

HIGGINS, Dave

Born Liverpool 19.8.61.   Ht 6 0   Wt 11 00
Defender. From Eagle.

Season	Club	App	Goals
1983–84	Tranmere R	20	—
1984–85		8	—
From S. Liverpool, Caernarfon			
1987–88	Tranmere R	33	1
1988–89		43	1
1989–90		45	1
1990–91		33	2
1991–92		33	1
1992–93		40	4

HIGNETT, Craig

Born Whiston 12.1.70.   Ht 5 10   Wt 11 00
Midfield.

Season	Club	App	Goals
1987–88	Crewe Alex	—	—
1988–89		1	—
1989–90		35	8
1990–91		38	13
1991–92		33	13
1992–93		14	8
1992–93	Middlesbrough	21	4

HILDERSLEY, Ron

Born Fife 6.4.65.   Ht 5 4   Wt 9 2
Forward. From Apprentice. Scotland
Schools.

Season	Club	App	Goals
1982–83	Manchester C	1	—
1983–84		—	—
1983–84	Chester C	9	—
1984–85	Chester C	9	—
1985–86	Rochdale	16	—
1986–87	Preston NE	33	2
1987–88		25	1
1987–88	Cambridge U	9	3
1988–89	Blackburn R	25	4
1989–90		5	—
1990–91	Wigan Ath	4	—
1991–92	Halifax T	18	—
1992–93		13	2

HILEY, Scott

Born Plymouth 27.9.68.   Ht 5 9   Wt 10 07
Midfield. From Trainee.

Season	Club	App	Goals
1986–87	Exeter C	—	—
1987–88		15	1
1988–89		37	5
1989–90		46	—
1990–91		46	2
1991–92		33	1
1992–93		33	3
1992–93	Birmingham C	7	—

HILL, Andy

Born Maltby 20.1.65.   Ht 5 10   Wt 12 00
Defender. From Apprentice. England
Youth.

Season	Club	App	Goals
1982–83	Manchester U	—	—
1983–84		—	—
1984–85	Bury	43	3
1985–86		35	2
1986–87		42	1
1987–88		43	2
1988–89		43	—
1989–90		46	2
1990–91		12	—
1990–91	Manchester C	8	1
1991–92		36	4
1992–93		24	1

HILL, Colin

Born Hillingdon 12.11.63.   Ht 5 11
Wt 12 08
Defender. From Apprentice. Northern
Ireland 6 full caps.

Season	Club	App	Goals
1981–82	Arsenal	—	—
1982–83		7	—
1983–84		37	1
1984–85		2	—
1985–86		—	—
1985–86	Brighton	—	—
From Maritimo.H			
1987–88	Colchester U	25	—
1988–89		44	—
1989–90	Sheffield U	43	—
1990–91		24	—

1991–92	....	15	1
1991–92	*Leicester C*	10	—
1992–93	Leicester C	46	—

HILL, Danny

Born Edmonton 1.10.74 Ht 5 9
Wt 11 00
Midfield. From Trainee.

| 1992–93 | Tottenham H .... | 4 | — |

HILL, David

Born Nottingham 6.6.66. Ht 5 11
Wt 12 04
Midfield. From Local.

1983–84	Scunthorpe U	2	—
1984–85	....	29	2
1985–86	....	42	2
1986–87	....	41	3
1987–88	....	26	3
1988–89	Ipswich T	36	—
1989–90	....	2	—
1990–91	....	23	—
1990–91	Scunthorpe U	9	1
1991–92	....	37	5
1992–93	....	19	—

HILL, Keith

Born Bolton 17.5.69. Ht 6 0 Wt 11 03
Defender. From Apprentice.

1986–87	Blackburn R	—	—
1987–88	....	1	—
1988–89	....	15	1
1989–90	....	25	—
1990–91	....	22	2
1991–92	....	32	1
1992–93	....	1	—
1992–93	Plymouth Arg	36	—

HILLIER, David

Born Blackheath 19.12.69. Ht 5 10
Wt 12 05
Midfield. From Trainee. England
Under-21.

| 1987–88 | Arsenal .... | — | — |

1988–89	....	—	—
1989–90	....	—	—
1990–91	....	16	—
1991–92	....	27	1
1992–93	....	30	1

HIMSWORTH, Gary

Born Appleton 19.12.69. Ht 5 7 Wt 9 08
Forward. From Trainee.

1987–88	York C	31	2
1988–89	....	32	2
1989–90	....	23	4
1990–91	....	2	—
1990–91	Scarborough	23	1
1991–92	....	36	4
1992–93	....	33	1

HINCHCLIFFE, Andy

Born Manchester 5.2.69. Ht 5 10
Wt 12 10
Defender. From Apprentice. England
Youth, Under-21.

1986–87	Manchester C	—	—
1987–88	....	42	1
1988–89	....	39	5
1989–90	....	31	2
1990–91	Everton	21	1
1991–92	....	18	—
1992–93	....	25	1

HINCHLEY, Gary

Born Guisborough 14.11.68. Ht 6 0
Wt 12 07
Defender.

1986–87	Darlington	9	—
1987–88	....	5	—
From Guisborough			
1991–92	Darlington	6	—
1992–93	....	7	1

HINDMARCH, Rob

Born Stannington 27.4.61. Ht 6 1
Wt 13 04
Defender. From Apprentice. England
Youth.

Season	Club	App	Goals
1977–78	Sunderland	2	—
1978–79		—	—
1979–80		21	—
1980–81		29	—
1981–82		36	2
1982–83		14	—
1983–84		13	—
1983–84	*Portsmouth*	2	—
1984–85	Derby Co	22	1
1985–86		39	6
1986–87		33	2
1987–88		19	—
1988–89		25	—
1989–90		26	—
1990–91	Wolverhampton W	40	2
1991–92		—	—
1992–93		—	—

HINE, Mark

Born Middlesbrough 18.5.64. Ht 5 8
Wt 10 08
Midfield. From Local.

Season	Club	App	Goals
1983–84	Grimsby T	—	—
1984–85		9	—
1985–86		13	1
1986–87	Darlington	43	2
1987–88		45	4
1988–89		40	2
1989–90		—	—
1989–90	Peterborough U	22	4
1990–91		33	4
1990–91	Scunthorpe U	12	2
1991–92		10	—
1992–93	Doncaster R	25	1

HIRST, David

Born Barnsley 7.12.67. Ht 5 11 Wt 13 01
Forward. From Apprentice. England
Youth, B, Under-21, 3 full caps.

Season	Club	App	Goals
1985–86	Barnsley	28	9

Season	Club	App	Goals
1986–87	Sheffield W	21	6
1987–88		24	3
1988–89		32	7
1989–90		38	14
1990–91		41	24
1991–92		33	18
1992–93		22	11

HIRST, Lee

Born Sheffield 26.1.69. Ht 6 2 Wt 12 07
Defender.

Season	Club	App	Goals
1989–90	Scarborough	10	—
1990–91		32	2
1991–92		30	2
1992–93		36	2

HISLOP, Neil

Born London 22.2.69. Ht 6 6 Wt 12 02
Goalkeeper. From USA.

Season	Club	App	Goals
1992–93	Reading	12	—

HITCHCOCK, Kevin

Born Custom House 5.10.62. Ht 6 1
Wt 12 02
Goalkeeper. From Barking.

Season	Club	App	Goals
1983–84	Nottingham F	—	—
1983–84	*Mansfield T*	14	—
1984–85	Mansfield T	43	—
1985–86		46	—
1986–87		46	—
1987–88		33	—
1987–88	Chelsea	8	—
1988–89		3	—
1989–90		—	—
1990–91		3	—
1990–91	*Northampton T*	17	—
1991–92	Chelsea	21	—
1992–93		20	—
1992–93	*West Ham U*	—	—

HOBSON, Gary

Born North Ferriby 12.11.72. Ht 6 2
Wt 12 10
Defender. From Trainee.

Season	Club	App	Goals
1990–91	Hull C	4	—

| 1991–92 | | 16 | — |
| 1992–93 | | 21 | — |

HOCKADAY, David

Born Billingham 9.11.57.   Ht 5 9
Wt 11 02
Defender. From Amateur.

1975–76	Blackpool	—	—
1976–77		5	—
1977–78		—	—
1978–79		18	4
1979–80		7	1
1980–81		36	4
1981–82		41	7
1982–83		40	8
1983–84	Swindon T	36	3
1984–85		22	1
1985–86		37	1
1986–87		40	1
1987–88		43	—
1988–89		44	—
1989–90		20	—
1990–91		3	—
1990–91	Hull C	35	1
1991–92		12	—
1992–93		25	1
1992–93	*Stoke C*	7	—

HODDER, Steve

Born Sheffield 18.10.71   Ht 5 9   Wt 11 03
Forward. From Nottingham F.

| 1991–92 | Notts Co | — | — |
| 1992–93 | Doncaster R | 2 | — |

HODDLE, Carl

Born Harlow 8.3.67.   Ht 6 4   Wt 11 00
Midfield. From Bishop's Stortford.

1989–90	Leyton Orient	26	2
1990–91		2	—
1991–92	Barnet	13	—
1992–93		5	2

HODDLE, Glenn

Born Hayes 27.10.57.   Ht 6 0   Wt 11 06
Midfield. From Apprentice. England
Youth, Under-21, B, 53 full caps.

1974–75	Tottenham	—	—
1975–76		7	1
1976–77		39	4
1977–78		41	12
1978–79		35	7
1979–80		41	19
1980–81		38	12
1981–82		34	10
1982–83		24	1
1983–84		24	4
1884–85		28	8
1985–86		31	7
1986–87		35	3
From Monaco			
1990–91	Chelsea	—	—
1991–92	Swindon T	22	—
1992–93		42	1

HODGE, John

Born Ormskirk 1.4.69.   Ht 5 6   Wt 10 00
Forward. From Exmouth.

| 1991–92 | Exeter C | 23 | 1 |
| 1992–93 | | 42 | 9 |

HODGE, Martin

Born Southport 4.2.59.   Ht 6 1   Wt 14 06
Goalkeeper. From Apprentice.

1976–77	Plymouth Arg	—	—
1977–78		5	—
1978–79		38	—
1979–80	Everton	23	—
1980–81		2	—
1981–82	*Preston NE*	28	—
1982–83	*Oldham Ath*	4	—
1982–83	*Gillingham*	4	—
1982–83	*Preston NE*	16	—
1983–84	Sheffield W	42	—
1984–85		42	—
1985–86		42	—
1986–87		42	—
1987–88		29	—

Season	Club	League Appearances/Goals	
1988–89	Leicester C	19	—
1989–90		46	—
1990–91		10	—
1991–92	Hartlepool U	40	—
1992–93		29	—

HODGE, Steve

Born Nottingham 25.10.62. Ht 5 8
Wt 9 11
Midfield. From Apprentice. England
Under-21, B, 24 full caps.

Season	Club		
1980–81	Nottingham F	—	—
1981–82		1	—
1982–83		39	8
1983–84		39	10
1984–85		42	12
1985–86		2	—
1985–86	Aston Villa	36	8
1986–87		17	4
1986–87	Tottenham H	19	4
1987–88		26	3
1988–89	Nottingham F	34	7
1989–90		34	10
1990–91		14	3
1991–92	Leeds U	23	7
1992–93		23	2

HODGES, David

Born Hereford 17.1.70. Ht 5 9   Wt 10 02
Midfield.

Season	Club		
1986–87	Mansfield T	3	—
1987–88		22	2
1988–89		39	4
1989–90		19	1
1990–91		2	—
1990–91	Torquay U	10	—
1991–92		6	—
1992–93	Shrewsbury T	1	—

HODGES, Glyn

Born Streatham 30.4.63.   Ht 6 0
Wt 12 03
Forward. From Apprentice. Wales Youth,
B, Under-21, 16 full caps.

Season	Club		
1980–81	Wimbledon	30	5

Season	Club		
1981–82		34	2
1982–83		37	9
1983–84		42	15
1984–85		22	3
1985–86		30	6
1986–87		37	9
1987–88	Newcastle U	7	—
1987–88	Watford	24	3
1988–89		27	5
1989–90		35	7
1990–91	Crystal Palace	7	—
1990–91	Sheffield U	12	4
1991–92		26	2
1992–93		31	4

HODGES, Kevin

Born Bridport 12.6.60.   Ht 5 8   Wt 10 08
Midfield. From Apprentice.

Season	Club		
1977–78	Plymouth Arg	—	—
1978–79		12	—
1979–80		44	5
1980–81		41	5
1981–82		46	11
1982–83		46	11
1983–84		43	4
1984–85		45	10
1985–86		46	16
1986–87		35	5
1987–88		37	6
1988–89		31	1
1989–90		44	4
1990–91		42	3
1991–92		14	—
1991–92	*Torquay U*	3	—
1992–93	Plymouth Arg	4	—
1992–93	Torquay U	8	1

HODGES, Lee

Born Epping 4.9.73.   Ht 5 9   Wt 11 06
Forward. From Trainee.

Season	Club		
1991–92	Tottenham H	—	—
1992–93		4	—
1992–93	*Plymouth Arg*	7	2

HODSON, Simeon

Born Lincoln 5.3.66. Ht 5 10 Wt 11 06
Defender. From Apprentice.

Season	Club	App	Goals
1983–84	Notts Co	13	—
1984–85		14	—
1984–85	Charlton Ath	5	—
1985–86		—	—
1985–86	Lincoln C	15	—
1986–87		41	—
1987–88	Newport Co	34	1
1987–88	WBA	7	—
1988–89		9	—
1989–90		10	—
1990–91		30	—
1991–92		25	—
1992–93		2	—
1992–93	Doncaster R	15	—
1992–93	Mansfield T	17	—

HOGG, Graeme

Born Aberdeen 17.6.64. Ht 6 1 Wt 13 01
Defender. From Apprentice. Scotland
Under-21.

Season	Club	App	Goals
1982–83	Manchester U	—	—
1983–84		16	1
1984–85		29	—
1985–86		17	—
1986–87		11	—
1987–88		10	—
1987–88	*WBA*	7	—
1988–89	Portsmouth	41	1
1989–90		39	1
1990–91		20	—
1991–92	Hearts	18	1
1992–93		22	2

HOLDEN, Rick

Born Skipton 9.9.64. Ht 5 11 Wt 12 07
Midfield.

Season	Club	App	Goals
1985–86	Burnley	1	—
1986–87	Halifax T	32	2
1987–88		35	10
1987–88	Watford	10	2
1988–89		32	6
1989–90	Oldham Ath	45	9

Season	Club	App	Goals
1990–91		42	5
1991–92		42	5
1992–93	Manchester C	41	3

HOLDEN, Steve

Born Luton 4.9.72. Ht 6 0 Wt 11 13
Forward. From Trainee.

Season	Club	App	Goals
1990–91	Leicester C	—	—
1991–92		1	—
1992–93	Carlisle U	21	1

HOLDSWORTH, David

Born London 8.11.68. Ht 6 1 Wt 12 04
Defender. From Trainee. England Youth,
Under-21.

Season	Club	App	Goals
1986–87	Watford	—	—
1987–88		—	—
1988–89		33	1
1989–90		44	3
1990–91		15	2
1991–92		33	2
1992–93		39	—

HOLDSWORTH, Dean

Born London 8.11.68. Ht 5 11 Wt 11 13
Forward. From Trainee.

Season	Club	App	Goals
1986–87	Watford	2	—
1987–88	*Carlisle U*	4	1
1987–88	*Port Vale*	6	2
1988–89	Watford	10	2
1988–89	*Swansea C*	5	1
1988–89	*Brentford*	7	1
1989–90	Watford	4	1
1989–90	Brentford	39	24
1990–91		30	5
1991–92		41	24
1992–93	Wimbledon	36	19

HOLLAND, Paul

Born Lincoln 8.7.73. Ht 5 11 Wt 12 05
Midfield. From School.

Season	Club	App	Goals
1990–91	Mansfield T	1	—

1991–92	....	38	6		
1992–93	....	39	3		

HOLLIDAY, John

Born Penrith 13.3.70. Ht 6 4 Wt 11 00
Defender.

1989–90	Carlisle U......................	—	—
1990–91	....	1	—
1991–92	....	16	—
1992–93	....	2	—
1992–93	Mansfield T..................	—	—
1992–93	Carlisle U......................	—	—

HOLLOWAY, Ian

Born Kingswood 12.3.63. Ht 5 8
Wt 10 10
Midfield. From Apprentice.

1980–81	Bristol R	1	—
1981–82	....	1	—
1982–83	....	31	7
1983–84	....	36	1
1984–85	....	42	6
1985–86	Wimbledon	19	2
1985–86	*Brentford*......................	13	2
1986–87	Brentford	16	—
1986–87	*Torquay U*......................	5	—
1987–88	....	1	—
1987–88	Bristol R	43	5
1988–89	....	44	6
1989–90	....	46	8
1990–91	....	46	7
1991–92	QPR	40	—
1992–93	....	24	2

HOLMES, Dan

Born Clophill 13.6.72
Defender. From Middlesbrough.

1992–93	Bournemouth..............	1	—

HOLMES, Matt

Born Luton 1.8.69. Ht 5 7 Wt 10 07
Forward. From Trainee.

1988–89	Bournemouth..............	4	1

1988–89	*Cardiff C*......................	1	—
1989–90	Bournemouth..............	22	2
1990–91	....	42	2
1991–92	....	46	3
1992–93	West Ham U	18	—

HOLMES, Micky

Born Blackpool 9.9.65. Ht 5 8 Wt 10 12
Midfield.

1984–85	Bradford C	5	—
1985–86	Burnley	—	—
1985–86	Wolverhampton W	26	3
1986–87	....	37	8
1987–88	....	20	2
1988–89	Huddersfield T...........	7	—
1988–89	Cambridge U	11	—
1989–90	Rochdale......................	38	2
1990–91	....	16	5
1990–91	Torquay U	22	2
1991–92	....	18	1
1991–92	Carlisle U......................	15	4
1992–93	....	19	7
1992–93	Northampton T	6	—

HOLMES, Paul

Born Wortley 18.2.68. Ht 5 10 Wt 11 03
Defender. From Apprentice.

1985–86	Doncaster R..............	5	1
1986–87	....	16	—
1987–88	....	26	—
1988–89	Torquay U	25	—
1989–90	....	44	2
1990–91	....	33	1
1991–92	....	36	1
1992–93	Birmingham C	12	—
1992–93	Everton	4	—

HOLSGROVE, Paul

Born Wellington 26.8.69. Ht 6 2
Wt 12 11
Midfield. From Trainee.

1986–87	Aldershot	—	—
1987–88	....	2	—
1988–89	....	1	—

1988–89	*Wimbledon*	—	—
1989–90	Aldershot	—	—
1989–90	*WBA*	—	—
From Wokingham			
1990–91	Luton T	1	—
1991–92		1	—
From Heracles			
1992–93	Millwall	11	—

HOLZMAN, Mark

Born Bracknell 22.2.73. Ht 5 7 Wt 10 07
Defender. From Trainee.

| 1991–92 | Reading | 16 | 1 |
| 1992–93 | | 16 | — |

HONOR, Chris

Born Bristol 5.6.68. Ht 5 9 Wt 10 09
Defender. From Apprentice.

1985–86	Bristol C	1	—
1986–87		2	—
1986–87	*Torquay U*	3	—
1987–88	Bristol C	17	—
1988–89		26	—
1989–90		14	1
1989–90	*Hereford U*	3	—
1990–91	Bristol C	—	—
1990–91	*Swansea C*	2	—
1991–92	Airdrieonians	30	—
1992–93		29	3

HONOUR, Brian

Born Horden 16.2.64. Ht 5 7 Wt 12 05
Midfield. From Apprentice.

1981–82	Darlington	1	—
1982–83		32	3
1983–84		41	1
From Peterlee			
1984–85	Hartlepool U	17	—
1985–86		46	8
1986–87		32	2
1987–88		44	—
1988–89		34	1
1989–90		9	—
1990–91		42	4

| 1991–92 | | 40 | 4 |
| 1992–93 | | 37 | 3 |

HOOPER, Michael

Born Bristol 10.2.64. Ht 6 2 Wt 13 05
Goalkeeper.

1983–84	Bristol C	—	—
1984–85		1	—
1984–85	*Wrexham*	20	—
1985–86	Wrexham	14	—
1985–86	Liverpool	—	—
1986–87		11	—
1987–88		2	—
1988–89		17	—
1989–90		—	—
1990–91		7	—
1990–91	*Leicester C*	14	—
1991–92	Liverpool	5	—
1992–93		9	—

HOPKIN, David

Born Greenock 21.8.70 Ht 5 9 Wt 10 03
Midfield. From Pt Glasgow R BC.

1989–90	Morton	8	—
1990–91		10	—
1991–92		—	—
1992–93	Chelsea	4	—

HOPKINS, Jeff

Born Swansea 14.4.64. Ht 6 0 Wt 12 12
Defender. From Apprentice. Wales Youth,
Under-21, 16 full caps.

1980–81	Fulham	1	—
1981–82		35	—
1982–83		41	1
1983–84		33	—
1984–85		40	2
1985–86		23	—
1986–87		20	1
1987–88		26	—
1988–89	Crystal Palace	43	—
1989–90		27	2
1990–91		—	—
1991–92		—	—

Season	Club		
1991–92	Plymouth Arg	8	—
1991–92	Bristol R	6	—
1992–93	Reading	36	1

HOPKINS, Robert

Born Birmingham 25.10.61. Ht 5 7
Wt 10 07
Midfield. From Apprentice.

Season	Club		
1979–80	Aston Villa	2	1
1980–81		—	—
1981–82		—	—
1982–83		1	—
1982–83	Birmingham C	11	2
1983–84		32	5
1984–85		39	9
1985–86		38	4
1986–87		3	1
1986–87	Manchester C	7	1
1986–87	WBA	25	4
1987–88		29	2
1988–89		29	5
1988–89	Birmingham C	9	—
1989–90		18	6
1990–91		23	3
1991–92	Shrewsbury T	27	3
1992–93		—	—
1992–93	Colchester U	14	1

HOPPER, Tony

Born Carlisle 31.5.76
Defender. From Trainee.

Season	Club		
1992–93	Carlisle U	1	—

HORLOCK, Kevin

Born Bexley 1.11.72   Ht 6 0   Wt 12 00
Defender. From Trainee.

Season	Club		
1991–92	West Ham U	—	—
1992–93		—	—
1992–93	Swindon T	14	1

HORNE, Barry

Born St. Asaph 18.5.62. Ht 5 10
Wt 12 02
Midfield. From Rhyl. Wales 38 full caps.

Season	Club		
1984–85	Wrexham	44	6
1985–86		46	3
1986–87		46	8
1987–88	Portsmouth	39	3
1988–89		31	4
1988–89	Southampton	11	—
1989–90		29	4
1990–91		38	1
1991–92		34	1
1992–93	Everton	34	1

HORNE, Brian

Born Billericay 5.10.67.   Ht 5 11
Wt 13 13
Goalkeeper. From Apprentice. England Youth, Under-21.

Season	Club		
1985–86	Millwall	—	—
1986–87		32	—
1987–88		43	—
1988–89		38	—
1989–90		22	—
1990–91		28	—
1991–92		—	—
1991–92	Watford	—	—
1992–93	Millwall	—	—
1992–93	Middlesbrough	4	—
1992–93	Stoke C	1	—
1992–93	Portsmouth	—	—

HORNER, Philip

Born Leeds 10.11.66.   Ht 6 1   Wt 12 07
Forward. From Lincoln C Schoolboy.

Season	Club		
1984–85	Leicester C	—	—
1985–86		—	—
1985–86	Rotherham U	4	—
1986–87	Leicester C	3	—
1987–88		7	—
1988–89	Halifax T	38	3
1989–90		34	1
1990–91	Blackpool	39	7
1991–92		27	4
1992–93		46	7

HORSEFIELD, Geoff

Born Barnsley 1.11.73
Midfield.

Season	Club		
1992–93	Scarborough	6	1

HORTON, Duncan

Born Maidstone 18.2.67. Ht 5 10
Wt 11 12
Midfield. From Maidstone U, Charlton
Ath, Welling U.

1991–92	Barnet	29	3
1992–93		28	—

HOUCHEN, Keith

Born Middlesbrough 25.7.60. Ht 6 2
Wt 12 08
Forward. From Chesterfield Amateur.

1977–78	Hartlepool U	13	4
1978–79		39	12
1979–80		41	14
1980–81		45	17
1981–82		32	18
1981–82	Orient	14	1
1982–83		32	10
1983–84		30	9
1983–84	York C	7	1
1984–85		35	12
1985–86		25	6
1985–86	Scunthorpe U	9	3
1986–87	Coventry C	20	2
1987–88		21	3
1988–89		13	2
1988–89	Hibernian	7	2
1989–90		29	8
1990–91		21	1
1991–92	Port Vale	21	4
1992–93		28	6

HOUGHTON, Ray

Born Glasgow 9.1.62.   Ht 5 7   Wt 10 10
Midfield. Amateur. Eire 53 full caps.

1979–80	West Ham U	—	—
1980–81		—	—
1981–82		1	—
1982–83	Fulham	42	5
1983–84		40	3
1984–85		42	8
1985–86		5	—
1985–86	Oxford U	35	4
1986–87		37	5

1987–88		11	1
1987–88	Liverpool	28	5
1988–89		38	7
1989–90		19	1
1990–91		32	7
1991–92		36	8
1992–93	Aston Villa	39	3

HOUGHTON, Scott

Born Hitchin 22.10.71. Ht 5 5   Wt 11 06
Midfield. From Trainee. England Schools,
Youth.

1990–91	Tottenham H	—	—
1990–91	Ipswich T	8	1
1991–92	Tottenham H	10	2
1992–93		—	—
1992–93	Cambridge U	—	—
1992–93	Gillingham	3	—
1992–93	Charlton Ath	6	—

HOULT, Russell

Born Leicester 22.11.72.   Ht 6 3
Wt 14 01
Goalkeeper. From Trainee.

1990–91	Leicester C	—	—
1991–92		—	—
1991–92	Lincoln C	2	—
1991–92	Blackpool	—	—
1992–93	Leicester C	10	—

HOWARD, Andy

Born Southport 15.3.72   Ht 5 6   Wt 10 02
Midfield. From Liverpool trainee.

1991–92	Blackpool	—	—
From Fleetwood			
1992–93	Rochdale	15	2

HOWARD, Jonathan

Born Sheffield 7.10.71.   Ht 6 0   Wt 12 02
Forward. From Trainee.

1990–91	Rotherham U	1	—
1991–92		10	3

Season			
1992–93	....	17	2

HOWARD, Terry

Born Stepney 26.2.66. Ht 6 1   Wt 11 07
Defender. From Apprentice. England
Youth.

Season	Club	App	Goals
1983–84	Chelsea	—	—
1984–85		4	—
1985–86		1	—
1985–86	*C Palace*	4	—
1986–87	Chelsea	1	—
1986–87	*Chester C*	2	—
1986–87	Orient	12	2
1987–88		41	2
1988–89		46	5
1989–90		45	7
1990–91		46	3
1991–92		45	4
1992–93		41	5

HOWARTH, Lee

Born Bolton 3.1.68. Ht 6 1   Wt 12 06
Defender. From Chorley.

Season	Club	App	Goals
1991–92	Peterborough U	7	—
1992–93		30	—

HOWELL, David

Born London 10.10.58. Ht 6 0   Wt 12 00
Defender. From Fulham, Hillingdon Bor,
Hounslow, Harrow Bor, Enfield.

Season	Club	App	Goals
1991–92	Barnet	34	3
1992–93		23	—

HOWELLS, David

Born Guildford 15.12.67. Ht 5 11
Wt 11 10
Forward. From Trainee. England Youth.

Season	Club	App	Goals
1984–85	Tottenham H	—	—
1985–86		1	1
1986–87		1	—
1987–88		11	—
1988–89		27	3

Season			
1989–90	....	34	5
1990–91	....	29	4
1991–92	....	31	1
1992–93	....	18	1

HOWEY, Lee

Born Sunderland 1.4.69. Ht 6 2   Wt 13 09
Forward. From AC Hemptinne Eghezee.

Season	Club	App	Goals
1992–93	Sunderland	1	—

HOWEY, Steve

Born Sunderland 26.10.71.   Ht 6 1
Wt 10 05
Midfield. From Trainee.

Season	Club	App	Goals
1988–89	Newcastle U	1	—
1989–90		—	—
1990–91		11	—
1991–92		21	1
1992–93		41	2

HOYLAND, Jamie

Born Sheffield 23.1.66. Ht 6 0   Wt 12 08
Midfield. From Apprentice. England
Youth.

Season	Club	App	Goals
1983–84	Manchester C	1	—
1984–85		1	—
1985–86		—	—
1986–87	Bury	36	2
1987–88		44	8
1988–89		46	9
1989–90		46	16
1990–91	Sheffield U	21	—
1991–92		26	4
1992–93		22	2

HOYLE, Colin

Born Derby 15.1.72. Ht 5 11   Wt 12 03
Forward. From Trainee.

Season	Club	App	Goals
1989–90	Arsenal	—	—
1989–90	*Chesterfield*	3	—
1990–91	Barnsley	—	—
1991–92		—	—

| 1992–93 | .... | — — |
| 1992–93 | Bradford C .... | 33 1 |

HUGHES, Anthony

Born Liverpool 3.10.73 Ht 6 0 Wt 12 05
Defender. From Trainee. England Youth.

| 1992–93 | Crewe Alex .... | 17 1 |

HUGHES, Ceri

Born Pontypridd 26.2.71. Ht 5 10
Wt 11 05
Midfield. From Trainee. Wales Youth,
Under-21, 1 full cap.

1989–90	Luton T	1 —
1990–91	....	17 1
1991–92	....	18 —
1992–93	....	29 2

HUGHES, Ian

Born Bangor 2.8.74. Ht 5 11 Wt 12 00
Defender. From Trainee. Wales Under-21.

1991–92	Bury	17 —
1992–93	....	15 —
1992–93	....	15 —

HUGHES, John

Born Edinburgh 9.9.64. Ht 6 0 Wt 13 07
Defender. From Newtongrange Star.

1988–89	Berwick R	27 10
1989–90	....	14 4
1989–90	Swansea C....................	24 4
1990–91	Falkirk	32 2
1991–92	....	38 2
1992–93	....	15 —

HUGHES, Ken

Born Barmouth 9.1.66. Ht 6 0 Wt 11 06
Goalkeeper.

| 1985–86 | Crystal Palace............. | — — |
| 1986–87 | Shrewsbury T.............. | 6 — |

1987–88	....	2 —
1988–89	....	7 —
1989–90	....	— —
1990–91	....	36 —
1991–92	....	23 —
1992–93	Wrexham	8 —

HUGHES, Mark

Born Port Talbot 3.2.62. Ht 6 0
Wt 12 08
Defender. From Apprentice. Wales Youth.

1979–80	Bristol R	1 —
1980–81	....	38 1
1981–82	....	22 2
1982–83	....	4 —
1982–83	*Torquay U*....................	9 1
1983–84	Bristol R	9 —
1984–85	Swansea C....................	12 —
1984–85	Bristol C	20 —
1985–86	....	2 —
1985–86	Tranmere R	32 —
1986–87	....	38 1
1987–88	....	20 —
1988–89	....	37 1
1989–90	....	45 4
1990–91	....	42 2
1991–92	....	33 1
1992–93	....	11 —

HUGHES, Mark

Born Wrexham 1.11.63. Ht 5 9 Wt 11 12
Forward. From Apprentice. Wales Youth,
Under-21, 50 full caps.

1980–81	Manchester U.............	— —
1981–82	....	— —
1982–83	....	— —
1983–84	....	11 4
1984–85	....	38 16
1985–86	....	40 17
From Barcelona, *Bayern Munich*		
1988–89	Manchester U.............	38 14
1989–90	....	37 13
1990–91	....	31 10
1991–92	....	39 11
1992–93	....	41 15

HUGHES, Michael

Born Larne 2.8.71. Ht 5 6 Wt 10 08
Forward. From Carrick R. Northern
Ireland Under-23, 11 full caps.

Season	Club		
1988–89	Manchester C	1	—
1989–90		—	—
1990–91		1	—
1991–92		24	1
To Strasbourg			

HUGHTON, Chris

Born West Ham 11.12.58. Ht 5 7
Wt 11 05
Defender. From Amateur. Eire Under-21,
53 full caps.

Season	Club		
1977–78	Tottenham H	—	—
1978–79		—	—
1979–80		39	1
1980–81		34	1
1981–82		37	2
1982–83		38	3
1983–84		34	3
1984–85		31	1
1985–86		33	1
1986–87		9	—
1987–88		13	—
1988–89		21	—
1989–90		8	—
1990–91		—	—
1990–91	West Ham U	32	—
1991–92		1	—
1991–92	Brentford	12	—
1992–93		20	—

HUISTRA, Pieter

Born Goenga 18.1.67. Ht 5 7 Wt 11 4
Forward. From FC Twente.

Season	Club		
1990–91	Rangers	27	4
1991–92		32	5
1992–93		30	4

HULME, Kevin

Born Farnworth 2.12.67. Ht 5 10
Wt 11 09
Forward. From Radcliffe Borough.

Season	Club		
1988–89	Bury	5	—
1989–90		19	1
1989–90	Chester C	4	—
1990–91	Bury	24	7
1991–92		30	4
1992–93		32	9

HUMES, Tony

Born Blyth 19.3.66. Ht 5 11 Wt 11 00
Defender. From Apprentice.

Season	Club		
1983–84	Ipswich T	—	—
1984–85		—	—
1985–86		—	—
1986–87		22	2
1987–88		27	—
1988–89		26	3
1989–90		24	3
1990–91		16	2
1991–92		5	—
1991–92	Wrexham	8	—
1992–93		38	—

HUMPHREY, John

Born Paddington 31.1.61. Ht 5 10
Wt 11 03
Defender. From Apprentice.

Season	Club		
1978–79	Wolverhampton W	—	—
1979–80		2	—
1980–81		12	—
1981–82		23	—
1982–83		42	3
1983–84		28	—
1984–85		42	—
1985–86	Charlton Ath	39	2
1986–87		39	—
1987–88		40	—
1988–89		38	1
1989–90		38	—
1990–91	Crystal Palace	38	1
1991–92		37	—
1992–93		32	—

HUMPHRIES, Glenn

Born Hull 11.8.64.   Ht 6 0   Wt 12 10
Defender. From Apprentice. England
Youth.

1980–81	Doncaster R	1	—
1981–82		14	—
1982–83		40	5
1983–84		44	2
1984–85		27	—
1985–86		29	—
1986–87		17	1
1986–87	*Lincoln C*	9	—
1987–88	Doncaster R	8	—
1987–88	Bristol C	24	—
1988–89		22	—
1989–90		37	—
1990–91		2	—
1990–91	Scunthorpe U	10	1
1991–92		32	3
1992–93		30	1

HUNT, Andy

Born Thurrock 9.6.70.   Ht 6 0   Wt 11 07
Forward. From Kettering T.

1990–91	Newcastle U	16	2
1991–92		27	9
1992–93		—	—
1992–93	*WBA*	10	9

HUNT, Jonathan

Born London 2.11.71.   Ht 5 10   Wt 11 00
Forward.

1991–92	Barnet	14	—
1992–93		19	—

HUNT, Paul

Born Swindon 8.10.71.   Ht 5 5   Wt 10 02
Forward. From Trainee.

1989–90	Swindon T	4	—
1990–91		2	—
1991–92		—	—
1992–93		5	—

HUNTER, Gordon

Born Wallyford 3.5.67.   Ht 5 10
Wt 10 05
Defender. From Musselburgh Windsor.
Scotland Youth, Under-21.

1983–84	Hibernian	1	—
1984–85		6	—
1985–86		25	—
1986–87		29	—
1987–88		35	—
1988–89		33	1
1989–90		34	—
1990–91		20	1
1991–92		37	2
1992–93		23	—

HUNTER, Paul

Born Kirkcaldy 30.8.68.   Ht 6 0
Wt 12 09
Forward. From Leven Royal Colts.

1984–85	East Fife	5	1
1985–86		20	7
1986–87		38	8
1987–88		39	17
1988–89		33	9
1989–90		29	14
1989–90	Hull C	9	3
1990–91		18	2
1991–92		15	—
1992–93		26	6

HUNTER, Roy

Born Cleveland 29.10.73.   Ht 5 9
Wt 11 00
Midfield. From Trainee.

1991–92	WBA	6	1
1992–93		1	—

HURLOCK, Terry

Born Hackney 22.9.58.   Ht 5 9   Wt 13 03
Midfield. From Leytonstone/Ilford.
England B.

1980–81	Brentford	42	4

Season	Club		Apps	Goals
1981–82			40	2
1982–83			39	3
1983–84			32	4
1984–85			40	3
1985–86			27	2
1985–86	Reading		16	—
1986–87			13	—
1986–87	Millwall		13	1
1987–88			28	4
1988–89			34	3
1989–90			29	—
1990–91	Rangers		29	2
1991–92			—	—
1991–92	Southampton		29	—
1992–93			30	—

HURST, Lee

Born Nuneaton 21.9.70. Ht 6 0
Wt 11 09
Midfield. From Trainee.

Season	Club		Apps	Goals
1989–90	Coventry C		—	—
1990–91			4	—
1991–92			10	—
1992–93			35	2

HUTCHINGS, Chris

Born Winchester 5.7.57. Ht 5 10
Wt 11 06
Defender. From Harrow Bor.

Season	Club		Apps	Goals
1980–81	Chelsea		12	1
1981–82			35	1
1982–83			36	—
1983–84			4	1
1983–84	Brighton		26	1
1984–85			42	1
1985–86			29	1
1986–87			36	—
1987–88			20	1
1987–88	Huddersfield T		23	—
1988–89			41	5
1989–90			46	5
1990–91	Walsall		40	—
1991–92	Rotherham U		41	4
1992–93			30	—

HUTCHISON, Don

Born Gateshead 9.5.71.   Ht 6 2   Wt 11 08
Forward. From Trainee.

Season	Club		Apps	Goals
1989–90	Hartlepool U		13	2
1990–91			11	—
1990–91	Liverpool		—	—
1991–92			3	—
1992–93			31	7

HUXFORD, Richard

Born Scunthorpe 25.7.69   Ht 5 10
Wt 11 06
Defender. From Kettering T.

Season	Club		Apps	Goals
1992–93	Barnet		33	1

HYDE, Graham

Born Doncaster 10.11.70.   Ht 5 7
Wt 11 07
Midfield. From Trainee.

Season	Club		Apps	Goals
1988–89	Sheffield W		—	—
1989–90			—	—
1990–91			—	—
1991–92			13	—
1992–93			20	1

HYSLOP, Christian

Born Watford 14.6.72.   Ht 5 11   Wt 11 07
Defender. From Trainee.

Season	Club		Apps	Goals
1989–90	Southend U		—	—
1990–91			11	—
1991–92			2	—
1992–93			6	—

IMPEY, Andrew

Born Hammersmith 13.9.71.   Ht 5 8
Wt 10 06
Forward. From Yeading. England
Under-21.

1990–91	QPR	—	—
1991–92		13	—
1992–93		40	2

INCE, Paul

Born Ilford 21.10.67.   Ht 5 10   Wt 11 07
Midfield. From Trainee. England Youth,
Under-21, B, 9 full caps.

1985–86	West Ham U	—	—
1986–87		10	1
1987–88		28	3
1988–89		33	3
1989–90		1	—
1989–90	Manchester U	26	—
1990–91		31	3
1991–92		33	3
1992–93		41	6

INGEBRITSEN, Kare

Born Rosenborg 11.11.65
Defender. From Rosenborg. Norway full
caps.

1992–93	Manchester C	7	—

INGLIS, John

Born Edinburgh 16.10.66.   Ht 6 0
Wt 13 0
Defender. From Hutchison Vale.

1983–84	East Fife	4	1
1984–85	9		—
1985–86		30	—
1986–87		13	—
1986–87	Brechin C	15	—
1987–88		26	3
1988–89		12	1
1988–89	Meadowbank T	12	1
1989–90		38	3

1990–91	St Johnstone	31	1
1991–92		40	—
1992–93		39	—

INGRAM, Godfrey

Born Luton 26.10.59.   Ht 5 7   Wt 10 03
Forward. From Apprentice. England
Schools, Youth.

1977–78	Luton T	3	1
1978–79		3	—
1979–80		1	—
1979–80	Northampton T	10	4
1980–81	Luton T	17	5
1981–82		—	—
From San Jose Earthquakes			
1982–83	Cardiff C	11	2
To San Jose Earthquakes			
1992–93	Peterborough U	1	—

IORFA, Dominic

Born Lagos 1.10.68.   Ht 6 1   Wt 12 12
Forward. From Antwerp. Nigeria full
caps.

1989–90	QPR	1	—
1990–91		6	—
1991–92		1	—
1992–93		—	—
1992–93	Peterborough U	26	1

IRELAND, Simon

Born Barnstaple 23.11.71.   Ht 5 11
Wt 11 12
Forward. From School.

1990–91	Huddersfield T	6	—
1991–92		9	—
1991–92	*Wrexham*	5	—
1992–93	Huddersfield T	4	—
1992–93	Blackburn R	1	—

IRONS, David

Born Glasgow 18.7.61.   Ht 6 0   Wt 11 04
Midfield. From Kello Rovers.

1984–85	Ayr U	34	6

1985–86	....	37	6
1986–87	....	4	1
1986–87	Clydebank....................	23	1
1987–88	....	31	6
1987–88	Dunfermline Ath	11	1
1988–89	....	36	2
1989–90	....	23	2
1990–91	....	34	4
1991–92	....	2	—
1991–92	Partick T.....................	41	8
1992–93	....	43	2

IRONS, Kenny

Born Liverpool 4.11.70. Ht 5 9   Wt 11 00
Forward. From Trainee.

1989–90	Tranmere R	3	—
1990–91	....	32	6
1991–92	....	43	7
1992–93	....	42	7

IRONSIDE, Ian

Born Sheffield 8.3.64.   Ht 6 2   Wt 13 00
Goalkeeper. From Barnsley Apprentice, N.
Ferriby U.

1987–88	Scarborough................	6	—
1988–89	....	28	—
1989–90	....	14	—
1990–91	....	40	—
1991–92	Middlesbrough............	1	—
1991–92	*Scarborough*	7	—
1992–93	Middlesbrough............	12	—

IRVINE, Brian

Born Bellshill 24.5.65.   Ht 6 2   Wt 13 0
Defender. From Victoria Park. Scotland 4
full caps.

1983–84	Falkirk	3	—
1984–85	....	35	—
1985–86	Aberdeen......................	1	—
1986–87	....	20	1
1987–88	....	16	1
1988–89	....	27	2
1989–90	....	31	1
1990–91	....	29	2

1991–92	....	41	4
1992–93	....	39	5

IRWIN, Denis

Born Cork 31.70.65.   Ht 5 8   Wt 11 00
Defender. From Apprentice. Eire Schools,
Youth, B, Under-21, 21 full caps.

1983–84	Leeds U	12	—
1984–85	....	41	1
1985–86	....	19	—
1986–87	Oldham Ath.................	41	1
1987–88	....	43	—
1988–89	....	41	2
1989–90	....	42	1
1990–91	Manchester U	34	—
1991–92	....	38	4
1992–93	....	40	5

ISAACS, Tony

Born Middlesbrough 8.4.73.   Ht 5 8
Wt 10 07
Midfield.

1991–92	Darlington	9	—
1992–93	....	22	1

JACK, Paul

Born Malaya 15.5.65.   Ht 5 10   Wt 11 7
Midfield. From Fallin Miners Welfare.

1985–86	Arbroath	14	—
1986–87		35	1
1987–88		31	—
1988–89		25	5
1989–90	Airdrieonians	26	2
1990–91		35	—
1991–92		24	1
1992–93		33	3

JACK, Ross

Born Inverness 21.3.59   Ht 5 11   Wt 12 0
Forward. From Apprentice.

1976–77	Everton	––	—
1977–78		—	—
1978–79		1	1
1979–80		—	—
1979–80	*Cardiff C*	—	—
1979–80	Norwich C	—	—
1980–81		11	—
1981–82		35	10
1982–83		10	—
1983–84	Lincoln C	36	9
1984–85		24	7
1985–86	Dundee	6	—
1986–87		28	4
1987–88		4	—
1987–88	Dunfermline Ath	25	4
1988–89		36	18
1989–90		36	16
1990–91		33	8
1991–92	Kilmarnock	37	8
1992–93		18	5
1992–93	Montrose	6	2

JACKSON, Chris

Born Barnsley 16.1.76   Ht 6 0   Wt 12 00
Forward. From Trainee.

| 1992–93 | Barnsley | 3 | — |

JACKSON, Christopher

Born Edinburgh 29.10.73   Ht 5 7
Wt 10 3
Midfield. From Salvesen BC.

| 1992–93 | Hibernian | 1 | — |

JACKSON, Darren

Born Edinburgh 25.7.66.   Ht 5 10
Wt 10 10
Forward. From Broxburn Am.

1985–86	Meadowbank T	39	17
1986–87		9	5
1986–87	Newcastle U	23	3
1987–88		31	2
1988–89		15	2
1988–89	Dundee U	1	—
1989–90		25	7
1990–91		33	12
1991–92		28	11
1992–93	Hibernian	36	13

JACKSON, Darren

Born Bristol 24.9.71.   Ht 6 1   Wt 12 08
Defender. From Trainee.

1989–90	Oxford U	1	—
1990–91		5	—
1991–92		5	—
1992–93		1	—
1992–93	*Reading*	5	—

JACKSON, Matthew

Born Leeds 19.10.71.   Ht 6 1   Wt 12 12
Defender. From School. England Schools,
Under-21.

1990–91	Luton T	—	—
1990–91	*Preston NE*	4	—
1991–92	Luton T	9	—
1991–92	Everton	30	1
1992–93		27	3

JACKSON, Michael

Born West Cheshire 4.12.73. Ht 5 11
Wt 11 10
Defender. From Trainee.

Season	Club		
1991–92	Crewe Alex	1	—
1992–93		4	—

JACKSON, Peter

Born Bradford 6.4.61. Ht 6 0 Wt 12 07
Defender. From Apprentice.

Season	Club		
1978–79	Bradford C	9	1
1979–80		12	—
1980–81		45	1
1981–82		32	8
1982–83		41	3
1983–84		42	3
1984–85		45	8
1985–86		42	—
1986–87		10	—
1986–87	Newcastle U	31	1
1987–88		28	2
1988–89		1	—
1988–89	Bradford C	32	3
1989–90		26	2
1990–91	Huddersfield T	38	1
1991–92		45	1
1992–93		39	1

JAKUB, Joe

Born Falkirk 7.12.56. Ht 5 6 Wt 9 06
Midfield. From Apprentice.

Season	Club		
1973–74	Burnley	—	—
1974–75		—	—
1975–76		1	—
1976–77		5	—
1977–78		—	—
1978–79		13	—
1979–80		23	—
1980–81		—	—
1981–82	Bury	33	1
1982–83		46	2
1983–84		46	3
1984–85		46	11
1985–86		40	3
1986–87		44	6

Season	Club		
1987–88		10	1
From AZ Alkmaar			
1988–89	Chester C	42	1
1989–90	Burnley	46	5
1990–91		46	3
1991–92		39	—
1992–93		32	—

JAMES, David

Born Welwyn 1.8.70. Ht 6 4 Wt 14 13
Goalkeeper. From Trainee. England
Youth, Under-21.

Season	Club		
1988–89	Watford	—	—
1989–90		—	—
1990–91		46	—
1991–92		43	—
1992–93	Liverpool	29	—

JAMES, Julian

Born Tring 22.3.70. Ht 5 10 Wt 11 10
Midfield. From Trainee. England
Under-21.

Season	Club		
1987–88	Luton T	3	—
1988–89		1	—
1989–90		20	1
1990–91		17	1
1991–92		28	2
1991–92	*Preston NE*	6	—
1992–93	Luton T	43	2

JAMES, Lutel

Born 2.6.72
Defender.

Season	Club		
1992–93	Scarborough	6	—

JAMES, Martin

Born Formby 18.5.71. Ht 5 10 Wt 11 07
Midfield. From Trainee.

Season	Club		
1989–90	Preston NE	—	—
1990–91		37	2
1991–92		36	4
1992–93		25	5

| 1992–93 | Stockport Co | 8 | — |

JAMES, Robbie

Born Swansea 23.3.57. Ht 5 11 Wt 13 0
Forward. From Apprentice. Wales Under-
21, 47 full caps.

1972–73	Swansea C	1	—
1973–74		29	2
1974–75		42	8
1975–76		45	8
1976–77		46	14
1977–78		42	16
1978–79		43	14
1979–80		29	6
1980–81		35	8
1981–82		42	14
1982–83		40	9
1983–84	Stoke C	40	6
1984–85		8	—
1984–85	QPR	20	2
1985–86		28	1
1986–87		39	1
1987–88	Leicester C	23	—
1987–88	Swansea C	19	3
1988–89		41	9
1989–90		30	4
1990–91	Bradford C	46	3
1991–92		43	3
1992–93	Cardiff C	42	2

JAMES, Tony

Born Sheffield 27.6.67. Ht 6 3 Wt 14 02
Defender. From Gainsborough T.

1988–89	Lincoln C	28	—
1989–90		1	—
1989–90	Leicester C	31	2
1990–91		38	8
1991–92		13	—
1992–93		16	—

JAMIESON, Willie

Born Barnsley 27.4.63. Ht 5 11 Wt 12 00
Defender. From Tynecastle BC.

| 1980–81 | Hibernian | 28 | 12 |

1981–82		12	5
1982–83		19	2
1983–84		33	4
1984–85		25	2
1985–86	Hamilton A	39	2
1986–87		15	—
1987–88		41	4
1988–89		34	1
1989–90	Dundee	14	—
1990–91		38	2
1991–92		38	4
1992–93	Partick T	28	3

JEFFERS, John

Born Liverpool 5.10.68. Ht 5 10
Wt 11 10
Forward. From Trainee. England Schools.

1986–87	Liverpool	—	—
1987–88		—	—
1988–89		—	—
1988–89	Port Vale	15	—
1989–90		40	1
1990–91		31	2
1991–92		33	3
1992–93		26	2

JEFFREY, Mike

Born Liverpool 11.8.71. Ht 5 11
Wt 11 06
Forward. From Trainee.

1988–89	Bolton W	9	—
1989–90		4	—
1990–91		—	—
1991–92		2	—
1991–92	*Doncaster R*	11	6
1992–93	Doncaster R	30	12

JEMSON, Nigel

Born Preston 10.8.69. Ht 5 10 Wt 11 10
Forward. From Trainee. England
Under-21.

1985–86	Preston NE	1	—
1986–87		4	3
1987–88		27	5

Season	Club	App	Goals
1987–88	Nottingham F	—	—
1988–89		—	—
1988–89	*Bolton W*	5	—
1988–89	*Preston NE*	9	2
1989–90	Nottingham F	18	4
1990–91		23	8
1991–92		6	1
1991–92	Sheffield W	20	4
1992–93		13	—

JENKINS, Iain

Born Prescot 24.11.72. Ht 5 11 Wt 11 07
Defender. From Trainee.

Season	Club	App	Goals
1990–91	Everton	1	—
1991–92		3	—
1992–93		1	—
1992–93	*Bradford C*	6	—

JENKINS, Steve

Born Merthyr 16.7.72. Ht 5 10 Wt 11 02
Defender. From Trainee. Wales Under-21.

Season	Club	App	Goals
1990–91	Swansea C	1	—
1991–92		34	—
1992–93		33	—

JENKINSON, Leigh

Born Thorne 9.7.69. Ht 6 0 Wt 12 02
Forward. From Trainee.

Season	Club	App	Goals
1987–88	Hull C	3	1
1988–89		11	—
1989–90		22	—
1990–91		26	—
1990–91	*Rotherham U*	7	—
1991–92	Hull C	42	8
1992–93		26	4
1992–93	Coventry C	5	—

JENNINGS, Jedd

Born Bermuda 15.10.71.
Forward. From Pembroke, Bermuda.

Season	Club	App	Goals
1991–92	Hereford U	11	—
1992–93		5	—

JENSEN, John

Born Denmark 3.5.65. Ht 5 10 Wt 12 06
Midfield. From Brondby. Denmark full
caps.

Season	Club	App	Goals
1992–93	Arsenal	32	—

JEPSON, Ron

Born Stoke 12.5.63. Ht 6 1 Wt 13 02
Forward. From Nantwich.

Season	Club	App	Goals
1988–89	Port Vale	2	—
1989–90		5	—
1989–90	*Peterborough U*	18	5
1990–91	Port Vale	15	—
1990–91	Preston NE	14	3
1991–92		24	5
1992–93	Exeter C	38	8

JESS, Eoin

Born Aberdeen 13.12.70. Ht 5 7
Wt 10 10
Forward. From Rangers S Form. Scotland
Under-21, 2 full caps.

Season	Club	App	Goals
1987–88	Aberdeen	—	—
1988–89		2	—
1989–90		11	3
1990–91		27	13
1991–92		39	12
1992–93		31	12

JEWELL, Paul

Born Liverpool 28.9.64. Ht 5 8 Wt 11 10
Forward. From Apprentice.

Season	Club	App	Goals
1982–83	Liverpool	—	—
1983–84		—	—
1984–85	Wigan Ath	26	9
1985–86		29	6
1986–87		39	9
1987–88		43	11
1988–89	Bradford C	39	4
1989–90		30	4
1990–91		38	4
1991–92		30	6
1992–93		46	16

JOACHIM, Julian

Born Peterborough 20.9.74 Ht 5 6
Wt 11 10
Forward. From Trainee. England Youth.

1992–93	Leicester C	26	10

JOBLING, Kevin

Born Sunderland 1.1.68. Ht 5 9
Wt 10 11
Midfield. From Apprentice.

1985–86	Leicester C	—	—
1986–87		3	—
1987–88		6	—
1987–88	Grimsby T	15	1
1988–89		32	4
1989–90		33	1
1990–91		45	—
1991–92		36	2
1992–93		14	—

JOBSON, Richard

Born Hull 9.5.63. Ht 6 1 Wt 13 05
Defender. From Burton Alb. England B.

1982–83	Watford	13	1
1983–84		13	2
1984–85		2	1
1984–85	Hull C	8	—
1985–86		36	7
1986–87		40	5
1987–88		44	2
1988–89		46	1
1989–90		45	2
1990–91		2	—
1990–91	Oldham Ath	44	1
1991–92		36	2
1992–93		40	2

JOHNROSE, Lenny

Born Preston 29.11.69. Ht 5 11 Wt 12 00
Forward. From Trainee.

1987–88	Blackburn R	1	—
1988–89		—	—
1989–90		8	3

1990–91		26	7
1991–92		7	1
1991–92	*Preston NE*	3	1
1991–92	Hartlepool U	15	2
1992–93		38	6

JOHNSEN, Erland

Born Fredrikstad (Norway) 5.4.67.
Ht 6 0 Wt 12 10
Defender. From Bayern Munich. Norway
full caps.

1989–90	Chelsea	18	—
1990–91		6	—
1991–92		7	—
1992–93		13	—

JOHNSON, Alan

Born Ince 19.2.71. Ht 5 11 Wt 11 12
Defender. From Trainee.

1988–89	Wigan Ath	8	1
1989–90		33	1
1990–91		43	5
1991–92		44	4
1992–93		36	1

JOHNSON, Andrew

Born Bath 2.5.74. Ht 5 11 Wt 11 06
Midfield. From Trainee.

1991–92	Norwich C	2	—
1992–93		2	1

JOHNSON, David

Born Rother Valley 29.10.70. Ht 6 2
Wt 13 08
Forward. From Trainee.

1989–90	Sheffield W	—	—
1990–91		—	—
1991–92		6	—
1991–92	*Hartlepool U*	7	2
1992–93	Sheffield W	—	—
1992–93	*Hartlepool U*	3	—

JOHNSON, Gavin

Born Eye 10.10.70   Ht 5 11   Wt 11 12
Defender. From Trainee.

Season	Club		
1988–89	Ipswich T	4	—
1989–90		6	—
1990–91		7	—
1991–92		42	5
1992–93		40	5

JOHNSON, Grant

Born Dundee 24.3.72. Ht 5 11   Wt 10 00
Midfield. From Broughty Ferry. Scotland
Under-21.

Season	Club		
1990–91	Dundee U	—	—
1991–92		10	1
1992–93		17	1

JOHNSON, Ian

Born Newcastle 14.2.69   Ht 6 2   Wt 13 08
Defender. From Whitley Bay.

Season	Club		
1992–93	Torquay U	9	1

JOHNSON, Marvin

Born Wembley 29.10.68. Ht 6 0
Wt 12 03
Defender. From Apprentice.

Season	Club		
1986–87	Luton T	—	—
1987–88		9	—
1988–89		16	—
1989–90		12	—
1990–91		26	—
1991–92		—	—
1992–93		40	3

JOHNSON, Michael

Born Nottingham 4.7.73. Ht 5 11
Wt 11 00
Defender. From Trainee.

Season	Club		
1991–92	Notts Co	5	—
1992–93		37	—

JOHNSON, Nigel

Born Rotherham 23.6.64.   Ht 6 2
Wt 13 13
Defender. From Apprentice.

Season	Club		
1982–83	Rotherham U	11	—
1983–84		43	1
1983–84	*Nottingham F*	—	—
1984–85	Rotherham U	35	—
1985–86	Manchester C	4	—
1986–87		—	—
1987–88	Rotherham U	23	—
1988–89		26	2
1989–90		43	2
1990–91		17	1
1991–92		35	2
1992–93		31	2

JOHNSON, Richard

Born Kurri, Kurri 27.4.74.   Ht 5 10
Wt 11 13
Midfield. From Trainee.

Season	Club		
1991–92	Watford	2	—
1992–93		1	—

JOHNSON, Tommy

Born Newcastle 15.1.71.   Ht 5 10
Wt 11 02
Forward. From Trainee. England
Under-21.

Season	Club		
1988–89	Notts Co	10	4
1989–90		40	18
1990–91		37	16
1991–92		31	9
1991–92	Derby Co	12	2
1992–93		35	8

JOHNSTON, Alan

Born Glasgow 14.12.73   Ht 5 7   Wt 9 7
Forward. From Tynecastle BC.

Season	Club		
1991–92	Hearts	—	—
1992–93		2	1

JOHNSTON, Forbes

Born Aberdeen 3.8.71. Ht 5 10 Wt 9 12
Defender. From Musselburgh Ath.
Scotland Under-21.

Season	Club	App	Goals
1990–91	Falkirk	—	—
1991–92		12	—
1992–93		22	1

JOHNSTON, Mo

Born Glasgow 30.4.63. Ht 5 9 Wt 10 06
Forward. From Milton Battlefield.
Scotland Under-21, 38 full caps.

Season	Club	App	Goals
1980–81	Partick T	—	—
1981–82		32	9
1982–83		39	22
1983–84		14	10
1983–84	Watford	29	20
1984–85		9	3
1984–85	Celtic	27	14
1985–86		32	15
1986–87		40	23
1987–88	Nantes	32	13
1988–89		34	9
1989–90	Rangers	36	15
1990–91		29	11
1991–92		11	5
1991–92	Everton	21	7
1992–93		13	3

JOHNSTON, Sammy

Born Glasgow 13.4.67. Ht 5 9 Wt 10 07
Midfield. From Bishopbriggs BC.

Season	Club	App	Goals
1984–85	St Johnstone	3	—
1985–86		27	2
1986–87		39	6
1987–88		39	11
1988–89		30	3
1989–90		37	7
1990–91		1	—
1991–92	Partick T	20	2
1992–93		15	1

JOHNSTONE, Glenn

Born Kenya 5.6.67 Ht 6 3 Wt 14 07
Goalkeeper. From Lancaster C.

Season	Club	App	Goals
1992–93	Preston NE	10	—

JONES, Alex

Born Blackburn 27.11.64. Ht 6 2
Wt 12 08
Defender. From Apprentice.

Season	Club	App	Goals
1982–83	Oldham Ath	2	—
1983–84		2	—
1984–85		5	—
1984–85	Stockport Co	3	—
1985–86	Oldham Ath	—	—
1986–87	Preston NE	46	1
1987–88		22	2
1988–89		30	—
1989–90		3	—
1989–90	Carlisle U	36	4
1990–91		26	—
1991–92	Rochdale	13	—
1991–92	Motherwell	12	1
1992–93		—	—
1992–93	Rochdale	29	2

JONES, Andy

Born Wrexham 9.1.63. Ht 5 11 Wt 13 06
Forward. From Rhyl. Wales 6 full caps.

Season	Club	App	Goals
1985–86	Port Vale	41	12
1986–87		43	31
1987–88		6	6
1987–88	Charlton Ath	25	6
1988–89		9	4
1988–89	Port Vale	17	3
1989–90	Charlton Ath	25	5
1989–90	Bristol C	4	1
1990–91	Charlton Ath	7	—
1990–91	Bournemouth	33	8
1991–92		7	—
1991–92	Leyton Orient	30	5
1992–93		29	8

JONES, Barry

Born Prescot 20.6.70   Ht 5 10   Wt 11 02
Defender. From Prescot T.

Season	Club	Apps	Goals
1988–89	Liverpool	—	—
1989–90		—	—
1990–91		—	—
1991–92		—	—
1992–93	Wrexham	42	2

JONES, David

Born Harrow 3.7.64   Ht 6 4   Wt 13 10
Forward.

Season	Club	Apps	Goals
1987–88	Chelsea	—	—
1988–89	Bury	1	—
1988–89	Leyton Orient	2	—
1988–89	Burnley	4	—
1989–90	Ipswich T	—	—
1989–90	Doncaster R	27	12
1990–91		13	2
1991–92	Bury	9	—
1992–93	Hull C	12	1

JONES, Keith

Born Dulwich 14.10.64.   Ht 5 9   Wt 11 02
Midfield. From Apprentice. England
Schools, Youth.

Season	Club	Apps	Goals
1982–83	Chelsea	2	—
1983–84		—	—
1984–85		19	2
1985–86		14	2
1986–87		17	3
1987–88		—	—
1987–88	Brentford	36	1
1988–89		40	3
1989–90		42	2
1990–91		45	6
1991–92		6	1
1991–92	Southend U	34	5
1992–93		29	1

JONES, Kevin

Born Wrexham 16.2.74.   Ht 5 10
Wt 11 00
Defender. From Trainee.

Season	Club	Apps	Goals
1991–92	Wrexham	1	—

Season	Club	Apps	Goals
1992–93		3	—

JONES, Lee

Born Wrexham 29.5.73.   Ht 5 8   Wt 10 08
Forward. From Trainee. Wales Under-21.

Season	Club	Apps	Goals
1990–91	Wrexham	18	5
1991–92		21	5
1991–92	Liverpool	—	—
1992–93		—	—

JONES, Murray

Born Bexley 7.10.64.   Ht 6 4   Wt 14 00
Forward. From Carshalton.

Season	Club	Apps	Goals
1989–90	Crystal Palace	—	—
1990–91	Bristol C	—	—
1990–91	Doncaster R	—	—
1990–91	Exeter C	20	3
1991–92	Grimsby T	28	3
1992–93	Brentford	16	—

JONES, Paul

Born Chirk 18.4.67   Ht 6 3   Wt 14 00
Goalkeeper. From Kidderminster H.

Season	Club	Apps	Goals
1991–92	Wolverhampton W	—	—
1992–93		16	—

JONES, Philip

Born Liverpool 1.12.69.   Ht 5 8   Wt 10 09
Defender. From Trainee.

Season	Club	Apps	Goals
1987–88	Everton	1	—
1988–89		—	—
1989–90		—	—
1989–90	Blackpool	6	—
1990–91	Everton	—	—
1990–91	Wigan Ath	20	1
1991–92		41	1
1992–93		27	—

JONES, Richard

Born Pontypool 26.4.69.   Ht 5 11
Wt 11 01
Defender.

Season	Club	Apps	Goals
1986–87	Newport Co	10	—

1987–88		31	1
1988–89	Hereford U	38	1
1989–90		19	3
1990–91		40	1
1991–92		16	1
1992–93		35	3

JONES, Rob

Born Wrexham 5.11.71. Ht 5 8   Wt 11 00
Defender. From Schoolboy, Trainee.
England Under-21 1 full cap.

1987–88	Crewe Alex	5	—
1988–89		19	1
1989–90		11	—
1990–91		32	1
1991–92		8	—
1991–92	Liverpool	28	—
1992–93		30	—

JONES, Ryan

Born Sheffield 23.7.73 Ht 6 1   Wt 11 10
Midfield. From Trainee.

1991–92	Sheffield W	—	—
1992–93		9	—

JONES, Steve

Born Cambridge 17.3.70   Ht 5 11
Wt 12 00
Forward. From Billericay.

1992–93	West Ham U	6	2

JONES, Steven

Born Teeside 31.1.74.   Ht 5 11   Wt 12 03
Goalkeeper. From Trainee.

1991–92	Hartlepool U	6	—
1992–93		3	—

JONES, Tommy

Born Aldershot 7.10.64.   Ht 5 10
Wt 11 07
Midfield. From Chelsea apprentice,
Farnborough, Weymouth.

1987–88	Aberdeen	28	3

1988–89		—	—
1988–89	Swindon T	40	6
1989–90		44	2
1990–91		43	—
1991–92		41	4
1992–93	Reading	21	1

JONES, Vaughan

Born Tonyrefail 2.9.59.   Ht 5 8   Wt 11 11
Defender. From Apprentice. Wales
Under-21.

1976–77	Bristol R	1	—
1977–78		—	—
1978–79		22	1
1979–80		23	1
1980–81		21	1
1981–82		34	—
1982–83	Newport Co	43	—
1983–84		25	4
1984–85	Cardiff C	11	—
1984–85	Bristol R	20	—
1985–86		32	—
1986–87		34	1
1987–88		46	3
1988–89		45	2
1989–90		46	2
1990–91		44	1
1991–92		1	—
1992–93		12	—

JONES, Vinny

Born Watford 5.1.65.   Ht 5 11   Wt 11 10
Midfield. From Wealdstone.

1986–87	Wimbledon	22	4
1987–88		24	2
1988–89		31	3
1989–90	Leeds U	45	5
1990–91		1	—
1990–91	Sheffield U	31	2
1991–92		4	—
1991–92	Chelsea	35	3
1992–93		7	1
1992–93	Wimbledon	27	1

JORDAN, Scott

Born Newcastle 19.7.75 Ht 5 10
Wt 11 02
Midfield. From Trainee.

| 1992–93 | York C | 1 | — |

JOSEPH, Roger

Born Paddington 24.12.65. Ht 5 11
Wt 11 10
Defender. From Juniors. England B.

1984–85	Brentford	1	—
1985–86		28	1
1986–87		32	1
1987–88		43	—
1988–89	Wimbledon	31	—
1989–90		19	—
1990–91		38	—
1991–92		26	—
1992–93		32	—

JOYCE, Joe

Born Consett 18.3.61. Ht 5 10 Wt 11 07
Defender. From School.

1979–80	Barnsley	8	—
1980–81		33	—
1981–82		20	—
1982–83		32	1
1983–84		40	1
1984–85		41	—
1985–86		40	—
1986–87		34	—
1987–88		38	2
1988–89		45	—
1989–90		—	—
1990–91		3	—
1990–91	Scunthorpe U	21	—
1991–92		40	2
1992–93		30	—

JOYCE, Sean

Born Doncaster 15.2.67. Ht 5 8
Wt 10 05
Midfield.

| 1985–86 | Doncaster R | 15 | — |

1986–87		14	—
1986–87	*Exeter C*	1	—
1987–88	Doncaster R	12	1
1988–89	Torquay U	30	3
1989–90		41	5
1990–91		25	3
1991–92		35	1
1992–93		27	3

JOYCE, Warren

Born Oldham 20.1.65. Ht 5 9 Wt 11 11
Midfield. Local.

1982–83	Bolton W	8	—
1983–84		45	3
1984–85		45	5
1985–86		31	4
1986–87		44	5
1987–88		11	—
1987–88	Preston NE	22	—
1988–89		40	9
1989–90		44	11
1990–91		42	9
1991–92		29	5
1992–93	Plymouth Arg	30	3

JUDGE, Alan

Born Kingsbury 14.5.60. Ht 5 11
Wt 11 06
Goalkeeper. From Amateur.

1977–78	Luton T	—	—
1978–79		—	—
1979–80		1	—
1980–81		2	—
1981–82		4	—
1982–83		4	—
1982–83	*Reading*	33	—
1983–84	Reading	41	—
1984–85		3	—
1984–85	Oxford U	—	—
1985–86		19	—
1985–86	*Lincoln C*	2	—
1986–87	Oxford U	9	—
1989–90		17	—
1987–88		9	—
1987–88	*Cardiff C*	8	—
1988–89	Oxford U	20	—

1989–90	....	17	—
1990–91	....	6	—
1991–92	Hereford U	24	—
1992–93	....	42	—

JULES, Mark

Born Bradford 5.9.71.   Ht 5 9
Forward. From Trainee.

1990–91	Bradford C	—	—
1991–92	Scarborough................	41	8
1992–93	....	36	8

JUPP, Duncan

Born Guildford 25.1.75   Ht 6 0   Wt 12 02
Defender. From Trainee.

| 1992–93 | Fulham .... | 3 | — |

JURYEFF, Ian

Born Gosport 24.11.62.   Ht 5 11   Wt 12 0
Forward. From Apprentice.

1980–81	Southampton	—	—
1981–82	....	—	—
1982–83	....	—	—
From Sweden			
1983–84	Southampton	2	—
1983–84	*Mansfield T*	12	5
1984–85	Southampton	—	—
1984–85	*Reading*	7	1
1984–85	Orient	19	7
1985–86	....	27	10
1986–87	....	13	2
1987–88	....	23	16
1988–89	....	29	9
1988–89	*Ipswich T*	2	—
1989–90	Halifax T	17	7
1989–90	Hereford U	25	3
1990–91	....	3	1
1990–91	Halifax T	34	9
1991–92	....	37	4
1992–93	....	1	—
1992–93	Darlington	33	6

KABIA, Jason

Born Sutton in Ashfield 28.5.69.
Forward. From Oakham United.

1991–92	Lincoln C....................	15	3
1992–93	....	13	1
1992–93	*Doncaster R*	5	—

KAMARA, Alan

Born Sheffield 15.7.58.   Ht 5 9   Wt 10 12
Defender. From Kiveton Park.

1979–80	York C........................	10	—
1980–81	Darlington	45	—
1981–82	....	43	—
1982–83	....	46	1
From York RI, Retford, Burton Alb			
1987–88	Scarborough................	29	—
1988–89	....	44	1
1989–90	....	45	1
1990–91	....	41	—
1991–92	Halifax T	35	—
1992–93	....	1	—

KAMARA, Chris

Born Middlesbrough 25.12.57.   Ht 6 1
Wt 12 00
Midfield. From Apprentice.

1975–76	Portsmouth	24	4
1976–77	....	39	3
1977–78	Swindon T	40	10
1978–79	....	28	2
1979–80	....	34	5
1980–81	....	45	4
1981–82	Portsmouth	11	—
1981–82	Brentford	31	5
1982–83	....	44	11
1983–84	....	38	6
1984–85	....	39	6
1985–86	Swindon T	20	1
1986–87	....	42	3
1987–88	....	25	2
1988–89	Stoke C	38	4
1989–90	....	22	1
1989–90	Leeds U	11	1
1990–91	....	7	—

Season	Club	Apps	Goals
1991–92		2	—
1991–92	Luton T	28	—
1992–93		21	—
1992–93	*Sheffield U*	8	—
1992–93	*Middlesbrough*	5	—

KANCHELSKIS, Andrei

Born Kirowgrad 23.1.69. Ht 5 10
Wt 12 04
Midfield. From Dynamo Kiev, Donezts.
USSR full caps.

Season	Club	Apps	Goals
1990–91	Manchester U	1	—
1991–92		34	5
1992–93		27	3

KANE, Paul

Born Edinburgh 20.6.65. Ht 5 8 Wt 9 09
Midfield. From Salvesen BC. Scotland
Youth.

Season	Club	Apps	Goals
1982–83	Hibernian	—	—
1983–84		13	1
1984–85		34	8
1985–86		32	5
1986–87		37	1
1987–88		44	10
1988–89		35	5
1989–90		31	3
1990–91		21	—
1990–91	Oldham Ath	17	—
1991–92		4	—
1991–92	Aberdeen	25	2
1992–93		27	4

KAVANAGH, Graham

Born Dublin 3.12.73 Ht 5 10
Midfield. From Home Farm.

Season	Club	Apps	Goals
1991–92	Middlesbrough	—	—
1992–93		10	—

KAVANAGH, Jason

Born Birmingham 23.11.71. Ht 5 9
Wt 11 00
Midfield. From Birmingham C schoolboys.
FA Schools. England Youth.

Season	Club	Apps	Goals
1988–89	Derby Co	—	—

KAY, John

Born Sunderland 29.1.64. Ht 5 10
Wt 11 06
Defender. From Apprentice.

Season	Club	Apps	Goals
1981–82	Arsenal	—	—
1982–83		7	—
1983–84		7	—
1984–85	Wimbledon	21	1
1984–85	*Middlesbrough*	8	—
1985–86	Wimbledon	26	1
1986–87		16	—
1987–88	Sunderland	46	—
1988–89		11	—
1989–90		32	—
1990–91		30	—
1991–92		41	—
1992–93		36	—

KEANE, Roy

Born Cork 10.8.71. Ht 5 10 Wt 11 03
Midfield. From Cobh Ramblers. Eire
Youth, Under-21, 16 full caps.

Season	Club	Apps	Goals
1990–91	Nottingham F	35	8
1991–92		39	8
1992–93		40	6

KEARNEY, Mark

Born Ormskirk 12.6.62. Ht 5 10
Wt 11 00
Midfield. From Marine.

Season	Club	Apps	Goals
1981–82	Everton	—	—
1982–83		—	—
1982–83	Mansfield T	11	1
1983–84		17	2
1984–85		38	4
1985–86		31	7
1986–87		43	10
1987–88		4	—
1988–89		45	2

Season	Club	League Appearances/Goals	
1989–90		41	3
1990–91		20	—
1990–91	*Bury*	13	1
1990–91	Bury	9	—
1991–92		43	1
1992–93		39	2

KEARTON, Jason

Born Ipswich (Australia) 9.7.69. Ht 6 1
Wt 11 10
Goalkeeper. From Brisbane Lions.

Season	Club		
1988–89	Everton	—	—
1989–90		—	—
1990–91		—	—
1991–92		—	—
1991–92	*Stoke C*	16	—
1991–92	*Blackpool*	14	—
1992–93	Everton	5	—

KEE, Paul

Born Belfast 8.11.69. Ht 6 3 Wt 12 05
Goalkeeper. From Ards. Northern Ireland
7 full caps.

Season	Club		
1988–89	Oxford U	—	—
1989–90		21	—
1990–91		13	—
1991–92		8	—
1992–93		11	—

KEEBLE, Matthew

Born Chipping Norton 8.9.72 Ht 5 9
Wt 10 00
Forward.

Season	Club		
1992–93	Oxford U	1	—

KEELEY, John

Born Plaistow 27.7.61. Ht 6 1 Wt 14 02
Goalkeeper. From Apprentice.

Season	Club		
1979–80	Southend U	4	—
1980–81		—	—
1981–82		27	—
1982–83		7	—

Season	Club		
1983–84		16	—
From Chelmsford C			
1986–87	Brighton	20	—
1987–88		46	—
1988–89		37	—
1989–90		35	—
1990–91	Oldham Ath	—	—
1991–92		1	—
1991–92	*Oxford U*	6	—
1991–92	*Reading*	6	—
1992–93	Oldham Ath	1	—
1992–93	*Chester C*	4	—

KEEN, Kevin

Born Amersham 25.2.67. Ht 5 6
Wt 10 03
Midfield. From Wycombe W and
Apprentice. England Schools, Youth.

Season	Club		
1983–84	West Ham U	—	—
1984–85		—	—
1985–86		—	—
1986–87		13	—
1987–88		23	1
1988–89		24	3
1989–90		44	10
1990–91		40	—
1991–92		29	—
1992–93		46	7

KEIZERWEERD, Orfeo

21.11.68
Forward. From Rodez.

Season	Club		
1992–93	Oldham Ath	1	—

KELLER, Kasey

Born Washington 27.11.69. Ht 6 1
Wt 13 07
Goalkeeper. From Portland University.
USA full caps.

Season	Club		
1991–92	Millwall	1	—
1992–93		45	—

KELLY, Alan

Born Preston 11.8.68. Ht 6 2 Wt 12 05
Goalkeeper. Eire Youth, Under-21, Under-23, 1 full cap.

Season	Club	Apps	Goals
1985–86	Preston NE	13	—
1986–87		22	—
1987–88		19	—
1988–89			
1989–90		42	—
1990–91		23	—
1991–92		23	—
1992–93	Sheffield U	33	—

KELLY, David

Born Birmingham 25.11.65. Ht 5 11
Wt 11 03
Forward. From Alvechurch. Eire B, Under-21, Under-23, 15 full caps.

Season	Club	Apps	Goals
1983–84	Walsall	6	3
1984–85		32	7
1985–86		28	10
1986–87		42	23
1987–88		39	20
1988–89	West Ham U	25	6
1989–90		16	1
1989–90	Leicester C	10	7
1990–91		44	14
1991–92		12	1
1991–92	Newcastle U	25	11
1992–93		45	24

KELLY, Gary

Born Fulwood 3.8.66. Ht 5 11 Wt 12 03
Goalkeeper. From Apprentice. Eire B, Under-21.

Season	Club	Apps	Goals
1984–85	Newcastle U	—	—
1985–86		—	—
1986–87		3	—
1987–88		37	—
1988–89		9	—
1988–89	*Blackpool*	5	—
1989–90	Newcastle U	4	—
1989–90	Bury	38	—
1990–91		46	—
1991–92		46	—

Season	Club	Apps	Goals
1992–93		42	—

KELLY, Gavin

Born Beverley 29.9.68. Ht 6 0 Wt 12 13
Goalkeeper.

Season	Club	Apps	Goals
1987–88	Hull C	—	—
1988–89		3	—
1989–90		8	—
1989–90	*Bristol R.*	—	—
1990–91	Bristol R	7	—
1991–92		3	—
1992–93		19	—

KELLY, Jimmy

Born Liverpool 14.2.73. Ht 5 7 Wt 11 10
Midfield. From Trainee.

Season	Club	Apps	Goals
1990–91	Wrexham	12	—
1991–92		9	—
1991–92	Wolverhampton W	3	—
1992–93		—	—
1992–93	*Walsall*	10	2

KELLY, John

Born Bebbington 20.10.60. Ht 5 10
Wt 10 09
Forward. From Cammell Laird. Eire Under-21.

Season	Club	Apps	Goals
1979–80	Tranmere R	28	4
1980–81		29	5
1981–82		7	—
1981–82	Preston NE	30	5
1982–83		29	2
1983–84		34	13
1984–85		37	7
1985–86	Chester C	43	8
1986–87		42	9
1987–88	Swindon T	7	1
1987–88	Oldham Ath	10	—
1988–89		42	6
1989–90	Walsall	26	1
1989–90	*Huddersfield T*	10	—
1990–91	Walsall	13	—
1990–91	Huddersfield T	4	—
1991–92		14	—

Season	Club	Apps	Goals
1992–93	Chester C	31	1

KELLY, Mark

Born Blackpool 7.10.66. Ht 5 9
Wt 10 05
Midfield.

Season	Club	Apps	Goals
1985–86	Shrewsbury T	—	—
1986–87		—	—
1987–88	Cardiff C	36	1
1988–89		28	—
1989–90		41	1
1990–91	Fulham	18	—
1991–92		21	1
1992–93		25	1

KELLY, Paul

Born Hillingdon 24.2.74. Ht 5 7
Wt 10 13
Midfield. From Trainee.

Season	Club	Apps	Goals
1991–92	Fulham	3	—
1992–93		—	—

KELLY, Tom

Born Bellshill 28.3.64. Ht 5 9 Wt 12 05
Defender. From Hibs.

Season	Club	Apps	Goals
1985–86	Hartlepool U	15	—
1986–87	Torquay U	38	—
1987–88		38	—
1988–89		44	—
1989–90	York C	35	2
1989–90	Exeter C	12	2
1990–91		22	1
1991–92		32	5
1992–93		22	1
1992–93	Torquay U	18	3

KELLY, Tony

Born Meridan 14.2.66. Ht 5 9 Wt 11 06
Forward.

Season	Club	Apps	Goals
1982–83	Bristol C	6	1
	From St Albans C		
1989–90	Stoke C	9	—

Season	Club	Apps	Goals
1990–91		29	3
1991–92		13	2
1991–92	Hull C	6	1
1992–93	Stoke C	7	—
1992–93	Cardiff C	5	1

KELLY, Tony

Born Prescot 1.10.64. Ht 5 10 Wt 11 09
Midfield. From Liverpool Apprentice.

Season	Club	Apps	Goals
1983–84	Derby Co	—	—
1983–84	Wigan Ath	29	2
1984–85		40	4
1985–86		32	9
1985–86	Stoke C	1	—
1986–87		35	4
1987–88	WBA	26	1
1988–89		—	—
1988–89	Chester C	5	—
1988–89	Colchester U	13	2
1988–89	Shrewsbury T	20	5
1989–90		43	5
1990–91		38	5
1991–92	Bolton W	31	2
1992–93		36	2

KENNA, Jeff

Born Dublin 27.8.70. Ht 5 11 Wt 11 09
Defender. From Trainee. Eire Youth,
Under-21.

Season	Club	Apps	Goals
1988–89	Southampton	—	—
1989–90		—	—
1990–91		2	—
1991–92		14	—
1992–93		29	2

KENNEDY, Andy

Born Stirling 8.10.64. Ht 6 2 Wt 13 00
Forward. From Sauchie Ath.

Season	Club	Apps	Goals
1983–84	Rangers	13	3
1984–85		2	—
1984–85	Birmingham C	7	4
1985–86		32	6
1986–87		9	1
1986–87	Sheffield U	9	1

Season	Club	Appearances	Goals
1987–88	Birmingham C	28	7
1988–89	Blackburn R	25	10
1989–90		34	13
1990–91	Watford	18	3
1991–92		7	1
1991–92	*Bolton W*	1	—
1992–93	Watford	—	—
1992–93	Brighton	30	8

KENNEDY, Mark

Born Dublin 15.5.76 Ht 5 11 Wt 11 09
Forward. From Trainee.

Season	Club	Appearances	Goals
1992–93	Millwall	1	—

KENNEDY, Mick

Born Salford 9.4.61. Ht 5 9 Wt 12 00
Midfield. From Apprentice. Eire Under-21,
2 caps.

Season	Club	Appearances	Goals
1978–79	Halifax T	30	—
1979–80		46	4
1980–81	Huddersfield T	42	2
1981–82		39	7
1982–83	Middlesbrough	38	5
1983–84		30	—
1984–85	Portsmouth	37	—
1985–86		39	2
1986–87		35	2
1987–88		18	—
1987–88	Bradford C	15	1
1988–89		30	1
1988–89	Leicester C	9	—
1989–90	Luton T	32	—
1990–91	Stoke C	32	3
1991–92		20	—
1992–93	Chesterfield	27	1

KENNY, William

Born Liverpool 19.9.73 Ht 5 07
Wt 10 10
Midfield. From Trainee. England
Under-21.

Season	Club	Appearances	Goals
1992–93	Everton	17	1

KENT, Kevin

Born Stoke 19.3.65. Ht 5 11 Wt 11 00
Forward. From Apprentice.

Season	Club	Appearances	Goals
1982–83	WBA	—	—
1983–84		2	—
1984–85	Newport Co	33	1
1985–86	Mansfield T	34	8
1986–87		46	6
1987–88		45	10
1988–89		39	5
1989–90		38	3
1990–91		27	4
1990–91	Port Vale	11	—
1991–92		23	—
1992–93		27	1

KEOWN, Martin

Born Oxford 24.7.66. Ht 6 1 Wt 12 04
Defender. From Apprentice. England
Youth, Under-21 B, 11 full caps.

Season	Club	Appearances	Goals
1983–84	Arsenal	—	—
1984–85		—	—
1984–85	*Brighton*	16	—
1985–86	Arsenal	22	—
1985–86	*Brighton*	7	1
1986–87	Aston Villa	36	—
1987–88		42	3
1988–89		34	—
1989–90	Everton	20	—
1990–91		24	—
1991–92		39	—
1992–93		13	—
1992–93	Arsenal	16	—

KERNAGHAN, Alan

Born Otley 25.4.67. Ht 6 2 Wt 13 00
Forward. From Apprentice. Eire 6 full
caps.

Season	Club	Appearances	Goals
1984–85	Middlesbrough	8	1
1985–86		6	—
1986–87		13	—
1987–88		35	6
1988–89		23	—
1989–90		37	4
1990–91		24	—

1990–91	*Charlton Ath*	13 —
1991–92	Middlesbrough	38 2
1992–93		22 2

KERR, David

Born Dumfries 6.9.74 Ht 5 11 Wt 11 00
Midfield. From Trainee.

| 1991–92 | Manchester C | — — |
| 1992–93 | | 1 — |

KERR, Dylan

Born Valetta 14.1.67. Ht 5 11 Wt 12 05
Defender. From Arcadia Shepherds.

1988–89	Leeds U	3 —
1989–90		5 —
1990–91		— —
1991–92		— —
1991–92	*Doncaster R*	7 1
1991–92	*Blackpool*	12 1
1992–93	Leeds U	5 —

KERR, John

Born Toronto 6.3.65 Ht 5 8 Wt 11 05
Forward. From Harrow Borough.

1987–88	Portsmouth	4 —
1987–88	*Peterborough U*	10 1
From San Diego Sockers		
1992–93	Millwall	6 1

KERR, Paul

Born Portsmouth 9.6.64. Ht 5 8
Wt 11 03
Forward. From Apprentice.

1982–83	Aston Villa	— —
1983–84		2 —
1984–85		10 —
1985–86		6 1
1986–87		6 2
1986–87	Middlesbrough	20 —
1987–88		44 5
1988–89		20 1
1989–90		17 1

1990–91		24 6
1990–91	Millwall	10 2
1991–92		34 12
1992–93	Port Vale	38 11

KERSLAKE, David

Born London 19.6.66. Ht 5 8 Wt 11 00
Midfield. From Apprentice. England
Schools, Youth, Under-21. Football
League.

1983–84	QPR	— —
1984–85		1 —
1985–86		14 1
1986–87		3 —
1987–88		18 5
1988–89		21 —
1989–90		1 —
1989–90	Swindon T	28 —
1990–91		37 —
1991–92		39 1
1992–93		31 —
1992–93	Leeds U	8 —

KEVAN, David

Born Wigtown 31.8.68. Ht 5 8 Wt 10 12
Midfield. From Apprentice.

1985–86	Notts Co	3 —
1986–87		33 1
1987–88		32 —
1988–89		18 2
1989–90		3 —
1989–90	*Cardiff C*	7 —
1989–90	Stoke C	17 —
1990–91		5 —
1990–91	*Maidstone U*	3 —
1991–92	Stoke C	43 1
1992–93		15 1

KHARINE, Dimitri

Born Moscow 16.8.68 Ht 6 2 Wt 12 04
Goalkeeper. From Moscow Torpedo,
Moscow Dynamo, CSKA Moscow. CIS
full caps.

| 1992–93 | Chelsea | 5 — |

KIDD, Ryan

Born Heywood 6.10.71.   Ht 6 0   Wt 11 07
Defender. From Trainee.

Season	Club		
1990–91	Port Vale	—	—
1991–92		1	—
1992–93	Preston NE	15	—

KIDD, Walter

Born Edinburgh 10.3.58.   Ht 5 11
Wt 12 03
Defender. From Newtongrange Star.

Season	Club		
1977–78	Hearts	23	—
1978–79		30	—
1979–80		34	2
1980–81		25	1
1981–82		30	—
1982–83		37	—
1983–84		31	1
1984–85		33	1
1985–86		28	—
1986–87		35	—
1987–88		18	—
1988–89		20	—
1989–90		17	1
1990–91		4	—
1991–92	Airdrieonians	32	—
1992–93		30	1

KIELY, Dean

Born Manchester 10.10.70.   Ht 6 0
Wt 12 08
Goalkeeper. From WBA schoolboy. FA
Schools. England Youth.

Season	Club		
1987–88	Coventry C	—	—
1988–89		—	—
1989–90		—	—
1989–90	*Ipswich T*	—	—
1989–90	*York C*	—	—
1990–91	York C	17	—
1991–92		21	—
1992–93		40	—

KILCLINE, Brian

Born Nottingham 7.5.62.   Ht 6 2
Wt 12 00
Defender. From Apprentice. England
Under-21.

Season	Club		
1979–80	Notts Co	16	1
1980–81		42	1
1981–82		36	3
1982–83		40	3
1983–84		24	1
1984–85	Coventry C	26	2
1985–86		32	7
1986–87		29	3
1987–88		28	8
1988–89		33	4
1989–90		11	1
1990–91		14	3
1991–92	Oldham Ath	8	—
1991–92	Newcastle U	12	—
1992–93		19	—

KILNER, Andy

Born Bolton 11.10.66.   Ht 6 0   Wt 11 12
Forward. From Apprentice.

Season	Club		
1985–86	Burnley	5	—
From Jonsered			
1990–91	Stockport Co	24	11
1991–92		18	3
1991–92	*Rochdale*	3	—
1992–93	Bury	5	1

KIMBLE, Alan

Born Poole 6.8.66.   Ht 5 8   Wt 11 00
Defender.

Season	Club		
1984–85	Charlton Ath	6	—
1985–86		—	—
1985–86	*Exeter C*	1	—
1986–87	Cambridge U	35	—
1987–88		41	2
1988–89		45	6
1989–90		44	8
1990–91		43	4
1991–92		45	—
1992–93		46	4

KING, Phil

Born Bristol 28.12.67.   Ht 5 8   Wt 11 09
Defender. From Apprentice. England B.

1984–85	Exeter C	16	—
1985–86		11	—
1986–87	Torquay U	24	3
1986–87	Swindon T	21	—
1987–88		44	1
1988–89		37	2
1989–90		14	1
1989–90	Sheffield W	25	—
1990–91		43	—
1991–92		39	1
1992–93		12	1

KINNAIRD, Paul

Born Glasgow 11.11.66.   Ht 5 8   Wt 10 10
Forward. From Apprentice.

1984–85	Norwich C	—	—
1985–86	Dundee U	—	—
1986–87		7	—
1987–88		11	—
1987–88	Motherwell	10	—
1988–89		24	—
1988–89	St Mirren	6	—
1989–90		25	—
1990–91		23	4
1991–92		3	—
1991–92	Partick T	13	2
1992–93		20	1
1992–93	Shrewsbury T	4	1
1992–93	St Johnstone	8	—

KINSELLA, Mark

Born Dublin 12.8.72   Ht 5 9   Wt 11 00
Midfield. From Home Farm.

1989–90	Colchester U	6	—
1990–91		11	—
1991–92		42	3
1992–93		38	6

KIRK, Steve

Born Kirkcaldy 3.1.63.   Ht 5 11
Wt 11 04
Midfield. From Buckhaven Hibs.

1979–80	East Fife	25	2
1980–81	Stoke C	—	—
1981–82		12	—
1982–83	Partick T	—	—
1982–83	East Fife	25	8
1983–84		33	5
1984–85		38	8
1985–86		39	14
1986–87	Motherwell	35	10
1987–88		38	4
1988–89		33	14
1989–90		34	8
1990–91		29	2
1991–92		38	6
1992–93		40	10

KIRKWOOD, David

Born St Andrews 27.8.67.   Ht 5 10
Wt 11 07
Midfield. From Leven Royal Colts.
Scotland Under-21.

1983–84	East Fife	14	2
1984–85		17	4
1985–86		34	2
1986–87		35	2
1987–88	Rangers	4	—
1988–89		2	—
1989–90	Hearts	19	—
1990–91		9	1
1991–92	Airdrieonians	36	9
1992–93		27	2

KITCHEN, Sam

Born Germany 11.6.67
Defender. From Frickley Ath.

1992–93	Leyton Orient	32	1

KITE, Phil

Born Bristol 26.10.62.   Ht 6 1   Wt 14 07
Goalkeeper. From Apprentice. England
Youth.

1980–81	Bristol R	4	—
1981–82		27	—
1982–83		46	—
1983–84		19	—
1983–84	*Tottenham H*	—	—
1984–85	Southampton	1	—
1985–86		3	—
1985–86	*Middlesbrough*	2	—
1986–87	Gillingham	17	—
1987–88		26	—
1988–89		27	—
1989–90	Bournemouth	7	—
1990–91	Sheffield U	7	—
1991–92		4	—
1991–92	*Mansfield T*	11	—
1992–93	Sheffield U	—	—
1992–93	*Plymouth Arg*	2	—
1992–93	*Rotherham U*	1	—
1992–93	*Crewe Alex*	5	—
1992–93	*Stockport Co*	5	—

KITSON, Paul

Born Co Durham 9.1.71.   Ht 5 11
Wt 10 12
Forward. From Trainee. England
Under-21.

1988–89	Leicester C	—	—
1989–90		13	—
1990–91		7	—
1991–92		30	6
1991–92	Derby Co	12	4
1992–93		44	17

KIWOMYA, Andrew

Born Huddersfield 1.10.67   Ht 5 9
Wt 10 10
Forward. From Trainee. England Youth.

1985–86	Barnsley	1	—
1986–87	Sheffield W	—	—
1987–88		—	—
1988–89		—	—

Retired injury

1992–93	Dundee	21	1

KIWOMYA, Chris

Born Huddersfield 2.12.69.   Ht 5 10
Wt 10 12
Forward.

1986–87	Ipswich T	—	—
1987–88		—	—
1988–89		26	2
1989–90		29	5
1990–91		37	10
1991–92		43	16
1992–93		38	10

KNIGHT, Alan

Born Balham 3.6.61.   Ht 6 0   Wt 13 00
Goalkeeper. From Apprentice. England
Youth, Under-21.

1977–78	Portsmouth	1	—
1978–79		—	—
1979–80		8	—
1980–81		1	—
1981–82		45	—
1982–83		46	—
1983–84		42	—
1984–85		42	—
1985–86		38	—
1986–87		42	—
1987–88		36	—
1988–89		32	—
1989–90		46	—
1990–91		22	—
1991–92		45	—
1992–93		46	—

KNIGHT, Craig

Born Wrexham 24.10.73.   Ht 6 1
Wt 12 00
Defender. From Trainee.

1991–92	Wrexham	1	—
1992–93		—	—

KNIGHT, Ian

Born Hartlepool 26.10.66.   Ht 6 2
Wt 12 04
Defender. From Apprentice. England
Under-21.

1984–85	Barnsley	—	—
1985–86	Sheffield W	4	—
1986–87		15	—
1987–88		—	—
1988–89		2	—
1989–90		—	—
1989–90	*Scunthorpe U*	2	—
1989–90	Grimsby T	9	1
1990–91		8	1
1991–92		4	—
1992–93	Carlisle U	1	—

KNIGHT, Richard

Born Burton 31.8.74   Ht 5 9   Wt 10 13
Defender. From Trainee.

1991–92	Walsall	—	—
1992–93		27	1

KNILL, Alan

Born Slough 8.10.64.   Ht 6 2   Wt 11 07
Defender. From Apprentice. Wales Youth,
1 full cap.

1982–83	Southampton	—	—
1983–84		—	—
1984–85	Halifax T	44	1
1985–86		33	2
1986–87		41	3
1987–88	Swansea C	46	1
1988–89		43	2
1989–90	Bury	43	1
1990–91		20	1
1991–92		35	1
1992–93		38	5

KNOWLES, Darren

Born Sheffield 8.10.70.   Ht 5 6   Wt 10 01
Midfield. From Trainee.

1989–90	Sheffield U	—	—

1989–90	Stockport Co	9	—
1990–91		12	—
1991–92		31	—
1992–93		11	—

KOPEL, Scott

Born Blackburn 25.2.70
Forward.

1992–93	Chesterfield	1	—

KOZMA, Istvan

Born Paszto, Hungary 3.12.64.   Ht 5 9
Wt 12 00
Midfield. From Ujpest Dozsa, Bordeaux.
Hungary full caps.

1989–90	Dunfermline Ath	33	6
1990–91		34	2
1991–92		23	—
1991–92	Liverpool	5	—
1992–93		1	—

KRISTENSEN, Bjorn

Born Malling 10.10.63.   Ht 6 1   Wt 12 05
Defender. From Aarhus. Denmark full
caps.

1988–89	Newcastle U	5	—
1989–90		33	3
1990–91		40	1
1991–92		2	—
1992–93		—	—
1992–93	*Bristol C*	4	—
1992–93	Portsmouth	10	1

KRIVOKAPIC, Miodrag

Born Niksic 6.9.59   Ht 6 1   Wt 12 12
Defender. From Red Star Belgrade.
Yugoslavia full caps.

1988–89	Dundee U	24	1
1989–90		26	—
1990–91		24	—
1991–92		—	—
1992–93		8	—

KROMHEER, Elroy

Born Amsterdam 15.1.70   Ht 6 2   Wt 11 0
Defender. From FC Volendam.

| 1992–93 | Motherwell | 12 | — |

KRUSZYNSKI, Detsi

Born Divschav 14.10.61.   Ht 6 0
Wt 12 12
Midfield. From Homburg.

1988–89	Wimbledon	16	—
1989–90		27	2
1990–91		27	2
1991–92		1	—
1991–92	*Brentford*	8	—
1992–93	Wimbledon	—	—
1992–93	Brentford	6	—

KUHL, Martin

Born Frimley 10.1.65.   Ht 5 11   Wt 11 13
Midfield. From Apprentice.

1982–83	Birmingham C	2	—
1983–84		22	1
1984–85		27	2
1985–86		37	1
1986–87		23	1
1986–87	Sheffield U	10	1
1987–88		28	3
1987–88	Watford	4	—
1988–89		—	—
1988–89	Portsmouth	32	1
1989–90		40	9
1990–91		41	13
1991–92		41	3
1992–93		3	1
1992–93	Derby Co	32	1

KUZNETSOV, Oleg

Born Kiev 2.3.63   Ht 6 2   Wt 12 08
Defender. From Dynamo Kiev. CIS full
caps.

1990–91	Rangers	2	—
1991–92		18	—
1992–93		9	—

LAKE, Michael

Born Manchester 6.11.66.   Ht 6 1
Wt 12 11
Midfield. From Macclesfield T.

1989–90	Sheffield U	4	—
1990–91		7	—
1991–92		18	4
1992–93		6	—
1992–93	Wrexham	26	5

LAKE, Paul

Born Manchester 28.10.68.   Ht 6 0
Wt 12 02
Midfield. From Trainee. England
Under-21.

1986–87	Manchester C	3	1
1987–88		33	3
1988–89		38	3
1989–90		31	—
1990–91		3	—
1991–92		—	—
1992–93		2	—

LAKIN, Barry

Born Dartford 19.9.73
Midfield. From Trainee.

| 1992–93 | Leyton Orient | 9 | 2 |

LAMB, Paul

Born Plumstead 12.9.74
Midfield. From Trainee.

| 1992–93 | Northampton T | 3 | — |

LAMBERT, James

Born Henley 14.9.73   Ht 5 7   Wt 10 04
Forward. From School.

| 1992–93 | Reading | 27 | 3 |

LAMBERT, Matthew

Born Morecambe 28.9.71.   Ht 6 2
Wt 13 01
Midfield. From Trainee.

| 1990–91 | Preston NE | 5 | — |

| 1991–92 | | 11 | 2 |
| 1992–93 | Bury | — | — |

LAMPKIN, Kevin

Born Liverpool 20.12.72 Ht 5 10
Wt 11 08
Midfield. From Trainee.

| 1991–92 | Liverpool | — | — |
| 1992–93 | Huddersfield T | 13 | — |

LANCASHIRE, Graham

Born Blackpool 19.10.72. Ht 5 10
Wt 11 12
Forward. From Trainee.

1990–91	Burnley	1	—
1991–92		25	8
1992–93		3	—
1992–93	*Halifax T*	2	—

LANCASTER, Dave

Born Preston 8.9.61. Ht 6 3 Wt 14 00
Forward. From Colne Dynamoes.

1990–91	Blackpool	8	1
1990–91	*Chesterfield*	12	4
1991–92	Chesterfield	29	7
1992–93		40	9

LANGE, Tony

Born London 10.12.64. Ht 6 0 Wt 12 09
Goalkeeper. From Apprentice.

1982–83	Charlton Ath	—	—
1983–84		6	—
1984–85		2	—
1985–86		4	—
1985–86	*Aldershot*	7	—
1986–87	Aldershot	45	—
1987–88		35	—
1988–89		45	—
1989–90	Wolverhampton W	5	—
1990–91		3	—
1990–91	*Aldershot*	2	—
1991–92	Wolverhampton W	—	—

1991–92	*Torquay U*	1	—
1991–92	*Portsmouth*	—	—
1992–93	WBA	14	—

LANGFORD, Craig

Born Solihull 12.3.75
Defender. From Trainee.

| 1992–93 | Hereford U | 1 | — |

LANGLEY, Kevin

Born St. Helens 24.5.64. Ht 6 1
Wt 10 03
Midfield. From Apprentice.

1981–82	Wigan Ath	2	—
1982–83		28	2
1983–84		44	1
1984–85		43	1
1985–86		43	2
1986–87	Everton	16	2
1986–87	*Manchester C*	9	—
1987–88	Manchester C	—	—
1987–88	*Chester C*	9	—
1987–88	Birmingham C	7	—
1988–89		36	2
1989–90		33	—
1990–91		—	—
1990–91	Wigan Ath	39	2
1991–92		45	2
1992–93		40	—

LAVIN, Gerard

Born Corby 5.2.74. Ht 5 9 Wt 10 07
Midfield. From Trainee.

| 1991–92 | Watford | 1 | — |
| 1992–93 | | 28 | — |

LAW, Bobby

Born Bellshill 24.12.65. Ht 5 9 Wt 11 00
Midfield. From Stonehouse Violet.

1984–85	Partick T	1	—
1985–86		16	3
1986–87		31	2

Season	Club	App	Goals
1987–88		21	1
1988–89		33	—
1989–90		28	1
1990–91		27	—
1991–92		31	2
1992–93		34	—

LAW, Brian

Born Merthyr 1.1.70. Ht 6 2 Wt 11 12
Defender. From Apprentice. Wales Under-21, 1 full cap.

Season	Club	App	Goals
1987–88	QPR	1	—
1988–89		6	—
1989–90		10	—
1990–91		3	—
1991–92		—	—
1992–93		—	—

LAW, Nicky

Born London 8.9.61. Ht 6 1 Wt 12 07
Defender. From Apprentice.

Season	Club	App	Goals
1979–80	Arsenal	—	—
1980–81		—	—
1981–82	Barnsley	19	—
1982–83		28	—
1983–84		31	1
1984–85		35	—
1985–86		1	—
1985–86	Blackpool	39	1
1986–87		27	—
1986–87	Plymouth Arg	12	2
1987–88		26	3
1988–89	Notts Co	44	4
1989–90		3	—
1989–90	*Scarborough*	12	—
1990–91	Rotherham U	32	2
1991–92		42	—
1992–93		44	2

LAWFORD, Craig

Born Dewsbury 25.11.72. Ht 5 10
Wt 11 10
Defender. From Trainee.

Season	Club	App	Goals
1989–90	Bradford C	1	—

Season	Club	App	Goals
1990–91		—	—
1991–92		—	—
1992–93		8	1

LAWRENCE, Alan

Born Edinburgh 19.8.62 Ht 5 7
Wt 10 06
Forward. From Easthouses BC.

Season	Club	App	Goals
1984–85	Meadowbank T	35	—
1985–86		38	17
1986–87		29	6
1986–87	Dundee	4	1
1987–88		22	1
1988–89		10	—
1988–89	Airdrieonians	7	2
1989–90		34	9
1990–91		38	13
1991–92		31	7
1992–93		35	2

LAWRENCE, George

Born London 14.9.62. Ht 5 10 Wt 12 02
Forward. From Apprentice.

Season	Club	App	Goals
1980–81	Southampton	—	—
1981–82		4	—
1981–82	*Oxford U*	15	4
1982–83	Southampton	6	1
1982–83	Oxford U	22	9
1983–84		34	9
1984–85		7	3
1984–85	Southampton	11	1
1985–86		21	2
1986–87		36	8
1987–88	Millwall	17	4
1988–89		11	—
1989–90	Bournemouth	33	3
1990–91		34	2
1991–92		8	—
From Weymouth			
1992–93	Portsmouth	12	—

LAWS, Brian

Born Wallsend 14.10.61. Ht 5 10
Wt 11 05
Defender. From Apprentice. England B.

Season	Club	App	Goals
1979–80	Burnley	1	—

Season	Club	League Appearances/Goals	
1980–81		42	2
1981–82		44	6
1982–83		38	4
1983–84	Huddersfield T	31	—
1984–85		25	1
1984–85	Middlesbrough	11	1
1985–86		42	2
1986–87		26	8
1987–88		28	1
1988–89	Nottingham F	22	1
1989–90		38	3
1990–91		32	—
1991–92		15	—
1992–93		33	—

LE SAUX, Graeme

Born Jersey 17.10.68.   Ht 5 9   Wt 12 00
Defender. From England B, Under-21.

Season	Club	League Appearances/Goals	
1987–88	Chelsea	—	—
1988–89		1	—
1989–90		7	1
1990–91		28	4
1991–92		40	3
1992–93		14	—
1992–93	Blackburn R	9	—

LE TISSIER, Matthew

Born Guernsey 14.10.68.   Ht 6 1
Wt 12 10
Forward. From Vale Recreation, Trainee.
England Youth, B.

Season	Club	League Appearances/Goals	
1986–87	Southampton	24	6
1987–88		19	—
1988–89		28	9
1989–90		35	20
1990–91		35	19
1991–92		32	6
1992–93		40	15

LEABURN, Carl

Born Lewisham 30.3.69.   Ht 6 3
Wt 11 03
Forward. From Apprentice. England
Youth.

Season	Club	League Appearances/Goals	
1986–87	Charlton Ath	3	1

Season	Club	League Appearances/Goals	
1987–88		12	—
1988–89		32	2
1989–90		13	—
1989–90	*Northampton T*	9	—
1990–91	Charlton Ath	20	1
1991–92		39	11
1992–93		39	5

LEADBITTER, Chris

Born Middlesbrough 17.10.67.   Ht 5 9
Wt 10 07
Forward. From Apprentice.

Season	Club	League Appearances/Goals	
1985–86	Grimsby T	—	—
1986–87	Hereford U	6	—
1987–88		30	1
1988–89	Cambridge U	31	6
1989–90		43	4
1990–91		39	1
1991–92		25	1
1992–93		38	6

LEANING, Andy

Born York 18.5.63.   Ht 6 1   Wt 14 07
Goalkeeper. From Rowntree Mackintosh.

Season	Club	League Appearances/Goals	
1984–85	York C	—	—
1985–86		30	—
1986–87		39	—
1987–88	Sheffield U	21	—
1988–89		—	—
1988–89	Bristol C	6	—
1989–90		19	—
1990–91		29	—
1991–92		20	—
1992–93		1	—

LEE, Chris

Born Halifax 18.6.71.   Ht 5 10   Wt 11 07
Midfield. From Trainee.

Season	Club	League Appearances/Goals	
1989–90	Bradford C	—	—
1990–91	Rochdale	26	2
1990–91	Scarborough	9	—
1991–92		41	2
1992–93		28	1

LEE, Dave

Born Manchester 5.11.67.   Ht 5 8
Wt 10 02
Midfield. From Blackburn Schools.

Season	Club	App	Goals
1984–85	Bury	—	—
1985–86		1	—
1986–87		30	4
1987–88		40	3
1988–89		45	4
1989–90		45	8
1990–91		45	15
1991–92		2	1
1991–92	Southampton	19	—
1992–93		1	—
1992–93	Bolton W	32	5

LEE, David

Born Kingswood 26.11.69.   Ht 6 3
Wt 13 12
Defender. From Trainee. England Youth,
Under-21.

Season	Club	App	Goals
1988–89	Chelsea	20	4
1989–90		30	1
1990–91		21	1
1991–92		1	—
1991–92	*Reading*	5	5
1991–92	*Plymouth Arg*	9	1
1992–93	Chelsea	25	2

LEE, Jason

Born Newham 9.5.71.   Ht 6 3   Wt 13 08
Forward. From Trainee.

Season	Club	App	Goals
1989–90	Charlton Ath	1	—
1990–91		—	—
1990–91	*Stockport Co*	2	—
1990–91	Lincoln C	17	3
1991–92		35	6
1992–93		41	12

LEE, Robert

Born West Ham 1.2.66.   Ht 5 10
Wt 11 13
Forward. From Hornchurch. England
Under-21.

Season	Club	App	Goals
1983–84	Charlton Ath	11	4

Season	Club	App	Goals
1984–85		39	10
1985–86		35	8
1986–87		33	3
1987–88		23	2
1988–89		31	5
1989–90		37	1
1990–91		43	13
1991–92		39	12
1992–93		7	1
1992–93	Newcastle U	36	10

LEGG, Andy

Born Neath 28.7.66.   Ht 5 8   Wt 10 07
Midfield. From Briton Ferry.

Season	Club	App	Goals
1988–89	Swansea C	6	—
1989–90		26	3
1990–91		39	5
1991–92		46	9
1992–93		46	12

LEIGHTON, Jim

Born Johnstone 24.7.58.   Ht 6 1
Wt 12 09
Goalkeeper. From Dalry Thistle. Scotland
Under-21, 58 full caps.

Season	Club	App	Goals
1978–79	Aberdeen	11	—
1979–80		1	—
1980–81		35	—
1981–82		36	—
1982–83		35	—
1983–84		36	—
1984–85		34	—
1985–86		26	—
1986–87		42	—
1987–88		44	—
1988–89	Manchester U	38	—
1989–90		35	—
1990–91		—	—
1990–91	*Arsenal*	—	—
1991–92	Manchester U	—	—
1991–92	*Reading*	8	—
1991–92	Dundee	13	—
1992–93		8	—

LEITCH, Grant

Born South Africa 31.10.72.   Ht 6 1
Wt 12 05
Forward.

Season	Club	Apps	Goals
1991–92	Blackpool	6	—
1992–93		17	1

LEMON, Paul

Born Middlesbrough 3.6.66.   Ht 5 11
Wt 11 06
Forward. From Apprentice.

Season	Club	Apps	Goals
1984–85	Sunderland	11	—
1984–85	*Carlisle U*	2	—
1985–86	Sunderland	5	—
1986–87		32	5
1987–88		41	9
1988–89		18	1
1989–90		—	—
1989–90	*Walsall*	2	—
1989–90	*Reading*	3	—
1990–91	Sunderland	—	—
1990–91	Chesterfield	39	2
1991–92		15	2
1992–93		31	6

LENNON, Daniel

Born Whitburn 6.4.69   Ht 5 5   Wt 9 05
Midfield. From Hutchison Vale BC.

Season	Club	Apps	Goals
1987–88	Hibernian	1	—
1988–89		1	—
1989–90		—	—
1990–91		6	—
1991–92		11	1
1992–93		13	—

LENNON, Neil

Born Lurgan 25.6.71.   Ht 5 9   Wt 11 06
Defender. From Trainee. Northern Ireland
Under-23.

Season	Club	Apps	Goals
1987–88	Manchester C	1	—
1988–89		—	—
1989–90		—	—
1990–91	Crewe Alex	34	3

Season	Club	Apps	Goals
1991–92		—	—
1992–93		24	—

LENNOX, Gary

Born Kilwinning 6.12.69.   Ht 5 8
Wt 10 00
Midfield. From Celtic BC.

Season	Club	Apps	Goals
1986–87	Queen's Park	7	—
1987–88		15	1
1988–89		28	2
1989–90	Dundee	—	—
1990–91		—	—
1990–91	Brechin C	12	2
1991–92	Falkirk	25	—
1992–93		20	2

LEONARD, Mark

Born St Helens 27.9.62.   Ht 5 11
Wt 11 10
Forward. From Witton Albion.

Season	Club	Apps	Goals
1981–82	Everton	—	—
1982–83		—	—
1982–83	*Tranmere R*	7	—
1983–84	Crewe Alex	38	10
1984–85		16	5
1984–85	Stockport Co	23	4
1985–86		44	20
1986–87		6	—
1986–87	Bradford C	24	3
1987–88		28	10
1988–89		44	7
1989–90		24	5
1990–91		18	4
1991–92		19	—
1991–92	Rochdale	9	1
1992–93	Preston NE	22	1

LEONARD, Mick

Born Carshalton 9.5.59.   Ht 5 11
Wt 11 00
Goalkeeper. From Epsom & Ewell.

Season	Club	Apps	Goals
1976–77	Halifax T	19	—
1977–78		20	—
1978–79		25	—

Season	Club	App	Goals
1979–80		5	—
1979–80	Notts Co	9	—
1980–81		4	—
1981–82		—	—
1982–83		6	—
1983–84		18	—
1984–85		31	—
1985–86		23	—
1986–87		41	—
1987–88		45	—
1988–89		27	—
1988–89	Chesterfield	16	—
1989–90		46	—
1990–91		30	—
1990–91	*Halifax T*	3	—
1991–92	Chesterfield	35	—
1992–93		17	—

LEVEIN, Craig

Born Dunfermline 22.10.64.   Ht 6 0
Wt 11 04
Defender. From Lochore Welfare.
Scotland Youth, Under-21, 11 full caps.

Season	Club	App	Goals
1981–82	Cowdenbeath	15	—
1982–83		30	—
1983–84		15	—
1983–84	Hearts	22	—
1984–85		36	1
1985–86		33	2
1986–87		12	—
1987–88		21	—
1988–89		9	—
1989–90		35	—
1990–91		33	4
1991–92		36	2
1992–93		37	3

LEVER, Mark

Born Beverley 29.3.70.   Ht 6 3   Wt 12 08
Defender. From Trainee.

Season	Club	App	Goals
1987–88	Grimsby T	1	—
1988–89		37	2
1989–90		38	2
1990–91		40	2
1991–92		36	—
1992–93		14	1

LEWIS, Dudley

Born Swansea 17.11.62.   Ht 5 11
Wt 10 10
Defender. From Apprentice. Wales
Schools, Under-21, 1 full cap.

Season	Club	App	Goals
1979–80	Swansea C	—	—
1980–81		12	—
1981–82		1	—
1982–83		23	1
1983–84		37	—
1984–85		43	1
1985–86		24	—
1986–87		32	—
1987–88		18	—
1988–89		40	—
1989–90	Huddersfield T	28	—
1990–91		6	—
1991–92		—	—
1991–92	*Halifax T*	11	—
1991–92	Wrexham	9	—
1992–93	Halifax T	13	—
1992–93	Torquay U	9	—

LEWIS, Junior

Born Middlesex 9.10.73   Ht 6 2   Wt 11 08
Midfield. From Trainee.

Season	Club	App	Goals
1992–93	Fulham	6	—

LEWIS, Mickey

Born Birmingham 15.2.65.   Ht 5 6
Wt 10 10
Midfield. From school. England Youth.

Season	Club	App	Goals
1981–82	WBA	4	—
1982–83		5	—
1983–84		14	—
1984–85		1	—
1984–85	Derby Co	22	—
1985–86		5	1
1986–87		—	—
1987–88		16	—
1988–89	Oxford U	36	—
1989–90		45	1
1990–91		34	1
1991–92		40	4
1992–93		41	—

LEWIS, Neil

Born Wolverhampton 28.6.74   Ht 5 7
Wt 10 09
Defender. From Trainee.

Season	Club		
1992–93	Leicester C	7	—

LIDDELL, Andrew

Born Leeds 28.6.73.   Ht 5 8   Wt 10.05
Midfield. From Trainee.

Season	Club		
1990–91	Barnsley	—	—
1991–92		1	—
1992–93		21	2

LIGHTBOURNE, Kyle

Born Bermuda 29.9.68
Midfield.

Season	Club		
1992–93	Scarborough	19	3

LIGHTFOOT, Chris

Born Wimwick 1.4.70.   Ht 6 1   Wt 12 00
Midfield. From Trainee.

Season	Club		
1987–88	Chester C	16	1
1988–89		36	7
1989–90		40	1
1990–91		37	2
1991–92		44	5
1992–93		39	2

LILWALL, Steve

Born Solihull 5.2.70   Ht 5 11   Wt 12 00
Defender. From Kidderminster H.

Season	Club		
1992–93	WBA	44	—

LIM, Harvey

Born Halesworth 30.8.67.   Ht 6 0
Wt 13 07
Goalkeeper. From Apprentice.

Season	Club		
1984–85	Norwich C	—	—
1985–86		—	—

Season	Club		
1985–86	*Plymouth Arg*	—	—
1986–87	Norwich C	—	—
1987–88		—	—
From Kettering T			
1989–90	Gillingham	4	—
1990–91		39	—
1991–92		39	—
1992–93		8	—

LIMBER, Nicholas

Born Doncaster 23.1.74.   Ht 5 9
Wt 11 01
Midfield. From Trainee.

Season	Club		
1990–91	Doncaster R	1	—
1991–92		12	1
1991–92	Manchester C	—	—
1992–93		—	—
1992–93	*Peterborough U*	2	—

LIMBERT, Mark

Born Hawarden 3.10.73
Defender. From Trainee.

Season	Club		
1992–93	Chester C	14	—

LIMPAR, Anders

Born Solna 24.9.65.   Ht 5 8   Wt 11 07
Forward. From Brommapojkarna,
Orgryte, Young Boys, Cremonese. Sweden
full caps.

Season	Club		
1990–91	Arsenal	34	11
1991–92		29	4
1992–93		23	2

LINEKER, Gary

Born Leicester 30.11.60.   Ht 5 9
Wt 11 10
Forward. From Apprentice. B, England 80
full caps.

Season	Club		
1978–79	Leicester C	7	1
1979–80		19	3
1980–81		9	2
1981–82		39	17

Season	Club		App	Goals
1982–83			40	26
1983–84			39	22
1984–85			41	24
1985–86	Everton		41	30
1986–87	Barcelona		37	22
1987–88			36	16
1988–89			26	6
1989–90	Tottenham H		38	24
1990–91			32	15
1991–92			35	28

To Grampus 8

LING, Martin

Born West Ham 15.7.66.　Ht 5 7　Wt 9 12
Forward. From Apprentice.

Season	Club	App	Goals
1983–84	Exeter C	29	—
1984–85		42	6
1985–86		45	8
1986–87	Swindon T	2	—
1986–87	Southend U	24	8
1987–88		42	7
1988–89		44	6
1989–90		25	10
1990–91		3	—
1990–91	*Mansfield T*	3	—
1990–91	*Swindon T*	1	—
1991–92	Swindon T	21	3
1992–93		43	3

LINGER, Paul

Born Tower Hamlets 20.12.74
Defender. From Trainee.

Season	Club	App	Goals
1992–93	Charlton Ath	2	—

LINIGHAN, Andy

Born Hartlepool 18.6.62.　Ht 6 4
Wt 13 10
Defender. From Smiths BC. England B.

Season	Club	App	Goals
1980–81	Hartlepool U	6	—
1981–82		17	—
1982–83		45	3
1983–84		42	1
1984–85	Leeds U	42	2
1985–86		24	1

Season	Club	App	Goals
1985–86	Oldham Ath	15	1
1986–87		40	3
1987–88		32	2
1987–88	Norwich C	12	2
1988–89		37	4
1989–90		37	2
1990–91	Arsenal	10	—
1991–92		17	—
1992–93		21	2

LINIGHAN, David

Born Hartlepool 9.1.65.　Ht 6 2　Wt 13 00
Defender. From Local.

Season	Club	App	Goals
1981–82	Hartlepool U	6	—
1982–83		6	1
1983–84		23	1
1984–85		17	2
1984–85	*Leeds* U	—	—
1985–86	Hartlepool U	39	1
1986–87	Derby Co	—	—
1986–87	Shrewsbury T	24	—
1987–88		41	1
1988–89	Ipswich T	41	2
1989–90		41	—
1990–91		45	3
1991–92		36	3
1992–93		42	1

LINTON, Des

Born Birmingham 5.9.71.　Ht 6 1
Wt 13 02
Defender. From Trainee.

Season	Club	App	Goals
1989–90	Leicester C	2	—
1990–91		8	—
1991–92		1	—
1991–92	Luton T	3	—
1992–93		20	1

LITTLEJOHN, Adrian

Born Wolverhampton 26.9.70.　Ht 5 10
Wt 10 04
Forward. From WBA Trainee.

Season	Club	App	Goals
1989–90	Walsall	11	—
1990–91		33	1

| 1991–92 | Sheffield U | 7 | — |
| 1992–93 | | 27 | 8 |

LIVETT, Simon

Born Newham 8.1.69　Ht 5 10　Wt 12 02
Midfield. From Trainee.

1986–87	West Ham U	—	—
1987–88		—	—
1988–89		—	—
1989–90		—	—
1990–91		1	—
1991–92		—	—
1992–93		—	—
1992–93	Leyton Orient	23	—

LIVINGSTONE, Steve

Born Middlesbrough 8.9.69.　Ht 6 1
Wt 11 04
Forward. From Trainee.

1986–87	Coventry C	3	—
1987–88		4	—
1988–89		1	—
1989–90		13	3
1990–91		10	2
1990–91	Blackburn R	18	9
1991–92		10	1
1992–93		2	—
1992–93	Chelsea	1	—

LLEWELLYN, Andy

Born Bristol 26.2.66.　Ht 5 7　Wt 11 00
Defender. From Apprentice. England
Youth.

1983–84	Bristol C	—	—
1984–85		22	—
1985–86		38	1
1986–87		31	—
1987–88		42	1
1988–89		16	1
1989–90		46	—
1990–91		42	—
1991–92		37	—
1992–93		12	—

LOCKE, Adam

Born Croydon 20.8.70.　Ht 5 10
Wt 12 02
Midfield. From Trainee.

1988–89	Crystal Palace	—	—
1989–90		—	—
1990–91	Southend U	28	4
1991–92		10	—
1992–93		27	—

LOCKE, Gary

Born Edinburgh 16.6.75　Ht 5 8　Wt 10 7
Midfield. From Whitehill Welfare.

| 1992–93 | Hearts | 1 | — |

LONGDEN, Paul

Born Wakefield 28.9.62.　Ht 5 7
Wt 11 00
Defender. From Apprentice.

1981–82	Barnsley	4	—
1982–83		1	—
1983–84	Scunthorpe U	43	—
1984–85		14	—
1985–86		31	—
1986–87		42	—
1987–88		44	—
1988–89		41	—
1989–90		46	—
1990–91		46	—
1991–92		41	—
1992–93		20	—

LORAM, Mark

Born Brixham 13.8.67.　Ht 6 0　Wt 12 00
Forward. From Brixham.

1984–85	Torquay U	14	2
1985–86		38	6
1985–86	*QPR*	—	—
1986–87	QPR	—	—
1986–87	*Torquay U*	13	4
1987–88	Torquay U	45	8
1988–89		37	4
1989–90		42	12

Season	Club	App	Goals
1990–91	....	41	7
1991–92	....	31	5
1991–92	*Stockport Co*	4	—
1992–93	Torquay U	—	—
1992–93	*Exeter C*	3	—

LORMOR, Tony

Born Ashington 29.10.70. Ht 6 1
Wt 12 03
Forward. From Trainee.

Season	Club	App	Goals
1987–88	Newcastle U	5	2
1988–89	....	3	1
1988–89	*Norwich C*	—	—
1989–90	Newcastle U	—	—
1989–90	Lincoln C	21	8
1990–91	....	34	12
1991–92	....	35	9
1992–93	....	—	—

LOVE, Graeme

Born Bathgate 7.12.73. Ht 5 10
Wt 11 08
Midfield. From Salvesen BC.

Season	Club	App	Goals
1991–92	Hibernian	1	—
1992–93	....	1	—

LOVELL, Steve

Born Swansea 16.7.60. Ht 5 10 Wt 11 10
Forward. From Apprentice. Wales 6 full caps.

Season	Club	App	Goals
1977–78	Crystal Palace	—	—
1978–79	....	—	—
1979–80	....	—	—
1979–80	*Stockport Co*	12	—
1980–81	Crystal Palace	25	2
1981–82	....	30	1
1982–83	....	19	—
1982–83	Millwall	17	1
1983–84	....	46	7
1984–85	....	41	22
1985–86	....	42	14
1986–87	....	—	—
1986–87	*Swansea C*	2	1
1986–87	Gillingham	6	1

Season	Club	App	Goals
1987–88	....	46	25
1988–89	....	39	14
1989–90	....	41	16
1990–91	....	46	19
1991–92	....	42	16
1992–93	....	13	3
1992–93	Bournemouth	3	—

LOVELL, Stuart

Born Sydney 9.1.72. Ht 5 10 Wt 10 06
Midfield. From Trainee.

Season	Club	App	Goals
1990–91	Reading	30	2
1991–92	....	24	4
1992–93	....	22	8

LOWE, David

Born Liverpool 30.8.65. Ht 5 10
Wt 11 10
Forward. From Apprentice. England Youth, Under-21.

Season	Club	App	Goals
1982–83	Wigan Ath	28	6
1983–84	....	40	8
1984–85	....	29	5
1985–86	....	46	5
1986–87	....	45	16
1987–88	Ipswich T	41	17
1988–89	....	32	6
1989–90	....	34	13
1990–91	....	13	—
1991–92	....	14	1
1991–92	*Port Vale*	9	2
1992–93	Leicester C	32	11

LOWE, Kenny

Born Sedgefield 6.11.64. Ht 6 1
Wt 11 04
Midfield. From Apprentice.

Season	Club	App	Goals
1981–82	Hartlepool U	4	—
1982–83	....	22	1
1983–84	....	28	2
From Barrow			
1987–88	Scarborough	4	—
1988–89	....	—	—
From Barrow			
1991–92	Barnet	36	3

Season	Club	Apps	Goals
1992–93	....	36	2

LOWE, Matthew

Born Birmingham 25.2.74.
Goalkeeper. From Trainee.

Season	Club	Apps	Goals
1991–92	Torquay U	7	—
1992–93	....	13	—

LUCAS, Richard

Born Sheffield 22.9.70.   Ht 5 10   Wt 11 04
Midfield. From Trainee.

Season	Club	Apps	Goals
1989–90	Sheffield U	—	—
1990–91	....	9	—
1991–92	....	1	—
1992–93	....	—	—
1992–93	Preston NE	26	—

LUCKETTI, Chris

Born Littleborough 28.9.71.
Defender. From Trainee.

Season	Club	Apps	Goals
1988–89	Rochdale	1	—
1989–90	....	—	—
1990–91	Stockport Co	—	—
1991–92	Halifax T	36	—
1992–93	....	42	2

LUDDEN, Dominic

Born Basildon 30.3.74
Midfield. From Trainee.

Season	Club	Apps	Goals
1992–93	Leyton Orient	24	1

LUKE, Noel

Born Birmingham 28.12.64.   Ht 5 11
Wt 10 11
Midfield. From School.

Season	Club	Apps	Goals
1981–82	WBA	—	—
1982–83	....	1	—
1983–84	....	8	1
1984–85	Mansfield T	36	6
1985–86	....	14	3

Season	Club	Apps	Goals
1986–87	Peterborough U	30	10
1987–88	....	43	7
1988–89	....	45	3
1989–90	....	43	5
1990–91	....	45	2
1991–92	....	43	—
1992–93	....	28	—
1992–93	Rochdale	3	—

LUKIC, John

Born Chesterfield 11.12.60.   Ht 6 4
Wt 13 13
Goalkeeper. From Apprentice. England
Youth, B, Under-21.

Season	Club	Apps	Goals
1978–79	Leeds U	—	—
1979–80	....	33	—
1980–81	....	42	—
1981–82	....	42	—
1982–83	....	29	—
1983–84	Arsenal........................	4	—
1984–85	....	27	—
1985–86	....	40	—
1986–87	....	36	—
1987–88	....	40	—
1988–89	....	38	—
1989–90	....	38	—
1990–91	Leeds U	38	—
1991–92	....	42	—
1992–93	....	39	—

LUND, Gary

Born Grimsby 13.9.64.   Ht 6 0   Wt 11 00
Forward. From school. England Youth.
Under-21.

Season	Club	Apps	Goals
1983–84	Grimsby T	7	4
1984–85	....	24	12
1985–86	....	29	8
1986–87	Lincoln C.....................	44	13
1987–88	Notts Co......................	40	20
1988–89	....	42	8
1989–90	....	40	9
1990–91	....	16	3
1991–92	....	13	2
1992–93	....	28	4
1992–93	*Hull C*	11	3

LUSCOMBE, Lee

Born Guernsey 16.7.71. Ht 6 0 Wt 12 04
Forward. From Trainee.

1990–91	Southampton	—	—
1991–92		—	—
1991–92	Brentford	13	3
1992–93		29	3

LYDERSEN, Pal

Born Odense 10.9.65. Ht 6 0 Wt 14 01
Defender. From IK Start. Norway full caps.

| 1991–92 | Arsenal | 7 | — |
| 1992–93 | | 8 | — |

LYDIATE, Jason

Born Manchester 29.10.71. Ht 5 11
Wt 12 07
Defender. From Trainee.

1989–90	Manchester U	—	—
1990–91		—	—
1991–92		—	—
1991–92	Bolton W	1	—
1992–93		6	—

LYNCH, Chris

Born Middlesbrough 18.11.74
Forward. From Halifax T trainee.

| 1992–93 | Hartlepool U | 1 | — |

LYNCH, Tommy

Born Limerick 10.10.64. Ht 6 0
Wt 12 06
Midfield. From Limerick.

1988–89	Sunderland	4	—
1989–90		—	—
1989–90	Shrewsbury T	22	—
1990–91		39	2
1991–92		40	2
1992–93		39	2

LYNCH, Tony

Born Paddington 20.1.66. Ht 5 8
Wt 10 08
Forward. From Maidstone U.

1983–84	Brentford	2	—
1984–85		10	—
1985–86		33	6
From Wealdstone			
1991–92	Barnet	6	—
1992–93		8	1

LYNE, Neil

Born Leicester 4.4.70. Ht 6 1 Wt 12 04
Forward. From Leicester U.

1989–90	Nottingham F	—	—
1989–90	*Walsall*	7	—
1990–91	Nottingham F	—	—
1990–91	*Shrewsbury T*	16	6
1991–92	Shrewsbury T	44	8
1992–93		20	3
1992–93	Cambridge U	14	—

LYONS, Andy

Born Blackpool 19.10.66
Forward. From Fleetwood.

| 1992–93 | Crewe Alex | 9 | 2 |

LYONS, Darren

Born Manchester 9.11.66. Ht 6 1
Wt 12 00
Forward. From Ashton U.

| 1991–92 | Bury | 10 | 4 |
| 1992–93 | | 26 | 3 |

LYTTLE, Des

Born Wolverhampton 24.9.71 Ht 5 9
Wt 12 00
Defender. From Worcester C.

| 1992–93 | Swansea C | 46 | 1 |

MABBUTT, Gary

Born Bristol 23.8.61. Ht 5 9 Wt 12 09
Defender . From Apprentice. England
Youth, Under-21, B, 16 full caps.

1978–79	Bristol R	11	—
1979–80		33	—
1980–81		42	5
1981–82		45	5
1982–83	Tottenham H	38	10
1983–84		21	2
1984–85		25	2
1985–86		32	3
1986–87		37	1
1987–88		37	2
1988–89		38	1
1989–90		36	—
1990–91		35	2
1991–92		40	2
1992–93		29	2

McALLISTER, Brian

Born Glasgow 30.11.70. Ht 5 11
Wt 12 05
Defender. From Trainee.

1988–89	Wimbledon	—	—
1989–90		3	—
1990–91		—	—
1990–91	*Plymouth Arg*	8	—
1991–92	Wimbledon	10	—
1992–93		27	—

McALLISTER, Gary

Born Motherwell 25.12.64. Ht 6 1
Wt 10 11
Midfield. From Fir Park BC. Scotland B,
Under-21, 22 full caps.

1981–82	Motherwell	1	—
1982–83		1	—
1983–84		21	—
1984–85		35	6
1985–86		1	—
1985–86	Leicester C	31	7
1986–87		39	10
1987–88		42	9

1988–89		46	11
1989–90		43	10
1990–91	Leeds U	38	2
1991–92		42	5
1992–93		32	5

McALLISTER, Kevin

Born Falkirk 8.11.62. Ht 5 5 Wt 11 0
Forward.

1983–84	Falkirk	35	11
1984–85		29	7
1985–86	Chelsea	20	—
1986–87		8	—
1987–88		5	—
1987–88	*Falkirk*	6	3
1988–89	Chelsea	36	6
1989–90		24	1
1990–91		13	—
1991–92	Falkirk	42	9
1992–93		41	3

McATEER, Jason

Born Liverpool 18.6.71. Ht 5 10
Wt 10 05
Midfield. From Marine.

| 1991–92 | Bolton W | — | — |
| 1992–93 | | 21 | — |

McAULEY, Sean

Born Sheffield 23.6.72. Ht 6 0 Wt 11 9
Defender. From trainee.

| 1991–92 | Manchester U | — | — |
| 1992–93 | St Johnstone | 26 | — |

MACAULEY, Steve

Born Lytham 4.3.69. Ht 6 1 Wt 12 00
Defender. From Fleetwood.

| 1991–92 | Crewe Alex | 9 | 1 |
| 1992–93 | | 25 | 3 |

McAVENNIE, Frank

Born Glasgow 22.11.59. Ht 5 9 Wt 11 0
Forward. From Johnstone Borough and
Partick T trialist. Scotland Under-21, 5
full caps.

Season	Club	App	Goals
1981–82	St Mirren	31	13
1982–83		36	9
1983–84		34	12
1984–85		34	16
1985–86	West Ham U	41	26
1986–87		36	7
1987–88		8	—
1987–88	Celtic	32	15
1988–89		23	12
1988–89	West Ham U	9	—
1989–90		5	—
1990–91		34	10
1991–92		20	6
1992–93	Aston Villa	3	—
1992–93	Celtic	19	9

McCALL, Ian

Born Dumfries 13.9.64. Ht 5 10
Wt 11 07
Midfield. From Motherwell Tech.

Season	Club	App	Goals
1983–84	Queen's Park	3	1
1984–85		28	—
1985–86		35	8
1986–87	Dunfermline Ath	43	8
1987–88		4	—
1987–88	Rangers	12	1
1988–89		5	1
1989–90		4	—
1989–90	Bradford C	12	1
1990–91	Dunfermline Ath	29	4
1991–92		9	1
1991–92	Dundee	27	9
1992–93	Falkirk	35	6

McCALL, Steve

Born Carlisle 15.10.60. Ht 5 11 Wt 12 06
Midfield. From Apprentice. England
Youth, Under-21, B.

Season	Club	App	Goals
1978–79	Ipswich T	—	—
1979–80		10	—

Season	Club	App	Goals
1980–81		31	1
1981–82		42	1
1982–83		42	4
1983–84		42	1
1984–85		31	—
1985–86		33	—
1986–87		26	—
1987–88	Sheffield W	5	—
1988–89		2	—
1989–90		3	—
1989–90	*Carlisle U*	6	—
1990–91	Sheffield W	19	2
1991–92		—	—
1991–92	Plymouth Arg	9	1
1992–93		35	1

McCALL, Stuart

Born Leeds 10.6.64. Ht 5 6 Wt 10 01
Midfield. From Apprentice. Scotland
Under-21, 23 full caps.

Season	Club	App	Goals
1982–83	Bradford C	28	4
1983–84		46	5
1984–85		46	8
1985–86		38	4
1986–87		36	7
1987–88		44	9
1988–89	Everton	33	—
1989–90		37	3
1990–91		33	3
1991–92	Rangers	36	1
1992–93		36	5

McCANCE, Daren

Born Consett 13.9.73 Ht 6 0 Wt 10 12
Defender. From Trainee.

Season	Club	App	Goals
1992–93	Reading	1	—

McCANN, Neil

Born Greenock 11.8.74 Ht 5 10 Wt 10 0
Midfield. From Port Glasgow BC.

Season	Club	App	Goals
1992–93	Dundee	3	—

McCARRISON, Dugald

Born Lanark 22.12.69 Ht 5 11 Wt 10 07
Forward. From Celtic BC.

Season	Club		
1987–88	Celtic	—	—
1988–89		1	—
1989–90		—	—
1990–91		1	—
1990–91	Ipswich T	—	—
1991–92	Celtic	—	—
1991–92	Darlington	5	2
1992–93	Celtic	1	—
1992–93	Kilmarnock	8	1

McCART, Chris

Born Motherwell 17.4.67. Ht 5 9
Wt 10 05
Midfield. From Fir Park BC.

Season	Club		
1984–85	Motherwell	—	—
1985–86		13	—
1986–87		—	—
1987–88		1	—
1988–89		26	—
1989–90		34	1
1990–91		36	—
1991–92		22	2
1992–93		29	3

McCARTHY, Alan

Born London 11.1.72. Ht 5 11 Wt 12 10
Defender. From Trainee.

Season	Club		
1989–90	QPR	—	—
1990–91		2	—
1991–92		3	—
1992–93		—	—

McCARTHY, Jon

Born Middlesbrough 18.8.70. Ht 5 10
Wt 11 01
Forward.

Season	Club		
1987–88	Hartlepool U	1	—
From Shepshed			
1990–91	York C	27	2
1991–92		42	6
1992–93		42	7

McCARTHY, Mick

Born Barnsley 7.2.59. Ht 6 2 Wt 13 12
Defender. From Apprentice. Eire 57 full
caps.

Season	Club		
1977–78	Barnsley	46	1
1978–79		46	2
1979–80		44	1
1980–81		43	1
1981–82		42	1
1982–83		39	1
1983–84		12	—
1983–84	Manchester C	24	1
1984–85		39	—
1985–86		38	—
1986–87		39	1
1987–88	Celtic	22	—
1988–89		26	—
From Lyon			
1989–90	Millwall	6	—
1990–91		12	—
1991–92		17	2
1992–93		—	—

McCARTHY, Paul

Born Cork 4.8.71. Ht 6 0 Wt 13 06
Defender. From Trainee. Eire Youth
Under-21.

Season	Club		
1989–90	Brighton	3	—
1990–91		21	—
1991–92		20	—
1992–93		30	—

McCARTHY, Sean

Born Bridgend 12.9.67. Ht 6 0 Wt 12 05
Forward. From Bridgend. Wales B.

Season	Club		
1985–86	Swansea C	22	3
1986–87		44	14
1987–88		25	8
1988–89	Plymouth Arg	38	8
1989–90		32	11
1990–91	Bradford C	42	13
1991–92		29	16

| 1992–93 | | 42 | 17 |

McCARTHY, Tony

Born Dublin 9.11.69 Ht 6 1 Wt 12 03
Defender. From Shelbourne.

| 1992–93 | Millwall | 7 | 1 |

MACCIOCHI, David

Born Harlow 14.1.72
Midfield. From Trainee.

| 1991–92 | QPR | — | — |
| 1992–93 | Brighton | 2 | — |

McCLAIR, Brian

Born Bellshill 8.12.63. Ht 5 9 Wt 12 00
Forward. From Apprentice. Scotland
Youth, B, Under-21, 30 full caps.

1980–81	Aston Villa	—	—
1981–82	Motherwell	11	4
1982–83		28	11
1983–84	Celtic	35	23
1984–85		32	19
1985–86		34	22
1986–87		44	35
1987–88	Manchester U	40	24
1988–89		38	10
1989–90		37	5
1990–91		36	13
1991–92		42	18
1992–93		42	9

McCLELLAND, John

Born Belfast 7.12.55. Ht 6 2 Wt 13 02
Defender. From Portadown. Northern
Ireland 53 full caps. Football League.

1973–74	Cardiff C	—	—
1974–75		4	1
From Bangor			
1978–79	Mansfield T	36	1
1979–80		43	1
1980–81		46	6
1981–82	Rangers	14	—

1982–83		35	2
1983–84		36	2
1984–85		11	—
1984–85	Watford	29	1
1985–86		31	1
1986–87		41	1
1987–88		40	—
1988–89		43	—
1989–90	Leeds U	3	—
1989–90	Watford	1	—
1990–91	Leeds U	3	—
1991–92		18	—
1991–92	Notts Co	6	—
1992–93	St Johnstone	26	—

McCLUSKEY, George

Born Hamilton 19.9.57 Ht 5 10 Wt 12 6
Forward. From Celtic BC. Scotland U-21.

1975–76	Celtic	4	—
1976–77		—	—
1977–78		15	6
1978–79		21	5
1979–80		23	10
1980–81		22	10
1981–82		35	21
1982–83		10	2
1983–84	Leeds U	32	8
1984–85		19	5
1985–86		22	3
1986–87	Hibernian	35	9
1987–88		31	4
1988–89		16	3
1989–90	Hamilton A	28	8
1990–91		35	14
1991–92		32	12
1992–93	Kilmarnock	31	11

McCOIST, Ally

Born Bellshill 24.9.62. Ht 5 10 Wt 12 00
Forward. From Fir Park BC. Scotland
Youth, Under-21, 46 full caps.

1978–79	St Johnstone	4	—
1979–80		15	—
1980–81		38	22
1981–82	Sunderland	28	2
1982–83		28	6

Season	Club		Apps	Goals
1983–84	Rangers		30	9
1984–85			25	12
1985–86			33	24
1986–87			44	33
1987–88			40	31
1988–89			19	9
1989–90			34	14
1990–91			26	11
1991–92			38	34
1992–93			34	34

McCORD, Brian

Born Derby 24.8.68. Ht 5 10 Wt 11 06
Midfield. From Apprentice.

Season	Club		Apps	Goals
1987–88	Derby Co		1	—
1988–89			—	—
1989–90			4	—
1989–90	Barnsley		16	1
1990–91			24	1
1991–92			3	—
1992–93			—	—
1992–93	*Mansfield T*		11	1
1992–93	Stockport Co		8	—

McCREERY, David

Born Belfast 16.9.57. Ht 5 6 Wt 10 07
Midfield. From Apprentice. Northern
Ireland Schools. Youth Under-21, 67 full
caps.

Season	Club		Apps	Goals
1974–75	Manchester U		2	—
1975–76			28	4
1976–77			25	2
1977–78			17	1
1978–79			15	—
1979–80	QPR		42	4
1980–81			15	—
From Tulsa R				
1982–83	Newcastle U		26	—
1983–84			40	—
1984–85			35	1
1985–86			41	—
1986–87			30	—
1987–88			35	1
1988–89			36	—
1989–90	Hearts		22	—
1990–91			7	—

Season	Club		Apps	Goals
1991–92	Hartlepool U		30	—
1992–93	Carlisle U		22	—

McCULLAGH, Paul

Born Brigg 6.2.74 Ht 5 11 Wt 11 04
Defender. From Trainee.

Season	Club		Apps	Goals
1992–93	Scunthorpe U		5	1

McCULLOCH, William

Born Baillieston 2.4.73. Ht 6 3 Wt 12 06
Goalkeeper. From Linlithgow Rose.

Season	Club		Apps	Goals
1991–92	Airdrieonians		1	—
1992–93			1	—

McDERMOTT, John

Born Middlesbrough 3.2.69. Ht 5 7
Wt 10 00
Defender.

Season	Club		Apps	Goals
1986–87	Grimsby T		13	—
1987–88			28	—
1988–89			38	1
1989–90			39	—
1990–91			43	—
1991–92			39	1
1992–93			38	2

McDONALD, Alan

Born Belfast 12.10.63. Ht 6 2 Wt 12 07
Defender. From Apprentice. Northern
Ireland Youth, 41 full caps.

Season	Club		Apps	Goals
1981–82	QPR		—	—
1982–83			—	—
1982–83	*Charlton Ath*		9	—
1983–84	QPR		5	—
1984–85			16	1
1985–86			42	—
1986–87			39	4
1987–88			36	3
1988–89			30	—
1989–90			34	—
1990–91			17	—
1991–92			28	—

Season	Club	App	Goals
1992–93		39	—

McDONALD, David

Born Dublin 2.1.71.   Ht 5 11   Wt 11 07
Defender. From Trainee. Eire Youth,
Under-21, B.

Season	Club	App	Goals
1989–90	Tottenham H	—	—
1990–91		—	—
1990–91	*Gillingham*	10	—
1991–92	Tottenham H	—	—
1992–93		2	—
1992–93	*Bradford C*	7	—
1992–93	*Reading*	11	—

MacDONALD, Kevin

Born Inverness 22.12.60.   Ht 6 1
Wt 12 06
Midfield. From Inverness Caley.

Season	Club	App	Goals
1980–81	Leicester C	20	2
1981–82		25	1
1982–83		42	4
1983–84		38	1
1984–85		13	—
1984–85	Liverpool	13	—
1985–86		17	1
1986–87		6	—
1987–88		1	—
1987–88	*Leicester C*	3	—
1988–89	Liverpool	3	—
1988–89	*Rangers*	3	—
1989–90	Coventry C	22	—
1990–91		9	—
1990–91	*Cardiff C*	8	—
1991–92	Walsall	20	3
1992–93		33	3

McDONALD, Neil

Born Wallsend 2.11.65.   Ht 5 11
Wt 11 04
Midfield. From Wallsend BC. England
Schools, Youth, Under-21.

Season	Club	App	Goals
1982–83	Newcastle U	24	4
1983–84		12	—
1984–85		36	6

Season	Club	App	Goals
1985–86		28	4
1986–87		40	7
1987–88		40	3
1988–89	Everton	25	1
1989–90		31	1
1990–91		29	2
1991–92		5	—
1991–92	Oldham Ath	17	1
1992–93		4	—

McDONALD, Rod

Born London 20.3.67.   Ht 5 10   Wt 12 07
Forward. From South Liverpool, Colne
Dynamoes.

Season	Club	App	Goals
1990–91	Walsall	36	5
1991–92		39	18
1992–93		39	12

McDONOUGH, Roy

Born Solihull 16.10.58   Ht 6 1   Wt 13 07
Forward. From Apprentice.

Season	Club	App	Goals
1976–77	Birmingham C	2	1
1977–78		—	—
1978–79		—	—
1978–79	Walsall	34	7
1979–80		42	7
1980–81		6	1
1980–81	Chelsea	—	—
1980–81	Colchester U	12	2
1981–82		40	14
1982–83		41	8
1983–84	Southend U	22	4
1983–84	Exeter C	16	—
1984–85		4	1
1984–85	Cambridge U	32	5
1985–86	Southend U	38	7
1986–87		33	4
1987–88		42	9
1988–89		40	5
1989–90		33	5
1990–91	Colchester U	*24*	*8*
1991–92		*40*	*26*
1992–93		25	9

McDOUGALL, Gordon

Born Bellshill 17.2.71. Ht 6 2 Wt 12 03
Goalkeeper. From Musselburgh Ath.

1990–91	Falkirk	—	—
1991–92		4	—
1992–93		5	—

McELHATTON, Michael

Born Co.Kerry 16.4.75
Defender. From Trainee.

1992–93	Bournemouth	1	—

McFARLANE, Andy

Born Wolverhampton 30.11.66. Ht 6 3
Wt 12 06
Forward. From Cradley T.

1990–91	Portsmouth	—	—
1991–92		2	—
1992–93	Swansea C	24	5

McGAVIN, Steve

Born North Walsham 24.1.69 Ht 5 8
Wt 11 00
Forward. From Sudbury.

1990–91	Colchester U	8	—
1991–92		39	20
1992–93		37	9

McGEACHIE, George

Born Bothkennar 5.2.59 Ht 5 11
Wt 11 12
Defender. From Bo'ness U.

1977–78	Dundee	15	2
1978–79		5	—
1979–80		28	1
1980–81		30	2
1981–82		29	3
1982–83		22	—
1983–84		23	—
1984–85		35	1
1985–86		2	—

1986–87		28	—
1987–88		14	1
1988–89		6	—
1989–90		2	—
1989–90	Raith R	14	—
1990–91		31	—
1991–92		18	—
1992–93		30	—

McGEE, Owen

Born Teesside 29.4.70. Ht 5 5 Wt 10 08
Defender. From Trainee.

1988–89	Middlesbrough	—	—
1989–90		13	—
1990–91		8	1
1991–92		—	—
1991–92	Scarborough	8	—
1992–93		16	—

McGEE, Paul

Born Dublin 17.5.68. Ht 5 6 Wt 9 10
Forward. From Bohemians. Eire
Under-21.

1988–89	Colchester U	3	—
1988–89	Wimbledon	1	1
1989–90		13	—
1990–91		27	6
1991–92		16	2
1992–93		3	—

McGHEE, Mark

Born Glasgow 25.5.57. Ht 5 10 Wt 12 00
Forward. From Apprentice. Scotland
Under-21, 4 full caps.

1974–75	Bristol C	—	—
1975–76	Morton	5	1
1976–77		39	20
1977–78		20	16
1977–78	Newcastle U	18	3
1978–79		10	2
1978–79	Aberdeen	11	4
1979–80		21	6
1980–81		36	13
1981–82		31	8

Season	Club	League Appearances/Goals	
1982–83		32	16
1983–84		33	16
1984–85	SV Hamburg	26	6
1985–86		4	1
1985–86	Celtic	18	4
1986–87		17	1
1987–88		24	6
1988–89		29	16
1989–90	Newcastle U	46	19
1990–91		21	5
1991–92	Reading	32	5
1992–93		13	2

McGINLAY, John

Born Inverness 8.4.64.   Ht 5 9   Wt 11 06
Forward. From Elgin C.

Season	Club	League Appearances/Goals	
1988–89	Shrewsbury T	16	5
1989–90		44	22
1990–91	Bury	25	9
1990–91	Millwall	2	—
1991–92		25	8
1992–93		7	2
1992–93	Bolton W	34	16

McGINLAY, Pat

Born Glasgow 30.5.67.   Ht 5 10   Wt 10 10
Midfield. From Scottish Junior.

Season	Club	League Appearances/Goals	
1985–86	Blackpool	—	—
1986–87		12	1
1987–88	Hibernian	—	—
1988–89		2	—
1989–90		28	3
1990–91		32	1
1991–92		43	9
1992–93		40	10

McGINNIS, Gary

Born Dundee 21.10.63.   Ht 5 11
Wt 10 03
Defender. From Dundee BC. Scotland
Schools, Youth, Under-21.

Season	Club	League Appearances/Goals	
1981–82	Dundee U	—	—
1982–83		—	—
1983–84		4	—

Season	Club	League Appearances/Goals	
1984–85		10	—
1985–86		4	—
1986–87		20	—
1987–88		11	—
1988–89		11	—
1989–90		7	—
1989–90	St Johnstone	11	—
1990–91		32	—
1991–92		29	—
1992–93		27	—

McGIVERN, Sam

Born Kilwinning 9.10.63   Ht 5 9
Wt 10 07
Midfield. From Glenfield.

Season	Club	League Appearances/Goals	
1981–82	Kilmarnock	28	2
1982–83		34	3
1983–84		37	7
1984–85		32	5
1985–86		36	11
1986–87		19	2
1986–87	Falkirk	16	3
1987–88		10	1
1988–89		34	8
1989–90		16	2
1990–91		30	15
1991–92		30	3
1992–93		1	—

McGLASHAN, Colin

Born Perth 17.3.64.   Ht 5 7   Wt 10 04
Forward. From Celtic BC.

Season	Club	League Appearances/Goals	
1980–81	Dundee	—	—
1981–82		—	—
1982–83		2	—
1983–84		9	1
1984–85		—	—
1984–85	Dunfermline Ath	16	1
1984–85	Cowdenbeath	11	5
1985–86		34	15
1986–87		15	7
1986–87	Clyde	21	5
1987–88		43	16
1988–89		37	16
1989–90		39	11
1990–91	Partick T	36	10

Season	Club	App	Goals
1991–92	....	44	18
1992–93	....	22	2

McGLASHAN, John

Born Dundee 3.6.67. Ht 6 1 Wt 12 00
Forward. From Dundee Violet.

Season	Club	App	Goals
1988–89	Montrose	35	2
1989–90	....	33	9
1990–91	Millwall	8	—
1991–92	....	8	—
1992–93		—	—
1992–93	*Cambridge U*	1	—
1992–93	*Fulham*	5	1
1992–93	Peterborough U	18	—

McGOLDRICK, Eddie

Born London 30.4.65. Ht 5 10 Wt 12 00
Midfield. From Nuneaton, Kettering T.
Eire 8 full caps.

Season	Club	App	Goals
1986–87	Northampton T	39	5
1987–88	....	46	2
1988–89	....	22	2
1988–89	Crystal Palace	21	—
1989–90	....	22	—
1990–91	....	26	—
1991–92	....	36	3
1992–93	....	42	8

McGORRY, Brian

Born Liverpool 16.4.70. Ht 5 10
Wt 11 00
Midfield. From Weymouth.

Season	Club	App	Goals
1991–92	Bournemouth	8	—
1992–93	....	37	8

McGOWAN, Gavin

Born Blackheath 16.1.76
Defender. From Trainee.

Season	Club	App	Goals
1992–93	Arsenal	2	—

McGOWAN, Jamie

Born Morecambe 5.12.70 Ht 6 0
Wt 11 1
Defender. From Morecambe.

Season	Club	App	Goals
1992–93	Dundee	21	1

McGOWNE, Kevin

Born Kilmarnock 16.12.69. Ht 6 0
Wt 11 04
Defender. From Hurlford U.

Season	Club	App	Goals
1989–90	St Mirren	2	—
1990–91	....	10	—
1991–92	....	36	1
1992–93	St Johnstone	26	1

McGRATH, Lloyd

Born Birmingham 24.2.65. Ht 5 5
Wt 11 06
Midfield. From Apprentice. England
Youth, Under-21.

Season	Club	App	Goals
1982–83	Coventry C	—	—
1983–84	....	1	—
1984–85	....	23	—
1985–86	....	32	—
1986–87	....	30	3
1987–88	....	17	—
1988–89	....	8	—
1989–90	....	13	—
1990–91	....	14	—
1991–92	....	40	1
1992–93	....	25	—

McGRATH, Paul

Born Greenford 4.12.59. Ht 6 2
Wt 14 00
Defender. From St Patrick's Ath. Eire 61
full caps. Football League.

Season	Club	App	Goals
1981–82	Manchester U	—	—
1982–83	....	14	3
1983–84	....	9	1
1984–85	....	23	—
1985–86	....	40	3
1986–87	....	35	2

Season	Club	Appearances	Goals
1987–88		22	2
1988–89		20	1
1989–90	Aston Villa	35	1
1990–91		35	—
1991–92		41	1
1992–93		42	4

McGRAW, Mark

Born Rutherglen 5.1.71 Ht 5 11
Wt 10 07
Forward. From Port Glasgow R.

Season	Club	Appearances	Goals
1988–89	Morton	1	—
1989–90		11	3
1990–91	Hibernian	13	—
1991–92		24	1
1992–93		2	—

McGRILLEN, Paul

Born Glasgow 19.8.71 Ht 5 8 Wt 10 05
Forward. From Motherwell BC.

Season	Club	Appearances	Goals
1990–91	Motherwell	2	—
1991–92		16	—
1992–93		22	6

McGUCKIN, Thomas

Born Middlesbrough 24.4.73. Ht 6 2
Wt 12 02
Defender. From Trainee.

Season	Club	Appearances	Goals
1991–92	Hartlepool U	7	—
1992–93		14	1

McGUGAN, Paul

Born Glasgow 17.7.64. Ht 6 2 Wt 12 00
Defender. From Eastercraigs.

Season	Club	Appearances	Goals
1980–81	Celtic	—	—
1981–82		—	—
1982–83		—	—
1983–84		1	—
1984–85		3	—
1985–86		21	2
1986–87		22	—
1987–88		2	—

Season	Club	Appearances	Goals
1987–88	Barnsley	29	1
1988–89		20	1
1989–90		—	—
1990–91		—	—
1990–91	Chesterfield	22	1
1991–92		37	3
1992–93		13	2

McHUGH, Michael

Born Donegal 3.4.71. Ht 5 11 Wt 11 00
Forward.

Season	Club	Appearances	Goals
1989–90	Bradford C	—	—
1990–91		1	—
1991–92		9	—
1992–93		16	4

McILHARGEY, Steve

Born Ferryhill 28.8.63. Ht 6 0 Wt 11 07
Goalkeeper. From Blantyre Celtic.
Scotland Schools.

Season	Club	Appearances	Goals
1987–88	Walsall	—	—
1988–89		—	—
1989–90	Blackpool	22	—
1990–91		44	—
1991–92		28	—
1992–93		3	—

McINALLY, Alan

Born Ayr 10.2.63. Ht 6 1 Wt 13 03
Forward. From Ayr U BC. Scotland 8 full
caps.

Season	Club	Appearances	Goals
1980–81	Ayr U	6	—
1981–82		17	9
1982–83		35	7
1983–84		35	16
1984–85	Celtic	11	1
1985–86		16	1
1986–87		38	15
1987–88	Aston Villa	25	4
1988–89		33	14

To Bayern Munich

McINALLY, Jim

Born Glasgow 19.2.64.   Ht 6 0   Wt 12 00
Midfield. From Celtic BC. Scottish Youth,
Under-21. 10 full caps.

1982–83	Celtic	1	—
1983–84		—	—
1983–84	*Dundee*	11	2
1984–85	Nottingham F	24	—
1985–86		12	—
1985–86	Coventry C	5	—
1986–87	Dundee U	32	1
1987–88		36	2
1988–89		29	1
1989–90		35	3
1990–91		33	1
1991–92		32	4
1992–93		32	—

McINTYRE, James

Born Dumbarton 24.5.72.   Ht 5 11
Wt 11 05
Forward. From Duntocher Boys.

1991–92	Bristol C	1	—
1992–93		—	—
1992–93	*Exeter C*	15	3

McINTYRE, Tom

Born Bellshill 26.12.63.   Ht 6 0   Wt 10 10
Defender. From Fir Park BC.

1983–84	Aberdeen	10	—
1984–85		—	—
1985–86		5	—
1986–87		4	—
1986–87	Hibernian	15	—
1987–88		25	—
1988–89		17	2
1989–90		—	—
1990–91		9	—
1991–92		37	6
1992–93		12	1

MACKAY, Gary

Born Edinburgh 23.1.64.   Ht 5 9
Wt 10 05
Midfield. From Salvesan BC. Scotland
Schools, Youth, 4 full caps.

1980–81	Hearts	12	—
1981–82		17	2
1982–83		34	6
1983–84		31	4
1984–85		17	2
1985–86		32	4
1986–87		37	7
1987–88		41	5
1988–89		29	2
1989–90		33	1
1990–91		30	3
1991–92		43	1
1992–93		37	2

McKEARNEY, David

Born Crosby 20.6.68.   Ht 5 10   Wt 11 02
Forward.

1987–88	Bolton W	—	—
1988–89		—	—
1989–90	Crewe Alex	17	1
1990–91		31	1
1991–92		31	4
1992–93		29	6

McKEE, Colin

Born Glasgow 22.8.73   Ht 5 10   Wt 11 00
Forward. From Trainee.

1991–92	Manchester U	—	—
1992–93		—	—
1992–93	*Bury*	2	—

MACKENZIE, Alan

Born Edinburgh 8.8.66   Ht 5 8   Wt 10 2
Forward. From Hutcheson Vale.

1984–85	Cowdenbeath	1	—
1985–86		19	—
1986–87	Berwick R	20	1
1987–88	HJK Finland	—	—

1987–88	Cowdenbeath	18	6
1988–89		19	6
1989–90		20	3
1990–91		33	15
1991–92	Raith R	22	3
1992–93		23	3

McKENZIE, Roger

Born Sheffield 27.1.73.
Forward. From Trainee.

| 1991–92 | Doncaster R | 17 | 1 |
| 1992–93 | Scarborough | 1 | — |

McKENZIE, Scott

Born Glasgow 7.7.70.   Ht 5 9   Wt 10 05
Forward. From Musselburgh Ath.

1990–91	Falkirk	—	—
1991–92		2	—
1992–93		3	—

MACKENZIE, Steve

Born Romford 23.11.61.   Ht 5 11
Wt 12 05
Midfield. From Apprentice. England
Youth, Under-21, B.

1979–80	Crystal Palace	—	—
1979–80	Manchester C	19	2
1980–81		39	6
1981–82	WBA	37	5
1982–83		1	—
1983–84		19	4
1984–85		38	8
1985–86		31	4
1986–87		22	2
1987–88	Charlton Ath	32	2
1988–89		36	3
1989–90		17	1
1990–91		15	1
1990–91	Sheffield W	12	2
1991–92		3	—
1991–92	Shrewsbury T	13	1
1992–93		8	—

McKEOWN, Gary

Born Oxford 19.10.70.   Ht 5 10   Wt 11 07
Midfield. From Trainee. FA Schools,
England Youth.

1988–89	Arsenal	—	—
1989–90		—	—
1990–91		—	—
1991–92		—	—
1991–92	Shrewsbury T	8	1
1992–93	Dundee	20	1

McKILLIGAN, Neil

Born Falkirk 2.1.74   Ht 5 10   Wt 11 0
Midfield. From Southampton trainee.

| 1992–93 | Partick T | 5 | — |

McKIMMIE, Stuart

Born Aberdeen 27.10.62.   Ht 5 8
Wt 10 07
Defender. From Banks o'Dee. Scotland
Under-21, 21 full caps.

1980–81	Dundee	17	—
1981–82		16	—
1982–83		31	—
1983–84		16	—
1983–84	Aberdeen	18	1
1984–85		34	3
1985–86		34	3
1986–87		37	—
1987–88		42	—
1988–89		35	—
1989–90		33	—
1990–91		26	1
1991–92		39	—
1992–93		14	—

McKINLAY, Billy

Born Glasgow 22.4.69.   Ht 5 9   Wt 9 13
Midfield. From Hamilton T. Scotland B,
Under-21.

1986–87	Dundee U	3	—
1988–89		30	1
1989–90		13	—

1990–91	....	34	2
1991–92	....	22	1
1992–93	....	37	1

McKINLAY, Tosh

Born Glasgow 3.12.64. Ht 5 7 Wt 10 03
Defender. From Celtic BC. Scotland
Youth, Under-21.

Season	Club		
1981–82	Dundee.........................	—	—
1982–83	....	1	—
1983–84	....	36	3
1984–85	....	34	3
1985–86	....	22	—
1986–87	....	32	2
1987–88	....	19	—
1988–89	....	18	—
1988–89	Hearts...........................	17	1
1989–90	....	29	1
1990–91	....	33	2
1991–92	....	39	2
1992–93	....	34	—

McKINNON, Ray

Born Dundee 5.8.70. Ht 5 8 Wt 9 11
Defender. From S form. Scotland
Under-21.

Season	Club		
1987–88	Dundee U.....................	—	—
1988–89	....	1	—
1989–90	....	10	—
1990–91	....	17	2
1991–92	....	25	4
1992–93	Nottingham F..............	6	1

McKINNON, Rob

Born Glasgow 31.7.66. Ht 5 11 Wt 11 01
Defender. From Rutherglen Glencairn.

Season	Club		
1984–85	Newcastle U.................	—	—
1985–86	....	1	—
1986–87	Hartlepool U	45	—
1987–88	....	42	2
1988–89	....	46	2
1989–90	....	46	1
1990–91	....	45	1
1990–91	*Manchester U*..............	—	—

1991–92	Hartlepool U	23	1
1991–92	Motherwell..................	16	1
1992–93	....	35	—

McLAREN, Alan

Born Edinburgh 4.1.71. Ht 5 11
Wt 11 06
Defender. From Cavalry Bank. Scotland
Under-21, 8 full caps.

Season	Club		
1987–88	Hearts..........................	1	—
1988–89	....	12	1
1989–90	....	27	1
1990–91	....	23	1
1991–92	....	38	1
1992–93	....	34	—

McLAREN, Andrew

Born Glasgow 5.6.73. Ht 5 10 Wt 10 06
Forward. From Rangers Amateur BC.

Season	Club		
1989–90	Dundee U	—	—
1990–91	....	—	—
1991–92	....	13	—
1992–93	....	5	—

MacLAREN, Ross

Born Edinburgh 14.4.62. Ht 5 10
Wt 12 12
Midfield. From Glasgow Rangers.

Season	Club		
1980–81	Shrewsbury T..............	4	—
1981–82	....	35	—
1982–83	....	40	5
1983–84	....	40	7
1984–85	....	42	6
1985–86	Derby Co	46	4
1986–87	....	42	—
1987–88	....	34	—
1988–89	Swindon T	37	4
1989–90	....	46	3
1990–91	....	45	1
1991–92	....	32	1
1992–93	....	22	—

McLAUGHLIN, Joe

Born Greenock 2.6.60. Ht 6 1 Wt 12 00
Defender. From school. Scotland
Under-21.

Season	Club	Apps	Goals
1977–78	Morton	—	—
1978–79		—	—
1979–80		30	2
1980–81		34	1
1981–82		36	—
1982–83		34	—
1983–84	Chelsea	41	—
1984–85		36	1
1985–86		40	1
1986–87		36	2
1987–88		36	1
1988–89		31	—
1989–90	Charlton Ath	31	—
1990–91	Watford	24	1
1991–92		22	1
1992–93		—	—
1992–93	Falkirk	8	1

McLAUGHLIN, Paul

Born Johnstone 9.12.65. Ht 5 11
Wt 11 09
Defender. From Anniesland U.

Season	Club	Apps	Goals
1983–84	Queen's Park	—	—
1984–85		33	—
1985–86		23	1
1986–87		30	—
1987–88		33	2
1988–89		34	1
1989–90	Celtic	—	—
1990–91		3	—
1991–92	Partick T	33	—
1992–93		23	—

McLEARY, Alan

Born London 6.10.64. Ht 6 0 Wt 11 11
Defender. From Apprentice. England
Youth, B, Under-21.

Season	Club	Apps	Goals
1981–82	Millwall	—	—
1982–83		3	1
1983–84		30	—
1984–85		21	—

Season	Club	Apps	Goals
1985–86		35	3
1986–87		42	—
1987–88		31	—
1988–89		38	1
1989–90		31	—
1990–91		42	—
1991–92		28	—
1992–93		6	—
1992–93	Sheffield U	3	—
1992–93	Wimbledon	4	—

McLEISH, Alex

Born Glasgow 21.1.59. Ht 6 1 Wt 12 04
Defender. From Glasgow United. Scotland
Under-21, 77 full caps.

Season	Club	Apps	Goals
1977–78	Aberdeen	1	—
1978–79		19	1
1979–80		35	2
1980–81		32	3
1981–82		32	5
1982–83		34	2
1983–84		32	2
1984–85		30	1
1985–86		34	3
1986–87		40	3
1987–88		36	1
1988–89		34	—
1989–90		32	2
1990–91		33	—
1991–92		7	—
1992–93		27	—

MacLEOD, Ian

Born Glasgow 19.11.59 Ht 5 11 Wt 11 6
Defender. From Claremont BC.

Season	Club	Apps	Goals
1977–78	Motherwell	5	—
1978–79		25	—
1979–80		24	—
1980–81		25	1
1981–82		37	—
1982–83		30	1
1983–84		29	—
1984–85		38	—
1985–86		29	1
1986–87	Falkirk	35	—
1987–88		33	—

Season	Club	Apps	Goals
1988–89		—	—
1989–90	Raith R	37	—
1990–91		26	1
1991–92		44	1
1992–93		36	2

McLEOD, Joe

Born Edinburgh 30.12.67. Ht 5 7
Wt 9 11
Forward. From Hutchison Vale BC.

Season	Club	Apps	Goals
1984–85	Dundee U	—	—
1985–86		—	—
1986–87	*Dumbarton*	5	—
1986–87	Dundee U	2	—
1987–88		10	1
1988–89		3	—
1989–90		2	—
1990–91		—	—
1991–92	Motherwell	14	—
1992–93		10	—

MacLEOD, Murdo

Born Glasgow 24.9.58. Ht 5 8   Wt 12 00
Midfield. From Glasgow Amateurs.
Scotland Under-21, 20 full caps.

Season	Club	Apps	Goals
1974–75	Dumbarton	—	—
1975–76		7	—
1976–77		27	7
1977–78		39	1
1978–79		14	1
1978–79	Celtic	23	3
1979–80		36	7
1980–81		18	8
1981–82		36	10
1982–83		35	11
1983–84		34	7
1984–85		31	3
1985–86		30	3
1986–87		38	4
From Borussia Dortmund			
1990–91	Hibernian	25	2
1991–92		22	—
1992–93		31	—

McLOUGHLIN, Alan

Born Manchester 20.4.67. Ht 5 8
Wt 10 00
Midfield. From Local. Eire B, 13 full caps.

Season	Club	Apps	Goals
1984–85	Manchester U	—	—
1985–86		—	—
1986–87	Swindon T	9	—
1986–87	Torquay U	16	1
1987–88		8	3
1987–88	Swindon T	8	—
1988–89		26	3
1989–90		46	12
1990–91		17	4
1990–91	Southampton	22	1
1991–92		2	—
1991–92	*Aston Villa*	—	—
1991–92	Portsmouth	14	2
1992–93		46	9

McLOUGHLIN, Paul

Born Bristol 23.12.63. Ht 5 10 Wt 11 11
Forward. From Bristol C and Gisborne C.

Season	Club	Apps	Goals
1984–85	Cardiff C	17	—
1985–86		32	4
From Gisborne C			
1987–88	Hereford U	29	1
1988–89		45	13
1989–90	Wolverhampton W	19	4
1990–91		6	—
1991–92		3	—
1991–92	*Walsall*	9	4
1991–92	*York C*	1	—
1991–92	Mansfield T	12	3
1992–93		26	4

McMAHON, Steve

Born Liverpool 20.8.61. Ht 5 9 Wt 11 08
Midfield. From Apprentice. England
Under-21, B, 17 full caps.

Season	Club	Apps	Goals
1979–80	Everton	—	—
1980–81		34	5
1981–82		32	2
1982–83		34	4
1983–84	Aston Villa	37	5
1984–85		35	2

Season	Club	App	Goals
1985–86	....	3	—
1985–86	Liverpool	23	6
1986–87	....	37	5
1987–88	....	40	9
1988–89	....	29	3
1989–90	....	38	5
1990–91	....	22	—
1991–92	....	15	1
1991–92	Manchester C	18	—
1992–93	....	27	1

McMAHON, Steven

Born Glasgow 22.4.70 Ht 6 4 Wt 14 03
Defender. From Ferguslie.

Season	Club	App	Goals
1991–92	Swansea C..................	—	—
1992–93	....	2	—

McMANAMAN, Steve

Born Liverpool 11.2.72. Ht 6 0 Wt 10 06
Forward. From School. England Youth,
Under-21.

Season	Club	App	Goals
1989–90	Liverpool	—	—
1990–91	....	2	—
1991–92	....	30	5
1992–93	....	31	4

McMANUS, Steven

Born Nottingham 8.3.75 Ht 5 11
Wt 11 07
Midfield. From Trainee.

Season	Club	App	Goals
1992–93	Walsall	1	—

McMARTIN, Grant

Born Linlithgow 31.12.70. Ht 5 10
Wt 10 00
Midfield. From Dunipace J.

Season	Club	App	Goals
1989–90	Dundee........................	4	—
1990–91	....	19	1
1991–92	....	25	1
1992–93	....	3	—

McMILLAN, Andy

Born Bloemfontein 22.6.68. Ht 5 11
Wt 11 04
Defender.

Season	Club	App	Goals
1987–88	York C........................	22	—
1988–89	....	2	—
1989–90	....	25	—
1990–91	....	45	1
1991–92	....	41	1
1992–93	....	42	—

McMINN, Ted

Born Castle Douglas 28.9.62. Ht 5 11
Wt 11 02
Forward. From Glenafton Athletic.

Season	Club	App	Goals
1982–83	Queen of the S............	22	1
1983–84	....	32	3
1984–85	....	8	1
1984–85	Rangers......................	20	1
1985–86	....	28	2
1986–87	....	15	1
From Seville			
1987–88	Derby Co	7	1
1988–89	....	32	4
1989–90	....	15	—
1990–91	....	13	—
1991–92	....	37	2
1992–93	....	19	2

McNAB, Neil

Born Greenock 4.6.57. Ht 5 7 Wt 11 00
Midfield. Scotland Schools. Under-21.

Season	Club	App	Goals
1972–73	Morton	3	—
1973–74	....	11	—
1973–74	Tottenham H..............	1	—
1974–75	....	2	—
1975–76	....	15	—
1976–77	....	10	—
1977–78	....	42	3
1978–79	....	2	—
1978–79	Bolton W	23	3
1979–80	....	12	1
1979–80	Brighton	16	—
1980–81	....	33	1
1981–82	....	40	3

Season	Club	Apps	Goals
1982–83	....	14	—
1982–83	Leeds U	5	—
1982–83	Portsmouth	—	—
1983–84	Manchester C	33	1
1984–85	....	18	—
1985–86	....	37	4
1986–87	....	42	4
1987–88	....	37	2
1988–89	....	42	5
1989–90	....	12	—
1989–90	Tranmere R	22	1
1990–91	....	40	3
1991–92	....	12	—
1991–92	Huddersfield T	11	—
1992–93	Tranmere R	31	2

McNALLY, Bernard

Born Shrewsbury 17.2.63.   Ht 5 7
Wt 10 12
Midfield. From Apprentice. Northern
Ireland 5 full caps.

Season	Club	Apps	Goals
1980–81	Shrewsbury T	1	—
1981–82	....	33	1
1982–83	....	25	1
1983–84	....	41	4
1984–85	....	42	2
1985–86	....	35	6
1986–87	....	40	5
1987–88	....	43	2
1988–89	....	22	2
1989–90	WBA	41	5
1990–91	....	25	1
1991–92	....	21	1
1992–93	....	40	3

McNALLY, Mark

Born Bellshill 10.3.71 Ht 5 9 Wt 10 07
Defender. From Celtic BC. Scotland
Under-21.

Season	Club	Apps	Goals
1987–88	Celtic	—	—
1988–89	....	—	—
1989–90	....	—	—
1990–91	....	19	—
1991–92	....	25	1
1992–93	....	27	—

McPARLAND, Ian

Born Edinburgh 4.10.61.   Ht 5 8
Wt 10 08
Forward. From Ormiston Primrose.

Season	Club	Apps	Goals
1980–81	Notts Co	2	—
1981–82	....	12	—
1982–83	....	11	1
1983–84	....	21	2
1984–85	....	20	—
1985–86	....	44	15
1986–87	....	45	24
1987–88	....	43	21
1988–89	....	23	6
1988–89	Hull C	11	1
1989–90	....	20	5
1990–91	....	16	1
1990–91	Walsall	11	6
1991–92	Dunfermline Ath	16	2
1992–93	Lincoln C	4	—
1992–93	Northampton T	11	3

MacPHAIL, John

Born Dundee 7.12.55.   Ht 6 0   Wt 12 03
Defender. From St. Columba's.

Season	Club	Apps	Goals
1975–76	Dundee	6	—
1976–77	....	25	—
1977–78	....	34	—
1978–79	....	3	—
1978–79	Sheffield U	15	1
1979–80	....	44	5
1980–81	....	39	—
1981–82	....	26	1
1982–83	....	11	—
1982–83	York C	12	2
1983–84	....	46	10
1984–85	....	42	5
1985–86	....	42	7
1986–87	Bristol C	26	1
1987–88	Sunderland	46	16
1988–89	....	45	4
1989–90	....	38	2
1990–91	....	1	—
1990–91	Hartlepool U	42	1
1991–92	....	41	1
1992–93	....	42	1

MacPHERSON, Angus

Born Glasgow 11.10.68   Ht 5 11   Wt 10 4
Defender. From S Form.

Season	Club		
1988–89	Rangers	—	—
1989–90		—	—
1989–90	*Exeter C*	11	1
1990–91	Kilmarnock	11	—
1991–92		43	3
1992–93		40	5

McPHERSON, David

Born Paisley 28.1.64.   Ht 6 3   Wt 11 11
Defender. From Gartcosh United.
Scotland Youth, B, Under-21, 27 full caps.

Season	Club		
1980–81	Rangers	—	—
1981–82		—	—
1982–83		18	1
1983–84		36	2
1984–85		31	—
1985–86		34	5
1986–87		42	7
1987–88		44	4
1988–89	Hearts	32	4
1989–90		35	4
1990–91		34	2
1991–92		44	2
1992–93	Rangers	34	2

McPHERSON, Keith

Born Greenwich 11.9.63.   Ht 5 11
Wt 10 11
Defender. From Apprentice.

Season	Club		
1981–82	West Ham U	—	—
1982–83		—	—
1983–84		—	—
1984–85		1	—
1985–86		—	—
1985–86	*Cambridge U*	11	1
1985–86	Northampton T	20	—
1986–87		46	5
1987–88		32	—
1988–89		41	2
1989–90		43	1
1990–91	Reading	46	3
1991–92		44	1

Season	Club		
1992–93		44	1

McQUEEN, Tommy

Born Bellshill 1.4.63.   Ht 5 11   Wt 11 00
Defender. From Gartcosh United.

Season	Club		
1981–82	Clyde	39	—
1982–83		35	—
1983–84		38	1
1984–85	Aberdeen	35	3
1985–86		17	1
1986–87		1	—
1986–87	West Ham U	9	—
1987–88		12	—
1988–89		2	—
1989–90		7	—
1990–91		—	—
1990–91	Falkirk	32	2
1991–92		26	1
1992–93		30	4

McQUILKEN, James

Born Glasgow 3.10.74   Ht 5 9   Wt 10 7
Defender. From Giffnock N BC.

Season	Club		
1992–93	Celtic	1	—

McQUILLAN, John

Born Stranraer 20.7.70.   Ht 5 10
Wt 10 07
Defender. From Stranraer Sch.

Season	Club		
1986–87	Stranraer	—	—
1987–88	Dundee	—	—
1988–89		—	—
1989–90		2	—
1990–91		14	1
1991–92		40	3
1992–93		29	—

McSKIMMING, Shaun

Born Stranraer 29.5.70   Ht 5 11   Wt 10 8
Defender. From Schools.

Season	Club		
1986–87	Stranraer	—	—
1987–88	Dundee	—	—

Season	Club	App	Goals
1988–89		—	—
1989–90		7	—
1990–91		16	3
1991–92	Kilmarnock	30	1
1992–93		35	5

McSTAY, John

Born Larkhall 24.12.65   Ht 5 9   Wt 10 12
Defender. From Gartcosh U.

Season	Club	App	Goals
1982–83	Motherwell	—	—
1983–84		1	—
1984–85		6	1
1985–86		10	—
1986–87		4	—
1987–88	Raith R	39	6
1988–89		37	5
1989–90		38	3
1990–91		36	1
1991–92		34	2
1992–93		41	5

McSTAY, Paul

Born Hamilton 22.10.64.   Ht 5 10
Wt 10 07
Midfield. From Celtic BC. Scotland
Schools, Youth, Under-21, 67 full caps.

Season	Club	App	Goals
1981–82	Celtic	10	1
1982–83		36	6
1983–84		34	3
1984–85		32	4
1985–86		34	8
1986–87		43	3
1987–88		44	5
1988–89		33	5
1989–90		35	3
1990–91		30	2
1991–92		31	7
1992–93		43	4

McSTAY, Willie

Born Hamilton 26.11.61   Ht 5 11
Wt 11 2
Defender. From Celtic BC. Scotland
Schools, Youth.

Season	Club	App	Goals
1979–80	Celtic	—	—

Season	Club	App	Goals
1980–81		—	—
1981–82		—	—
1982–83		1	—
1983–84		19	1
1984–85		14	1
1985–86		18	—
1986–87		16	—
1986–87	Huddersfield T	1	—
1987–88		8	—
1987–88	Notts Co	9	—
1988–89		33	1
1989–90		3	—
1989–90	*Hartlepool U*	3	—
1989–90	*Partick T*	5	—
1990–91	Kilmarnock	20	—
1991–92		9	—
1992–93		1	—

McSWEGAN, Gary

Born Glasgow 24.9.70.   Ht 5 7   Wt 10 09
Forward. From Rangers Amateur BC.

Season	Club	App	Goals
1986–87	Rangers	—	—
1987–88		1	—
1988–89		1	—
1989–90		—	—
1990–91		3	—
1991–92		4	—
1992–93		9	4

McVICAR, Don

Born Perth 6.11.62.   Ht 5 9   Wt 11 06
Defender. From Blairgowrie Jun.

Season	Club	App	Goals
1981–82	St Johnstone	13	—
1982–83		26	—
1983–84		21	—
1984–85		26	1
1985–86	Tranmere R	7	—
1985–86	Montrose	12	—
1986–87	St Johnstone	23	2
1987–88		38	1
1988–89		28	3
1989–90		35	3
1990–91		23	1
1991–92		4	—
1991–92	Partick T	10	—
1992–93		38	—

McWALTER, Mark

Born Arbroath 20.6.68.   Ht 5 11
Wt 10 09
Forward. From Arbroath Lads Club.

1984–85	Arbroath	14	2
1985–86		37	14
1986–87		19	4
1987–88	St Mirren	4	—
1988–89		31	5
1989–90		22	—
1990–91		22	3
1991–92	Partick T	7	—
1992–93		12	—

MADDEN, Lawrie

Born London 28.9.55.   Ht 5 11   Wt 13 01
Defender. From Arsenal Amateur.

1974–75	Mansfield T	7	—
1975–76		3	—
From Manchester Univ			
1977–78	Charlton Ath	4	—
1978–79		38	3
1979–80		36	1
1980–81		28	1
1981–82		7	2
1981–82	Millwall	10	—
1982–83		37	2
1983–84	Sheffield W	38	1
1984–85		19	—
1985–86		25	—
1986–87		35	1
1987–88		38	—
1988–89		27	—
1989–90		25	—
1990–91		5	—
1990–91	*Leicester C*	3	—
1991–92	Wolverhampton W	43	1
1992–93		24	—

MADDICK, Kevin

Born Newcastle 18.9.74
Midfield. From Trainee.

1992–93	Darlington	1	—

MADDISON, Lee

Born Bristol 5.10.72.   Ht 5 11   Wt 11 00
Defender. From Trainee.

1991–92	Bristol R	10	—
1992–93		12	—

MADDISON, Neil

Born Darlington 2.10.69.   Ht 5 10
Wt 10 07
Midfield. From Trainee.

1987–88	Southampton	—	—
1988–89		5	2
1989–90		2	—
1990–91		4	—
1991–92		6	—
1992–93		37	4

MADDIX, Danny

Born Ashford 11.10.67.   Ht 5 10
Wt 11 07
Defender. From Apprentice.

1985–86	Tottenham H	—	—
1986–87		—	—
1986–87	*Southend U*	2	—
1987–88	QPR	9	—
1988–89		33	2
1989–90		32	3
1990–91		32	1
1991–92		19	—
1992–93		14	—

MAGEE, Kevin

Born Bangour 10.4.71.   Ht 5 10   Wt 11 04
Forward. From Armadale Th.

1991–92	Partick T	6	—
1992–93		5	—

MAGILTON, John

Born Belfast 6.5.69.   Ht 5 10   Wt 12 07
Midfield. From Apprentice. Northern
Ireland Under-23, 15 full caps. Football
League.

1986–87	Liverpool	—	—

Season	Club	App	Goals
1987–88		—	—
1988–89		—	—
1989–90		—	—
1990–91		—	—
1990–91	Oxford U	37	6
1991–92		44	12
1992–93		40	11

MAGUIRE, Gavin

Born Hammersmith 24.11.67. Ht 5 10
Wt 11 08
Midfield. From Apprentice. Wales B, 7 full
caps.

Season	Club	App	Goals
1985–86	QPR	—	—
1986–87		14	—
1987–88		18	—
1988–89		8	—
1988–89	Portsmouth	18	—
1989–90		29	—
1990–91		23	—
1991–92		—	—
1991–92	*Newcastle U*	3	—
1992–93	Portsmouth	21	—
1992–93	Millwall	9	—

MAIL, David

Born Bristol 12.9.62. Ht 5 11 Wt 11 12
Defender. From Apprentice.

Season	Club	App	Goals
1980–81	Aston Villa	—	—
1981–82	Blackburn R	—	—
1982–83		34	—
1983–84		11	1
1984–85		4	—
1985–86		18	1
1986–87		38	—
1987–88		36	—
1988–89		40	—
1989–90		25	2
1990–91	Hull C	36	1
1991–92		37	1
1992–93		39	—

MAIN, Alan

Born Elgin 5.12.67. Ht 5 11 Wt 12 03
Goalkeeper. From Elgin C. Scotland
Under-21.

Season	Club	App	Goals
1986–87	Dundee U	2	—
1987–88		8	—
1988–89		—	—
1988–89	*Cowdenbeath*	3	—
1988–89	*East Stirling*	2	—
1989–90	Dundee U	27	—
1990–91		31	—
1991–92		17	—
1992–93		43	—

MAKEL, Lee

Born Sunderland 11.1.73. Ht 5 10
Wt 9 10
Midfield. From Trainee.

Season	Club	App	Goals
1990–91	Newcastle U	3	—
1991–92		9	1
1992–93	Blackburn R	1	—

MAKIN, Chris

Born Manchester 8.5.73
Defender. From Trainee.

Season	Club	App	Goals
1991–92	Oldham Ath	—	—
1992–93		—	—
1992–93	*Wigan Ath*	15	2

MALKIN, Chris

Born Bebington 4.6.67. Ht 6 0 Wt 10 12
Forward. From Stork, Overpool.

Season	Club	App	Goals
1987–88	Tranmere R	5	—
1988–89		20	4
1989–90		40	18
1990–91		25	4
1991–92		35	3
1992–93		36	7

MALPAS, Maurice

Born Dunfermline 3.8.62. Ht 5 8
Wt 10 11
Defender. 'S' Form. Scotland Schools,
Youth, Under-21, 55 full caps.

Season	Club	Apps	Goals
1979–80	Dundee U	—	—
1980–81		—	—
1981–82		19	—
1982–83		34	1
1983–84		34	2
1984–85		35	2
1985–86		36	2
1986–87		36	—
1987–88		44	—
1988–89		36	1
1989–90		30	2
1990–91		36	1
1991–92		44	3
1992–93		37	—

MANNING, Paul

Born Lewisham 21.1.74. Ht 5 8 Wt 10 12
Midfield. From Trainee.

Season	Club	Apps	Goals
1991–92	Millwall	—	—
1992–93		1	—

MANUEL, Billy

Born Hackney 28.6.69. Ht 5 5 Wt 10 00
Defender. From Apprentice.

Season	Club	Apps	Goals
1987–88	Tottenham H	—	—
1988–89		—	—
1988–89	Gillingham	17	1
1989–90		32	4
1990–91		38	—
1991–92	Brentford	35	—
1992–93		41	1

MARDENBOROUGH, Steve

Born Birmingham 11.9.64. Ht 5 8
Wt 11 09
Forward. From Apprentice.

Season	Club	Apps	Goals
1982–83	Coventry C	—	—

Season	Club	Apps	Goals
1983–84	Wolverhampton W	9	1
1983–84	*Cambridge U*	6	—
1984–85	Swansea C	36	7
1985–86	Newport Co	39	7
1986–87		25	4
1986–87	Cardiff C	11	1
1987–88		21	—
1988–89	Hereford U	27	—
1989–90	Darlington	*17*	*1*
1990–91		35	1
1991–92		29	6
1992–93		42	11

MARDON, Paul

Born Bristol 14.9.69. Ht 6 0 Wt 11 10
Defender. From Trainee.

Season	Club	Apps	Goals
1987–88	Bristol C	8	—
1988–89		20	—
1989–90		7	—
1990–91		7	—
1990–91	*Doncaster R*	3	—
1991–92	Birmingham C	35	—
1992–93		21	1

MARGERISON, Lee

Born Bradford 10.9.73.
Midfield. From Trainee.

Season	Club	Apps	Goals
1992–93	Bradford C	3	—

MARGETSON, Martyn

Born West Glamorgan 8.9.71. Ht 6 0
Wt 13 10
Goalkeeper. From Trainee. Wales
Under-21.

Season	Club	Apps	Goals
1990–91	Manchester C	2	—
1991–92		3	—
1992–93		1	—

MARGINSON, Karl

Born Manchester 11.11.70. Ht 6 0
Wt 11 00
Midfield.

Season	Club	Apps	Goals
1992–93	Rotherham U	1	—

MARKER, Nick

Born Exeter 3.5.65.   Ht 6 1   Wt 13 00
Defender. From Apprentice.

Season	Club		
1981–82	Exeter C	14	1
1982–83		18	1
1983–84		31	—
1984–85		45	—
1985–86		40	—
1986–87		43	1
1987–88		11	—
1987–88	Plymouth Arg	26	1
1988–89		43	6
1989–90		43	1
1990–91		39	2
1991–92		44	1
1992–93		7	2
1992–93	Blackburn R	15	—

MARPLES, Chris

Born Chesterfield 3.8.64.   Ht 6 0
Wt 13 03
Goalkeeper. From Sutton T and Goole.

Season	Club		
1984–85	Chesterfield	38	—
1985–86		32	—
1986–87		14	—
1986–87	Stockport Co	13	—
1987–88		44	—
1988–89	York C	45	—
1989–90		46	—
1990–91		29	—
1991–92		16	—
1991–92	*Scunthorpe U*	1	—
1992–93	York C	2	—
1992–93	Chesterfield	25	—

MARRIOTT, Andrew

Born Nottingham 11.10.70.   Ht 6 0
Wt 12 07
Goalkeeper. From Trainee. FA Schools,
England Youth, Under-21.

Season	Club		
1988–89	Arsenal	—	—
1989–90	Nottingham F	—	—
1989–90	*WBA*	3	—
1989–90	*Blackburn R*	2	—
1989–90	*Colchester U*	10	—

Season	Club		
1990–91	Nottingham F	—	—
1991–92		6	—
1991–92	*Burnley*	15	—
1992–93	Nottingham F	5	—

MARSDEN, Chris

Born Sheffield 3.1.69.   Ht 5 11   Wt 10 12
Midfield. From Trainee.

Season	Club		
1986–87	Sheffield U	—	—
1987–88		16	1
1988–89	Huddersfield T	14	1
1989–90		32	2
1990–91		43	5
1991–92		23	1
1992–93		7	—

MARSH, Chris

Born Dudley 14.1.70.   Ht 5 10   Wt 12 11
Midfield. From Trainee.

Season	Club		
1987–88	Walsall	3	—
1988–89		13	—
1989–90		9	—
1990–91		23	2
1991–92		37	1
1992–93		33	3

MARSH, Mike

Born Liverpool 21.7.69.   Ht 5 8   Wt 11 00
Forward. From Kirkby T.

Season	Club		
1987–88	Liverpool	—	—
1988–89		1	—
1989–90		2	—
1990–91		2	—
1991–92		34	—
1992–93		28	1

MARSHALL, Dwight

Born Jamaica 3.10.65.   Ht 5 7   Wt 10 10
Forward. From Grays Ath.

Season	Club		
1991–92	Plymouth Arg	44	14
1992–93		24	1
1992–93	*Middlesbrough*	3	—

MARSHALL, Gordon

Born Edinburgh 19.4.64.   Ht 6 2
Wt 12 00
Goalkeeper. From Schools. Scotland 1 full
cap.

Season	Club	Apps	Goals
1982–83	East Stirling	15	—
1982–83	East Fife	10	—
1983–84		34	—
1984–85		39	—
1985–86		39	—
1986–87		36	—
1986–87	Falkirk	10	—
1987–88		44	—
1988–89		39	—
1989–90		39	—
1990–91			—
1986–87		36	—
1986–87	Falkirk	10	—
1987–88		44	—
1988–89		39	—
1989–90		39	—
1990–91		39	—
1991–92	Celtic	25	—
1992–93		11	—

MARSHALL, Ian

Born Oxford 20.3.66.   Ht 6 1   Wt 12 12
Forward. From Apprentice.

Season	Club	Apps	Goals
1983–84	Everton	—	—
1984–85		—	—
1985–86		9	—
1986–87		2	1
1987–88		4	—
1987–88	Oldham Ath	10	—
1988–89		41	4
1989–90		25	3
1990–91		26	17
1991–92		41	10
1992–93		27	2

MARSHALL, John

Born Surrey 18.8.64.   Ht 5 10   Wt 12 01
Defender. From Apprentice.

Season	Club	Apps	Goals
1982–83	Fulham	—	—
1983–84		25	—

Season	Club	Apps	Goals
1984–85		32	1
1985–86		42	3
1986–87		29	4
1987–88		25	2
1988–89		41	7
1989–90		36	4
1990–91		35	2
1991–92		41	—
1992–93		41	2

MARSHALL, Scott

Born Edinburgh 1.5.73   Ht 6 1   Wt 12 05
Defender. From Trainee.

Season	Club	Apps	Goals
1992–93	Arsenal	2	—

MARTIN, Alvin

Born Bootle 29.7.58.   Ht 6 1   Wt 13 07
Defender. From Apprentice. England
Youth, B, 17 full caps.

Season	Club	Apps	Goals
1976–77	West Ham U	—	—
1977–78		7	1
1978–79		22	1
1979–80		40	2
1980–81		41	1
1981–82		28	4
1982–83		38	3
1983–84		29	3
1984–85		40	1
1985–86		40	4
1986–87		16	2
1987–88		15	—
1988–89		27	1
1989–90		31	—
1990–91		20	1
1991–92		7	—
1992–93		23	1

MARTIN, Brian

Born Bellshill 24.2.63.   Ht 6 0   Wt 13 00
Midfield. From Shotts Bon Accord.

Season	Club	Apps	Goals
1985–86	Falkirk	25	1
1986–87		34	1
1986–87	Hamilton A	7	—
1987–88		23	—

Season	Club	League Appearances/Goals
1987–88	St Mirren	12 1
1988–89		34 2
1989–90		35 2
1990–91		31 2
1991–92		17 2
1991–92	Motherwell	25 —
1992–93		44 3

MARTIN, David

Born East Ham 25.4.63.   Ht 6 1
Wt 13 01
Midfield. From Apprentice. England
Youth.

Season	Club	League Appearances/Goals
1979–80	Millwall	3 —
1980–81		33 1
1981–82		38 1
1982–83		33 1
1983–84		31 3
1984–85		2 —
1984–85	Wimbledon	20 2
1985–86		15 1
1986–87	Southend U	32 2
1987–88		41 —
1988–89		37 1
1989–90		39 3
1990–91		41 11
1991–92		5 1
1992–93		26 1

MARTIN, Dean

Born Halifax 9.9.67.   Ht 5 11   Wt 11 10
Midfield. From Local.

Season	Club	League Appearances/Goals
1984–85	Halifax T	— —
1985–86		— —
1986–87		16 1
1987–88		40 3
1988–89		32 2
1989–90		37 —
1990–91		28 1
1991–92	Scunthorpe U	37 2
1992–93		38 3

MARTIN, Dean

Born London 31.8.72.   Ht 5 8   Wt 10 06
Forward. From Fisher Ath.

Season	Club	League Appearances/Goals
1991–92	West Ham U	2 —

Season	Club	League Appearances/Goals
1992–93		— —
1992–93	Colchester U	8 2

MARTIN, Eliot

Born Plumstead 27.9.72.   Ht 5 6
Wt 10 00
Defender. From Trainee.

Season	Club	League Appearances/Goals
1990–91	Gillingham	— —
1991–92		22 —
1992–93		22 1

MARTIN, John

Born Edinburgh 27.10.58.   Ht 6 1
Wt 12 00
Goalkeeper. From Tranent J.

Season	Club	League Appearances/Goals
1980–81	Airdrieonians	22 —
1981–82		27 —
1982–83		39 1
1983–84		39 —
1984–85		36 —
1985–86		36 —
1986–87		44 —
1987–88		44 —
1988–89		36 —
1989–90		39 —
1990–91		38 —
1991–92		41 —
1992–93		43 —

MARTIN, Lee

Born Huddersfield 9.9.68.   Ht 6 0
Wt 13 00
Goalkeeper. From Trainee. England
Schools.

Season	Club	League Appearances/Goals
1987–88	Huddersfield T	18 —
1988–89		— —
1989–90		25 —
1990–91		4 —
1991–92		7 —
1992–93	Blackpool	24 —

MARTIN, Lee

Born Hyde 5.2.68.   Ht 5 11   Wt 11 05
Defender. England Under-21.

Season	Club	League Appearances/Goals
1986–87	Manchester U	— —

Season	Club		App	Goals
1987–88			1	—
1988–89			24	1
1989–90			32	—
1990–91			14	—
1991–92			1	—
1992–93			—	—

MARTINDALE, Dave

Born Liverpool 9.4.64. Ht 5 11 Wt 11 10
Midfield. From Liverpool Apprentice,
Southport, Caernarfon.

Season	Club	App	Goals
1987–88	Tranmere R	34	4
1988–89		32	1
1989–90		19	2
1990–91		11	—
1991–92		31	—
1992–93		26	2

MARTYN, Nigel

Born St Austell 11.8.66. Ht 6 2 Wt 14 00
Goalkeeper. From St Blazey. England B,
Under-21, 3 full caps.

Season	Club	App	Goals
1987–88	Bristol R	39	—
1988–89		46	—
1989–90		16	—
1989–90	Crystal Palace	25	—
1990–91		38	—
1991–92		38	—
1992–93		42	—

MARWOOD, Brian

Born Seaham Harbour 5.2.60. Ht 5 7
Wt 11 06
Midfield. From Apprentice. England 1 full
cap.

Season	Club	App	Goals
1977–78	Hull C	—	—
1978–79		—	—
1979–80		6	—
1980–81		31	4
1981–82		42	12
1982–83		40	19
1983–84		39	16
1984–85	Sheffield W	41	7
1985–86		37	13

Season	Club	App	Goals
1986–87		32	5
1987–88		18	2
1987–88	Arsenal	4	1
1988–89		31	9
1989–90		17	6
1990–91		—	—
1990–91	Sheffield U	17	2
1991–92		5	1
1991–92	*Middlesbrough*	3	—
1992–93	Sheffield U	—	—
1992–93	Swindon T	11	1

MASEFIELD, Paul

Born Birmingham 21.10.70. Ht 6 1
Wt 12 12
Defender. From Trainee.

Season	Club	App	Goals
1989–90	Birmingham C	—	—
1990–91		—	—
1991–92	Preston NE	—	—
1991–92	Exeter C	1	—
1992–93	Stockport Co	7	—
1992–93	Doncaster R	9	—

MASKELL, Craig

Born Aldershot 10.4.68. Ht 5 10
Wt 11 04
Forward. From Apprentice. Football
League.

Season	Club	App	Goals
1985–86	Southampton	2	1
1986–87		4	—
1986–87	*Swindon T*	—	—
1987–88	Southampton	—	—
1988–89	Huddersfield T	46	28
1989–90		41	15
1990–91	Reading	38	10
1991–92		34	16
1992–93	Swindon T	33	19

MASKREY, Steve

Born Edinburgh 16.8.62. Ht 5 6
Wt 10 00
Forward. From Strathbrock Jun.

Season	Club	App	Goals
1984–85	East Stirling	37	12
1985–86		21	12

Season	Club		League Appearances	Goals
1985–86	Queen of the S............		12	2
1986–87	....		31	2
1987–88	St Johnstone		33	5
1988–89	....		31	12
1989–90	....		29	11
1990–91	....		34	7
1991–92	....		24	2
1992–93	....		19	2

MASON, Paul

Born Liverpool 3.9.63. Ht 5 8 Wt 11 09
Midfield. From Groningen.

Season	Club	League Appearances	Goals
1988–89	Aberdeen......................	28	4
1989–90	....	34	9
1990–91	....	26	3
1991–92	....	31	7
1992–93	....	39	4

MASSEY, Stuart

Born Crawley 17.11.64 Ht 5 10 Wt 10 10
Midfield. From Sutton U.

Season	Club	League Appearances	Goals
1992–93	Crystal Palace	1	—

MASTERS, Neil

Born Lisburn 25.5.72 Ht 6 1 Wt 13 03
Defender. From Trainee.

Season	Club	League Appearances	Goals
1992–93	Bournemouth	20	—

MATHERS, Paul

Born Aberdeen 17.1.70. Ht 5 11
Wt 10 07
Goalkeeper. From Sunnybank A.

Season	Club	League Appearances	Goals
1989–90	Dundee......................	8	—
1990–91	....	6	—
1991–92	....	31	—
1992–93	....	36	—

MATHIE, Alex

Born Bathgate 20.12.68 Ht 5 10
Wt 10 07
Forward. From Celtic BC.

Season	Club	League Appearances	Goals
1987–88	Celtic............................	—	—

Season	Club	League Appearances	Goals
1988–89	....	1	—
1989–90	....	6	—
1990–91	....	4	—
1991–92	Morton	42	18
1992–93	....	32	13
1992–93	*Port Vale*....................	3	—

MATTHEW, Damian

Born Islington, London 23.9.70. Ht 5 11
Wt 10 10
Midfield. From Trainee. England
Under-21.

Season	Club	League Appearances	Goals
1989–90	Chelsea......................	2	—
1990–91	....	8	—
1991–92	....	7	—
1992–93	....	4	—
1992–93	*Luton T*......................	5	—

MATTHEWS, Mike

Born Hull 25.9.60. Ht 5 9 Wt 11 03
Midfield. From Apprentice.

Season	Club	League Appearances	Goals
1978–79	Wolverhampton W	—	—
1979–80	....	—	—
1980–81	....	1	—
1981–82	....	32	2
1982–83	....	40	5
1983–84	....	3	—
1983–84	Scunthorpe U	25	1
1984–85	....	22	3
1985–86	....	11	1
1986–87	Halifax T	39	4
1987–88	....	45	3
1988–89	....	15	1
1988–89	Scarborough..............	7	1
1988–89	Stockport Co	19	1
1989–90	....	16	2
1989–90	Scarborough	21	3
1990–91	....	45	1
1991–92	Hull C.....................	16	2
1992–93	Halifax T	23	2

MATTHEWS, Neil

Born Grimsby 19.9.66. Ht 6 0 Wt 12 12
Forward.

Season	Club	League Appearances	Goals
1984–85	Grimsby T	4	1

Season	Club	Apps	Goals
1985–86	Scunthorpe U	4	—
1985–86	*Scunthorpe U*	1	—
1986–87	Grimsby T	3	—
1986–87	*Halifax T*	9	2
1986–87	*Bolton W*	1	—
1987–88	Halifax T	32	10
1988–89		34	7
1989–90		39	12
1990–91	Stockport Co	29	14
1991–92		9	1
1991–92	*Halifax T*	3	—
1992–93	Stockport Co	5	—
1992–93	Lincoln C	24	11

MATTHEWS, Neil

Born Manchester 3.12.67. Ht 6 0
Wt 11 07
Defender. From Apprentice.

Season	Club	Apps	Goals
1985–86	Blackpool	1	—
1986–87		22	—
1987–88		27	—
1988–89		14	1
1989–90		12	—
1990–91	Cardiff C	37	1
1991–92		15	—
1992–93		14	1

MATTHEWS, Rob

Born Slough 14.10.70. Ht 6 0 Wt 12 05
Forward. From Loughborough Univ.

Season	Club	Apps	Goals
1991–92	Notts Co	5	3
1992–93		8	2

MATTHEWSON, Trevor

Born Sheffield 12.2.63. Ht 6 1 Wt 12 05
Defender. From Apprentice.

Season	Club	Apps	Goals
1980–81	Sheffield W	1	—
1981–82		1	—
1982–83		1	—
1983–84		—	—
1983–84	Newport Co	32	—
1984–85		43	—
1985–86	Stockport Co	35	—
1986–87		45	—

Season	Club	Apps	Goals
1987–88	Lincoln C	40	6
1988–89		43	2
1989–90	Birmingham C	46	1
1990–91		46	3
1991–92		36	6
1992–93		40	2

MAUCHLEN, Ally

Born Kilwinning 29.6.60. Ht 5 8
Wt 13 07
Midfield. From Irvine Meadow.

Season	Club	Apps	Goals
1978–79	Kilmarnock	20	—
1979–80		30	2
1980–81		31	3
1981–82		37	4
1982–83		2	1
1982–83	Motherwell	25	3
1983–84		20	—
1984–85		30	1
1985–86		1	—
1985–86	Leicester C	37	2
1986–87		30	1
1987–88		36	2
1988–89		38	3
1989–90		38	1
1990–91		40	1
1991–92		20	1
1991–92	*Leeds U*	—	—
1992–93	Hearts	18	—

MAUGE, Ron

Born Islington 10.3.69 Ht 5 10 Wt 10 06
Defender. From Trainee.

Season	Club	Apps	Goals
1987–88	Charlton Ath	—	—
1988–89	Fulham	13	—
1989–90		37	2
1990–91	Bury	29	6
1991–92		22	—
1991–92	*Manchester C*	—	—
1992–93	Bury	13	1

MAXWELL, Ally

Born Hamilton 16.2.65. Ht 6 1 Wt 12 07
Goalkeeper. From Fir Park BC.

Season	Club	Apps	Goals
1981–82	Motherwell	—	—

Season	Club	App	Goals
1982–83	....	—	—
1983–84	....	4	—
1984–85	....	15	—
1985–86	....	4	—
1986–87	....	21	—
1987–88	....	1	—
1987–88	Clydebank	1	—
1988–89	Motherwell............	17	—
1989–90	....	36	—
1990–91	....	36	—
1991–92	....	—	—
1991–92	Liverpool	—	—
1991–92	Bolton W................	3	—
1992–93	Rangers................	10	—

MAXWELL, Jason

Born 1.9.72 Ht 6 0 Wt 12 10
Forward.

Season	Club	App	Goals
1992–93	Scunthorpe U	2	—

MAY, Andy

Born Bury 26.2.64. Ht 5 8 Wt 11 10
Midfield. From Apprentice. England
Under-21.

Season	Club	App	Goals
1980–81	Manchester C	1	—
1981–82	....	6	—
1982–83	....	8	—
1983–84	....	42	5
1984–85	....	39	3
1985–86	....	37	—
1986–87	....	17	—
1987–88	Huddersfield T............	28	3
1987–88	Bolton W................	10	2
1988–89	Huddersfield T............	45	2
1989–90	....	41	—
1990–91	Bristol C	45	3
1991–92	....	45	1
1992–93	Millwall................	35	1

MAY, David

Born Oldham 24.6.70. Ht 6 0 Wt 11 07
Defender. From Trainee.

Season	Club	App	Goals
1988–89	Blackburn R	1	—
1989–90	....	17	—

Season	Club	App	Goals
1990–91	....	19	1
1991–92	....	12	—
1992–93	....	34	1

MAY, Edward

Born Edinburgh 30.8.67. Ht 5 7
Wt 10 03
Forward. From Hutchison Vale BC.
Scotland Youth, Under-21.

Season	Club	App	Goals
1983–84	Dundee U	—	—
1984–85	....	—	—
1984–85	Hibernian	—	—
1985–86	....	19	1
1986–87	....	30	5
1987–88	....	35	2
1988–89	....	25	2
1989–90	Brentford	30	8
1990–91	....	17	2
1990–91	Falkirk	13	6
1991–92	....	36	9
1992–93	....	42	6

MAY, Leroy

Born Wolverhampton 12.8.69. Ht 6 1
Wt 11 07
Forward. From Tividale.

Season	Club	App	Goals
1991–92	Walsall................	4	—
From Tividale			
1992–93	Hereford U................	14	2

MEAKER, Michael

Born Greenford 18.8.71. Ht 5 11
Wt 11 05
Midfield. From Trainee.

Season	Club	App	Goals
1989–90	QPR................	—	—
1990–91	....	8	—
1991–92	....	1	—
1991–92	Plymouth Arg................	4	—
1992–93	QPR................	3	—

MEAN, Scott

Born Crawley 13.12.73 Ht 5 11 Wt 11 11
Midfield. From Trainee.

Season	Club	App	Goals
1992–93	Bournemouth............	15	1

MEARA, Jim

Born London 7.10.72 Ht 5 7 Wt 10 06
Midfield. From Trainee.

Season	Club	Apps	Goals
1991–92	Watford	—	—
1992–93		2	—

MEASHAM, Ian

Born Barnsley 14.12.64. Ht 5 11
Wt 11 08
Defender. From Apprentice.

Season	Club	Apps	Goals
1982–83	Huddersfield T	—	—
1983–84		—	—
1984–85		17	—
1985–86		—	—
1985–86	*Lincoln C*	6	—
1985–86	*Rochdale*	12	—
1986–87	Cambridge U	46	—
1987–88		—	—
1988–89		—	—
1988–89	Burnley	30	1
1989–90		35	—
1990–91		45	—
1991–92		27	1
1992–93		39	—

MEGSON, Gary

Born Manchester 2.5.59. Ht 5 10
Wt 12 00
Midfield. From Apprentice.

Season	Club	Apps	Goals
1977–78	Plymouth Arg	24	2
1978–79		42	8
1979–80		12	—
1979–80	Everton	12	1
1980–81		10	1
1981–82	Sheffield W	40	5
1982–83		41	4
1983–84		42	4
1984–85	Nottingham F	—	—
1984–85	Newcastle U	20	1
1985–86		4	—
1985–86	Sheffield W	20	3
1986–87		35	6
1987–88		37	2
1988–89		18	1
1988–89	Manchester C	22	1

Season	Club	Apps	Goals
1989–90		19	—
1990–91		19	1
1991–92		22	—
1992–93	Norwich C	23	1

MEGSON, Kevin

Born Halifax 1.7.71 Ht 5 11 Wt 11 00
Forward. From Trainee.

Season	Club	Apps	Goals
1989–90	Bradford C	23	—
1990–91		4	—
1990–91	Halifax T	5	—
1991–92		10	—
1992–93		26	1

MEHEW, David

Born Camberley 29.10.67. Ht 5 11
Wt 12 06
Forward.

Season	Club	Apps	Goals
1984–85	Leeds U	—	—
1985–86	Bristol R	4	—
1986–87		21	10
1987–88		18	8
1988–89		31	7
1989–90		46	18
1990–91		41	8
1991–92		37	9
1992–93		24	3

MELLON, Michael

Born Paisley 18.3.72. Ht 5 8 Wt 11 03
Midfield. From Trainee.

Season	Club	Apps	Goals
1989–90	Bristol C	9	—
1990–91		—	—
1991–92		16	—
1992–93		10	1
1992–93	WBA	17	3

MELVILLE, Andy

Born Swansea 29.11.68. Ht 6 0 Wt 12 00
Defender. From school. Wales B, Under-
21, 15 full caps.

Season	Club	Apps	Goals
1985–86	Swansea C	5	—

1986–87	....	42	3
1987–88	....	37	4
1988–89	....	45	10
1989–90	....	46	5
1990–91	Oxford U	46	3
1991–92	....	45	4
1992–93	....	44	6

MENDONCA, Clive

Born Tullington 9.9.68.   Ht 5 10
Wt 10 07
Forward. From Apprentice.

1986–87	Sheffield U	2	—
1987–88	....	11	4
1987–88	*Doncaster R*	2	—
1987–88	Rotherham U	8	2
1988–89	....	10	1
1989–90	....	32	14
1990–91	....	34	10
1991–92	Sheffield U	10	1
1991–92	*Grimsby T*	10	3
1992–93	Grimsby T	42	10

MERCER, William

Born Liverpool 22.5.69.   Ht 6 1   Wt 13 05
Goalkeeper. From Trainee.

1987–88	Liverpool	—	—
1988–89	....	—	—
1988–89	Rotherham U	—	—
1989–90	....	2	—
1990–91	....	13	—
1991–92	....	35	—
1992–93	....	36	—

MERSON, Paul

Born London 20.3.68.   Ht 6 0   Wt 13 02
Forward. From Apprentice. England
Youth, Under-21 B, 12 full caps.

1985–86	Arsenal.......................	—	—
1986–87	....	7	3
1986–87	*Brentford*	7	—
1987–88	Arsenal.......................	15	5
1988–89	....	37	10
1989–90	....	29	7

1990–91	....	37	13
1991–92	....	42	12
1992–93	....	33	6

METHVEN, Colin

Born India 10.12.55.   Ht 6 2   Wt 12 07
Defender. From Leven Royals.

1974–75	East Fife	1	—
1975–76	....	26	1
1976–77	....	39	—
1977–78	....	39	2
1978–79	....	39	11
1979–80	Wigan Ath	35	2
1980–81	....	46	2
1981–82	....	46	9
1982–83	....	44	1
1983–84	....	39	—
1984–85	....	43	—
1985–86	....	43	7
1986–87	Blackpool....................	46	5
1987–88	....	40	2
1988–89	....	42	1
1989–90	....	45	3
1990–91	....	—	—
1990–91	*Carlisle U*	12	—
1990–91	Walsall	32	1
1991–92	....	42	2
1992–93	....	23	—

METTIOUI, Ahmed

Born Tangier 3.11.65
Forward. From Fath Union SC.

1992–93	Crewe Alex	3	—

MEYER, Adrian

Born Bristol 22.9.70.   Ht 6 0   Wt 14 00
Defender. From Trainee.

1989–90	Scarborough................	18	2
1990–91	....	17	1
1991–92	....	30	5
1992–93	....	—	—

MICKLEWHITE, Gary

Born Southwark 21.3.61. Ht 5 7
Wt 10 04
Forward. From Apprentice.

Season	Club	App	Goals
1977–78	Manchester U	—	—
1978–79		—	—
1979–80	QPR	—	—
1980–81		1	—
1981–82		26	2
1982–83		34	6
1983–84		30	2
1984–85		15	1
1984–85	Derby Co	19	4
1985–86		46	11
1986–87		42	6
1987–88		16	1
1988–89		26	3
1989–90		18	2
1990–91		35	2
1991–92		32	2
1992–93		6	—

MIDDLETON, Craig

Born Nuneaton 10.9.70. Ht 5 9
Wt 11 00
Forward. From Trainee.

Season	Club	App	Goals
1989–90	Coventry C	1	—
1990–91		—	—
1991–92		1	—
1992–93		1	—

MIKE, Adie

Born Manchester 16.11.73. Ht 6 0
Wt 11 06
Forward. From Trainee. England Youth.

Season	Club	App	Goals
1991–92	Manchester C	2	1
1992–93		3	—
1992–93	*Bury*	7	1

MIKHAILICHENKO, Alexei

Born Kiev 30.3.63. Ht 6 2 Wt 13 03
Midfield. From Sampdoria. USSR, CIS
full caps.

Season	Club	App	Goals
1991–92	Rangers	27	10

Season	Club	App	Goals
1992–93		29	5

MIKLOSKO, Ludek

Born Ostrava 9.12.61. Ht 6 5 Wt 14 00
Goalkeeper. From Banik Ostrava.
Czechoslovakia full caps.

Season	Club	App	Goals
1989–90	West Ham U	18	—
1990–91		46	—
1991–92		36	—
1992–93		46	—

MILLAR, John

Born Lanark 8.12.66. Ht 5 10 Wt 10 00
Midfield.

Season	Club	App	Goals
1984–85	Chelsea	—	—
1985–86		7	—
1986–87		4	—
1986–87	*Hamilton A*	10	—
1986–87	*Northampton T*	1	—
1987–88	Blackburn R	15	—
1988–89		38	—
1989–90		39	1
1990–91		34	—
1991–92	Hearts	41	7
1992–93		24	—

MILLAR, Paul

Born Belfast 16.11.66. Ht 6 2 Wt 12 07
Forward. From Portadown. Northern
Ireland Under-23.

Season	Club	App	Goals
1988–89	Port Vale	—	—
1989–90		23	4
1990–91		17	1
1990–91	*Hereford U*	5	2
1991–92	Cardiff C	15	—
1992–93		33	3

MILLAR, Robert

Born Manchester 3.11.72. Ht 6 0
Wt 11 10
Defender. From Trainee.

Season	Club	App	Goals
1991–92	Oldham Ath	—	—

1992–93	Hull C	25	—

MILLEN, Keith

Born Croydon 26.9.66.   Ht 6 2   Wt 12 04
Defender. From Juniors.

1984–85	Brentford	17	—
1985–86		32	2
1986–87		39	2
1987–88		40	3
1988–89		36	3
1989–90		32	—
1990–91		32	2
1991–92		34	1
1992–93		43	4

MILLER, Allan

Born Epping 29.3.70.   Ht 6 3   Wt 14 07
Goalkeeper. From Trainee. FA Schools,
England Under-21.

1987–88	Arsenal	—	—
1988–89		—	—
1988–89	*Plymouth Arg*	13	—
1989–90	Arsenal	—	—
1990–91		—	—
1991–92		—	—
1991–92	*WBA*	3	—
1991–92	*Birmingham C*	15	—
1992–93	Arsenal	4	—

MILLER, David

Born Burnley 8.1.64.   Ht 5 11   Wt 11 12
Midfield. From Apprentice.

1981–82	Burnley	—	—
1982–83		1	—
1982–83	*Crewe Alex*	3	—
1983–84	Burnley	17	2
1984–85		14	1
1985–86	Tranmere R	29	1
1986–87	Preston NE	15	—
1987–88		28	2
1988–89		12	—
1988–89	*Burnley*	4	—
1989–90	Preston NE	3	—
1989–90	Carlisle U	42	3

1990–91		41	4
1991–92		26	—
1991–92	Stockport Co	3	—
1992–93		37	1

MILLER, Graeme

Born Glasgow 21.2.73.   Ht 5 7   Wt 9 5
Midfield. From Tynecastle BC.

1992–93	Hibernian	1	—

MILLER, Joe

Born Glasgow 8.12.67.   Ht 5 8   Wt 9 12
Forward. 'S' Form. Scotland Schools,
Youth, Under-21.

1984–85	Aberdeen	1	—
1985–86		18	3
1986–87		27	6
1987–88		14	4
1987–88	Celtic	27	3
1988–89		22	8
1989–90		24	5
1990–91		30	8
1991–92		26	2
1992–93		23	2

MILLER, Kevin

Born Falmouth 15.3.69.   Ht 6 1   Wt 12 10
Goalkeeper. From Newquay.

1988–89	Exeter C	3	—
1989–90		28	—
1990–91		46	—
1991–92		42	—
1992–93		44	—

MILLER, Paul

Born Bisley 31.1.68.   Ht 6 0   Wt 11 00
Forward. From Trainee.

1987–88	Wimbledon	5	—
1987–88	*Newport Co*	6	2
1988–89	Wimbledon	18	5
1989–90		15	2
1989–90	*Bristol C*	3	—

Season	Club	League Appearances/Goals	
1990–91	Wimbledon	1	—
1991–92		22	2
1992–93		19	1

MILLER, William

Born Edinburgh 1.11.69. Ht 5 8
Wt 10 06
Defender. From Edina Hibs BC. Scotland
Under-21.

1989–90	Hibernian	11	—
1990–91		25	1
1991–92		30	—
1992–93		34	—

MILLIGAN, Mike

Born Manchester 20.2.67. Ht 5 8
Wt 11 00
Midfield. Eire Under-21 B, 1 full cap.

1984–85	Oldham Ath	—	—
1985–86		5	1
1986–87		38	2
1987–88		39	1
1988–89		39	6
1989–90		41	7
1990–91	Everton	17	1
1991–92	Oldham Ath	36	3
1992–93		42	3

MILLS, Gary

Born Northampton 11.11.61. Ht 5 9
Wt 11 10
Forward. From Apprentice. England
Schools, Youth, Under-21.

1978–79	Nottingham F	4	1
1979–80		13	1
1980–81		27	5
1981–82		14	1
From Seattle S			
1982–83	Derby Co	18	1
From Seattle S			
1983–84	Nottingham F	7	—
1984–85		26	4
1985–86		14	—
1986–87		32	—

1987–88	Notts Co	46	5
1988–89		29	3
1988–89	Leicester C	13	—
1989–90		29	4
1990–91		45	5
1991–92		46	6
1992–93		43	

MILLS, Simon

Born Sheffield 16.8.64. Ht 5 8 Wt 11 04
Defender. From Apprentice. England
Youth.

1982–83	Sheffield W	1	—
1983–84		2	—
1984–85		2	—
1985–86	York C	36	2
1986–87		45	1
1987–88		18	2
1987–88	Port Vale	19	5
1988–89		43	—
1989–90		45	1
1990–91		41	—
1991–92		33	2
1992–93		3	—

MILNE, Callum

Born Edinburgh 27.8.65. Ht 5 8
Wt 10 07
Defender. From Salvesen BC.

1983–84	Hibernian	—	—
1984–85		1	—
1985–86		7	—
1986–87		2	—
1987–88		3	—
1988–89		19	—
1989–90		3	—
1990–91		21	—
1991–92		8	—
1992–93		15	—

MILNER, Andy

Born Kendal 10.2.67. Ht 5 11 Wt 11 07
Forward. From Netherfield.

1988–89	Manchester C	—	—

1989–90	....	—	—
1989–90	Rochdale......................	16	4
1990–91	....	35	5
1991–92	....	33	10
1992–93	....	18	4

MILTON, Simon

Born London 23.8.63.   Ht 5 10   Wt 11 05
Midfield. From Bury St Edmunds.

1987–88	Ipswich T......................	8	1
1987–88	*Exeter C*......................	2	3
1987–88	*Torquay U*....................	4	1
1988–89	Ipswich T......................	35	10
1989–90	....	41	10
1990–91	....	31	6
1991–92	....	34	7
1992–93	....	12	2

MIMMS, Bobby

Born York 12.10.63.   Ht 6 2   Wt 12 13
Goalkeeper. From Halifax T Apprentice.
England Under-21.

1981–82	Rotherham U	2	—
1982–83	....	13	—
1983–84	....	22	—
1984–85	....	46	—
1985–86	Everton	10	—
1985–86	*Notts Co*......................	2	—
1986–87	Everton	11	—
1986–87	*Sunderland*....................	4	—
1986–87	*Blackburn R*	6	—
1987–88	Everton	8	—
1987–88	*Manchester C*..............	3	—
1987–88	Tottenham H	13	—
1988–89	....	20	—
1989–90	....	4	—
1989–90	*Aberdeen*	6	—
1990–91	Tottenham H..............	—	—
1990–91	Blackburn R	22	—
1991–92	....	45	—
1992–93	....	42	—

MINETT, Jason

Born Peterborough 12.8.71.   Ht 5 10
Wt 10 02
Midfield. From Trainee.

1989–90	Norwich C..................	—	—
1990–91	....	2	—
1991–92	....	—	—
1992–93	....	1	—
1992–93	*Exeter C*......................	12	—

MINTO, Scott

Born Cheshire 6.8.71.   Ht 5 10   Wt 10 00
Defender. From Trainee. England Youth,
Under-21.

1988–89	Charlton Ath	3	—
1989–90	....	23	2
1990–91	....	43	1
1991–92	....	33	1
1992–93	....	36	1

MINTON, Jeffrey

Born Hackney 28.12.73.   Ht 5 5
Wt 11 07
Forward. From Trainee.

| 1991–92 | Tottenham H.............. | 2 | 1 |
| 1992–93 | .... | — | — |

MITCHELL, Alistair

Born Kirkcaldy 3.12.68   Ht 5 7   Wt 11 0
Forward. From Ballingry Rovers.

1988–89	East Fife	18	4
1989–90	....	35	12
1990–91	....	34	7
1991–92	Kilmarnock................	42	10
1992–93	....	32	6

MITCHELL, Brian

Born Stonehaven 16.7.63.   Ht 6 1
Wt 13 01
Defender. From King St. Scotland
Schools.

| 1981–82 | Aberdeen...................... | 1 | — |

Season	Club	Apps	Goals
1982–83		1	—
1983–84		9	—
1984–85		14	1
1985–86		23	—
1986–87		17	—
1986–87	Bradford C	16	—
1987–88		42	6
1988–89		45	1
1989–90		35	2
1990–91		20	—
1991–92		20	—
1992–93	Bristol C	16	—

MITCHELL, David

Born Glasgow 13.6.62. Ht 6 1 Wt 12 07
Forward. From Australia full caps.

Season	Club	Apps	Goals
1983–84	Rangers	12	2
1984–85		14	4
From Feyenoord			
1988–89	Chelsea	6	—
1989–90		—	—
1990–91		1	—
1990–91	*Newcastle U*	2	1
1991–92	Swindon T	27	5
1992–93		41	11

MITCHELL, Graham

Born Glasgow 2.11.62. Ht 5 10 Wt 11 08
Defender. From Auchengill BC.

Season	Club	Apps	Goals
1980–81	Hamilton A	4	—
1981–82		37	—
1982–83		32	1
1983–84		21	1
1984–85		30	—
1985–86		32	6
1986–87		23	1
1986–87	Hibernian	17	1
1987–88		41	1
1988–89		20	—
1989–90		31	—
1990–91		28	—
1991–92		27	—
1992–93		41	—

MITCHELL, Graham

Born Shipley 16.2.68. Ht 6 0 Wt 11 05
Defender. From Apprentice.

Season	Club	Apps	Goals
1986–87	Huddersfield T	17	—
1987–88		29	1
1988–89		34	—
1989–90		37	1
1990–91		46	—
1991–92		43	—
1992–93		4	—

MITCHELL, Neil

Born Lytham 7.11.74.
Midfield. From Trainee.

Season	Club	Apps	Goals
1991–92	Blackpool	1	—
1992–93		12	1

MITCHELL, Paul

Born Bournemouth 20.10.71. Ht 5 10
Wt 12 00
Defender. From Trainee.

Season	Club	Apps	Goals
1990–91	Bournemouth	2	—
1991–92		5	—
1992–93		5	—

MOCKLER, Andrew

Born Stockton 18.11.70. Ht 5 11
Wt 11 13
Midfield. From Trainee.

Season	Club	Apps	Goals
1988–89	Arsenal	—	—
1989–90		—	—
1990–91	Scarborough	34	5
1991–92		24	4
1992–93		10	1

MOHAN, Nicky

Born Middlesbrough 6.10.70. Ht 6 2
Wt 12 00
Defender. From Trainee.

Season	Club	Apps	Goals
1987–88	Middlesbrough	—	—
1988–89		6	—

1989–90		22	—
1990–91		—	—
1991–92		27	2
1992–93		18	2
1992–93	Hull C	5	1

MOLBY, Jan

Born Kolding 4.7.63. Ht 6 1 Wt 14 07
Midfield. From Kolding, Ajax. Denmark
Youth, Under-21, full caps.

1984–85	Liverpool	22	1
1985–86		39	14
1986–87		34	7
1987–88		7	—
1988–89		13	2
1989–90		17	1
1990–91		25	9
1991–92		26	3
1992–93		10	3

MONCUR, John

Born Stepney 22.9.66. Ht 5 7 Wt 9 10
Midfield. From Apprentice.

1984–85	Tottenham H	—	—
1985–86		—	—
1986–87		1	—
1986–87	Cambridge U	4	—
1986–87	Doncaster R	4	—
1987–88	Tottenham H	5	—
1988–89		1	—
1988–89	Portsmouth	7	—
1989–90	Tottenham H	5	1
1989–90	Brentford	5	1
1990–91	Tottenham H	9	—
1991–92	Ipswich T	6	—
1991–92	Nottingham F	—	—
1991–92	Swindon T	3	—
1992–93		14	1

MONINGTON, Mark

Born Bilsthorpe 21.10.70. Ht 6 1
Wt 13 00
Midfield. From Schoolboy.

| 1988–89 | Burnley | 8 | 1 |

1989–90		13	—
1990–91		—	—
1991–92		12	1
1992–93		31	2

MONKOU, Kenneth

Born Surinam 29.11.64. Ht 6 3 Wt 14 05
Defender. From Feyenoord. Holland
Under-21.

1988–89	Chelsea	2	—
1989–90		34	1
1990–91		27	1
1991–92		31	—
1992–93		—	—
1992–93	Southampton	33	1

MONTGOMERIE, Ray

Born Irvine 17.4.61 Ht 5 8 Wt 11 7
Defender. From Saltcoats Vic.

1980–81	Newcastle U	—	—
1981–82	Dumbarton	20	5
1982–83		25	2
1983–84		39	1
1984–85		6	—
1985–86		24	—
1986–87		35	—
1987–88		31	—
1988–89	Kilmarnock	31	2
1989–90		35	3
1990–91		37	—
1991–92		30	1
1992–93		42	—

MOODY, Paul

Born Portsmouth 13.6.67. Ht 6 3
Wt 14 03
Forward. From Waterlooville.

1991–92	Southampton	4	—
1992–93		3	—
1992–93	Reading	5	1

MOONEY, Brian

Born Dublin 2.2.66. Ht 5 10 Wt 11 02
Midfield. From Home Farm. Eire Youth,
B, Under-23.

| 1983–84 | Liverpool | — | — |

Season	Club	App	Goals
1984–85		—	—
1985–86		—	—
1985–86	*Wrexham*	9	2
1986–87	Liverpool	—	—
1987–88		—	—
1987–88	Preston NE	34	3
1988–89		40	6
1989–90		45	9
1990–91	*Sheffield W*	—	—
1990–91	Preston NE	9	2
1990–91	Sunderland	6	—
1991–92		9	—
1992–93		12	1
1992–93	*Burnley*	6	—

MOONEY, Tom

Born Newry 14.12.73 Ht 5 11 Wt 11 02
Midfield. From Trainee.

1992–93	Huddersfield T	1	—

MOONEY, Tommy

Born Teesside North 11.8.71. Ht 5 10
Wt 12 05
Forward. From Trainee.

1989–90	Aston Villa	—	—
1990–91	Scarborough	27	13
1991–92		40	8
1992–93		40	9

MOORE, Alan

Born Dublin 25.11.74 Ht 5 10 Wt 11 00
Midfield. From Rivermount.

1991–92	Middlesbrough	—	—
1992–93		2	—

MOORE, Allan

Born Glasgow 23.12.64. Ht 5 6 Wt 9 10
Forward. From Possil YM.

1983–84	Dumbarton	4	—
1984–85		4	—
1985–86		33	4
1986–87		18	3

1986–87	Hearts	10	—
1987–88		7	1
1988–89		12	2
1989–90	St Johnstone	33	13
1990–91		31	5
1991–92		21	1
1992–93		17	3

MOORE, Darren

Born Birmingham 22.4.74. Ht 6 2
Wt 15 00
Defender. From Trainee.

1991–92	Torquay U	5	1
1992–93		31	2

MOORE, Kevin

Born Grimsby 29.4.58. Ht 6 0 Wt 13 00
Defender. From Local. England Schools.

1976–77	Grimsby T	28	—
1977–78		42	—
1978–79		46	6
1979–80		41	4
1980–81		41	1
1981–82		36	4
1982–83		38	—
1983–84		41	1
1984–85		31	4
1985–86		31	2
1986–87		25	5
1986–87	Oldham Ath	13	1
1987–88	Southampton	35	3
1988–89		25	3
1989–90		21	1
1990–91		19	1
1991–92		16	—
1991–92	*Bristol R*	7	—
1992–93	Southampton	18	2
1992–93	*Bristol R*	4	1

MOORE, Neil

Born Liverpool 21.9.72 Ht 6 1 Wt 12 02
Defender. From Trainee.

1991–92	Everton	—	—
1992–93		1	—

MORAH, Ollie

Born Islington 3.9.72. Ht 5 11 Wt 13 02
Forward. From Trainee.

Season	Club	App	Goals
1991–92	Tottenham H	—	—
1991–92	*Hereford U*	2	—
1992–93	Tottenham H	—	—
1992–93	Swindon T	—	—

MORALEE, Jamie

Born Wandsworth 2.12.71. Ht 5 11
Wt 11 05
Forward. From Trainee.

Season	Club	App	Goals
1989–90	Crystal Palace	—	—
1990–91		—	—
1991–92		6	—
1992–93		—	—
1992–93	Millwall	37	15

MORAN, Kevin

Born Dublin 29.4.56. Ht 5 11 Wt 12 09
Defender. From Pegasus-Eire Gaelic
Football. Eire 66 full caps.

Season	Club	App	Goals
1977–78	Manchester U	—	—
1978–79		1	—
1979–80		9	1
1980–81		32	—
1981–82		30	7
1982–83		29	2
1983–84		38	7
1984–85		19	4
1985–86		19	—
1986–87		33	—
1987–88		21	—
From Sporting Gijon			
1989–90	Blackburn R	19	2
1990–91		32	1
1991–92		41	2
1992–93		36	4

MORAN, Paul

Born Enfield 22.5.68. Ht 5 10 Wt 11 00
Forward. From Trainee.

Season	Club	App	Goals
1984–85	Tottenham H	—	—

Season	Club	App	Goals
1985–86		—	—
1986–87		1	—
1987–88		13	1
1988–89		8	—
1988–89	*Portsmouth*	3	—
1989–90	Tottenham H	5	1
1989–90	*Leicester C*	10	1
1990–91	Tottenham H	1	—
1990–91	*Newcastle U*	1	—
1990–91	*Southend U*	1	—
1991–92	Tottenham H	—	—
1992–93		3	—
1992–93	*Cambridge U*	—	—

MORAN, Steve

Born Croydon 10.1.61. Ht 5 8 Wt 11 03
Forward. From Amateur. England
Under-21.

Season	Club	App	Goals
1979–80	Southampton	1	1
1980–81		31	18
1981–82		18	9
1982–83		36	10
1983–84		34	21
1984–85		32	11
1985–86		28	8
1986–87		—	—
1986–87	Leicester C	27	9
1987–88		16	5
1987–88	Reading	28	7
1988–89		34	4
1989–90		28	11
1990–91		26	8
1991–92	Exeter C	34	19
1992–93		23	8

MORGAN, Jamie

Born Plymouth 1.10.75 Ht 5 11
Wt 11 00
Midfield. From Trainee.

Season	Club	App	Goals
1992–93	Plymouth Arg	3	—

MORGAN, Nicky

Born East Ham 30.10.59. Ht 5 10
Wt 13 10
Forward. From Apprentice.

Season	Club	App	Goals
1977–78	West Ham U	—	—

Season	Club	App	Goals
1978–79		2	—
1979–80		6	1
1980–81		6	1
1981–82		—	—
1982–83		7	—
1982–83	Portsmouth	6	1
1983–84		25	9
1984–85		30	8
1985–86		30	14
1986–87		4	—
1986–87	Stoke C	29	10
1987–88		28	5
1988–89		18	5
1989–90		13	1
1989–90	Bristol C	7	4
1990–91		44	13
1991–92		19	3
1992–93		10	3
1992–93	*Bournemouth*	6	1

MORGAN, Simon

Born Birmingham 5.9.66. Ht 5 10
Wt 11 07
Defender. From England Under-21.

Season	Club	App	Goals
1984–85	Leicester C	—	—
1985–86		30	—
1986–87		41	1
1987–88		40	—
1988–89		32	—
1989–90		17	2
1990–91		—	—
1990–91	Fulham	32	—
1991–92		36	3
1992–93		39	8

MORGAN, Steve

Born Oldham 19.9.68. Ht 5 11 Wt 13 00
Defender. From Apprentice. England
Youth.

Season	Club	App	Goals
1985–86	Blackpool	5	—
1986–87		11	—
1987–88		46	6
1988–89		44	3
1989–90		38	1
1990–91	Plymouth Arg	40	3
1991–92		45	2

Season	Club	App	Goals
1992–93		36	1

MORLEY, Trevor

Born Nottingham 20.3.61. Ht 5 11
Wt 12 01
Forward. From Derby Co, Corby T,
Nuneaton.

Season	Club	App	Goals
1985–86	Northampton T	43	13
1986–87		37	16
1987–88		27	10
1987–88	Manchester C	15	4
1988–89		40	12
1989–90		17	2
1989–90	West Ham U	19	10
1990–91		38	12
1991–92		24	2
1992–93		41	20

MORRELL, Paul

Born Poole 23.3.61. Ht 5 11 Wt 13 05
Defender. From Poole, Bath &
Weymouth.

Season	Club	App	Goals
1983–84	Bournemouth	22	2
1984–85		44	1
1985–86		38	1
1986–87		45	2
1987–88		42	—
1988–89		44	—
1989–90		21	—
1990–91		42	1
1991–92		24	1
1992–93		21	—

MORRIS, Andy

Born Sheffield 17.11.67. Ht 6 4 Wt 15 07
Forward.

Season	Club	App	Goals
1984–85	Rotherham U	1	—
1985–86		—	—
1986–87		6	—
1987–88		—	—
1987–88	Chesterfield	10	—
1988–89		42	9
1989–90		43	4
1990–91		15	4

1991–92	....	8	2	1990–91	....	14	—
1991–92	*Exeter C*	7	2	1991–92	Bournemouth	43	3
1992–93	Chesterfield	40	10	1992–93	....	43	1

MORRIS, Chris

Born Newquay 24.12.63.   Ht 5 10
Wt 10 08
Defender. From England Schools. Eire 35
full caps.

1982–83	Sheffield W	—	—
1983–84	....	13	1
1984–85	....	14	—
1985–86	....	30	—
1986–87	....	17	—
1987–88	Celtic	44	3
1988–89	....	33	3
1989–90	....	32	1
1990–91	....	19	—
1991–92	....	32	1
1992–93	....	3	—
1992–93	Middlesbrough	25	1

MORRIS, David

Born Plumstead 19.11.71.   Ht 5 11
Wt 12 00
Midfield. From Trainee.

1990–91	Bournemouth	1	—
1991–92	....	—	—
1992–93	Hereford U	11	—

MORRIS, Mark

Born Morden 26.9.62.   Ht 6 1   Wt 13 08
Defender. From Apprentice.

1980–81	Wimbledon	—	—
1981–82	....	33	1
1982–83	....	26	3
1983–84	....	39	3
1984–85	....	29	1
1985–86	....	20	1
1985–86	*Aldershot*	14	—
1986–87	Wimbledon	21	—
1987–88	Watford	39	1
1988–89	....	2	—
1989–90	Sheffield U	42	3

MORRIS, Mark

Born Chester 1.8.68.   Ht 6 0   Wt 12 00
Goalkeeper.

1985–86	Wrexham	3	—
1986–87	....	—	—
1987–88	....	6	—
1988–89	....	3	—
1989–90	....	3	—
1990–91	....	40	—
1991–92	....	8	—
1992–93	....	34	—

MORRIS, Paul

Born Bolton 6.2.75
Defender. From Trainee.

1992–93	Bury	1	—

MORRISON, Andy

Born Inverness 30.7.70.   Ht 5 11
Wt 12 00
Midfield. From Trainee.

1987–88	Plymouth Arg	1	—
1988–89	....	2	—
1989–90	....	19	1
1990–91	....	32	2
1991–92	....	30	3
1992–93	....	29	—

MORRISSEY, John

Born Liverpool 8.3.65.   Ht 5 8   Wt 11 09
Midfield. From Apprentice. England
Youth.

1982–83	Everton	—	—
1983–84	....	—	—
1984–85	....	1	—
1985–86	Wolverhampton W	10	1
1985–86	Tranmere R	32	5
1986–87	....	38	7

1987–88		39	4
1988–89		42	4
1989–90		27	4
1990–91		40	9
1991–92		40	5
1992–93		43	5

MORROW, Grant

Born Glasgow 4.10.70. Ht 5 10 Wt 11 07
Forward. From Rowntree Mackintosh.

1989–90	Doncaster R	7	2
1990–91		14	1
1991–92		20	—
1992–93		23	4

MORROW, Steve

Born Belfast 2.7.70. Ht 5 11 Wt 12 02
Defender. From Bangor, Arsenal Trainee.
Northern Ireland Youth, Under-23, 10 full
caps.

1987–88	Arsenal	—	—
1988–89		—	—
1989–90		—	—
1990–91	*Reading*	10	—
1991–92	Arsenal	2	—
1991–92	*Watford*	8	—
1991–92	*Reading*	3	—
1991–92	*Barnet*	1	—
1992–93	Arsenal	16	—

MORTIMER, Paul

Born London 8.5.68. Ht 5 11 Wt 11 03
Midfield. From Fulham Apprentice.
England Under-21.

1987–88	Charlton Ath	12	—
1988–89		33	5
1989–90		36	5
1990–91		32	7
1991–92	Aston Villa	12	1
1991–92	Crystal Palace	21	2
1992–93		1	—
1992–93	*Brentford*	6	—

MORTON, Neil

Born Congleton 21.12.68. Ht 5 9
Wt 10 07
Forward. From Trainee.

1986–87	Crewe Alex	2	—
1987–88		24	1
1988–89		5	—
From Northwich Vic			
1990–91	Chester C	34	7
1991–92		34	2
1992–93		27	4

MOSS, David

Born Doncaster 15.11.68
Midfield. From Boston U.

| 1992–93 | Doncaster R | 9 | 3 |

MOSS, Neil

Born New Milton 10.5.75 Ht 6 1
Wt 12 11
Goalkeeper. From Trainee.

| 1992–93 | Bournemouth | 1 | — |

MOULDEN, Paul

Born Farnworth 6.9.67. Ht 5 8 Wt 11 03
Forward. From Apprentice. England
Youth.

1984–85	Manchester C	—	—
1985–86		2	—
1986–87		20	5
1987–88		6	—
1988–89		36	13
1989–90	Bournemouth	32	13
1989–90	Oldham Ath	8	—
1990–91		24	3
1991–92		2	1
1992–93		4	—
1992–93	*Brighton*	11	5
1992–93	Birmingham C	13	5

MOUNTFIELD, Derek

Born Liverpool 2.11.62. Ht 6 1 Wt 12 07
Defender. From Apprentice. England B,
Under-21.

1980–81	Tranmere R	5	—
1981–82		21	1
1982–83	Everton	1	—
1983–84		31	3
1984–85		37	10
1985–86		15	3
1986–87		13	3
1987–88		9	—
1988–89	Aston Villa	24	1
1989–90		32	4
1990–91		32	4
1991–92		2	—
1991–92	Wolverhampton W	28	1
1992–93		36	2

MOWBRAY, Tony

Born Saltburn 22.11.63. Ht 6 1 Wt 13 00
Defender. From Apprentice. England B.

1981–82	Middlesbrough	—	—
1982–83		26	—
1983–84		35	1
1984–85		40	2
1985–86		35	4
1986–87		46	7
1987–88		44	3
1988–89		37	3
1989–90		28	2
1990–91		40	3
1991–92		17	—
1991–92	Celtic	15	2
1992–93		26	2

MOYLON, Craig

Born Munster 16.10.72 Ht 5 10
Wt 10 10
Defender. From Trainee.

1991–92	Preston NE	—	—
1992–93		1	—

MUDD, Paul

Born Hull 13.11.70. Ht 5 8 Wt 11 02
Defender. From Trainee.

1988–89	Hull C	1	—
1989–90		—	—
1990–91	Scarborough	24	—
1991–92		36	1
1992–93		38	1

MUGGLETON, Carl

Born Leicester 13.9.68. Ht 6 2 Wt 13 07
Goalkeeper. From Apprentice. England
Under-21.

1986–87	Leicester C	—	—
1987–88		—	—
1987–88	*Chesterfield*	17	—
1987–88	*Blackpool*	2	—
1988–89	Leicester C	3	—
1988–89	*Hartlepool U*	8	—
1989–90	Leicester C	—	—
1989–90	*Stockport Co*	4	—
1990–91	Leicester C	22	—
1990–91	*Liverpool*	—	—
1991–92	Leicester C	4	—
1992–93		17	—

MUIR, Ian

Born Coventry 5.5.63. Ht 5 8 Wt 11 00
Forward. From Apprentice. England
Youth.

1980–81	QPR	2	2
1981–82		—	—
1982–83		—	—
1982–83	*Burnley*	2	1
1983–84	Birmingham C	1	—
1983–84	Brighton	2	—
1984–85		2	—
1984–85	*Swindon T*	2	—
1985–86	Tranmere R	32	14
1986–87		46	20
1987–88		43	27
1988–89		46	21
1989–90		46	23
1990–91		35	13
1991–92		20	5

1992–93	....	11	2

MUIR, John

Born Sedgley 26.4.63.   Ht 6 2   Wt 14 06
Forward. From Dudley T.

1989–90	Doncaster R................	16	4
1990–91	....	39	13
1991–92	....	20	1
1991–92	Stockport Co	4	—
1992–93	....	9	3
1992–93	*Torquay U*................	12	—

MULRAIN, Steve

Born Lambeth 23.10.72   Ht 5 10
Wt 11 07
Forward. From Trainee.

1991–92	Leeds U	—	—
1992–93	Rochdale	6	2

MUNDAY, Stuart

Born London 28.9.72.   Ht 5 11   Wt 11 00
Defender. From Trainee.

1990–91	Brighton......................	—	—
1991–92	....	14	1
1992–93	....	7	—

MUNDEE, Denny

Born Swindon 10.10.68.   Ht 5 10
Wt 11 00
Forward. From Apprentice.

1986–87	QPR	—	—
1986–87	Swindon T	—	—
1987–88	Bournemouth..............	—	—
1988–89	....	2	—
1989–90	....	10	—
1989–90	*Torquay U*....................	9	—
1990–91	Bournemouth..............	21	2
1991–92	....	41	2
1992–93	....	26	2

MUNGALL, Steve

Born Bellshill 22.5.58.   Ht 5 8   Wt 11 05
Defender.

1976–77	Motherwell..................	3	—

1977–78	....	13	—
1978–79	....	4	—
1979–80	Tranmere R	24	—
1980–81	....	38	3
1981–82	....	44	1
1982–83	....	31	1
1983–84	....	26	—
1984–85	....	23	—
1985–86	....	46	1
1986–87	....	46	—
1987–88	....	45	—
1988–89	....	42	1
1989–90	....	17	1
1990–91	....	33	1
1991–92	....	18	—
1992–93	....	35	3

MUNRO, Stuart

Born Falkirk 15.9.62.   Ht 5 8   Wt 10 05
Defender. From Bo'ness United. Scotland
B.

1980–81	St Mirren	1	—
1981–82	....	—	—
1982–83	Alloa	39	5
1983–84	....	21	1
1983–84	Rangers......................	5	—
1984–85	....	13	—
1985–86	....	29	—
1986–87	....	43	—
1987–88	....	17	—
1988–89	....	22	2
1989–90	....	36	1
1990–91	....	14	—
1991–92	Blackburn R	1	—
1992–93	....	—	—
1992–93	Bristol C	16	—

MUNSON, Nathan

Born Colchester 10.11.74
Goalkeeper. From Trainee.

1992–93	Colchester U..............	1	—

MURDOCH, Andrew

Born Greenock 20.7.68.   Ht 5 11
Wt 11 00
Goalkeeper. From Johnstone Burgh.

Season	Club		
1987–88	Celtic	—	—
1988–89		—	—
1988–89	*Partick T*	13	—
1989–90	Celtic	—	—
1989–90	*Partick T*	13	—
1990–91	Celtic	—	—
1990–91	Partick T	18	—
1991–92		32	—
1992–93		17	—

MURPHY, Aidan

Born Manchester 17.9.67.   Ht 5 10
Wt 11 03
Midfield. From Apprentice. England
Schools, Youth.

Season	Club		
1984–85	Manchester U	—	—
1985–86		—	—
1986–87		—	—
1986–87	*Lincoln C*	2	—
1986–87	*Oldham Ath*	—	—
1987–88	Crewe Alex	20	2
1988–89		35	5
1989–90		35	3
1990–91		16	2
1991–92		7	1
1992–93	Scarborough	8	—

MURPHY, Jamie

Born Manchester 25.2.73   Ht 6 1
Wt 13 00
Defender. From Trainee.

Season	Club		
1991–92	Blackpool	—	—
1992–93		33	—

MURPHY, Matthew

Born Northampton 20.8.71
Forward. From Corby.

Season	Club		
1992–93	Oxford U	2	—

MURPHY, Shaun

Born Sydney 5.11.70   Ht 6 0   Wt 12 00
Defender. From Perth Italia.

Season	Club		
1992–93	Notts Co	8	1

MURRAY, Mark

Born Manchester 13.6.73.   Ht 5 8
Wt 10 12
Defender. From Trainee.

Season	Club		
1990–91	Blackpool	—	—
1991–92		2	—
1992–93		1	—

MURRAY, Neil

Born Bellshill 21.2.73   Ht 5 9   Wt 10 10
Midfield. From Rangers Ams.

Season	Club		
1989–90	Rangers	—	—
1990–91		—	—
1991–92		—	—
1992–93		16	—

MURRAY, Robert

Born Hammersmith 31.10.74   Ht 5 11
Wt 11 07
Forward. From Trainee. Scotland
Under-21.

Season	Club		
1992–93	Bournemouth	25	4

MURRAY, Shaun

Born Newcastle 7.2.70.   Ht 5 8   Wt 11 02
Forward. From Trainee. England Youth.

Season	Club		
1987–88	Tottenham H	—	—
1988–89		—	—
1989–90	Portsmouth	—	—
1990–91		25	1
1991–92		2	—
1992–93		7	—

MUSSELWHITE, Paul

Born Portsmouth 22.12.68.   Ht 6 2
Wt 12 07
Goalkeeper.

Season	Club		
1987–88	Portsmouth	—	—

Season	Club	Apps	Goals
1988–89	Scunthorpe U	41	—
1989–90		29	—
1990–91		38	—
1991–92		24	—
1992–93	Port Vale	41	—

MUSTOE, Robbie

Born Oxford 28.8.68.   Ht 5 10   Wt 10 08
Midfield.

Season	Club	Apps	Goals
1986–87	Oxford U	3	—
1987–88		17	—
1988–89		33	3
1989–90		38	7
1990–91	Middlesbrough	41	4
1991–92		30	2
1992–93		23	1

MUTCH, Andy

Born Liverpool 28.12.63.   Ht 5 10
Wt 11 00
Forward. From Southport. England B,
Under-21.

Season	Club	Apps	Goals
1985–86	Wolverhampton W	15	7
1986–87		41	12
1987–88		46	19
1988–89		45	21
1989–90		37	11
1990–91		29	8
1991–92		37	10
1992–93		39	9

MYALL, Stuart

Born Eastbourne 12.11.74
Defender. From Trainee.

Season	Club	Apps	Goals
1992–93	Brighton	7	—

MYERS, Andy

Born Hounslow 3.11.73.   Ht 5 8   Wt 9 10
Midfield. From Trainee. England Youth.

Season	Club	Apps	Goals
1990–91	Chelsea	3	—
1991–92		11	1
1992–93		3	—

MYERS, Chris

Born Yeovil 1.4.69.   Ht 5 10   Wt 11 10
Midfield. From Apprentice.

Season	Club	Apps	Goals
1986–87	Torquay U	9	‡
From local			
1990–91	Torquay U	29	2
1991–92		39	4
1992–93		28	1

NARBETT, Jon

Born Birmingham 21.11.68.   Ht 5 10
Wt 10 08
Midfield. From Apprentice.

Season	Club	App	Goals
1986–87	Shrewsbury T	1	—
1987–88		25	3
1988–89		—	—
1988–89	Hereford U	36	7
1989–90		36	5
1990–91		44	11
1991–92		33	8
1991–92	*Leicester C*	—	—
1992–93	Oxford U	14	—

NAREY, David

Born Dundee 21.6.56.   Ht 6 0   Wt 12 06
Defender. 'S' Form. Scotland Youth,
Under-21, Under-23, 35 full caps.

Season	Club	App	Goals
1973–74	Dundee U	12	—
1974–75		31	6
1975–76		33	—
1976–77		32	2
1977–78		35	—
1978–79		36	5
1979–80		35	1
1980–81		32	—
1981–82		34	1
1982–83		36	5
1983–84		34	1
1984–85		29	1
1985–86		35	—
1986–87		33	—
1987–88		39	—
1988–89		33	—
1989–90		31	—
1990–91		4	—
1991–92		24	—
1992–93		28	—

Nayim (Mohamed Ali Amar)

Born Morocco 5.11.66.   Ht 5 8   Wt 11 08
Midfield. From Barcelona. Spain Youth,
Under-21.

Season	Club	App	Goals
1988–89	Tottenham H	11	2

Season	Club	App	Goals
1989–90		19	—
1990–91		33	5
1991–92		31	1
1992–93		18	3

NAYLOR, Dominic

Born Watford 12.8.70.   Ht 5 9   Wt 11 07
Defender. From Trainee.

Season	Club	App	Goals
1988–89	Watford	—	—
1989–90		—	—
1989–90	Halifax T	6	1
To Barnet			
1991–92	Barnet	26	—
1992–93		25	—

NAYLOR, Glenn

Born York 11.8.72.   Ht 5 11   Wt 11 02
Forward. From Trainee.

Season	Club	App	Goals
1989–90	York C	1	—
1990–91		20	5
1991–92		21	8
1992–93		4	—

NAYLOR, Stuart

Born Wetherby 6.12.62.   Ht 6 4   Wt 12 02
Goalkeeper. From Yorkshire A. England
Youth, B.

Season	Club	App	Goals
1980–81	Lincoln C	—	—
1981–82		3	—
1982–83		1	—
1982–83	*Peterborough U*	8	—
1983–84	Lincoln C	—	—
1983–84	*Crewe Alex*	38	—
1984–85	*Crewe Alex*	17	—
1984–85	Lincoln C	25	—
1985–86		20	—
1985–86	WBA	12	—
1986–87		42	—
1987–88		35	—
1988–89		44	—
1989–90		39	—
1990–91		28	—
1991–92		34	—
1992–93		32	—

NAYLOR, Tony

Born Manchester 29.3.67.   Ht 5 8
Wt 10 08
Forward. From Droylsden.

Season	Club	Apps	Goals
1989–90	Crewe Alex	2	—
1990–91		14	1
1991–92		34	15
1992–93		35	16

NDAH, George

Born Camberwell 23.12.74   Ht 6 1
Wt 10 00
Midfield. From Trainee.

Season	Club	Apps	Goals
1992–93	Crystal Palace	13	—

NDLOVU, Peter

Born Zimbabwe 25.2.73.   Ht 5 8
Wt 10 02
Forward. From Highlanders.

Season	Club	Apps	Goals
1991–92	Coventry C	23	2
1992–93		32	7

NEBBELING, Gavin

Born Johannesburg 15.5.63.   Ht 6 0
Wt 12 10
Defender. From Arcadia Shepherds.

Season	Club	Apps	Goals
1981–82	Crystal Palace	1	—
1982–83		28	1
1983–84		16	—
1984–85		16	—
1985–86		14	—
1985–86	*Northampton T*	11	—
1986–87	Crystal Palace	23	—
1987–88		39	6
1988–89		14	1
1989–90	Fulham	36	—
1990–91		6	—
1991–92		16	—
1991–92	*Hereford U*	3	—
1992–93	Fulham	30	2

NEILL, Warren

Born Acton 21.11.62.   Ht 5 9   Wt 11 05
Defender. From Apprentice. England
Schools.

Season	Club	Apps	Goals
1980–81	QPR	4	—
1981–82		11	—
1982–83		39	2
1983–84		41	1
1984–85		18	—
1985–86		16	—
1986–87		29	—
1987–88		23	—
1988–89	Portsmouth	43	—
1989–90		37	—
1990–91		30	—
1991–92		38	—
1992–93		28	—

NEILSON, Alan

Born Wegburg 26.9.72.   Ht 5 11
Wt 11 07
Defender. From Trainee. Wales Under-21,
1 full cap.

Season	Club	Apps	Goals
1990–91	Newcastle U	3	—
1991–92		16	1
1992–93		3	—

NELSON, Craig

Born Coatbridge 28.5.71.   Ht 6 1
Wt 13 00
Goalkeeper. From Ashfield.

Season	Club	Apps	Goals
1990–91	Partick T	1	—
1991–92		11	—
1992–93		27	—

NELSON, Garry

Born Braintree 16.1.61.   Ht 5 10
Wt 11 04
Forward. From Amateur.

Season	Club	Apps	Goals
1979–80	Southend U	22	2
1980–81		22	3
1981–82		40	4
1982–83		45	8

Season	Club	App	Goals
1983–84	Swindon T	36	4
1984–85		43	3
1985–86	Plymouth Arg	42	13
1986–87		32	7
1987–88	Brighton	42	22
1988–89		46	15
1989–90		33	4
1990–91		23	5
1990–91	*Notts Co*	2	—
1991–92	Charlton Ath	41	6
1992–93		44	6

NETHERCOTT, Stuart

Born Chadwell Heath 21.3.73. Ht 6 0
Wt 12 04
Defender. From Trainee.

Season	Club	App	Goals
1991–92	Tottenham H	—	—
1991–92	*Maidstone U*	13	1
1991–92	*Barnet*	3	—
1992–93	Tottenham H	5	—

NEVIN, Pat

Born Glasgow 6.9.63. Ht 5 6 Wt 11 09
Forward. From Gartcosh U. Scotland,
Youth, Under-21, B, 17 full caps.

Season	Club	App	Goals
1981–82	Clyde	34	12
1982–83		39	5
1983–84	Chelsea	38	14
1984–85		41	4
1985–86		40	7
1986–87		37	5
1987–88		37	6
1988–89	Everton	25	2
1989–90		30	4
1990–91		37	8
1991–92		17	2
1991–92	*Tranmere R*	8	—
1992–93	Tranmere R	43	13

NEWELL, Mike

Born Liverpool 27.1.65. Ht 6 1 Wt 11 00
Forward. From Liverpool Amateur.
England, B, Under-21.

Season	Club	App	Goals
1983–84	Crewe Alex	3	—

Season	Club	App	Goals
1983–84	Wigan Ath	9	—
1984–85		39	9
1985–86		24	16
1985–86	Luton T	16	6
1986–87		42	12
1987–88		5	—
1987–88	Leicester C	36	8
1988–89		45	13
1989–90	Everton	26	7
1990–91		29	7
1991–92		13	1
1991–92	Blackburn R	20	6
1992–93		40	13

NEWELL, Paul

Born Greenwich 23.2.69. Ht 6 1
Wt 11 05
Goalkeeper. From Trainee.

Season	Club	App	Goals
1987–88	Southend U	13	—
1988–89		2	—
1989–90		—	—
1990–91	Leyton Orient	8	—
1991–92		10	—
1992–93		3	—
1992–93	*Colchester U*	14	—

NEWHOUSE, Aidan

Born Wallasey 23.5.72. Ht 6 2 Wt 13 05
Midfield. From Schoolboy, Trainee.
England Youth.

Season	Club	App	Goals
1987–88	Chester C	1	—
1988–89		25	2
1989–90		18	4
1989–90	Wimbledon	2	—
1990–91		8	1
1991–92		12	1
1992–93		1	—

NEWLAND, Ray

Born Liverpool 19.7.71 Ht 6 1 Wt 12 01
Goalkeeper. From Everton trainee.

Season	Club	App	Goals
1992–93	Plymouth Arg	21	—

NEWMAN, Ricky

Born Guildford 5.8.70.   Ht 5 10
Wt 11 00
Midfield.

1987–88	Crystal Palace	—	—
1998–89		—	—
1989–90		—	—
1990–91		—	—
1991–92		—	—
1991–92	*Maidstone U*	10	1
1992–93	Crystal Palace	2	—

NEWMAN, Rob

Born Bradstone-on-Avon 13.12.63.
Ht 6 0   Wt 13 00
Defender. From Apprentice.

1981–82	Bristol C	21	3
1982–83		43	3
1983–84		30	1
1984–85		34	3
1985–86		39	3
1986–87		45	6
1987–88		44	11
1988–89		46	6
1989–90		46	8
1990–91		46	8
1991–92	Norwich C	41	7
1992–93		18	2

NEWSOME, Jon

Born Sheffield 6.9.70.   Ht 6 2   Wt 13 11
Defender. From Trainee.

1989–90	Sheffield W	6	—
1990–91		1	—
1991–92	Leeds U	10	2
1992–93		37	—

NEWSON, Mark

Born Stepney 7.12.60.   Ht 5 10   Wt 12 06
Defender. From Apprentice.

1979–80	Charlton Ath	—	—
From Maidstone U			
1985–86	Bournemouth	46	5

1986–87		46	7
1987–88		29	3
1988–89		40	7
1989–90		16	1
1989–90	Fulham	16	—
1990–91		31	1
1991–92		26	3
1992–93		29	—

NEWTON, Eddie

Born Hammersmith 13.12.71.   Ht 5 11
Wt 11 02
Forward. From Trainee. England
Under-21.

1990–91	Chelsea	—	—
1991–92		1	1
1991–92	*Cardiff C*	18	4
1992–93	Chelsea	34	5

NEWTON, Shaun

Born Camberwell 20.8.75   Ht 5 8
Wt 10 04
Midfield. From Trainee.

| 1992–93 | Charlton Ath | 2 | — |

NICHOLAS, Charlie

Born Glasgow 30.12.61.   Ht 5 10
Wt 11 00
Forward. From Celtic BC. Scotland
Youth. Under-21, 20 full caps.

1980–81	Celtic	29	16
1981–82		10	3
1982–83		35	29
1983–84	Arsenal	41	11
1984–85		38	9
1985–86		41	10
1986–87		28	4
1987–88		3	—
1987–88	Aberdeen	16	3
1988–89		29	16
1989–90		33	11
1990–91	Celtic	14	6
1991–92		37	21
1992–93		16	2

NICHOLL, Jimmy

Born Hamilton,Canada 20.12.56
Ht 5 10   Wt 11 10
Defender. From Apprentice. Northern
Ireland U-21, 73 full caps.

Season	Club	Appearances	Goals
1973–74	Manchester U	—	—
1974–75		1	—
1975–76		20	—
1976–77		30	—
1977–78		37	2
1978–79		21	—
1979–80		42	—
1980–81		36	1
1981–82		1	—
1981–82	Sunderland	3	—

From Toronto B.

Season	Club	Appearances	Goals
1982–83	Sunderland	29	—

From Toronto B.

Season	Club	Appearances	Goals
1983–84	Rangers	17	—
1984–85	WBA	27	—
1985–86		29	—
1986–87	Rangers	42	—
1987–88		22	—
1988–89		1	—
1989–90	Dunfermline Ath	17	—
1990–91		7	—
1990–91	Raith R	10	—
1991–92		32	1
1992–93		38	5

NICHOLSON, Max

Born Leeds 3.10.71.
Forward. From Trainee.

Season	Club	Appearances	Goals
1989–90	Doncaster R	2	—
1990–91		1	—
1991–92		24	2
1992–93	Hereford U	36	3

NICHOLSON, Shane

Born Newark 3.6.70.   Ht 5 10   Wt 11 00
Defender. From Trainee.

Season	Club	Appearances	Goals
1986–87	Lincoln C	7	—
1987–88		*33*	*1*
1988–89		34	1
1989–90		23	—

Season	Club	Appearances	Goals
1990–91		40	4
1991–92		29	1
1991–92	Derby Co	—	—
1992–93		17	—

NICOL, Steve

Born Irvine 11.12.61.   Ht 5 10   Wt 12 00
Midfield. From Ayr U. BC. Scotland
Under-21, 27 full caps.

Season	Club	Appearances	Goals
1979–80	Ayr U	20	2
1980–81		39	3
1981–82		11	2
1981–82	Liverpool	—	—
1982–83		4	—
1983–84		23	5
1984–85		31	5
1985–86		34	4
1986–87		14	3
1987–88		40	6
1988–89		38	2
1989–90		23	6
1990–91		35	3
1991–92		34	1
1992–93		32	—

NIELSEN, Kent

Born Frederiksberg 28.12.61.   Ht 6 2
Wt 14 01
Defender. From Brondby. Denmark full
caps.

Season	Club	Appearances	Goals
1989–90	Aston Villa	36	2
1990–91		37	2
1991–92		6	—

To Aarhus

NIJHOLT, Luc

Born Zaandam 29.7.61   Ht 5 11
Wt 12 01
Defender. From BSC Old Boys Basel.

Season	Club	Appearances	Goals
1990–91	Motherwell	23	—
1991–92		39	5
1992–93		34	—

NILSSON, Roland

Born Helsingborg 27.11.63.   Ht 6 0
Wt 11 06
Defender. From IFK Gothenburg. Sweden
full caps.

1989–90	Sheffield W	20	—
1990–91		22	—
1991–92		39	1
1992–93		32	1

NISBET, Scott

Born Edinburgh 30.1.68.   Ht 6 1
Wt 11 08
Defender. From Salvesen BC. Scotland
Schools, Youth, Under-21.

1985–86	Rangers	5	—
1986–87		1	—
1986–87	*East Fife*	6	—
1987–88	Rangers	25	—
1988–89		7	1
1989–90		7	—
1990–91		15	—
1991–92		20	5
1992–93		10	—

NIXON, Eric

Born Manchester 4.10.62.   Ht 6 2
Wt 14 03
Goalkeeper. From Curzon Ashton.

1983–84	Manchester C	—	—
1984–85		—	—
1985–86		28	—
1986–87		5	—
1986–87	*Wolverhampton W*	16	—
1986–87	*Bradford C*	3	—
1986–87	*Southampton*	4	—
1986–87	*Carlisle U*	16	—
1987–88	Manchester C	25	—
1987–88	*Tranmere R*	8	—
1988–89	Tranmere R	45	—
1989–90		46	—
1990–91		43	—
1991–92		46	—
1992–93		45	—

NOBBS, Keith

Born Bishop Auckland 19.9.61.   Ht 5 10
Wt 11 10
Defender. From Apprentice.

1979–80	Middlesbrough	—	—
1980–81		1	—
1981–82		—	—
1982–83	Halifax T	46	1
1983–84		41	—
From Bishop Auckland			
1985–86	Hartlepool U	39	1
1986–87		40	—
1987–88		43	—
1988–89		18	—
1989–90		32	—
1990–91		40	—
1991–92		41	—
1992–93		27	—

NOGAN, Kurt

Born Cardiff 9.9.70.   Ht 5 11   Wt 12 07
Forward. From Trainee. Wales Under-21.

1989–90	Luton T	10	2
1990–91		9	—
1991–92		14	1
1992–93	Peterborough U	—	—
1992–93	Brighton	30	20

NOGAN, Lee

Born Cardiff 21.5.69.   Ht 5 10   Wt 11 00
Forward. From Apprentice. Wales B,
Under-21, 1 full cap.

1986–87	Oxford U	—	—
1986–87	*Brentford*	11	2
1987–88	Oxford U	3	—
1987–88	*Southend U*	6	1
1988–89	Oxford U	3	—
1989–90		4	—
1990–91		32	5
1991–92		22	5
1991–92	Watford	23	5
1992–93		42	11

NOLAN, Ian

Born Liverpool 9.7.70.   Ht 6 0   Wt 11 10
Defender. From Preston NE Trainee,
Northwich V, Marine.

Season	Club		
1991–92	Tranmere R	34	1
1992–93		14	—

NORBURY, Mike

Born Hemsworth 22.1.69.   Ht 6 1
Wt 11 10
Forward. From Ossett, Scarborough,
Bridlington.

Season	Club		
1991–92	Cambridge U	14	2
1992–93		12	1
1992–93	Preston NE	21	8

NORMAN, John

Born Birkenhead 26.6.71
Midfield.

Season	Club		
1992–93	Bury	2	—

NORMAN, Tony

Born Mancot 24.2.58.   Ht 6 2   Wt 13 10
Goalkeeper. From Amateur. Wales B, 5
full caps.

Season	Club		
1976–77	Burnley	—	—
1977–78		—	—
1978–79		—	—
1979–80		—	—
1979–80	Hull C	17	—
1980–81		42	—
1981–82		36	—
1982–83		36	—
1983–84		46	—
1984–85		46	—
1985–86		42	—
1986–87		42	—
1987–88		44	—
1988–89		21	—
1988–89	Sunderland	24	—
1989–90		28	—
1990–91		37	—
1991–92		44	—

Season	Club		
1992–93		33	—

NORRIS, Steve

Born Coventry 22.9.61   Ht 5 10   Wt 10 10
Forward. From Telford.

Season	Club		
1988–89	Scarborough	31	9
1989–90		14	4
1989–90	*Notts Co*	1	—
1989–90	Carlisle U	24	3
1990–91		5	2
1990–91	Halifax T	39	30
1991–92		17	5
1991–92	Chesterfield	21	10
1992–93		30	11

NORTON, David

Born Cannock 3.3.65.   Ht 5 7   Wt 11 03
Midfield. From Apprentice. England
Youth.

Season	Club		
1982–83	Aston Villa	—	—
1983–84		—	—
1984–85		2	—
1985–86		20	2
1986–87		20	—
1987–88		2	—
1988–89	Notts Co	8	—
1989–90		15	1
1990–91		4	—
1990–91	*Rochdale*	9	—
1990–91	*Hull C*	15	—
1991–92	Hull C	45	2
1992–93		45	1

NOTEMAN, Kevin

Born Preston 15.10.69.   Ht 5 10   Wt 11 12
Forward. From Trainee.

Season	Club		
1987–88	Leeds U	1	—
1988–89		—	—
1989–90		—	—
1989–90	Doncaster R	30	3
1990–91		42	7
1991–92		34	10
1991–92	Mansfield T	6	—
1992–93		24	4

NTAMARK, Charlie

Born Cameroon 22.7.64.   Ht 5 8
Wt 11 12
Midfield. Cameroon full caps.

1990–91	Walsall	42	3
1991–92		41	3
1992–93		41	4

NUGENT, Kevin

Born Edmonton 10.4.69.   Ht 6 1
Wt 12 04
Forward. From Trainee. Eire Youth.

1987–88	Leyton Orient	11	3
1988–89		3	—
1988–89	*Cork C*	—	—
1989–90	Leyton Orient	11	—
1990–91		33	5
1991–92		36	12
1991–92	Plymouth Arg	4	—
1992–93		45	11

NUGENT, Stephen

Born Wigan 7.5.73.   Ht 5 10   Wt 12 06
Forward. From Trainee.

1989–90	Wigan Ath	1	—
1990–91		1	—
1991–92		2	—
1992–93		9	—

OAKES, Scott

Born Leicester 5.8.72.   Ht 5 11   Wt 11 04
Forward. From Trainee.

1989–90	Leicester C	2	—
1990–91		—	—
1991–92		1	—
1991–92	Luton T	21	2
1992–93		44	5

OBEBO, Godfrey

Born Lagos 16.4.66
Forward.

1992–93	Halifax T	3	—

O'BRIEN, Liam

Born Dublin 5.9.64.   Ht 6 1   Wt 13 03
Midfield. From Shamrock R. Eire Youth,
10 full caps.

1986–87	Manchester U	11	—
1987–88		17	2
1988–89		3	—
1988–89	Newcastle U	20	4
1989–90		19	2
1990–91		33	3
1991–92		40	4
1992–93		33	6

O'CALLAGHAN, Kevin

Born London 19.10.61.   Ht 5 8   Wt 11 00
Midfield. From Apprentice. Eire Youth,
Under-21, 20 full caps.

1978–79	Millwall	10	—
1979–80		10	3
1979–80	Ipswich T	4	—
1980–81		24	—
1981–82		19	1
1982–83		28	—
1983–84		25	2
1984–85		15	—
1984–85	Portsmouth	15	2
1985–86		39	11
1986–87		33	3

1987–88	Millwall	22	7
1988–89		34	5
1989–90		—	—
1990–91		20	2
1991–92	Southend U	8	—
1992–93		13	1

O'CONNELL, Brendan

Born London 12.11.66.   Ht 5 10
Wt 10 09
Forward.

1984–85	Portsmouth	—	—
1985–86		—	—
1986–87	Exeter C	42	8
1987–88		39	11
1988–89	Burnley	43	13
1989–90		21	4
1989–90	*Huddersfield T*	11	1
1989–90	Barnsley	11	2
1990–91		45	9
1991–92		36	4
1992–93		40	6

O'CONNOR, Mark

Born Rochdale 10.3.63.   Ht 5 7   Wt 10 02
Midfield. From Apprentice. Eire Under-21.

1980–81	QPR	—	—
1981–82		1	—
1982–83		2	—
1983–84		—	—
1983–84	*Exeter C*	38	1
1984–85	Bristol R	46	8
1985–86		34	2
1985–86	Bournemouth	9	1
1986–87		43	7
1987–88		37	2
1988–89		33	2
1989–90		6	—
1989–90	Gillingham	15	1
1990–91		41	3
1991–92		39	3
1992–93		21	1

O'CONNOR, Martyn

Born Walsall 10.12.67   Ht 5 8   Wt 10 08
Midfield. From Bromsgrove R.

1992–93	Crystal Palace	—	—
1992–93	*Walsall*	10	1

O'DONNELL, Phillip

Born Bellshill 25.3.72   Ht 5 10   Wt 10 05
Midfield. From X Form. Scotland
Under-21.

1990–91	Motherwell	12	—
1991–92		42	4
1992–93		32	4

O'DRISCOLL, Sean

Born Wolverhampton 1.7.57.   Ht 5 8
Wt 11 03
Midfield. From Alvechurch. Eire Under-
21, 3 full caps.

1979–80	Fulham	10	1
1980–81		42	2
1981–82		42	7
1982–83		42	3
1983–84		12	—
1983–84	*Bournemouth*	19	1
1984–85	Bournemouth	44	1
1985–86		46	5
1986–87		46	5
1987–88		39	4
1988–89		41	—
1989–90		39	—
1990–91		45	2
1991–92		44	1
1992–93		42	—

OGDEN, Neil

Born Billinge 29.11.75   Ht 5 10   Wt 10 04
Defender. From Trainee.

1992–93	Wigan Ath	2	—

OGHANI, George

Born Manchester 2.9.60 Ht 5 11
Wt 12 01
Forward. From Hyde.

Season	Club		
1983–84	Bolton W	3	—
1984–85		41	16
1985–86		36	7
1986–87		19	4
1986–87	*Wrexham*	7	—
1987–88	Burnley	37	14
1988–89		37	7
1989–90	Stockport Co	8	2
1989–90	Hereford U	8	2
1989–90	Scarborough	14	4
1990–91		36	14
From Evagoras			
1992–93	Carlisle U	39	15

OGRIZOVIC, Steve

Born Mansfield 12.9.57. Ht 6 5 Wt 15 00
Goalkeeper. From ONRYC.

Season	Club		
1977–78	Chesterfield	16	—
1977–78	Liverpool	2	—
1978–79		—	—
1979–80		1	—
1980–81		1	—
1981–82		—	—
1982–83	Shrewsbury T	42	—
1983–84		42	—
1984–85	Coventry C	42	—
1985–86		42	—
1986–87		42	1
1987–88		40	—
1988–89		38	—
1989–90		37	—
1990–91		37	—
1991–92		38	—
1992–93		33	—

O'HANLON, Kelham

Born Saltburn 16.5.62. Ht 6 1 Wt 13 01
Goalkeeper. From Apprentice. Eire
Under-21, 1 full cap.

Season	Club		
1980–81	Middlesbrough	—	—
1981–82		—	—

Season	Club		
1982–83		19	—
1983–84		30	—
1984–85		38	—
1985–86	Rotherham U	46	—
1986–87		40	—
1987–88		40	—
1988–89		46	—
1989–90		43	—
1990–91		33	—
1991–92	Carlisle U	42	—
1992–93		41	—

O'HARA, Steve

Born Lanark 21.2.71. Ht 6 1 Wt 12 02
Defender. From Trainee.

Season	Club		
1989–90	Walsall	18	—
1990–91		20	—
1991–92		37	3
1992–93		26	1

OKAI, Stephen

Born Ghana 3.12.73.
Midfield. From Schoolboy.

Season	Club		
1991–92	Leyton Orient	1	1
1992–93		13	1

O'KEEFE, Vince

Born Birmingham 2.4.57. Ht 6 2
Wt 13 00
Goalkeeper. From Local.

Season	Club		
1975–76	Birmingham C	—	—
1975–76	*Peterborough U*	—	—
1976–77	Walsall	—	—
From AP Leamington			
1978–79	Exeter C	33	—
1979–80		20	—
1979–80	Torquay U	16	—
1980–81		46	—
1981–82		46	—
1982–83	Blackburn R	9	—
1983–84		12	—
1983–84	*Bury*	2	—
1984–85	Blackburn R	5	—
1985–86		10	—

Season	Club	App	Goals
1986–87	....	25	—
1986–87	*Blackpool*	1	—
1987–88	Blackburn R	5	—
1988–89	....	2	—
1988–89	*Blackpool*	6	—
1989–90	Wrexham	43	—
1990–91	....	6	—
1991–92	....	34	—
1992–93	Exeter C	2	—

OLDFIELD, David

Born Perth, Australia 30.5.68. Ht 5 11
Wt 13 02
Midfield. From Apprentice. England
Under-21.

Season	Club	App	Goals
1986–87	Luton T	—	—
1987–88	....	8	3
1988–89	....	21	1
1988–89	Manchester C	11	3
1989–90	....	15	3
1989–90	Leicester C	20	5
1990–91	....	42	7
1991–92	....	41	4
1992–93	....	44	5

O'LEARY, David

Born London 2.5.58. Ht 6 1 Wt 13 09
Defender. From Apprentice. Eire Youth,
67 full caps.

Season	Club	App	Goals
1975–76	Arsenal	27	—
1976–77	....	33	2
1977–78	....	41	1
1978–79	....	37	2
1979–80	....	34	1
1980–81	....	24	1
1981–82	....	40	1
1982–83	....	36	1
1983–84	....	36	—
1984–85	....	36	—
1985–86	....	35	—
1986–87	....	39	—
1987–88	....	23	—
1988–89	....	26	—
1989–90	....	34	—
1990–91	....	21	1
1991–92	....	25	—

Season	Club	App	Goals
1992–93	....	11	—

OLIVER, Darren

Born Liverpool 1.11.71 Ht 5 8 Wt 10 05
Defender.

Season	Club	App	Goals
1991–92	Bolton W	—	—
1992–93	....	3	—

OLIVER, Gavin

Born Felling 6.9.62. Ht 6 0 Wt 12 10
Defender. From Apprentice.

Season	Club	App	Goals
1980–81	Sheffield W	2	—
1981–82	....	—	—
1982–83	....	2	—
1982–83	*Tranmere R*	17	1
1983–84	Sheffield W	6	—
1984–85	....	10	—
1985–86	....	—	—
1985–86	*Brighton*	16	—
1985–86	Bradford C	27	1
1986–87	....	40	—
1987–88	....	43	—
1988–89	....	39	1
1989–90	....	22	—
1990–91	....	46	5
1991–92	....	10	—
1992–93	....	40	2

OLIVER, Neil

Born Berwick 11.4.67. Ht 5 11 Wt 11 10
Defender. From Coldstream.

Season	Club	App	Goals
1985–86	Berwick R	5	—
1986–87	....	37	—
1987–88	....	12	—
1988–89	....	39	—
1989–90	Blackburn R	3	—
1990–91	....	3	—
1991–92	Falkirk	35	—
1992–93	....	25	—

OLLERENSHAW, Scott

Born Sydney 9.2.68 Ht 5 10 Wt 11 07
Forward. From Sydney Olympic.

Season	Club	App	Goals
1992–93	Walsall	20	4

OLNEY, Ian

Born Luton 17.12.69. Ht 6 1 Wt 11 00
Forward. From Trainee. England
Under-21.

Season	Club		
1988–89	Aston Villa	15	2
1989–90		35	9
1990–91		18	3
1991–92		20	2
1992–93	Oldham Ath	34	12

OLSEN, Jesper

Born Fakse 20.3.61. Ht 5 6 Wt 9 09
Forward. From Naestved and Ajax.
Denmark full caps.

Season	Club		
1984–85	Manchester U	36	5
1985–86		28	11
1986–87		28	3
1987–88		37	2
1988–89		10	—

To Bordeaux

OLSSON, Paul

Born Hull 24.12.65. Ht 5 8 Wt 10 11
Midfield. From Apprentice.

Season	Club		
1983–84	Hull C	—	—
1984–85		—	—
1985–86		—	—
1986–87		—	—
1986–87	*Exeter C*	8	—
1987–88	Exeter C	35	2
1988–89	Scarborough	32	4
1989–90		16	1
1989–90	Hartlepool U	23	2
1990–91		31	1
1991–92		46	6
1992–93		39	2

O'NEIL, Brian

Born Paisley 6.9.72. Ht 6 1 Wt 12 04
Midfield. From X form. Scotland
Under-21.

Season	Club		
1991–92	Celtic	28	1
1992–93		17	3

O'NEIL, John

Born Bellshill 6.7.71. Ht 5 7 Wt 10 02
Midfield. From Fir Park BC. Scotland
Under-21.

Season	Club		
1988–89	Dundee U	1	—
1989–90		10	—
1990–91		15	—
1991–92		12	—
1992–93		28	3

O'NEILL, Michael

Born Portadown 5.7.69. Ht 5 11
Wt 10 10
Forward. From Coleraine. Northern
Ireland 22 full caps.

Season	Club		
1987–88	Newcastle U	21	12
1988–89		27	3
1989–90	Dundee U	18	5
1990–91		13	—
1991–92		8	4
1992–93		25	2

ONUORA, Iffy

Born Glasgow 28.7.67. Ht 5 10 Wt 11 10
Forward. From British Universities.

Season	Club		
1989–90	Huddersfield T	20	3
1990–91		43	7
1991–92		41	8
1992–93		39	6

ONWERE, Udo

Born Hammersmith 9.11.71. Ht 6 0
Wt 11 07
Midfield. From Trainee.

Season	Club		
1990–91	Fulham	7	1
1991–92		27	3
1992–93		29	3

ORD, Richard

Born Easington 3.3.70. Ht 6 2 Wt 12 08
Defender. From Trainee. England
Under-21.

Season	Club		
1987–88	Sunderland	8	—

Season	Club	Apps	Goals
1988–89		34	1
1989–90		7	1
1989–90	*York C*	3	—
1990–91	Sunderland	14	—
1991–92		6	—
1992–93		24	—

O'REGAN, Kieran

Born Cork 9.11.63. Ht 5 8 Wt 10 12
Midfield. From Tramore Ath. Eire Youth,
Under-21, 4 full caps.

Season	Club	Apps	Goals
1982–83	Brighton	1	—
1983–84		31	1
1984–85		15	—
1985–86		15	1
1986–87		24	—
1987–88	Swindon T	26	1
1988–89	Huddersfield T	36	2
1989–90		37	3
1990–91		46	11
1991–92		39	4
1992–93		41	5

O'RIORDAN, Don

Born Dublin 14.5.57. Ht 6 0 Wt 12 08
Midfield. From Apprentice. Eire Youth,
Under-21.

Season	Club	Apps	Goals
1975–76	Derby Co	—	—
1976–77		1	—
1977–78		5	1
1977–78	*Doncaster R*	2	—
From TulsaH			
1978–79	Preston NE	32	—
1979–80		18	—
1980–81		21	—
1981–82		46	4
1982–83		41	4
1983–84	Carlisle U	42	8
1984–85		42	10
1985–86	Middlesbrough	41	2
1986–87	Grimsby T	40	6
1987–88		46	8
1988–89	Notts Co	43	3
1989–90		17	—
1989–90	*Mansfield T*	6	—
1990–91	Notts Co	31	1

Season	Club	Apps	Goals
1991–92		1	—
1992–93		17	1
1992–93	Torquay U	16	—

ORLYGSSON, Thorvaldur

Born Odense 2.8.66. Ht 5 11 Wt 10 08
Midfield. From FC Akureyri. Iceland full
caps.

Season	Club	Apps	Goals
1989–90	Nottingham F	12	1
1990–91		—	—
1991–92		5	—
1992–93		20	1

ORMONDROYD, Ian

Born Bradford 22.9.64. Ht 6 4 Wt 13 05
Forward. From Thackley.

Season	Club	Apps	Goals
1985–86	Bradford C	12	3
1986–87		13	4
1986–87	*Oldham Ath*	10	1
1987–88	Bradford C	37	9
1988–89		25	4
1988–89	Aston Villa	12	1
1989–90		25	4
1990–91		18	1
1991–92		1	—
1991–92	Derby Co	25	8
1991–92	Leicester C	14	1
1992–93		26	2

ORMSBY, Brendan

Born Birmingham 1.10.60. Ht 5 11
Wt 11 12
Defender. From Apprentice. England
Schools, Youth.

Season	Club	Apps	Goals
1978–79	Aston Villa	2	—
1979–80		23	—
1980–81		—	—
1981–82		12	—
1982–83		—	—
1983–84		34	2
1984–85		32	2
1985–86		14	—
1985–86	Leeds U	12	1
1986–87		33	4

Season	Club	App	Goals
1987–88	....	—	—
1988–89	....	1	—
1989–90	....	—	—
1989–90	*Shrewsbury T*	1	—
1990–91	Doncaster R.	43	4
1991–92	....	35	3
1992–93	Scarborough	16	1

ORR, Neil

Born Airdrie 13.5.59.   Ht 5 10   Wt 12 02
Midfield. Scotland Under-21.

Season	Club	App	Goals
1975–76	Morton	4	—
1976–77	....	24	—
1977–78	....	39	—
1978–79	....	35	—
1979–80	....	35	1
1980–81	....	33	—
1981–82	....	16	—
1981–82	West Ham U	24	1
1982–83	....	14	—
1983–84	....	29	—
1984–85	....	20	—
1985–86	....	36	2
1986–87	....	22	1
1987–88	....	1	—
1987–88	Hibernian	38	1
1988–89	....	33	—
1989–90	....	29	1
1990–91	....	17	—
1991–92	....	28	—
1992–93	....	21	—

OSBORN, Simon

Born New Addington 19.1.72.   Ht 5 10
Wt 11 04
Midfield. From Apprentice.

Season	Club	App	Goals
1989–90	Crystal Palace	—	—
1990–91	....	4	—
1991–92	....	14	2
1992–93	....	31	2

OSBORNE, Lawrence

Born London 20.10.67.   Ht 5 10
Wt 11 11
Forward. From Apprentice.

Season	Club	App	Goals
1985–86	Arsenal	—	—

Season	Club	App	Goals
1986–87	....	—	—
1987–88	Newport Co.	15	—
From Redbridge Forest			
1990–91	Maidstone U.	37	4
From Redbridge Forest			
1990–91	Maidstone U.	37	4
1991–92	....	16	4
1991–92	Gillingham	5	—
1992–93	....	1	1

O'SHAUGHNESSY, Steve

Born Wrexham 13.10.67.   Ht 6 2
Wt 13 01
Defender. Wales Youth.

Season	Club	App	Goals
1984–85	Leeds U	—	—
1985–86	....	—	—
1985–86	Bradford C	—	—
1986–87	....	—	—
1987–88	....	1	—
1988–89	Rochdale	41	6
1989–90	....	30	8
1990–91	....	38	2
1991–92	Exeter C.	3	—
1991–92	Darlington	15	1
1992–93	....	41	1

O'SHEA, Danny

Born Kennington 26.3.63.   Ht 6 0
Wt 12 08
Defender. From Apprentice.

Season	Club	App	Goals
1980–81	Arsenal	—	—
1981–82	....	—	—
1982–83	....	6	—
1983–84	....	—	—
1983–84	*Charlton Ath*	9	—
1984–85	Exeter C.	45	2
1985–86	Southend U.	35	9
1986–87	....	41	2
1987–88	....	22	—
1988–89	....	20	1
1989–90	Cambridge U	26	—
1990–91	....	40	—
1991–92	....	31	1
1992–93	....	37	—

OSMAN, Russell

Born Repton 14.2.59.   Ht 5 11   Wt 12 01
Defender. From Apprentice. England
Under-21, B, 11 full caps.

1975–76	Ipswich	—	—
1976–77		—	—
1977–78		28	—
1978–79		39	2
1979–80		42	2
1980–81		42	1
1981–82		39	2
1982–83		38	4
1983–84		37	3
1984–85		29	3
1985–86	Leicester C	40	—
1986–87		31	3
1987–88		37	5
1988–89	Southampton	36	—
1989–90		35	5
1990–91		20	1
1991–92		5	—
1991–92	Bristol C	31	2
1992–93		34	—

O'TOOLE, Pat

Born Dublin 2.1.65.   Ht 5 7   Wt 11 00
Midfield. From Shelbourne.

1989–90	Leicester C	—	—
1990–91		—	—
1990–91	Exeter C	6	—
1990–91	Shrewsbury T	11	—
1991–92		27	—
1992–93		8	1

OTTO, Ricky

Born London 9.11.67.   Ht 5 10   Wt 11 00
Midfield. From Dartford.

1990–91	Leyton Orient	1	—
1991–92		32	5
1992–93		23	8

OVERSON, Vince

Born Kettering 15.5.62.   Ht 6 0   Wt 14 10
Defender. From Apprentice.

1979–80	Burnley	22	—

1980–81		39	1
1981–82		36	4
1982–83		6	—
1983–84		38	—
1984–85		42	1
1985–86		28	—
1986–87	Birmingham C	34	1
1987–88		37	—
1988–89		41	—
1989–90		30	—
1990–91		40	2
1991–92	Stoke C	35	3
1992–93		43	1

OWEN, Gareth

Born Chester 21.10.71.   Ht 5 7   Wt 11 10
Midfield. From Trainee. Wales Under-21.

1989–90	Wrexham	13	—
1990–91		27	2
1991–92		36	7
1992–93		41	3

OWERS, Gary

Born Newcastle 3.10.68.   Ht 5 10
Wt 11 10
Midfield. From Apprentice.

1986–87	Sunderland	—	—
1987–88		37	4
1988–89		38	3
1989–90		43	9
1990–91		38	1
1991–92		30	4
1992–93		33	1

OXBROW, Darren

Born Ipswich 1.9.69.   Ht 6 1   Wt 12 06
Defender. From Trainee.

1988–89	Ipswich T	—	—
1989–90	Maidstone U	24	—
1990–91		30	1
1991–92		31	1
1992–93	Colchester U	16	4
1992–93	Barnet	1	—

PAATELAINEN, Mixu

Born Helsinki 3.2.67.   Ht 6 0   Wt 13 11
Forward. From Valkeakosken Haka.
Finland full caps.

1987–88	Dundee U	19	9
1988–89		33	10
1989–90		31	7
1990–91		20	1
1991–92		30	6
1991–92	Aberdeen	6	1
1992–93		33	16

PAGE, Don

Born Manchester 18.1.64   Ht 5 10
Wt 11 03
Forward. From Runcorn.

1988–89	Wigan Ath	15	2
1989–90		25	—
1990–91		34	13
1991–92	Rotherham U	31	11
1992–93		24	2
1992–93	*Rochdale*	4	1

PAINTER, Robert

Born Ince 26.1.71.   Ht 5 11   Wt 11 00
Midfield. From Trainee.

1987–88	Chester C	2	—
1988–89		8	1
1989–90		32	4
1990–91		42	3
1991–92	Maidstone U	30	5
1991–92	Burnley	9	2
1992–93		17	—

PALIN, Leigh

Born Worcester 12.9.65.   Ht 5 9
Wt 11 07
Midfield. From Apprentice. England
Youth.

1983–84	Aston Villa	—	—
1984–85		—	—
1984–85	*Shrewsbury T*	2	—

1985–86	Aston Villa	—	—
1985–86	Nottingham F	—	—
1986–87		—	—
1986–87	Bradford C	21	3
1987–88		20	3
1988–89		30	4
1989–90		—	—
1989–90	Stoke C	19	3
1989–90	Hull C	9	1
1990–91		35	5
1991–92		13	1
1991–92	*Rochdale*	3	—
1992–93	Burnley	1	—
1992–93	Halifax T	—	—
1992–93	Partick T	5	—

PALLISTER, Gary

Born Ramsgate 30.6.65.   Ht 6 4   Wt 13 04
Defender. England B, 9 full caps.

1984–85	Middlesbrough	—	—
1985–86		28	—
1985–86	*Darlington*	7	—
1986–87	Middlesbrough	44	1
1987–88		44	3
1988–89		37	1
1989–90		3	—
1989–90	Manchester U	35	3
1990–91		36	—
1991–92		40	1
1992–93		42	1

PALMER, Carlton

Born West Bromwich 5.12.65.   Ht 6 2
Wt 12 04
Defender. From Trainee. England B,
Under-21, 17 full caps.

1984–85	WBA	—	—
1985–86		20	—
1986–87		37	1
1987–88		38	3
1988–89		26	—
1988–89	Sheffield W	13	1
1989–90		34	—
1990–91		45	2
1991–92		42	5
1992–93		34	1

PALMER, Charlie

Born Aylesbury 10.7.63.   Ht 6 0
Wt 12 03
Defender. From Apprentice.

Season	Club		
1981–82	Watford	—	—
1982–83		—	—
1983–84		10	1
1984–85	Derby Co	33	2
1985–86		18	—
1986–87		—	—
1986–87	Hull C	17	—
1987–88		35	—
1988–89		18	1
1988–89	Notts Co	11	—
1989–90		37	5
1990–91		40	1
1991–92		41	—
1992–93		31	—

PALMER, Lee

Born Gillingham 19.9.70   Ht 5 11
Wt 13 00
Defender. From Trainee.

Season	Club		
1987–88	Gillingham	1	—
1988–89		—	—
1989–90		39	3
1990–91		21	1
1991–92		11	—
1992–93		10	—

PALMER, Roger

Born Manchester 30.1.59.   Ht 5 10
Wt 11 00
Forward. From Apprentice.

Season	Club		
1976–77	Manchester C	—	—
1977–78		5	3
1978–79		14	4
1979–80		7	1
1980–81		5	1
1980–81	Oldham Ath	21	6
1981–82		37	7
1982–83		42	15
1983–84		42	13
1984–85		36	9
1985–86		41	15

1986–87		42	16
1987–88		42	17
1988–89		46	15
1989–90		42	16
1990–91		29	9
1991–92		21	3
1992–93		17	—

PALMER, Steve

Born Brighton 31.3.68.   Ht 6 1   Wt 12 13
Midfield. From Cambridge University.

Season	Club		
1989–90	Ipswich T	5	—
1990–91		23	1
1991–92		23	—
1992–93		7	—

PAPE, Andy

Born London 22.3.62.   Ht 6 0   Wt 12 00
Goalkeeper. From QPR, Charlton Ath,
Enfield.

Season	Club		
1991–92	Barnet	36	—
1992–93		—	—

PARDEW, Alan

Born Wimbledon 18.7.61.   Ht 5 10
Wt 11 00
Midfield. From Yeovil.

Season	Club		
1986–87	Crystal Palace	—	—
1987–88		20	—
1988–89		45	1
1989–90		36	6
1990–91		19	1
1991–92		8	—
1991–92	Charlton Ath	24	2
1992–93		30	9

PARKER, Carl

Born Burnley 25.3.71.   Ht 6 0   Wt 12 00
Midfield. From Rossendale United.

Season	Club		
1991–92	Rochdale	6	1
1992–93		10	—

PARKER, Garry

Born Oxford 7.9.65.   Ht 5 11   Wt 12 05
Midfield. From Apprentice. England
Youth, B, Under-21.

1982–83	Luton T	1	—
1983–84		13	2
1984–85		20	1
1985–86		8	—
1985–86	Hull C	12	—
1986–87		38	—
1987–88		34	8
1987–88	Nottingham F	2	—
1988–89		22	7
1989–90		37	6
1990–91		36	3
1991–92		6	1
1991–92	Aston Villa	25	1
1992–93		37	9

PARKER, Paul

Born Essex 4.4.64.   Ht 5 7   Wt 10 13
Defender. From Apprentice. England
Youth, B, Under-21, 17 full caps.

1980–81	Fulham	1	—
1981–82		5	—
1982–83		16	—
1983–84		34	—
1984–85		36	—
1985–86		30	—
1986–87		31	2
1987–88	QPR	40	—
1988–89		36	—
1989–90		32	—
1990–91		17	1
1991–92	Manchester U	26	—
1992–93		31	1

PARKER, Richard

Born Wolverhampton 6.7.73   Ht 6 1
Wt 12 02
Forward. From Trainee.

| 1992–93 | Walsall | 1 | — |

PARKER, Sean

Born Newcastle 23.8.73.
Defender. From Trainee.

| 1991–92 | Northampton T | 6 | — |
| 1992–93 | | 4 | — |

PARKIN, Brian

Born Birkenhead 12.10.65.   Ht 6 1
Wt 12 00
Goalkeeper. From Local.

1982–83	Oldham Ath	—	—
1983–84		5	—
1984–85		1	—
1984–85	*Crewe Alex*	12	—
1985–86	Crewe Alex	39	—
1986–87		44	—
1987–88		3	—
1987–88	*Crystal Palace*	—	—
1988–89	Crystal Palace	19	—
1989–90		1	—
1989–90	Bristol R	30	—
1990–91		39	—
1991–92		43	—
1992–93		26	—

PARKIN, Steve

Born Mansfield 7.11.65.   Ht 5 6   Wt 11 07
Defender. From Apprentice. England
Schools, Youth, Under-21.

1982–83	Stoke C	2	—
1983–84		1	—
1984–85		13	1
1985–86		12	1
1986–87		38	—
1987–88		43	3
1988–89		4	—
1989–90	WBA	14	1
1990–91		25	1
1991–92		9	—
1992–93	Mansfield T	16	—

PARKIN, Tim

Born Penrith 31.12.57.   Ht 6 2   Wt 13 02
Defender. From Apprentice.

| 1976–77 | Blackburn R | 1 | — |

1977–78	....	—	—
1978–79	....	12	—
1979–80	....	—	—

From Malmo and Almondsbury Greenway

1981–82	Bristol R	40	2
1982–83	....	41	3
1983–84	....	39	2
1984–85	....	43	3
1985–86	....	43	2
1986–87	Swindon T	32	2
1987–88	....	40	2
1988–89	....	32	1
1989–90	....	6	1
1989–90	Port Vale....................	12	1
1990–91	....	29	—
1991–92	....	7	—
1991–92	*Shrewsbury T*	5	—
1992–93	Darlington	40	2

PARKINSON, Gary

Born Middlesbrough 10.1.68.   Ht 5 10
Wt 11 06
Defender. From Everton Amateur.

1985–86	Middlesbrough....................	—	—
1986–87	....	46	—
1987–88	....	38	—
1988–89	....	36	2
1989–90	....	41	2
1990–91	....	10	1
1991–92	,....................	27	—
1992–93	....	4	—
1992–93	*Southend U*	6	—
1992–93	Bolton W	2	—

PARKINSON, Joe

Born Eccles 11.6.71.   Ht 5 11   Wt 12 02
Defender. From Trainee.

1988–89	Wigan Ath	12	1
1989–90	....	33	2
1990–91	....	25	—
1991–92	....	36	3
1992–93	....	13	—

PARKINSON, Philip

Born Chorley 1.12.67.   Ht 6 0   Wt 11 06
Midfield. From Apprentice.

1985–86	Southampton	—	—
1986–87	....	—	—
1987–88	....	—	—
1987–88	Bury	8	1
1988–89	....	39	—
1989–90	....	22	2
1990–91	....	44	2
1991–92	....	32	—
1992–93	Reading....................	39	4

PARKINSON, Steve

Born Lincoln 27.8.74.   Ht 5 11   Wt 11 11
Midfield. From Trainee.

1992–93	Lincoln C....................	2	—

PARKS, Tony

Born Hackney 26.1.63.   Ht 5 11
Wt 10 08
Goalkeeper. From Apprentice.

1980–81	Tottenham H	—	—
1981–82	....	2	—
1982–83	....	1	—
1983–84	....	16	—
1984–85	....	—	—
1985–86	....	—	—
1986–87	....	2	—
1986–87	*Oxford U*	5	—
1987–88	Tottenham H	16	—
1987–88	*Gillingham*	2	—
1988–89	Brentford	33	—
1989–90	....	37	—
1990–91	....	1	—
1990–91	*QPR*	—	—
1990–91	Fulham	2	—
1991–92	West Ham U	6	—
1992–93	Stoke C	2	—
1992–93	Falkirk	15	—

PARLOUR, Ray

Born Romford 7.3.73.   Ht 5 10   Wt 11 12
Midfield. From Trainee. England
Under-21.

Season	Club		
1990–91	Arsenal	—	—
1991–92		6	1
1992–93		21	1

PARRIS, George

Born Ilford 11.9.64.   Ht 5 9   Wt 13 00
Defender. From Apprentice. England
Schools.

Season	Club		
1982–83	West Ham U	—	—
1983–84		—	—
1984–85		1	—
1985–86		26	1
1986–87		36	2
1987–88		30	1
1988–89		27	1
1989–90		38	2
1990–91		44	5
1991–92		21	—
1992–93		16	—
1992–93	Birmingham C	13	—

PARSLEY, Neil

Born Liverpool 25.4.66.   Ht 5 10
Wt 10 11
Defender. From Witton Alb.

Season	Club		
1988–89	Leeds U	—	—
1989–90		—	—
1989–90	*Chester C*	6	—
1990–91	Huddersfield T	8	—
1990–91	*Doncaster R*	3	—
1991–92	Huddersfield T	5	—
1992–93		44	—

PARSONS, Mark

Born Luton 24.2.75.
Defender.

Season	Club		
1991–92	Northampton T	13	—
1992–93		19	—

PARTNER, Andy

Born Colchester 21.10.74   Ht 6 1
Wt 12 10
Defender. From Trainee.

Season	Club		
1992–93	Colchester U	1	—

PARTRIDGE, Scott

Born Grimsby 13.10.74
Forward. From Trainee.

Season	Club		
1992–93	Bradford C	4	—

PASCOE, Colin

Born Port Talbot 9.4.65.   Ht 5 9
Wt 10 00
Forward. From Apprentice. Wales Youth,
Under-21, 10 full caps.

Season	Club		
1982–83	Swansea C	7	1
1983–84		32	2
1984–85		41	9
1985–86		19	3
1986–87		41	11
1987–88		34	13
1987–88	Sunderland	9	4
1988–89		39	10
1989–90		33	1
1990–91		25	5
1991–92		20	2
1992–93		—	—
1992–93	*Swansea C*	15	4

PASKIN, John

Born Capetown 1.2.62.   Ht 6 2   Wt 12 05
Forward. From Seiko.

Season	Club		
1988–89	WBA	25	5
1989–90	Wolverhampton W	17	2
1990–91		15	1
1991–92		2	—
1991–92	*Stockport Co*	5	1
1991–92	*Birmingham C*	10	3
1991–92	*Shrewsbury T*	1	—
1991–92	Wrexham	17	3
1992–93		19	8

PATERSON, Craig

Born South Queensferry 2.10.59 Ht 6 2
Wt 12 12
Defender. From Bonnyrigg Rose. Scotland
U-21.

Season	Club		
1978–79	Hibernian	—	—
1979–80		30	—
1980–81		38	3
1981–82		36	1
1982–83	Rangers	20	—
1983–84		21	1
1984–85		22	2
1985–86		18	1
1986–87		2	—
1986–87	Motherwell	16	—
1987–88		44	2
1988–89		33	1
1989–90		33	3
1990–91		32	2
1991–92	Kilmarnock	28	—
1992–93		21	1

PATERSON, Garry

Born Dunfermline 10.11.69 Ht 6 4
Wt 13 10
Midfield. From Lochore Welfare.

Season	Club		
1992–93	Dundee	20	2

PATES, Colin

Born Mitcham 10.8.61. Ht 6 0 Wt 13 00
Defender. From Apprentice. England
Youth.

Season	Club		
1979–80	Chelsea	16	—
1980–81		15	—
1981–82		42	1
1982–83		35	4
1983–84		42	—
1984–85		36	1
1985–86		35	1
1986–87		33	2
1987–88		17	—
1988–89		10	1
1988–89	Charlton Ath	21	—
1989–90		17	—
1989–90	Arsenal	2	—

Season	Club		
1990–91		1	—
1990–91	*Brighton*	17	—
1991–92	Arsenal	11	—
1992–93		7	—

PATMORE, Warren

Born Kingsbury 14.8.71
Midfield.

Season	Club		
1992–93	Cambridge U	1	—

PATTERSON, Jamie

Born Dumfries 26.4.73. Ht 5 5 Wt 9 07
Forward. From Trainee.

Season	Club		
1990–91	Halifax T	6	1
1991–92		15	2
1992–93		23	2

PATTERSON, Mark

Born Darwen 24.5.65. Ht 5 6 Wt 10 10
Forward. From Apprentice.

Season	Club		
1983–84	Blackburn R	29	7
1984–85		9	—
1985–86		26	10
1986–87		24	1
1987–88		13	2
1988–89	Preston NE	42	15
1989–90		13	4
1989–90	Bury	20	4
1990–91		22	6
1990–91	Bolton W	19	2
1991–92		36	2
1992–93		37	2

PATTERSON, Mark

Born Leeds 13.9.68. Ht 5 10 Wt 11 05
Defender. From Trainee.

Season	Club		
1986–87	Carlisle U	6	—
1987–88		16	—

Season	Club	App	Goals
1987–88	Derby Co	—	—
1988–89		1	—
1989–90		9	—
1990–91		11	1
1991–92		12	2
1992–93		18	—

PAYNE, Derek

Born Edgware 26.4.67. Ht 5 7 Wt 10 01
Midfield. From Kingsbury T, Burnham,
Hayes.

Season	Club	App	Goals
1991–92	Barnet	14	1
1992–93		37	5

PAYNE, Mark

Born Cheltenham 3.8.60 Ht 5 9
Wt 11 09
Midfield. From Cambuur.

Season	Club	App	Goals
1988–89	Stockport Co	22	1
1989–90		34	6
1990–91		31	9
1991–92	Rochdale	34	2
1992–93		28	6

PAYTON, Andy

Born Burnley 23.10.66. Ht 5 9 Wt 10 06
Midfield. From Apprentice.

Season	Club	App	Goals
1985–86	Hull C	—	—
1986–87		2	—
1987–88		22	2
1988–89		28	4
1989–90		39	17
1990–91		43	25
1991–92		10	7
1991–92	Middlesbrough	19	3
1992–93	Celtic	29	13

PEACOCK, Darren

Born Bristol 3.2.68. Ht 6 2 Wt 12 06
Defender. From Apprentice.

Season	Club	App	Goals
1984–85	Newport Co	—	—
1985–86		18	—
1986–87		5	—
1987–88		5	—
1988–89	Hereford U	8	—
1989–90		36	3
1990–91		15	1
1990–91	QPR	19	—
1991–92		39	1
1992–93		38	2

PEACOCK, Gavin

Born Kent 18.11.67. Ht 5 8 Wt 11 08
Midfield. England School, Youth. Football
League.

Season	Club	App	Goals
1984–85	QPR	—	—
1985–86		—	—
1986–87		12	1
1987–88		5	—
1987–88	Gillingham	26	2
1988–89		44	9
1989–90	Bournemouth	41	4
1990–91		15	4
1990–91	Newcastle U	27	7
1991–92		46	16
1992–93		32	12

PEAKE, Andy

Born Market Harborough 1.11.61.
Ht 5 10 Wt 12 00
Midfield. From Apprentice. England
Youth, Under-21.

Season	Club	App	Goals
1978–79	Leicester C	18	2
1979–80		25	3
1980–81		24	1
1981–82		31	2
1982–83		4	—
1983–84		24	4
1984–85		21	1
1985–86	Grimsby T	36	4
1986–87		3	—
1986–87	Charlton Ath	29	—

Season	Club	Appearances	Goals
1987–88		16	—
1988–89		31	1
1989–90		36	—
1990–91		45	4
1991–92		20	—
1991–92	Middlesbrough	23	—
1992–93		33	—

PEAKE, Jason

Born Leicester 29.9.71. Ht 5 9 Wt 11 05
Midfield. From Trainee. England Youth.

Season	Club	Appearances	Goals
1989–90	Leicester C	—	—
1990–91		8	1
1991–92		—	—
1991–92	*Hartlepool U*	6	1
1992–93	Halifax T	33	1

PEAKE, Trevor

Born Nuneaton 10.2.57. Ht 6 0
Wt 12 10
Defender. From Nuneaton Bor.

Season	Club	Appearances	Goals
1979–80	Lincoln C	45	1
1980–81		43	1
1981–82		37	4
1982–83		46	1
1983–84	Coventry C	33	3
1984–85		35	1
1985–86		37	1
1986–87		39	—
1987–88		31	—
1988–89		32	—
1989–90		33	—
1990–91		36	1
1991–92		2	—
1991–92	Luton T	38	—
1992–93		40	—

PEARCE, Andy

Born Bradford 20.4.66. Ht 6 4 Wt 13 00
Defender. From Halesowen.

Season	Club	Appearances	Goals
1990–91	Coventry C	11	1
1991–92		36	2
1992–93		24	1

PEARCE, Chris

Born Newport 7.8.61. Ht 6 0 Wt 11 04
Goalkeeper. From Wolverhampton W.
Apprentice. Wales Schools, Youth.

Season	Club	Appearances	Goals
1979–80	Blackburn R	—	—
1980–81	*Rochdale*	5	—
1981–82	*Barnsley*	—	—
1982–83	Rochdale	36	—
1983–84	Port Vale	7	—
1984–85		36	—
1985–86		5	—
1986–87	Wrexham	25	—
1987–88	Burnley	46	—
1988–89		39	—
1989–90		39	—
1990–91		43	—
1991–92		14	—
1992–93	Bradford C	9	—

PEARCE, Ian

Born Bury St Edmunds 7.5.74. Ht 6 1
Wt 12 04
Defender. From Schoolboy. England
Youth.

Season	Club	Appearances	Goals
1990–91	Chelsea	1	—
1991–92		2	—
1992–93		1	—

PEARCE, Stuart

Born London 24.4.62. Ht 5 10 Wt 12 09
Defender. From Wealdstone. England
Under-21, 53 full caps.

Season	Club	Appearances	Goals
1983–84	Coventry C	23	—
1984–85		28	4
1985–86	Nottingham F	30	1
1986–87		39	6
1987–88		34	5
1988–89		36	6
1989–90		34	5
1990–91		33	11
1991–92		30	5
1992–93		23	2

PEARCEY, Jason

Born Leamington Spa 2.7.71.   Ht 6 1
Wt 13 06
Goalkeeper. From Trainee.

1988–89	Mansfield T	1	—
1989–90		5	—
1990–91		4	—
1991–92		22	—
1992–93		33	—

PEARS, Steve

Born Brandon 22.1.62.   Ht 6 0   Wt 12 11
Goalkeeper. From Apprentice.

1978–79	Manchester U	—	—
1979–80		—	—
1980–81		—	—
1981–82		—	—
1982–83		—	—
1983–84		—	—
1983–84	*Middlesbrough*	12	—
1984–85	Manchester U	4	—
1985–86	Middlesbrough	38	—
1986–87		46	—
1987–88		43	—
1988–89		26	—
1989–90		25	—
1990–91		27	—
1991–92		45	—
1992–93		26	—

PEARSON, John

Born Sheffield 1.9.63.   Ht 6 3   Wt 13 00
Forward. From Apprentice. England
Youth.

1980–81	Sheffield W	15	4
1981–82		24	7
1982–83		30	7
1983–84		27	4
1984–85		9	2
1985–86	Charlton Ath	42	14
1986–87		19	1
1986–87	Leeds U	18	4
1987–88		28	6
1988–89		33	1
1989–90		7	—

1990–91		13	1
1990–91	*Rotherham U*	11	5
1991–92	Barnsley	10	1
1991–92	*Hull C*	15	—
1992–93	Barnsley	22	3

PEARSON, Nigel

Born Nottingham 21.8.63.   Ht 6 1
Wt 13 03
Defender. From Heanor T.

1981–82	Shrewsbury T	—	—
1982–83		39	1
1983–84		26	—
1984–85		—	—
1985–86		35	1
1986–87		42	3
1987–88		11	—
1987–88	Sheffield W	19	2
1988–89		37	2
1989–90		33	1
1990–91		39	6
1991–92		31	2
1992–93		16	1

PEEBLES, Gary

Born Johnstone 6.2.67.   Ht 6 0   Wt 11 00
Midfield. From Gleniffer Th.

1984–85	St Mirren	—	—
1985–86		—	—
1986–87		7	—
1987–88		1	—
1988–89		—	—
1988–89	Partick T	12	1
1989–90		24	1
1990–91		33	3
1991–92		2	—
1992–93		9	—

PEEL, Nathan

Born Blackburn 17.5.72.   Ht 6 1
Wt 12 07
Forward. From Trainee.

| 1990–91 | Preston NE | 10 | 1 |
| 1991–92 | Sheffield U | 1 | — |

Season	Club	App	Goals
1992–93		—	—
1992–93	*Halifax T*	3	—

PEER, Dean

Born Dudley 8.8.69. Ht 6 2 Wt 12 00
Midfield. From Trainee.

Season	Club	App	Goals
1986–87	Birmingham C	2	—
1987–88		—	—
1988–89		17	1
1989–90		27	3
1990–91		40	2
1991–92		21	1
1992–93		13	1
1992–93	*Mansfield T*	10	—

PEJIC, Mel

Born Chesterton 27.4.59. Ht 5 9
Wt 10 13
Defender. From Local.

Season	Club	App	Goals
1977–78	Stoke C	—	—
1978–79		—	—
1979–80		1	—
1980–81	Hereford U	13	—
1981–82		27	—
1982–83		45	1
1983–84		44	—
1984–85		46	1
1985–86		45	1
1986–87		31	—
1987–88		44	1
1988–89		18	3
1989–90		38	5
1990–91		46	1
1991–92		15	1
1991–92	Wrexham	7	—
1992–93		39	2

PEMBERTON, John

Born Oldham 18.11.64. Ht 5 11
Wt 12 03
Defender. From Chadderton.

Season	Club	App	Goals
1984–85	Rochdale	1	—
1984–85	Crewe Alex	6	—
1985–86		41	—

Season	Club	App	Goals
1986–87		43	—
1987–88		31	1
1987–88	Crystal Palace	2	—
1988–89		42	1
1989–90		34	1
1990–91	Sheffield U	21	—
1991–92		20	1
1992–93		19	—

PEMBRIDGE, Mark

Born Methyr Tydfil 29.11.70. Ht 5 7
Wt 11 01
Midfield. From Trainee. Wales B, Under-21, 7 full caps.

Season	Club	App	Goals
1989–90	Luton T	—	—
1990–91		18	1
1991–92		42	5
1992–93	Derby Co	42	8

PENDER, John

Born Luton 19.11.63. Ht 6 0 Wt 12 03
Defender. From Apprentice. Eire Youth, Under-21.

Season	Club	App	Goals
1981–82	Wolverhampton W	8	—
1982–83		39	1
1983–84		34	1
1984–85		36	1
1985–86	Charlton Ath	38	—
1986–87		1	—
1987–88		2	—
1987–88	Bristol C	28	2
1988–89		45	1
1989–90		10	—
1990–91		—	—
1990–91	Burnley	40	—
1991–92		39	3
1992–93		44	4

PENNEY, David

Born Wakefield 17.8.64. Ht 5 8
Wt 10 07
Forward. From Pontefract.

Season	Club	App	Goals
1985–86	Derby Co	—	—
1986–87		1	—

1987–88		9 —
1988–89		9 —
1989–90	Oxford U	29 2
1990–91		9 1
1990–91	*Swansea C*	12 3
1991–92	Oxford U	23 4
1992–93		33 6

PENNEY, Steve

Born Ballymena 16.1.64. Ht 5 8
Wt 10 07
Midfield. From Ballymena U. Northern
Ireland 17 full caps.

1983–84	Brighton	25 1
1984–85		26 4
1985–86		37 3
1986–87		27 3
1987–88		13 3
1988–89		10 1
1989–90		— —
1990–91		— —
1991–92	Hearts	9 —
1992–93	Burnley	11 3

PENNOCK, Adrian

Born Ipswich 27.3.71. Ht 5 11 Wt 12 01
Defender. From Trainee.

1989–90	Norwich C	1 —
1990–91		— —
1991–92		— —
1992–93	Bournemouth	43 1

PENNOCK, Tony

Born Swansea 10.4.71. Ht 5 11 Wt 10 09
Goalkeeper. From School.

1990–91	Stockport Co	— —
1990–91	*Wigan Ath*	2 —
1991–92	Wigan Ath	— —
1992–93		8 —

PENNYFATHER, Glenn

Born Billericay 11.2.63. Ht 5 8 Wt 11 05
Midfield. From Apprentice.

1980–81	Southend U	1 —

1981–82		33 4
1982–83		34 1
1983–84		33 4
1984–85		41 7
1985–86		41 7
1986–87		38 10
1987–88		17 3
1987–88	Crystal Palace	19 1
1988–89		15 —
1989–90		— —
1989–90	Ipswich T	8 1
1990–91		— —
1991–92		3 —
1992–93		4 —
1992–93	*Bristol C*	14 1

PENRICE, Gary

Born Bristol 23.3.64. Ht 5 8 Wt 10 06
Forward. From Bristol C. Apprentice.

1984–85	Bristol R	5 1
1985–86		39 5
1986–87		43 7
1987–88		46 18
1988–89		43 20
1989–90		12 3
1989–90	Watford	29 13
1990–91		14 5
1990–91	Aston Villa	12 —
1991–92		8 1
1991–92	QPR	19 3
1992–93		15 6

PEPPER, Nigel

Born Rotherham 25.4.68. Ht 5 10
Wt 11 05
Midfield. From Apprentice.

1985–86	Rotherham U	7 —
1986–87		2 —
1987–88		15 —
1988–89		2 —
1989–90		19 1
1990–91	York C	39 3
1991–92		35 4
1992–93		34 8

PERKINS, Chris

Born Nottingham 9.1.74   Ht 5 11
Wt 10 09
Defender. From Trainee.

1992–93	Mansfield T	5	—

PERRY, Jason

Born Newport 2.4.70.   Ht 5 11   Wt 10 04
Defender. Wales B, Under-21.

1986–87	Cardiff C	1	—
1987–88		3	—
1988–89		—	—
1989–90		36	—
1990–91		43	—
1991–92		36	—
1992–93		39	3

PERRY, Mark

Born Aberdeen 7.2.71   Ht 6 1   Wt 11 0
Defender. From Cove R.

1988–89	Dundee U	—	—
1989–90		—	—
1990–91		—	—
1991–92		—	—
1992–93		18	1

PESCHISOLIDO, Paul

Born Canada 25.5.71
Forward. From Toronto Blizzards.
Canada full caps.

1992–93	Birmingham C	19	7

PETERS, Mark

Born St Asaph 6.7.72   Ht 6 0   Wt 11 03
Defender. From Trainee. Wales Under-21.

1991–92	Manchester C	—	—
1992–93	Norwich C	—	—

PETERS, Rob

Born Kensington 18.5.71.   Ht 5 8
Wt 11 02
Defender. From Trainee.

1989–90	Brentford	2	—

1990–91		6	1
1991–92		9	—
1992–93		1	—

PETTERSON, Andrew

Born Fremantle 26.9.69   Ht 6 1   Wt 14 10
Goalkeeper.

1988–89	Luton T	—	—
1988–89	*Swindon T*	—	—
1989–90	Luton T	—	—
1990–91		—	—
1991–92		—	—
1991–92	*Ipswich T*	—	—
1992–93	Luton T	14	—
1992–93	*Ipswich T*	1	—

PEVERELL, Nick

Born Middlesbrough 28.4.73   Ht 5 11
Wt 11 10
Forward. From Trainee.

1991–92	Middlesbrough	—	—
1992–93	Hartlepool U	19	1

PEYTON, Gerry

Born Birmingham 20.5.56.   Ht 6 2
Wt 13 09
Goalkeeper. From Atherstone T. Eire
Under-21, 33 full caps.

1975–76	Burnley	20	—
1976–77		10	—
1976–77	Fulham	23	—
1977–78		42	—
1978–79		40	—
1979–80		31	—
1980–81		28	—
1981–82		44	—
1982–83		42	—
1983–84		27	—
1983–84	*Southend U*	10	—
1984–85	Fulham	32	—
1985–86		36	—
1986–87	Bournemouth	46	—
1987–88		42	—
1988–89		39	—

1989–90		39	—
1990–91		36	—
1991–92	Everton	—	—
1991–92	*Bolton W*	1	—
1991–92	*Norwich C*	—	—
1992–93	Everton	—	—
1992–93	*Brentford*	19	—
1992–93	*Chelsea*	1	—

PHELAN, Mike

Born Nelson 24.9.62. Ht 5 11 Wt 11 01
Defender. From Apprentice. England
Youth, 1 full cap.

1980–81	Burnley	16	2
1981–82		23	1
1982–83		42	3
1983–84		44	2
1984–85		43	1
1985–86	Norwich C	42	3
1986–87		40	4
1987–88		37	—
1988–89		37	2
1989–90	Manchester U	38	1
1990–91		33	1
1991–92		18	—
1992–93		11	—

PHELAN, Terry

Born Manchester 16.3.67. Ht 5 8
Wt 10 00
Defender. Eire Youth, B, Under-21,
Under-23, 15 full caps.

1984–85	Leeds U	—	—
1985–86		14	—
1986–87	Swansea C	45	—
1987–88	Wimbledon	30	—
1988–89		29	—
1989–90		34	—
1990–91		29	—
1991–92		37	1
1992–93		—	—
1992–93	Manchester C	37	—

PHILLIBEN, John

Born Stirling 14.3.64. Ht 5 10 Wt 11 00
Defender. From Gairdoch U. Scotland
Youth.

1980–81	Stirling A	15	—
1981–82		37	1
1982–83		34	—
1983–84		23	—
1983–84	Doncaster R	12	—
1984–85		36	1
1985–86		22	—
1985–86	*Cambridge U*	6	—
1986–87	Doncaster R	1	—
1986–87	Motherwell	37	—
1987–88		35	2
1988–89		19	—
1989–90		24	—
1990–91		11	1
1991–92		32	1
1992–93		31	—

PHILLIPS, David

Born Wegberg 29.7.63. Ht 5 10
Wt 11 02
Midfield. From Apprentice. Wales Under-
21, 46 full caps.

1981–82	Plymouth Arg	8	1
1982–83		23	8
1983–84		42	6
1984–85	Manchester C	42	12
1985–86		39	1
1986–87	Coventry C	39	4
1987–88		35	2
1988–89		26	2
1989–90	Norwich C	38	4
1990–91		38	4
1991–92		34	1
1992–93		42	9

PHILLIPS, Gary

Born St Albans 20.9.61. Ht 6 0 Wt 14 00
Goalkeeper. England Schools.

| 1979–80 | WBA | — | — |
| 1980–81 | | — | — |
| From Barnet |
| 1884–85 | Brentford | 21 | — |

Season	Club	Apps	Goals
1985–86	....	43	—
1986–87	....	44	—
1987–88	....	35	—
1988–89	....	—	—
1988–89	Reading.........................	24	—
1989–90	....	—	—
1989–90	Hereford U	6	—
1990–91	Barnet	—	—
1991–92	....	6	—
1992–93	....	42	—

PHILLIPS, Ian

Born Edinburgh 23.4.59 Ht 5 Wt 11 12
Defender. From Ipswich T apprentice.

Season	Club	Apps	Goals
1977–78	Mansfield T.................	18	—
1978–79	....	5	—
1979–80	Peterborough U...........	39	1
1980–81	....	41	—
1981–82	....	17	2
1982–83	Northampton T..........	42	1
1983–84	....	—	—
1983–84	Colchester U...............	43	5
1984–85	....	37	1
1985–86	....	37	2
1986–87	....	33	2
1987–88	Aldershot	32	—
1988–89	....	30	—
1989–90	....	44	2
From Kettering T			
1991–92	Colchester U...............	6	—
1992–93	....	1	—

PHILLIPS, Jimmy

Born Bolton 8.2.66. Ht 6 0 Wt 12 00
Defender. From Apprentice.

Season	Club	Apps	Goals
1983–84	Bolton W	1	—
1984–85	....	40	1
1985–86	....	33	1
1986–87	....	34	—
1986–87	Rangers........................	6	—
1987–88	....	19	—
1988–89	Oxford U	45	5
1989–90	....	34	3
1989–90	Middlesbrough.............	12	—
1990–91	....	44	2
1991–92	....	43	2

Season	Club	Apps	Goals
1992–93	....	40	2

PHILLIPS, Les

Born Lambeth 7.1.63. Ht 5 8 Wt 10 06
Midfield. From Apprentice.

Season	Club	Apps	Goals
1980–81	Birmingham C.............	—	—
1981–82	....	11	1
1982–83	....	13	2
1983–84	....	20	—
1983–84	Oxford U	6	—
1984–85	....	3	—
1985–86	....	28	2
1986–87	....	35	—
1987–88	....	30	4
1988–89	....	26	2
1989–90	....	8	—
1990–91	....	25	1
1991–92	....	7	—
1992–93	....	11	—

PHILLIPS, Martin

Born Exeter 13.3.76
Defender. From Trainee.

Season	Club	Apps	Goals
1992–93	Exeter C......................	6	—

PHILLIPS, Wayne

Born Bangor 15.12.70. Ht 5 10 Wt 11 00
Midfield. From Trainee.

Season	Club	Apps	Goals
1989–90	Wrexham	5	—
1990–91	....	28	—
1991–92	....	30	3
1992–93	....	15	—

PHILLISKIRK, Tony

Born Sunderland 10.2.65. Ht 6 1
Wt 12 02
Forward. From Amateur. England
Schools.

Season	Club	Apps	Goals
1983–84	Sheffield U	21	8
1984–85	....	23	2
1985–86	....	4	—
1986–87	....	6	1

Season	Club	Apps	Goals
1986–87	*Rotherham U*	6	1
1987–88	Sheffield U	26	9
1988–89	Oldham Ath	10	1
1988–89	Preston NE	14	6
1989–90	Bolton W	45	18
1990–91		43	19
1991–92		43	12
1992–93		10	2
1992–93	Peterborough U	32	11

PHILPOTT, Lee

Born Barnet 21.2.70. Ht 5 9   Wt 12 00
Forward. From Trainee.

Season	Club	Apps	Goals
1987–88	Peterborough U	1	—
1988–89		3	—
1989–90	Cambridge U	42	5
1990–91		45	5
1991–92		31	5
1992–93		16	2
1992–93	Leicester C	27	3

PICKARD, Owen

Born Barnstaple 18.11.69.   Ht 5 10
Wt 11 03
Forward. From Trainee.

Season	Club	Apps	Goals
1988–89	Plymouth Arg	2	—
1989–90		5	—
1990–91		7	1
1991–92		2	—
1992–93	Hereford U	37	9

PICKERING, Ally

Born Manchester 22.6.67.   Ht 5 11
Wt 11 01
Defender. From Buxton.

Season	Club	Apps	Goals
1989–90	Rotherham U	10	—
1990–91		1	—
1991–92		27	—
1992–93		38	1

PICKERING, Nick

Born Newcastle 4.8.63.   Ht 6 0   Wt 11 10
Midfield. From Apprentice. England
Youth, Under-21, 1 full cap.

Season	Club	Apps	Goals
1981–82	Sunderland	37	3

Season	Club	Apps	Goals
1982–83		39	7
1983–84		42	1
1984–85		37	2
1985–86		24	5
1985–86	Coventry C	15	4
1986–87		36	5
1987–88		27	—
1988–89	Derby Co	8	—
1989–90		23	3
1990–91		13	—
1991–92		1	—
1991–92	Darlington	29	5
1992–93		28	2
1992–93	Burnley	4	—

PIECHNIK, Torben

Born Copenhagen 21.5.63   Ht 6 0
Wt 12 04
Defender. From Copenhagen. Denmark
full caps.

Season	Club	Apps	Goals
1992–93	Liverpool	16	—

PIGGOTT, Gary

Born Warley 1.4.69.   Ht 5 11   Wt 12 02
Forward. From Dudley T.

Season	Club	Apps	Goals
1990–91	WBA	—	—
1991–92		5	—
1992–93		—	—
1992–93	Shrewsbury T	4	—

PIKE, Chris

Born Cardiff 19.10.61.   Ht 6 2   Wt 13 07
Forward. From Barry T.

Season	Club	Apps	Goals
1984–85	Fulham	—	—
1985–86		26	4
1986–87		13	—
1986–87	*Cardiff C*	6	2
1987–88	Fulham	3	—
1988–89		—	—
1989–90	Cardiff C	41	18
1990–91		39	14
1991–92		40	21
1992–93		28	12

PIKE, Martin

Born South Shields 21.10.64.   Ht 5 11
Wt 11 07
Defender. From Apprentice.

Season	Club		
1982–83	WBA	—	—
1983–84	Peterborough U	35	2
1984–85		45	4
1985–86		46	2
1986–87	Sheffield U	42	—
1987–88		39	—
1988–89		45	5
1989–90		3	—
1989–90	*Tranmere R*	2	—
1989–90	*Bolton W*	5	1
1989–90	Fulham	20	2
1990–91		46	3
1991–92		45	2
1992–93		46	6

PILLING, Andy

Born Wigan 30.6.69.   Ht 5 10   Wt 11 04
Midfield. From Trainee.

Season	Club		
1985–86	Preston NE	1	—
1986–87		—	—
1987–88	Wigan Ath	20	3
1988–89		39	2
1989–90		26	6
1990–91		13	3
1991–92		27	2
1992–93		31	4

PITCHER, Darren

Born London 12.10.69.   Ht 5 9   Wt 12 02
Defender. From Trainee.

Season	Club		
1987–88	Charlton Ath	—	—
1988–89		—	—
1988–89	*Galway*	—	—
1989–90	Charlton Ath	—	—
1990–91		44	3
1991–92		46	2
1992–93		41	2

PITTMAN, Stephen

Born N Carolina 18.7.67   Ht 5 10
Wt 12 5
Defender. From Broxburn J.

Season	Club		
1986–87	East Fife	11	—
1987–88		31	2
1988–89		25	8
1988–89	Shrewsbury T	12	—
1989–90		20	2
1990–91		—	
1991–92		—	
1992–93	Dundee	20	1

PLATNAUER, Nicky

Born Leicester 10.6.61.   Ht 5 11
Wt 12 10
Defender. From Northampton T Amateur
and Bedford T.

Season	Club		
1982–83	Bristol R	24	7
1983–84	Coventry C	34	6
1984–85		10	—
1984–85	Birmingham C	11	1
1985–86		17	1
1985–86	*Reading*	7	—
1986–87	Cardiff C	38	3
1987–88		38	1
1988–89		39	2
1989–90	Notts Co	44	—
1990–91		13	1
1990–91	*Port Vale*	14	—
1991–92	Leicester C	29	—
1992–93		6	—
1992–93	Scunthorpe U	14	2

PLATT, David

Born Chadderton 10.6.66.   Ht 5 10
Wt 11 12
Forward. From Chadderton. England B,
Under-21, 42 full caps.

Season	Club		
1984–85	Manchester U	—	—
1984–85	Crewe Alex	22	5
1985–86		43	8
1986–87		43	23
1987–88		26	19
1987–88	Aston Villa	11	5

Season	Club	Apps	Goals
1988–89		38	7
1989–90		37	19
1990–91		35	19
1991–92	Bari	29	11

To Juventus

POINTON, Neil

Born Church Warsop 28.11.64. Ht 5 10
Wt 11 00
Defender. From Apprentice.

Season	Club	Apps	Goals
1981–82	Scunthorpe U	5	—
1982–83		46	1
1983–84		45	1
1984–85		46	—
1985–86		17	—
1985–86	Everton	15	—
1986–87		12	1
1987–88		33	3
1988–89		23	—
1989–90		19	1
1990–91	Manchester C	35	1
1991–92		39	1
1992–93	Oldham Ath	34	3

POLLITT, Michael

Born Bolton 29.2.72 Ht 6 4 Wt 14 00
Goalkeeper. From Trainee.

Season	Club	Apps	Goals
1990–91	Manchester U	—	—
1990–91	*Oldham Ath*	—	—
1991–92	Bury	—	—
1992–93	Lincoln C	27	—

POLLOCK, Jamie

Born Stockton 16.2.74. Ht 6 0 Wt 11 12
Midfield. From Trainee. England Youth.

Season	Club	Apps	Goals
1990–91	Middlesbrough	1	—
1991–92		26	1
1992–93		22	1

POLSTON, John

Born London 10.6.68. Ht 5 11 Wt 11 03
Defender. From Apprentice. England
Youth.

Season	Club	Apps	Goals
1985–86	Tottenham H	—	—

Season	Club	Apps	Goals
1986–87		6	—
1987–88		2	—
1988–89		3	—
1989–90		13	1
1990–91	Norwich C	27	4
1991–92		19	1
1992–93		34	1

POOLE, Gary

Born Stratford 11.9.67. Ht 6 0 Wt 11 00
Defender. From Arsenal Schoolboys.

Season	Club	Apps	Goals
1984–85	Tottenham H	—	—
1985–86		—	—
1986–87		—	—
1987–88	Cambridge U	42	—
1988–89		1	—

To Barnet

Season	Club	Apps	Goals
1991–92	Barnet	40	2
1992–93	Plymouth Arg	39	5

POOLE, Kevin

Born Bromsgrove 21.7.63. Ht 5 10
Wt 12 06
Goalkeeper. From Apprentice.

Season	Club	Apps	Goals
1981–82	Aston Villa	—	—
1982–83		—	—
1983–84		—	—
1984–85		7	—
1984–85	*Northampton T*	3	—
1985–86	Aston Villa	11	—
1986–87		10	—
1987–88	Middlesbrough	1	—
1988–89		12	—
1989–90		21	—
1990–91		—	—
1990–91	*Hartlepool U*	12	—
1991–92	Leicester C	42	—
1992–93		19	—

PORTEOUS, Ian

Born Glasgow 21.11.64. Ht 5 7 Wt 10 6
Midfield. From Eastercraigs. Scotland
Youth.

Season	Club	Apps	Goals
1981–82	Aberdeen	—	—

Season	Club	App	Goals
1982–83		1	—
1983–84		14	3
1984–85		13	1
1985–86		6	—
1986–87		9	2
1987–88		3	1
1988–89		—	—
1988–89	*Swansea C*	—	—
From Herfolge FC, Denmark			
1990–91	Kilmarnock	—	—
1991–92		24	1
1992–93		20	6

PORTER, Andy

Born Manchester 17.9.68.   Ht 5 9
Wt 11 02
Midfield. From Trainee.

Season	Club	App	Goals
1986–87	Port Vale	1	—
1987–88		6	—
1988–89		14	1
1989–90		36	1
1990–91		40	1
1991–92		32	1
1992–93		17	1

PORTER, Gary

Born Sunderland 6.3.66.   Ht 5 6
Wt 10 06
Midfield. From Apprentice. England
Youth, Under-21.

Season	Club	App	Goals
1983–84	Watford	2	—
1984–85		9	—
1985–86		8	1
1986–87		26	4
1987–88		40	3
1988–89		42	10
1989–90		32	4
1990–91		45	4
1991–92		44	8
1992–93		33	—

POTTER, Graham

Born Solihull 20.5.75
Defender. From Trainee.

Season	Club	App	Goals
1992–93	Birmingham C	18	2

POTTS, Craig

Born Carlisle 25.2.74.   Ht 5 10   Wt 11 00
Defender. From Trainee.

Season	Club	App	Goals
1991–92	Carlisle U	6	—
1992–93		8	—

POTTS, Steven

Born Hartford (USA) 7.5.67.   Ht 5 7
Wt 10 11
Defender. From Apprentice. England
Youth.

Season	Club	App	Goals
1984–85	West Ham U	1	—
1985–86		1	—
1986–87		8	—
1987–88		8	—
1988–89		28	—
1989–90		32	—
1990–91		37	1
1991–92		34	—
1992–93		46	—

POUNDER, Tony

Born Yeovil 11.3.66.   Ht 5 8   Wt 11 00
Forward. From Westland Sports and
Weymouth.

Season	Club	App	Goals
1990–91	Bristol R	45	3
1991–92		40	4
1992–93		18	1

POWELL, Chris

Born Lambeth 8.9.69.   Ht 5 8   Wt 11 03
Defender.

Season	Club	App	Goals
1987–88	Crystal Palace	—	—
1988–89		3	—
1989–90		—	—
1989–90	*Aldershot*	11	—
1990–91	Southend U	45	1
1991–92		44	—
1992–93		42	2

POWELL, Darryl

Born Lambeth 15.1.71.   Ht 6 0   Wt 12 03
Forward. From Trainee.

Season	Club	App	Goals
1988–89	Portsmouth	3	—

Season	Club	App	Goals
1989–90		—	—
1990–91		8	—
1991–92		36	6
1992–93		23	—

POWELL, Gary

Born Holylake 2.4.69.   Ht 5 10   Wt 10 02
Forward. From Trainee.

Season	Club	App	Goals
1987–88	Everton	—	—
1988–89		—	—
1989–90		—	—
1990–91		—	—
1990–91	*Lincoln C*	11	—
1990–91	*Scunthorpe U*	4	1
1990–91	*Wigan Ath*	14	4
1991–92	Wigan Ath	34	7
1992–93		36	6

POWELL, Lee

Born Newport 2.6.73.   Ht 5 5   Wt 9 00
Forward. From Trainee. Wales Under-21.

Season	Club	App	Goals
1990–91	Southampton	—	—
1991–92		4	—
1992–93		2	—

POWER, Lee

Born Lewisham 30.6.72.   Ht 5 11
Wt 11 02
Forward. From Trainee. Eire Youth,
Under-21, B.

Season	Club	App	Goals
1989–90	Norwich C	1	—
1990–91		16	3
1991–92		4	1
1992–93		18	6
1992–93	*Charlton Ath*	5	—

PREECE, Andy

Born Evesham 27.3.67.   Ht 6 1   Wt 12 00
Midfield.

Season	Club	App	Goals
1988–89	Northampton T	1	—
From Worcester C.			
1989–90	Wrexham	7	1

Season	Club	App	Goals
1990–91		34	4
1991–92		10	2
1991–92	Stockport Co	25	13
1992–93		29	8

PREECE, David

Born Bridgnorth 28.5.63.   Ht 5 6
Wt 11 05
Midfield. From Apprentice. England B.

Season	Club	App	Goals
1980–81	Walsall	8	—
1981–82		8	—
1982–83		42	2
1983–84		41	3
1984–85		12	—
1984–85	Luton T	21	2
1985–86		41	2
1986–87		14	—
1987–88		13	—
1988–89		26	—
1989–90		32	1
1990–91		37	1
1991–92		38	3
1992–93		43	3

PREECE, Roger

Born Much Wenlock 9.6.69.   Ht 5 9
Wt 10 12
Midfield. From Coventry C Apprentice.

Season	Club	App	Goals
1986–87	Wrexham	7	2
1987–88		40	4
1988–89		31	5
1989–90		32	1
1990–91	Chester C	35	—
1991–92		29	—
1992–93		23	—

PRESSLEY, Steven

Born Elgin 11.10.73.   Ht 6 0   Wt 11 00
Defender. From Inverkeithling BC.
Scotland Under-21.

Season	Club	App	Goals
1991–92	Rangers	1	—
1992–93		8	—

PRESSMAN, Kevin

Born Fareham 6.11.67.   Ht 6 1   Wt 14 02
Goalkeeper. From Apprentice. England
Schools, Youth, Under-21.

Season	Club		
1985–86	Sheffield W	—	—
1986–87		—	—
1987–88		11	—
1988–89		9	—
1989–90		15	—
1990–91		23	—
1991–92		1	—
1991–92	*Stoke C*	4	—
1992–93	Sheffield W	3	—

PRESTON, Allan

Born Edinburgh 16.8.68.   Ht 5 10
Wt 10 01
Midfield. From Hutchison Vale BC.

Season	Club		
1985–86	Dundee U	—	—
1986–87		—	—
1987–88		2	—
1988–89		9	1
1989–90		8	—
1990–91		3	—
1991–92		2	—
1991–92		2	—
1992–93	Hearts	21	2

PRICE, Chris

Born Hereford 30.3.60.   Ht 5 7   Wt 10 02
Defender. From Apprentice. England
Youth.

Season	Club		
1976–77	Hereford U	2	—
1977–78		13	—
1978–79		29	—
1979–80		42	—
1980–81		42	2
1981–82		41	10
1982–83		42	5
1983–84		37	1
1984–85		41	5
1985–86		41	4
1986–87	Blackburn R	40	1
1987–88		43	10
1988–89	Aston Villa	36	—

Season	Club		
1989–90		34	1
1990–91		38	1
1991–92		2	—
1991–92	Blackburn R	13	3
1992–93		6	—
1992–93	Portsmouth	13	—

PRIMUS, Linvoy

Born Stratford 14.9.73   Ht 5 10   Wt 12 04
Defender. From Trainee.

Season	Club		
1992–93	Charlton Ath	4	—

PRINDIVILLE, Steve

Born Harlow 26.12.68.   Ht 5 9   Wt 11 07
Defender. From Apprentice.

Season	Club		
1986–87	Leicester C	—	—
1987–88		1	—
1988–89	Chesterfield	43	1
1989–90	Mansfield T	22	—
1990–91		6	—
1991–92	Doncaster R	16	—
1992–93		42	2

PRINS, Jason

Born Wisbech 1.11.74.
Midfield.

Season	Club		
1991–92	Carlisle U	4	—
1992–93		9	—

PRIOR, Spencer

Born Rochford 22.4.71.   Ht 6 1   Wt 12 09
Defender. From Trainee.

Season	Club		
1988–89	Southend U	14	1
1989–90		15	1
1990–91		19	—
1991–92		42	1
1992–93		45	—

PROCTOR, Mark

Born Middlesbrough 30.1.61.   Ht 5 10
Wt 11 13
Midfield. From Apprentice. England
Youth, Under-21.

Season	Club		
1978–79	Middlesbrough	33	9

Season	Club	App	Goals
1979–80		38	2
1980–81		38	1
1981–82	Nottingham F	37	1
1982–83		27	4
1982–83	*Sunderland*	5	—
1983–84	Sunderland	41	2
1984–85		17	2
1985–86		19	7
1986–87		31	8
1987–88		4	—
1987–88	Sheffield W	35	2
1988–89		24	2
1988–89	Middlesbrough	10	—
1989–90		45	4
1990–91		18	—
1991–92		36	2
1992–93		11	—
1992–93	*Tranmere R*	13	1

PROUDLOCK, Paul

Born Hartlepool 25.10.65.   Ht 5 10
Wt 11 00
Forward. From Local.

Season	Club	App	Goals
1984–85	Hartlepool U	14	—
1985–86		1	—
1986–87	Middlesbrough	3	1
1987–88		1	—
1988–89		1	—
1988–89	Carlisle U	10	3
1989–90		40	6
1990–91		45	7
1991–92		34	1
1992–93		26	3
1992–93	*Hartlepool U*	6	—

PRUDHOE, Mark

Born Washington 8.11.63.   Ht 6 0
Wt 13 00
Goalkeeper. From Apprentice.

Season	Club	App	Goals
1981–82	Sunderland	—	—
1982–83		7	—
1983–84		—	—
1983–84	*Hartlepool U*	3	—
1984–85	Sunderland	—	—
1984–85	Birmingham C	1	—
1985–86	Walsall	16	—

Season	Club	App	Goals
1986–87		10	—
1986–87	*Doncaster R*	5	—
1986–87	*Sheffield W*	—	—
1986–87	*Grimsby T*	8	—
1987–88	Walsall	—	—
1987–88	*Hartlepool U*	13	—
1987–88	*Bristol C*	3	—
1987–88	Carlisle U	22	—
1988–89		12	—
1988–89	Darlington	12	—
1989–90		34	—
1990–91		46	—
1991–92		46	—
1992–93		42	—

PUGH, David

Born Liverpool 19.9.64.   Ht 5 10
Wt 11 02
Midfield. From Runcorn.

Season	Club	App	Goals
1989–90	Chester C	35	3
1990–91		37	3
1991–92		35	—
1992–93		35	5

PUGH, Stephen

Born Bangor 27.11.73   Ht 5 10   Wt 11 00
Forward. From Trainee. Wales Under-21.

Season	Club	App	Goals
1992–93	Wrexham	3	—

PUTNEY, Trevor

Born Harold Hill 11.2.61.   Ht 5 9
Wt 11 08
Midfield. From Brentwood & W.

Season	Club	App	Goals
1980–81	Ipswich T	—	—
1981–82		—	—
1982–83		20	3
1983–84		35	2
1984–85		27	2
1985–86		21	1
1986–87	Norwich C	23	4
1987–88		26	1
1988–89		33	4
1989–90	Middlesbrough	25	—
1990–91		23	1

1991–92	Watford	28	2
1992–93		24	—

PUTTNAM, David

Born Leicester 3.2.67. Ht 5 10 Wt 11 09
Midfield. From Leicester U.

1988–89	Leicester C	3	—
1989–90		4	—
1989–90	Lincoln C	23	1
1990–91		43	6
1991–92		39	6
1992–93		37	2

QUIGLEY, Mike

Born Manchester 2.10.70. Ht 5 6
Wt 9 04
Midfield. From Trainee.

1990–91	Manchester C	—	—
1991–92		5	—
1992–93		5	—

QUINLAN, Paul

Born Madrid 17.4.71. Ht 5 7 Wt 10 02
Forward. From Trainee.

1989–90	Everton	—	—
1990–91		—	—
1990–91	*Huddersfield T*	8	2
1991–92	Everton	—	—
1992–93	Doncaster R	9	—

QUINN, James

Born Coventry 15.12.74
Forward. From Trainee.

1992–93	Birmingham C	4	—

QUINN, Jimmy

Born Belfast 18.11.59. Ht 6 0 Wt 12 07
Forward. From Oswestry T. Northern
Ireland 34 full caps.

1981–82	Swindon T	4	—
1982–83		13	3
1983–84		32	7
1984–85	Blackburn R	25	10
1985–86		31	4
1986–87		15	3
1986–87	Swindon T	22	9
1987–88		42	21
1988–89	Leicester C	31	6
1988–89	Bradford C	12	8
1989–90		23	6
1989–90	West Ham U	21	12
1990–91		26	6
1991–92	Bournemouth	43	19
1992–93	Reading	42	17

QUINN, Mick

Born Liverpool 2.5.62.   Ht 5 9   Wt 13 00
Forward. From Derby Co Apprentice.

1979–80	Wigan Ath	4	1
1980–81		36	14
1981–82		29	4
1982–83	Stockport Co	39	24
1983–84		24	15
1983–84	Oldham Ath	14	5
1984–85		40	18
1985–86		26	11
1985–86	Portsmouth	11	6
1986–87		39	22
1987–88		32	8
1988–89		39	18
1989–90	Newcastle U	45	32
1990–91		43	18
1991–92		22	7
1992–93		5	2
1992–93	Coventry C	26	17

QUINN, Niall

Born Dublin 6.10.66.   Ht 6 3   Wt 13 10
Forward. From Eire Youth, B, Under-21,
Under-23, 39 full caps.

1983–84	Arsenal	—	—
1984–85		—	—
1985–86		12	1
1986–87		35	8
1987–88		11	2
1988–89		3	1
1989–90		6	2
1989–90	Manchester C	9	4
1990–91		38	20
1991–92		35	12
1992–93		39	9

RADOSAVLJEVIC, Predrag

Born Belgrade 24.6.63   Ht 5 11   Wt 12 10
Forward. From St Louis Storms.

1992–93	Everton	23	3

RAE, Alex

Born Glasgow 30.9.69.   Ht 5 9   Wt 11 05
Midfield. From Bishopbriggs. Scotland
Under-21.

1987–88	Falkirk	12	—
1988–89		37	12
1989–90		34	8
1990–91	Millwall	39	10
1991–92		38	11
1992–93		30	6

RAESIDE, Robert

Born South Africa 7.7.72   Ht 6 0
Wt 11 10
Defender. St Andrews University.

1990–91	Raith R	14	—
1991–92		13	—
1992–93		10	—

RAMAGE, Craig

Born Derby 30.3.70.   Ht 5 9   Wt 11 08
Forward. From Trainee. England
Under-21.

1988–89	Derby Co	—	—
1988–89	*Wigan Ath*	10	2
1989–90	Derby Co	12	1
1990–91		17	1
1991–92		7	2
1992–93		1	—

RAMMELL, Andy

Born Nuneaton 10.2.67.   Ht 5 10
Wt 11 07
Forward. From Atherstone U.

1989–90	Manchester U	—	—

Season	Club			
1990–91	Barnsley	40	12	
1991–92		37	8	
1992–93		30	7	

RAMSEY, Paul

Born Londonderry 3.9.62. Ht 5 11
Wt 13 00
Defender. From Apprentice. Northern
Ireland 14 full caps.

1979–80	Leicester C	—	—
1980–81		3	—
1981–82		10	—
1982–83		40	1
1983–84		33	1
1984–85		39	—
1985–86		13	1
1986–87		29	6
1987–88		42	1
1988–89		22	—
1989–90		35	3
1990–91		24	—
1991–92	Cardiff C	39	3
1992–93		30	4

RANDALL, Adrian

Born Amesbury 10.11.68. Ht 5 11
Wt 10 11
Forward. From Apprentice. England
Youth.

1985–86	Bournemouth	2	—
1986–87		—	—
1987–88		1	—
1988–89		—	—
1988–89	Aldershot	37	2
1989–90		34	2
1990–91		36	8
1991–92		9	—
1991–92	Burnley	18	2
1992–93		23	1

RANKINE, Mark

Born Doncaster 30.9.69. Ht 5 10
Wt 11 01
Midfield. From Trainee.

1987–88	Doncaster R	18	2

1988–89		46	11
1989–90		36	2
1990–91		40	2
1991–92		24	3
1991–92	Wolverhampton W	15	1
1992–93		27	—

RANSON, Ray

Born St. Helens 12.6.60. Ht 5 9
Wt 11 12
Defender. From Apprentice. England
Schools, Youth, Under-21.

1978–79	Manchester C	8	—
1979–80		40	—
1980–81		33	1
1981–82		36	—
1982–83		40	—
1983–84		26	—
1984–85		—	—
1984–85	Birmingham C	28	—
1985–86		37	—
1986–87		17	—
1987–88		38	—
1988–89		17	—
1988–89	Newcastle U	14	1
1989–90		33	—
1990–91		27	—
1991–92		6	—
1992–93		3	—
1992–93	Manchester C	17	—

RATCLIFFE, Kevin

Born Mancot 12.11.60. Ht 5 11
Wt 12 07
Defender. From Apprentice. Wales
Schools, Youth, Under-21, 59 caps.

1978–79	Everton	—	—
1979–80		2	—
1980–81		21	—
1981–82		25	—
1982–83		29	1
1983–84		38	—
1984–85		40	—
1985–86		39	1
1986–87		42	—
1987–88		24	—

Season	Club	App	Goals
1988–89	....	30	—
1989–90	....	24	—
1990–91	....	36	—
1991–92	....	9	—
1992–93	Dundee....................	4	—
1992–93	Everton	—	—
1992–93	Cardiff C...................	19	1

RATCLIFFE, Simon

Born Davyhulme 8.2.67. Ht 5 11
Wt 11 09
Defender. From Apprentice. England
Schools, Youth.

Season	Club	App	Goals
1984–85	Manchester U.............	—	—
1985–86	....	—	—
1986–87	....	—	—
1987–88	Norwich C	9	—
1988–89	....	—	—
1988–89	Brentford	9	1
1989–90	....	35	2
1990–91	....	38	2
1991–92	....	34	2
1992–93	....	30	2

RAVEN, Paul

Born Salisbury 28.7.70. Ht 6 0 Wt 12 03
Defender. From School. England Schools,
Youth.

Season	Club	App	Goals
1987–88	Doncaster R................	17	3
1988–89	....	35	1
1988–89	WBA.........................	3	—
1989–90	....	7	—
1990–91	....	13	—
1991–92	....	7	1
1991–92	*Doncaster R*	7	—
1992–93	WBA.........................	44	7

RAYNES, Steven

Born Edinburgh 6.9.71. Ht 5 9 Wt 9 09
Midfield. From Hutcheson Vale BC.

Season	Club	App	Goals
1991–92	Hibernian...................	1	—
1992–93	....	2	—

RAYNOR, Paul

Born Nottingham 29.4.66. Ht 6 0
Wt 11 04
Forward. From Apprentice.

Season	Club	App	Goals
1983–84	Nottingham F.............	—	—
1984–85	....	3	—
1984–85	*Bristol R*......................	8	—
1985–86	Huddersfield T...........	30	5
1986–87	....	20	4
1986–87	Swansea C.................	12	1
1987–88	....	44	8
1988–89	....	26	5
1988–89	*Wrexham*.....................	6	—
1989–90	Swansea C.................	40	6
1990–91	....	43	5
1991–92	....	26	2
1991–92	Cambridge U..............	8	—
1992–93	....	41	2

READY, Karl

Born Neath 14.8.72. Ht 6 1 Wt 12 00
Defender. Wales Under-21.

Season	Club	App	Goals
1990–91	QPR...........................	—	—
1991–92	....	1	—
1992–93	....	3	—

REDDISH, Shane

Born Bolsover 5.5.71. Ht 5 10 Wt 11 10
Midfield. From Mansfield T Trainee and
Doncaster R Trainee.

Season	Club	App	Goals
1989–90	Doncaster R................	1	—
1990–91	....	11	—
1991–92	....	17	2
1992–93	....	31	1

REDFEARN, Neil

Born Dewsbury 20.6.65. Ht 5 10
Wt 12 09
Midfield. From Nottingham F Apprentice.

Season	Club	App	Goals
1982–83	Bolton W	10	—
1983–84	....	25	1
1983–84	*Lincoln C*	10	1
1984–85	Lincoln C...................	45	4

1985–86	....	45	8
1986–87	Doncaster R..............	46	14
1987–88	Crystal Palace	42	8
1988–89	....	15	2
1988–89	Watford	12	2
1989–90	....	12	1
1989–90	Oldham Ath..............	17	2
1990–91	....	45	14
1991–92	Barnsley	36	4
1992–93	....	46	3

REDFERN, David

Born Sheffield 8.11.62.   Ht 6 2   Wt 13 12
Goalkeeper. From School.

1981–82	Sheffield W..................	—	—
1982–83	....	—	—
1983–84	....	—	—
1984–85	....	—	—
1984–85	*Doncaster R*	—	—
1984–85	*Rochdale*......................	19	—
1985–86	Rochdale.....................	46	—
1986–87	....	22	—
1987–88	....	—	—
From Gainsborough T			
1989–90	Stockport Co	11	—
1990–91	....	24	—
1991–92	....	7	—
1992–93	....	6	—

REDFORD, Ian

Born Perth 5.4.60.   Ht 5 11   Wt 11 10
Midfield. From Errol Rovers. Scotland
Youth, Under-21.

1976–77	Dundee......................	1	—
1977–78	....	34	10
1978–79	....	37	15
1979–80	....	13	9
1979–80	Rangers.....................	13	—
1980–81	....	35	9
1981–82	....	32	2
1982–83	....	34	3
1983–84	....	32	4
1984–85	....	26	5
1985–86	Dundee U	30	4
1986–87	....	37	8
1987–88	....	25	6

1988–89	....	9	2
1988–89	Ipswich T	24	2
1989–90	....	18	2
1990–91	....	26	4
1991–92	St Johnstone	28	3
1992–93	....	16	2

REDKNAPP, Jamie

Born Barton on Sea 25.6.73.   Ht 6 0
Wt 12 00
Midfield. From Tottenham H Schoolboy,
Bournemouth Trainee. England Youth,
Under-21.

1989–90	Bournemouth..............	4	—
1990–91	....	9	—
1990–91	Liverpool	—	—
1991–92	....	6	1
1992–93	....	29	2

REDMOND, Steven

Born Liverpool 2.11.67.   Ht 5 11
Wt 12 13
Defender. From Apprentice. England
Youth, Under-21.

1984–85	Manchester C	—	—
1985–86	....	9	—
1986–87	....	30	2
1987–88	....	44	—
1988–89	....	46	1
1989–90	....	38	—
1990–91	....	37	3
1991–92	....	31	1
1992–93	Oldham Ath................	31	—

REDWOOD, Toby

Born Newton Abbot 7.10.73.
Defender. From Trainee.

| 1991–92 | Exeter C...................... | 1 | — |
| 1992–93 | .... | 6 | — |

REECE, Andy

Born Shrewsbury 5.9.62.   Ht 5 11
Wt 12 04
Midfield. From Walsall, Worcester C,
Willenhall.

Season	Club		
1987–88	Bristol R	40	1
1988–89		42	7
1989–90		43	2
1990–91		46	1
1991–92		42	4
1992–93		26	2
1992–93	*Walsall*	9	1

REECE, Paul

Born Nottingham 16.7.68.   Ht 5 11
Wt 12 07
Goalkeeper. From Kettering T.

Season	Club		
1988–89	Grimsby T	14	—
1989–90		15	—
1990–91		—	—
1991–92		25	—
1992–93	Doncaster R	1	—
1992–93	Oxford U	35	—

REED, John

Born Rotherham 27.8.72.   Ht 5 10
Wt 10 11
Forward. From Trainee.

Season	Club		
1990–91	Sheffield U	—	—
1990–91	*Scarborough*	14	6
1991–92	Sheffield U	1	—
1991–92	*Scarborough*	6	—
1992–93	Sheffield U	—	—
1992–93	*Darlington*	10	2

REES, Jason

Born Pontypridd 22.12.69.   Ht 5 5
Wt 9 10
Midfield. From Trainee. Wales Schools,
Youth, B, Under-21, 1 full cap.

Season	Club		
1988–89	Luton T	—	—
1989–90		14	—
1990–91		21	—

1991–92		5	—
1992–93		32	—

REES, Mel (Deceased)

Born Cardiff 25.1.67.   Ht 6 2   Wt 12 02
Goalkeeper. From Plymouth Arg
Schoolboy and Trainee. Wales Youth.

Season	Club		
1984–85	Cardiff C	1	—
1985–86		9	—
1986–87		21	—
1987–88	Watford	3	—
1988–89		—	—
1989–90		—	—
1989–90	*Crewe Alex*	6	—
1989–90	*Southampton*	—	—
1989–90	*Leyton Orient*	9	—
1990–91	Watford	—	—
1990–91	WBA	18	—
1991–92		—	—
1991–92	*Norwich C*	—	—
1991–92	Sheffield U	8	—
1992–93		—	—
1992–93	*Chesterfield*	—	—

REES, Tony

Born Merthyr Tydfil 1.8.64.   Ht 5 9
Wt 11 13
Forward. From Apprentice. Wales Youth,
Under-21, 1 full cap.

Season	Club		
1982–83	Aston Villa	—	—
1983–84	Birmingham C	25	2
1984–85		9	2
1985–86		8	2
1985–86	*Peterborough U*	5	2
1985–86	*Shrewsbury T*	2	—
1986–87	Birmingham C	30	4
1987–88		23	4
1987–88	Barnsley	14	2
1988–89		17	1
1989–90	Grimsby T	35	13
1990–91		36	10
1991–92		23	5
1992–93		31	5

REEVES, Alan

Born Birkenhead 19.11.67.   Ht 6 0
Wt 12 00.
Defender.

Season	Club	App	Goals
1988–89	Norwich C	—	—
1988–89	*Gillingham*	18	—
1989–90	Chester C	30	2
1990–91		10	—
1991–92	Rochdale	34	3
1992–93		41	3

REEVES, David

Born Birkenhead 19.11.67.   Ht 6 0
Wt 11 05
Forward. From Heswall.

Season	Club	App	Goals
1986–87	Sheffield W	—	—
1986–87	*Scunthorpe U*	4	2
1987–88	Sheffield W	—	—
1987–88	*Scunthorpe U*	6	4
1987–88	*Burnley*	16	8
1988–89	Sheffield W	17	2
1989–90	Bolton W	41	10
1990–91		44	10
1991–92		35	8
1992–93		14	1
1992–93	Notts Co	9	2

REGIS, Cyrille

Born French Guyana 9.2.58.   Ht 6 0
Wt 13 04
Forward. From Moseley, Hayes. England
Under-21, B, 5 full caps.

Season	Club	App	Goals
1977–78	WBA	34	10
1978–79		39	13
1979–80		26	8
1980–81		38	14
1981–82		37	17
1982–83		26	9
1983–84		30	10
1984–85		7	1
1984–85	Coventry C	31	5
1985–86		34	5
1986–87		40	12
1987–88		31	10
1988–89		34	7

Season	Club	App	Goals
1989–90		34	4
1990–91		34	4
1991–92	Aston Villa	39	11
1992–93		13	1

REGIS, Dave

Born Paddington 3.3.64.   Ht 6 1
Wt 13 08
Forward. From Barnet.

Season	Club	App	Goals
1990–91	Notts Co	37	15
1991–92		9	—
1991–92	Plymouth Arg	24	2
1992–93		7	2
1992–93	*Bournemouth*	6	2
1992–93	Stoke C	25	5

REID, Andrew

Born Manchester 4.7.62   Ht 6 0   Wt 13 01
Midfield. From Altrincham.

Season	Club	App	Goals
1992–93	Bury	29	—

REID, Brian

Born Paisley 15.6.70   Ht 6 2   Wt 11 12
Defender. From Renfrew Waverley.

Season	Club	App	Goals
1988–89	Morton	2	—
1989–90		36	1
1990–91		19	—
1990–91	Rangers	3	—
1991–92		—	—
1992–93		2	—

REID, Chris

Born Edinburgh 4.11.71.   Ht 5 11
Wt 11 06
Goalkeeper. From Hutcheson Vale BC.
Scotland Under-21.

Season	Club	App	Goals
1989–90	Hibernian	2	—
1990–91		1	—
1991–92		9	—
1992–93		14	—

REID, Nicky

Born Ormston 30.10.60.   Ht 5 10
Wt 12 00
Defender. From Apprentice. England
Under-21.

1978–79	Manchester C	8	—
1979–80		23	—
1980–81		37	—
1981–82		36	—
1982–83		25	—
1983–84		19	2
1984–85		32	—
1985–86		30	—
1986–87		7	—
1987–88	Blackburn R	44	1
1988–89		37	1
1989–90		42	4
1990–91		30	2
1991–92		21	1
1992–93		—	—
1992–93	*Bristol C*	4	—
1992–93	WBA	15	—

REID, Paul

Born Warley 19.1.68.   Ht 5 8   Wt 10 08
Forward. From Apprentice.

1985–86	Leicester C	—	—
1986–87		6	—
1987–88		26	5
1988–89		45	6
1989–90		40	8
1990–91		33	2
1991–92		12	—
1991–92	*Bradford C*	7	—
1992–93	Bradford C	44	6

REID, Peter

Born Huyton 20.6.56.   Ht 5 8   Wt 10 07
Midfield. From Apprentice. England
Under-21, 13 full caps.

1974–75	Bolton W	27	—
1975–76		42	2
1976–77		42	5
1977–78		38	9
1978–79		14	—

1979–80		17	3
1980–81		18	2
1981–82		12	1
1982–83		15	1
1982–83	Everton	7	—
1983–84		35	2
1984–85		36	2
1985–86		15	1
1986–87		16	1
1987–88		32	1
1988–89		18	1
1988–89	QPR	14	1
1989–90		15	—
1989–90	Manchester C	18	1
1990–91		30	—
1991–92		31	—
1992–93		20	—

REID, Shaun

Born Huyton 13.10.65.   Ht 5 8   Wt 11 10
Midfield. From Local.

1983–84	Rochdale	17	—
1984–85		21	1
1985–86		8	—
1985–86	*Preston NE*	3	—
1986–87	Rochdale	41	1
1987–88		28	—
1988–89		18	2
1988–89	York C	24	2
1989–90		25	4
1990–91		29	—
1991–92		28	1
1992–93	Rochdale	40	4

REID, Wesley

Born Lewisham 10.9.68.   Ht 5 8
Wt 11 03
Midfield. From Trainee.

1986–87	Arsenal	—	—
1987–88	Millwall	—	—
1988–89		1	—
1989–90		5	—
1990–91		—	—
1990–91	Bradford C	16	—
1991–92		19	3
1991–92	Airdrieonians	7	—

1992–93		25	—

REILLY, Mark

Born Bellshill 30.3.69   Ht 5 8   Wt 10 0
Defender. From Wishaw J.

1988–89	Motherwell	—	—
1989–90		4	—
1990–91		—	—
1991–92	Kilmarnock	19	—
1992–93		19	3

REINELT, Robert

Born Epping 11.3.74.   Ht 5 10   Wt 11 13
Forward. From Trainee.

1990–91	Aldershot	5	—
1991–92		*11*	—
1992–93	Gillingham	—	—

RENNIE, David

Born Edinburgh 29.8.64.   Ht 6 0
Wt 12 00
Defender. From Apprentice. Scotland
Youth.

1982–83	Leicester C	—	—
1983–84		15	—
1984–85		3	1
1985–86		3	—
1985–86	Leeds U	16	2
1986–87		24	—
1987–88		28	2
1988–89		33	1
1989–90	Bristol C	45	4
1990–91		32	2
1991–92		27	2
1991–92	Birmingham C	17	2
1992–93		18	2
1992–93	Coventry C	9	—

RENNIE, Paul

Born Nantwich 26.10.71.   Ht 5 9
Wt 11 04
Defender. From Trainee.

1989–90	Crewe Alex	2	—

1990–91	Stoke C	3	—
1991–92		1	—
1992–93		—	—

RETALLICK, Graham

Born Cambridge 8.2.70
Midfield.

1992–93	Peterborough U	5	—

RHODES, Andy

Born Doncaster 23.8.64.   Ht 6 1
Wt 13 06
Goalkeeper. From Apprentice.

1982–83	Barnsley	—	—
1983–84		31	—
1984–85		5	—
1985–86		—	—
1985–86	Doncaster R	30	—
1986–87		41	—
1987–88		35	—
1987–88	Oldham Ath	11	—
1988–89		27	—
1989–90		31	—
1990–91	Dunfermline Ath	35	—
1991–92		44	—
1992–93	St Johnstone	44	—

RICE, Brian

Born Glasgow 11.10.63.   Ht 6 0   Wt 12 04
Midfield. From Whitburn Central.
Scotland Youth, Under-21.

1980–81	Hibernian	1	—
1981–82		1	—
1982–83		22	2
1983–84		25	5
1984–85		35	4
1985–86	Nottingham F	19	3
1986–87		3	1
1986–87	*Grimbsy T*	4	—
1987–88		30	2
1988–89		20	1
1988–89	*WBA*	3	—
1989–90	Nottingham F	18	2
1990–91		1	—

1990–91	*Stoke C*	18 —
1991–92	Falkirk	16 1
1992–93		17 2

RICHARDS, Dean

Born Bradford 9.6.74.
Defender. From Trainee.

1991–92	Bradford C	7 1
1992–93		3 —

RICHARDS, Steve

Born Dundee 24.10.61. Ht 6 1 Wt 13 00
Defender. From Apprentice.

1979–80	Hull C	1 —
1980–81		25 1
1981–82		29 1
1982–83		3 —
From Gainsborough T.		
1984–85	York C	7 —
1985–86	Lincoln C	21 —
1985–86	Cambridge U	4 2
1986–87	Scarborough	— —
1987–88		42 5
1988–89		42 1
1989–90		35 4
1990–91		45 3
1991–92	Halifax T	25 —
1992–93	Doncaster R	38 3

RICHARDSON, Barry

Born Willington Key 5.8.69. Ht 6 0
Wt 12 00
Goalkeeper. From Trainee.

1987–88	Sunderland	— —
1988–89	Scunthorpe U	— —
1989–90	Scarborough	24 —
1990–91		6 —
1991–92	Northampton T	27 —
1992–93		42 —

RICHARDSON, Kevin

Born Newcastle 4.12.62. Ht 5 7
Wt 11 07
Midfield. From Apprentice.

1980–81	Everton	— —

1981–82		18 2
1982–83		29 3
1983–84		28 4
1984–85		15 4
1985–86		18 3
1986–87		1 —
1986–87	Watford	39 2
1987–88	Arsenal	29 4
1988–89		34 1
1989–90		33 —
From Real Sociedad		
1991–92	Aston Villa	42 6
1992–93		42 2

RICHARDSON, Lee

Born Halifax 12.3.69. Ht 5 11 Wt 11 00
Midfield.

1986–87	Halifax T	1 —
1987–88		30 1
1988–89		25 1
1988–89	Watford	9 —
1989–90		32 1
1990–91	Blackburn R	38 2
1991–92		24 1
1992–93		— —
1992–93	Aberdeen	29 2

RICHARDSON, Neil

Born Sunderland 3.3.68. Ht 5 11
Wt 13 02
Defender. From Brandon U.

1989–90	Rotherham U	2 —
1990–91		16 2
1991–92		18 2
1992–93		14 —

RICHARDSON, Nick

Born Halifax 11.4.67. Ht 6 0 Wt 12 07
Midfield. From Local.

1988–89	Halifax T	7 —
1989–90		27 6
1990–91		26 3
1991–92		41 8
1992–93	Cardiff C	39 4

RICHARDSON, Steve

Born Slough 11.2.62.   Ht 5 5   Wt 10 03
Defender. From Apprentice.

Season	Club	App	Goals
1979–80	Southampton	—	—
1980–81		—	—
1981–82		—	—
1982–83	Reading	40	1
1983–84		34	—
1984–85		43	—
1985–86		32	—
1986–87		37	1
1987–88		27	—
1988–89		39	—
1989–90		43	—
1990–91		32	—
1991–92		38	1
1992–93		15	—

RIDEOUT, Paul

Born Bournemouth 14.8.64.   Ht 5 11
Wt 12 01
Forward. From Apprentice. England
Schools, Youth, Under-21.

Season	Club	App	Goals
1980–81	Swindon T	16	4
1981–82		35	14
1982–83		44	20
1983–84	Aston Villa	25	5
1984–85		29	14
1985–86	Bari	28	6
1986–87		34	10
1987–88		37	7
1988–89	Southampton	24	6
1989–90		31	7
1990–91		16	6
1990–91	*Swindon T*	9	1
1991–92	Southampton	4	—
1991–92	Notts Co	11	3
1991–92	Rangers	11	1
1992–93		1	—
1992–93	Everton	24	3

RIDINGS, David

Born Farnworth 27.2.70
Forward.

Season	Club	App	Goals
1992–93	Halifax T	21	4

RIGBY, Tony

Born Ormskirk 10.8.72   Ht 5 10
Wt 12 01
Midfield. From Barrow.

Season	Club	App	Goals
1992–93	Bury	21	2

RIMMER, Neill

Born Liverpool 13.11.67.   Ht 5 6
Wt 10 03
Midfield. From Apprentice. England
Schools, Youth.

Season	Club	App	Goals
1984–85	Everton	1	—
1985–86	Ipswich T	2	—
1986–87		1	—
1987–88		19	3
1988–89	Wigan Ath	25	3
1989–90		38	1
1990–91		34	2
1991–92		9	—
1992–93		1	—

RIMMER, Stuart

Born Southport 12.10.64.   Ht 5 8
Wt 11 00
Forward. From Apprentice. England
Youth.

Season	Club	App	Goals
1981–82	Everton	2	—
1982–83		—	—
1983–84		1	—
1984–85		—	—
1984–85	Chester C	24	14
1985–86		18	16
1986–87		38	13
1987–88		34	24
1987–88	Watford	9	1
1988–89		1	—
1988–89	Notts Co	4	2
1988–89	Walsall	20	8
1989–90		41	10
1990–91		27	13
1990–91	Barnsley	15	1
1991–92	Chester C	44	13
1992–93		43	20

RIPLEY, Stuart

Born Middlesbrough 20.11.67. Ht 5 11
Wt 12 06
Forward. From Apprentice. England
Youth, Under-21.

Season	Club		
1984–85	Middlesbrough	1	—
1985–86		8	—
1985–86	*Bolton W*	5	1
1986–87	Middlesbrough	44	4
1987–88		43	8
1988–89		36	4
1989–90		39	1
1990–91		39	6
1991–92		39	3
1992–93	Blackburn R	40	7

RITCHIE, Andy

Born Manchester 28.11.60. Ht 5 10
Wt 11 11
Forward. From Apprentice. England
Schools, Youth, Under-21.

Season	Club		
1977–78	Manchester U	4	—
1978–79		17	10
1979–80		8	3
1980–81		4	—
1980–81	Brighton	26	5
1981–82		39	13
1982–83		24	5
1982–83	Leeds U	10	3
1983–84		38	7
1984–85		28	12
1985–86		29	11
1986–87		31	7
1987–88	Oldham Ath	36	19
1988–89		31	14
1989–90		38	15
1990–91		31	15
1991–92		14	3
1992–93		12	3

RITCHIE, Paul

Born St Andrews 25.1.69. Ht 5 11
Wt 12 00
Forward. From Kirkcaldy YMCA.

Season	Club		
1986–87	Dundee	—	—

Season	Club		
1987–88		—	—
1987–88	*Brechin C*	8	3
1988–89	Dundee	—	—
1988–89	*Brechin C*	18	7
1989–90	Brechin C	38	9
1990–91		38	14
1991–92		24	12
1991–92	Dundee	6	1
1992–93		19	3
1992–93	*Gillingham*	6	3

RIX, Graham

Born Doncaster 23.10.57. Ht 5 9
Wt 11 00
Forward. From Apprentice. England
Under-21, 17 full caps.

Season	Club		
1974–75	Arsenal	—	—
1975–76		—	—
1976–77		7	1
1977–78		39	2
1978–79		39	3
1979–80		38	4
1980–81		35	5
1981–82		39	9
1982–83		36	6
1983–84		34	4
1984–85		18	2
1985–86		38	3
1986–87		18	2
1987–88		10	—
1987–88	*Brentford*	6	—

From Caen, Le Havre

Season	Club		
1992–93	Dundee	14	2

ROBERTS, Andy

Born Dartford 20.3.74. Ht 5 10
Wt 13 00
Midfield. From Trainee.

Season	Club		
1991–92	Millwall	7	—
1992–93		45	—

ROBERTS, Darren

Born Birmingham 12.10.69 Ht 6 0
Wt 12 10
Forward. From Burton Alb.

Season	Club		
1991–92	Wolverhampton W	—	—

1992–93 21   5

ROBERTS, Iwan

Born Bangor 26.6.68. Ht 6 3 Wt 12 06
Forward. Wales Youth, 3 full caps.

Season	Club	App	Goals
1985–86	Watford	4	—
1986–87		3	1
1987–88		25	2
1988–89		22	6
1989–90		9	—
1990–91	Huddersfield T	44	13
1991–92		46	24
1992–93		37	9

ROBERTS, Jamie

Born Doncaster 11.4.74
Forward. From Trainee.

Season	Club	App	Goals
1992–93	Doncaster R	2	—

ROBERTS, Mark

Born Irvine 29.10.75 Ht 5 9 Wt 9 10
Forward. From Bellfield BC.

Season	Club	App	Goals
1991–92	Kilmarnock	1	—
1992–93		5	—

ROBERTS, Paul

Born London 27.4.62 Ht 5 9 Wt 11 13
Defender. From Apprentice.

Season	Club	App	Goals
1978–79	Millwall	2	—
1979–80		27	—
1980–81		45	—
1981–82		41	—
1982–83		31	—
1983–84		—	—
1983–84	Brentford	34	—
1984–85		28	—
1985–86	Swindon T	27	—
1986–87	Southend U	38	—
1987–88	Aldershot	39	—
1988–89	Exeter C	3	—
1988–89	Southend U	23	—
1989–90		31	—

From Fisher Ath

Season	Club	App	Goals
1991–92	Colchester U	*31*	*1*
1992–93		42	1

ROBERTS, Tony

Born Bangor 4.8.69. Ht 6 0
Goalkeeper. From Trainee. Wales Under-21, 1 full cap.

Season	Club	App	Goals
1987–88	QPR	1	—
1988–89		—	—
1989–90		5	—
1990–91		12	—
1991–92		1	—
1992–93		28	—

ROBERTSON, Alexander

Born Edinburgh 26.4.71. Ht 5 9
Wt 10 07
Midfield. From S Form. Scotland
Under-21.

Season	Club	App	Goals
1987–88	Rangers	—	—
1988–89		2	—
1989–90		1	—
1990–91		15	1
1991–92		6	—
1992–93		2	—

ROBERTSON, David

Born Aberdeen 17.10.68. Ht 5 11
Wt 11 00
Defender. From Deeside BC. Scotland
Under-21, 1 full cap.

Season	Club	App	Goals
1986–87	Aberdeen	34	—
1987–88		23	—
1988–89		23	—
1989–90		20	1
1990–91		35	1
1991–92	Rangers	42	1
1992–93		39	3

ROBERTSON, John

Born Edinburgh 2.10.64.   Ht 5 7
Wt 11 06
Forward. From Edina Hibs. Scotland B,
Under-21, 12 full caps.

1980–81	Hearts	—	—
1981–82		1	—
1982–83		23	19
1983–84		35	15
1984–85		33	8
1985–86		35	20
1986–87		37	16
1987–88		39	26
1987–88	Newcastle U	—	—
1988–89		12	—
1988–89	Hearts	15	4
1989–90		32	17
1990–91		31	12
1991–92		42	14
1992–93		42	11

ROBERTSON, John

Born Liverpool 8.1.74   Ht 6 2   Wt 13 02
Defender. From Trainee.

1992–93	Wigan Ath	24	1

ROBERTSON, Lee

Born Edinburgh 25.8.73.   Ht 5 7   Wt 9 06
Midfield. From Salvesen BC.

1990–91	Rangers	—	—
1991–92		1	—
1992–93		1	—

ROBERTSON, Paul

Born Stockport 5.2.72.   Ht 5 7   Wt 11 06
Defender. From York C Trainee.

1989–90	Stockport Co	9	—
1990–91		1	—
1991–92	Bury	5	—
1992–93		3	—

ROBINS, Mark

Born Ashton-under-Lyme. 22.12.69.
Ht 5 7   Wt 10 04
Forward. From Apprentice. England
Under-21.

1986–87	Manchester U	—	—
1987–88		—	—
1988–89		10	—
1989–90		17	7
1990–91		19	4
1991–92		2	—
1992–93	Norwich C	37	15

ROBINSON, David

Born Newcastle 27.11.69.   Ht 6 0
Wt 13 02
Forward. From Trainee.

1988–89	Newcastle U	1	—
1989–90		1	—
1990–91		3	—
1990–91	*Peterborough U*	7	3
1991–92	Newcastle U	3	—
1991–92	Reading	8	—
1992–93	Blackpool	14	2

ROBINSON, David

Born Cleveland 14.1.65.   Ht 6 0   Wt 13 00
Defender.

1983–84	Hartlepool U	7	—
1984–85		38	—
1985–86		21	1
1986–87	Halifax T	10	—
1987–88		32	—
1988–89		30	1
1989–90	Peterborough U	45	4
1990–91		6	2
1991–92		43	3
1992–93		1	—
1992–93	Notts Co	1	—

ROBINSON, Jamie

Born Liverpool 26.2.72   Ht 6 0   Wt 12 03
Defender. From Trainee.

1991–92	Liverpool	—	—

1992–93 Barnsley .... 8 —

ROBINSON, John

Born Bulawayo, Rhodesia 29.8.71.
Ht 5 10   Wt 11 05
Midfield. From Apprentice. Wales
Under-21.

1989–90	Brighton	5	—
1990–91		15	—
1991–92		36	6
1992–93		6	—
1992–93	Charlton Ath	15	2

ROBINSON, Les

Born Mansfield 1.3.67.   Ht 5 8   Wt 11 01
Defender. From Local.

1984–85	Mansfield T	6	—
1985–86		7	—
1986–87		2	—
1986–87	Stockport Co	30	1
1987–88		37	2
1987–88	Doncaster R	7	1
1988–89		43	3
1989–90		32	8
1989–90	Oxford U	1	—
1990–91		43	—
1991–92		27	—
1992–93		16	—

ROBINSON, Liam

Born Bradford 29.12.65.   Ht 5 7   Wt 11 05
Forward. From Nottingham F Schoolboy.

1983–84	Huddersfield T	5	1
1984–85		15	1
1985–86		1	—
1985–86	*Tranmere R*	4	3
1986–87	Bury	33	13
1987–88		43	19
1988–89		43	20
1989–90		45	17
1990–91		43	4
1991–92		41	10
1992–93		14	6

ROBINSON, Mark

Born Manchester 21.11.68.   Ht 5 9
Wt 11 08
Midfield. From Trainee.

1985–86	WBA	1	—
1986–87		1	—
1987–88	Barnsley	3	—
1988–89		18	2
1989–90		24	—
1990–91		22	1
1991–92		41	2
1992–93		29	1
1992–93	Newcastle U	9	—

ROBINSON, Phil

Born Stafford 6.1.67.   Ht 5 10   Wt 10 10
Midfield. From Apprentice.

1984–85	Aston Villa	—	—
1985–86		—	—
1986–87		3	1
1987–88	Wolverhampton W	41	5
1988–89		30	3
1989–90	Notts Co	46	2
1990–91		19	3
1990–91	Birmingham	9	—
1991–92	Notts Co	1	—
1992–93		—	—
1992–93	Huddersfield T	36	4

ROBINSON, Ronnie

Born Sunderland 22.10.66.   Ht 5 9
Wt 11 05
Defender.

1984–85	Ipswich T	—	—
From Vaux Breweries			
1985–86	Leeds U	16	—
1986–87		11	—
1986–87	Doncaster R	12	—
1987–88		37	1
1988–89		29	4
1988–89	WBA	1	—
1989–90	Rotherham U	43	1
1990–91		38	—
1991–92		5	1
1991–92	Peterborough U	27	—

1992–93		20 —

ROBSON, Bryan

Born Chester-le-Street 11.1.57. Ht 5 10
Wt 11 11
Midfield. From Apprentice. England
Schools, Youth, Under-21, B, 90 full caps.

1974–75	WBA	3	2
1975–76		16	1
1976–77		23	8
1977–78		35	3
1978–79		41	7
1979–80		34	8
1980–81		40	10
1981–82		5	—
1981–82	Manchester U	32	5
1982–83		33	10
1983–84		33	12
1984–85		33	9
1985–86		21	7
1986–87		30	7
1987–88		36	11
1988–89		34	4
1989–90		20	2
1990–91		17	1
1991–92		27	4
1992–93		14	1

ROBSON, Gary

Born Durham 6.7.65. Ht 5 7 Wt 10 12
Midfield. From Apprentice.

1982–83	WBA	2	—
1983–84		7	—
1984–85		11	—
1985–86		14	—
1986–87		5	1
1987–88		31	1
1988–89		38	8
1989–90		25	5
1990–91		31	2
1991–92		32	9
1992–93		22	2

ROBSON, Mark

Born Newham 22.5.69. Ht 5 7 Wt 10 05
Forward. From Trainee.

1986–87	Exeter C	26	7
1987–88	Tottenham H	—	—
1987–88	*Reading*	7	—
1988–89	Tottenham H	5	—
1989–90		3	—
1989–90	*Watford*	1	—
1989–90	*Plymouth Arg*	7	—
1990–91	Tottenham H	—	—
1991–92		—	—
1991–92	*Exeter C*	8	1
1992–93	West Ham U	44	8

ROBSON, Stewart

Born Billericay 6.11.64. Ht 5 11
Wt 12 04
Midfield. From Apprentice. England
Youth, Under-21.

1981–82	Arsenal	20	2
1982–83		31	2
1983–84		28	6
1984–85		40	2
1985–86		27	4
1986–87		5	—
1986–87	West Ham U	18	1
1987–88		37	2
1988–89		6	—
1989–90		7	1
1990–91		1	—
1990–91	*Coventry C*	4	—
1991–92	Coventry C	37	3
1992–93		15	—

ROCASTLE, David

Born Lewisham 2.5.67. Ht 5 9 Wt 11 12
Forward. From Apprentice. England
Under-21, B, 14 full caps.

1984–85	Arsenal	—	—
1985–86		16	1
1986–87		36	2
1987–88		40	7
1988–89		38	6
1989–90		33	2

Season	Club	App	Goals
1990–91		16	2
1991–92		39	4
1992–93	Leeds U	18	1

ROCHE, David

Born Newcastle 13.12.70. Ht 5 11
Wt 12 01
Defender. From Trainee.

Season	Club	App	Goals
1988–89	Newcastle U	2	—
1989–90		—	—
1990–91		8	—
1991–92		26	—
1992–93		—	—
1992–93	Peterborough U	4	—

RODDIE, Andrew

Born Glasgow 4.11.71. Ht 5 9 Wt 11 00
Midfield. S Form. Scotland Under-21.

Season	Club	App	Goals
1988–89	Aberdeen	—	—
1989–90		—	—
1990–91		—	—
1991–92		10	2
1992–93		11	2

RODGER, Graham

Born Glasgow 1.4.67. Ht 6 2 Wt 11 13
Defender. From Apprentice. England
Under-21.

Season	Club	App	Goals
1983–84	Wolverhampton W	1	—
1984–85	Coventry C	—	—
1985–86		10	—
1986–87		6	—
1987–88		12	1
1988–89		8	1
1989–90	Luton T	2	—
1990–91		14	2
1991–92		12	—
1991–92	Grimsby T	16	—
1992–93		30	7

RODGER, Simon

Born Shoreham 3.10.71. Ht 5 9
Wt 11 07
Defender. From Trainee.

Season	Club	App	Goals
1989–90	Crystal Palace	—	—

Season	Club	App	Goals
1990–91		—	—
1991–92		22	—
1992–93		23	2

RODGERSON, Ian

Born Hereford 9.4.66. Ht 5 10 Wt 10 07
Midfield. From Pegasus Juniors.

Season	Club	App	Goals
1984–85	Hereford U	—	—
1985–86		19	2
1986–87		44	1
1987–88		37	3
1988–89	Cardiff C	40	—
1989–90		45	4
1990–91		14	—
1990–91	Birmingham C	25	2
1991–92		39	9
1992–93		31	2

RODWELL, Tony

Born Southport 26.8.62. Ht 5 11
Wt 11 02
Forward. From Colne Dynamoes.

Season	Club	App	Goals
1990–91	Blackpool	45	7
1991–92		40	8
1992–93		20	1

ROEDER, Glenn

Born Woodford 13.12.55. Ht 6 2
Wt 13 09
Defender. From Apprentice. England B.

Season	Club	App	Goals
1974–75	Orient	6	—
1975–76		25	2
1976–77		42	2
1977–78		42	—
1978–79	QPR	27	4
1979–80		40	9
1980–81		39	2
1981–82		41	2
1982–83		9	—
1983–84		1	—
1983–84	Notts Co	4	—
1983–84	Newcastle U	23	—
1984–85		36	—
1985–86		42	6

Season	Club	App	Goals
1986–87		37	1
1987–88		37	1
1988–89		18	—
1989–90	Watford	45	1
1990–91		33	1
1991–92	Leyton Orient	8	—
1992–93	Gillingham	6	—

ROGAN, Anton

Born Belfast 25.3.66. Ht 5 11 Wt 12 06
Defender. From Distillery. Northern
Ireland, 17 full caps.

Season	Club	App	Goals
1986–87	Celtic	10	1
1987–88		33	1
1988–89		34	1
1989–90		18	—
1990–91		27	1
1991–92		5	—
1991–92	Sunderland	33	1
1992–93		13	—

ROGERS, Darren

Born Birmingham 9.4.71. Ht 5 10
Wt 11 02
Defender. From Trainee.

Season	Club	App	Goals
1988–89	WBA	—	—
1989–90		—	—
1990–91		4	—
1991–92		10	1
1992–93	Birmingham C	17	—

ROGERS, Lee

Born Doncaster 21.10.66. Ht 5 11
Wt 12 01
Defender. From Doncaster R.

Season	Club	App	Goals
1986–87	Chesterfield	36	—
1987–88		43	—
1988–89		24	—
1989–90		32	—
1990–91		34	—
1991–92		18	—
1992–93		35	1

ROGERS, Paul

Born Portsmouth 21.3.65. Ht 6 0
Wt 12 05
Midfield. From Sutton U.

Season	Club	App	Goals
1991–92	Sheffield U	13	—
1992–93		27	3

ROSARIO, Robert

Born Hammersmith 4.3.66. Ht 6 3
Wt 12 01
Forward. From Hillingdon Bor. England
Youth.

Season	Club	App	Goals
1983–84	Norwich C	8	1
1984–85		4	1
1985–86		8	2
1985–86	*Wolverhampton W*	2	1
1986–87	Norwich C	25	3
1987–88		14	2
1988–89		27	4
1989–90		31	5
1990–91		9	—
1990–91	Coventry C	2	—
1991–92		29	4
1992–93		28	4
1992–93	Nottingham F	10	1

ROSE, Kevin

Born Evesham 23.11.60. Ht 6 1
Wt 13 03
Goalkeeper. From Ledbury T.

Season	Club	App	Goals
1979–80	Lincoln C	—	—
1980–81		—	—
From Ledbury T			
1982–83	Hereford U	15	—
1983–84		46	—
1984–85		46	—
1985–86		46	—
1986–87		46	—
1987–88		46	—
1988–89		23	—
1989–90	Bolton W	6	—
1989–90	*Halifax T*	—	—
1989–90	*Carlisle U*	11	—
1990–91	Bolton W	—	—
1990–91	*Rochdale*	3	—

Season	Club	App	Goals
1991–92	Bolton W	4	—
1991–92	*Rochdale*	28	—
1992–93	Rochdale	40	—

ROSENIOR, Leroy

Born London 24.3.64. Ht 6 1 Wt 11 10
Forward. From School. England Schools.

Season	Club	App	Goals
1982–83	Fulham	1	—
1983–84		23	8
1984–85		30	8
1985–86	QPR	18	3
1986–87		20	4
1987–88	Fulham	34	20
1987–88	West Ham U	9	5
1988–89		28	7
1989–90		5	2
1990–91		2	—
1990–91	*Fulham*	11	3
1991–92	West Ham U	9	1
1991–92	*Charlton Ath*	3	—
1991–92	Bristol C	8	5
1992–93		38	7

ROSENTHAL, Ronny

Born Haifa 11.10.63. Ht 5 11 Wt 12 00
Forward. From Maccabi Haifa, FC
Brugge, Standard Liege. Israel full caps.

Season	Club	App	Goals
1989–90	*Luton T*	—	—
1989–90	*Liverpool*	8	7
1990–91	Liverpool	16	5
1991–92		20	3
1992–93		27	6

ROSTRON, Wilf

Born Sunderland 29.9.56. Ht 5 6
Wt 11 01
Defender. England Schools. From
Apprentice.

Season	Club	App	Goals
1973–74	Arsenal	—	—
1974–75		6	2
1975–76		5	—
1976–77		6	—
1977–78	Sunderland	34	6
1978–79		34	11

Season	Club	App	Goals
1979–80		8	—
1979–80	Watford	31	3
1980–81		27	1
1981–82		27	2
1982–83		42	3
1983–84		39	4
1984–85		38	3
1985–86		30	5
1986–87		39	1
1987–88		37	
1988–89		7	—
1988–89	Sheffield W	7	—
1989–90	Sheffield U	26	3
1990–91		10	
1990–91	Brentford	22	2
1991–92		18	
1992–93		2	

ROUND, Steve

Born Buxton 9.11.70. Ht 5 10 Wt 11 00
Defender. From Trainee.

Season	Club	App	Goals
1990–91	Derby Co	—	—
1991–92		3	—
1992–93		6	—

ROWBOTHAM, Darren

Born Cardiff 22.10.66. Ht 5 10 Wt 11 05
Midfield. From Trainee.

Season	Club	App	Goals
1984–85	Plymouth Arg	7	—
1985–86		14	1
1986–87		16	1
1987–88		9	—
1987–88	Exeter C	23	2
1988–89		45	20
1989–90		32	21
1990–91		13	3
1991–92		5	1
1991–92	Torquay U	14	3
1991–92	Birmingham C	22	4
1992–93		14	2
1992–93	*Hereford U*	8	2
1992–93	*Mansfield T*	4	—

ROWBOTHAM, Jason

Born Cardiff 3.1.69   Ht 5 9   Wt 11 00
Midfield. From Trainee.

Season	Club		
1987–88	Plymouth Arg	4	—
1988–89		5	—
1989–90		—	—
1990–91		—	—
1991–92	Shrewsbury T	—	—
1992–93	Hereford U	5	1

ROWE, Brian

Born Sunderland 24.10.71.   Ht 5 9
Wt 10 12
Midfield. From Trainee.

Season	Club		
1990–91	Doncaster R	4	—
1991–92		25	—
1992–93		25	1

ROWETT, Gary

Born Bromsgrove 6.3.74.   Ht 6 0
Wt 12 10
Forward. From Trainee.

Season	Club		
1991–92	Cambridge U	13	2
1992–93		21	2

ROWLAND, Keith

Born Portadown 1.9.71.   Ht 5 10
Wt 10 00
Midfield. From Trainee.

Season	Club		
1990–91	Bournemouth	—	—
1991–92		37	—
1992–93		35	2
1992–93	*Coventry C*	2	—

ROYCE, Simon

Born Forest Gate 9.9.71.   Ht 6 2
Wt 11 07
Goalkeeper. From Heybridge Swifts.

Season	Club		
1991–92	Southend U	1	—
1992–93		3	—

RUDDOCK, Neil

Born London 9.5.68.   Ht 6 2   Wt 12 06
Defender. From Apprentice. England
Youth, Under-21.

Season	Club		
1985–86	Millwall	—	—
1985–86	Tottenham H	—	—
1986–87		4	—
1987–88		5	—
1988–89	Millwall	2	1
1988–89	Southampton	13	3
1989–90		29	3
1990–91		35	3
1991–92		30	—
1992–93	Tottenham H	38	3

RUSH, David

Born Sunderland 15.5.71.   Ht 5 11
Wt 10 10
Forward. From Trainee.

Season	Club		
1989–90	Sunderland	—	—
1990–91		11	2
1991–92		25	4
1991–92	*Hartlepool U*	8	2
1992–93	Sunderland	18	6

RUSH, Ian

Born St. Asaph 20.10.61.   Ht 6 0
Wt 12 06
Forward. From Apprentice. Wales
Schools, Under-21, 60 full caps.

Season	Club		
1978–79	Chester	1	—
1979–80		33	14
1979–80	Liverpool	—	—
1980–81		7	—
1981–82		32	17
1982–83		34	24
1983–84		41	32
1984–85		28	14
1985–86		40	22
1986–87		42	30
1987–88	Juventus	29	7
1988–89	Liverpool	24	7
1989–90		36	18
1990–91		37	16
1991–92		18	4

Season	Club	App	Goals
1992–93		32	14

RUSH, Matthew

Born Dalston 6.8.71.   Ht 5 11   Wt 12 10
Midfield. From Trainee. Eire Under-21.

Season	Club	App	Goals
1990–91	West Ham U	5	—
1991–92		10	2
1992–93		—	—
1992–93	*Cambridge U*	10	—

RUSSELL, Kevin

Born Portsmouth 6.12.66.   Ht 5 8
Wt 10 12
Forward. From Brighton Apprentice.
England Youth.

Season	Club	App	Goals
1984–85	Portsmouth	—	—
1985–86		1	—
1986–87		3	1
1987–88	Wrexham	38	21
1988–89		46	22
1989–90	Leicester C	10	—
1990–91		13	5
1990–91	*Peterborough U*	7	3
1990–91	*Cardiff C*	3	—
1991–92	Leicester C	20	5
1991–92	*Hereford U*	3	1
1991–92	*Stoke C*	5	1
1992–93	Stoke C	40	5

RUSSELL, Lee

Born Southampton 3.9.69.   Ht 5 11
Wt 11 04
Defender. From Trainee.

Season	Club	App	Goals
1988–89	Portsmouth	2	—
1989–90		3	—
1990–91		19	1
1991–92		9	—
1992–93		14	—

RYAN, Darren

Born Oswestry 3.7.72.   Ht 5 9   Wt 11 00
Midfield. From Trainee.

Season	Club	App	Goals
1990–91	Shrewsbury T	2	—

Season	Club	App	Goals
1991–92		2	—
1992–93	Chester C	17	2
1992–93	Stockport Co	4	—

RYAN, John

Born Ashton 18.2.62.   Ht 5 10   Wt 11 07
Defender. From Apprentice. England
Under-21.

Season	Club	App	Goals
1979–80	Oldham Ath	—	—
1980–81		—	—
1981–82		37	—
1982–83		40	8
1983–84	Newcastle U	22	1
1984–85		6	—
1984–85	Sheffield W	8	1
1985–86	Oldham Ath	22	—
1986–87		1	—
1987–88		—	—
1987–88	Mansfield T	32	1
1988–89		30	—
1989–90	Chesterfield	43	4
1990–91		39	2
1991–92	Rochdale	32	2
1992–93		26	—

RYAN, Tim

Born Stockport 10.12.74
Defender. From Trainee.

Season	Club	App	Goals
1992–93	Scunthorpe U	1	—

RYAN, Vaughan

Born Westminster 2.9.68.   Ht 5 8
Wt 10 12
Midfield.

Season	Club	App	Goals
1986–87	Wimbledon	1	—
1987–88		22	1
1988–89		5	—
1988–89	*Sheffield U*	3	—
1989–90	Wimbledon	31	—
1990–91		2	—
1991–92		21	2
1992–93	Leyton Orient	20	—

RYDER, Stuart

Born Sutton Coldfield 6.11.73   Ht 6 0
Wt 12 01
Defender. From Trainee.

1992–93	Walsall	22	—

SAGE, Mel

Born Gillingham 24.3.64.   Ht 5 8
Wt 10 04
Defender. From Apprentice.

1981–82	Gillingham	1	—
1982–83		9	—
1983–84		40	2
1984–85		36	1
1985–86		46	2
1986–87	Derby Co	26	2
1987–88		13	—
1988–89		16	1
1989–90		34	—
1990–91		34	1
1991–92		17	—
1992–93		—	—

SALAKO, John

Born Nigeria, 11.2.69.   Ht 5 9   Wt 11 00
Forward. From Trainee. England 5 full caps.

1986–87	Crystal Palace	4	—
1987–88		31	—
1988–89		28	—
1989–90		17	2
1989–90	*Swansea C*	13	3
1990–91	Crystal Palace	35	6
1991–92		10	2
1992–93		13	—

SALE, Mark

Born Burton-on-Trent 27.2.72.   Ht 6 5
Wt 13 08
Forward. From Trainee.

1989–90	Stoke C	2	—
1990–91	—		—
1991–92	Cambridge U	—	—
1991–92	Birmingham C	6	—
1992–93		15	—
1992–93	*Torquay U*	11	2

SALMAN, Danis

Born Cyprus 12.3.60.   Ht 5 10   Wt 12 02
Defender. From Apprentice. England
Youth.

1975–76	Brentford	6	—
1976–77		18	1
1977–78		37	—
1978–79		40	1
1979–80		41	3
1980–81		38	—
1981–82		40	—
1982–83		1	—
1983–84		21	—
1984–85		43	3
1985–86		40	—
1986–87	Millwall	31	2
1987–88		36	1
1988–89		19	1
1989–90		7	—
1989–90	Plymouth Arg	11	—
1990–91		35	3
1991–92		28	1
1991–92	*Peterborough U*	1	—
1992–93	Torquay U	20	—

SALMON, Mike

Born Leyland 14.7.64.   Ht 6 2   Wt 13 00
Goalkeeper. From Local.

1981–82	Blackburn R	1	—
1982–83		—	—
1982–83	*Chester C*	16	—
1983–84	Stockport Co	46	—
1984–85		46	—
1985–86		26	—
1986–87	Bolton W	26	—
1986–87	*Wrexham*	17	—
1987–88	Wrexham	40	—
1988–89		43	—
1989–90	Charlton Ath	—	—
1990–91		7	—
1991–92		—	—
1992–93		19	—

SALTON, Darren

Born Edinburgh 16.3.72.   Ht 6 2
Wt 13 00
Forward. From Trainee. Scotland Schools,
Youth, Under-21.

1988–89	Luton T	—	—
1989–90		—	—
1990–91		—	—
1991–92		3	—
1992–93		15	—

SAMPSON, Ian

Born Wakefield 14.11.68.   Ht 6 2
Wt 12 08
Defender. From Goole T.

1990–91	Sunderland	—	—
1991–92		8	—
1992–93		5	1

SAMWAYS, Mark

Born Doncaster 11.11.68.   Ht 6 2
Wt 13 10
Goalkeeper. From Trainee.

1987–88	Doncaster R	11	—
1988–89		12	—
1989–90		46	—
1990–91		26	—
1991–92		26	—
1991–92	*Scunthorpe U*	8	—
1992–93	Scunthorpe U	31	—

SAMWAYS, Vinny

Born Bethnal Green 27.10.68.   Ht 5 8
Wt 11 00
Midfield. From Apprentice. England
Youth, Under-21.

1985–86	Tottenham H	—	—
1986–87		2	—
1987–88		26	—
1988–89		19	3
1989–90		23	3
1990–91		23	1
1991–92		27	1

Season	Club	App	Goals
1992–93		34	—

SANCHEZ, Lawrie

Born Lambeth 22.10.59.   Ht 5 11
Wt 12 00
Midfield. From Thatcham. Northern
Ireland 3 caps.

Season	Club	App	Goals
1977–78	Reading	8	1
1978–79		39	4
1979–80		46	5
1980–81		37	2
1981–82		35	3
1982–83		37	1
1983–84		45	10
1984–85		15	2
1984–85	Wimbledon	20	5
1985–86		42	9
1986–87		29	—
1987–88		38	4
1988–89		36	5
1989–90		18	1
1990–91		29	—
1991–92		16	3
1992–93		27	4

SANDEMAN, Bradley

Born Northampton 24.2.70.   Ht 5 10
Wt 10 08
Midfield. From Trainee.

Season	Club	App	Goals
1987–88	Northampton T	2	—
1988–89		22	2
1989–90		29	1
1990–91		5	—
1990–91	Maidstone U	20	1
1991–92		37	7
1992–93	Port Vale	22	1

SANDFORD, Lee

Born Basingstoke 22.4.68.   Ht 6 1
Wt 12 02
Defender. From Apprentice. England
Youth.

Season	Club	App	Goals
1985–86	Portsmouth	7	—
1986–87		—	—
1987–88		21	1
1988–89		31	—
1989–90		13	—
1989–90	Stoke C	23	2
1990–91		32	2
1991–92		38	—
1992–93		42	2

SANDISON, James

Born Edinburgh 22.6.65.   Ht 6 0
Wt 11 02
Defender. From Edinburgh Emmet.

Season	Club	App	Goals
1983–84	Hearts	—	—
1984–85		3	—
1985–86		3	—
1986–87		13	—
1987–88		2	—
1988–89		14	—
1989–90		12	2
1990–91		25	1
1991–92	Airdrieonians	40	—
1992–93		38	—

SANSOM, Kenny

Born Camberwell 26.9.58.   Ht 5 7
Wt 10 04
Defender. From Apprentice. England
Schools, Youth, Under-21, B, 86 full caps.
Football League.

Season	Club	App	Goals
1974–75	Crystal Palace	1	—
1975–76		6	—
1976–77		46	—
1977–78		41	2
1978–79		42	—
1979–80		36	1
1980–81	Arsenal	42	3
1981–82		42	—
1982–83		40	—
1983–84		40	1
1984–85		39	1
1985–86		42	—
1986–87		35	—
1987–88		34	1
1988–89		—	—
1988–89	Newcastle U	20	—
1989–90	QPR	36	—

Season	Club	App	Goals
1990–91	....	28	—
1990–91	Coventry C	9	—
1991–92	....	21	—
1992–93	....	21	—
1992–93	Everton	7	1
1992–93	Brentford	8	—

SANSOME, Paul

Born N. Addington 6.10.61.   Ht 6 0
Wt 13 07
Goalkeeper. From Crystal Palace
Apprentice.

Season	Club	App	Goals
1979–80	Millwall	—	—
1980–81	....	—	—
1981–82	....	8	—
1982–83	....	24	—
1983–84	....	31	—
1984–85	....	46	—
1985–86	....	36	—
1986–87	....	10	—
1987–88	....	1	—
1987–88	Southend U	6	—
1988–89	....	44	—
1989–90	....	46	—
1990–91	....	46	—
1991–92	....	45	—
1992–93	....	43	—

SAUNDERS, Carl

Born Marston Green 26.11.64.   Ht 5 8
Wt 11 02
Forward. From Local.

Season	Club	App	Goals
1982–83	Stoke C	1	—
1983–84	....	—	—
1984–85	....	23	2
1985–86	....	37	2
1986–87	....	31	13
1987–88	....	17	3
1988–89	....	33	2
1989–90	....	22	1
1989–90	Bristol R	20	5
1990–91	....	38	16
1991–92	....	36	10
1992–93	....	41	11

SAUNDERS, Dean

Born Swansea 21.6.64.   Ht 5 8   Wt 10 06
Forward. From Apprentice. Wales 40 full
caps.

Season	Club	App	Goals
1982–83	Swansea C	—	—
1983–84	....	19	3
1984–85	....	30	9
1984–85	Cardiff C	4	—
1985–86	Brighton	42	15
1986–87	....	30	6
1986–87	Oxford U	12	6
1987–88	....	37	12
1988–89	....	10	4
1988–89	Derby Co	30	14
1989–90	....	38	11
1990–91	....	38	17
1991–92	Liverpool	36	10
1992–93	....	6	1
1992–93	Aston Villa	35	13

SAUNDERS, Wes

Born Sunderland 23.2.63.   Ht 6 0
Wt 11 11
Defender. From School.

Season	Club	App	Goals
1981–82	Newcastle U	29	—
1982–83	....	13	—
1983–84	....	16	—
1984–85	....	21	—
1984–85	Bradford C	4	—
1985–86	Carlisle U	35	3
1986–87	....	37	3
1987–88	....	25	5
1987–88	Dundee	11	—
1988–89	....	30	1
1989–90	....	9	1
1990–91	Torquay U	37	3
1991–92	....	18	3
1992–93	....	6	—

SAVILLE, Andrew

Born Hull 12.12.64.   Ht 6 0   Wt 12 06
Forward. From local.

Season	Club	App	Goals
1983–84	Hull C	1	—
1984–85	....	4	1
1985–86	....	9	1

Season	Club		App	Goals
1986–87	....		35	9
1987–88	....		31	6
1988–89	....		20	1
1988–89	Walsall		12	4
1989–90	....		26	1
1989–90	Barnsley		15	3
1990–91	....		45	12
1991–92	....		22	6
1991–92	Hartlepool U		1	—
1992–93	....		36	13
1992–93	Birmingham C		10	7

SCALES, John

Born Harrogate 4.7.66.   Ht 6 2   Wt 12 07
Defender.

Season	Club		App	Goals
1984–85	Leeds U		—	—
1985–86	Bristol R		29	1
1986–87	....		43	1
1987–88	Wimbledon		25	1
1988–89	....		38	5
1989–90	....		28	2
1990–91	....		36	2
1991–92	....		41	—
1992–93	....		32	1

SCHMEICHEL, Peter

Born Glodsone 18.11.68.   Ht 6 4
Wt 13 06
Goalkeeper. From Hvidovre, Brondby.
Denmark full caps.

Season	Club		App	Goals
1991–92	Manchester U		40	—
1992–93	....		42	—

SCHOFIELD, Jon

Born Barnsley 16.5.65.   Ht 5 11   Wt 11 03
Midfield. From Gainsborough T.

Season	Club		App	Goals
1988–89	Lincoln C		29	2
1989–90	....		29	2
1990–91	....		42	3
1991–92	....		39	1
1992–93	....		40	—

SCOTT, Andy

Born Epsom 2.8.72   Ht 6 1   Wt 11 05
Midfield. From Sutton U.

Season	Club		App	Goals
1992–93	Sheffield U		2	1

SCOTT, Ian

Born Radcliffe 20.9.67.   Ht 5 9   Wt 11 04
Forward. From Apprentice. England
Schools.

Season	Club		App	Goals
1985–86	Manchester C		—	—
1986–87	....		—	—
1987–88	....		23	3
1988–89	....		1	—
1989–90	Stoke C		19	1
1990–91	....		2	—
1990–91	*Crewe Alex*		12	1
1991–92	Stoke C		9	1
1992–93	Bury		9	2

SCOTT, Kevin

Born Easington 17.12.66.   Ht 6 2
Wt 11 06
Defender.

Season	Club		App	Goals
1984–85	Newcastle U		—	—
1985–86	....		—	—
1986–87	....		3	1
1987–88	....		4	1
1988–89	....		29	—
1989–90	....		42	3
1990–91	....		42	—
1991–92	....		44	1
1992–93	....		45	2

SCOTT, Martin

Born Sheffield 7.1.68.   Ht 5 8   Wt 10 10
Midfield. From Apprentice.

Season	Club		App	Goals
1984–85	Rotherham U		3	—
1985–86	....		—	—
1986–87	....		12	—
1987–88	....		19	—
1987–88	*Nottingham F*		—	—
1988–89	Rotherham U		19	1
1989–90	....		28	1

1990–91	....	13	1
1990–91	Bristol C	27	1
1991–92	....	46	3
1992–93	....	35	3

SCOTT, Morrys

Born Swansea 17.12.70. Ht 6 3   Wt 12 06
Forward. From Swansea C Trainee and
Cardiff C Trainee.

1989–90	Cardiff C.....................	9	—
From Colchester U			
1990–91	Southend U.................	—	—
1991–92	Plymouth Arg.............	6	—
1992–93	Northampton T	17	2

SCOTT, Peter

Born London 1.10.63.   Ht 5 9   Wt 11 12
Midfield. From Apprentice.

1981–82	Fulham	1	—
1982–83	....	—	—
1983–84	....	32	4
1984–85	....	19	1
1985–86	....	32	5
1986–87	....	30	6
1987–88	....	23	2
1988–89	....	37	3
1989–90	....	41	3
1990–91	....	23	2
1991–92	....	39	1
1992–93	Bournemouth..............	10	—

SCOTT, Philip

Born Perth 14.11.74.   Ht 5 8   Wt 10 2
Midfield. From Scone Thistle.

1992–92	St Johnstone	—	—
1992–93	....	3	—

SCOTT, Richard

Born Dudley 29.9.74
Defender. From Trainee.

1992–93	Birmingham C	1	—

SCULLY, Pat

Born Dublin 23.6.70.   Ht 6 1   Wt 13 02
Defender. Eire Schools, Youth, B, Under-
21, Under-23, 1 full cap.

1987–88	Arsenal.........................	—	—
1988–89	....	—	—
1989–90	....	—	—
1989–90	*Preston NE*	13	1
1990–91	Arsenal.........................	—	—
1990–91	*Northampton T*............	15	—
1990–91	Southend U.................	21	—
1991–92	....	44	3
1992–93	....	42	3

SEABURY, Kevin

Born Shrewsbury 24.11.73   Ht 5 9
Wt 11 06
Midfield. From Trainee.

1992–93	Shrewsbury T..............	1	—

SEAGRAVES, Mark

Born Bootle 22.10.66.   Ht 6 1   Wt 12 10
Defender. England Schools, Youth.

1983–84	Liverpool	—	—
1984–85	....	—	—
1985–86	....	—	—
1986–87	....	—	—
1986–87	*Norwich C*...................	3	—
1987–88	Liverpool	—	—
1987–88	Manchester C	17	—
1988–89	....	23	—
1989–90	....	2	—
1990–91	Bolton W	32	—
1991–92	....	40	1
1992–93	....	37	5

SEALEY, Les

Born Bethnal Green 29.9.57.   Ht 6 1
Wt 13 06
Goalkeeper. From Apprentice.

1975–76	Coventry C.................	—	—
1976–77	....	11	—
1977–78	....	2	—

Season	Club	League Appearances/Goals
1978–79	....	36 —
1979–80		20 —
1980–81		35 —
1981–82		15 —
1982–83		39 —
1983–84	Luton T	42 —
1984–85		26 —
1984–85	*Plymouth Arg*	6 —
1985–86	Luton T	35 —
1986–87		41 —
1987–88		31 —
1988–89		32 —
1989–90		— —
1989–90	*Manchester U*	2 —
1990–91	Manchester U	31 —
1991–92	Aston Villa	18 —
1991–92	*Coventry C*	2 —
1992–93	Aston Villa	— —
1992–93	*Birmingham C*	12 —

SEAMAN, David

Born Rotherham 19.9.63.   Ht 6 4
Wt 14 10
Goalkeeper. From Apprentice. England B,
Under-21, 9 full caps.

Season	Club	League Appearances/Goals
1981–82	Leeds U	— —
1982–83	Peterborough U	38 —
1983–84		45 —
1984–85		8 —
1984–85	Birmingham C	33 —
1985–86		42 —
1986–87	QPR	41 —
1987–88		32 —
1988–89		35 —
1989–90		33 —
1990–91	Arsenal	38 —
1991–92		42 —
1992–93		39 —

SEARLE, Damon

Born Cardiff 26.10.71.   Ht 5 11   Wt 10 04
Defender. From Trainee. Wales Youth,
Under-21.

Season	Club	League Appearances/Goals
1990–91	Cardiff C	35 —
1991–92		42 1
1992–93		42 1

SEDGLEY, Steve

Born Enfield 26.5.68.   Ht 6 1   Wt 13 03
Midfield. From Apprentice. England
Under-21.

Season	Club	League Appearances/Goals
1986–87	Coventry C	26 —
1987–88		27 2
1988–89		31 1
1989–90	Tottenham H	32 —
1990–91		34 —
1991–92		34 —
1992–93		22 3

SEGERS, Hans

Born Eindhoven 30.10.61.   Ht 5 11
Wt 12 12
Goalkeeper. From PSV Eindhoven.

Season	Club	League Appearances/Goals
1984–85	Nottingham F	28 —
1985–86		11 —
1986–87		14 —
1986–87	*Stoke C*	1 —
1987–88	Nottingham F	5 —
1987–88	*Sheffield U*	10 —
1987–88	*Dunfermline Ath*	4 —
1988–89	Nottingham F	— —
1988–89	Wimbledon	33 —
1989–90		38 —
1990–91		37 —
1991–92		41 —
1992–93		41 —

SELLARS, Scott

Born Sheffield 27.11.65.   Ht 5 7   Wt 9 10
Midfield. From Apprentice. England
Under-21.

Season	Club	League Appearances/Goals
1982–83	Leeds U	1 —
1983–84		19 3
1984–85		39 7
1985–86		17 2
1986–87	Blackburn R	32 4
1987–88		42 7
1988–89		46 2
1989–90		43 14
1990–91		9 1
1991–92		30 7
1992–93	Leeds U	7 —

1992–93 Newcastle U................ 13 2

SELLEY, Ian

Born Chertsey 14.6.74 Ht 5 9 Wt 10 01
Midfield. From Trainee. England Youth.

1992–93 Arsenal........................ 9 —

SENDALL, Richard

Born Stamford 10.7.67. Ht 5 10
Wt 11 06
Forward. From Watford Apprentice.

1985–86	Blackpool....................	8	—
1986–87	....	3	—
1987–88	....	—	—
1988–89	Carlisle U....................	29	6
1989–90	....	19	4
1989–90	*Cardiff C*	4	—
1990–91	Carlisle U....................	25	2
1991–92	....	1	1
1992–93	....	10	1

SERTORI, Mark

Born Manchester 1.9.67. Ht 6 1
Wt 13 00
Defender.

1986–87	Stockport Co	3	—
1987–88	....	1	—
1987–88	Lincoln C....................	28	6
1988–89	....	26	4
1989–90	....	24	5
1989–90	Wrexham	18	2
1990–91	....	29	—
1991–92	....	36	—
1992–93	....	12	—

SHAIL, Mark

Born Sweden 15.10.63
Defender. From Yeovil.

1992–93 Bristol C .... 4 —

SHAKESPEARE, Craig

Born Birmingham 26.10.63. Ht 5 10
Wt 12 05
Midfield. From Apprentice.

1981–82	Walsall	—	—
1982–83	....	31	4
1983–84	....	46	6
1984–85	....	41	9
1985–86	....	32	4
1986–87	....	44	11
1987–88	....	45	8
1988–89	....	45	3
1989–90	Sheffield W.................	17	—
1989–90	WBA............................	18	1
1990–91	....	36	1
1991–92	....	44	8
1992–93	....	14	2

SHARP, Graeme

Born Glasgow 16.10.60. Ht 6 1 Wt 11 09
Forward. From Eastercraigs. Scotland
Under-21, 12 full caps.

1978–79	Dumbarton	6	1
1979–80	....	34	16
1979–80	Everton	2	—
1980–81	....	4	—
1981–82	....	29	15
1982–83	....	41	15
1983–84	....	28	7
1984–85	....	36	21
1985–86	....	37	19
1986–87	....	27	5
1987–88	....	32	13
1988–89	....	26	7
1989–90	....	33	6
1990–91	....	27	3
1991–92	Oldham Ath...............	42	12
1992–93	....	21	7

SHARP, Kevin

Born Canada 19.9.74
Midfield. From Auxerre. England Youth.

1992–93 Leeds U .... 4 —

SHARPE, Lee

Born Halesowen 25.7.71.   Ht 5 11
Wt 11 04
Midfield. From Trainee. England Under-
21, B, 6 full caps.

1987–88	Torquay U	14	3
1988–89	Manchester U	22	—
1989–90		18	1
1990–91		23	2
1991–92		14	1
1992–93		27	1

SHARRATT, Chris

Born West Kirby 13.8.70.   Ht 5 7
Wt 11 04
Forward. From Stalybridge.

1991–92	Wigan Ath	4	—
1992–93		20	3

SHAW, George

Born Glasgow 10.2.69.   Ht 5 7   Wt 9 02
Forward. From Ayresome N.

1987–88	St Mirren	2	—
1988–89		10	1
1989–90		23	2
1990–91		33	1
1991–92	Partick T	43	9
1992–93		31	10

SHAW, Graham

Born Stoke 7.6.67.   Ht 5 8   Wt 10 05
Forward. From Apprentice.

1985–86	Stoke C	20	5
1986–87		18	2
1987–88		33	6
1988–89		28	5
1989–90	Preston NE	31	5
1990–91		44	10
1991–92		46	14
1992–93	Stoke C	29	5

SHAW, Greg

Born Dumfries 15.2.70   Ht 6 0   Wt 10 12
Forward. From Dalbeattie Star.

1988–89	Ayr U	2	—
1989–90		3	—
1990–91		9	—
1991–92		39	10
1992–93		5	—
1992–93	Falkirk	6	2

SHAW, Richard

Born Brentford 11.9.68.   Ht 5 9   Wt 11 08
Defender. From Apprentice.

1986–87	Crystal Palace	—	—
1987–88		3	—
1988–89		14	—
1989–90		21	—
1989–90	*Hull C*	4	—
1990–91	Crystal Palace	36	1
1991–92		10	—
1992–93		33	—

SHAW, Simon

Born Teeside 21.9.73.   Ht 6 0   Wt 12 00
Midfield. From Trainee.

1991–92	Darlington	1	—
1992–93		23	4

SHEARER, Alan

Born Newcastle 13.8.70.   Ht 5 11
Wt 11 03
Forward. From Trainee. England Youth,
Under-21 B, 6 full caps.

1987–88	Southampton	5	3
1988–89		10	—
1989–90		26	3
1990–91		36	4
1991–92		41	13
1992–93	Blackburn R	21	16

SHEARER, Duncan

Born Fort William 28.8.62.   Ht 5 10
Wt 10 09
Forward. From Inverness Clach.

Season	Club	League Appearances	Goals
1983–84	Chelsea	—	—
1984–85		—	—
1985–86		2	1
1985–86	Huddersfield T	8	7
1986–87		42	21
1987–88		33	10
1988–89	Swindon T	36	14
1989–90		42	20
1990–91		44	22
1991–92		37	22
1991–92	Blackburn R	6	1
1992–93	Aberdeen	34	22

SHEARER, Peter

Born Birmingham 4.2.67.   Ht 6 0
Wt 11 06
Forward. From Apprentice.

Season	Club	League Appearances	Goals
1984–85	Birmingham C	4	—
1985–86		—	—
1986–87	Rochdale	1	—
From Cheltenham T			
1988–89	Bournemouth	4	1
1989–90		34	4
1990–91		5	—
1991–92		8	1
1992–93		34	4

SHEEDY, Kevin

Born Builth Wells 21.10.59.   Ht 5 9
Wt 10 11
Midfield. From Apprentice. Eire Youth,
Under-21, 45 full caps.

Season	Club	League Appearances	Goals
1975–76	Hereford U	1	—
1976–77		16	1
1977–78		34	3
1978–79	Liverpool	—	—
1979–80		—	—
1980–81		1	—
1981–82		2	—
1982–83	Everton	40	11
1983–84		28	4

Season	Club	League Appearances	Goals
1984–85		29	11
1985–86		31	5
1986–87		28	13
1987–88		17	1
1988–89		26	8
1989–90		37	9
1990–91		22	4
1991–92		16	1
1991–92	Newcastle U	13	1
1992–93		24	3

SHEFFIELD, Jon

Born Bedworth 1.2.69.   Ht 5 11   Wt 11 07
Goalkeeper.

Season	Club	League Appearances	Goals
1986–87	Norwich C	—	—
1987–88		—	—
1988–89		1	—
1989–90		—	—
1989–90	Aldershot	11	—
1989–90	Ipswich T	—	—
1990–91	Norwich C	—	—
1990–91	Aldershot	15	—
1990–91	Cambridge U	2	—
1991–92	Cambridge U	13	—
1992–93		13	—

SHELTON, Gary

Born Nottingham 21.3.58.   Ht 5 7
Wt 10 12
Midfield. From Apprentice. England
Under-21.

Season	Club	League Appearances	Goals
1975–76	Walsall	2	—
1976–77		10	—
1977–78		12	—
1977–78	Aston Villa	—	—
1978–79		19	7
1979–80		4	—
1979–80	Notts Co	8	—
1980–81	Aston Villa	—	—
1981–82		1	—
1981–82	Sheffield W	9	1
1982–83		40	4
1983–84		40	5
1984–85		41	4
1985–86		31	1
1986–87		37	3

Season	Club	Appearances	Goals
1987–88	Oxford U	32	—
1988–89		33	1
1989–90	Bristol C	43	9
1990–91		43	8
1991–92		19	3
1992–93		42	4

SHEPHERD, Tony

Born Glasgow 16.11.66. Ht 5 9 Wt 10 07
Midfield. From Celtic BC. Scotland
Schools, Youth.

Season	Club	Appearances	Goals
1983–84	Celtic	—	—
1984–85		—	—
1985–86		1	—
1986–87		21	2
1987–88		6	1
1988–89		—	—
1988–89	Bristol C	3	—
1989–90	Carlisle U	31	2
1990–91		44	6
1991–92	Motherwell	5	—
1992–93		5	—

SHEPPARD, Simon

Born Clevedon 7.8.73. Ht 6 4 Wt 14 03
Goalkeeper. From Trainee. England
Youth.

Season	Club	Appearances	Goals
1991–92	Watford	—	—
1992–93		5	—

SHEPSTONE, Paul

Born Coventry 8.11.70. Ht 5 8 Wt 10 06
Midfield. From FA Schools.

Season	Club	Appearances	Goals
1987–88	Coventry C	—	—
1988–89		—	—
1989–90	Birmingham C	—	—
1989–90	Blackburn R	—	—
From Atherstone U			
1990–91		25	1
1991–92		1	—
1991–92	York C	2	—
1992–93	Motherwell	1	—

SHERIDAN, John

Born Manchester 1.10.64. Ht 5 9
Wt 10 08
Midfield. From Local. Eire Youth, Under-
21, Under-23, B, 15 full caps.

Season	Club	Appearances	Goals
1981–82	Leeds U	—	—
1982–83		27	2
1983–84		11	1
1984–85		42	6
1985–86		32	4
1986–87		40	15
1987–88		38	12
1988–89		40	7
1989–90	Nottingham F	—	—
1989–90	Sheffield W	27	2
1990–91		46	10
1991–92		24	6
1992–93		25	3

SHERIDAN, Tony

Born Dublin 21.10.74. Ht 6 0 Wt 11 08
Forward.

Season	Club	Appearances	Goals
1991–92	Coventry C	—	—
1992–93		1	—

SHERINGHAM, Teddy

Born Highams Park 2.4.66. Ht 6 0
Wt 12 05
Forward. From Apprentice. England
Youth, 2 full caps.

Season	Club	Appearances	Goals
1983–84	Millwall	7	1
1984–85		—	—
1984–85	Aldershot	5	—
1985–86	Millwall	18	4
1986–87		42	13
1987–88		43	22
1988–89		33	11
1989–90		31	9
1990–91		46	33
1991–92	Nottingham F	39	13
1992–93		3	1
1992–93	Tottenham H	38	21

SHERON, Mike

Born Liverpool 11.1.72. Ht 5 9 Wt 11 03
Midfield. From Trainee. England
Under-21.

1990–91	Manchester C	—	—
1990–91	*Bury*	5	1
1991–92	Manchester C	29	7
1992–93		38	11

SHERWOOD, Steve

Born Selby 10.12.53. Ht 6 4 Wt 14 07
Goalkeeper. From Apprentice.

1970–71	Chelsea	—	—
1971–72		1	—
1972–73		3	—
1973–74		—	—
1973–74	*Brighton*	—	—
1973–74	*Millwall*	1	—
1973–74	*Brentford*	16	—
1974–75	Chelsea	—	—
1974–75	*Brentford*	46	—
1975–76	Chelsea	12	—
1976–77		—	—
1976–77	Watford	8	—
1977–78		16	—
1978–79		16	—
1979–80		4	—
1980–81		22	—
1981–82		41	—
1982–83		42	—
1983–84		40	1
1984–85		9	—
1985–86		2	—
1986–87		11	—
1987–88	Grimsby T	46	—
1988–89		32	—
1989–90		31	—
1990–91		46	—
1991–92		21	—
1992–93		7	—

SHERWOOD, Tim

Born St Albans 6.2.69. Ht 6 1 Wt 11 04
Midfield. From Trainee. England
Under-21.

1986–87	Watford	—	—

1987–88		13	—
1988–89		19	2
1989–90	Norwich C	27	3
1990–91		37	7
1991–92		7	—
1991–92	Blackburn R	11	—
1992–93		39	3

SHILTON, Peter

Born Leicester 18.9.49. Ht 6 0 Wt 14 00
Goalkeeper. From Apprentice. England
Schools, Youth, Under-23, 125 full caps.
Football League.

1965–66	Leicester C	1	—
1966–67		4	—
1967–68		35	1
1968–69		42	—
1969–70		39	—
1970–71		40	—
1971–72		37	—
1972–73		41	—
1973–74		42	—
1974–75		5	—
1974–75	Stoke C	25	—
1975–76		42	—
1976–77		40	—
1977–78		3	—
1977–78	Nottingham F	37	—
1978–79		42	—
1979–80		42	—
1980–81		40	—
1981–82		41	—
1982–83	Southampton	39	—
1983–84		42	—
1984–85		41	—
1985–86		37	—
1986–87		29	—
1987–88	Derby Co	40	—
1988–89		38	—
1989–90		35	—
1990–91		31	—
1991–92		31	—
1991–92	Plymouth Arg	7	—
1992–93		23	—

SHIPPERLEY, Neil

Born Chatham 30.10.74
Forward. From Trainee.

1992–93	Chelsea	3	1

SHIRTLIFF, Peter

Born Barnsley 6.4.61. Ht 5 11 Wt 12 02
Defender. From Apprentice.

1978–79	Sheffield W	26	1
1979–80		3	—
1980–81		28	—
1981–82		31	2
1982–83		8	—
1983–84		36	1
1984–85		35	—
1985–86		21	—
1986–87	Charlton Ath	33	3
1987–88		36	2
1988–89		34	2
1989–90	Sheffield W	33	2
1990–91		39	2
1991–92		12	—
1992–93		20	—

SHORT, Chris

Born Munster 9.5.70. Ht 5 10 Wt 12 02
Defender.

1988–89	Scarborough	2	—
1989–90		41	1
1990–91		—	—
1990–91	*Manchester U*	—	—
1990–91	Notts Co	15	1
1991–92		27	—
1992–93		31	1

SHORT, Craig

Born Bridlington 25.6.68. Ht 6 2
Wt 12 03
Defender. From Pickering T. England
Schools.

1987–88	Scarborough	21	2
1988–89		42	5
1989–90	Notts Co	44	2

1990–91		—	—
1990–91		43	—
1991–92		38	3
1992–93		3	1
1992–93	Derby Co	38	3

SHOWLER, Paul

Born Doncaster 10.10.66. Ht 5 10
Wt 11 06
Forward. From Sheffield W, Sunderland,
Colne D, Altrincham.

1991–92	Barnet	39	7
1992–93		32	5

SHUTT, Carl

Born Sheffield 10.10.61. Ht 5 10
Wt 11 13
Forward. From Spalding U.

1984–85	Sheffield W	—	—
1985–86		19	9
1986–87		20	7
1987–88		1	—
1987–88	Bristol C	22	9
1988–89		24	1
1988–89	Leeds U	3	4
1989–90		20	2
1990–91		28	10
1991–92		14	1
1992–93		14	—

SIDDALL, Barry

Born Ellesmere Port 12.9.54. Ht 6 1
Wt 14 02
Goalkeeper. From Apprentice. England
Youth.

1971–72	Bolton W	—	—
1972–73		4	—
1973–74		42	—
1974–75		42	—
1975–76		42	—
1976–77		7	—
1976–77	Sunderland	34	—
1977–78		42	—
1978–79		41	—

Season	Club	App	Goals
1979–80		12	—
1980–81		15	—
1980–81	*Darlington*	8	—
1981–82	Sunderland	23	—
1982–83	Port Vale	33	—
1983–84		39	—
1983–84	*Blackpool*	7	—
1984–85	Port Vale	9	—
1984–85	Stoke C	15	—
1985–86		5	—
1985–86	*Tranmere R*	12	—
1985–86	*Manchester C*	6	—
1986–87	Blackpool	37	—
1987–88		38	—
1988–89		35	—
1989–90	Stockport Co	21	—
1989–90	Hartlepool U	11	—
1990–91	WBA	—	—
1990–91	Carlisle U	24	—
1991–92	Chester C	9	—
1992–93	Preston NE	1	—

SIMKIN, Darren

Born Walsall 24.3.70. Ht 6 0 Wt 12 00
Defender. From Blakenhall.

Season	Club	App	Goals
1991–92	Wolverhampton W	—	—
1992–93		7	—

SIMPSON, Fitzroy

Born Trowbridge 26.2.70. Ht 5 8
Wt 10 07
Midfield. From Trainee.

Season	Club	App	Goals
1988–89	Swindon T	7	—
1989–90		30	2
1990–91		38	3
1991–92		30	4
1991–92	Manchester C	11	1
1992–93		29	1

SIMPSON, Neil

Born London 15.11.61. Ht 5 10
Wt 11 06
Midfield. From Middlefield Wasps.
Scotland Youth, Under-21, 4 full caps.

Season	Club	App	Goals
1978–79	Aberdeen	—	—
1979–80		—	—
1980–81		16	2
1981–82		29	4
1982–83		33	5
1983–84		24	2
1984–85		33	4
1985–86		22	1
1986–87		9	—
1987–88		15	1
1988–89		16	—
1989–90		9	—
1990–91	Newcastle U	4	—
1991–92	Motherwell	21	—
1992–93		12	1

SIMPSON, Paul

Born Carlisle 26.7.66. Ht 5 7 Wt 11 04
Forward. From Apprentice. England
Youth, Under-21.

Season	Club	App	Goals
1982–83	Manchester C	3	—
1983–84		—	—
1984–85		10	6
1985–86		37	8
1986–87		32	3
1987–88		38	1
1988–89		1	—
1988–89	Oxford U	25	8
1989–90		42	9
1990–91		46	17
1991–92		31	9
1991–92	Derby Co	16	7
1992–93		35	12

SINCLAIR, David

Born Dunfermline 6.10.69 Ht 5 11
Wt 12 10
Midfield. From Kelty U21.

Season	Club	App	Goals
1990–91	Raith R	23	1
1991–92		22	1
1992–93	*Portadown*	—	—
1992–93	Raith R	32	—

SINCLAIR, Frank

Born Lambeth 3.12.71. Ht 5 8 Wt 11 02
Defender. From Trainee.

Season	Club	App	Goals
1989–90	Chelsea	—	—

Season	Club	App	Goals
1990–91		4	—
1991–92		8	1
1991–92	*WBA*	6	1
1992–93	Chelsea	32	—

SINCLAIR, Ron

Born Stirling 19.11.64. Ht 5 10 Wt 11 13
Goalkeeper. From Apprentice. Scotland
Schools, Youth.

Season	Club	App	Goals
1982–83	Nottingham F	—	—
1983–84		—	—
1983–84	*Wrexham*	11	—
1984–85	Nottingham F	—	—
1984–85	*Derby Co*	—	—
1985–86	Nottingham F	—	—
1985–86	*Sheffield U*	—	—
1985–86	*Leeds U*	—	—
1986–87	Leeds U	8	—
1986–87	*Halifax T*	4	—
1987–88	Leeds U	—	—
1988–89		—	—
1988–89	*Halifax T*	10	—
1989–90	Leeds U	—	—
1989–90	Bristol C	27	—
1990–91		17	—
1991–92		—	—
1991–92	*Walsall*	10	—
1991–92	Stoke C	26	—
1992–93		29	—

SINCLAIR, Trevor

Born Dulwich 2.3.73. Ht 5 10 Wt 11 02
Midfield. From Trainee.

Season	Club	App	Goals
1989–90	Blackpool	9	—
1990–91		31	1
1991–92		27	3
1992–93		45	11

SINNOTT, Lee

Born Pelsall 12.7.65. Ht 6 1 Wt 12 07
Defender. From Apprentice. England
Youth, Under-21.

Season	Club	App	Goals
1981–82	Walsall	4	—
1982–83		32	2
1983–84		4	—
1983–84	Watford	20	—
1984–85		30	—
1985–86		18	2
1986–87		10	—
1987–88	Bradford C	42	1
1988–89		42	2
1989–90		45	2
1990–91		44	1
1991–92	Crystal Palace	36	—
1992–93		19	—

SINTON, Andy

Born Newcastle. 19.3.66. Ht 5 8
Wt 10 10
Midfield. From Apprentice. England
Schools, B, 10 full caps.

Season	Club	App	Goals
1982–83	Cambridge U	13	5
1983–84		34	6
1984–85		26	2
1985–86		20	—
1985–86	Brentford	26	3
1986–87		46	5
1987–88		46	11
1988–89		31	9
1988–89	QPR	10	3
1989–90		38	6
1990–91		38	3
1991–92		38	3
1992–93		36	7

SKEDD, Tony

Born North Cleveland 19.5.75
Midfield. From Trainee.

Season	Club	App	Goals
1992–93	Hartlepool U	1	—

SKILLING, Mark

Born Irvine 6.10.72 Ht 5 9 Wt 10 13
Midfield. From Saltcoats Victoria.

Season	Club	App	Goals
1992–93	Kilmarnock	40	4

SKINNER, Craig

Born Bury 21.10.70. Ht 5 8 Wt 11 00
Forward. From Trainee.

Season	Club	App	Goals
1989–90	Blackburn R	—	—

1990–91		7	—
1991–92		9	—
1992–93	Plymouth Arg	13	1

SKINNER, Justin

Born London 30.1.69. Ht 6 0 Wt 11 03
Midfield. From Apprentice.

1986–87	Fulham	3	—
1987–88		32	6
1988–89		38	8
1989–90		30	4
1990–91		32	5
1991–92	Bristol R	42	3
1992–93		12	—

SKINNER, Justin

Born London 17.9.72 Ht 5 7 Wt 11 00
Defender. From Trainee.

1991–92	Wimbledon	—	—
1992–93		1	—

SKIPPER, Peter

Born Hull 11.4.58. Ht 6 0 Wt 13 08
Defender. From Local.

1978–79	Hull C	17	2
1979–80		6	—
1979–80	*Scunthorpe U*	1	—
1980–81	Darlington	46	2
1981–82		45	2
1982–83	Hull C	46	4
1983–84		46	1
1984–85		46	5
1985–86		40	1
1986–87		41	4
1987–88		43	2
1988–89		3	—
1988–89	Oldham Ath	27	1
1989–90	Walsall	40	1
1990–91		41	1
1991–92	Wrexham	2	—
1991–92	Wigan Ath	18	—
From Stafford R			
1992–93	Wigan Ath	32	1

SLATER, Stuart

Born Sudbury 27.3.69. Ht 5 9 Wt 10 04
Forward. From Apprentice. England B,
Under-21.

1986–87	West Ham U	—	—
1987–88		2	—
1988–89		18	1
1989–90		40	7
1990–91		40	3
1991–92		41	—
1992–93	Celtic	39	2

SLAVEN, Bernie

Born Paisley 13.11.60. Ht 5 11 Wt 12 00
Forward. Eire 7 full caps.

1981–82	Morton	13	1
1982–83		9	—
1983–84	Airdrie	2	—
1983–84	Queen of the South	2	—
1983–84	Albion R	3	—
1984–85		39	27
1985–86	Middlesbrough	32	8
1986–87		46	17
1987–88		44	21
1988–89		37	15
1989–90		46	21
1990–91		46	16
1991–92		38	16
1992–93		18	4
1992–93	Port Vale	10	2

SLAWSON, Stephen

Born Nottingham 13.11.72. Ht 6 0
Wt 12 06
Forward. From Trainee.

1991–92	Notts Co	13	1
1992–93		20	3
1992–93	*Burnley*	5	2

SLOAN, Scott

Born Wallsend 14.12.67. Ht 5 10
Wt 11 06
Forward. From Ponteland.

1988–89	Berwick R	26	4

Season	Club		A/G	
1989–90	....	35	16
1990–91	Newcastle U..............	16	1
1991–92	....	—	—
1991–92	Falkirk..............	23	4
1992–93	....	29	6

SMALL, Bryan

Born Birmingham 15.11.71. Ht 5 9
Wt 11 09
Defender. From Trainee. England
Under-21.

1989–90	Aston Villa..................	—	—
1990–91	....	—	—
1991–92	....	8	—
1992–93	....	14	—

SMALL, Mike

Born Birmingham 2.3.62. Ht 6 0
Wt 13 05
Forward.

1980–81	Luton T	—	—
1981–82	....	3	—
1982–83	....	—	—
Twente, Standard Liege			
1982–83	Peterborough U..........	4	1
From Go Ahead Eagles/PAOK Salonika			
1990–91	Brighton......................	39	15
1991–92	West Ham U	40	13
1992–93	....	9	—

SMART, Gary

Born Totnes 29.4.64. Ht 5 9 Wt 11 03
Defender. From Wokingham.

1988–89	Oxford U	17	—
1989–90	....	40	—
1990–91	....	15	—
1991–92	....	39	—
1992–93	....	41	—

SMART, Jason

Born Rochdale 15.2.69. Ht 6 0 Wt 12 10
Defender. From Trainee.

1985–86	Rochdale......................	1	—

1986–87	....	38	1
1987–88	....	36	3
1988–89	....	42	—
1989–90	Crewe Alex	41	2
1990–91	....	37	—
1991–92	....	11	—
1992–93	....	—	—

SMILLIE, Neil

Born Barnsley 19.7.58. Ht 5 6 Wt 10 07
Forward. From Apprentice.

1975–76	Crystal Palace.............	—	—
1976–77	....	1	—
1976–77	*Brentford*..................	3	—
1977–78	Crystal Palace............	1	—
1978–79	....	8	1
1979–80	....	8	1
1980–81	....	24	2
1981–82	....	41	3
1982–83	Brighton..................	25	—
1983–84	....	26	2
1984–85	....	24	—
1985–86	Watford	16	3
1986–87	....	—	—
1986–87	Reading..................	16	—
1987–88	....	23	—
1988–89	Brentford	28	2
1989–90	....	43	5
1990–91	....	36	3
1991–92	....	44	7
1992–93	....	21	1

SMITH, Alan

Born Birmingham 21.11.62. Ht 6 3
Wt 12 13
Forward. From Alvechurch. England B,
13 full caps. Football League.

1982–83	Leicester C..................	39	13
1983–84	....	40	15
1984–85	....	39	12
1985–86	....	40	19
1986–87	....	33	14
1986–87	*Leicester C*...............	9	3
1987–88	Arsenal......................	39	11
1988–89	....	36	23
1989–90	....	38	10

1990–91	....	37	22
1991–92	....	39	12
1992–92	....	31	3

SMITH, Andrew

Born Aberdeen 22.11.68 Ht 6 1
Wt 12 07
Midfield. From Peterhead.

1990–91	Airdrieonians	28	3
1991–92	....	28	4
1992–93	....	34	4

SMITH, Anthony

Born Sunderland 21.9.71. Ht 5 10
Wt 11 04
Defender. From Trainee. England Youth.

1990–91	Sunderland	9	—
1991–92	....	2	—
1991–92	*Hartlepool U*	5	—
1992–93	Sunderland	7	—

SMITH, Barry

Born Paisley 19.2.74. Ht 5 10 Wt 12 00
Defender. From Giffnock N. Scotland
Under-21.

1991–92	Celtic	3	—
1992–93	....	6	—

SMITH, David

Born Liverpool 26.12.70. Ht 5 9
Wt 11 12
Midfield. From Trainee.

1989–90	Norwich C	1	—
1990–91	....	3	—
1991–92	....	1	—
1992–93	....	6	—

SMITH, David

Born Sidcup 25.6.61. Ht 5 11 Wt 12 00
Forward. From Welling U.

1986–87	Gillingham	27	1

1987–88	....	35	7
1988–89	....	42	2
1989–90	Bristol C	45	4
1990–91	....	34	5
1991–92	Plymouth Arg	18	2
1992–93	Notts Co	37	8

SMITH, David

Born Gloucester 29.3.68. Ht 5 8
Wt 10 02
Midfield. England Under-21.

1986–87	Coventry C	—	—
1987–88	....	16	4
1988–89	....	35	3
1989–90	....	37	6
1990–91	....	36	1
1991–92	....	24	4
1992–93	....	6	1
1992–93	*Bournemouth*	1	—
1992–93	Birmingham C	13	1

SMITH, Dean

Born West Bromwich 19.3.71. Ht 6 0
Wt 12 01
Defender. From Trainee.

1988–89	Walsall	15	—
1989–90	....	7	—
1990–91	....	33	—
1991–92	....	9	—
1992–93	....	42	1

SMITH, Gary

Born Glasgow 25.3.71 Ht 6 0 Wt 10 04
Defender. From Duntocher BC.

1988–89	Falkirk	3	—
1989–90	....	36	—
1990–91	....	31	—
1991–92	Aberdeen	16	1
1992–93	....	40	—

SMITH, Henry

Born Lanark 10.3.56. Ht 6 2 Wt 12 00
Goalkeeper. From school. Scotland
Under-21, 3 full caps.

1978–79	Leeds U	—	—

Season	Club	App	Goals
1979–80		—	—
1980–81		—	—
1981–82	Hearts	33	—
1982–83		39	—
1983–84		36	—
1984–85		36	—
1985–86		36	—
1986–87		43	—
1987–88		44	—
1988–89		36	—
1989–90		36	—
1990–91		23	—
1991–92		44	—
1992–93		25	—

SMITH, Kevan

Born Eaglescliffe 13.12.59.   Ht 6 3
Wt 12 07
Defender. From Stockton.

Season	Club	App	Goals
1979–80	Darlington	35	1
1980–81		39	2
1981–82		45	1
1982–83		46	3
1983–84		44	2
1984–85		36	2
1985–86	Rotherham U	43	3
1986–87		16	1
1986–87	Coventry C	—	—
1987–88		6	—
1987–88	York C	—	—
1988–89		31	5
1989–90	Darlington	*39*	*3*
1990–91		46	4
1991–92		39	1
1992–93		13	—
1992–93	*Hereford U*	6	—

SMITH, Mark

Born Sheffield 21.3.60.   Ht 6 2   Wt 13 11
Defender. From Apprentice. England
Under-21.

Season	Club	App	Goals
1977–78	Sheffield W	2	—
1978–79		21	—
1979–80		44	9
1980–81		41	1
1981–82		41	—

Season	Club	App	Goals
1982–83		41	2
1983–84		27	2
1984–85		36	2
1985–86		13	—
1986–87		16	—
1987–88	Plymouth Arg	41	6
1988–89		35	—
1989–90		6	—
1989–90	Barnsley	25	3
1990–91		37	6
1991–92		38	1
1992–93		4	—
1992–93	Notts Co	5	—
1992–93	*Chesterfield*	6	1
1992–93	*Huddersfield T*	5	—
1992–93	*Port Vale*	6	—

SMITH, Mark

Born Sheffield 19.12.61.   Ht 5 9   Wt 12 02
Forward.

Season	Club	App	Goals
1979–80	Sheffield U	—	—
1980–81		—	—
1981–82		—	—
From Worksop, Gainsborough T.			
1985–86	Scunthorpe U	1	—
From Kettering			
1988–89	Rochdale	27	7
1988–89	Huddersfield T	20	2
1989–90		44	7
1990–91		32	2
1990–91	Grimsby T	11	—
1991–92		40	4
1992–93		26	—

SMITH, Mark

Born Bellshill 16.12.64.   Ht 5 9   Wt 10 04
Midfield. From St Mirren BC.

Season	Club	App	Goals
1983–84	Queen's Park	15	2
1984–85		36	2
1985–86		31	3
1986–87	Celtic	6	—
1987–88	Dunfermline Ath	30	5
1988–89		23	1
1989–90	*Stoke C*	2	—
1989–90	Nottingham F	—	—
1990–91		—	—

Season	Club	League Appearances/Goals	
1990–91	*Reading*	3	—
1991–92	Nottingham F	—	—
1992–93	Shrewsbury T	31	1

SMITH, Mark

Born Birmingham 2.1.73 Ht 6 1
Wt 13 09
Goalkeeper. From Trainee.

Season	Club	League Appearances/Goals	
1991–92	Nottingham F	—	—
1992–93		—	—
1992–93	Crewe Alex	7	—

SMITH, Neil

Born London 30.9.71. Ht 5 9 Wt 12 00
Midfield. From Trainee.

Season	Club	League Appearances/Goals	
1990–91	Tottenham H	—	—
1991–92		—	—
1991–92	Gillingham	26	2
1992–93		59	3

SMITH, Nicky

Born Berkley 28.1.69 Ht 5 7 Wt 10 00
Midfield.

Season	Club	League Appearances/Goals	
1986–87	Southend U	1	—
1987–88		34	5
1988–89		11	—
1989–90		14	1
1990–91	Colchester U	*34*	—
1991–92		*42*	*8*
1992–93		42	4

SMITH, Nigel

Born Leeds 21.12.69. Ht 5 7 Wt 10 04
Midfield. From Leeds U.

Season	Club	League Appearances/Goals	
1989–90	Burnley	11	—
1990–91		2	—
1991–92	Bury	34	3
1992–93	Shrewsbury T	2	—

SMITH, Paul

Born Currie 2.11.62 Ht 5 11 Wt 11 04
Defender. From Edinburgh BC.

Season	Club	League Appearances/Goals	
1980–81	Dundee	—	—

Season	Club	League Appearances/Goals	
1981–82		—	—
1982–83	Dundee U	—	—
1982–83	Raith R	16	2
1983–84		38	8
1984–85		38	19
1985–86		35	21
1986–87	Motherwell	44	9
1987–88		30	4
1988–89		4	—
1988–89	Dunfermline Ath	35	5
1989–90		33	4
1990–91		31	2
1991–92	Falkirk	32	2
1992–93		19	1

SMITH, Paul

Born Rotherham 9.11.64. Ht 5 10
Wt 10 09
Forward. From Apprentice.

Season	Club	League Appearances/Goals	
1982–83	Sheffield U	7	—
1983–84		3	—
1984–85		8	1
1985–86		18	—
1985–86	*Stockport Co*	7	5
1986–87	Port Vale	42	7
1987–88		2	—
1987–88	Lincoln C	*33*	*8*
1988–89		28	10
1989–90		33	5
1990–91		46	6
1991–92		39	3
1992–93		33	3

SMITH, Paul

Born Lenham 18.9.71. Ht 5 11 Wt 14 00
Midfield. From Trainee.

Season	Club	League Appearances/Goals	
1989–90	Southend U	10	1
1990–91		2	—
1991–92		—	—
1992–93		8	—

SMITH, Richard

Born Leicester 3.10.70. Ht 5 11
Wt 12 10
Defender. From Trainee.

Season	Club	League Appearances/Goals	
1988–89	Leicester C	—	—

1989–90	....	4	—
1989–90	*Cambridge U*	4	—
1990–91	Leicester C	4	—
1991–92	....	25	1
1992–93	....	44	—

SMITH, Shaun

Born Leeds 9.4.71. Ht 5 10 Wt 11 00
Defender. From Trainee.

1988–89	Halifax T	1	—
1989–90	....	6	—
1990–91	....	—	—
1991–92	Crewe Alex	10	—
1992–93	....	36	4

SMITH, Thomas

Born Glasgow 12.10.73. Ht 5 8 Wt 11 7
Midfield. 'S' Form.

| 1991–92 | Partick T .... | — | — |
| 1992–93 | .... | 2 | — |

SNEDDON, Alan

Born Baillieston 12.3.58. Ht 5 11
Wt 12 03
Defender. From Larkhall Thistle. Scotland
Under-21.

1977–78	Celtic	15	—
1978–79	....	4	—
1979–80	....	32	1
1980–81	....	15	—
1980–81	Hibernian	14	—
1981–82	....	36	—
1982–83	....	36	—
1983–84	....	35	1
1984–85	....	36	2
1985–86	....	31	2
1986–87	....	26	—
1987–88	....	32	—
1988–89	....	26	—
1989–90	....	29	2
1990–91	....	6	—
1991–92	....	5	—
1992–93	Motherwell	16	—

SNELDERS, Theo

Born Westervoort 7.12.63. Ht 6 2
Wt 14 02
Goalkeeper. From Twente. Holland full
caps.

1988–89	Aberdeen	36	—
1989–90	....	23	—
1990–91	....	21	—
1991–92	....	42	—
1992–93	....	41	—

SNODIN, Glynn

Born Rotherham 14.2.60. Ht 5 6
Wt 9 05
Midfield. From Apprentice.

1976–77	Doncaster R	4	—
1977–78	....	22	2
1978–79	....	34	3
1979–80	....	41	1
1980–81	....	44	3
1981–82	....	40	7
1982–83	....	38	14
1983–84	....	43	13
1984–85	....	43	18
1985–86	Sheffield W	28	1
1986–87	....	31	—
1987–88	Leeds U	35	7
1988–89	....	35	3
1989–90	....	4	—
1990–91	....	20	—
1991–92	....	—	—
1991–92	*Oldham Ath*	8	1
1991–92	Rotherham U	3	—
1991–92	Hearts	7	—
1992–93	....	27	—

SNODIN, Ian

Born Rotherham 15.8.63. Ht 5 7
Wt 9 01
Midfield. From Apprentice. England
Youth, Under-21.

1979–80	Doncaster R	9	1
1980–81	....	32	2
1981–82	....	33	2
1982–83	....	34	3

Season	Club		
1983–84	....	39	9
1984–85	....	41	8
1985–86	Leeds U	37	5
1986–87	....	14	1
1986–87	Everton	16	—
1987–88	....	31	2
1988–89	....	23	—
1989–90	....	25	—
1990–91	....	1	—
1991–92	....	—	—
1992–93	....	20	1

SNOWDEN, Trevor

Born Sunderland 4.10.73   Ht 5 8
Wt 11 00
Midfield. From Seaham Red Star.

Season	Club		
1992–93	Rochdale	13	—

SOLOMAN, Jason

Born Welwyn 6.10.70.   Ht 6 0   Wt 11 10
Defender. From Trainee. England Youth.

Season	Club		
1988–89	Watford	—	—
1989–90	....	—	—
1990–91	....	8	—
1991–92	....	29	—
1992–93	....	36	2

SOMMER, Jurgen

Born New York 27.2.64.   Ht 6 4
Wt 15 12
Goalkeeper.

Season	Club		
1991–92	Luton T	—	—
1991–92	Brighton	*1*	—
1992–93	Luton T	—	—
1992–93	*Torquay U*	10	—

SONNER, Danny

Born Wigan 9.1.72.   Ht 5 10   Wt 11 00
Forward. From Wigan Ath.

Season	Club		
1990–91	Burnley	2	—
1991–92	....	3	—
1992–93	....	1	—

Season	Club		
1992–93	*Bury*	5	3

SORRELL, Tony

Born London 17.10.66.   Ht 5 11
Wt 12 04
Midfield. From Barking and Bishop's
Stortford (1988).

Season	Club		
1989–90	Maidstone U	28	3
1990–91	....	27	5
1991–92	....	—	—
1992–93	Peterborough U	—	—
1992–93	Colchester U	5	1
1992–93	Barnet	8	2

SOUTHALL, Neville

Born Llandudno 16.9.58.   Ht 6 1
Wt 12 01
Goalkeeper. From Winsford. Wales
Under-21, 68 full caps.

Season	Club		
1980–81	Bury	39	—
1981–82	Everton	26	—
1982–83	....	17	—
1982–83	*Port Vale*	9	—
1983–84	Everton	35	—
1984–85	....	42	—
1985–86	....	32	—
1986–87	....	31	—
1987–88	....	32	—
1988–89	....	38	—
1989–90	....	38	—
1990–91	....	38	—
1991–92	....	42	—
1992–93	....	40	—

SOUTHALL, Nicky

Born Teeside 28.1.72.   Ht 5 10   Wt 11 02
Forward.

Season	Club		
1990–91	Hartlepool U	—	—
1991–92	....	22	3
1992–93	....	39	6

SOUTHGATE, Gareth

Born Watford 3.9.70.   Ht 5 10   Wt 11 12
Defender. From Trainee.

Season	Club		
1988–89	Crystal Palace	—	—

Season	Club	App	Goals
1989–90		—	—
1990–91		1	—
1991–92		30	—
1992–93		33	3

SOUTHON, Jamie

Born Hornchurch 13.10.74   Ht 5 9
Wt 11 09
Midfield. From Trainee.

Season	Club	App	Goals
1992–93	Southend U	1	—

SPACKMAN, Nigel

Born Romsey 2.12.60.   Ht 6 1   Wt 13 02
Midfield. From Andover.

Season	Club	App	Goals
1980–81	Bournemouth	44	3
1981–82		35	3
1982–83		40	4
1983–84	Chelsea	40	3
1984–85		42	1
1985–86		39	7
1986–87		20	1
1986–87	Liverpool	12	—
1987–88		27	—
1988–89		12	—
1988–89	QPR	16	1
1989–90		13	—
1989–90	Rangers	21	1
1990–91		35	—
1991–92		42	—
1992–93		2	—
1992–93	Chelsea	6	—

SPEAK, Chris

Born Preston 20.8.73   Ht 6 0   Wt 12 04
Forward. From Trainee.

Season	Club	App	Goals
1992–93	Blackpool	1	—

SPEARING, Tony

Born Romford 7.10.64.   Ht 5 9   Wt 10 12
Defender. From Apprentice. England Youth.

Season	Club	App	Goals
1982–83	Norwich C	—	—

Season	Club	App	Goals
1983–84		4	—
1984–85		—	—
1984–85	*Stoke C*	9	—
1984–85	*Oxford U*	5	—
1985–86	Norwich C	8	—
1986–87		39	—
1987–88		18	—
1988–89	Leicester C	36	—
1989–90		20	1
1990–91		17	—
1991–92	Plymouth Arg	30	—
1992–93		5	—
1992–93	Peterborough U	22	—

SPEED, Gary

Born Hawarden 8.9.69.   Ht 5 9   Wt 10 06
Midfield. From Trainee. Wales Under-21, 20 full caps.

Season	Club	App	Goals
1988–89	Leeds U	1	—
1989–90		25	3
1990–91		38	7
1991–92		41	7
1992–93		39	7

SPEEDIE, David

Born Glenrothes 20.2.60.   Ht 5 7
Wt 11 01
Forward. From Amateur. Scotland Under-21, 10 full caps.

Season	Club	App	Goals
1978–79	Barnsley	10	—
1979–80		13	—
1980–81	Darlington	44	4
1981–82		44	17
1982–83	Chelsea	34	7
1983–84		37	13
1984–85		35	10
1985–86		34	14
1986–87		22	3
1987–88	Coventry C	36	6
1988–89		36	14
1989–90		32	8
1990–91		18	3
1990–91	Liverpool	12	6
1991–92	Blackburn R	36	23
1992–93	Southampton	11	—
1992–93	*Birmingham C*	10	2

| 1992–93 | *WBA* | 7 | 2 |
| 1992–93 | *West Ham U* | 11 | 4 |

SPENCER, John

Born Glasgow 11.9.70. Ht 5 6 Wt 10 00
Forward. From Rangers Am BC. Scotland
Under-21.

1986–87	Rangers	—	—
1987–88		—	—
1988–89		—	—
1988–89	*Morton*	4	1
From Lisburn, HK			
1990–91	Rangers	5	1
1991–92		8	1
1992–93	Chelsea	23	7

SPINK, Dean

Born Birmingham 22.1.67. Ht 5 11
Wt 13 08
Forward. From Halesowen.

1989–90	Aston Villa	—	—
1989–90	*Scarborough*	3	2
1989–90	*Bury*	6	1
1989–90	Shrewsbury T	13	5
1990–91		43	6
1991–92		40	1
1992–93		23	1

SPINK, Nigel

Born Chelmsford 8.8.58. Ht 6 2
Wt 14 08
Goalkeeper. From Chelmsford C. England
B, 1 full cap.

1976–77	Aston Villa	—	—
1977–78		—	—
1978–79		—	—
1979–80		1	—
1980–81		—	—
1981–82		—	—
1982–83		22	—
1983–84		28	—
1984–85		19	—
1985–86		31	—
1986–87		32	—

1987–88		44	—
1988–89		34	—
1989–90		38	—
1990–91		34	—
1991–92		23	—
1992–93		25	—

SPOONER, Nicky

Born Manchester 5.6.71. Ht 5 8
Wt 11 00
Defender. From Trainee.

1990–91	Bolton W	—	—
1991–92		15	1
1992–93		6	1

SPOONER, Steve

Born London 25.1.61. Ht 5 10 Wt 12 00
Midfield. From Apprentice.

1978–79	Derby Co	1	—
1979–80		1	—
1980–81		2	—
1981–82		4	—
1981–82	Halifax T	29	2
1982–83		43	11
1983–84	Chesterfield	20	3
1984–85		41	6
1985–86		32	5
1986–87	Hereford U	42	11
1987–88		42	8
1988–89	York C	31	5
1989–90		41	6
1990–91	Rotherham U	19	1
1990–91	Mansfield T	12	—
1991–92		31	2
1992–93		15	1
1992–93	Blackpool	2	—

SRNICEK, Pavel

Born Ostrava 10.3.68. Ht 6 2 Wt 14 09
Goalkeeper. From Banik Ostrava.
Czechoslovakia full caps.

1990–91	Newcastle U	7	—
1991–92		13	—
1992–93		32	—

STAINROD, Simon

Born Sheffield 1.2.59.   Ht 5 10   Wt 12 09
Forward. From Apprentice. England
Youth.

Season	Club		
1975–76	Sheffield U	7	2
1976–77		21	3
1977–78		25	6
1978–79		14	3
1978–79	Oldham Ath	14	5
1979–80		37	11
1980–81		18	5
1980–81	QPR	15	4
1981–82		39	17
1982–83		31	9
1983–84		41	13
1984–85		19	5
1984–85	Sheffield W	9	1
1985–86		6	1
1985–86	Aston Villa	30	10
1986–87		29	6
1987–88		4	—
1987–88	Stoke C	12	2
1988–89		16	4
From Strasbourg			
1990–91	Falkirk	37	16
1991–92		23	5
1991–92	Dundee	13	2
1992–93		20	7

STALLARD, Mark

Born Derby 24.10.74.   Ht 6 0   Wt 12 06
Forward. From Trainee.

1991–92	Derby Co	3	—
1992–93		5	—

STAMPS, Scott

Born Edgbaston 20.3.75   Ht 5 11
Wt 11 00
Defender. From Trainee.

1992–93	Torquay U	2	—

STANCLIFFE, Paul

Born Sheffield 5.5.58.   Ht 6 2   Wt 13 05
Defender. From Apprentice.

1975–76	Rotherham U	42	2

1976–77		46	—
1977–78		32	3
1978–79		33	—
1979–80		33	1
1980–81		44	—
1981–82		42	2
1982–83		13	—
1983–84	Sheffield U	43	1
1984–85		33	1
1985–86		40	1
1986–87		36	2
1987–88		41	3
1988–89		42	3
1989–90		40	1
1990–91		3	—
1990–91	*Rotherham U*	5	—
1990–91	Wolverhampton W	17	—
1991–92	York C	18	1
1992–93		41	1

STANISLAUS, Roger

Born Hammersmith 2.11.68.   Ht 5 9
Wt 12 06
Defender. From Trainee.

1986–87	Arsenal	—	—
1987–88	Brentford	37	2
1988–89		43	1
1989–90		31	1
1990–91	Bury	44	2
1991–92		40	3
1992–93		24	—

STANNARD, Jim

Born London 6.10.62.   Ht 6 2   Wt 14 12
Goalkeeper. From Local.

1980–81	Fulham	17	—
1981–82		2	—
1982–83		—	—
1983–84		15	—
1984–85		7	—
1984–85	*Charlton Ath*	1	—
1984–85	*Southend U*	17	—
1985–86	Southend U	46	—
1986–87		46	—
1987–88	Fulham	46	—
1988–89		45	—

Season	Club	Appearances	Goals
1989–90	....	44	1
1990–91	....	42	—
1991–92	....	46	—
1992–93	....	43	—

STANT, Phil

Born Bolton 13.10.62.   Ht 6 1   Wt 12 07
Forward. From Camberley.

Season	Club	Appearances	Goals
1982–83	Reading	4	2
From Army			
1986–87	Hereford U	9	1
1987–88	....	39	9
1988–89	....	41	28
1989–90	Notts Co	22	6
1990–91	....	—	—
1990–91	*Blackpool*	12	5
1990–91	*Lincoln C*	4	—
1990–91	*Huddersfield T*	5	1
1990–91	Fulham	19	5
1991–92	Mansfield T	40	26
1992–93	....	17	6
1992–93	Cardiff C	24	11

STAPLETON, Frank

Born Dublin 10.7.56.   Ht 6 0   Wt 13 01
Forward. From Apprentice. Eire Youth, 70 full caps.

Season	Club	Appearances	Goals
1973–74	Arsenal	—	—
1974–75	....	1	—
1975–76	....	25	4
1976–77	....	40	13
1977–78	....	39	13
1978–79	....	41	17
1979–80	....	39	14
1980–81	....	40	14
1981–82	Manchester U	41	13
1982–83	....	41	14
1983–84	....	42	13
1984–85	....	24	6
1985–86	....	41	7
1986–87	....	34	7
1987–88	Ajax	4	—
1987–88	Derby Co	10	1
From Le Havre			
1989–90	Blackburn R	43	3
1990–91	....	38	10

Season	Club	Appearances	Goals
1991–92	Aldershot	1	—
1991–92	Huddersfield T	5	—
1991–92	Bradford C	27	—
1992–93	....	13	2

STARBUCK, Philip

Born Nottingham 24.11.68.   Ht 5 10
Wt 10 13
Forward. From Apprentice.

Season	Club	Appearances	Goals
1986–87	Nottingham F	5	2
1987–88	....	10	—
1987–88	*Birmingham C*	3	—
1988–89	Nottingham F	7	—
1989–90	....	2	—
1989–90	*Hereford U*	6	—
1990–91	Nottingham F	12	—
1990–91	*Blackburn R*	6	1
1991–92	Huddersfield T	44	14
1992–93	....	38	9

STARK, Billy

Born Glasgow 1.12.56   Ht 6 1   Wt 11 11
Midfield. From Anniesland W. Scotland U-21.

Season	Club	Appearances	Goals
1975–76	St Mirren	21	6
1976–77	....	35	11
1977–78	....	33	7
1978–79	....	32	9
1979–80	....	36	8
1980–81	....	34	5
1981–82	....	33	10
1982–83	....	31	4
1983–84	Aberdeen	14	6
1984–85	....	32	15
1985–86	....	30	8
1986–87	....	35	12
1987–88	Celtic	37	8
1988–89	....	25	9
1989–90	....	2	—
1990–91	Kilmarnock	21	6
1991–92	....	1	—
1991–92	Hamilton A	14	—
1992–93	Kilmarnock	28	3

STATHAM, Brian

Born Zimbabwe 21.5.69.   Ht 5 11
Wt 11 00
Defender. From Apprentice. England
Youth, Under-21.

Season	Club		
1987–88	Tottenham H	18	—
1988–89		6	—
1989–90		—	—
1990–91		—	—
1990–91	*Reading*	8	—
1991–92	Tottenham H	—	—
1991–92	*Bournemouth*	2	—
1991–92	*Brentford*	18	—
1992–93	Brentford	45	—

STATHAM, Derek

Born Wolverhampton 24.3.59.   Ht 5 5
Wt 11 05
Defender. From Apprentice. England
Youth, Under-21, B, 3 full caps.

Season	Club		
1976–77	WBA	16	1
1977–78		40	—
1978–79		39	1
1979–80		16	—
1980–81		31	—
1981–82		35	—
1982–83		32	2
1983–84		16	—
1984–85		30	4
1985–86		37	—
1986–87		6	—
1987–88		1	—
1987–88	Southampton	38	—
1988–89		26	2
1989–90	Stoke C	19	—
1990–91		22	1
1991–92	Walsall	29	—
1992–93		21	—

STAUNTON, Steve

Born Drogheda 19.1.69.   Ht 6 0
Wt 12 04
Defender. From Dundalk. Eire Under-21,
41 full caps.

Season	Club		
1986–87	Liverpool	—	—

Season	Club		
1987–88		—	—
1987–88	*Bradford C*	8	—
1988–89	Liverpool	21	—
1989–90		20	—
1990–91		24	—
1991–92	Aston Villa	37	4
1992–93		42	2

STEELE, Tim

Born Coventry 1.2.67.   Ht 5 9   Wt 11 00
Forward. From Apprentice.

Season	Club		
1985–86	Shrewsbury T	2	—
1986–87		11	1
1987–88		33	3
1988–89		15	1
1988–89	Wolverhampton W	11	1
1989–90		15	1
1990–91		28	2
1991–92		17	3
1991–92	*Stoke C*	7	1
1992–93	Wolverhampton W	4	—

STEIN, Brian

Born S. Africa 19.10.57.   Ht 5 10
Wt 11 08
Forward. From Edgware T. England
Under-21, 1 full cap.

Season	Club		
1977–78	Luton T	24	3
1978–79		34	10
1979–80		42	8
1980–81		42	18
1981–82		42	21
1982–83		21	15
1983–84		42	9
1984–85		42	9
1985–86		33	14
1986–87		38	12
1987–88		28	9
From Caen			
1991–92	Luton T	39	3
1992–93	Barnet	40	8

STEIN, Edwin

Born Cape Town 28.6.55. Ht 5 10
Wt 11 00
Midfield. From Luton T, Edgware,
Harrow Bor, Dagenham.

1991–92	Barnet	1	—
1992–93		—	—

STEIN, Mark

Born S. Africa 28.1.66. Ht 5 6   Wt 11 02
Forward. England Youth.

1983–84	Luton T	1	—
1984–85		1	—
1985–86		6	—
1985–86	*Aldershot*	2	1
1986–87	Luton T	21	8
1987–88		25	11
1988–89	QPR	31	4
1989–90		2	—
1989–90	Oxford U	41	9
1990–91		34	8
1991–92		7	1
1991–92	Stoke C	36	16
1992–93		46	26

STEJSKAL, Jan

Born Czechoslovakia 15.1.62. Ht 6 3
Wt 12 00
Goalkeeper. From Sparta Prague.
Czechoslovakia full caps.

1990–91	QPR	26	—
1991–92		41	—
1992–93		15	—

STEPHENSON, Paul

Born Wallsend 2.1.68. Ht 5 10   Wt 12 02
Forward. From Apprentice. England
Youth.

1985–86	Newcastle U	22	1
1986–87		24	—
1987–88		7	—
1988–89		8	—
1989–90	Millwall	12	1

1989–90		23	2
1990–91		30	1
1991–92		28	2
1992–93		5	—
1992–93	*Gillingham*	12	2
1992–93	Brentford	11	—

STERLAND, Mel

Born Sheffield 1.10.61. Ht 6 0   Wt 13 05
Defender. From Apprentice. England
Under-21, B, 1 full cap. Football League.

1978–79	Sheffield W	2	1
1979–80		2	—
1980–81		22	2
1981–82		27	—
1982–83		35	—
1983–84		39	8
1984–85		24	2
1985–86		38	8
1986–87		30	2
1987–88		38	8
1988–89		22	6
1988–89	Rangers	9	3
1989–90	Leeds U	42	5
1990–91		38	5
1991–92		31	6
1992–93		3	—

STERLING, Worrell

Born Bethnal Green 8.6.65. Ht 5 7
Wt 10 11
Midfield. From Apprentice.

1982–83	Watford	3	—
1983–84		10	1
1984–85		15	4
1985–86		24	3
1986–87		18	4
1987–88		21	2
1988–89		3	—
1988–89	Peterborough U	12	3
1989–90		46	5
1990–91		46	9
1991–92		45	4
1992–93		44	8

STEVEN, Trevor

Born Berwick 21.9.63. Ht 5 8 Wt 10 09
Midfield. From Apprentice. England
Under-21, 36 full caps.

1980–81	Burnley	1	—
1981–82		36	3
1982–83		39	8
1983–84	Everton	27	1
1984–85		40	12
1985–86		41	9
1986–87		41	14
1987–88		36	6
1988–89		29	6
1989–90	Rangers	34	3
1990–91		19	2
1991–92		2	1
1991–92	Marseille	27	3
1992–93	Rangers	24	5

STEVENS, Gary

Born Barrow 27.3.63. Ht 5 11 Wt 10 11
Defender. From Apprentice. England 46
full caps.

1980–81	Everton	—	—
1981–82		19	1
1982–83		28	—
1983–84		27	1
1984–85		37	3
1985–86		41	1
1986–87		25	2
1987–88		31	—
1988–89	Rangers	35	1
1989–90		35	1
1990–91		36	4
1991–92		43	2
1992–93		9	—

STEVENS, Ian

Born Malta 21.10.66. Ht 5 9 Wt 12 00
Forward. From Trainee.

1984–85	Preston NE	4	1
1985–86		7	1
1986–87	Stockport Co	2	—
From Lancaster C			
1986–87	Bolton W	8	2

1987–88		9	—
1988–89		21	5
1989–90		4	—
1990–91		5	—
1991–92	Bury	45	17
1992–93		32	14

STEVENS, Keith

Born Merton 21.6.64. Ht 6 0 Wt 12 10
Defender. From Apprentice.

1980–81	Millwall	1	—
1981–82		7	—
1982–83		26	—
1983–84		17	—
1984–85		41	—
1985–86		33	1
1986–87		35	1
1987–88		35	1
1988–89		23	—
1989–90		28	—
1990–91		42	1
1991–92		27	—
1992–93		31	2

STEVENSON, Andy

Born Scunthorpe 29.9.67. Ht 6 0
Wt 13 05
Midfield. From School.

1985–86	Scunthorpe U	2	—
1986–87		7	—
1987–88		8	—
1988–89		26	—
1989–90		24	1
1990–91		9	—
1991–92		2	—
1991–92	*Doncaster R*	1	—
1992–93	Scunthorpe U	25	3

STEWART, Billy

Born Liverpool 1.1.65. Ht 5 11 Wt 11 07
Goalkeeper. From Apprentice.

1982–83	Liverpool	—	—
1983–84		—	—
1984–85	Wigan Ath	6	—
1985–86		8	—

1986–87	Chester C	29	—
1987–88		27	—
1988–89		46	—
1989–90		46	—
1990–91		38	—
1991–92		37	—
1992–93		42	—

STEWART, Marcus

Born Bristol 7.11.72. Ht 5 10 Wt 10 03
Forward. From Trainee. Football League.

| 1991–92 | Bristol R | 33 | 5 |
| 1992–93 | | 38 | 11 |

STEWART, Paul

Born Manchester 7.10.64. Ht 5 11
Wt 11 03
Forward. From Apprentice. England
Youth, B, Under-21, 3 full caps.

1981–82	Blackpool	14	3
1982–83		38	7
1983–84		44	10
1984–85		31	7
1985–86		42	8
1986–87		32	21
1986–87	Manchester C	11	2
1987–88		40	24
1988–89	Tottenham H	30	12
1989–90		28	8
1990–91		35	3
1991–92		38	5
1992–93	Liverpool	24	1

STEWART, Sandy

Born Bellshill 14.10.65. Ht 5 9 Wt 10 10
Midfield. From Pollok J.

1987–88	Hearts	—	—
1988–89		—	—
1988–89	Kilmarnock	7	1
1989–90	Airdrieonians	8	3
1990–91		25	—
1991–92		41	1
1992–93		43	1

STEWART, Simon

Born Leeds 1.11.73. Ht 6 1 Wt 11 00
Defender. From Trainee.

| 1992–93 | Sheffield W | 6 | — |

STIMSON, Mark

Born Plaistow 27.12.67. Ht 5 11
Wt 11 00
Defender. From Trainee.

1984–85	Tottenham H	—	—
1985–86		—	—
1986–87		1	—
1987–88		—	—
1987–88	Leyton Orient	10	—
1988–89	Tottenham H	1	—
1988–89	Gillingham	18	—
1989–90	Newcastle U	37	1
1990–91		23	1
1991–92		24	—
1992–93		2	—
1992–93	Portsmouth	4	—

STOCKWELL, Mick

Born Chelmsford 14.2.65. Ht 5 9
Wt 11 04
Midfield. From Apprentice.

1982–83	Ipswich T	—	—
1983–84		—	—
1984–85		—	—
1985–86		8	—
1986–87		21	1
1987–88		43	1
1988–89		23	2
1989–90		34	3
1990–91		44	6
1991–92		46	2
1992–93		39	4

STOKER, Gareth

Born Bishop Auckland 22.2.73. Ht 5 9
Wt 10 03
Midfield. From Leeds U Trainee.

| 1991–92 | Hull C | 24 | 2 |

1992–93 .... 6 —

STONE, Steven

Born Gateshead 20.8.71. Ht 5 9
Wt 11 03
Midfield. From Trainee.

1989–90	Nottingham F.............	—	—
1990–91	....	—	—
1991–92	....	1	—
1992–93	....	12	1

STONEMAN, Paul

Born Whitley Bay 26.2.73. Ht 6 1
Wt 13 06
Defender. From Trainee.

1991–92	Blackpool.....................	19	—
1992–93	....	10	—

STORER, Stuart

Born Harborough 16.1.67. Ht 5 11
Wt 11 08
Forward. From Local.

1983–84	Mansfield T.................	1	—
1984–85	Birmingham C............	—	—
1985–86	....	2	—
1986–87	....	6	—
1986–87	Everton	—	—
1987–88	....	—	—
1987–88	Wigan Ath.................	12	—
1987–88	Bolton W	15	1
1988–89	....	23	2
1989–90	....	38	4
1990–91	....	35	5
1991–92	....	9	—
1992–93	....	3	—
1992–93	Exeter C......................	10	4

STOWE, Dean

Born Burnley 27.3.75. Ht 5 9 Wt 11 02
Midfield. From Trainee.

1992–93	Hull C........................	1	—

STOWELL, Mike

Born Preston 19.4.65. Ht 6 2 Wt 11 10
Goalkeeper. From Leyland Motors.

1984–85	Preston NE.................	—	—
1985–86	....	—	—
1985–86	Everton	—	—
1986–87	....	—	—
1987–88	Chester C	14	—
1987–88	York C	6	—
1987–88	Manchester C.............	14	—
1988–89	Everton	—	—
1988–89	Port Vale.....................	7	—
1988–89	Wolverhampton W.......	7	—
1989–90	Everton	—	—
1989–90	Preston NE.................	2	—
1990–91	Wolverhampton W	39	—
1991–92	....	46	—
1992–93	....	26	—

STRACHAN, Gordon

Born Edinburgh 9.2.57. Ht 5 6 Wt 10 06
Midfield. Scotland Youth, Under-21, 50
full caps.

1974–75	Dundee.......................	1	—
1975–76	....	23	6
1976–77	....	36	7
1977–78	Aberdeen....................	12	2
1978–79	....	31	5
1979–80	....	33	10
1980–81	....	20	6
1981–82	....	30	7
1982–83	....	32	12
1983–84	....	25	13
1984–85	Manchester U.............	41	15
1985–86	....	28	5
1986–87	....	34	4
1987–88	....	36	8
1988–89	....	21	1
1988–89	Leeds U	11	3
1989–90	....	46	16
1990–91	....	34	7
1991–92	....	36	4
1992–93	....	31	4

STRANDLI, Frank

Born Norway 16.5.72
Forward. From IK Start. Norway full
caps.

1992–93	Leeds U	10	2

STRINGFELLOW, Ian

Born Nottingham 8.5.69.   Ht 5 9
Wt 11 04
Forward. From Apprentice.

1985–86	Mansfield T	3	—
1986–87		22	4
1987–88		30	8
1988–89		8	1
1989–90		19	3
1990–91		24	2
1991–92		17	2
1992–93		30	5
1992–93	*Blackpool*	3	1

STRODDER, Gary

Born Leeds 1.4.65.   Ht 6 1   Wt 12 06
Defender. From Apprentice.

1982–83	Lincoln C	8	—
1983–84		22	1
1984–85		26	2
1985–86		43	1
1986–87		33	2
1986–87	West Ham U	12	—
1987–88		30	1
1988–89		7	—
1989–90		16	1
1990–91	WBA	34	1
1991–92		37	3
1992–93		29	1

STUART, Graham

Born Tooting, London 24.10.70.   Ht 5 8
Wt 11 06
Forward. From Trainee. FA Schools.
England Under-21.

1989–90	Chelsea	2	1
1990–91		19	4
1991–92		27	—
1992–93		39	9

STUART, Mark

Born Hammersmith 15.12.66.   Ht 5 10
Wt 11 03
Forward. From QPR Schoolboy.

1984–85	Charlton Ath	6	1
1985–86		30	12
1986–87		36	9
1987–88		31	6
1988–89		4	—
1988–89	Plymouth Arg	32	5
1989–90		25	6
1989–90	*Ipswich T*	5	2
1990–91	Bradford C	13	2
1991–92		16	3
1992–93		—	—
1992–93	Huddersfield T	15	3

STUBBS, Alan

Born Kirkby 6.10.71.   Ht 6 2   Wt 12 12
Defender. From Trainee.

1990–91	Bolton W	23	—
1991–92		32	1
1992–93		42	2

STURGESS, Paul

Born Dartford 4.8.75
Midfield. From Trainee.

1992–93	Charlton Ath	4	—

STURRIDGE, Dean

Born Birmingham 26.7.73.   Ht 5 7
Wt 10 10
Forward. From Trainee.

1991–92	Derby Co	1	—
1992–93		10	—

STURRIDGE, Simon

Born Birmingham 9.12.69.   Ht 5 5
Wt 10 07
Forward. From Trainee.

1988–89	Birmingham C	21	3

Season	Club	App	Goals
1989–90		31	10
1990–91		38	6
1991–92		40	10
1992–93		20	1

SUCKLING, Perry

Born Leyton 12.10.65. Ht 6 2 Wt 13 02
Goalkeeper. From Apprentice. England
Youth, Under-21.

Season	Club	App	Goals
1982–83	Coventry C	3	—
1983–84		24	—
1984–85		—	—
1985–86		—	—
1986–87	Manchester C	37	—
1987–88		2	—
1987–88	Crystal Palace	17	—
1988–89		27	—
1989–90		12	—
1989–90	*West Ham U*	6	—
1990–91	Crystal Palace	—	—
1991–92		3	—
1991–92	*Brentford*	8	—
1992–93	Watford	37	—

SULLEY, Chris

Born Camberwell 3.12.59. Ht 5 8
Wt 10 00
Defender. From Apprentice.

Season	Club	App	Goals
1978–79	Chelsea	—	—
1979–80		—	—
1980–81		—	—
1980–81	Bournemouth	8	—
1981–82		46	—
1982–83		46	1
1983–84		46	2
1984–85		23	—
1985–86		37	—
1986–87	Dundee U	7	—
1986–87	Blackburn R	13	—
1987–88		34	—
1988–89		19	—
1989–90		36	—
1990–91		25	3
1991–92		7	—
1992–93	Port Vale	40	1

SULLIVAN, Neil

Born Sutton 24.2.70. Ht 6 0 Wt 12 01
Goalkeeper. From Trainee.

Season	Club	App	Goals
1988–89	Wimbledon	—	—
1989–90		—	—
1990–91		1	—
1991–92		1	—
1991–92	*Crystal Palace*	1	—
1992–93	Wimbledon	1	—

SUMMERBEE, Nicky

Born Altrincham 26.8.71. Ht 5 11
Wt 11 08
Forward. From Trainee. England
Under-21.

Season	Club	App	Goals
1989–90	Swindon T	1	—
1990–91		7	—
1991–92		27	—
1992–93		39	3

SUMMERFIELD, Kevin

Born Walsall 7.1.59. Ht 5 11 Wt 11 00
Midfield. From Apprentice.

Season	Club	App	Goals
1976–77	WBA	—	—
1977–78		—	—
1978–79		2	1
1979–80		3	1
1980–81		—	—
1981–82		4	2
1982–83	Birmingham C	5	1
1982–83	Walsall	21	9
1983–84		33	8
1984–85	Cardiff C	10	1
1984–85	Plymouth Arg	17	2
1985–86		26	7
1986–87		28	9
1987–88		37	5
1988–89		20	2
1989–90		10	1
1989–90	*Exeter C*	4	—
1990–91	Plymouth Arg	1	—
1990–91	Shrewsbury T	32	5
1991–92		44	7
1992–93		35	7

SUNLEY, Mark

Born Stockton 13.10.71. Ht 6 1
Wt 12 07
Defender.

Season	Club	App	Goals
1990–91	Middlesbrough	—	—
1991–92	Darlington	15	—
1992–93		2	—

SUSSEX, Andy

Born Enfield 23.11.64. Ht 6 0   Wt 13 11
Forward. From Apprentice.

Season	Club	App	Goals
1981–82	Orient	8	1
1982–83		24	2
1983–84		29	6
1984–85		19	2
1985–86		36	4
1986–87		20	1
1987–88		8	1
1988–89	Crewe Alex	25	4
1989–90		33	9
1990–91		44	11
1991–92	Southend U	15	3
1992–93		23	4

SUTCH, Daryl

Born Lowestoft 11.9.71. Ht 6 0
Wt 12 00
Midfield. From Trainee. England Youth,
Under-21.

Season	Club	App	Goals
1989–90	Norwich C	—	—
1990–91		4	—
1991–92		9	—
1992–93		22	2

SUTTON, Chris

Born Nottingham 10.3.73. Ht 6 3
Wt 12 01
Forward. From Trainee. England
Under-21.

Season	Club	App	Goals
1990–91	Norwich C	2	—
1991–92		21	2
1992–93		38	8

SUTTON, Steve

Born Hartington 16.4.61. Ht 6 1
Wt 13 07
Goalkeeper. From Apprentice.

Season	Club	App	Goals
1980–81	Nottingham F	1	—
1980–81	*Mansfield T*	8	—
1981–82	Nottingham F	1	—
1982–83		17	—
1983–84		6	—
1984–85		14	—
1984–85	*Derby Co*	14	—
1985–86	Nottingham F	31	—
1986–87		28	—
1987–88		35	—
1988–89		36	—
1989–90		30	—
1990–91		—	—
1990–91	*Coventry C*	1	—
1991–92	Nottingham F	—	—
1991–92	*Luton T*	14	—
1991–92	Derby Co	10	—
1992–93		25	—

SWALES, Steve

Born Whitby 26.12.73.
Defender. From Trainee.

Season	Club	App	Goals
1991–92	Scarborough	4	—
1992–93		3	—

SWAN, Peter

Born Leeds 29.9.66. Ht 6 0   Wt 12 00
Forward. From Local.

Season	Club	App	Goals
1984–85	Leeds U	—	—
1985–86		16	3
1986–87		7	—
1987–88		25	8
1988–89		1	—
1988–89	Hull C	11	1
1989–90		31	11
1990–91		38	12
1991–92	Port Vale	33	3
1992–93		38	2

SWANN, Gary

Born York 11.4.62.   Ht 5 11   Wt 11 13
Midfield. From Apprentice.

Season	Club	Apps	Goals
1980–81	Hull C	20	2
1981–82		20	—
1982–83		25	—
1983–84		41	2
1984–85		32	3
1985–86		39	2
1986–87		9	—
1986–87	Preston NE	30	5
1987–88		46	12
1988–89		18	2
1989–90		46	8
1990–91		30	5
1991–92		29	5
1992–93	York C	38	—

1992–93		41	2

SWEENEY, Paul

Born Glasgow 10.1.65   Ht 5 8   Wt 11 5
Midfield. From St Kentigern's Acad.

Season	Club	Apps	Goals
1981–82	Raith R	—	—
1982–83		2	—
1983–84		29	1
1984–85		32	—
1985–86		37	3
1986–87		38	—
1987–88		39	2
1988–89		28	2
1988–89	Newcastle U	8	—
1989–90		19	—
1990–91		9	—
1990–91	St Johnstone	8	—
1991–92		—	—
1992–93		2	—

SYMONS, Kit

Born Basingstoke 8.3.71.   Ht 6 1
Wt 10 10
Defender. From Trainee. Wales Under-21,
10 full caps.

Season	Club	Apps	Goals
1988–89	Portsmouth	2	—
1989–90		1	—
1990–91		1	—
1991–92		46	1

TAGGART, Craig

Born Glasgow 17.1.73.   Ht 5 10   Wt 11 00
Midfield.

| 1991–92 | Falkirk | 8 | — |
| 1992–93 | | 5 | — |

TAGGART, Gerry

Born Belfast 18.10.70.   Ht 6 1   Wt 12 03
Defender. From Trainee. Northern Ireland
Under-23, 21 full caps.

1988–89	Manchester C	11	1
1989–90		1	—
1989–90	Barnsley	21	2
1990–91		30	2
1991–92		38	3
1992–93		44	4

TAIT, Mick

Born Wallsend 30.9.56.   Ht 5 11
Wt 12 05
Midfield. From Apprentice.

1974–75	Oxford U	4	—
1975–76		37	12
1976–77		23	11
1976–77	Carlisle U	13	3
1977–78		43	10
1978–79		46	7
1979–80		4	—
1979–80	Hull C	33	3
1980–81	Portsmouth	38	8
1981–82		35	9
1982–83		44	6
1983–84		36	3
1984–85		33	1
1985–86		26	2
1986–87		28	1
1987–88		—	—
1987–88	Reading	35	2
1988–89		36	4
1989–90		28	3
1990–91	Darlington	45	2
1991–92		34	—
1992–93	Hartlepool U	35	1

TAIT, Paul

Born Sutton Coldfield 31.1.71.   Ht 6 1
Wt 10 00
Midfield. From Trainee.

1987–88	Birmingham C	1	—
1988–89		10	—
1989–90		14	2
1990–91		17	3
1991–92		12	—
1992–93		28	2

TAIT, Thomas

Born Ayr 8.9.67   Ht 5 10   Wt 11 7
Midfield. From Valspar BC.

1986–87	Clyde	30	1
1987–88		21	2
1988–89		31	3
1989–90	Kilmarnock	38	6
1990–91		36	3
1991–92		23	3
1992–93		5	1
1992–93	Stirling Albion	27	2

TALBOYS, Steve

Born Bristol 18.9.66   Ht 5 11   Wt 11 10
Midfield. From Gloucester C.

| 1991–92 | Wimbledon | — | — |
| 1992–93 | | 7 | — |

TALIA, Frank

Born Melbourne 20.7.72
Goalkeeper. From Sunshine George Cross.

| 1992–93 | Blackburn R | — | — |
| 1992–93 | *Hartlepool U* | 14 | — |

TANKARD, Allen

Born Fleet 21.5.69.   Ht 5 10   Wt 11 07
Defender. From Trainee. England Youth.

1985–86	Southampton	3	—
1986–87		2	—
1987–88		—	—

1988–89	Wigan Ath	33	1
1989–90		45	1
1990–91		46	1
1991–92		44	—
1992–93		41	1

TANNER, Nick

Born Bristol 24.5.65. Ht 6 2 Wt 13 07
Defender. From Mangotsfield.

1984–85	Bristol R	—	—
1985–86		37	2
1986–87		44	1
1987–88		26	—
1988–89	Liverpool	—	—
1989–90		4	—
1989–90	Norwich C	6	—
1990–91	Liverpool	—	—
1990–91	Swindon T	7	—
1991–92	Liverpool	32	1
1992–93		4	—

TAYLOR, Alex

Born Baillieston 13.6.62. Ht 5 7
Wt 10 11
Midfield. From Blantyre St J.

1982–83	Dundee U	3	—
1983–84		9	1
1984–85		21	5
1985–86		—	—
1986–87	Hamilton A	25	1
1987–88		41	4
1988–89	Walsall	13	3
1989–90		32	3
1990–91		—	—
1990–91	Falkirk	29	2
1991–92		22	1
1992–93		8	1
1992–93	Partick T	8	1

TAYLOR, Andy

Born Rawmarsh 19.1.73. Ht 5 8
Wt 10 13
Defender. From Trainee.

1990–91	Rotherham U	5	—

1991–92		6	—
1992–93		7	—

TAYLOR, Bob

Born Horden 3.2.67. Ht 5 10 Wt 11 09
Forward. From Horden CW.

1985–86	Leeds U	2	—
1986–87		2	—
1987–88		32	9
1988–89		6	—
1988–89	Bristol C	12	8
1989–90		37	27
1990–91		39	11
1991–92		18	4
1991–92	WBA	19	8
1992–93		46	30

TAYLOR, Colin

Born Liverpool 25.12.71. Ht 6 0
Wt 12 07
Forward. From Trainee. England Youth.

1989–90	Wolverhampton W	—	—
1990–91		15	2
1991–92		3	—
1991–92	Wigan Ath	7	2
1992–93	Wolverhampton W	1	—
1992–93	Preston NE	4	—
1992–93	Doncaster R	2	—

TAYLOR, Craig

Born Plymouth 24.1.74 Ht 6 1 Wt 12 00
Defender. From Trainee.

1992–93	Exeter C	5	—

TAYLOR, Gareth

Born Weston-Super-Mare 25.2.73.
Ht 6 2 Wt 12 05
Defender. From Southampton Trainee.

1991–92	Bristol R	1	—
1992–93		—	—

TAYLOR, Ian

Born Birmingham 4.6.68 Ht 6 1
Wt 12 00
Midfield. From Moor Green.

1992–93	Port Vale	41	15

TAYLOR, John

Born Norwich 24.10.64. Ht 6 2 Wt 11 12
Forward. From Local.

1982–83	Colchester U	—	—
1983–84		—	—
1984–85		—	—
From Sudbury			
1988–89	Cambridge U	40	12
1989–90		45	15
1990–91		40	14
1991–92		35	5
1991–92	Bristol R	8	7
1992–93		42	14

TAYLOR, Mark

Born Hartlepool 20.11.64. Ht 5 7
Wt 11 00
Midfield. From Local.

1982–83	Hartlepool U	—	—
1983–84		6	—
1984–85		36	4
1985–86		5	—
1985–86	Crewe Alex	3	—
1986–87	Blackpool	40	14
1987–88		41	21
1988–89		9	3
1989–90		—	—
1990–91		—	—
1990–91	Cardiff C	6	3
1991–92	Blackpool	10	2
1991–92	Wrexham	9	—
1992–93		19	2

TAYLOR, Mark

Born Walsall 22.2.66. Ht 5 8 Wt 11 08
Midfield. From Local.

1984–85	Walsall	4	—

1985–86		18	2
1986–87		17	—
1987–88		40	1
1988–89		34	1
1989–90	Sheffield W	9	—
1990–91	Shrewsbury T	19	2
1991–92	Shrewsbury T	29	2
1992–93		42	5

TAYLOR, Martin

Born Tamworth 9.12.66. Ht 5 11
Wt 12 04
Goalkeeper. From Mile Oak R.

1986–87	Derby Co	—	—
1987–88		—	—
1987–88	Carlisle U	10	—
1987–88	Scunthorpe U	8	—
1988–89	Derby Co	—	—
1989–90		3	—
1990–91		7	—
1991–92		5	—
1992–93		21	—

TAYLOR, Robert

Born Norwich 30.4.71. Ht 6 0 Wt 11 07
Forward. From Trainee.

1989–90	Norwich C	—	—
1990–91		—	—
1990–91	Leyton Orient	3	1
1991–92	Birmingham C	—	—
1991–92	Leyton Orient	11	1
1992–93		39	18

TAYLOR, Scott

Born Portsmouth 23.11.70. Ht 5 9
Wt 11 00
Midfield. From Trainee.

1988–89	Reading	3	—
1989–90		29	2
1990–91		32	1
1991–92		29	2
1992–93		32	5

TAYLOR, Shaun

Born Plymouth 26.3.63.   Ht 6 1   Wt 13 00
Defender. From Bideford.

Season	Club		
1986–87	Exeter C	23	—
1987–88		41	1
1988–89		46	6
1989–90		45	5
1990–91		45	4
1991–92	Swindon T	42	4
1992–93		46	11

TEALE, Shaun

Born Southport 10.3.64.   Ht 6 0
Wt 13 10
Defender. From Southport, Northwich
Vics, Weymouth.

Season	Club		
1988–89	Bournemouth	20	—
1989–90		34	—
1990–91		46	4
1991–92	Aston Villa	42	—
1992–93		39	1

TELFER, Paul

Born Edinburgh 21.10.71.   Ht 5 9
Wt 11 06
Midfield. From Trainee. Scotland
Under-21.

Season	Club		
1988–89	Luton T	—	—
1989–90		—	—
1990–91		1	—
1991–92		20	1
1992–93		32	2

TEN CAAT, Theo

Born Scheveld 8.12.64.   Ht 5 11   Wt 11 00
Midfield. From Groningen.

Season	Club		
1991–92	Aberdeen	30	5
1992–93		15	—

TERRY, Steve

Born Clapton 14.6.62.   Ht 6 1   Wt 13 05
Defender. From Apprentice.

Season	Club		
1979–80	Watford	2	—

Season	Club		
1980–81		5	—
1981–82		26	2
1982–83		7	1
1983–84		17	1
1984–85		38	4
1985–86		41	4
1986–87		18	2
1987–88		6	—
1988–89	Hull C	33	1
1989–90		29	3
1989–90	Northampton T	17	2
1990–91		46	6
1991–92		37	3
1992–93		42	5

THACKERAY, Andy

Born Huddersfield 13.2.68.   Ht 5 9
Wt 11 00
Midfield.

Season	Club		
1985–86	Manchester C	—	—
1986–87	Huddersfield T	2	—
1986–87	Newport Co	11	3
1987–88		43	1
1988–89	Wrexham	35	2
1989–90		34	7
1990–91		41	2
1991–92		42	3
1992–93	Rochdale	41	6

THEODOSIOU, Andy

Born Stoke Newington 30.10.70.   Ht 6 0
Wt 12 10
Defender. From Tottenham H Trainee.

Season	Club		
1989–90	Norwich C	—	—
1990–91		—	—
1991–92	Hereford U	33	1
1992–93		9	1

THOMAS, Dean

Born Bedworth 19.12.61.   Ht 5 10
Wt 11 08
Defender. From Nuneaton Borough.

Season	Club		
1981–82	Wimbledon	18	—
1982–83		24	5

Season	Club	Apps	Goals
1983–84	....	15	3
From Fortuna Dusseldorf			
1988–89	Northampton T	43	9
1989–90	....	31	2
1989–90	Notts Co	10	1
1990–91	....	44	3
1991–92	....	36	1
1992–93	....	37	3

THOMAS, Geoff

Born Manchester 5.8.64.   Ht 5 10
Wt 10 07
Midfield. From Local. England B, 9 full
caps.

Season	Club	Apps	Goals
1981–82	Rochdale	—	—
1982–83	....	1	—
1983–84	....	10	1
1983–84	Crewe Alex	8	1
1984–85	....	40	4
1985–86	....	37	6
1986–87	....	40	9
1987–88	Crystal Palace	41	6
1988–89	....	22	5
1989–90	....	35	1
1990–91	....	38	6
1991–92	....	30	6
1992–93	....	29	2

THOMAS, Glen

Born Hackney 6.10.67.   Ht 6 1   Wt 12 07
Defender. From Apprentice.

Season	Club	Apps	Goals
1985–86	Fulham	—	—
1986–87	....	1	—
1987–88	....	27	—
1988–89	....	40	1
1989–90	....	17	1
1990–91	....	34	1
1991–92	....	45	3
1992–93	....	43	—

THOMAS, John

Born Wednesbury 5.8.58.   Ht 5 8
Wt 11 03
Forward.

Season	Club	Apps	Goals
1978–79	Everton	—	—

Season	Club	Apps	Goals
1978–79	*Tranmere R*	11	2
1979–80	Everton	—	—
1979–80	*Halifax T*	5	—
1980–81	Bolton W	17	5
1981–82	....	5	1
1982–83	Chester	44	20
1983–84	Lincoln C	37	15
1984–85	....	30	5
1985–86	Preston NE	40	17
1986–87	....	38	21
1987–88	Bolton W	44	22
1988–89	....	29	9
1989–90	WBA	18	1
1989–90	Preston NE	11	3
1990–91	....	5	1
1991–92	....	11	2
1991–92	Hartlepool U	7	1
1992–93	Halifax T	12	—

THOMAS, Kevin

Born Edinburgh 25.4.75   Ht 5 8   Wt 12 0
Forward. From Links U.

Season	Club	Apps	Goals
1992–93	Hearts	4	2

THOMAS, Martin

Born Caerphilly 28.11.59.   Ht 6 1
Wt 13 00
Goalkeeper. From Apprentice. Wales
Under-21, 1 full cap.

Season	Club	Apps	Goals
1976–77	Bristol R	1	—
1977–78	....	37	—
1978–79	....	42	—
1979–80	....	38	—
1980–81	....	25	—
1981–82	....	19	—
1982–83	*Cardiff C*	15	—
1982–83	*Tottenham H*	—	—
1982–83	*Southend U*	6	—
1982–83	*Newcastle U*	3	—
1983–84	Newcastle U	23	—
1984–85	....	18	—
1984–85	*Middlesbrough*	4	—
1985–86	Newcastle U	32	—
1986–87	....	39	—
1987–88	....	3	—
1988–89	....	—	—

Season	Club	Apps	Goals
1988–89	Birmingham C	36	—
1989–90		42	—
1990–91		45	—
1991–92		16	—
1992–93		5	—
1992–93	*Crystal Palace*	—	—
1992–93	*Aston Villa*	—	—

THOMAS, Michael

Born Lambeth 24.8.67. Ht 5 9 Wt 12 06
Midfield. From Apprentice. England
Schools, Youth, B, Under-21, 2 full caps.

Season	Club	Apps	Goals
1985–86	Arsenal	—	—
1986–87		12	—
1986–87	*Portsmouth*	3	—
1987–88	Arsenal	37	9
1988–89		37	7
1989–90		36	5
1990–91		31	2
1991–92		10	1
1991–92	Liverpool	17	3
1992–93		8	1

THOMAS, Mickey

Born Mochdre 7.7.54. Ht 5 6 Wt 10 07
Midfield. From Amateur. Wales Under-23,
51 full caps.

Season	Club	Apps	Goals
1971–72	Wrexham	20	3
1972–73		26	—
1973–74		19	4
1974–75		31	5
1975–76		30	2
1976–77		45	6
1977–78		43	7
1978–79		16	6
1978–79	Manchester U	25	1
1979–80		35	8
1980–81		30	2
1981–82	Everton	10	—
1981–82	Brighton	20	—
1982–83	Stoke C	41	11
1983–84		16	3
1983–84	Chelsea	17	4
1984–85		27	5
1985–86		—	—
1985–86	WBA	20	—

Season	Club	Apps	Goals
1985–86	*Derby Co*	9	—
From Wichita W			
1988–89	Shrewsbury T	40	1
1989–90	Leeds U	3	—
1989–90	*Stoke C*	5	—
1990–91	Stoke C	38	7
1991–92	Wrexham	26	1
1992–93		8	1

THOMAS, Mitchell

Born Luton 2.10.64. Ht 6 0 Wt 12 00
Defender. From Apprentice. England
Youth, B, Under-21.

Season	Club	Apps	Goals
1982–83	Luton T	4	—
1983–84		26	—
1984–85		36	—
1985–86		41	1
1986–87	Tottenham H	39	4
1987–88		36	—
1988–89		25	1
1989–90		26	1
1990–91		31	—
1991–92	West Ham U	35	3
1992–93		3	—

THOMAS, Rod

Born London 10.10.70. Ht 5 6 Wt 10 10
Forward. From Trainee. England Youth,
Under-21.

Season	Club	Apps	Goals
1987–88	Watford	4	—
1988–89		18	2
1989–90		32	6
1990–91		24	1
1991–92		5	—
1991–92	*Gillingham*	8	1
1992–93	Watford	1	—

THOMAS, Tony

Born Liverpool 12.7.71. Ht 5 11
Wt 12 05
Defender. From Trainee.

Season	Club	Apps	Goals
1988–89	Tranmere R	9	2
1989–90		42	2
1990–91		33	3

1991–92	....	30	3
1992–93	....	16	—

THOMPSON, Alan

Born Newcastle 22.12.73.   Ht 6 0
Wt 12 05
Midfield. From Trainee. England Youth.

1990–91	Newcastle U................	—	—
1991–92	....	14	—
1992–93	....	2	—

THOMPSON, Andy

Born Carnock 9.11.67.   Ht 5 4   Wt 10 06
Midfield. From Apprentice.

1985–86	WBA.........................	15	1
1986–87	....	9	—
1986–87	Wolverhampton W	29	8
1987–88	....	42	2
1988–89	....	46	6
1989–90	....	33	4
1990–91	....	44	3
1991–92	....	17	—
1992–93	....	20	—

THOMPSON, David

Born Manchester 27.5.62.   Ht 5 11
Wt 12 10
Forward. From Local.

1981–82	Rochdale......................	2	—
1982–83	....	46	5
1983–84	....	40	4
1984–85	....	40	2
1985–86	....	27	2
1985–86	*Manchester U.*.............	—	—
1986–87	Notts Co.....................	46	7
1987–88	....	9	1
1987–88	Wigan Ath	27	2
1988–89	....	42	7
1989–90	....	39	5
1990–91	Preston NE.................	21	2
1991–92	....	25	2
1992–93	Chester C...................	39	3

THOMPSON, David

Born Ashington 20.11.68.   Ht 6 3
Wt 12 07
Defender. From Trainee.

1986–87	Millwall......................	—	—
1987–88	....	—	—
1988–89	....	15	1
1989–90	....	27	2
1990–91	....	17	3
1991–92	....	33	—
1992–93	Bristol C	17	—

THOMPSON, Garry

Born Birmingham 7.10.59.   Ht 6 1
Wt 14 00
Forward. From Apprentice. England
Under-21.

1977–78	Coventry C	6	2
1978–79	....	20	8
1979–80	....	17	6
1980–81	....	35	8
1981–82	....	36	10
1982–83	....	20	4
1982–83	WBA	12	7
1983–84	....	37	13
1984–85	....	42	19
1985–86	Sheffield W................	36	7
1986–87	Aston Villa.................	31	6
1987–88	....	24	11
1988–89	....	5	—
1988–89	Watford	21	7
1989–90	....	13	1
1989–90	Crystal Palace............	9	2
1990–91	....	11	1
1991–92	QPR	15	1
1992–93	....	4	—

THOMPSON, Les

Born Cleethorpes 23.9.68.   Ht 5 10
Wt 11 00
Forward.

1986–87	Hull C........................	—	—
1987–88	....	7	2
1988–89	....	7	—
1988–89	*Scarborough*	3	1

Season	Club	App	Goals
1989–90	Hull C	1	—
1990–91		20	2
1991–92	Maidstone U	38	—
1992–93	Burnley	3	—

THOMPSON, Neil

Born Beverley 2.10.63.   Ht 5 11   Wt 13 08
Defender. From Nottingham F
Apprentice.

Season	Club	App	Goals
1981–82	Hull C	23	—
1982–83		8	—
To Scarborough			
1987–88	Scarborough	41	6
1988–89		46	9
1989–90	Ipswich T	45	3
1990–91		38	6
1991–92		45	6
1992–93		31	3

THOMPSON, Paul

Born Newcastle 17.4.73   Ht 5 11
Wt 11 10
Forward. From Trainee.

Season	Club	App	Goals
1991–92	Hartlepool U	—	—
1992–93		2	1

THOMPSON, Simon

Born Sheffield 27.2.70.   Ht 5 9   Wt 10 06
Forward. From Trainee.

Season	Club	App	Goals
1988–89	Rotherham U	1	—
1989–90		11	—
1990–91		16	—
1991–92		—	—
1991–92	Scarborough	23	3
1992–93		37	—

THOMPSON, Steve

Born Oldham 2.11.64.   Ht 5 10   Wt 12 00
Midfield. From Apprentice.

Season	Club	App	Goals
1982–83	Bolton W	3	—
1983–84		40	3
1984–85		34	4

Season	Club	App	Goals
1985–86		35	8
1986–87		44	7
1987–88		44	7
1988–89		43	9
1989–90		45	6
1990–91		45	5
1991–92		2	—
1991–92	Luton T	5	—
1991–92	Leicester C	34	3
1992–93		44	8

THOMPSTONE, Ian

Born Manchester 17.1.71.   Ht 6 1
Wt 13 02
Midfield. From Trainee.

Season	Club	App	Goals
1987–88	Manchester C	1	1
1988–89		—	—
1989–90		—	—
1990–91	Oldham Ath	—	—
1991–92		—	—
1991–92	Exeter C	15	3
1992–93	Halifax T	31	9
1992–93	Scunthorpe U	11	2

THOMSON, Billy

Born Linwood 10.2.58.   Ht 6 2   Wt 12 03
Goalkeeper. From Glasgow United.
Scotland Under-21, 7 full caps.

Season	Club	App	Goals
1975–76	Partick T	—	—
1976–77		—	—
1977–78		—	—
1978–79	St Mirren	34	—
1979–80		36	—
1980–81		36	—
1981–82		35	—
1982–83		35	—
1983–84		30	—
1984–85	Dundee U	11	—
1985–86		28	—
1986–87		42	—
1987–88		36	—
1988–89		36	—
1989–90		7	—
1990–91		5	—
1991–92	Motherwell	43	—
1992–93		9	—

THOMSON, Ian

Born Coatbridge 24.9.65   Ht 6 0   Wt 11 7
Midfield. From Dunipace J.

Season	Club		
1985–86	Stenhousemuir	4	1
1986–87		26	1
1987–88		37	4
1988–89	Partick T	25	2
1989–90	Queen of the S	27	2
1990–91		29	2
1991–92		34	10
1992–93	Raith R	34	4

THOMSON, Scott

Born Aberdeen 29.1.72   Ht 5 10   Wt 11 2
Midfield. From Shrewsbury T trainee.

1990–91	Brechin C	30	3
1991–92		11	3
1991–92	Aberdeen	—	—
1992–93		2	—

THORN, Andy

Born Carshalton 12.11.66.   Ht 6 0
Wt 11 05
Defender. From Apprentice. England
Under-21.

1984–85	Wimbledon	10	—
1985–86		28	—
1986–87		34	2
1987–88		35	—
1988–89	Newcastle U	26	1
1989–90		10	1
1989–90	Crystal Palace	17	1
1990–91		34	1
1991–92		33	—
1992–93		34	1

THORNBER, Stephen

Born Dewsbury 11.10.65.   Ht 5 10
Wt 11 02
Midfield. From Local.

1983–84	Halifax T	4	1
1984–85		31	3
1985–86		18	—

1986–87		16	—
1987–88		35	—
1988–89	Swansea C	31	—
1989–90		34	1
1990–91		19	1
1991–92		33	4
1992–93	Blackpool	24	—

THORPE, Jeff

Born Whitehaven 17.11.72.   Ht 5 10
Wt 12 06
Midfield. From Trainee.

1990–91	Carlisle U	13	—
1991–92		28	1
1992–93		28	—

THORSTVEDT, Erik

Born Stavanger 28.10.62   Ht 6 4
Wt 14 03
Goalkeeper. From IFK Gothenburg.
Norway full caps.

1988–89	Tottenham H	18	—
1989–90		34	—
1990–91		37	—
1991–92		24	—
1992–93		27	—

TIERLING, Lee

Born Wegberg 25.10.72   Ht 5 7   Wt 11 08
Forward. From Trainee.

1991–92	Portsmouth	—	—
1992–93	Fulham	5	—

TIERNEY, Francis

Born Liverpool 10.9.75
Midfield. From Trainee.

1992–93	Crewe Alex	1	—

TIERNEY, Grant

Born Falkirk 11.10.61.   Ht 6 0   Wt 11 06
Defender. From Bainsford F.

1978–79	Hearts	—	—

Season	Club	Apps	Goals
1979–80		—	—
1980–81	Cowdenbeath	32	1
1981–82		32	2
1982–83		32	2
1983–84		35	1
1984–85		25	3
1984–85	Meadowbank T	8	—
1985–86		35	4
1986–87		36	4
1987–88		36	2
1988–89		18	—
1988–89	Dunfermline Ath	18	1
1989–90		33	2
1990–91	Partick T	28	1
1991–92		13	1
1992–93		16	2

TILER, Carl

Born Sheffield 11.2.70. Ht 6 2 Wt 13 00
Defender. From Trainee. England
Under-21.

Season	Club	Apps	Goals
1987–88	Barnsley	1	—
1988–89		4	—
1989–90		21	1
1990–91		45	2
1991–92	Nottingham F	26	1
1992–93		37	—

TILLEY, Darren

Born Bristol 15.3.67. Ht 6 2 Wt 13 07
Forward. From Yate T.

Season	Club	Apps	Goals
1991–92	York C	15	—
1992–93		6	—

TILLSON, Andy

Born Huntingdon 30.6.66. Ht 6 2
Wt 12 07
Defender. From Kettering T.

Season	Club	Apps	Goals
1988–89	Grimsby T	45	2
1989–90		42	3
1990–91		18	—
1990–91	QPR	19	2
1991–92		10	—
1992–93		—	—

Season	Club	Apps	Goals
1992–93	*Grimsby T*	4	—
1992–93	Bristol R	29	—

TILSON, Steve

Born Essex 27.7.66. Ht 5 11 Wt 12 05
Forward. From Burnham.

Season	Club	Apps	Goals
1988–89	Southend U	16	2
1989–90		16	—
1990–91		38	8
1991–92		46	7
1992–93		31	3

TINKLER, John

Born Trimdon 24.8.68. Ht 5 8 Wt 11 07
Midfield.

Season	Club	Apps	Goals
1986–87	Hartlepool U	2	—
1987–88		20	—
1988–89		38	3
1989–90		45	2
1990–91		26	2
1991–92		39	—
1992–93	Preston NE	24	2

TINKLER, Mark

Born Bishop Auckland 24.10.74
Midfield. From Trainee. England Youth.

Season	Club	Apps	Goals
1991–92	Leeds U	—	—
1992–93		7	—

TINNION, Brian

Born Stanley 23.2.68. Ht 5 11 Wt 11 05
Defender. From Apprentice.

Season	Club	Apps	Goals
1985–86	Newcastle U	—	—
1986–87		3	—
1987–88		16	1
1988–89		13	1
1988–89	Bradford C	14	1
1989–90		37	5
1990–91		41	5
1991–92		26	8
1992–93		27	3
1992–93	Bristol C	11	2

TISDALE, Paul

Born Malta 14.1.73   Ht 5 9   Wt 10 08
Midfield. From School.

Season	Club		
1991–92	Southampton	—	—
1992–93		—	—
1992–93	*Northampton T*	5	—

TITTERTON, David

Born Hatton 25.9.71.   Ht 5 11   Wt 10 09
Midfield. From Trainee. England Youth.

Season	Club		
1989–90	Coventry C	1	—
1990–91		1	—
1991–92		—	—
1991–92	Hereford U	25	1
1992–93		26	—

TODD, Lee

Born Hartlepool 7.3.72.   Ht 5 5   Wt 10 03
Forward. From Hartlepool U Trainee.

Season	Club		
1990–91	Stockport Co	14	—
1991–92		19	—
1992–93		39	—

TODD, Mark

Born Belfast 4.12.67.   Ht 5 8   Wt 10 04
Midfield. From Trainee. Northern Ireland
Under-23.

Season	Club		
1985–86	Manchester U	—	—
1986–87		—	—
1987–88	Sheffield U	12	—
1988–89		39	4
1989–90		16	1
1990–91		3	—
1990–91	*Wolverhampton W*	7	
1991–92	Sheffield U	—	—
1991–92	Rotherham U	23	2
1992–93		16	4

TOLSON, Neil

Born Wordley 25.10.73.   Ht 6 1   Wt 10 07
Forward. From Trainee.

Season	Club		
1991–92	Walsall	9	1

Season	Club		
1991–92	Oldham Ath	—	—
1992–93		3	—

TOMAN, Andy

Born Northallerton 7.3.62.   Ht 5 10
Wt 11 07
Midfield. From Bishop Auckland.

Season	Club		
1985–86	Lincoln C	24	4
1986–87	Hartlepool U	21	5
1987–88		46	17
1988–89		45	6
1989–90	Darlington	40	7
1990–91		43	5
1991–92		43	4
1992–93		29	1
1992–93	*Scarborough*	6	—

TOMLINSON, Michael

Born Lambeth 15.9.72.   Ht 5 9   Wt 11 00
Midfield. From Trainee.

Season	Club		
1990–91	Leyton Orient	1	1
1991–92		1	—
1992–93		8	—

TOMLINSON, Paul

Born Brierley Hill 22.2.64.   Ht 6 2
Wt 13 12
Goalkeeper. From Middlewood R.

Season	Club		
1983–84	Sheffield U	30	—
1984–85		2	—
1985–86		—	—
1986–87		5	—
1986–87	*Birmingham C*	11	—
1987–88	Bradford C	42	—
1988–89		38	—
1989–90		41	—
1990–91		43	—
1991–92		45	—
1992–93		24	—

TONGE, Alan

Born Bury 25.2.72.   Ht 5 8   Wt 11 11
Defender. From Trainee.

Season	Club		
1990–91	Manchester U	—	—

Season	Club	App	Goals
1991–92	Exeter C	3	—
1992–93		15	1

TORFASON, Gudmundor

Born Westann Isles 13.12.61. Ht 6 1
Wt 13 02
Forward. From RSC Genk. Iceland full
caps.

Season	Club	App	Goals
1989–90	St Mirren	29	12
1990–91		18	4
1991–92		29	8
1992–93	St Johnstone	10	4

TORPEY, Stephen

Born Islington 8.12.70. Ht 6 2 Wt 12 11
Forward. From Trainee.

Season	Club	App	Goals
1988–89	Millwall	—	—
1989–90		7	—
1990–91		—	—
1990–91	Bradford C	29	7
1991–92		43	10
1992–93		24	5

TORTOLANO, Joe

Born Stirling 6.4.66. Ht 5 8 Wt 11 02
Forward. From Apprentice. Scotland
Under-21.

Season	Club	App	Goals
1983–84	WBA	—	—
1984–85		—	—
1985–86	Hibernian	20	3
1986–87		33	—
1987–88		21	4
1988–89		25	—
1989–90		7	—
1990–91		18	1
1991–92		25	1
1992–93		21	3

TOWNSEND, Andy

Born Maidstone 23.7.63. Ht 5 11
Wt 12 13
Midfield. From Welling and Weymouth.
Eire 39 full caps.

Season	Club	App	Goals
1984–85	Southampton	5	—

Season	Club	App	Goals
1985–86		27	1
1986–87		14	1
1987–88		37	3
1988–89	Norwich C	36	5
1989–90		35	3
1990–91	Chelsea	34	2
1991–92		35	6
1992–93		41	4

TRACEY, Simon

Born Woolwich 9.12.67. Ht 6 0
Wt 12 00
Goalkeeper. From Apprentice.

Season	Club	App	Goals
1985–86	Wimbledon	—	—
1986–87		—	—
1987–88		—	—
1988–89		1	—
1988–89	Sheffield U	7	—
1989–90		46	—
1990–91		31	—
1991–92		29	—
1992–93		10	—

TREANOR, Mark

Born Glasgow 1.4.63. Ht 6 0 Wt 11 00
Defender. From Eastercraigs.

Season	Club	App	Goals
1979–80	Clydebank	1	—
1980–81		16	—
1981–82		35	—
1982–83		36	3
1983–84		18	1
1984–85		38	1
1985–86		32	—
1986–87		33	—
1987–88		37	3
1988–89		27	5
1988–89	St Johnstone	3	—
1989–90		30	4
1990–91		30	4
1991–92		33	2
1992–93		9	1
1992–93	Falkirk	3	—

TREVITT, Simon

Born Dewsbury 20.12.67.   Ht 5 11
Wt 11 02
Defender. From Apprentice.

Season	Club	App	Goals
1986–87	Huddersfield T	11	—
1987–88	....	37	1
1988–89	....	39	—
1989–90	....	7	—
1990–91	....	38	—
1991–92	....	41	1
1992–93	....	—	—

TROLLOPE, Paul

Born Swindon 3.6.72.   Ht 6 0   Wt 12 02
Midfield. From Trainee.

Season	Club	App	Goals
1989–90	Swindon T	—	—
1990–91	....	—	—
1991–92	....	—	—
1991–92	*Torquay U*	10	—
1992–93	Torquay U	36	2

TROTTER, Michael

Born Hartlepool 27.10.69.   Ht 6 0
Wt 12 12
Midfield. From Trainee.

Season	Club	App	Goals
1987–88	Middlesbrough	—	—
1988–89	....	—	—
1988–89	*Doncaster R*	3	—
1989–90	Middlesbrough	—	—
1990–91	Darlington	24	2
1991–92	....	5	—
1991–92	Leicester C	2	—
1992–93	....	1	—

TUCKER, Mark

Born Woking 27.4.72.   Ht 6 0   Wt 11 07
Defender. From Trainee.

Season	Club	App	Goals
1990–91	Fulham	—	—
1991–92	....	2	—
1992–93	....	2	—

TUPLING, Steve

Born Wensleydale 11.7.64.   Ht 6 0
Wt 11 03
Midfield. From Apprentice.

Season	Club	App	Goals
1982–83	Middlesbrough	—	—
1983–84	....	—	—
1984–85	*Carlisle U*	1	—
1984–85	Darlington	39	4
1985–86	....	40	4
1986–87	....	32	—
1987–88	Newport Co	33	2
1988–89	Cardiff C	4	—
1988–89	*Torquay U*	3	—
1988–89	*Exeter C*	9	1
1989–90	Cardiff C	1	—
1989–90	Hartlepool U	26	1
1990–91	....	42	2
1991–92	....	21	—
1992–93	Darlington	11	—

TURNBULL, Lee

Born Teesside 27.9.67.   Ht 6 0   Wt 11 09
Midfield. From Local.

Season	Club	App	Goals
1985–86	Middlesbrough	2	—
1986–87	....	14	4
1987–88	....	—	—
1987–88	Aston Villa	—	—
1987–88	Doncaster R	30	1
1988–89	....	32	4
1989–90	....	42	10
1990–91	....	19	6
1990–91	Chesterfield	19	9
1991–92	....	27	7
1992–93	....	33	8

TURNER, Andy

Born Woolwich 23.3.75   Ht 5 9   Wt 11 00
Forward. From Trainee.

Season	Club	App	Goals
1991–92	Tottenham H	—	—
1992–93	....	18	3

TURNER, Chris

Born Sheffield 15.9.58. Ht 5 11 Wt 11 12
Goalkeeper. From Apprentice. England
Youth.

Season	Club		
1976–77	Sheffield W	45	—
1977–78		23	—
1978–79		23	—
1978–79	*Lincoln C*	5	—
1979–80	Sunderland	30	—
1980–81		27	—
1981–82		19	—
1982–83		35	—
1983–84		42	—
1984–85		42	—
1985–86	Manchester U	17	—
1986–87		23	—
1987–88		24	—
1988–89		—	—
1988–89	Sheffield W	29	—
1989–90		23	—
1989–90	*Leeds U*	2	—
1990–91	Sheffield W	23	—
1991–92		—	—
1991–92	Leyton Orient	34	—
1992–93		17	—

TURNER, Mark

Born Bebbington 4.10.72 Ht 6 0
Wt 11 01
Midfield. From Trainee.

Season	Club		
1991–92	Wolverhampton W	—	—
1992–93		1	—

TURNER, Phil

Born Sheffield 12.2.62. Ht 5 9 Wt 10 13
Midfield. From Apprentice.

Season	Club		
1979–80	Lincoln C	14	1
1980–81		38	4
1981–82		28	1
1982–83		40	3
1983–84		42	3
1984–85		36	3
1985–86		43	4
1986–87	Grimsby T	34	3
1987–88		28	5

Season	Club		
1987–88	Leicester C	8	—
1988–89		16	2
1988–89	Notts Co	16	2
1989–90		44	6
1990–91		38	1
1991–92		29	1
1992–93		20	1

TURNER, Robert

Born Durham 18.9.66. Ht 6 3 Wt 14 01
Midfield. From Apprentice.

Season	Club		
1984–85	Huddersfield T	1	—
1985–86	Cardiff C	34	7
1986–87		5	1
1986–87	*Hartlepool U*	7	1
1986–87	Bristol R	17	1
1987–88		9	1
1987–88	Wimbledon	4	—
1988–89		6	—
1988–89	Bristol C	19	6
1989–90		33	6
1990–91	Plymouth Arg	39	14
1991–92		25	3
1992–93		2	—
1992–93	Notts Co	8	1
1992–93	*Shrewsbury T*	9	—

TURNER, Tommy

Born Johnstone 11.10.63. Ht 5 9
Wt 10 07
Midfield. From Glentyan Thistle.

Season	Club		
1983–84	Morton	—	—
1984–85		13	1
1985–86		34	7
1986–87		38	4
1987–88		29	1
1988–89		31	10
1989–90		30	6
1990–91	St Johnstone	28	3
1991–92		33	3
1992–93		28	1

TUTILL, Steve

Born Derwent 1.10.69. Ht 6 0 Wt 12 02
Defender. From Trainee. England Schools.

Season	Club		
1987–88	York C	21	—

356

Season	Club	Apps	Goals
1988–89		22	1
1989–90		42	—
1990–91		42	—
1991–92		39	1
1992–93		8	—

TUTTLE, David

Born Reading 6.2.72.   Ht 5 9   Wt 12 10
Defender. From Trainee. England Youth.

Season	Club	Apps	Goals
1989–90	Tottenham H	—	—
1990–91		6	—
1991–92		2	—
1992–93		5	—
1992–93	*Peterborough U*	7	—

TWEED, Steven

Born Edinburgh 8.8.72.   Ht 6 3   Wt 13 02
Defender. From Hutcheson Vale. Scotland
Under-21.

Season	Club	Apps	Goals
1991–92	Hibernian	1	—
1992–93		14	—

TWENTYMAN, Geoff

Born Liverpool 10.3.59.   Ht 6 1   Wt 13 02
Defender. From Southport, Maghull,
Formby and Chorley.

Season	Club	Apps	Goals
1983–84	Preston NE	28	2
1984–85		44	2
1985–86		26	—
1986–87	Bristol R	43	—
1987–88		38	1
1988–89		46	1
1989–90		46	3
1990–91		46	—
1991–92		25	1
1992–93		8	—

ULLATHORNE, Robert

Born Wakefield 11.10.71.   Ht 5 8
Wt 10 00
Defender. From Trainee.

Season	Club	Apps	Goals
1989–90	Norwich C	—	—
1990–91		2	—
1991–92		20	3
1992–93		—	—

UNSWORTH, David

Born Preston 16.10.73.   Ht 5 11   Wt 12 02
Forward. From Trainee. England Youth.

Season	Club	Apps	Goals
1991–92	Everton	2	1
1992–93		3	—

VALENTINE, Peter

Born Huddersfield 16.6.63.   Ht 5 10
Wt 12 00
Defender. From Apprentice.

Season	Club	Apps	Goals
1980–81	Huddersfield T	—	—
1981–82		14	1
1982–83		5	—
1983–84	Bolton W	42	1
1984–85		26	—
1985–86	Bury	46	3
1986–87		46	2
1987–88		42	2
1988–89		30	1
1989–90		38	—
1990–91		42	2
1991–92		39	3
1992–93		36	3

VAN DE KAMP, Guido

Born Den Bosch 8.2.64.   Ht 6 2   Wt 13 01
Goalkeeper. From Den Bosch.

Season	Club	Apps	Goals
1991–92	Dundee U	27	—
1992–93		1	—

VAN DE VEN, Peter

Born Hunsel 8.1.61   Ht 6 1   Wt 13 05
Defender. From Willem II.

Season	Club	Apps	Goals
1990–91	Aberdeen	—	—
1991–92		23	2
1992–93	Hearts	37	—

VAN DEN HAUWE, Pat

Born Dendermonde 16.12.60.   Ht 5 11
Wt 11 10
Defender. From Apprentice. Wales 13 full
caps.

Season	Club	Apps	Goals
1978–79	Birmingham C	8	—
1979–80		1	—
1980–81		4	—
1981–82		31	—
1982–83		31	1
1983–84		42	—

Season	Club	Apps	Goals
1984–85		6	—
1984–85	Everton	31	—
1985–86		40	1
1986–87		11	1
1987–88		28	—
1988–89		25	—
1989–90		—	—
1989–90	Tottenham H	31	—
1990–91		32	—
1991–92		35	—
1992–93		18	—

VAN DER HOORN, Freddy

Born Den Bosch 12.10.63.   Ht 6 0
Wt 12 06
Defender. From Den Bosch.

Season	Club	Apps	Goals
1989–90	Dundee U	31	2
1990–91		32	1
1991–92		41	1
1992–93		32	1

VAN DER LAAN, Robin

Born Schiedam 5.9.68.   Ht 5 11   Wt 12 05
Forward. From Wageningen.

Season	Club	Apps	Goals
1990–91	Port Vale	18	4
1991–92		43	5
1992–93		38	6

VARADI, Imre

Born Paddington 8.7.59.   Ht 5 10
Wt 12 00
Forward. From Letchworth GC.

Season	Club	Apps	Goals
1977–78	Sheffield U	—	—
1978–79		10	4
1978–79	Everton	—	—
1979–80		4	—
1980–81		22	6
1981–82	Newcastle U	42	18
1982–83		39	21
1983–84	Sheffield W	38	17
1984–85		38	16
1985–86	WBA	32	9
1986–87		—	—

Season	Club	App	Goals
1986–87	Manchester C	30	9
1987–88		32	17
1988–89		3	—
1988–89	Sheffield W	20	3
1989–90		2	—
1989–90	Leeds U	13	2
1990–91		6	2
1991–92		3	—
1991–92	*Luton T*	6	1
1992–93	Leeds U	4	1
1992–93	*Oxford U*	5	—
1992–93	Rotherham U	11	4

VATA, Rudi

Born Shkoder,Albania. 13.2.69   Ht 6 1
Wt 12 5
Midfield. From Dinamo Tirana.

Season	Club	App	Goals
1992–93	Celtic	22	2

VAUGHAN, John

Born Isleworth 26.6.64.   Ht 5 10
Wt 13 01
Goalkeeper. From Apprentice.

Season	Club	App	Goals
1981–82	West Ham U	—	—
1982–83		—	—
1983–84		—	—
1984–85		—	—
1984–85	*Charlton Ath*	6	—
1985–86		—	—
1985–86	*Bristol R*	6	—
1985–86	*Wrexham*	4	—
1985–86	*Bristol C*	2	—
1986–87	Fulham	44	—
1987–88		—	—
1987–88	*Bristol C*	3	—
1988–89	Cambridge U	29	—
1989–90		46	—
1990–91		43	—
1991–92		33	—
1992–93		27	—

VAUGHAN, John

Born Liverpool 18.2.72
Defender.

Season	Club	App	Goals
1992–93	Crewe Alex	7	—

VENISON, Barry

Born Consett 16.8.64.   Ht 5 10   Wt 11 09
Defender. From Apprentice. England
Youth, Under-21.

Season	Club	App	Goals
1981–82	Sunderland	20	1
1982–83		37	—
1983–84		41	—
1984–85		39	1
1985–86		36	—
1986–87	Liverpool	33	—
1987–88		18	—
1988–89		15	—
1989–90		25	—
1990–91		6	—
1991–92		13	1
1992–93	Newcastle U	44	—

VENUS, Mark

Born Hartlepool 6.4.67.   Ht 6 0   Wt 11 08
Defender.

Season	Club	App	Goals
1984–85	Hartlepool U	4	—
1985–86	Leicester C	1	—
1986–87		39	—
1987–88		21	1
1987–88	Wolverhampton W	4	—
1988–89		35	—
1989–90		44	2
1990–91		6	—
1991–92		46	1
1992–93		12	—

VERHEUL, Bart

Born Arnhem 23.11.71.   Ht 5 10
Wt 10 07
Forward. From Go Ahead Eagles.

Season	Club	App	Goals
1991–92	Motherwell	3	—
1992–93		1	—

VERVEER, Etienne

Born Surinam 22.9.67.   Ht 5 11   Wt 11 12
Midfield. From Chur.

Season	Club	App	Goals
1991–92	Millwall	25	2
1992–93		1	—

VEYSEY, Ken

Born Hackney 8.6.67. Ht 5 11   Wt 11 08
Goalkeeper. From Arsenal Apprentice.

Season	Club		
1987–88	Torquay U	—	—
1988–89		25	—
1989–90		46	—
1990–91		1	—
1990–91	Oxford U	25	—
1991–92		32	—
1992–93		—	—
1992–93	Sheffield U	—	—

VICKERS, Steve

Born Bishop Auckland 13.10.67.   Ht 6 2
Wt 12 00
Defender. From Spennymoor U.

Season	Club		
1985–86	Tranmere R	3	—
1986–87		36	2
1987–88		46	1
1988–89		46	3
1989–90		42	3
1990–91		42	1
1991–92		43	1
1992–93		42	—

VINNICOMBE, Chris

Born Exeter 20.10.70   Ht 5 9   Wt 10 04
Midfield. England Under-21.

Season	Club		
1988–89	Exeter C	25	—
1989–90		14	1
1989–90	Rangers	7	—
1990–91		10	1
1991–92		2	—
1992–93		—	—

VIVEASH, Adrian

Born Swindon 30.9.69.   Ht 6 1   Wt 11 12
Forward. From Trainee.

Season	Club		
1988–89	Swindon T	—	—
1989–90		—	—
1990–91		25	1
1991–92		10	—
1992–93		5	—

Season	Club		
1992–93	Reading	5	—

VONK, Michael

Born Holland 28.10.68.   Ht 6 3   Wt 13 03
Defender. From SVV/Dordrecht.

Season	Club		
1991–92	Manchester C	9	—
1992–93		26	3

VRTO, Dusan

Born Banksa Stiavnica 29.10.65   Ht 6 0
Wt 11 12
Midfield. From Banik Ostrava.

Season	Club		
1992–93	Dundee	32	1

WADDLE, Chris

Born Hepworth 14.12.60. Ht 6 0
Wt 11 05
Forward. From Tow Law T. England
Under-21, 62 full caps. Football League.

Season	Club	App	Goals
1980–81	Newcastle U	13	1
1981–82		42	7
1982–83		37	7
1983–84		42	18
1984–85		36	13
1985–86	Tottenham H	39	11
1986–87		39	6
1987–88		22	2
1988–89		38	14
1989–90	Marseille	37	9
1990–91		35	6
1991–92		35	7
1992–93	Sheffield W	33	1

WADDOCK, Gary

Born Alperton 17.3.62. Ht 5 10
Wt 11 12
Midfield. From Apprentice. Eire Youth B,
Under-21, Under-23, 20 full caps.

Season	Club	App	Goals
1979–80	QPR	16	1
1980–81		33	3
1981–82		35	—
1982–83		33	—
1983–84		36	3
1984–85		31	1
1985–86		15	—
1986–87		4	—
1987–88		—	—
From Charleroi			
1989–90	Millwall	18	—
1990–91		40	2
1991–92	QPR	—	—
1991–92	*Swindon T*	6	—
1992–93	QPR	—	—
1992–93	Bristol R	31	—

WADE, Meashach

Born Bermuda 23.1.73.
Midfield. From Pembroke, Bermuda.

Season	Club	App	Goals
1991–92	Hereford U	10	—

Season	Club	App	Goals
1992–93		7	—

WALKER, Alan

Born Mossley 17.12.59. Ht 6 2 Wt 12 11
Defender. From Stockport Co and Telford
U.

Season	Club	App	Goals
1983–84	Lincoln C	33	2
1984–85		42	2
1985–86	Millwall	26	3
1986–87		40	1
1987–88		26	4
1987–88	Gillingham	7	—
1988–89		22	1
1989–90		38	1
1990–91		44	4
1991–92		40	1
1992–93	Plymouth Arg	2	1
1992–93	Mansfield T	22	1

WALKER, Andy

Born Glasgow 6.4.65. Ht 5 8 Wt 10 07
Forward. From Baillieston Juniors.
Scotland, Under-21, 1 full cap.

Season	Club	App	Goals
1984–85	Motherwell	11	3
1985–86		22	4
1986–87		43	10
1987–88	Celtic	42	16
1988–89		22	8
1989–90		32	6
1990–91		11	—
1991–92		1	—
1991–92	*Newcastle U*	2	—
1991–92	Bolton W	24	15
1992–93		32	26

WALKER, Clive

Born Oxford 26.5.57. Ht 5 7 Wt 11 09
Forward. From Apprentice. England
Schools.

Season	Club	App	Goals
1974–75	Chelsea	—	—
1975–76		—	—
1976–77		1	—
1977–78		23	7
1978–79		30	4

Season	Club	Apps	Goals
1979–80		36	13
1980–81		37	11
1981–82		36	16
1982–83		29	6
1983–84		6	3
1984–85	Sunderland	38	10
1985–86		12	—
1985–86	QPR	5	1
1986–87		16	—
1987–88		—	—
1987–88	Fulham	26	8
1988–89		38	8
1989–90		45	13
1990–91	Brighton	45	3
1991–92		23	2
1992–93		38	3

WALKER, Des

Born Hackney 26.11.65.   Ht 5 10
Wt 11 05
Defender. From Apprentice. England
Under-21, 58 full caps.

Season	Club	Apps	Goals
1983–84	Nottingham F	4	—
1984–85		3	—
1985–86		39	—
1986–87		41	—
1987–88		35	—
1988–89		34	—
1989–90		38	—
1990–91		37	—
1991–92		33	1

To Sampdoria

WALKER, Ian

Born Watford 31.10.71.   Ht 6 1   Wt 11 09
Goalkeeper. From Trainee. England
Youth, Under-21.

Season	Club	Apps	Goals
1989–90	Tottenham H	—	—
1990–91		1	—
1990–91	Oxford U	2	—
1990–91	Ipswich T	—	—
1991–92	Tottenham H	18	—
1992–93		17	—

WALKER, Keith

Born Edinburgh 17.4.66.   Ht 6 0
Wt 11 09
Midfield. From ICI Juveniles.

Season	Club	Apps	Goals
1984–85	Stirling Albion	38	6
1985–86		32	5
1986–87		21	6
1987–88	St Mirren	19	3
1988–89		14	1
1989–90		10	2
1989–90	Swansea C	13	—
1990–91		24	—
1991–92		32	1
1992–93		42	2

WALKER, Nicky

Born Aberdeen 29.9.62.   Ht 6 2   Wt 11 12
Goalkeeper. From Elgin C. Scotland
Youth, 1 full cap.

Season	Club	Apps	Goals
1980–81	Leicester C	—	—
1981–82		6	—
1982–83	Motherwell	16	—
1983–84		15	—
1983–84	Rangers	8	—
1984–85		14	—
1985–86		34	—
1986–87		2	—
1987–88		5	—
1987–88	Dunfermline Ath	1	—
1988–89	Rangers	12	—
1989–90	Hearts	—	—
1990–91		13	—
1991–92		—	—
1991–92	Burnley	6	—
1992–93	Hearts	18	—

WALKER, Ray

Born North Shields 28.9.63.   Ht 5 10
Wt 11 12
Midfield. From Apprentice. England
Youth.

Season	Club	Apps	Goals
1981–82	Aston Villa	—	—
1982–83		1	—
1983–84		8	—
1984–85		7	—

1984–85	*Port Vale*	15	1
1985–86	Aston Villa	7	—
1986–87	Port Vale	45	4
1987–88		42	6
1988–89		43	5
1989–90		40	—
1990–91		45	6
1991–92		26	2
1992–93		35	9

WALKER, Richard

Born Derby 9.11.71   Ht 6 0   Wt 12 00
Defender. From Trainee.

1991–92	Notts Co	—	—
1992–93		12	3

WALLACE, Danny

Born London 21.1.64.   Ht 5 4   Wt 10 04
Forward. From Apprentice. England
Youth, Under-21, 1 full cap.

1980–81	Southampton	2	—
1981–82		7	—
1982–83		35	12
1983–84		41	11
1984–85		35	7
1985–86		35	8
1986–87		31	8
1987–88		33	11
1988–89		31	5
1989–90		5	2
1989–90	Manchester U	26	3
1990–91		19	3
1991–92		—	—
1992–93		2	—
1992–93	*Millwall*	3	—

WALLACE, Michael

Born Farnworth 5.10.70   Ht 5 8
Wt 10 02
Midfield. From Trainee.

1991–92	Manchester C	—	—
1992–93	Stockport Co	8	—

WALLACE, Ray

Born Lewisham 2.10.69.   Ht 5 6
Wt 10 02
Defender. From Trainee, England
Under-21.

1987–88	Southampton	—	—
1988–89		26	—
1989–90		9	—
1990–91		—	—
1991–92	Leeds U	—	—
1991–92	*Swansea C*	2	—
1992–93	Leeds U	6	—

WALLACE, Rodney

Born Lewisham 2.10.69.   Ht 5 7
Wt 10 01
Forward. From Trainee. England B,
Under-21.

1987–88	Southampton	15	1
1988–89		38	12
1989–90		38	18
1990–91		37	14
1991–92	Leeds U	34	11
1992–93		32	7

WALLING, Dean

Born Leeds 17.4.69.   Ht 6 0   Wt 12 00
Defender.

1986–87	Leeds U	—	—
1987–88	Rochdale	12	2
1988–89		34	3
1989–90		19	3
From Guiseley			
1991–92	Carlisle U	37	5
1992–93		23	—

WALSH, Colin

Born Hamilton 22.7.62.   Ht 5 9   Wt 10 11
Midfield. From Apprentice. Scotland
Youth, Under-21.

1979–80	Nottingham F	—	—
1980–81		16	4
1981–82		15	3

Season	Club		League App./Goals
1982–83		37	5
1983–84		38	13
1984–85		13	1
1985–86		20	6
1986–87		—	—
1986–87	Charlton Ath	33	6
1987–88		11	3
1988–89		5	—
1988–89	*Peterborough U*	5	1
1989–90	Charlton Ath	27	2
1990–91		13	—
1990–91	*Middlesbrough*	13	1
1991–92	Charlton Ath	42	4
1992–93		42	1

WALSH, Derek

Born Hamilton 24.10.67.   Ht 5 7
Wt 11 05
Midfield. From Apprentice.

Season	Club		League App./Goals
1984–85	Everton	1	—
1985–86		—	—
1986–87		—	—
1987–88	Hamilton A	2	—
1988–89	Carlisle U	35	3
1989–90		28	3
1990–91		19	—
1991–92		15	—
1992–93		24	1

WALSH, Gary

Born Wigan 21.3.68.   Ht 6 1   Wt 13 01
Goalkeeper. England Under-21.

Season	Club		League App./Goals
1984–85	Manchester U	—	—
1985–86		—	—
1986–87		14	—
1987–88		16	—
1988–89		—	—
1988–89	*Airdrie*	3	—
1989–90	Manchester U	—	—
1990–91		5	—
1991–92		2	—
1992–93		—	—

WALSH, Paul

Born Plumstead 1.10.62.   Ht 5 7
Wt 10 08
Forward. From Apprentice. England
Youth, Under-21, 3 full caps.

Season	Club		League App./Goals
1979–80	Charlton Ath	9	—
1980–81		40	11
1981–82		38	13
1982–83	Luton T	41	13
1983–84		39	11
1984–85	Liverpool	26	8
1985–86		20	11
1986–87		23	6
1987–88		8	—
1987–88	Tottenham H	11	1
1988–89		33	6
1989–90		26	2
1990–91		29	7
1991–92		29	3
1991–92	*QPR*	2	—
1992–93	Portsmouth	43	9

WALSH, Steve

Born Fulwood 3.11.64.   Ht 6 2   Wt 13 13
Defender. From Local.

Season	Club		League App./Goals
1982–83	Wigan Ath	31	—
1983–84		42	1
1984–85		40	2
1985–86		13	1
1986–87	Leicester C	21	—
1987–88		32	7
1988–89		30	2
1989–90		34	3
1990–91		35	3
1991–92		43	7
1992–93		40	15

WALTER, David

Born Barnstaple 3.9.64.   Ht 6 3   Wt 13 03
Goalkeeper. From Bideford T.

Season	Club		League App./Goals
1988–89	Exeter C	26	—
1989–90		18	—
1989–90	*Plymouth Arg*	—	—
1990–91	Plymouth Arg	10	—
1991–92		5	—

Season	Club	League Appearances/Goals
1992–93	Torquay U	1 —

WALTERS, Mark

Born Birmingham 12.1.61. Ht 5 9
Wt 11 08
Forward. From Apprentice. England
Youth, B, Under-21, 1 full cap.

Season	Club	League Appearances/Goals	
1981–82	Aston Villa	1	—
1982–83		22	1
1983–84		37	8
1984–85		36	10
1985–86		40	10
1986–87		21	3
1987–88		24	7
1987–88	Rangers	18	7
1988–89		31	8
1989–90		27	5
1990–91		30	12
1991–92	Liverpool	25	3
1992–93		34	11

WALTERS, Steve

Born Plymouth 9.1.72. Ht 5 10 Wt 11 08
Forward. From Schoolboy, Trainee. FA
Schools.

Season	Club	League Appearances/Goals	
1987–88	Crewe Alex	1	—
1988–89		22	1
1989–90		30	1
1990–91		4	—
1991–92		35	3
1992–93		23	3

WANLESS, Paul

Born Banbury 14.12.73. Ht 6 1 Wt 13 04
Midfield. From Trainee.

Season	Club	League Appearances/Goals	
1991–92	Oxford U	6	—
1992–93		7	—

WARBURTON, Ray

Born Rotherham 7.10.67. Ht 6 0
Wt 12 09
Defender. From Apprentice.

Season	Club	League Appearances/Goals	
1984–85	Rotherham U	1	—

Season	Club	League Appearances/Goals	
1985–86		—	—
1986–87		3	—
1987–88		—	—
1988–89		—	—
1989–90	York C	43	2
1990–91		22	4
1991–92		9	—
1992–93		10	3

WARD, Ashley

Born Manchester 24.11.70. Ht 6 1
Wt 11 07
Forward. From Trainee.

Season	Club	League Appearances/Goals	
1989–90	Manchester C	1	—
1990–91		—	—
1990–91	*Wrexham*	4	2
1991–92	Leicester C	10	—
1992–93		—	—
1992–93	*Blackpool*	2	1
1992–93	Crewe Alex	20	4

WARD, Darren

Born Worksop 11.5.74 Ht 5 11 Wt 12 09
Goalkeeper. From Trainee.

Season	Club	League Appearances/Goals	
1992–93	Mansfield T	13	—

WARD, Derek

Born Birkenhead 17.5.72 Ht 5 10
Wt 11 03
Midfield.

Season	Club	League Appearances/Goals	
1992–93	Bury	25	—

WARD, Gavin

Born Sutton Coldfield 30.6.70. Ht 6 2
Wt 12 12
Goalkeeper. From Aston Villa Trainee.

Season	Club	League Appearances/Goals	
1988–89	Shrewsbury T	—	—
1989–90	WBA	—	—
1989–90	Cardiff C	2	—
1990–91		1	—
1991–92		24	—
1992–93		32	—

WARD, Mark

Born Prescot 10.10.62. Ht 5 6 Wt 9 12
Midfield. From Everton Apprentice and
Northwich Vic.

1983–84	Oldham Ath	42	6
1984–85		42	6
1985–86	West Ham U	42	3
1986–87		37	1
1987–88		37	1
1988–89		30	2
1989–90		19	5
1989–90	Manchester C	19	3
1990–91		36	11
1991–92	Everton	37	4
1992–93		19	1

WARD, Mitch

Born Sheffield 18.6.71. Ht 5 8 Wt 10 12
Defender. From Trainee.

1989–90	Sheffield U	—	—
1990–91		4	—
1990–91	*Crewe Alex*	4	1
1991–92	Sheffield U	6	2
1992–93		26	—

WARD, Paul

Born Sedgefield 15.9.63. Ht 5 11
Wt 12 05
Midfield. From Apprentice.

1981–82	Chelsea	—	—
1982–83	Middlesbrough	15	—
1983–84		28	1
1984–85		30	—
1985–86		3	—
1985–86	Darlington	35	2
1986–87		44	1
1987–88		45	6
1988–89	Leyton Orient	28	1
1989–90		3	—
1989–90	Scunthorpe U	25	4
1990–91		30	2
1990–91	Lincoln C	9	—
1991–92		29	—
1992–93		1	—

WARD, Peter

Born Durham 15.10.64. Ht 6 0 Wt 11 10
Forward. From Chester-le-Street.

1986–87	Huddersfield T	7	—
1987–88		26	2
1988–89		4	—
1989–90	Rochdale	40	5
1990–91		44	5
1991–92	Stockport Co	44	1
1992–93		35	3

WARDEN, Danny

Born London 11.4.73 Ht 5 8 Wt 10 10
Forward. From Arsenal.

1992–93	Charlton Ath	3	—

WARE, Paul

Born Congleton 7.11.70. Ht 5 9
Wt 11 05
Midfield. From Trainee.

1987–88	Stoke C	1	—
1988–89		11	1
1989–90		16	—
1990–91		34	2
1991–92		24	3
1992–93		28	4

WARHURST, Paul

Born Stockport 26.9.69. Ht 6 1 Wt 14 00
Defender. From Trainee. England
Under-21.

1987–88	Manchester C	—	—
1988–89	Oldham Ath	4	—
1989–90		30	1
1990–91		33	1
1991–92	Sheffield W	33	—
1992–93		29	6

WARK, John

Born Glasgow 4.8.57. Ht 5 11 Wt 12 12
Defender. From Apprentice. Scotland
Under-21, 29 full caps.

| 1974–75 | Ipswich T | 3 | — |

Season	Club	Appearances	Goals
1975–76		3	—
1976–77		33	10
1977–78		18	5
1978–79		42	6
1979–80		41	12
1980–81		40	18
1981–82		42	18
1982–83		42	20
1983–84		32	5
1983–84	Liverpool	9	2
1984–85		40	18
1985–86		9	3
1986–87		11	5
1987–88		1	—
1987–88	Ipswich T	7	—
1988–89		41	13
1989–90		41	10
1990–91	Middlesbrough	32	2
1991–92	Ipswich T	37	3
1992–93	Ipswich T	37	6

WARREN, Lee

Born Manchester 28.2.69.   Ht 6 0
Wt 11 13
Midfield. From Trainee.

Season	Club	Appearances	Goals
1987–88	Leeds U	—	—
1987–88	Rochdale	31	1
1988–89	Hull C	28	—
1989–90		10	—
1990–91		15	—
1990–91	*Lincoln C*	3	1
1991–92	Hull C	31	1
1992–93		36	—

WARREN, Mark

Born Clapton 12.11.74.
Midfield. From Trainee.

Season	Club	Appearances	Goals
1991–92	Leyton Orient	1	—
1992–93		14	—

WARZYCHA, Robert

Born Poland 20.6.63.   Ht 5 8   Wt 11 10
Forward. From Gornik Zabrze. Poland
full caps.

Season	Club	Appearances	Goals
1990–91	Everton	8	2

Season	Club	Appearances	Goals
1991–92		37	3
1992–93		20	1

WASSALL, Darren

Born Edgbaston 27.6.68.   Ht 5 11
Wt 11 09
Defender.

Season	Club	Appearances	Goals
1987–88	Nottingham F	3	—
1987–88	*Hereford U*	5	—
1988–89	Nottingham F	—	—
1988–89	*Bury*	7	1
1989–90	Nottingham F	3	—
1990–91		7	—
1991–92		14	—
1992–93	Derby Co	24	—

WATKIN, Steve

Born Wrexham 16.6.71.   Ht 5 10
Wt 10 05
Forward. From School.

Season	Club	Appearances	Goals
1989–90	Wrexham	—	—
1990–91		9	1
1991–92		28	8
1992–93		33	18

WATSON, Alex

Born Liverpool 5.4.68.   Ht 6 0   Wt 11 09
Defender. From Apprentice. England
Youth.

Season	Club	Appearances	Goals
1984–85	Liverpool	—	—
1985–86		—	—
1986–87		—	—
1987–88		2	—
1988–89		2	—
1989–90		—	—
1990–91		—	—
1990–91	*Derby Co*	5	—
1990–91	Bournemouth	23	3
1991–92		15	—
1992–93		46	1

WATSON, Andy

Born Huddersfield 1.4.67. Ht 5 9
Wt 11 02
Defender. From Harrogate T.

Season	Club	App	Goals
1988–89	Halifax T	45	5
1989–90		38	10
1990–91	Swansea C	14	1
1991–92		—	—
1991–92	Carlisle U	35	14
1992–93		21	8
1992–93	Blackpool	15	2

WATSON, Dave

Born Liverpool 20.11.61. Ht 6 0
Wt 11 12
Defender. From Amateur. England Under-21, 12 full caps.

Season	Club	App	Goals
1979–80	Liverpool	—	—
1980–81		—	—
1980–81	Norwich C	18	3
1981–82		38	3
1982–83		35	1
1983–84		40	1
1984–85		39	—
1985–86		42	3
1986–87	Everton	35	4
1987–88		37	4
1988–89		32	3
1989–90		29	1
1990–91		32	2
1991–92		35	3
1992–93		40	1

WATSON, David

Born Barnsley 10.11.73. Ht 5 11
Wt 12 00
Goalkeeper. From Trainee. England Youth.

Season	Club	App	Goals
1992–93	Barnsley	5	—

WATSON, Gordon

Born Kent 20.3.71. Ht 6 0 Wt 12 00
Forward. From Trainee. England Under-21.

Season	Club	App	Goals
1988–89	Charlton Ath	—	—

Season	Club	App	Goals
1989–90		9	—
1990–91		22	7
1990–91	Sheffield W	5	—
1991–92		4	—
1992–93		11	1

WATSON, John

Born Edinburgh 13.2.59. Ht 6 0
Wt 12 06
Forward. From Hong Kong R.

Season	Club	App	Goals
1983–84	Dunfermline Ath	21	3
1984–85		37	15
1985–86		37	24
1986–87		40	13
1987–88		25	3
1988–89		35	14
1989–90	Fulham	14	—
1989–90	Airdrieonians	11	1
1990–91		30	4
1991–92		22	4
1992–93		8	—

WATSON, John

Born South Shields 14.4.74. Ht 5 9
Wt 10 10
Midfield. From Trainee.

Season	Club	App	Goals
1990–91	Newcastle U	1	—
1991–92		—	—
1992–93		—	—

WATSON, Kevin

Born Hackney 3.1.74. Ht 5 9 Wt 12 06
Midfield. From Trainee.

Season	Club	App	Goals
1991–92	Tottenham H	—	—
1992–93		5	—

WATSON, Liam

Born Liverpool 21.5.70. Ht 5 11
Wt 11 10
Forward. From Warrington T.

Season	Club	App	Goals
1992–93	Preston NE	8	3

WATSON, Paul

Born Hastings 4.1.75   Ht 5 8   Wt 10 10
Defender. From Trainee.

Season	Club		
1992–93	Gillingham	1	—

WATSON, Stephen

Born Liverpool 4.4.73   Ht 5 11   Wt 11 4
Defender. From Maudsley.

Season	Club		
1990–91	Rangers	—	—
1991–92		—	—
1992–93		3	—

WATSON, Steve

Born North Shields 1.4.74.   Ht 6 0
Wt 12 07
Defender. From Trainee. England Youth,
Under-21.

Season	Club		
1990–91	Newcastle U	24	—
1991–92		28	1
1992–93		2	—

WATSON, Tommy

Born Liverpool 29.9.69.   Ht 5 8   Wt 10 10
Midfield. From Trainee.

Season	Club		
1987–88	Grimsby T	19	—
1988–89		21	4
1989–90		16	1
1990–91		41	9
1991–92		17	2
1992–93		24	4

WATT, Michael

Born Aberdeen 27.11.70.   Ht 6 1
Wt 11 10
Goalkeeper. From Cove R. Scotland
Under-21.

Season	Club		
1989–90	Aberdeen	7	—
1990–91		10	—
1991–92		2	—
1992–93		3	—

WATTS, Grant

Born Croydon 5.11.73   Ht 6 0   Wt 11 02
Forward. From Trainee.

Season	Club		
1992–93	Crystal Palace	4	—

WATTS, Julian

Born Sheffield 17.3.71.   Ht 6 3   Wt 12 01
Defender.

Season	Club		
1990–91	Rotherham U	10	—
1991–92		10	1
1991–92	Sheffield W	—	—
1992–93		4	—
1992–93	*Shrewsbury T*	9	—

WAUGH, Keith

Born Sunderland 27.10.56.   Ht 6 1
Wt 13 00
Goalkeeper. From Apprentice.

Season	Club		
1974–75	Sunderland	—	—
1975–76		—	—
1976–77	Peterborough U	32	—
1977–78		26	—
1978–79		46	—
1979–80		46	—
1980–81		45	—
1981–82	Sheffield U	45	—
1982–83		28	—
1983–84		16	—
1984–85		10	—
1984–85	*Bristol C*	3	—
1984–85	*Cambridge U*	4	—
1985–86	Bristol C	44	—
1986–87		46	—
1987–88		40	—
1988–89		37	—
1989–90	Coventry C	1	—
1990–91		—	—
1990–91	Watford	—	—
1991–92		3	—
1992–93		4	—

WDOWCZYK, Dariusz

Born Warsaw 21.9.62. Ht 5 11 Wt 11 11
Defender. From Legia Warsaw. Poland
full caps.

1989–90	Celtic	23	1
1990–91		24	—
1991–92		19	—
1992–93		25	3

WEBB, Neil

Born Reading 30.7.63. Ht 6 0 Wt 13 07
Midfield. From Apprentice. England
Youth, B, Under-21, 26 full caps. Football
League.

1979–80	Reading	5	—
1980–81		27	7
1981–82		40	15
1982–83	Portsmouth	42	8
1983–84		40	10
1984–85		41	16
1985–86	Nottingham F	38	14
1986–87		32	14
1987–88		40	13
1988–89		36	6
1989–90	Manchester U	11	2
1990–91		32	3
1991–92		31	3
1992–93		1	—
1992–93	Nottingham F	9	—

WEBSTER, Simon

Born Earl Shilton 20.1.64. Ht 6 0
Wt 11 07
Defender. From Apprentice.

1981–82	Tottenham H	—	—
1982–83		2	—
1983–84		1	—
1983–84	*Exeter C*	26	—
1984–85	Tottenham H	—	—
1984–85	*Norwich C*	—	—
1984–85	Huddersfield T	16	1
1985–86		41	2
1986–87		39	1
1987–88		22	—
1987–88	Sheffield U	5	1

1988–89		12	2
1989–90		20	—
1990–91	Charlton Ath	40	—
1991–92		44	5
1992–93		43	2

WEGERLE, Roy

Born South Africa 19.3.64. Ht 5 11
Wt 11 00
Forward. From Tampa Bay R. USA full
caps.

1986–87	Chelsea	12	2
1987–88		11	1
1987–88	*Swindon T*	7	1
1988–89	Luton T	30	8
1989–90		15	2
1989–90	QPR	19	6
1990–91		35	18
1991–92		21	5
1991–92	Blackburn R	12	2
1992–93		22	4
1992–93	Coventry C	6	—

WEIR, David

Born Falkirk 10.5.70 Ht 6 2 Wt 13 7
Defender. From Celtic BC.

| 1992–93 | Falkirk | 30 | 1 |

WEIR, Michael

Born Edinburgh 16.1.66. Ht 5 4 Wt 9 02
Midfield. From Portobello Thistle.

1982–83	Hibernian	—	—
1983–84		—	—
1984–85		12	—
1985–86		7	—
1986–87		24	4
1987–88		5	1
1987–88	Luton T	8	—
1987–88	Hibernian	13	2
1988–89		7	—
1989–90		18	3
1990–91		20	1
1991–92		31	11
1992–93		33	5

WELCH, Keith

Born Bolton 3.10.68.   Ht 6 0   Wt 12 0
Goalkeeper. From Trainee.

1986–87	Bolton W	—	—
1986–87	Rochdale	24	—
1987–88		46	—
1988–89		46	—
1989–90		46	—
1990–91		43	—
1991–92	Bristol C	26	—
1992–93		45	—

WELLS, Mark

Born Leicester 15.10.71.   Ht 5 9
Wt 10 10
Midfield. From Trainee.

1990–91	Notts Co	—	—
1991–92		1	—
1992–93		1	—

WELSH, Brian

Born Edinburgh 23.2.69.   Ht 6 2
Wt 12 01
Defender. From Tynecastle BC.

1986–87	Dundee U	1	—
1987–88		1	1
1988–89		1	—
1989–90		5	—
1990–91		17	—
1991–92		11	1
1992–93		15	1

WELSH, Steve

Born Glasgow 19.4.68.   Ht 6 0   Wt 12 03
Defender. From Army.

1989–90	Cambridge U	—	—
1990–91		1	—
1991–92	Peterborough U	42	—
1992–93		45	1

WEST, Colin

Born Wallsend 13.11.62.   Ht 6 0
Wt 13 11
Forward. From Apprentice.

1980–81	Sunderland	—	—
1981–82		18	6
1982–83		23	3
1983–84		38	9
1984–85		23	3
1984–85	Watford	12	7
1985–86		33	13
1986–87	Rangers	9	2
1987–88		1	—
1987–88	Sheffield W	25	7
1988–89		20	1
1988–89	WBA	17	8
1989–90		21	4
1990–91		28	8
1991–92		7	2
1991–92	*Port Vale*	5	1
1992–93	Swansea C	33	12

WEST, Colin

Born Middlesbrough 19.9.67.   Ht 5 8
Wt 11 10
Forward. From Apprentice.

1985–86	Chelsea	—	—
1986–87		7	1
1986–87	*Partick T*	24	10
1987–88	Chelsea	9	3
1988–89		—	—
1988–89	*Swansea C*	14	3
1989–90	Chelsea	—	—
1990–91	Dundee	19	3
1991–92		9	3
1992–93		7	—

WEST, Dean

Born Wakefield 5.12.72.   Ht 5 10
Wt 11 07
Defender. From Leeds U Schoolboy.

1990–91	Lincoln C	1	1
1991–92		32	3
1992–93		19	3

WEST, Gary

Born Scunthorpe 25.8.64. Ht 6 2
Wt 13 02
Defender. From Apprentice. England
Youth.

Season	Club		
1982–83	Sheffield U	26	1
1983–84		24	—
1984–85		25	—
1985–86	Lincoln C	38	2
1986–87		45	2
1987–88	Gillingham	42	2
1988–89		10	1
1988–89	Port Vale	14	1
1989–90		3	—
1990–91		—	—
1990–91	*Lincoln C*	3	—
1990–91	*Gillingham*	1	—
1991–92	Lincoln C	18	1
1992–93		—	—
1992–93	*Walsall*	9	1

WESTLEY, Shane

Born Canterbury 16.6.65. Ht 6 2
Wt 13 08
Defender. From Apprentice.

Season	Club		
1983–84	Charlton Ath	8	—
1984–85		—	—
1984–85	Southend U	12	—
1985–86		36	5
1986–87		32	—
1986–87	*Norwich C*	—	—
1987–88	Southend U	36	5
1988–89		28	—
1989–90	Wolverhampton W	37	—
1990–91		5	1
1991–92		—	—
1992–93		8	1
1992–93	Brentford	17	1

WESTWATER, Ian

Born Loughborough 8.11.63. Ht 6 0
Wt 13 00
Goalkeeper. From Salvesen BC.

Season	Club		
1980–81	Hearts	2	—
1981–82		—	—
1982–83		—	—
1983–84		—	—
1984–85		—	—
1984–85	Dunfermline Ath	8	—
1985–86		38	—
1986–87		42	—
1987–88		28	—
1988–89		39	—
1989–90		36	—
1990–91		1	—
1991–92	Falkirk	40	—
1992–93		24	—

WETHERALL, David

Born Sheffield 14.3.71. Ht 6 3 Wt 12 00
Defender. From School.

Season	Club		
1989–90	Sheffield W	—	—
1990–91		—	—
1991–92	Leeds U	1	—
1992–93		13	1

WHALLEY, Gareth

Born Manchester 19.12.73 Ht 5 10
Wt 11 00
Midfield. From Trainee.

Season	Club		
1992–93	Crewe Alex	25	1

WHALLEY, Neil

Born Liverpool 29.10.65 Ht 6 0
Wt 12 09
Midfield. From Warrington T.

Season	Club		
1992–93	Preston NE	14	—

WHEELER, Paul

Born Caerphilly 3.1.65. Ht 5 9 Wt 11 00
Forward. From Apprentice.

Season	Club		
1982–83	Bristol R	—	—
1983–84		—	—
From Aberaman			
1985–86	Cardiff C	21	2
1986–87		37	7
1987–88		16	—

Season	Club	Apps	Goals
1988–89	....	27	1
1989–90	....	—	—
1989–90	Hull C....................................	5	—
1989–90	Hereford U	21	8
1990–91	....	33	4
1991–92	Stockport Co	22	5
1992–93	....	1	—
1992–93	*Scarborough*	7	1
1992–93	Chester C....................	14	—

WHELAN, Noel

Born Leeds 30.12.74
Forward. From Trainee.

Season	Club	Apps	Goals
1992–93	Leeds U	1	—

WHELAN, Phil

Born Stockport 7.8.72. Ht 6 4 Wt 14 01
Defender. England Under-21.

Season	Club	Apps	Goals
1989–90	Ipswich T	—	—
1990–91	....	—	—
1991–92	....	8	2
1992–93	....	32	—

WHELAN, Ronnie

Born Dublin 25.9.61. Ht 5 9 Wt 10 13
Midfield. From Home Farm. Eire Schools,
Youth, Under-21, 45 full caps.

Season	Club	Apps	Goals
1979–80	Liverpool	—	—
1980–81	....	1	1
1981–82	....	32	10
1982–83	....	28	2
1983–84	....	23	4
1984–85	....	37	7
1985–86	....	39	10
1986–87	....	39	3
1987–88	....	28	1
1988–89	....	37	4
1989–90	....	34	1
1990–91	....	14	1
1991–92	....	10	—
1992–93	....	17	1

WHELAN, Spencer

Born Liverpool 17.9.71. Ht 6 1 Wt 11 13
Defender. From Liverpool.

Season	Club	Apps	Goals
1990–91	Chester C....................	11	—
1991–92	....	32	—
1992–93	....	28	—

WHISTON, Peter

Born Widnes 4.1.68. Ht 6 0 Wt 11 06
Forward.

Season	Club	Apps	Goals
1987–88	Plymouth Arg.............	—	—
1988–89	....	2	—
1989–90	....	8	—
1989–90	*Torquay U*....................	8	1
1990–91	Torquay U....................	28	—
1991–92	....	4	—
1991–92	Exeter C......................	36	3
1992–93	....	27	3

WHITBREAD, Adrian

Born Epping 22.10.71. Ht 6 2 Wt 11 13
Defender. From Trainee.

Season	Club	Apps	Goals
1989–90	Leyton Orient	8	—
1990–91	....	38	—
1991–92	....	43	1
1992–93	....	36	1

WHITE, Chris

Born Chatham 11.12.70. Ht 5 11
Wt 11 10
Defender. From Trainee.

Season	Club	Apps	Goals
1988–89	Portsmouth	—	—
1989–90	....	—	—
1990–91	....	—	—
1991–92	Peterborough U	8	—
1992–93	....	5	—
1992–93	*Doncaster R*	6	—
1992–93	Exeter C......................	11	—

WHITE, David

Born Manchester 30.10.67.   Ht 6 1
Wt 12 09
Forward. England Youth, B, Under-21, 1
full cap.

1985–86	Manchester C	—	—
1986–87		24	1
1987–88		44	13
1988–89		45	6
1989–90		37	8
1990–91		38	16
1991–92		39	18
1992–93		42	16

WHITE, Devon

Born Nottingham 2.3.64.   Ht 6 3
Wt 14 00
Forward. From Arnold T.

1984–85	Lincoln C	7	1
1985–86		22	3
1986–87		—	—
From Boston U			
1987–88	Bristol R	39	15
1988–89		40	5
1989–90		43	12
1990–91		45	11
1991–92		35	10
1991–92	Cambridge U	2	—
1992–93		20	4
1992–93	QPR	7	2

WHITE, Jason

Born Meriden 19.10.71.   Ht 6 0   Wt 12 10
Forward. From Derby Co Trainee.

1991–92	Scunthorpe U	22	11
1992–93		37	5

WHITE, Steve

Born Chipping Sodbury 2.1.59.   Ht 5 10
Wt 11 04
Forward. From Mangotsfield U.

1977–78	Bristol R	8	4
1978–79		27	10

1979–80		15	6
1979–80	Luton T	9	—
1980–81		21	7
1981–82		42	18
1982–83	Charlton Ath	29	12
1982–83	*Lincoln C*	3	—
1982–83	*Luton T*	4	—
1983–84	Bristol R	43	9
1984–85		18	3
1985–86		40	12
1986–87	Swindon T	35	15
1987–88		25	11
1988–89		43	13
1989–90		43	18
1990–91		35	9
1991–92		23	10
1992–93		34	7

WHITE, Winston

Born Leicester 26.10.58.   Ht 5 10
Wt 10 12
Forward. From Apprentice.

1976–77	Leicester C	4	—
1977–78		6	1
1978–79		2	—
1978–79	Hereford U	15	3
1979–80		34	2
1980–81		43	5
1981–82		46	8
1982–83		37	3
1983–84	Chesterfield	1	—
1983–84	Port Vale	1	—
1983–84	Stockport Co	4	—
1983–84	Bury	29	1
1984–85		46	4
1985–86		43	5
1986–87		7	1
1986–87	*Rochdale*	4	—
1986–87	Colchester U	14	1
1987–88		41	7
1988–89		10	—
1988–89	Burnley	35	5
1989–90		40	7
1990–91		29	2
1990–91	WBA	6	1
1991–92		10	—
1992–93	Bury	2	—
1992–93	Carlisle U	6	—

| 1992–93 | Doncaster R | 4 | 2 |
| 1992–93 | Wigan Ath | 10 | 2 |

WHITEHALL, Steve

Born Bromborough 8.12.66. Ht 5 9
Wt 10 11
Forward. From Southport.

| 1991–92 | Rochdale | 34 | 8 |
| 1992–93 | | 42 | 14 |

WHITEHEAD, Philip

Born Halifax 17.12.69. Ht 6 3 Wt 13 07
Goalkeeper. From Trainee.

1986–87	Halifax T	12	—
1987–88		—	—
1988–89		11	—
1989–90		19	—
1989–90	Barnsley	—	—
1990–91		—	—
1990–91	Halifax T	9	—
1991–92	Barnsley	3	—
1991–92	Scunthorpe U	8	—
1992–93	Barnsley	13	—
1992–93	Scunthorpe U	8	—
1992–93	Bradford C	6	—

WHITEHEAD, Scott

Born Doncaster 20.4.74. Ht 5 9
Wt 11 10
Midfield. From Trainee.

| 1991–92 | Chesterfield | 5 | — |
| 1992–93 | | 4 | — |

WHITEHOUSE, Dane

Born Sheffield 14.10.70. Ht 5 9 Wt 10 13
Midfield. From Trainee.

1988–89	Sheffield U	5	—
1989–90		12	1
1990–91		4	—
1991–92		34	7
1992–93		14	5

WHITLOW, Mike

Born Northwich 13.1.68. Ht 5 11
Wt 12 03
Defender. From Witton Alb.

1988–89	Leeds U	20	1
1989–90		29	1
1990–91		18	1
1991–92		10	1
1991–92	Leicester C	5	—
1992–93		24	1

WHITTINGHAM, Guy

Born Evesham 10.11.64. Ht 5 10
Wt 11 12
Forward. From Yeovil and Army.

1989–90	Portsmouth	42	23
1990–91		37	12
1991–92		35	11
1992–93		46	42

WHITTON, Steve

Born East Ham 4.12.60. Ht 6 1
Wt 13 06
Forward. From Apprentice.

1978–79	Coventry C	—	—
1979–80		7	—
1980–81		1	—
1981–82		28	9
1982–83		38	12
1983–84	West Ham U	22	5
1984–85		17	1
1985–86		—	—
1985–86	Birmingham C	8	2
1986–87	Birmingham C	39	9
1987–88		33	14
1988–89		23	5
1988–89	Sheffield W	12	3
1989–90		19	1
1990–91		1	—
1990–91	Ipswich T	10	2
1991–92		43	9
1992–93		24	3

WHYTE, Chris

Born London 2.9.61.   Ht 6 1   Wt 11 10
Defender. From Amateur. England
Under-21.

Season	Club	Apps	Goals
1979–80	Arsenal	—	—
1980–81		—	—
1981–82		32	2
1982–83		36	3
1983–84		15	2
1984–85		—	—
1984–85	Crystal Palace	13	—
1985–86	Arsenal	7	1
From Los Angeles R			
1988–89	WBA	40	3
1989–90		44	4
1990–91	Leeds U	38	3
1991–92		41	1
1992–93		34	1

WHYTE, Derek

Born Glasgow 31.8.68.   Ht 5 11   Wt 11 05
Defender. From Celtic BC. Scotland
Schools, Youth, B, Under-21, 6 full caps.

Season	Club	Apps	Goals
1985–86	Celtic	11	—
1986–87		42	—
1987–88		41	3
1988–89		22	—
1989–90		35	1
1990–91		24	2
1991–92		40	1
1992–93		1	—
1992–93	Middlesbrough	35	—

WIDDRINGTON, Tommy

Born Newcastle 21.11.71.   Ht 5 10
Wt 11 07
Midfield. From Trainee.

Season	Club	Apps	Goals
1989–90	Southampton	—	—
1990–91		—	—
1991–92		3	—
1991–92	Wigan Ath	6	—
1992–93	Southampton	12	—

WIEGHORST, Morten

Born Glostrup, Denmark 25.2.71   Ht 6 3
Wt 14 0
Midfield. From Lyngby.

Season	Club	Apps	Goals
1992–93	Dundee	23	2

WILCOX, Jason

Born Bolton 15.7.71.   Ht 5 10   Wt 11 06
Forward. From Trainee.

Season	Club	Apps	Goals
1989–90	Blackburn R	1	—
1990–91		18	—
1991–92		38	4
1992–93		33	4

WILCOX, Russell

Born Hemsworth 25.3.64.   Ht 6 0
Wt 11 10
Defender. From Apprentice.

Season	Club	Apps	Goals
1980–81	Doncaster R	1	—
From Cambridge U, Frickley Ath.			
1986–87	Northampton T	35	1
1987–88		46	4
1988–89		11	1
1989–90		46	3
1990–91	Hull C	31	1
1991–92		40	4
1992–93		29	2

WILDER, Chris

Born Wortley 23.9.67.   Ht 5 11   Wt 11 02
Defender. From Apprentice.

Season	Club	Apps	Goals
1985–86	Southampton	—	—
1986–87	Sheffield U	11	—
1987–88		25	—
1988–89		29	1
1989–90		8	—
1989–90	Walsall	4	—
1990–91	Sheffield U	16	—
1990–91	Charlton Ath	1	—
1991–92	Sheffield U	4	—
1991–92	Charlton Ath	2	—
1991–92	Leyton Orient	16	1
1992–93	Rotherham U	32	8

WILKIN, Kevin

Born Cambridge 1.10.67
Forward. From Cambridge C.

Season	Club	Apps	Goals
1990–91	Northampton T	9	2
1991–92		—	—
1992–93		41	4

WILKINS, Dean

Born Hillingdon 12.7.62. Ht 5 10
Wt 12 04
Midfield. From Apprentice.

Season	Club	Apps	Goals
1980–81	QPR	2	—
1981–82		1	—
1982–83		3	—
1983–84	Brighton	2	—
1983–84	*Orient*	10	—
From PEC Zwolle			
1987–88	Brighton	44	3
1988–89		43	1
1989–90		46	6
1990–91		46	7
1991–92		26	—
1992–93		35	3

WILKINS, Ray

Born Hillingdon 14.9.56. Ht 5 8
Wt 11 02
Midfield. From Apprentice. England
Under-21, Under-23, 84 full caps. Football
League.

Season	Club	Apps	Goals
1973–74	Chelsea	6	—
1974–75		21	2
1975–76		42	11
1976–77		42	7
1977–78		33	7
1978–79		35	3
1979–80	Manchester U	37	2
1980–81		13	—
1981–82		42	1
1982–83		26	1
1983–84		42	3
1984–85	AC Milan	28	—
1985–86		29	2
1986–87		16	—
From Paris St Germain			
1987–88	Rangers	24	1

Season	Club	Apps	Goals
1988–89		31	1
1989–90		15	—
1989–90	QPR	23	1
1990–91		38	2
1991–92		27	1
1992–93		27	2

WILKINS, Richard

Born London 28.5.65. Ht 6 0 Wt 12 00
Midfield. From Haverhill R.

Season	Club	Apps	Goals
1986–87	Colchester U	23	2
1987–88		46	9
1988–89		40	7
1989–90		43	4
1990–91	Cambridge U	41	3
1991–92		32	4
1992–93		1	—

WILKINSON, Darron

Born Reading 24.11.69 Ht 5 11
Wt 12 08
Midfield. From Wokingham.

Season	Club	Apps	Goals
1992–93	Brighton	27	3

WILKINSON, Paul

Born Louth 30.10.64. Ht 6 0 Wt 11 09
Forward. From Apprentice. England
Under-21.

Season	Club	Apps	Goals
1982–83	Grimsby T	4	1
1983–84		37	12
1984–85		30	14
1984–85	Everton	5	2
1985–86		4	1
1986–87		22	4
1986–87	Nottingham F	8	—
1987–88		26	5
1988–89	Watford	45	19
1989–90		43	15
1990–91		46	18
1991–92	Middlesbrough	46	15
1992–93		41	14

WILKINSON, Steve

Born Lincoln 1.9.68. Ht 6 0 Wt 11 02
Forward. From Apprentice.

Season	Club	App	Goals
1986–87	Leicester C	1	—
1987–88		5	1
1988–89		1	—
1988–89	*Rochdale*	—	—
1988–89	*Crewe Alex*	5	2
1989–90	Leicester C	2	—
1989–90	Mansfield T	37	15
1990–91		39	11
1991–92		30	14
1992–93		43	11

WILLIAMS, Adrian

Born Reading 16.8.71. Ht 5 10 Wt 11 00
Defender. From Trainee.

Season	Club	App	Goals
1988–89	Reading	8	—
1989–90		16	2
1990–91		7	—
1991–92		40	4
1992–93		31	4

WILLIAMS, Andy

Born Birmingham 29.7.62. Ht 6 0
Wt 11 09
Midfield. From Dudley and Solihull B.

Season	Club	App	Goals
1985–86	Coventry C	8	—
1986–87		1	—
1986–87	Rotherham U	36	4
1987–88		36	6
1988–89		15	3
1988–89	Leeds U	18	1
1989–90		16	2
1990–91		12	—
1991–92		—	—
1991–92	*Port Vale*	5	—
1991–92	Notts Co	15	1
1992–93		22	1

WILLIAMS, Bill

Born Rochdale 7.10.60. Ht 5 10
Wt 12 11
Defender. From Local.

Season	Club	App	Goals
1981–82	Rochdale	6	—

Season	Club	App	Goals
1982–83		37	—
1983–84		27	2
1984–85		25	—
1985–86	Stockport Co	22	—
1986–87		30	—
1987–88		45	1
1988–89		7	—
1988–89	Manchester C	1	—
1988–89	Stockport Co	28	2
1989–90		37	—
1990–91		18	1
1991–92		35	2
1992–93		22	1

WILLIAMS, Brett

Born Dudley 19.3.68. Ht 5 10 Wt 11 12
Defender. From Apprentice.

Season	Club	App	Goals
1985–86	Nottingham F	11	—
1986–87		3	—
1986–87	*Stockport Co*	2	—
1987–88	Nottingham F	4	—
1987–88	*Northampton T*	4	—
1988–89	Nottingham F	2	—
1989–90		1	—
1989–90	*Hereford U*	14	—
1990–91	Nottingham F	4	—
1991–92		9	—
1991–92	*Oxford U*	7	—
1992–93	Nottingham F	9	—

WILLIAMS, David

Born Liverpool 18.9.68. Ht 6 0 Wt 12 00
Goalkeeper. From Trainee.

Season	Club	App	Goals
1987–88	Oldham Ath	—	—
1987–88	Burnley	—	—
1988–89		7	—
1989–90		7	—
1990–91		3	—
1991–92		5	—
1991–92	*Rochdale*	6	—
1992–93	Burnley	2	—
1992–93	*Crewe Alex*	—	—

WILLIAMS, David

Born Cardiff 11.3.55 Ht 5 10 Wt 11 08
Midfield. From Clifton Ath. Wales Under-23, Under-21, 5 full caps.

Season	Club	App	Goals
1975–76	Bristol R	41	2
1976–77		39	10
1977–78		33	8
1978–79		42	10
1979–80		40	4
1980–81		25	3
1981–82		46	11
1982–83		25	9
1983–84		24	3
1984–85		37	6
1985–86	Norwich C	39	8
1986–87		12	3
1987–88		9	—
1988–89		—	—
1989–90		—	—
1990–91		—	—
1991–92		—	—
1992–93	Bournemouth	1	—

WILLIAMS, Gareth

Born Isle of Wight 12.3.67. Ht 5 10
Wt 11 08
Forward. From Gosport Borough.

Season	Club	App	Goals
1987–88	Aston Villa	1	—
1988–89		1	—
1989–90		10	—
1990–91		—	—
1991–92	Barnsley	17	—
1992–93		8	5
1992–93	*Hull C*	4	—

WILLIAMS, Gary

Born Wolverhampton 17.6.60. Ht 5 9
Wt 11 12
Defender. From Apprentice.

Season	Club	App	Goals
1978–79	Aston Villa	23	—
1979–80		2	—
1979–80	*Walsall*	9	—
1980–81	Aston Villa	22	—
1981–82		28	—
1982–83		36	—

Season	Club	App	Goals
1983–84		40	—
1984–85		38	—
1985–86		25	—
1986–87		26	—
1987–88	Leeds U	31	3
1988–89		8	—
1989–90		—	—
1989–90	Watford	18	—
1990–91		24	—
1991–92		—	—
1991–92	Bradford C	22	—
1992–93		31	3

WILLIAMS, Geraint

Born Treorchy 5.1.62. Ht 5 7 Wt 10 06
Midfield. From Apprentice. Wales Youth, Under-21, 12 full caps.

Season	Club	App	Goals
1979–80	Bristol R	—	—
1980–81		28	1
1981–82		16	—
1982–83		35	3
1983–84		34	4
1984–85		28	—
1984–85	Derby Co	12	—
1985–86		40	4
1986–87		40	1
1987–88		40	1
1988–89		37	1
1989–90		38	—
1990–91		31	—
1991–92		39	2
1992–93	Ipswich T	37	—

WILLIAMS, John

Born Liverpool 3.10.60. Ht 6 1 Wt 13 12
Defender. From Amateur.

Season	Club	App	Goals
1978–79	Tranmere R	1	—
1979–80		3	—
1980–81		27	2
1981–82		44	6
1982–83		35	—
1983–84		20	1
1984–85		43	4
1985–86	Port Vale	36	2
1986–87		14	—
1986–87	Bournemouth	26	3

Season	Club	Apps	Goals
1987–88		38	2
1988–89		37	2
1989–90		16	2
1990–91		—	—
1991–92		—	—
1991–92	*Wigan Ath*	4	—
1991–92	Cardiff C	5	—
1992–93		1	—

WILLIAMS, John

Born Birmingham 11.5.68. Ht 6 2
Wt 12 04
Midfield. From Cradley T.

Season	Club	Apps	Goals
1991–92	Swansea C	39	11
1992–93	Coventry C	41	8

WILLIAMS, Lee

Born Birmingham 3.2.73 Ht 5 7
Wt 11 00
Midfield. From Trainee.

Season	Club	Apps	Goals
1991–92	Aston Villa	—	—
1992–93		—	—
1992–93	*Shrewsbury T*	3	—

WILLIAMS, Mark

Born Bangor 10.12.73. Ht 5 10 Wt 12 07
Forward. From Trainee.

Season	Club	Apps	Goals
1991–92	Shrewsbury T	1	—
1992–93		2	—

WILLIAMS, Mark

Born Cheshire 28.9.70. Ht 6 0 Wt 13 00
Defender. From Newtown.

Season	Club	Apps	Goals
1991–92	Shrewsbury T	3	—
1992–93		28	1

WILLIAMS, Martin

Born Luton 12.7.73. Ht 5 9 Wt 11 12
Forward. From Leicester C Trainee.

Season	Club	Apps	Goals
1991–92	Luton T	1	—

Season	Club	Apps	Goals
1992–93		22	1

WILLIAMS, Mike

Born Bradford 21.11.69. Ht 5 8 Wt 10 11
Midfield. From Maltby.

Season	Club	Apps	Goals
1991–92	Sheffield W	—	—
1992–93		3	—
1992–93	*Halifax T*	9	1

WILLIAMS, Neil

Born Waltham Abbey 23.10.64. Ht 5 11
Wt 11 04
Midfield. From Apprentice. England
Youth.

Season	Club	Apps	Goals
1982–83	Watford	—	—
1983–84		—	—
1984–85	Hull C	17	3
1985–86		19	3
1986–87		30	2
1987–88		25	2
1988–89	Preston NE	41	2
1989–90		41	3
1990–91		13	—
1991–92		26	1
1992–93	Carlisle U	19	1

WILLIAMS, Paul

Born Leicester 11.9.69. Ht 5 7 Wt 10 00
Forward. From Trainee.

Season	Club	Apps	Goals
1988–89	Leicester C	—	—
1989–90	Stockport Co	7	—
1990–91		24	2
1991–92		13	1
1992–93		26	1

WILLIAMS, Paul

Born Burton 26.3.71. Ht 5 11 Wt 12 00
Midfield. From Trainee. England
Under-21.

Season	Club	Apps	Goals
1989–90	Derby Co	10	1
1989–90	*Lincoln C*	3	—
1990–91	Derby Co	19	4

1991–92	....	41	13
1992–93	....	19	4

WILLIAMS, Paul

Born London 16.8.65.   Ht 5 7   Wt 10 03
Forward. From Woodford T. England B,
Under-21.

1986–87	Charlton Ath	—	—
1987–88	....	12	—
1987–88	*Brentford*	7	3
1988–89	Charlton Ath	32	13
1989–90	....	38	10
1990–91	Sheffield W	46	15
1991–92	....	40	9
1992–93	....	7	1
1992–93	Crystal Palace	18	—

WILLIAMS, Paul

Born Sheffield 8.9.63.   Ht 6 3   Wt 14 06
Forward. From Distillery, Leeds U,
Grenaker R, Nuneaton. Northern Ireland
1 full cap.

1986–87	Preston NE	1	—
1987–88	Newport Co	26	3
1987–88	Sheffield U	6	—
1988–89	....	2	—
1989–90	Hartlepool U	8	—
1990–91	Stockport Co	24	14
1990–91	WBA	10	—
1991–92	....	34	5
1992–93	....	—	—
1992–93	*Coventry C*	2	—
1992–93	Stockport Co	16	3

WILLIAMS, Scott

Born Bangor 7.8.74   Ht 6 0   Wt 11 00
Defender. From Trainee.

1992–93	Wrexham	1	—

WILLIAMS, Steve

Born London 12.7.58.   Ht 5 9   Wt 11 04
Midfield. From Apprentice. England
Under-21, B, 6 full caps.

1974–75	Southampton	—	—

1975–76	....	1	—
1976–77	....	33	—
1977–78	....	39	5
1978–79	....	39	—
1979–80	....	32	2
1980–81	....	33	4
1981–82	....	21	—
1982–83	....	39	3
1983–84	....	27	3
1984–85	....	14	1
1984–85	Arsenal	15	1
1985–86	....	17	—
1986–87	....	34	2
1987–88	....	29	1
1988–89	Luton T	10	—
1989–90	....	14	1
1990–91	....	16	—
1991–92	Exeter C	36	—
1992–93	....	12	—

WILLIAMS, Steven

Born Mansfield 18.7.70.   Ht 5 11
Wt 10 06
Midfield. From Trainee.

1986–87	Mansfield T	4	—
1987–88	....	4	—
1988–89	....	3	—
1989–90	Chesterfield	11	1
1990–91	....	25	4
1991–92	....	31	2
1992–93	....	31	5

WILLIAMS, Wayne

Born Delford 17.11.63.   Ht 5 11
Wt 11 09
Defender. From Apprentice.

1981–82	Shrewsbury T	—	—
1982–83	....	42	4
1983–84	....	40	—
1984–85	....	28	—
1985–86	....	30	1
1986–87	....	40	—
1987–88	....	31	2
1988–89	....	10	—
1988–89	Northampton T	26	1
1989–90	....	15	—

1990–91	....	14	—
1991–92	Walsall	42	—
1992–93	....	14	1

WILLIAMSON, Bobby

Born Glasgow 13.8.61   Ht 5 8   Wt 12 9
Forward. From Auchengill BC.

1980–81	Clydebank	2	—
1981–82	....	12	1
1982–83	....	39	23
1983–84	....	17	4
1983–84	Rangers	17	6
1984–85	....	1	—
1985–86	....	23	6
1986–87	WBA	31	8
1987–88	....	22	3
1988–89	Rotherham U	42	27
1989–90	....	42	19
1990–91	....	9	3
1990–91	Kilmarnock	23	14
1991–92	....	36	9
1992–93	....	33	6

WILLIAMSON, Trevor

Born Portadown 7.11.71   Ht 5 10
Wt 11 4
Forward. From Portadown.

1991–92	Raith R	25	2
1992–93	....	2	—

WILLIS, Jimmy

Born Liverpool 12.7.68.   Ht 6 0   Wt 12 02
Defender. From Blackburn R.

1986–87	Halifax T	—	—
1987–88	Stockport Co	10	—
1987–88	Darlington	9	—
1988–89	....	41	2
1989–90	....	*38*	2
1990–91	....	28	2
1991–92	....	12	2
1991–92	Leicester C	10	—
1991–92	*Bradford C*	9	1
1992–93	Leicester C	—	—

WILLIS, Roger

Born Sheffield 17.6.67.   Ht 6 1   Wt 11 06
Defender.

1989–90	Grimsby T	9	—
To Barnet			
1991–92	Barnet	38	12
1992–93	....	6	1
1992–93	Watford	32	2

WILMOT, Rhys

Born Newport 21.2.62.   Ht 6 1   Wt 12 00
Goalkeeper. From Apprentice. Wales
Youth, Under-21.

1979–80	Arsenal	—	—
1980–81	....	—	—
1981–82	....	—	—
1982–83	....	—	—
1982–83	*Hereford U*	9	—
1983–84	Arsenal	—	—
1984–85	*Orient*	46	—
1985–86	Arsenal	2	—
1986–87	....	6	—
1987–88	....	—	—
1988–89	....	—	—
1988–89	*Swansea C*	16	—
1988–89	*Plymouth Arg*	17	—
1989–90	Plymouth Arg	46	—
1990–91	....	36	—
1991–92	....	34	—
1992–93	Grimsby T	33	—

WILMOTT, Richard

29.8.69   Ht 6 4   Wt 13 07
Goalkeeper. From Stevenage.

1992–93	Scunthorpe U	3	—

WILSON, Clive

Born Manchester 13.11.61.   Ht 5 7
Wt 10 00
Midfield. From Local.

1979–80	Manchester C	—	—
1980–81	....	—	—
1981–82	....	4	—

Season	Club	Apps	Goals
1982–83	....	—	—
1982–83	*Chester*	21	2
1983–84	Manchester C	11	—
1984–85	....	27	4
1985–86	....	25	5
1986–87	....	31	—
1986–87	Chelsea......................	—	—
1986–87	*Manchester C*	11	—
1987–88	Chelsea......................	31	2
1988–89	....	32	3
1989–90	....	18	—
1990–91	QPR..........................	13	1
1991–92	....	40	3
1992–93	....	41	3

WILSON, Danny

Born Wigan 1.1.60.   Ht 5 6   Wt 11 00
Midfield. From Wigan Ath. Northern
Ireland 25 full caps.

Season	Club	Apps	Goals
1977–78	Bury	12	1
1978–79	....	46	7
1979–80	....	32	—
1980–81	Chesterfield	33	3
1981–82	....	43	3
1982–83	....	24	7
1982–83	Nottingham F.............	10	1
1983–84	*Scunthorpe U*	6	3
1983–84	Brighton......................	26	10
1984–85	....	38	5
1985–86	....	33	11
1986–87	....	38	7
1987–88	Luton T	38	8
1988–89	....	37	9
1989–90	....	35	7
1990–91	Sheffield W..................	36	6
1991–92	....	36	3
1992–93	....	26	2

WILSON, Darren

Born Manchester 30.9.71.   Ht 5 11
Wt 12 07
Defender.

Season	Club	Apps	Goals
1988–89	Manchester C	—	—
1989–90	....	—	—
1990–91	....	—	—
1991–92	Bury	32	1

Season	Club	Apps	Goals
1992–93	....	—	—

WILSON, David

Born Burnley 20.3.69.   Ht 5 9   Wt 10 10
Midfield. From Apprentice.

Season	Club	Apps	Goals
1986–87	Manchester U	—	—
1987–88	....	—	—
1988–89	....	4	—
1989–90	....	—	—
1990–91	....	—	—
1990–91	*Charlton Ath*	7	2
1990–91	*Lincoln C*	3	—
1991–92	Bristol R	3	—
1992–93	....	8	—

WILSON, Gus

Born Manchester 11.4.63.   Ht 5 11
Wt 12 00
Defender. From Runcorn.

Season	Club	Apps	Goals
1991–92	Crewe Alex	41	—
1992–93	....	35	—

WILSON, Ian

Born Aberdeen 27.3.58.   Ht 5 6   Wt 11 10
Midfield. From Elgin C. Scotland 5 full
caps.

Season	Club	Apps	Goals
1978–79	Leicester C..................	—	—
1979–80	....	24	2
1980–81	....	40	1
1981–82	....	35	—
1982–83	....	36	8
1983–84	....	41	—
1984–85	....	39	1
1985–86	....	25	2
1986–87	....	37	1
1987–88	....	8	2
1987–88	Everton	16	—
1988–89	....	18	1
From Besiktas			
1990–91	Derby Co.....................	11	—
1991–92	Bury...........................	24	1
1992–93	Wigan Ath..................	5	—

WILSON, Kevin

Born Banbury 18.4.61.   Ht 5 7   Wt 10 10
Forward. From Banbury U. Northern
Ireland 32 full caps.

Season	Club	Apps	Goals
1979–80	Derby Co	4	—
1980–81		27	7
1981–82		24	9
1982–83		22	4
1983–84		32	2
1984–85		13	8
1984–85	Ipswich T	17	7
1985–86		39	7
1986–87		42	20
1987–88	Chelsea	25	5
1988–89		46	13
1989–90		37	14
1990–91		22	7
1991–92		22	3
1991–92	Notts Co	8	1
1992–93		32	1

WILSON, Lee

Born Mansfield 23.5.72
Forward.

Season	Club	Apps	Goals
1992–93	Mansfield T	4	—

WILSON, Marvyn

Born Bellshill 1.12.73   Ht 5 7   Wt 10 0
Defender. From Motherwell BC.

Season	Club	Apps	Goals
1990–91	Hearts	—	—
1991–92		—	—
1992–93	Airdrieonians	4	—

WILSON, Paul

Born Bradford 2.8.68.   Ht 5 10   Wt 13 00
Defender. From Trainee.

Season	Club	Apps	Goals
1985–86	Huddersfield T	7	—
1986–87		8	—
1987–88	Norwich C	—	—
1987–88	Northampton T	15	1
1988–89		39	1
1989–90		27	—
1990–91		44	3

Season	Club	Apps	Goals
1991–92		16	1
1991–92	Halifax T	23	5
1992–93		22	2
1992–93	Burnley	20	—

WILSON, Paul

Born London 26.9.64.   Ht 5 9   Wt 11 04
Defender. From West Ham U, Billericay,
Barking.

Season	Club	Apps	Goals
1991–92	Barnet	25	1
1992–93		9	—

WILSON, Steve

Born Hull 24.4.74.   Ht 5 11   Wt 11 00
Goalkeeper. From Trainee.

Season	Club	Apps	Goals
1990–91	Hull C	2	—
1991–92		3	—
1992–93		26	—

WILSON, Terry

Born Broxburn 8.2.69.   Ht 6 0   Wt 10 10
Midfield. From Apprentice. Scotland
Under-21.

Season	Club	Apps	Goals
1986–87	Nottingham F	—	—
1987–88		36	5
1988–89		27	1
1989–90		21	—
1990–91		15	3
1991–92		1	—
1991–92	Newcastle U	2	—
1992–93	Nottingham F	5	—

WILSON, Tommy

Born Paisley 2.8.61.   Ht 5 8   Wt 9 07
Defender. From School. Scotland
Under-21.

Season	Club	Apps	Goals
1979–80	Queens Park	1	—
1980–81		1	—
1981–82		30	—
1982–83	St Mirren	36	—
1983–84		1	—
1984–85		35	—

Season	Club	App	Goals
1985–86		27	—
1986–87		25	1
1987–88		35	—
1988–89		31	—
1989–90		9	—
1989–90	Dunfermline Ath	15	—
1990–91		28	—
1991–92		16	—
1992–93	Kilmarnock	19	—

WIMBLETON, Paul

Born Havant 13.11.64. Ht 5 8 Wt 10 12
Midfield. From Apprentice. England
Schools, Youth.

Season	Club	App	Goals
1981–82	Portsmouth	8	—
1982–83		—	—
1983–84		2	—
1984–85		—	—
1985–86		—	—
1986–87	Cardiff C	46	8
1987–88		37	9
1988–89		36	—
1989–90	Bristol C	16	2
1989–90	Shrewsbury T	16	—
1990–91		18	1
1990–91	*Maidstone U*	2	1
1991–92	Shrewsbury T	—	—
1991–92	Exeter C	36	4
1992–93	Swansea C	15	1

WINDASS, Dean

Born Hull 1.4.69. Ht 5 9 Wt 12 03
Midfield.

Season	Club	App	Goals
1991–92	Hull C	32	6
1992–93		41	7

WINNIE, David

Born Glasgow 26.10.66. Ht 5 1 Wt 10 07
Defender. S Form. Scotland Schools,
Youth, Under-21.

Season	Club	App	Goals
1983–84	St Mirren	8	—
1984–85		30	3
1985–86		20	1
1986–87		14	—
1987–88		26	2
1988–89		30	—
1989–90		17	—
1990–91		1	—
1991–92	Aberdeen	28	1
1992–93		21	—

WINSTANLEY, Mark

Born St. Helens 22.1.68. Ht 6 1
Wt 12 04
Defender. From Trainee.

Season	Club	App	Goals
1984–85	Bolton W	—	—
1985–86		3	—
1986–87		13	—
1987–88		8	1
1988–89		44	—
1989–90		43	1
1990–91		32	—
1991–92		27	—
1992–93		29	1

WINTER, Steven

Born Bristol 26.10.73. Ht 5 7 Wt 10 03
Midfield. From Trainee.

Season	Club	App	Goals
1991–92	Walsall	16	—
1992–93		2	—

WINTERBURN, Nigel

Born Coventry 11.12.63. Ht 5 8
Wt 11 04
Defender. From Local. England Youth, B,
Under-21, 2 full caps.

Season	Club	App	Goals
1981–82	Birmingham C	—	—
1982–83		—	—
1983–84	Oxford U	—	—
1983–84	Wimbledon	43	1
1984–85		41	4
1985–86		39	1
1986–87		42	2
1987–88	Arsenal	17	—
1988–89		38	3
1989–90		36	—
1990–91		38	—
1991–92		41	1

1992–93		29	1

WISE, Dennis

Born Kensington 15.12.66. Ht 5 6
Wt 9 05
Forward. From Southampton Apprentice.
England B, Under-21, 5 full caps.

Season	Club	App	Goals
1984–85	Wimbledon	1	—
1985–86		4	—
1986–87		28	4
1987–88		30	10
1988–89		37	5
1989–90		35	8
1990–91	Chelsea	33	10
1991–92		38	10
1992–93		27	3

WISHART, Fraser

Born Johnstone 1.3.65. Ht 5 8 Wt 10 00
Defender. From Pollok.

Season	Club	App	Goals
1983–84	Motherwell	6	—
1984–85		—	—
1985–86		26	—
1986–87		44	3
1987–88		43	1
1988–89		35	1
1989–90	St Mirren	20	—
1990–91		22	—
1991–92		9	—
1992–93	Falkirk	24	2

WITHE, Chris

Born Liverpool 25.9.62. Ht 5 10
Wt 11 12
Defender. From Apprentice.

Season	Club	App	Goals
1980–81	Newcastle U	2	—
1981–82		—	—
1982–83		—	—
1983–84	Bradford C	45	1
1984–85		45	—
1985–86		33	—
1986–87		18	1
1987–88		2	—
1987–88	Notts Co	35	2

Season	Club	App	Goals
1988–89		45	1
1989–90	Bury	31	1
1990–91		—	—
1990–91	Chester C	2	—
1990–91	Mansfield T	11	—
1990–91	Mansfield T	10	—
1991–92		10	1
1992–93		45	4

WOAN, Ian

Born Wirrall 14.12.67. Ht 5 10 Wt 11 09
Midfield. From Runcorn.

Season	Club	App	Goals
1989–90	Nottingham F	—	—
1990–91		12	3
1991–92		21	5
1992–93		28	3

WOOD, Paul

Born Middlesbrough 1.11.64. Ht 5 9
Wt 10 01
Forward. From Apprentice.

Season	Club	App	Goals
1982–83	Portsmouth	—	—
1983–84		8	1
1984–85		6	1
1985–86		25	4
1986–87		8	—
1987–88		—	—
1987–88	Brighton	31	4
1988–89		35	1
1989–90		26	3
1989–90	Sheffield U	17	3
1990–91		7	—
1990–91	Bournemouth	21	—
1991–92	Sheffield U	4	—
1991–92	Bournemouth	35	9
1992–93		27	4

WOOD, Steve

Born Bracknell 2.2.63. Ht 6 1 Wt 12 04
Defender. From Apprentice.

Season	Club	App	Goals
1979–80	Reading	2	—
1980–81		6	—
1981–82		32	—
1982–83		18	—

Season	Club	League Appearances/Goals	
1983–84		37	3
1984–85		46	1
1985–86		46	4
1986–87		32	1
1987–88	Millwall	22	—
1988–89		35	—
1989–90		21	—
1990–91		25	—
1991–92		7	—
1991–92	Southampton	15	—
1992–93		4	—

WOOD, Trevor

Born Jersey 3.11.68. Ht 5 11 Wt 13 00
Goalkeeper. From Apprentice.

Season	Club	League Appearances/Goals	
1986–87	Brighton	—	—
1987–88		—	—
1988–89	Port Vale	2	—
1989–90		3	—
1990–91		32	—
1991–92		—	—
1992–93		5	—

WOODS, Chris

Born Boston 14.11.59. Ht 6 2 Wt 12 08
Goalkeeper. From Apprentice. England B,
Under-21, 43 full caps.

Season	Club	League Appearances/Goals	
1976–77	Nottingham F	—	—
1977–78		—	—
1978–79		—	—
1979–80	QPR	41	—
1980–81		22	—
1980–81	Norwich C	10	—
1981–82	Norwich C	42	—
1982–83		42	—
1983–84		42	—
1984–85		38	—
1985–86		42	—
1986–87	Rangers	42	—
1987–88		39	—
1988–89		24	—
1989–90		32	—
1990–91		36	—
1991–92	Sheffield W	41	—
1992–93		39	—

WOODS, Neil

Born York 30.7.66. Ht 6 0 Wt 12 11
Forward. From Apprentice.

Season	Club	League Appearances/Goals	
1982–83	Doncaster R	4	—
1983–84		7	1
1984–85		6	2
1985–86		30	7
1986–87		18	6
1986–87	Rangers	3	—
1987–88	Ipswich T	19	4
1988–89		1	—
1989–90		7	1
1989–90	Bradford C	14	2
1990–91		—	—
1990–91	Grimsby T	44	12
1991–92		37	8
1992–93		30	4

WOODS, Ray

Born Birkenhead 7.6.65. Ht 5 11
Wt 10 00
Forward. From Apprentice.

Season	Club	League Appearances/Goals	
1982–83	Tranmere R	1	—
1983–84		6	2
	From Colne D.		
1988–89	Wigan Ath	8	—
1989–90		—	—
1990–91		20	3
1990–91	Coventry C	12	1
1991–92		9	—
1992–93		—	—
1992–93	Wigan Ath	13	—

WOODTHORPE, Colin

Born Ellesmere Pt 13.1.69. Ht 5 11
Wt 11 08
Defender. From Apprentice.

Season	Club	League Appearances/Goals	
1986–87	Chester C	30	2
1987–88		35	—
1988–89		44	3
1989–90		46	1
1990–91	Norwich C	1	—
1991–92		15	1
1992–93		7	—

WOODWARD, Andy

Born Stockport 23.9.73
Defender. From Trainee.

1992–93 Crewe Alex .... 6 —

WORBOYS, Gavin

Born Doncaster 14.7.74. Ht 6 0
Wt 11 00
Forward. From Trainee.

1991–92 Doncaster R................ 7 2
1992–93 Notts Co..................... — —

WORSLEY, Graeme

Born Liverpool 4.1.69. Ht 5 10 Wt 11 02
Defender. From Bootle.

1988–89 Shrewsbury T.............. 6 —
1989–90 .... 15 —
1990–91 .... 31 1
1991–92 .... 25 1
1992–93 .... 28 2

WORTHINGTON, Gary

Born Cleethorpes 10.11.66. Ht 5 10
Wt 10 05
Forward. From Apprentice. England
Youth.

1984–85 Manchester U.............. — —
1985–86 .... — —
1986–87 Huddersfield T............ — —
1987–88 Darlington 9 3
1988–89 .... 31 12
1989–90 Wrexham 42 12
1990–91 .... 30 6
1990–91 Wigan Ath................... 12 5
1991–92 .... 41 15
1992–93 .... 10 —

WORTHINGTON, Nigel

Born Ballymena 4.11.61. Ht 5 11
Wt 12 05
Defender. From Ballymena U. Northern
Ireland Youth, 44 full caps.

1981–82 Notts Co..................... 2 —

1982–83 .... 41 3
1983–84 .... 24 1
1983–84 Sheffield W................. 14 1
1984–85 .... 38 1
1985–86 .... 15 —
1986–87 .... 35 —
1987–88 .... 38 —
1988–89 .... 28 —
1989–90 .... 32 2
1990–91 .... 33 1
1991–92 .... 34 5
1992–93 .... 40 1

WRATTEN, Paul

Born Middlesbrough 29.11.70 Ht 5 7
Wt 10 00
Midfield. From Trainee. England Youth.

1988–89 Manchester U............. — —
1989–90 .... — —
1990–91 .... 2 —
1991–92 .... — —
1992–93 Hartlepool U 15 1

WRIGHT, Alan

Born Ashton-under-Lyme 28.9.71.
Ht 5 4 Wt 9 04
Midfield. From Schoolboy, Trainee.
England Schools, Youth, Under-21.

1987–88 Blackpool.................... 1 —
1988–89 .... 16 —
1989–90 .... 24 —
1990–91 .... 45 —
1991–92 .... 12 —
1991–92 Blackburn R 33 1
1992–93 .... 24 —

WRIGHT, George

Born South Africa 22.12.69. Ht 5 7
Wt 10 02
Defender. From Hutcheson Vale BC.

1987–88 Hearts .... — —
1988–89 .... — —
1989–90 .... 1 —
1990–91 .... 17 2

| 1991–92 | | 24 | 1 |
| 1992–93 | | 12 | — |

WRIGHT, Ian

Born Lichfield 10.3.72. Ht 6 1   Wt 12 08
Defender. From Trainee.

1989–90	Stoke C	1	—
1990–91		1	—
1991–92		3	—
1992–93		1	—

WRIGHT, Ian

Born Woolwich 3.11.63.   Ht 5 9
Wt 11 08
Forward. From Greenwich Borough.
England B, 13 full caps.

1985–86	Crystal Palace	32	9
1986–87		38	8
1987–88		41	20
1988–89		42	24
1989–90		26	8
1990–91		38	15
1991–92		8	5
1991–92	Arsenal	30	24
1992–93		31	15

WRIGHT, Keith

Born Edinburgh 17.5.65.   Ht 5 11
Wt 11 00
Forward. From Melbourne Th. Scotland 1
full cap.

1983–84	Raith R	37	5
1884–85		38	22
1985–86		39	21
1986–87		17	13
1986–87	Dundee	20	10
1987–88		42	15
1988–89		35	8
1989–90		34	11
1990–91		36	18
1991–92	Hibernian	40	9
1992–93		42	11

WRIGHT, Mark

Born Manchester 29.1.70.   Ht 5 11
Wt 10 12
Defender. From Trainee.

1988–89	Everton	—	—
1989–90		1	—
1990–91		—	—
1990–91	Blackpool	3	—
1990–91	Huddersfield	10	1
1991–92	Huddersfield T	8	—
1992–93		14	—

WRIGHT, Mark

Born Dorchester 1.8.63.   Ht 6 2   Wt 13 03
Defender. From Amateur. England Under-
21, 43 full caps.

1980–81	Oxford U	—	—
1981–82		10	—
1981–82	Southampton	3	—
1982–83		39	2
1983–84		29	1
1984–85		36	—
1985–86		33	3
1986–87		30	1
1987–88		—	—
1987–88	Derby Co	38	3
1988–89		33	1
1989–90		36	6
1990–91		37	—
1991–92	Liverpool	21	—
1992–93		33	2

WRIGHT, Paul

Born East Kilbride 17.8.67.   Ht 5 8
Wt 10 08
Forward. S Form. Scotland Youth,
Under-21.

1983–84	Aberdeen	1	—
1984–85		—	—
1985–86		10	2
1986–87		25	4
1987–88		9	4
1988–89		23	6
1989–90	QPR	15	5
1989–90	Hibernian	3	1

Season	Club	League Appearances/Goals	
1990–91	....	33	6
1991–92	St Johnstone	41	18
1992–93	....	42	14

WRIGHT, Paul

Born London 29.7.69
Forward.

Season	Club	League Appearances/Goals	
1992–93	Halifax T	1	—

WRIGHT, Stephen

Born Bellshill 27.8.71.   Ht 5 10   Wt 10 10
Defender. From Aberdeen Lads. Scotland
Under-21, 2 full caps.

Season	Club	League Appearances/Goals	
1987–88	Aberdeen...................	—	—
1988–89	....	—	—
1989–90	....	1	—
1990–91	....	17	1
1991–92	....	23	—
1992–93	....	36	—

WRIGHT, Tommy

Born Belfast 29.8.63.   Ht 6 1   Wt 13 05
Goalkeeper. From Linfield. Northern
Ireland 15 full caps. Football League.

Season	Club	League Appearances/Goals	
1987–88	Newcastle U................	—	—
1988–89	....	9	—
1989–90	....	14	—
1990–91	....	—	—
1990–91	*Hull C*	6	—
1991–92	Newcastle U................	33	—
1992–93	....	14	—

WRIGHT, Tommy

Born Dunfermline 10.1.66.   Ht 5 7
Wt 9 10
Forward. From Apprentice. Scotland
Under-21.

Season	Club	League Appearances/Goals	
1982–83	Leeds U	4	1
1983–84	....	25	8
1984–85	....	42	14
1985–86	....	10	1
1986–87	....	—	—

Season	Club	League Appearances/Goals	
1986–87	Oldham Ath................	28	7
1987–88	....	41	9
1988–89	....	43	7
1989–90	Leicester C..................	41	3
1990–91	....	44	7
1991–92	....	44	12
1992–93	Middlesbrough............	36	5

YALLOP, Frank

Born Watford 4.4.64. Ht 5 11 Wt 12 00
Defender. From Apprentice. England
Youth, Canada full caps.

Season	Club	Apps	Goals
1981–82	Ipswich T	—	—
1982–83		—	—
1983–84		6	—
1984–85		10	—
1985–86		34	—
1986–87		31	—
1987–88		41	2
1988–89		40	2
1989–90		31	—
1990–91		45	—
1991–92		17	—
1992–93		6	2

YATES, Dean

Born Leicester 26.10.67. Ht 6 1
Wt 12 00
Defender. From Apprentice. England
Under-21.

Season	Club	Apps	Goals
1984–85	Notts Co	8	—
1985–86		44	4
1986–87		42	9
1987–88		46	2
1988–89		41	6
1989–90		45	6
1990–91		41	4
1991–92		25	2
1992–93		—	—

YATES, Mark

Born Birmingham 24.1.70. Ht 5 11
Wt 11 09
Midfield. From Trainee.

Season	Club	Apps	Goals
1987–88	Birmingham C	3	—
1988–89		20	3
1989–90		20	2
1990–91		9	1
1991–92		2	—
1991–92	Burnley	17	1
1992–93		1	—
1992–93	Lincoln C	14	—

YATES, Steve

Born Bristol 29.1.70. Ht 5 11 Wt 11 00
Defender. From Trainee.

Season	Club	Apps	Goals
1986–87	Bristol R	2	—
1987–88		—	—
1988–89		35	—
1989–90		42	—
1990–91		34	—
1991–92		39	—
1992–93		44	—

YORKE, Dwight

Born Tobago 3.12.71. Ht 5 11 Wt 11 13
Forward. From St Clair's Coaching
School, Tobago.

Season	Club	Apps	Goals
1989–90	Aston Villa	2	—
1990–91		18	2
1991–92		32	11
1992–93		27	6

YOUDS, Edward

Born Liverpool 3.5.70. Ht 6 1 Wt 13 03
Defender. From Trainee.

Season	Club	Apps	Goals
1988–89	Everton	—	—
1989–90		—	—
1989–90	Cardiff C	1	—
1989–90	Wrexham	20	2
1990–91	Everton	8	—
1991–92		—	—
1991–92	Ipswich T	1	—
1992–93		16	—

YOUNG, Eric

Born Singapore 25.3.60. Ht 6 2
Wt 13 00
Defender. From Slough Town. Wales 16
full caps.

Season	Club	Apps	Goals
1982–83	Brighton	—	—
1983–84		30	4
1984–85		35	3
1985–86		32	2
1986–87		29	1
1987–88	Wimbledon	29	3
1988–89		35	1

1989–90	....	35	5
1990–91	Crystal Palace	34	3
1991–92	....	30	1
1992–93	....	38	6

YOUNG, Kenneth

Born Edinburgh 6.5.74   Ht 5 6   Wt 10 7
Forward. From Links U.

| 1992–93 | Falkirk .... | 1 | — |

YOUNG, Stuart

Born Hull 16.12.72.   Ht 5 11   Wt 12 00
Forward. From Arsenal Trainee.

1991–92	Hull C	15	2
1992–93	....	4	—
1992–93	Northampton T	8	2

ZORICICH, Chris

Born New Zealand 3.5.69.   Ht 5 11
Wt 11 10
Defender.

1989–90	Leyton Orient	—	—
1990–91	....	28	—
1991–92	....	22	—
1992–93	....	12	1